THE ART OF

AJANTA AND SOPOĆANI

A Comparative Study

(AN ENQUIRY IN PRĀṆA AESTHETICS)

OM D. UPADHYA

MOTILAL BANARSIDASS PUBLISHERS
PRIVATE LIMITED • DELHI

First Edition: Delhi, 1994

ISBN: 81-208-0990-4

Also available at:

MOTILAL BANARSIDASS

41 U.A. Bungalow Road, Jawahar Nagar, Delhi 110 007
120 Royapettah High Road, Mylapore, Madras 600 004
16 St. Mark's Road, Bangalore 560 001
Ashok Rajpath, Patna 800 004
Chowk, Varanasi 221 001

PRINTED IN INDIA
BY JAINENDRA PRAKASH JAIN AT SHRI JAINENDRA PRESS,
A-45, NARAINA, PHASE I, NEW DELHI 110 028
AND PUBLISHED BY NARENDRA PRAKASH JAIN FOR
MOTILAL BANARSIDASS PUBLISHERS PVT. LTD.,
BUNGALOW ROAD, DELHI 110 007

DEDICATED TO MAA & JI

CONTENTS

(The political conditions described in the book are those mostly existing prior to 1985.)

PREFACE

During my two years of stay in Yugoslavia (1964-66) I studied the mural techniques and availed myself of ample opportunities to examine Byzantine murals at almost every centre in Europe, including Mt. Athos. It is worth-recording that I found in them many pictorial syntax common with Ajanta murals. The living patterns of monks at Mt. Athos[1] and many social customs in Yugoslavia impressed upon the mind a similarity between the environments of these two distant lands, which distilled into the contents of their respective arts. Further, I discovered that the culmination of such distillation was achieved in the murals of Sopoćani (pronounced Sopotchani) regarded as 'the most beautiful work of Serbian art.'[2] The Byzantine art specialists vehemently argue that the art of Sopoćani has influenced the formation of the Italian Renaissance.

On return, I again undertook to study the murals of Ajanta on site. It now clearly occurred to me that a fruitful comparison could be made between the works of Ajanta and those of Sopoćani. This idea was also supported by the enthusiasm of Ajanta admirers who had compared its best works with those of the Italian Renaissance. Stella Kramrisch's penetrating insights into the nature of Indian art and of Ajanta in particular served as a beacon-light to me. Besides, Professor R.V. Sakhalkar, to whom I owe my initiation in the field of art, gave me full, sympathetic encouragement. My further studies began to clearly show a relationship between the 'inner-light' as manifested in the 'projected-image' of the works of Byzantine art since the Justinian period[3] and the conception of *prāṇa* in the 'forthcoming'[4] of Ajanta, which Kramrisch (1937, 1955) expounded with the evidences of scriptures. To me it was a pleasant discovery to find the *ūrṇā*[5] mark between the eyebrows of St. John the Divine at Sopoćani (plate 97) along with the resemblance between Ushkar terracotta-heads of Bodhisattvas (plate 88) and those of Christ. I also discovered an aesthetic similarity between the Deogarh reliefs (plate 87) and the angels of St. Sophia at Ohrid in Yugoslavia (plate 86). All this kept up my enthusiasm for further research.

Finally, I decided upon a formal research programme to find out a systematic answer to the similarities and dissimilarities apparent in the best manifestations of the 'inner light' conception of Byzantine art at Sopoćani and those at Ajanta. Withal, the venture gave rise to the quest for the origin of this concept. The constraints and causes behind the difference in achieving the consummation of the similar inspiration were also to be investigated. Accordingly, the research was taken up following a form meaning-expression model comprising the comparative study of the general, factual and interpretative categories along with the study of artist and patron and above all, the analysis of the style and technique specifically examining the plastic and formal factors with artist's subjective visualization of the inner essence. The form-meaning study is elaborated fully in the main body of the thesis and the summary-conclusion stands with specific delineation of 'expression' rearranged in five parts. The importance, scope and further investigative possibilities also find a place there.

The pioneering work done in the field of comparative studies of the traditional arts of India and the Medieval art of Europe by Anand K. Coomaraswamy (1939) was based on the concept of 'art was religion and religion art.' Stella Kramrisch's expounding of Indian art maintaining no difference between the secular and the religious, found an echo in the stand taken by Niharranjan Ray[6] against Coomaraswamy's comparative 'conception.' Examined on a broader perspective the art of medieval Yugoslavian frescoes opens up pictorial configurations ranging from the 'temple of graces' to the stories of *Jātakas* including primitive and folk aspirations and the documentation of contemporary history. So it must be inferred that for these 'Hellas' the 'Holy-state' comprised cultural, social and political welfare as well. As such, it seems that N. Ray handled, only in a restricted sense, Coomaraswamy's (1935) basic propositions giving a broader base of *Paurāṇic* conception to the comparative iconographic studies. I had an opportunity to meet late Dr. Ray at Varanasi (3rd March, 1981). Having explained to him my propositions and discussed its implications and scope, I received his blessings in my venture. (It is needless to add that his concept of *prāṇa* in the appreciation of Indian sculptures (1973) deeply impressed me.) Further, the above idea of universal 'poetic minds' finds absolute confirmation by today's most perceptive art-historian Meyer Schapiro.[7]

A clearer perspective of my problem along with its solutions was provided by my studies of Mario Bussagli's (1963) and Benjamin Rowland's (1967) delineations of Ajanta's II Indian manner of aesthetics of inner-light influencing Central Asian works and such conceptions of the Byzantine art since the Ravenna mosaics. On the theoretical ground it flowered into Hesychast meditation of Buddhistic type and the works of Domentian, whose lauds influenced the plasticity of Sopoćani's works. Ernst Kitzinger (1977) proposed that such plasticity of 'projected composition' was handed down to Justinian-Byzantine art through the prescriptive aesthetics of the East Mediterranean floor mosaics transforming, with water-cosmology, the conception of extendible foil of grid surface into rinceaux growth or the 'creeper' motif—a motif in which the artists of Ajanta coded the aesthetics of *prāṇa* propounded by Indian scriptures.[8] Professor John F. Moffitt's insight into tectonic structures of pictorial space expressing artist's intentions has inspired me for bringing out a clearer definition of the styles as enumerated in *Citrasūtra.* I owe a great deal to S. Radhakrishnan's (1939) comparative studies in religions and philosophy and K.C. Pandey's (1956) comparative aesthetics. The latter's comparisons of *Mānasara* canons with those of Vitruvius works on Roman architecture were centainly revealing.

The importance and scope of the present research lies in providing a further link into the comparative study of the arts of the East and West, especially in the sphere of creativity where similar aesthetic module brings about similarities in the configurations of the art of two distant lands notwithstanding the differences and constraints which bar the consummation of the initial stimuli provided by the unit of comparison. This, however, does not restrict the investigations into the traditional arts but extends to the whole history of art in systematic comparative studies with a view to verifying the *prāṇa* aesthetics or 'Eastern influence' working behind the Western art. Such studies will also enable us to find out the causes standing in the way of consummation of the aesthetic idea and the dissimilarities caused by the constraints. In the contemporary art such comparisons become all the more significant owing to its reductivistic tendencies (Clement Greenberg, 1962) straining the visual arts to a stage of catabolic dissolution which is metaphorically envisaged as 'entropy' by Rudolf Arnheim (1971) and which requires to be qualified in the context of anabolic spirit of *prāṇa* aesthetics which has shown at Ajanta a way by giving a tactile configuration to the 'flux' reached in the Buddhistic dialectics. Professor Arnheim's writings and his concept of dynamic direction in visual-perception (1960) have helped me in scientifically finding out a suitable vocabulary for explaining the 'flux' and its perception in *kṣayavṛddhi* (diminution and augmentation).

I am indebted beyond measure to my revered 'guru' Professor R.V. Sakhalkar for his unreserved help, constant guidance, encouragement and inspiration. I really do not know whether I would ever have achieved success as a practising artist or completed this work without his blessings. To Dr. Vishnu Chandra, Deptt. of English, I owe deep gratitude for his valuable guidance and for sparing time to go through the manuscript. My heartfelt thanks are due to Mr. Madanjeet Singh who has very kindly allowed to reproduce coloured and black and white photographs, and drawings from his memorable monograph on Ajanta (1965). I received immense help from the libraries of the universities of Rajasthan (Jaipur and Udaipur), the University of Fine Art, Belgrade, National Museum, New Delhi and the NID, Ahmedabad. I cannot also forget the sincere interest taken in my work by Shri Vinayak Karnik, Librarian, British Council, Ahmedabad. I hereby express my cordial thanks to the members of the staff of these libraries.

Some very useful research papers, photographs and journals were received from Yugoslavia. My hearty thanks are due to Dr. Nada Komnenovic and Mr Peter Ignjatovic who made this possible. I feel obliged for having received two excellent colour transparencies of Sopoćani for the publication from Mr Branislav Strugar (courtesy Yugoslovenska Autorska Agencija, Beograd). My thanks are due to Mr. Danko Prokic, Attache (Press and Culture), the Embassy of SFR of Yugoslavia, New Delhi, for procuring photographs of the frescoes of Sopoćani and other monuments in Yugoslavia. I most respectfully acknowledge my deep sense of gratitude to Dr. Vojislav J. Djurić for his blessings and permission to reproduce illustrations from his classic monograph on Sopoćani (1963). Late Professor Milo Milunović had kindly initiated me into the plastic study of Byzantine art; Professor Božidar Prodanović gave me rare insight into its techniques and encouraged my comparative point of view; I remember both with deepest gratitude.

It is my bounden duty to thank Dr. Yash Pal, Chairman, University Grants Commission, New Delhi, and to the members of the staff there who have helped in expediting the release of the subsidy grant because of which only the publication of the thesis could be materialized. To the publishers, M/s Motilal Banarsidass Publishers Private Ltd., Delhi, especially to their Director, Mr. N.P. Jain, I express my deep indebtedness for his patience and encouraging me throughout the long period of struggle for arranging the means of publication. And the book, in its final form, owes much to the meticulous editorial skill and visual sensibility of their publication staff. To all of them I feel thankful, as also to many friends and relatives for help in writing and publishing the thesis.

Lastly, this study could never have been possible without the unceasing support of my wife, Mrs. Vimla. I am conscious of the serious strain she has undergone in the completion of the thesis and later in preparing the index for its publication. The burden of having put up with our very busy schedule has been now shared by my little son Vyom, as earlier, too, it was done by my daughter Vyoma along with Jyoti, my sister-in-law who helped us immensely in managing the typing affair. This will all remain unforgettable.

Udaipur, 1990

Om Datt Upadhya

REFERENCES

1. One cannot fail to discern a similarity between the monasteries built by the Tibetan Buddhist Monks and those by the Byzantines at Mt. Athos. Likewise, the holy-grottoes of Syria and the cave-cells of Buddhist monks in Ceylon have a strong resemblance. It may be pointed out that Mongolians had imbibed the Tibetan art which through Siyah Qalem reached Turkey (plate 90) and beyond in the late fourteenth—early fifteenth centuries.
2. Svetozar Radojčić, *Yugoslavia — Mediaeval Frescoes*, UNESCO, 1956, p. 22.
3. A concrete proof of this is given in the investigations of D.T. Rice (1935, 1972) and Vojislav J. Djurić on Sopoćani, 1963.
4. See Glossary.
5. See Glossary.
6. S. Shankar Menon's reporting on N. Ray's two lectures given on 21st and 22nd August, 1979, (*Financial Express*, Sept. 9, 1979) on 'What is Religious in Indian Art' sponsored by the Coomaraswamy Memorial Foundation.
7. *Late Antique, Early Christian and Mediaeval Art*, 1979, p. xv.
8. See Glossary.

ACKNOWLEDGEMENTS

Author and the publishers gratefully acknowledge the indebtedness and express their sincere thanks to the following :

A. K. Coomaraswamy, Munshiram Manoharlal, New Delhi (pls. 11, 113) ; Aleksa Čelebonvić, Publishing House, 'Jugoslavija' (pl. 151); Archaeological Survey of India, New Delhi (pls. 1, 13, 27, 29, 31, 34, 39, 41, 43, 46, 47, 50, 51, 54, 57, 61, 82, 87, 89, 95, 105, 116, 120, 122, 124, 125, 128, 133, 135, 136, 143, 144, 145, 148, 153, 155, 160, 163); Archeological Museum, Athens, Greece (pl. 85); Benjamin Rowland, Penguin Books and Staatliche Museen, Berlin-Dahlem (pl. 149); Branislav Strugar, Jugoslovenska Autorska Agencija, Beograd (colour pls., 142, 161); D.T. Rice, Oxford University Press, London (pls. 112, 99, 93; courtesy, Vetican Library, 10, 112); Erich Newman, Routledge and Kegan Paul Ltd., London (courtesy, National Museum, Belgrade, pls. 109, 110); F.D.K. Bosch, Mouton & Co., S-Gravenhage (pl. 22); H.A. Groenewegen-Frankfort and Bernard Ashmole. The New American Library, Inc., New York, (courtesy, Louvre, Paris, pl. 84); Hallade Madaleine, and Thames and Hudson, London (pl. 88); Madanjeet Singh, and Thames and Hudson, London (colour pls. 141 and 157; pls. 53, 59, 65, 71, 72, 75, 76 118, 121, 127, 134, 139, 146); Musée National Suisse, Zürich, Switzerland (pl. 104); National Gallery of Modern Art, New Delhi (pl. 95); National Museum, New Delhi (pls., 96, 132, 152); Radislav M. Grujić, Tkalčićev Zbornik-I, Zagreb, 1955 (pl. 101); S.P. Gupta, B.R. Publishing Corp., Delhi (courtesy, Patna Museum, Patna, pl. 108); The Embassy of SFR of Yogoslavia, New Delhi, and Republički Zavod, Zaštitu Spomenika Kulture, Beograd (pls. 5, 35, 54, 82, 86, 100, 103, 106, 111, 114, 115, 119, 123, 129, 130, 138, 139, 154, 157, 158, 164, 165); The Embassy of USSR, New Delhi (pl. 91); The Gallery of Frescoes of the National Museum, Belgrade (pl. 3); The Graphis Press, Zürich, Switzerland (courtesy Topkapi Sarayi Muzesi, Istanbul, pl. 90); Vojislav J. Djurić, and Srpska Khiževna Zadruga, Izdavačko Preduzeće, Procveta, Beograd (pls. 4, 12, 15, 16, 28, 30, 32, 33, 37, 38, 40, 42, 45, 48, 49, 52, 55, 58, 60, 62, 64, 67, 68, 70, 97, 126, 131, 140, 150, 156, 166); and all the authors quoted, along with the publishers.

LIST OF ILLUSTRATIONS

24. Kottayam, Valiya Palli (India): The Nestorian Cross (Cross Botonée).
25. Kottayam: The Manichean Cross (Cross Botonée) with the Dove.
26. Madras (India): St. Thomas Mount; similar to the above cross with 'Makara-toran'.
27. Ajanta: 'Miracle of Śrāvastī' (the Thousand Buddhas) (cave 7).
28. Sopoćani: Unidentified Stylite on pillar (nave).
29. Sanchi: Adorned Sun-pillar having male figure on right and female on left (railing of Stūpa 2, early 1st cent. B.C.).
30. Sopoćani: 'Tree of Jesse' (Narthex A.D. 1263-68).
31. Sanchi: Creeper issuing from the navel of Yakṣa (railing of Stūpa 2, early 1st cent. B.C.).
32. Sopoćani: Potipher's wife enticing Joseph in the 'Story of Joseph' (Narthex).
33. Sopoćani: The Last Judgment and the Hell (Narthex).
34. Ajanta: Composite man and animal, part of the scene of the worship of Buddha (cave 17).
35. Studenica (Yugoslavia), The Kings Church: 'The presentation of the virgin in the Temple' (detail, completed by A.D. 1314).
36. Sopoćani: Grid-system with the unit of head and a 'norm' of nose-length shown over 'The Dormition' (nave).
37. Sopoćani: Angular interstices becoming consistent form in the glory-halo in 'Transfiguration' (nave).
38. Sopoćani: Agitated folds in 'The Appearance of Christ to the Apostles after the Resurrection' (sanctuary, nave).
39. Ajanta: Five basic perceptual devices of planer structuring coded in the decorative patterns of the ceiling (cave 2).
    Curtained opening as a referent uniting the frame with the framed 'surface'.
40. Sopoćani: 'The Nativity of the Virgin' (prothesis, A.D. 1263-68).
41. Ajanta: 'Mahāhaṁsa Jātaka' (cave 17).
    Pillars uniting upper and lower edges making total area of the frame as the perceptual concern.
42. Sopoćani: 'Christ among the doctors' (nave).
43. Ajanta: 'The Consecration of Nanda' (cave 1).
    'Bust motif' and its use as a referent uniting the frame with the framed surface.
44. Ajanta: *Gavākṣa* window; Avalokiteśvara mural (cave 1).
45. Sopoćani: Medallions and busts on the base of cupola, pendentives and below (nave).
46. Ajanta: Grid-module on the ceiling decoration (cave 17).
47. Ajanta: Rectangular impost harmonised with the round capital of the pillar by the luxuriant growth of creeper of *pūrṇa-ghaṭa* (cave 23).
48. Sopoćani: Rock-cliff edges, 'Saving Three Dukes' (chapel of St. Nichola, A.D. 6th or 7th decade of 14th cent.).
49. Sopoćani: Wainscoating figures, 'Parable of the Richman' exo-narthex, c. A.D. 1331-46).

CHAPTER I

INTRODUCTION: AJANTA AND SOPOĆANI

Ajanta

Walter M. Spink looks upon Ajanta as 'one of the most remarkable creative achievements in man's history.'[1] That 'it has by now deservedly reached a fame outstripping the restricted milieu of the specialists' is another befitting eulogy paid by the celebrated art-historian, Maurizio Taddei.[2]

The first descriptions and the first graphic presentations of Ajanta reaching us (although through foreigners) are those given by Indians. The earliest reference describing Ajanta comes to us, written in the first half of 7th century A.D., as it was told (by Indians) to Hiuen Tsang at Badami, and drawings done and lithographed by 'a native', Fide Jesus (sent by Wathen in *c.*1836 to Ajanta to do them),[3] were published in 1847 in Dr. Bird's account. Both represent Ajanta in the mystique-overtures which, in Herringham's words, are 'of a primitive nature and like mediaeval drawings.'[4] Such mystic-feelings are best experienced in the lower storey of cave 6 at Ajanta or in Brahmanical caves of Ellora with their multipillared spaces, which are in contrast with usual Buddhist caves having pillars on the sides leaving open space in the nave. To a sensibility nurtured by 'facts' these mystique-overtures would be 'inaccuracies of the drawings,' as Burgess[5] writes about these lithographs published by Bird, though Griffiths, too, didn't deny the 'mystique' as he entered the sanctuary of cave 2 with a light finding that 'the effect produced is one of extreme richness, the floating figures in the spandrels standing out with startling effect.'[6] These drawings are as 'inaccurate' and are done with having 'filled up the small holes, for the sake of the beauty of the composition and of intelligibility,'[7] as were the facsimile copies published by Lady Herringham in 1915 about which A. Ghosh remarked 'insipid and mostly lacking the feel of the Ajanta Style.'[8] Incidentally, Syed Ahmed's copies in this portfolio have 'exhibition of the painter's knowledge of anatomy' which Axel Jarl does not accept, nor does he find 'any offence against anatomy,'[9] barring a few exceptions at Ajanta. There is no surprise, thus, that this very portfolio inspired Laurence Binyon to write about Ajanta paintings being 'in essence allied to Western than to Eastern Art.'[10]

Thus, study through portfolios seems to be a tradition taken up quite early and this 'museum without walls' is seriously taken up by contemporary scholars like Dr. Ratan Parimoo who refers to Yazdani's portfolios[11] as these were also referred to by Coomaraswamy.[12] This trend seems to be the outcome of (apart from the reference purposes) the 'hazards' in studying the works at first hand, the foremost being the present vestigial remains of masterpieces, for example, one can hardly make out the 'Dying Princess' now. (The history of their disintegration and mutation starts within a few years of their discovery in a 'decent state of preservation'[13] by officers of the Madras army in 1819.) The other 'hazards' are recorded since Hiuen Tsang who had written that 'the hill people changed their feelings and did not cease to show their violence and anger. Travellers no longer dared to go to the convent....'[14] In 1822, James E. Alexander was forewarned of tigers and 'stony hearted Bhils'[15] on his way to these paintings. Further, the students accompanying Griffiths fell sick and the superintendent of the School of Art reported it to 'illustrate the dangers and difficulties under which researches of the sort are carried out.'[16] These 'hazards' have now metamorphosed into long awaiting queues of 'art-lovers' and limited minutes of spotlights.[17] (Similar are the contentions of the researcher sandwiched between the never ending stream of masses of 'art-lovers' pouring into Sistine Chapel, and the misery really increases when he is asked to study paintings at that height). This justifies the study through portfolios and facsimile copies. The latter in original sizes are exhibited at various places especially at Ajanta itself and at Bahavalpur House, New Delhi. These, however, lack that textural and tactile quality which Krishna Chaitanya has aptly pointed out while contrasting them with the facsimile-copies of Yugoslavian frescoes where these factors have been maintained.[18] Actually, the first artist doing 'facsimile copies' was Fide Jesus, the 'native artist' of Wathen. Robert Gill sketched and painted in oils 'in the best tradition of the ancient Ajanta artists.'[19] Right from 1844 he devoted twenty-seven years of his life at Ajanta, and died there. Unfortunately, a very few copies done by him have survived the fire at Crystal Palace, London, in 1866. Besides, only a limited number of woodcuts made out of several tracings of them have reached us. In 1885, the copies by Griffiths and his students of Bombay School of Art done during 1872 to 1885 met the same fate. The remaining ones, with a few recopied, were published in two volumes of *Paintings in the Buddhist Cave Temples of Ajanta* in 1896-97. The third session of copying was done by Lady Herringham from 1909 to 1911 with her assistants. A few of them were published in her *Ajanta Frescoes*, in 1915. Further copies were also produced especially those by Syed Ahmed.

The photography done by Goloubew in 1911 started the exact documenting of Ajanta works. Vassey's photographs produced the excellent portfolios by Yazdani (*Ajanta*, four volumes 1930, 1933, 1946 and 1955). And this 'documentation with fidelity' gave us the UNESCO portfolio and some others by the Archaeological Survey and Lalit Kala Academy; superb details of 'varṇika-baṅga', i.e., 'execution', of various styles are given in Madanjeet Singh's monograph of 1965.

The descriptive and critical survey of Ajanta, which is voluminous, started with William Erskine reading a paper to the Bombay Literary Society in 1822, and with the publication of James E. Alexander's survey in the transactions of Royal Asiatic Society in 1829. Specialized eruditions began with James Fergusson's paper which he read at the Royal Asiatic Society of Great Britain and Ireland in 1843. The aesthetic aspects of Ajanta paintings have remarkably been expounded in Stella Kramrisch's book, *A Survey of Painting in the Deccan*, published in 1937. However, a scholar like Jagdish Mittal still feels that further studies over the aesthetic quality and the analysis of the various pictorial components needs be done 'by a scholar sensitive to their pictorial qualities.'[20] These should be aided, especially in comparative studies, with the current trends in applying 'divergent scientific knowledge as psychology, physiology, gnosiology, the theory of information, linguistics, cybernetics, sociology, ethics, pedagogics etc., as apparatuses, in analysing various aspects of art and aesthetics,' as is pointed out by A.K. Bhattacharya.

In aesthetic appreciation, Ajanta has had all the changing perspectives of its critics and prevalent norms of art criticism, as if to fulfil what Solomon Gladstone said 'the point to marvel at is that the frescoes can impress from so many standpoints'.[21] These were started literally in the spirit of 'Toros, Toros,' of little Maria (daughter of Sautuola who found, in 1879, bisons of Altamira), as the memorandum of Captain Morgan speaks stating the reactions of officers of Madras army saying 'seated figures with curled wigs.' These officers named Ajanta after the nearby village. The nineteenth century opinions, as Partha Mitter justly explains, express the impact of Indian art, religion and philosophy on the European mind and sensibility, although their appreciation was no more than unfolding 'as yet uncertain, subjective and speculative... dominated and conditioned by Western ideas and attitudes.'[22] Some of these opinions even parallel those expressed about India by the admirals of Alexander: '... they speak of people ten feet long and six feet wide ... where brass rains from the sky in brazen drops ....'[23]

Ajanta can never forget Robert Gill's fervent and unfaltering dedication to the reliving of this art. And if one goes by the theory ascribing the whole of the Mahāyāna phase of Ajanta to the late fifth century, then Gill's gigantic endeavour must be equated with the master Sthavira Achala Muni of Ajanta. His visions and interpretations of Ajanta art are now as rarely available as the appreciations in the inscriptions at Ajanta itself, which are limited to expressions like 'beautiful picture-galleries'—'Suvīthi'— or 'attractive'—'Manobhirāmam'— or 'brilliance'—'prabhā'—etc., (Cave 16, on left end wall outside the verandah).[24] Artist's persistent endeavour to project worthwhile interpretation of Ajanta, thus, started from Gill and culminated in Amrita Sher-Gil, who deserves the credit of making Ajanta contemporary. It is in the same vein in which Picasso's formal interpretations have made us feel classical art more than the volumes written by Winckelmann.

Mitter's synthesis of the European reaction and the same fact of colonial and post-colonial mentality surfaces often. It was under such zeitgeist that the frequent comparison with Italian Renaissance work was bestowed upon Ajanta. What Griffiths admired as 'the principles of Decorative Arts in its highest and noblest sense,'[25] was also in the spirit of 'great practical value to the students'[26] of the school of art run on the traditions of South Kensington workshops. Griffiths' stress on decorative designs, published in his portfolios, could testify it. Beaconlights to illuminate the 'spirit' of Ajanta, are, through the perceptive writings of Stella Kramrisch, and through the graphic presentation of Amrita Sher-Gil. The latter's paintings not only connect Ajanta with Rajput miniatures but make it relevant to the present-day India.[27] Gladstone Solomon's jottings vivify the verves of an Ajantian artist. In the tradition of literary analogists A.K. Coomaraswamy's contribution through comparative insights is undeniable, and that of Dr. C. Sivaramamurti has an abiding interest.

In the realm of proper understanding of Buddhist art from various points of view, efforts of Fergusson, Cunningham, Burgess, Cousens, Foucher, Grünwedel, Rhys Davids, Jouveau-Dubreuil, Macdonell, Havell, Vincent Smith, Mallmann, Bhattacharya, Agrawala, Spink, Ray, Anand and Bussagli are indelible.

Before closing this panorama of source introduction to Ajanta it is worth mentioning that the present state of sculpture and painting must give a very much muted image of what it was when the caves were 'filled with the sound of cow-tails (*cauris*)'[28] (inscriptions on cave 26), and with plastered and coloured sculptures[29]—vestiges of which are clear in the small standing figure on the left wall of antechamber, finely covered with lime-coat—'Sudhā'—appearing as if made of marble (cave 6 upper storey). The current appreciation of these works amounts parallel to the appreciation of originally coloured Greek sculptures having come down to us in pure white. The appreciation of Dr. Snellgrove for the sculptures of cave 19 as 'porous stone lends spongy softness,'[30] has relevance to today's condition and not to the days when Buddhas in sanctum were painted red, yellow and golden.[31] The aesthetic aroma must have been, then, like what we get in the scattered Buddhist monasteries in the Himalaya region, or, of eighteenth century Bavarian church as D. Barrett would agree.[32]

The above mutations 'in time' have made Ajanta more relevant to today's aesthetics. (Incidentally, many syntactical effacements have given an individual dominance to various factors, culminating into the formalistic appreciation, for example, plate 13 (p. 26) of Madanjeet Singh's *Ajanta* brings out the tachistic tendencies in almost a Zen Buddhist master's way[33] to appreciate the values of the art of Ajanta). Permutations and additions to this growing 'tree' of Ajanta into space 'nourishing and getting nourished, speaking with the tongues of many Nations,'[34] creates a style of art reaching beyond the confines of Asia. And all this radiates back for its own proper feeling and understanding in the dialectical relationship.

Descriptive Survey of the Site and the Works of Art:

Inscriptions found on the Ajanta painting and stones reveal all that the aesthete might have thought in selecting the place and the artist for transcendence through art. These inscriptions convey a sense through the syntax of language which sounds parallel to the pictorial syntax, mutilations on both are reticent in the same manner as they are suggestively eloquent.

On the front of the *Caitya* cave 26, the seventeenth line of inscription over the right side door reads as follows:[35]

> This temple is established for the welfare, tuneful with the notes of various birds, and whose caves are filled with the sound of cow-tails (*cauris*)... and which is inhabited by the *yogiśvaras*....

On cave 16, a *vihāra*, there is an inscription in Sanskrit verse on the left end wall outside the verandah, the last part of which reads as under:[35a]

> On the best of mountains on which hang multitudes of water-laden clouds, which is inhabited by the lords serpents... in the thickest of the slopes

of which... by the lord of the goddess of heroism.

Which is adorned with windows, doors, beautiful picture-galleries, ledges, statues of the nymphs of Indra and the like, which is ornamented with beautiful pillars and stairs and has a temple of the Buddha inside.

Which is situated on the top, appears attractive... a canopy, which is provided with a large reservoir of abundant water and with shrine of the lord of the Nagas and the like.

... Various pleasures... in a fierce wind blowing all round... warmed by the heat of the rays of the summer sun and affording enjoyment of wellknown comforts in all seasons.

(Which resembles)... the palaces of the lord of gods and is similar to a cave in the lovely Mandara mountain... as desired by the people.

Which... shines on this matchless mountain... since it removes fatigue.

The cave on this... clothed in the brilliance of Indra's crown, which the people, with their love expanding through joy and gratification, have named—Visala.

Having presented with devotion to the community of monks, Varāhadeva together with the multitude of his relatives, having enjoyed royal pleasures, rules righteously being praised by Sugata (i.e. Buddha). As long as... with the multitude of the hoods of serpents resemble crowding clouds... as long as the sun with rays reddish like fresh red arsenic, even so long may this spotless cave containing an excellent hall dedicated to the three ratnas be enjoyed.

... this mountain, the peak of which contains various caves, which is inhabited by great people... and may the whole world also, getting rid of its manifold sins, enter that tranquil, and noble state, free from sorrow and pain.

To complete the vivid account of Ajanta it is necessary to add what Hiuen Tsang heard of it when he was at Badami (*c.* A.D. 642):[36]

... In the middle was seventy feet stone statue of Buddha, and over the statue, hanging without any apparent support, were seven stone canopies about three feet apart, kept up, it was said, by the power of Lohan's (Arhat's) prayers.... Round the monastery were sculptured stone walls (depicting the event of Buddha's life)... Outside the convent gates, to the left and right, were stone elephants, which at times were said to utter frightful cries and shake the earth.

A mutilated Rāṣṭrakūṭa inscription in the court of cave 26 testifies to the use of caves till the ninth century.[37] These caves (thirty in all, discovered so far) lie at a distance of sixty-seven miles from Aurangabad in Maharashtra. They were excavated on the semicircular scarp of a steep rock of Sahyadri hills, running from east-south to almost south. Today they stand desolate, bereft of all the charm and grandeur of which the inscription on cave 16 'spake'. There is no more Bamiyan-like huge statue nor those shrieking elephants, except the two preserved ones silently guarding the base of the stairway leading to cave 16. Centuries of neglect of this 550 metre long trail of excavation, 'sculptures of space', in the heart of about 76 metre high rock have left only slight remains of those magnificent facades, pathways and ledges. Down below flows the stream Waghera in this narrow sinuous gorge, descending at the end of cave 28 in a waterfall of seven leaps (*sat-kund*). Now the caves have been linked with a terraced path at the lowest level of cave 8 and the highest at 29, and are under the care of the Archaeological Survey of India. Nature still takes abundant care of these with its verdant lush 'tuneful with the notes of various birds' which might have inspired those creators, the 'giant in execution,' who, it seems magnified the kaleidoscopic interiors of the plentiful, lovely stone found there.

The five sanctuaries (*caitya*-caves) and the rest monasteries (*vihāras*), are divided into the distinct trends of Buddhist rock-cut architecture said to have been influenced by ancient wooden prototypes. The *caitya*-caves 9 and 10 and *vihāras* 8, 12, 13 and 15-A are akin to those of Bhaja and Nasik etc., in Western Deccan. The *caitya*-cave 10, which dates from *c.* second century B.C., is considered to be the earliest of this group belonging to Hīnayāna School of Buddhism.

The second group belonging to Mahāyāna School started after a break of about four centuries. The latest of this group is cave 21 according to Walter Spink.[38] The initial experimentations seem to have been done in cave 11.[39] Later appeared the standardization of the plan of *vihāra*—a congregation hall with the monk-cells carved in the walls of side-aisles—to which was added a shrine chamber with the image of Buddha facing the door. Thus, the *vihāra*, monastery, also started serving the purpose of a sanctuary. On the basis of evolution of architectural features Spink assigns the lower storey of cave 6 as the earliest of this group.[40] On palaeographical grounds cave 26 has been assigned to a period between A.D. 450 and 525. Cave 4 is the largest *vihāra* and cave 16 has a novel feature of having two-side-aisles in the shrine. Caves 29 (unfinished), 19 and 26 are *caitya*-caves. These are planned with a central nave out of which side-aisles are divided by pillars. Behind the apse, which is a '*caitya*' or *stūpa*, the aisles continue to provide space for circumambulation. With vaulted ceiling these *caitya*-caves are provided with a huge horseshoe-shape *caitya* window on the facades. These might have a combined symbolic meaning of a rose-window with hoof ensuring silence for the goal of meditation, the purpose for which the happy gods held the hooves of the horse of Siddhārtha on the 'Departure.' The evolution of the shape of the *caitya*-window has a relationship with the '*gavākṣa*' motif also.[41] The Hīnayāna *caitya*-caves have aniconic '*uddeśika*' *stūpas* while those of Mahayana have the image in *pralambapādāsana*, seated in European fashion, on a lion throne,[42] (in cave 26) and standing in '*abhayamudrā*' (in cave 19). Cave 2 with throne and halo attached to a monolithic *stūpa* represents the transition between *stūpa* and image worship.[43] As ascertained from unfinished caves, the process of cutting into the rocks must have started with finishing the facade first. Then, having shaped the entire ceiling and continuing 'downwards by cutting deep alleys with sharp and heavy instruments like the pick-axe, followed by breaking of the intervening ridges, leaving solid blocks, for pillars, where necessary, till the floor was reached which was the last to receive the attention.'[44] With hammer and chisel the quarried blocks of granite rocks were given dressing and finishing simultaneously with coating of thin plaster and painting over them.

The cult images of Buddha in the shrine chambers are usually seated in *vajrāsana* and with hands in *dharmacakra-pravartana mudrā* (preaching -of-the-law-pose) flanked by whisk bearing Bodhisattvas and with other iconographic details. According to Spink, the images in caves 11, 16 and 6 are the earliest, as they can be circumambulated. In the case of cave 3, owing to the Buddha's throne attached to the back wall, it is inferred by him that it belongs to a later period.[45] 'Walking' or standing images are treated serving as edifying decorative pieces on facades. There is a colossi in *Parinirvāṇa mudrā* in cave 26 and the 'temptation of Māra' has *Bhūmisparśa mudrā* of the Buddha. The emphasis on sculpture in this cave starts a new phase in the Ajanta Art. Other sculptured principal figures of Buddhist pantheon with decorative motives, symbols and narrative details, adorning the pillars, bracket-capitals, door-jambs and lintels (especially in the caves of the second group) give Ajanta a completion and meaning which is almost lost in the remains of paintings in a few caves.

Painting is taken to be the art 'par excellence' in these series of caves at Ajanta which Burgess called 'more complete and more interesting than any other in India.'[46] It is, however, regrettable that substantial remains of paintings are only in caves 1, 2, 16 and 17 of the Mahāyāna period. The paintings of cave 6 are presently under the process of cleaning and restoration, and should show one of the most remarkable phase, when completed. There are interesting remains of paintings in *caitya* 19—which is referred to as *Gandhakuṭi* in the inscription of cave 17 and is 'singularly well-proportioned' and 'one of the most perfect specimens of Buddhist rock-cut architecture.'[47] This cave should be taken to be a house of innovations. It first introduced Buddha image on votive *stūpa* taking the shape of *sarvatobhadra* type of votive shrine which might have been the source of Buddhist votive temples found in Bangladesh mentioned by Saraswati.[48] Over the *stūpa* there is an *harmikā* with three diminishing *chatrāvalis* in grandiose form almost reminding Hiuen Tsang's description of Colossi Buddha with seven canopies. The conception of Buddha figure developed here foreshadows those in cave 1 and 2 and in cave 4 at Bagh,[49] and reached Tibet and Mongolia through east. A few of the symbols, very important for the present study, are first used in this *caitya*, i.e., flying *gaṇas*, with crown, *toraṇa* issuing from *makara* and the globular dome of the votive *stūpa*. Cave 9 and 10 are having the oldest Buddhist paintings but have subsequent repainting done at many places. The scenes here are painted as to be read clockwise by the circumambulating devotee. These are conditioned by frame whereas in other caves the *Jātaka* and *Avadāna* stories are rendered with no such frames and consideration of sequence. D. Barrett, however, considers that the 'scale of the wall surface imposes a definite frame.'[50] On the basis of circumambulating rite apparent in caves 6, 11, 16, 17 as proved by the shrine images as such,[51] and as the paintings present a continuum with these rites in cave 9 and 10,[52] it is easy to deduce the fact of a scheme of painting meant for *vihāras* and *caityas*. Such a scheme of decoration had been in vogue in the Veṅgi area according to the description in Mahāvaṁśa,[53] and in the *dulva* (for *vihāra*) as pointed out by Grünwedel.[54] The presentation of the 'Wheel of Life' on the left wall of 'the Zodiac verandah' of cave 17, which Grünwedel calls, 'Pictorial cycle of existence,'[55] representing the doctrine of 'Causation' and *nidānas* is a clue to the scheme of pictorial representation and their underlying meaning explained by Ānanda to Nanda, as M.N. Deshpande points out.[56] E. Neumann, on the basis of Jung's theory of archetypes, explains that 'the wheel of life' is 'the great round' in which the Feminine, the Great Mother, with its elementary and transformative characters first becomes visible during its ascending realms of symbols reaching the stage of 'Prajñāpāramitā' or Sophia.[57] Thus the narrations of *Jātakas* and *Avadānas* have been codified on different planes of symbolism by which 'the Sarnath Buddha' as a whole becomes the icon, so eloquent in expressing Mahāyāna philosophy. Randomly handled and condensed syntax of narratives also confirm to a certain level of symbolic meaning in these wall paintings. Sivaramamurti aptly remarks that through these 'the great quality of sacrifice of the bodhisattva is eulogized.'[58]

Cave 1 is having the frescoes of *Jātaka* narrations and those of *Avadānas*, especially of the 'Temptation of Māra', the 'Miracle of Srāvasti' (on the left and right side walls of the antechamber respectively) and 'Conversion of Nanda.'

It has Bodhisattvas on both the sides of the shrine chamber, and Shakti Pandara on its right. These could also be called the respective Buddhas (as for 'Padamapāṇi', Sivaramamurti suggests calling it Sidhārtha)[59] accepting Spink's explanation that the replacing of Buddhas by Boddhisattvas as *dvārapālas* is a very late conception.[60] The bull fight painting is on the bracket-capital of a pillar and the Bacchanalian scene forms part of the ceiling decoration divided into grids with panels. The controversial 'Persian Embassy' scene is to the right of the main doorway.

Cave 2 has the presentations of *Avadānas*, especially of Māyā's dream and birth of Sidhārtha on the start of left wall of the hall in conformity with Buddhistic perambulation from left to right. In and around the shrine are painted 'the thousand Buddhas.' *Jātakas* are depicted alongwith the two groups of women votaries in the right side 'Hārīti Chapel' and the left side chapel to the antechamber. The ceiling decoration in concentric circles and girding is well preserved in this *vihāra*. The wall of the portico to the left of the verandah has verses inscribed from *Kṣāntivadi Jātaka*, though the panel of painting has almost entirely perished. The noteworthy point in this *Jātaka* is that Bodhisattva Kundakakumāra's story bears resemblance to the 'Passion' cycle of Christ's life, especially, the Garden, Accusation of Blasphemy, Thorns and Flagellation, Execution (with word of utmost faith), Resurrection and Ascension (to Himalayas.)[61] In this *vihāra*, flanking the shrine on the left of the doorway is the presentation of Avalokiteśvara as saviour of mankind threatened with the eight great perils of lion, elephant, fire, snake, robber, water, fetters and demon. This cave has a wealth of plastic elements and style and art propositions which are of the extreme use for this present research.

Cave 6 is a double-storey *vihāra*. On the lower storey the 'Miracle of Srāvasti' and 'Temptation of Māra' are painted on the left and right walls of the antechamber. The upper storey has the kneeling figure of a devotee near the feet of a relief of the Buddha.

Cave 9 has, at places, two layers of paintings. There are paintings of six Buddhas, Buddhas painted on pillars, procession of devotees, and the animal hunt panel (now almost obliterated). On the front wall, inside above the door is inscribed the name of Śākya Bhikṣu Saṅgha-priya[62] written close to the painted head of a Bhikṣu. Madanjeet Singh records that this head along with the other one nearby is similar to the one of Bodhisattva in cave 2,[63] the style of painting is also identical with the Buddha painted on the triforium above the VI pillar on the right side.

Cave 10, too, has earlier and later groups of paintings. Madanjeet Singh considers them as belonging to the transitional periods,[64] the earlier to the change from archaic to classic and the latter from classic to baroque. The 'Worship of Bodhi Tree and Stūpa,' and *Sāmas Jātaka* and *Chadanta Jātaka* are also depicted. This *caitya*-cave is adjudged to be the earliest and of the *c.* first half of the second century B.C., and contains the oldest paintings.

Cave 16 has a few surviving pieces. Among them 'the Dying Princes,' 'Nanda's conversion' and 'Sujātā's offering,' 'Sage Asita,' 'Gautama's archery-practice and schooling' etc., are painted out of the *Avadāna* stories. *Jātakas* are also painted on the verandah. The Buddha's life scenes start from left in accordance with Buddhist-perambulation rite.

Cave 17 preserves the greatest number of murals. In verandah are painted 'the flying Indra with *apsarās*,' the *Jātakas*, 'Wheel of Life' and the 'Litany to Avalokiteśvara.' The hall is painted with *Avadānas*, particularly the 'Buddha in Kapilvastu' (with begging-bowl before Yaśodharā and Rāhula), and 'the Buddha preaching to his mother in the Tushita-heaven.' Here the maximum number of *Jātakas* are depicted alongwith 'the lady at her toilet' scene. The decoration of the ceiling is in designs arranged into a unified pattern. This *vihāra* has panels divided vertically, one of those is on the left of the antechamber door of the back aisle, and the other, just in front of it towards the left of the main door. Here, again, the usual circumambulation rite is maintained. Beginning on the left side of the porch verandah are presented the 'Wheel of Life' and the *Vessantara Jātaka*, the latter having the basic theme of alms-giving which is the first of the ten perfections of the Buddhist faith. Madanjeet Singh points out that because of its prime significance this *Jātaka* is repeated inside the hall on left side aisle wall and is frequently painted at Ajanta.[65] Burgess recorded sixty-one distinct scenes embellishing this cave, out of which quite a few are obliterated now.

Cave 19 has innovative Buddha figures painted over the walls foreshadowing perfection of those in caves 1 and 2. Snellgrove and others accept the compositional mastery in the 'Return to Kapilvastu' painted on the left wall.[66]

Cave 26 has very curious drawings on left and right aisle-walls (V.7. UNESCO *Archealogical Survey of India*, New Delhi) which at once connect Ajanta with the figures drawn in Ellora caves.

Cave 27 has some painted figures at the right end of the front aisle of its hall. The figures have names from *Śibi Jātaka*. There is a painted inscription here suggesting that the monk-painter Śākya Bhikṣu Masharsalia attained transcendental personage through painting images of Buddha.[67]

It is interesting to note further that the *Jātakas* related to elephants have been given first place on the left sides of the main entrance of the halls in caves 16 and 17. This symbolic conception becomes clear when one finds that *Avadānas*, related to Buddha's life, are treated on every starting point, as they are in cave 16 on the left end of the porch verandah, and on the left wall of the hall in cave 2. These *Avadānas* start with (bottom left) Māyā's dream having white elephant entering her body, alongwith the 'Nativity' scenes. On right side of the antechamber the back-aisle wall starts with scenes of 'Nativity' and Gautama's schooling in cave 16. Alternatively, these points would start with the scenes of 'conversion' like that of Nanda in cave 16 highlighting 'spiritual rebirth' against its worldly causal relevance in the so called 'Dying Princess' or 'the agony of Nanda's wife.' The Bodhisattva Avalokiteśvara (holding a flask in his hand) in the role of saviour of mankind, painted on the left of the shrine in cave 2 has the same connotations as are carried over on the left side in the verandah of cave 17 in Buddha's litany against eight great perils. The scenes of 'Votaries approaching the stūpa' on the left wall in cave 9 and 10 have the same point of view in the placement of scene. The placing of 'thousand Buddhas' on the left and right sides of the antechamber and on the shrine walls of cave 2 and again the repetition of it on the continuation of back-aisle on the right side do convey the miraculous effect of an endless emanation. This 'miracle of Śrāvasti' is also painted on the right side of the antechamber in cave 1 and on the left in cave 6. The position of the golden geese placed between the left wall and the adjoining pilaster on the back-aisle in *Haṃsa Jātaka* (cave 17) intensifies the image of a trap from which the birds are frantically struggling to escape.[68] This justifies the concept of appropriate placement of scenes.

Descriptive details are best documented in the portfolios of Yazdani. It is interesting to note that one of the earliest descriptive records looks upon the figures of Ajanta paintings as 'chiefs and chiefs' wives,' 'Chief ministers' sons, servants' along with 'European in colour and expression' and the 'red of lower tribes.'[69] Added to such comments are the records like 'the body in soft and rounded with little muscle' and 'the dress was almost always of the thinnest gauze' with ornaments throwing 'light on life in India between A.D. 300 to 800.' Besides, mention is made of the 'rooms with blue cushions and stuffed seats,' and 'ladies' beds like the modern coat,' in the houses or palaces 'conventionally drawn' of 'wood and two storeys height.'

Other records are like those of Rothenstein: 'so true is the psychological character of these paintings, so remarkable the delineation of human and animal forms, so profound the spiritual portrayal of Indian life, that they may till today serve in the absence of contemporaneous works of the kind, to represent the culture and character, rapidly changing though they now be, of the Indian people.'[70] Or, like Rene Grousset who takes only gestures of the hands to be sufficiently expressive—a point to which others have also alluded[71]—saying that 'this naturalistic art remains passionately mystical and is constantly lifted above itself by the most fervent *bhakti* (piety) as well as by the loftiest idealism.'[72] Hence, archaeologists, restorers, historians, critics, philosophers and artists—all have enriched the multisided documentations of these works.

Phases of the art of Ajanta (Chronology)

The dating of the Ajanta paintings has been sought to be established or refuted on the study of the rock surfaces and paint layers, stylistic and iconographic trends, ethnological and paleographical studies. Most of the paintings have been subjected to the various chronological changes except for those in cave 10 which are considered as the earliest.

The paintings of cave 2 show stylistic trends of late fourth or early fifth century.[73] But on the paleographical basis these have been assigned to the first half of the sixth century[74] which is rather confirmed by the style of the letters of the inscriptions.[75] Paintings of the 'Hārīti Shrine' also belong to early fifth century as C. Fabri has maintained comparing them with Garhwa relievo having inscription of *c.* A.D. 417.[76] Burgess puts them in the seventh century.[77] Madanjeet Singh points to the stylistic paradox in the fresco of 'Horses in a Procession' which exhibit 'elements from almost all the periods and styles of Ajanta paintings' and puts it into the transitional period.[78] Walter Spink also, on the basis of sculptural-iconography, ascribes it to that period.[79] It could even prove the eclecticism[80] of a master working in the first half of sixth century of the 'Baroque' and 'Mannerist'[81] periods of Ajanta.

Thus, it is evident that the chronology of Ajanta paintings has been attempted through varied methods. Out of the various disputes the most suitable period division, as generally accepted, is to base these paintings on a general programme of work taken up in different periods of political history,[82] although there still exist the overlappings, reverberations and stylistic interminglings. As Stella Kramrisch has aptly remarked: "the geographical term 'southern' and the chronological term medieval indicate continuity and adaptation of the pictorial tradition."[83] Art historians have also tried to divide the works according to the progressive accomplishment of religious expressions or 'inner content' in plastic terms. To the present researcher, however, an expression of wide open eye in the earliest works of cave 10 is in no way aesthetically inferior or 'archaic' to the half-closed eyes of cave 1. Considering the historical, cultural and more formal, meaning-oriented and personality expressing values, they are the outcomes of two different artists of the same capacity working on two different models.

The generally accepted chronologies are enumerated below:

(a) *Sātavāhana and the earlier period (c. second century* B.C.*-second century* A.D.*)*: There is no difference of opinion regarding caves 9 and 10 belonging to the Sātavāhana period of Ajanta. But since overlapping layers of paintings have been found in both of the *caityas*, there is the same controversy regarding at least two panels, i.e., 'Chadanta Jātaka' in cave 10 and the Animal-frieze above the left colonade of the nave in cave 9. Sivaramamurti adjudges the period of the first to be the second century B.C.[84] while Goetz puts it not later than first century A.D. on the basis of its maturity and presentation. On these grounds Nair (Krishna Chaitanya) shifts the time to fifth century A.D.[85] and Yazdani assigns it not earlier than third century A.D. Benjamin Rowland compares its plastic presentation to that of the panel on the west gate of Sanchi (first century A.D.),[86] hence he extends the tradition of the 'Chadanta Jātaka' panel. Sivaramamurti finds the motif of 'the fainting queen' of this Jātaka two centuries afterwards at Goli and three centuries later in the 'Dying Princess' of cave 16 in Vākāṭaka phase, which also proves the persistence of Sātavāhana traditions.[87] Jouveau-Dubreuil finds this Sātavāhana tradition at Bedsa cave (late second century A.D.), resembling the fourth period of Amaravati carvings.[88] Sivaramamurti also compares it to the 'maiden in the lotus pool,' *Dandan-uilik*. B. Rowland finds in this 'river goddess' the eastward extension of the provincial style of Indian painting at Bamyan.[89] As Jouveau-Dubreuil discovered terracottas of Sātavāhana art at Pondicherry,[90] the versatility of this phase becomes more evident. Ajit Ghosh with his detailed study has already established the affinities of Sātavāhana art with Bharhut.[91] Coomaraswamy had pointed out affinities of cave 10 with Sātavāhana traditions of the Sanchi and Bharhut carvers dating the *caitya* to 175 B.C. Continuity of the tradition of 'reading' the panel while circumambulating from left to right also echoes in the 'rotating' perspective found in Bharhut sculptures by Mario Bussagli who connects this to Gandhara as well.[92] To inscribe the pictorial representation is also a tradition of Bharhut where almost all the works are inscribed.

The second controversial panel the 'Animal frieze,' now quite obliterated, has significant value for the present study. This panel of cave 9 is important since it belongs to the intervening period of the art of Ajanta. Its analogy with Mathura and Gandhara motif (which Yazdani calls Krishna and cows) or with Syrian or those of Miran frescoes,[93] proves, in a way, Taranath's observation that after third century A.D. till fifth century, 'it seems as if the knowledge of art had vanished from among man.' Corresponding to the period of Sātavāhana is the Yakṣa (third century B.C.) and the Nāga style (early third century A.D.) as conceived by Taranath. D.N. Shukla places the first during Aśoka's time and the second during Nāgārjuna's.[94] Karl Khandalavala observes the competence to the artists of the caves 9 and 10 in simplified memory portraits.[95] This finds support in *Vinaya-āgama* and other contemporary works. The inscriptions referring to carved portraits are also found at the Nānāghāt caves of this period.[96] Karl Khandalavala doesn't agree with Taranath calling it a Buddhist style of Hīnayāna period, rather he labels it as the style of the period itself.[97] Mulk Raj Anand puts the period of caves 9 and 10 from *c.* 100 B.C. to A.D.100.

(b) *Gupta Period (c. fourth-sixth centuries A.D.)*: C. Sivaramamurti maintains that it is 'fantastic' to find Gupta influence on Ajanta works.[98] He is at one with D. Barrett[99] that guided by old traditions Gupta art flourished in the north and Vākāṭaka art in the south separately. To stress his point he has also worked out a chart of parallel figure-motif in Amaravati and Ajanta.[100] Scholars like Bussagli discover that Gupta figural arts' 'colonial' expansion was held in 'preference' even by 'south central regions.' R.N. Mishra also observes the influence of Kuṣāṇa-Mathura School on Amaravati through Kanheri etc.[101] (The influence of the art of Sanchi and Bharhut over the art of Amaravati is of course undisputed). To Karl Khandalavala also the theory of 'no Gupta influence' is not acceptable. He argues that the Gupta influence on Vākāṭaka was not confined to the main branch[102] (to which Prabhāvatī Guptā, the daughter of Chandragupta-II, and the queen-regent belonged). It extended also to Vatsagulma branch to which belonged King Hariṣeṇa whose minister Varāhadeva had got constructed the Buddhist *caitya* in cave 16 (vide CII, V, 103ff.) Spink's theory of all the Mahāyāna caves pertaining to the reign of Hariṣeṇa and his son[103] supports that of Sivaramamurti. However, there seems to be an anomaly in this stand. Sivaramamurti accepts Gupta influence over Bagh,[104] including its cave 4,[105] but since Snellgrove and others, alongwith Mulk Raj Anand[106], accept the Buddha figure at Bagh (cave 4) having kinship with that of cave 1 at Ajanta and not with its cave 19,[107] the argument of sticking to Vākāṭaka art only loses its force. Recent scholarship has accepted many provincial variations of Gupta art in which Deccan Gupta is regarded as having developed separately influenced by the fourth period of Amaravati and Ikṣvāku of Nāgārjunakoṇḍa and Goli.[108] It continued till the eighth century. In Ajanta it started with Mahāyāna group of caves. R.N. Misra looks upon the works in caves 26, 19, 16 and 1 as belonging to Deccan Gupta done during Vākāṭaka dynasty.[109] As for Krishna Chaitanya, he almost rejects the Gupta influence and supports the full-fledged Vākāṭaka art, the tradition of which had already matured at Ajanta itself before that.[110]

Thus, the influence of Gupta plastic tradition being in straits, its aesthetics and literary taste influencing the works of Ajanta is acceptable to all the art-historians.[111] Sivaramamurti[112] finds it percolating into the Buddha figures of Ajanta expressing compassion (*karuṇā*) and wisdom (*prajñā*).[113] Sarnath Buddhas' influence on the Buddha images on the facade of caves 9 and 10 is recognized by Snellgrove and others.[114] One finds *chef-d'oeuvre* of Ajanta artists 'Padmapāṇi' in kinship with the sculptures of Deogarh, Ahichhatra and Buddha heads of Ushkar and Akhnur as hinted by Hallade.[115]

(c) *Vākāṭaka period (c. fourth–sixth centuries A.D.)*: As is clear from the above, this period has been taken up in two different connotations: the first being Deccan Gupta during the regime of Vākāṭaka kings, the other, Vākāṭaka, embracing all the Mahāyāna caves within the creative activity of barely 35 years or so during the reign of Hariṣeṇa. The inscriptions confirm that caves 16, 20, 26 belong to the second. About cave 1, its period is usually related to Chalukya King Pulakeśin II (A.D. 610-42), receiving an embassy from the Sassanian King Khusrau-II (A.D. 596-626) of Persia. The inference is based on the identity of this scene painted inside the cave. The other source of dating this cave is related to its being inspired by the style of the Ghaṭotkaca cave group near Ajanta. As the said cave is placed in the last part of Hariṣeṇa's regime, it is presumed that this cave and cave 2 belong to his time or his son's (*c.* second quarter of sixth century A.D.). These dates become more plausible in the light of the inscription in cave 4, and the decoration of the main door which is similar to that of cave 1. But on the basis of development of style, the paintings of these caves are taken up even to the seventh century.[116] Karl Khandalavala thinks that the paintings in cave 16 and 17 were the base for the style in the first two caves of the same guild of artists with a generation gap of about twenty years.[117] Spink is of the opinion that the last decade of fifth century, being a period of haste and confusion, was period of decline in artistic vitality.[118] On the contrary, Karl Khandalavala considers the work of this period as the height of perfection of the Vākāṭaka art and for it he bestows credit to the royal guild workers.[119] Nair thinks that in the early period here 'accents were made more eloquent by a cultured urban mentality.'[120] The later period of Vākāṭaka art is generally accepted to have 'Manneristic' and 'Baroque' trends (of course, not in their full sense as in the history of Western art).

(d) *Later and survival period*: This phase starts with the decline of Vākāṭaka hold and the spread of Chalukyas' power in Deccan whence the Ajanta trend was taken over by Western Chalukyas at Badami. The trends of the seventh century, as apparent in the sketches found in cave 26, directly connect this art to that of Ellora. Before the later chronological phase of Ajanta is taken up, it is pertinent to look into a few facts. The first of these is that 'sculptures and paintings are the work of the same artists' and that 'in many cases, a story runs on from a painting and is taken up in the sculpture and painting.'[121] It conforms to the traditions in *Śilpa* and *Vāstu Śāstras.* This is verified by combination of the two in Hārīti Shrine (cave 2). The sketches in cave 26, which also has the masterpieces of sculptures like 'Assault and Temptation of Māra,' substantiate the aesthetic standing (of *śilpa* traditions) of the *sthavira* of this cave.

The point to derive is that there was a new emphasis on sculpture starting with this late *caitya* cave. By this time, sculptures had become the oeuvre of the *sthaviras* like Achala Muni,[122] for they had come to be regarded as important in being *Pūrṇa Citra*; withal, they served the purpose of decoration too—a fact confirmed by the *stūpa* proper becoming ornamental member of the wall. Thus, the art of Ajanta finds a channel of becoming later Brahmanical art of Ellora and Elephanta. The channel ran through Aurangabad and Jogeshwari caves embracing all the major motifs, as elaborated by W. Spink.[123] Ratan Parimoo, too, finds the Elephanta sculptor putting into high relief what had been gained by the painters of Ajanta.[124]

Coming to what Taranath had noted as Kashmir School of Buddhist Art,[125] we have already traced a thread of Gupta aesthetics working behind the faces of the 'Padmapāṇi', and Ushkar heads. Thence its delineation is traced to 'Irano-Buddhist' style in which Roman-Syrian and Irano-Sassanian art mingled with Gandhara and Gupta.[126] Since Hindu Kush area was directly and constantly in contact with Sassanids, Hallade presumes this as a channel for Indian influence in the seventh century at Piandzikent.[127] This accounts for the influence of post-Gupta sculpture found by Bussagli in the wooden caryatids of Pianjikent. He also finds types and figures in the murals there 'that can be traced back to the traditional Indian iconography.'[128] He quotes M.M. Diakonov who, in the Piandzikent school of the seventh century, finds 'one entire linking Byzantine or Transcaucasian art. Christian architecture is also represented in some scenes.'[129] Since we have touched Sogdiana, it is important to note a saturation point of Buddhist art—rather of Ajanta art of Bamiyan. In the first half of third century A.D., Mani[130]—the painter-founder of Manichaeanism—studied art possibly at Bamiyan,[131] a vital centre of art over the Silk Route. Bussagli calls this art 'Sassano-Gupta'—a term given by the French School of archaeologists.[132] Bazin accepts the affinities of the oldest Sassanian paintings at Bamiyan and of later Mongolian Persia with the wall paintings and manuscripts painted by

Uigur Turks and Manichaeans.[133] It was through Sogdian merchants that Manicheanism spread to Central Asia.[134] S.K. Saraswati accepts the vital role of the Manichaean element in the art of Central Asia.[135] Sogdiana art (especially its two-dimensional space, motifs and iconographic schemes)[136] alongwith the art of Turfan and Kuca 'left a deep impression on Ghaznavid art, on the Abbasid paintings of Samarra and on the Fatimid painting in the Palatine chapel of Palermo.'[137] Relationship between the arts of Palmyra and Gandhara in decorative motifs, ornamental designs and costumes has been established.[138] Sassano-Gupta art shaped certain stylistic trends of Irano-Buddhist art of the Hindu Kush region and the art of Serindia, Afghanistan and Tibet.[139] Bussagli finds these stylistic currents and their novelty of aesthetic principles in 'striking correspondences with Classical, Byzantine and medieval art of the west.'[140] Further, Niharranjan Ray points out that the Greek formal trends were incorporated in the Indian art during the Mauryan period owing to similar aesthetic attitude of the contemporary sculptors in feeling cubistic-throbbing in conventional forms.[141] This should be regarded as a very preceptive aspect of Indian art since subsequently in the 'forthcoming' movement or in the 'colour as form' at Ajanta,[142] this ultimately becomes acme of Indian tradition. It is further expressed as '*prāṇa*' or the 'breath' volume of chest and in the 'space-sculptures' of the caves. It is this 'Doric' assimilation which is discernible in the formal simplicity of Hīnayāna caves 9 and 10 at Ajanta (plate 559). It also helps to bring out the monumental simplicity of 'the Buddha with Begging-bowl' in cave 17 (plate 560). It is the same aesthetics which (in Mathura-Gupta or Sarnath-Gupta styles) shaped the Buddha of Sultanganj; it also echoes in the colossi of Buddha in 'Parinirvāṇa' at Ajanta (cave 26). This strain of aesthetics, which is Greco-Parthian as well as Gupta, has common lineage with the monumental art of Sopoćani. In *Citrasūtra* it is 'Ghan' technique. This '*Ghan*' plasticity, with open wide eyes, is found in Miran frescoes which reminds B. Rowland 'of grave portraits of Roman Egypt;'[143] besides, Malraux gives the clue to the present comparative study maintaining that 'the Fayum portrait ended in the icon, and the Palmyra bas-reliefs in figures of apostles.'[144] R.N. Misra calls it 'square' configuration of earlier Veṅgi style of Ajanta which later gave way to 'globular' grace.[145] This aesthetics of 'square' growing into 'the canon of immobility,' to which Bussagli refers as *sampadasthānaka* implying 'security and lack of outside stimuli,'[146] as an anti-classical taste of Kushans, was found in Mathura statues reflecting 'figural trends of Iranian-Central Asian type.'[147] Malraux asserts that 'the history of Buddhist art is primarily that of the conquest of immobility'[148] and Parimoo supports it.[149] This 'hieratic' arrangement of figures is called

'Parthian' by Aestovtzev but T. Rice insists on calling it 'Syrian style.'[150] Malraux calls it 'white barbarians' which tally with the figures on the geometric vases of the Greek art and its 'last traces in some Kouri draped in a curiously Romanesque manner.'[151] Both met in Tibet where the concentration of Mongols and Nestorians is worth-noticing.[152] Alongwith these, the survival of the Buddhist art of Ajanta in eleventh-thirteenth century, fresco cycles of Tabo[153] and those of Gyantse (fifteenth century A.D.)[154] confirms the channel of influences.

The second channel of the survival of Ajanta art is well delineated by Snellgrove and others. It reaches the east via Bagh (a fact supported by the types of letters used in the painted inscription in cave 27[155]) thence to Tibet and Mongolia. Pāla palm-leaf miniatures are a part of this migration which later turn into Tantric-Buddhist scrolls of Nepal and Tibet and blank sheet of Zen Masters, representing '*śūnya.*'[156]

However, in this channel there is a vein of Roman influence received in the 4th period of Amarāvati art which subsequently distilled into the Vākāṭaka art of Ajanta. Snellgrove and others strongly support this influence, Jouveau-Dubreuil also takes note of the 'Chubby Roman aspect of Buddha's face in Amaravati's first to third century A.D. style.'[157]

It is an accepted fact supported by the evidences of Roman trade and findings of Roman pottery, seals, coins and bronzes at the sites of Roman settlements.[158] Connecting the gift of Roman art as *lāvaṇya,* i.e., infusion of grace and artistic representation, we are able to comprehend more fully the 'courtly grace' and the 'grace of urban culture' being the height of perfection of Vākāṭaka's art in this phase of Ajanta art created by 'royal guilds.' Bussagli labels it as 'Dravido-Alexandrian synthesis.'[159] This *lāvaṇya* survives in the 'votaries' of Hārīti shrine and in 'the lady at the court of Saudasa' in Sutasoma Jātaka, cave 17 of Ajanta,[160] and in many other such graces which are equated with those of the 'Italian Renaissance.' In the north, it survives in Ushkar terracotta of the seventh and eighth centuries. To Bussagli they are 'reminiscent of the Gallic Hellenistic Roman types' of Kashmir school of Buddhist art,[161] which is also called 'Rococo' and Rommano-Buddhist style by Hallade.[162] The channel of this 'globular' style returned through the nomadic tribes of Central Asia. T. Rice mentions that Strzygowski was the first to point out the importance of this influence in the medieval art of the west.[163] Stella Kramrisch, quoting Strzygowski, stresses that this geometric art of curve and dot influenced the structure of Ellora and subsequent southern schools.[164] It is the same aesthetics of *varṇikabhaṅgam*—'the brushing'—which Malraux found in Gandhara terracottas having modelling as if cut with sharp-edged knife ('the incisive drawing and modelling assumed the function that the 'touch' was to have in modern painting'.)[165] The same 'touch' of modelling persisting since the terracottas of Harappa, becomes 'the decor of serenity'[166] at Angkorwat (twelfth century A.D.).

The channel of this classical 'Vakāṭaka grace' is traced in the south at Badami in the Western Chalukyan style (sixth century A.D.), and at Sigiria (Ceylon) in the wall paintings of A.D. 479-97. Basing his findings on the canonical *Śilpa-śāstra* principles of *Citralakṣaṇa*, A.K. Bhattacharya traces it till seventeenth century A.D. in the late medieval Kerala paintings. Starting from Tirunandikkara (ninth century A.D. strikingly similar to those of Qizil—fifth to seventh century A.D. and representing Sittanvasal tradition of sixth century A.D.), coming to the paintings of Mattachuri palace (sixteenth to eighteenth century A.D.) at Trichur, he traces it till late eighteenth century A.D. in Śrīpadmanābhasvāmī temple at Trivandrum, with 'ingenious combinations of classic grandeur and popular element'.[167] Kramrisch has traced these elements in the Mughal art in south. It may be added that the Buddhistic-tradition of assimilating heterodox influences with the intensity of producing a unified style was revived in Akbar's atelier.

On the western side, this classical trend is found on wooden cover boxes (*patlis*) of Jain miniatures carrying forward the tradition of decoration at Ajanta.[168] With the admixture of Ellora trend the miniature tradition of Western India and Gujarat is traced back to Ajanta. This tradition finds further metamorphosis into the Rajput and Pahari miniature paintings till its incorporation in the folk tradition. The finding of pictorial space as a void in 'colour volume' in Pahari miniatures by Geeta Kapur[169] and of mural tradition in 'popular Mughal Paintings' and Rajasthani miniature paintings by Dr. Parimoo[170] and J. Mittal,[171] are clear proofs to testify this mural tradition of Ajanta surviving till the present century. The Lamas in Himachal still paint Buddhist murals in the monasteries. It is the echo of the same arrangements of 'space-sculptures' of Ajanta caves arranged on base line—'horizon'—to give a transcendental sense, which is found in the 'solid sculptures' of *chatries* arranged on the roof-lines of Rajasthani architecture. In the miniatures of Ahar school (Udaipur) the formal simplicity for preserving the monumental tradition was kept alive (*Caurpañcāśikā*). This miniaturized tradition is continued till today as taken up by copyists almost all over India—at the tourist centres, especially the pilgrimage centres.

(e) *Revival period*: The dialectical spirit of Buddhism asserted itself in the revival of its art as well. First, it was brought to light by the West. It is clearly exemplified in Malraux's owning Buddhism,[172] in Philip Rawson's eulogy to Ajanta[173] and in Roberto S. Matta's feeling inner expansion through 'Tantra.'[174] Secondly, through post-impressionistic and formalistic approaches and through

Abstract-expressionism[175] and Tachīst's art, the Buddhist art got into the subconscious stream of modern art.

It should be recorded that Gauguin, having bought photographs of the reliefs of Borobudur Stupa from Exposition Universells 1889, painted 'Eve' in Paris (1890) which was based on one of the motifs in the said reliefs. M. Sullivan even notes motifs of figures taken from these photographs in several of his Tahiti works.[176] Gauguin's concepts were so Buddhist that on Van Gogh's death he wrote to E. Bernard '. . . another life, he will reap the reward for his good conduct in this world. . . .'[177] During his last years, he placed 'a Buddha' of baked clay in a dark corner of his hut.[178] Amrita Sher-Gil, not unlike Gauguin, expressed 'Sadness is my vocation' and found India in the 'sad-eyes' of the natives seen through formalistic-syntax of post-Impressionists (plate 95). Her studies in Paris gave her that 'art world' in which forms were being 'discovered' and through Cézanne and Gauguin she found the painter of Ajanta embodying Indian life. 'Ajanta seemed to her,' K.G. Subramanyan says, 'to hold in unison a succinct humanism and pictorial independence.'[179] It was an approach taken up by the Sātavāhana painter of the cave 10, by the painter of Bodhisattva Vajrapāṇi (cave 1) and by the painter of Bodhisattva in Bagh caves presumably recreating 'from among the aboriginal Bhil population of the forest.'[180] The genius of the painter of Ajanta in recreating 'live' surrounding is musingly substantiated by the comment of G. Kapur that 'a beautiful painting such as the Brahmacharis Amrita retracted from Ajanta.'[181]

It was a period which in its actual beginning centred in the south at Madras. Apart from Annie Besant's revival of India's spirituality, from here itself Lord Napier's advice (1871) to paint age-old themes and portraits 'with all the powers of European art'[182] got acceptance. It gave birth to the 'Company school' and bore fruits in the artists like Ravi Verma. He, like Ajanta painters, used the theatre for his compositions—a trend which Hussain used in borrowing from folk festivals of dance and drama.[183] These trends were assimilated in the contemporaneity of Hebbar, and in the artists like Piraji Sagara using the folk tradition of Gujarat. The other trend of opening schools of art and craft was also started from Madras on the impetus of Sir Charls Trevelyan (1850). From here E.B. Havell went to Calcutta school with his programme of reviving Indian painting through spiritual and 'transcendental' aesthetics. There the response came from Abanindranath Tagore, an eclectic painter deriving from many sources including Ajanta. His subtle modelling emphasized Ajantaesque grace in linear rhythms. Nandlal Bose, copying and studying Ajanta, revived the mural tradition.[184] Then, sprang the whole Bengal School movement—with constructivistic trends (recalling the 'cubism' of Ajanta) in Gaganendranath and Klee like search of 'soul of the

Universe' in Rabindranath Tagore. Withal, the whole group of Abanindranath's disciples started painting 'Ajantaesque' figures.[185] This group spread the trend in the form of 'affected linearism' in all the four corners of India. This tradition alongwith that of the Bagh artists in vivifying the form using 'Bhils' as models is continued till today by Goverdhan Joshi of Rajasthan. In Shailoz Mukherji, 'the power of European art' was his expressionistic handling of the canvas with village figures rendered in the linear punctuations. In the same vein, Almelkar combined folk paintings of Maharashtra, a subsequent development of later Southern Schools.

It is in the works of the artists like Ramkinkar Baij and Binod Bihari Mukherji that the tradition of *prāṇa* aesthetics was revived gaining the 'pulsating life' in the emerging forms.[186] The latter, being 'essentially a mural painter,'[187] painted the 'Medieval Hindu Saints'(plate 94) bringing forth the conception of Ajanta '*Bhikku*' into the 'monumental grandeur' of Sopoćani's apostles. In the works of R.V. Sakhalkar the vein of aesthetics of mystic-joy has emerged.

Scholasticism and Havell's 'transcendental' contact, as was apparent in the use of Tantric 'wheel of life' at Ajanta, were taken by the third generation of the artists. Probably in the tradition peculiarly suited to the Indian artist as 'diviner,' S.B. Palshikar started the revival of contemporary 'Tantric' art in a more 'smelling the earth' nostalgic forms. To this was given 'Picassism'[188] by G.R. Santosh, and J. Swaminathan made it nearer to the romantic mysticism in a more clear syntax of Pahari painters.[189] S.H. Raza carries over the colours having a 'resonance, reminiscent of Mewar Painting.'[190] K.G. Subramanyan inclined towards mural and contributing to the problems of art 'language,'[191] assimilated modern idiom from Persianism of Matisse together with Agnes Martin's (and Ajanta's) grid, and from the 'Company School' he imbibed the 'native soil.' This is the 'eclectic' tradition of Ajanta artist in the spirit of producing a 'unified style which is absolutely obvious, condensed sui generis and nothing else.' P. Rawson visualises this possibility in Indian art.[192] In figural tradition, inspired by *nṛtya*, S. Chavda adopted the 'fluent curvy lines' of dancers.[193] Ramchandran revives the monumental figure tradition of ancient murals, specifically from Mattanchery.[194] Myth making Indian psyche is found to be reasserting, as Ratan Parimoo finds in the works of the current generation, i.e., of Bikas Bhattacharjee, Ganesh Pyne, Ramanujan, Jeram Patel and Laxman Gaud.[195]

Art journals and periodicals right from *Rupam* (1919) to *Marg, Lalit Kala* and *Modern Review* etc., are justly accredited for playing a role in this revival by continuing the tradition of investigating Indian art.

Sopoćani

The phenomenon of 'Byzantine' has undergone a rapid conceptual change. In contrast to its nineteenth century view as an 'intrigue of priests' and 'perpetual patricides' (W.H. Lucky),[196] we have a poet's ecstatic vision of it as an 'artifice of eternity' (W.B. Yeats)[197]. Herbert Read's critical perception conceived it as 'the melting pot out of which the whole of modern art was to emerge.'[198] A structural analysis of Byzantine Art is highlighted in Kitzinger's scholarly study. Rice's account and appreciation of it are a landmark and an invaluable source material.

In the early eighteenth century Montesquien, and later, Gibbon wrote the history of Byzantine art in a general way. Writing on this art picked up momentum with Robert Curzon and a Russian, N.P. Kondakov (1891); the account of the Byzantine painter at work was given by Didron (1845).

An artist's appreciation of Byzantine works and inspiration from them are found in the creations of Ronault and Yugoslavs Mestrović and Milunović. Roger Fry, with his formalistic approach, found that 'it had great power in penetrating the inner recesses of thought.'[199] This opinion corresponds to the seventh century concept that in an icon 'The Holy Ghost which dwelt in the saint overshadow his image.'[200] It is surprising that, although icons were mentioned, medieval chronicles did not contain descriptions or explanations of mural paintings.[201]

Since the middle of this century study of Byzantine art has acquired the distinction of a separate discipline in universities and many foundations (like Dumberton Oaks), and research centres are now devoted to it. UNESCO published a special portfolio on Yugoslavian Medieval Fresco in 1956. Significant contribution has been made by erudite scholars like Demus, Graber, Millet, Michelis, Malraux, Radojčić, Toynbee, Chatzidakis and others.

Sopoćani was brought into focus in the middle of the nineteenth century when Gilferding, a Russian traveller and antiquarian, gave a brief account of it. Jovan Cvijić, a Yugoslav geographer, followed up with an account of these monuments. Truly serious enquiry with first-hand study began with a French scholar, Gabrial Millet, at the end of the nineteenth century.[202] These scientific investigations led to research in the history, architecture and painting of the monastery of Sopoćani, enriched by the scholarship of Vladimir Petković, Nikoloi Okunev, Svetozar Radojčić, Djurić and Deroko.

Since the exhibition of the facsimile copies held in Paris at the Palais Chaillot in 1950, numerous such exhibitions have been arranged throughout the world during the last two decades, including some in India.[203] Today any serious study of medieval Byzantine and European art is incomplete without giving 'a distinguished place to Sopoćani and especially to its XIIIth century frescoes.'[204] To Bazin these frescoes belong to 'the best school of fresco-painters'[205] found in Byzantine Art. Demus talks about their 'peak of cubic massiveness'[206] and considers them as 'most classical formulations hardly ever to be surpassed in grandeur and dignity.'[207] Rice eulogizing the 'Dormition' fresco in Sopoćani exclaims: 'one might say that here God has come down to earth, and that the paintings try to show that God was there to benefit the life of man.'[208] Mila Rajković, paying a glowing tribute to the 'Dormition', calls it 'a symphony of Beethoven on the dignity of sorrow.'[209] There are numerous studies, impressive publications and papers on the art of Sopoćani, the most comprehensive being the great monograph by Vojislav Djurić (1963).

Descriptive Survey of the Site and the Works of Art:

Built near the source of Raška river in District of Novi Pazar in Western Serbia, the monastery of Sopoćani was surrounded with well-planned monastery buildings and small paracletory chapels, all enclosed within walls.[210] Now, just a lone survivor of the battle with ravages and vagaries of time, it 'looks like an old, dilapidated and rather rusty boat... rolling on the green waves of the hills, anchored in port under the shelter of three mountains which the folk call 'Krisi, Juzac and Golac,'[211] which Djurić says, 'is one of its charms.'[212] The devastation of the monastery at the hands of Turks in 1689, coupled with long years of exposure to weather and human desecration, resulted in the effacement of the earliest paintings in the cupola and the upper zones along with the gold background. It also brought about damage to other masterpieces. Extensive restoration and conservation was done between 1925-29 and 1949-58. The existing frescoes, well illuminated by natural light, speak of the glory, however scarred it be.

Sopoćani was meant to be both a mausoleum and a cathedral. This conception finds expression in an architecture having features of both—open narthex and bell-tower, suggesting a cathedral, and the rest being 'severe and reminiscent of Ravena's Basilica.'[213] Considered an outstanding example of the Raška school of architecture, the exterior of Sopoćani presents extreme simplicity in a 'Romanesque style in its Serbian interpretation.'[214] Western influence is evident in the sculptural decoration of the two Romanesque portals of the Church.[215]

The same dual function is also apparent in the painted decoration inside this monument aptly termed 'the Sistine chapel of the Serbian middle ages.'[216] The 'Dormition' being the main theme[217] in the epic narrative form, as it used to be in Roman basilicas,[218] is accompanied by liturgical and signitive sarcophagi[219] type of portrayals of not only 'general Christian saints, but also national ones.'[220] And there are episcopal and illuminative narratives in the narthex, like in cathedrals, containing 'Tree of Jesses' and 'Oecumenical councils' etc.,[221] having 'left to right' order of narration.

The entire painting programme of Sopoćani has been well identified and presented in the monograph of Djurić,[222] which is as follows:

> *The Nave*: Base of cupola, pendentives: St. Matthew the Evangelist (South-East), the Patriarch Noah, St. Mark the Evangelist (South-West), unidentified Prophet, St. Luke the Evangelist (North-West), the Patriarch Seth, St. John the Evangelist (North-East), unidentified Prophet.
>
> Rim of dome: Inscription relating to the date of decoration of Church.
>
> Below: Prophets and Patriarchs on corresponding arches of central square.
>
> North-east and south-east pilasters: The Archangel Gabriel of the Annunciation, the Prophet Solomon, unidentified High Priest, St. Polycarp, the Prophet David, the Virgin of Annunciation (upper zone); the Patriarch Abraham, unidentified Patriarch, St. Babilas, St. Anthimus, two unidentified Patriarchs (middle zone); unidentified High Priest, St. Eleutherius, St. Spiridion, unidentified High Priest (lower zone).
>
> North-west and south-west pilasters: Six unidentified Martyrs (upper zone); five unidentified Martyrs and St. Menas (middle zone); unidentified Holy Warrior, St. Demetrius, unidentified Apostle, St. John the Evangelist, St. George, Christ Enthroned from the Presentation of the Donor (lower zone).
>
> Sanctuary: North Wall: The Entombment, the Holy Woman at the Tomb, the Appearance of Christ to the Apostles after the Resurrection, Archbishop, Arsenius I and Archbishop Sava II (from above downwards). Apse: Pentecost (head of apsidal arch); the Communion of the Apostles, the Adoration of the Sacrament (from above downwards). South Wall: The appearance of Christ to the Woman after the Resurrection, the Incredulity of Thomas, St. Sava of Serbia and St. Ignatius of Antioch (from above downwards).
>
> North transept: The Forty Martyrs of Sabaste (upper zone); The Apostle Thomas, unidentified Apostle, the Apostle John, St. Mark the Evangelist, St. Luke the Evangelist, unidentified Medical Saint (medallion); unidentified Apostle, Mandilion, the Apostle Peter (lower zone).
>
> South transept: The Holy Trinity—Abraham's Hospitality, the Baptism (upper zone); the Apostle Paul, St. Mathew the Evangelist, six unidentified Apostles, unidentified Medical saint (medallion); St. Panteleimon and unidentified Medical Saint (lower zone).

South Wall: The Presentation of Christ, Christ among the Doctors, John the Baptist and unidentified Stylite (central square, from above downwards); the Raising of Lazarus, the Crucifixion, the Presentation of the Donor; the Virgin, Simeon Nemanja, Stephen Provovenčani (the Monk Simeon) and King Uroš I (from above downwards).

West Wall: The Death of Virgin (Dormition) (upper zone); Prince Dragutin, Prince Milutin, unidentified Holy Warrior, Christ (head and shoulders), three unidentified Holy warriors (lower zone).

North Wall: The Entry into Jerusalem, the Descent into Limbo, four unidentified Warrior-Saints and Martyrs (from above downwards); the Nativity, the Transfiguration, unidentified Stylite and St. Stephen (central square from above downwards).

Narthex: East and South-Walls: Seven Oecumenical councils, the Council of Stephen Nemanja, the Last Supper, the Tree of Jesse (upper zone); Christ Enthroned, Christ (head and shoulders), the Virgin with Christ, King Uroš I with his son Dragutin, Queen Helena with her son Milutin, St. Macarius(?), Simeon Nemanja (head and shoulders), four Holy Monks (lower zone).

West and North Walls: The story of Joseph and the Last Judgment (upper zone); the Holy Hermits, St. Paul of the Thebaid, three Jewish youths (head and shoulders), Emperor Constantine and Empress Helena, the Death of Queen Anna Dandolo; St. Stephen (head and shoulders), and the Holy Monks (lower zone).

Prothesis: East, South and West Walls: The Annunciation, the Nativity of the Virgin, the Caressing of the Virgin, the First steps of the Virgin (upper zone); Archdeacon Stephen, the Virgin with Christ (head and shoulders), the Christ on Paten between two Angels, the Deacon Romanus, St. Florus, St. Sylvester (head and shoulders), St. Nicholas (head and shoulders), St. Stephen Novus, St. John the Divine (lower zone).

Diaconicon: East, West and North Walls: The Deesis with St. Nicholas, John the Baptist, St. Mandilion, St. John the Divine (with Ūrṇa) (east wall, from above downwards); the Consecration of St. Nicholas (west wall, above); the Birth of St. Nicholas (north wall, upper zone).

Chapel of St. Stephen: East, South and West Walls: Three scenes from the life of St. Stephen (upper zone); the Virgin with Christ 'Acheiropoietos,' unidentified Deacon, the Archangel Michael as 'Defender of the Holy Trinity,' St. Hermolaus (head and shoulders), St. Panteleimon, unidentified Martyr, Mandilion (lower zone).

Chapel of St. Simeon Nemanja: East and South walls: The departure of Simeon Nemanja to Mount Athos (?), the Arrival of Simeon Nemanja at

Mount Athos (upper zone); two Angels and the Virgin with Christ (head and shoulders) (middle zone); St. Nicholas, Christ on Paten between two Angels, St. Gregory the Theologian, four High Priests, unidentified Martyr (lower zone); lowest zone is decorative border with the motif based on Greek anthemion or rinceaux, in-between valances; the upper most has the decorative design with the motif of step-pyramid in diaper grid pattern.

North and West Walls: The Transfer of Nemanja's relics, the Death of Simeon Nemanja (upper zone); St. Tryphon, St. Mercurius (head and shoulders), St. Simeon Nemanja, St. Basil the Great, St. Demetrius, St. Panteleimon(?), St. George (lower zone), decorative design of rinceaux on the border (lower zone), and a border design in the middle.

Exo-narthex: North, East, South and West Walls: The Virgin with Christ among the Poor, the Healing of the Palsied Man, the Healing of the Blind Man, the Deesis (head and shoulder fragments), Daniel in the Lion's Den (damaged), unidentified Saint (medallion), Christ and the Woman of Samaria, St. Stephen, Simeon Nemanja (head and shoulders), Parable of the Rich Man and his Barns (upper zone); three unidentified Saints, Queen Helena as a nun, King Uroš I as a monk, St. Simeon Nemanja, the Virgin, the Last Supper, Christ, King Dušan, Prince Uroš, Queen Helena, three unidentified Martyrs, inscription (illegible), Archbishop Joanikije II (lower zone), with creeper, diamond and other borders framing the pictures, lowest zone has bordered rectangles (a few have circles inside) intermittently joined by pilasteral units.

Chapel of St. George: North and South Walls: The Beheading of St. George, the Scattering of St. George's Remains (upper zone); the Prophet Elisha, unidentified Prophet, the Prophet Zechariah, the Prophet David, the Prophet Solomon, the Prophet Moses, the Prophet Aaron, St. Demetrius, St. Procopius, St. Tryphon (belt of Medallions), Archdeacon Stephen, the Virgin with Christ, St. Gregory(?), St. Sabas of Jerusalem, St. Sava of Serbia, St. Arsenius of Serbia, Christ, John the Baptist, St. Nicholas (lower zone).

Chapel of St. Nicholas: South and North Walls: Nicholas becomes a priest, St. Nicholas becomes a bishop, St. Nicholas saves three dukes from the sword, St. Nicholas cuts down a tree with devils (upper zone); the Virgin presents a stole to St. Nicholas, St. Nicholas, Christ presents the Gospels to St. Nicholas, St. Gregory the Theologian. St. John Chrysostom, St. Basil the Great, St. Athanasius of Alexandria, St. John the Baptist, St. George (lower zone); wainscoting motifs on window.

PHASES OF THE ART OF SOPOĆANI (CHRONOLOGY)

In settling the chronology of the works, attempts were made to read their history through the study of the personages presented, inscriptions, the styles, specially in relation with those in Eastern Mediterranean, the technique, and the additions to the main building. Earlier attempts of studying the works led to the basic premises of the years of paintings being in between the inception of the fourteenth century and the fifteenth.[223]

(a) *Paintings completed between A.D. 1263–1268*: The Nave, Diaconicon, Prothesis, inner Narthex and the Chapels dedicated to St. Stephon (north), and St. Siemon Nemanja (south).

Since King Uroš I, the founder of the Monastery, ascended the throne in the year A.D. 1242, the construction of the oldest architectural work must have been completed between A.D. 1245 and 1260.[224] Thus it can be inferred that the painting work was taken up thereafter. The painting of Uroš' sons, Dragutin, and Milutin, and certain related chronological data led Petković and Okunev to base their dating of these works as having been executed between A.D. 1264 and 1265. Purković and Radojčić take the year of Queen Anna's death (A.D. 1256 or 1258) as the year of the painting of these works. Serbian Archbishop Sava II's representation in the sanctuary fresco gives Mandić a clue for the year of the painting being A.D. 1263, that being the year of The Archbishop's coming into office. Djurić has taken into consideration Mandić's clue as well as Dragutin's marriage as the deciding factor, to which he adds a period of about five years, between A.D. 1263 and 1268, which is substantiated by the evidence of the portraits of the ageing king and his son. Taking into account the fact that the technique of fresco painting demands a start from the top, the fact of Sava II's appearance on the lower zone automatically suggests that the paintings done on cupola[225] (now lost) belong to an earlier period.

King Uroš I's mother, Queen Anna Dandolo, died during the construction of the building and was buried under the fresco of the Last Judgment in the narthex—the so-called 'women's part of the Church.' Above the sarcophagus was painted the scene of her death.[226]

(b) *Painting done in exo-narthex during the reign of King Dušan C.A.D. 1331-46*: In accordance with the wishes of Uroš to give the mausoleum the character of a cathedral, exo-narthex with the tower was added during the time of King Dušan and Archbishop Joanikije II.[227] The time decided for the decoration of exo-narthex is dated between A.D. 1338 and 1346.[228]

(c) *Painting done c. sixth or seventh decade of the fourteenth century in the Paracletory chapels (side chapels of the nave), dedicated to St. Nicolas and St.*

George: Since the frescoes of these chapels were painted two or three decades after those of exo-narthex,[229] it is presumed that the painting in Sopoćani was completed during the time of Tsar Uroš (A.D. 1335–71). This chronology is supported by the existence of paintings done in a similar style at Salonika and a subtler form at places like Zaum and Šiševo.[230]

(d) *Painting between c. A.D. 1370–75*: The lower zone and the south-west part of the nave were repainted during this period. The artist of this work seems to have come from Hilandar.[231] In copying the earlier work of the nave he became the first follower of the monumental style of Sopoćani, and played an important part in extending the style to Gradac and Arilej.

Before the final catastrophy in A.D. 1689, it is recorded that in A.D. 1625, the front fountain of the monastery was restored bespeaking of the revival of good old days.[232]

(e) *Later survival of the style of Gradac and Arilej*: The unity of the whole complex of medieval art of Yugoslavia becomes apparent with a proper placing of its position as 'a specific stage in the history of Byzantine Art.'[233] This explains the phenomenon of plethora of related styles flourishing in the churches ranging in grandeur of a palace like that of Dečani, to those of humble wooden churches thickly strewn all over Yugoslavia.[234]

The art of Sopoćani finds a direct relation with the style of Gradac in a part of the frescoes of St. Peter at Ras, in Arilja,[235] and in the Church of Virgin at Šušica.[236] Djurić, in giving these descendants of the 'Court style' of Sopoćani, finds its other vein of 'Monastic' (archaic) style having an affinity with the Salonika area, specially the Monastery of Protaton on Mt. Athos which influenced the younger generation. In iconography and composition he finds Sopoćani's affinities with the Virgin of Peribleptos at Ohrid, works of Palaeologue renaissance.[237] One would be tempted to conjecture that this influenced young Michael and Eutychios, who were later responsible for decorating many of the Macedonian, Serbian and Greek Churches.[238]

Apart from the affinities drawn with 'Court' and 'Monastic' styles of Raška and Morava schools respectively,[239] it is pertinent to point out that the choice of the painter was imposed upon by the ruler or the archbishop.[240] The portrait of Archbishop Joanikije painted in the exo-narthex of Sopoćani, and the fact of his being instrumental in the decoration of the church of St. Demetrius in the Patriarchate of Peć indicates the possibility of a similar authorship (or workshop) of the works.[241] Djruić finds works of 'similar spirit' to that of exo-narthex, at Dečani, Treskavac, Ljuboten, the upper floor of the narthex of St. Sophia at Ohrid etc.[242] And, even within the church of St. Demetrius itself the traces of this influence lurk in the seventeenth century works of retouching and additions.[243]

A special branch of research to trace the influence of Byzantine art as a whole, and Yugoslavian in particular, on the art of the Renaissance has been taken up by experts. Speaking of Sopoćani, Demus opines that 'we have good reasons to assume that something like this art was transferred to Italy by Greek painters of the kind mentioned by Vasari' and finds in Cavallini 'the type of wise old man, a true father image,'[244] presented at Sopoćani. Rajković succinctly expresses the Yugoslavian opinion saying that 'insofar as one may speak of an element in Byzantine art which vividly suggests the Renaissance, in the spirit of Masaccio and Michaelangelo, the appearance of Sopoćani alone brings the recognition to life.'[245] The 'flux' in the creeper rhythms, achieved through the aesthetics of 'inner light' at Sopoćani is thus echoed in the Renaissance,[246] finding its perpetuation in the 'swelling' forms in Baroque. Creeper rhythm, 'swelling' forms and forthcoming find their adherents in Modern Yugoslavian sculptors, e.g., Kršinić's 'Contemplative Young ladies' (1959), Bakić's 'Blossom forms' (1958), Hadži-Boškov's 'Meditation' (1959), Bešlić's figurative-abstractions (1959), Ribnkar's 'Recumbent Nudes' (1959–60) and Jančić's 'Transformations' (1960).[247] Logically enough, this 'creeper' aesthetics culminating in Baroque's 'involvement aesthetics', reaches the contemporary Minimal-Art.

(f) *Revival phase*: The cultural interconnection between the religion of 'Mother of God' and the vision of the Serbian Nation initiated by St. Sava, reasserted itself with the nationalistic resurgence. The conscious kinship was adopted, as Zoran puts, with 'means that in earlier times spoke of large permanent things, of human existence in a tortured time that endlessly transforms itself.'[248] Thus, talking about Pregelj's 'the stiff ritual poses' recalling 'a living Byzantium'[249] the author asserts that all this 'continues to live in the consciousness of the descendants of Byzantium just as it is possible to find elements and reflections of ancient icons in the works of certain of the most modern artists.'[250]

The initiation of the 'spirit of spreading medieval monuments all over Yugoslavia' (like the biological growth of a creeper),[251] finds manifestation in Bogdanović's 'aesthetic sanctuaries.'[252] The search for finding symbols for 'basic human coordinates of existence' was taken up by the first generation of modern artists in a revivalist's spirit, e.g., in the great Ivan Mestrović's religious works. The second generation's 'cubistic' studies and aesthetic liking of Medieval works gave birth to the 'subjective realism' of Belgrade school.[253] The spirit of master John of Peć (St. Demetrus) seems to have been reborn in Čelebonović's 'process of subjective discovery' which approximates to the synoptic 'fragments of reality' of landscapes and seascapes in Milunović's works.[254] The latter's mosaics were as direct a descendant of northern religious art and formal discoveries of Mediterranean culture as are the surrealist works of Veličković.[255] Hegadušić's two divisions of the plane, parallel to those of Master John's 'horizontal sections,'[256] convey peasant philosophy showing a profound interest in human destiny.[257] The third generation, till late thirties, carried over the 'moral principles' of the second in 'intensely personal feeling for solitude' as manifested in the work of Gvozdenović[258] in a kind of 'hermetic emblems' (Haftsmann). The fourth generation of the late forties kept the spiritual values based on the perception of objective world, while the spirit of modern eclecticism paved way for the fifth.[259] In this post-war group Divjak's figures remind one of later icons of medieval school—the seventeenth century Peć and the eighteenth century Krušedol—showing 'the possibility of enriching their art with elements and significance of tradition.'[260] Vozarević and Tomašević were inspired by medieval frescoes, whereas Vujakliya's inspiration lay in peasant reliefs on tombstones. Protić started grappling with conflicts of 'luminosity' and 'illumination,' later replacing it by 'meditations on plastic elements.'[261] His learning from Milunović[262] also implied the relation with Medieval frescoes. These 'Decemberists' while admitting the tactonic flat surface, had 'spontaneity' of execution as the real verve of creation which took Ćelic ultimately to reduce the 'well developed national school of landscape painting' to synoptic signs as that of the John of Peć. 'Associative Lyricism' of abstract means, which created atmosphere in the interiors of churches and peasant dwellings, gave Murtić the 'hermetic emblems,' as Haftsmann terms them with reference to Kandinsky.[263] Aleska recognizes in Murtić the 'importance of tradition and the national element.'[264] 'Dense poetry' inspired 'March' group of Zagrab, as is evident in the works of Petlevaski,[265] who vivifies 'man's dialogues with his inner world.'[266] Ravenna art's exemplification of such dialogues in an 'archaic' language were revived by Prodanović[267] in his mosaics with images of archangels of St. Sophia (Ohrid) distilled into the Greeco-Turkish folk traditions.

The sixth group in 1958 started, as is evident in the works of 'Mediala' group, with conviction that 'in form they should attempt a synthesis of cultural heritage'[268] having 'a kind of esotericism nearer to the medieval than to the classical.' Vozarević, earlier inspired by Serbian medieval frescoes, now has affinity with icons, 'patina and sooty films, haunted by the idea of ageing of things and the transformation of life into darkness.'[269] This relationship with the past is the theme of textural surfaces and engraved lines of Bernik. Srbinović's mosaics have 'authentic Byzantine technical excellence'[270] plus what Dr. Amrozić calls 'life as a magic circuit,'[271] in his bizarre figures bearing striking resemblance to Central Asian experiments with 'innerlight' in the figure of Arhat from Qizil.[272]

In the mosaics of Karanović the same spirit is manifested in a Mediterranean form.[273]

The work of Berber, exhibited in the Triannale of India, (awarded Gold Medal in the fourth for his 'Chronicle of Sarajevo II'), using the traditional medium of wood-cut, 'almost reinvents the medium of a truly major form of art' with traditional iconography and 'distinct overtones of Byzantine monastic art.'[274]

The actual copying and making of facsimiles has become a specialised task and copies of Sopoćani's murals done by Perić, Zivković and Mandić, alongwith other works, were recently (1979) exhibited at New Delhi[275] and in other cities of India. The tradition of painting frescoes in medieval vein in the churches and monasteries continues till today carried on by monk painters like Nahum Andrić and painters like M. Arsich.[276]

REFERENCES

1. Walter M. Spink, 'Ajanta's Chronology: Politics and Patronage', in *Kalādarśana*, Joanna G. Williams, ed., 1981, p. 109.
2. Maurizio Taddei, *Monuments of Civilization India*, 1977, p. 131.
3. J. Bird, *Historical Research on the Origin and Principles of the Buddha and Jain Religions*, 1847, p. 131.
4. *Guide to Ajanta Frescoes*, 1927, p. 6.
5. J. Fergusson and Burgess, *The Cave Temples of India*, reprint , 1969, p. 281.
6. Ibid., p. 335.
7. A. Gosh, (ed.), *Ajanta Murals*, 1967, p. 4, note.
8. Ibid., p. 4.
9. *Guide to Ajanta Frescoes*, p. 16.
10. Ibid., p. 11.
11. R. Parimoo, 'Elephanta in the Context of Evolution and Significance of Saiva Sculpture,' in *Journal of the Oriental Institute*, Vol. XXVI, No. 1, Sept '76, p. 349 note 75.
12. A.K. Coomaraswamy, *Elements of Buddhist Iconography*, 1972, p. 78, note 76.
13. J. Fergusson and J. Burgess, op. cit., p. 7.
14. *Gazetteer of Bombay Presidency*, XII, 1880, p. 480.
15. Ibid., p. 481.
16. *The Indian Antiquary, A Journal of Oriental Research*, Vol. IV, 1875, p. 252.
17. It is because there is total darkness in the caves to be relieved by adaptation of corneal reflex. The progressive movement of the sun, too, sheds little light in almost all the caves.
18. 'Yugoslav Frescoes,' *The Hindustan Times*, Jan. 12, 1979, p. 16.
19. Madanjeet Singh, *The Cave Paintings of Ajanta*, 1965, p. 8.
20. 'Review of Research and Proposed New Areas of Research on the Pictorial Art of the Deccan and South India,' in *Proceedings of Workshop in History of Art, 1977*, ed., Ratan Parimoo, p. 167.

21. W.E. Solomon Gladstone, *Jottings at Ajanta*, 1923, p. 9.
22. Review of *Much Maligned Monsters: History of European Reaction to Indian Art*, by Niharranjan Ray, *The Hindustan Times Weekly*, Sunday, Sept. 24, 1978, p. iv.
23. Romila Thapar, *A History of India*, Part I, 1974, p. 61.
24. Ramesh Shanker Gupte and B.D. Mahajan, *Ajanta, Ellora and Aurangabad Caves*, 1962, p. 256.
Vasudev Vishnu Mirashi, (ed.,) *Corpus Inscriptionum Indicarum*, Vol. V, *Inscriptions of the Vākāṭakas*, pp. 109, 111, vs. 24, 25, 29.
25. *The Indian Antiquary*, Vol. II, 1873, p. 153.
26. Ibid., Vol. IV, 1875, p. 253.
27. Geeta Kapur, *Contemporary Indian Artists*, 1978, pp. 20, 143.
28. Ramesh Shanker Gupte and B.D. Mahajan, op. cit., p. 261.
29. *Gazetteer of Bombay Presidency*, XII, 1880, p. 491.
30. David L. Snellgrove, Gen. ed., *The Image of the Buddha*, 1978, p. 108.
31. J. Bird, op. cit., pp. 14, 15, 16. Moti Chandra too notes the 'golden hue,' in *Studies in Early Indian Painting*, 1970, p. 15.
32. D. Barrett and B. Gray, *Wall Paintings* (*Second to Sixth Century*), *Indian Paintings*, 1978, p. 22.
33. David L. Snellgrove, (Gen. ed.,) op. cit., p. 434.
34. W.E. Solomon Gladstone, *The Bombay Revival of Indian Art*, 1924, p. 46.
35. Ramesh Shanker Gupte and B.D. Mahajan, op. cit., pp. 256, 257.
Vasudev Vishnu Mirashi, (ed.,) op. cit., p. 111, vs. 23-32.
36. *Gazetteer of Bombay Presidency*, XII, 1880, p. 480.
37. Debala Mitra, *Ajanta*, 1974, p. 7.
38. 'Ajanta to Ellora,' *Prāchi-Jyoti*, Dec., 1967, Vol. V, Part 2, pp. 335-36.
39. Debala Mitra, op. cit., p. 7.
40. *Prāchi-Jyoti*, Dec., 1967, vol. V, Part 2, pp. 335-36.
41. C. Sivaramamurti, *The Art of India*, 1977, illus. on p. 547.
42. Ibid., p. 554.
43. Walter M. Spink, *Ajanta to Ellora*, pp. 332-36, (cf., ref. 38.)
44. Debala Mitra, op. cit., p. 8.
45. Walter Spink, op. cit., pp. 336, 337.
46. J. Fergusson and J. Burgess, op. cit., p. 283.
47. Walter Spink, op. cit., pp. 341-42.
48. S.K. Saraswati, 'Sectarian Approach to Indian Art How Far Valid,' *Proceedings of Workshop in History of Art*, p. 99.
49. David L. Snellgrove (Gen. ed.,) op. cit., p. 109.
50. D. Barrett and B. Gray, op. cit., p. 27.
51. Walter Spink, op. cit., pp. 336-37.
52. D. Barrett and B.Gray, op. cit., p. 24.
53. R.N. Mishra, *Bhārtiya Murtikalā*, 1978, pp. 63, 118.
54. Albert Grünwedel, *Buddhist Art in India*, (revised), 1972, p. 46.
55. *The Indian Antiquary*, Vol. XXII, 1893, p. 8.
56. A. Ghosh (ed.,), *Ajanta Murals*, 1969, p. 38.
57. Erich Newmann, *The Great Mother*, pp. 232-39.

58. C. Sivaramamurti, op. cit., p. 470.
59. Ibid., p. 468.
60. Walter Spink, op. cit., pp. 334-37.
61. Madanjeet Singh, op. cit., p. 56.
62. Ramesh Shanker Gupte and B.D. Mahajan, op. cit., p. 263.
63. Madanjeet Singh, op. cit., p. 179.
64. Ibid., p. 181.
65. Ibid., p. 185.
66. David L. Snellgrove (Gen. ed.,), op. cit., p. 109.
67. Ramesh Shanker Gupte and B.D. Mahajan, op. cit., p. 267.
68. Madanjeet Singh, op. cit, p. 186.
69. *Gazetteer of Bombay Presidency*, XII, 1880, pp. 485-95.
70. *Guide to Ajanta Frescoes*, 1927, p. 12.
71. David L. Snellgrove (Gen. ed.,), op. cit., p. 404.
72. S.N. Dasgupta, *Fundamentals of Indian Art*, 1960, p. 102.
73. Madanjeet Singh, op. cit., 1965, p. 179.
74. Debala Mitra, *Ajanta*, 1974, p. 27.
75. Ramesh Shanker Gupte and B.D. Mahajan, op. cit., p. 262.
76. Madanjeet Singh, op. cit., p. 176.
77. J. Fergusson and J. Burgess, op. cit., p. 335.
78. Madanjeet Singh, op. cit., p. 176.
79. 'Ajanta to Ellora', *Prāchi-Jyoti*, Dec., 1967, Vol. V, Part 2, pp. 336, 337.
80. Karl Khandalavala, *The Development of Style in Indian Painting*, 1974, p. 22.
81. Madanjeet Singh, op. cit., p. 22.
82. Ramesh Shanker Gupte has divided Ajanta excavations as those during Sātavāhanas between —225 B.C. to A.D. 225, Vākāṭakas—A.D. 250 to 450, Guptas—A.D. 320 to 500 and during Chalùkyas—A.D. 500 to 757: p. 46. According to Walter Spink some twenty-five of Mahāyāna caves were chiselled during Harisena's rule of about two decades starting in A.D. 465: 'Ajanta's Chronology Politics and Patronage,' *Kalādarśana*, (ed.,) Joanna G. Williams, 1981, p. 109.
83. Stella Kramrisch, *Survey of Painting in the Deccan*, 1937, p. 73.
84. C. Sivaramamurti, *South Indian Paintings*, 1968, p. 41.
85. Krishna Chaitanya, *The History of Indian Paintings, The Mural Tradition*, 1976, p. 35.
86. Benjamin Rowland, *The Art and Architecture of India*, 1970, p. 104.
87. C. Sivaramamurti, op. cit., 1968, pp. 41, 42.
88. As opposed to this, Snellgrove and others strongly refute the influence of the aesthetics of Mathura or Gandhara over the 4th pd. of Amarāvati and favour strong Roman influence, *The Image of the Buddha*, (Gen. ed.,), David L. Snellgrove, 1978, p. 78.
89. M. Bussagli, C. Sivaramamurti, *5000 Years of the Art of India*, p. 187.
90. Ibid., p. 113.
91. Krishna Chaitanya, op. cit., p. 34.
92. M. Bussagli, C. Sivaramamurti, op. cit., p. 91.
93. Madanjeet Singh, op. cit., p. 91.
94. D.N. Shukla, *Vāstu-śāstra*, Vol. II, 1967, p. 441.
95. Karl Khandalavala, op. cit., p. 25.

96. C. Sivaramamurti, op. cit., p. 39.
97. Karl Khandalavala, op. cit., p. 24.
98. C. Sivaramamurti, op. cit., p. 44.
99. "... rather later paintings at Bagh in Western Malwa, the only group of wall paintings of the classical period in North India, seems to represent a different tradition from those of Ajanta. Though there is a gap of three centuries between the Satavahana and Vakataka paintings it seems best to consider the latter as a continuation of the local northern Deccan style, which had completely assimilated such influences as may have been felt from Malwa by the fifth century": D. Barrett and B. Gray, *Wall Paintings (2nd to 6th Century), Indian Painting,* 1978, p. 31.
100. Ibid., p. 47, 48, Fig. 9.
101. R.N. Mishra, *Bhartiya Murtikalā,* p. 104.
102. Karl Khandalavala, op. cit., p. 28.
103. 'Ajanta to Ellora,' op. cit., p. 331, 332.
104. C. Sivaramamurti, *South Indian Paintings,* 1968, p. 44.
105. C. Sivaramamurti, *Indian Painting,* 1970, p. 30.
106. *Marg,* Vol. XXV, No. 4, Sept., 1972, p. 57.
107. *The Image of the Buddha,* 1978, op. cit., p. 109.
108. R. N. Misra, op. cit., pp. 126-36.
109. Ibid., p. 136.
110. Krishna Chaitanya, op. cit., p. 36.
111. Karl Khandalavala, op. cit., p. 33.
112. *Vessantara Jātaka,* Cave 17—'the painter could be graphic in his portrayal of a loving royal couple, the princess resting shyly almost in the lap of her lover (fig. 7) (plate 133), as Kālidāsa has described them in *Raghuvaṃsa* (vi.43). He could present the charm of a darting glance, or the neck, entwined by the arm (fig. 8 Simhala Avadāna), recalling the lines of *Meghdūta* (i, 3) ... 'C. Sivaramamurti, *South Indian Paintings,* 1968, p. 46.
113. C. Sivaramamurti, *The Art of India,* 1977, p. 67.
114. David L. Snellgrove (Gen. ed.,) op. cit., p. 109.
115. Madeleine Hallade, *The Gandhara Style and the Evolution of Buddhist Art,* 1968, pp. 212, 222.
116. Krishna Chaitanya, op. cit., p. 39.
117. Karl Khandalavala, op. cit., p. 38.
118. 'Ajanta to Ellora,' op. cit., p. 341, 342.
119. Karl Khandalavala, op. cit, p. 138; C. Sivaramamurti, *South Indian Paintings,* 1968, p. 44.
120. Krishna Chaitanya, op. cit., p. 36.
121. John Griffiths, in *Gazetteer of Bombay Presidency* XII, 1880, p. 497.
122. Ramesh Shanker Gupte and B.D. Mahajan, op. cit., p. 260.
123. 'Ajanta to Ellora,' op. cit, pp. 335, 345.
124. Ratan Parimoo, 'Elephanta in the Context of Evolution and Significance of Śaiva Sculptures,' in *Journal of the Oriental Institute,* No. 1, Sept., 1976, p. 296.
125. *Gazetteer of Bombay Presidency,* XII, 1880, p. 497.
126. Madeleine Hallade, op. cit., p. 153.
127. Ibid., p. 161.

128. M. Bussagli, C. Sivaramamurti, op. cit, p. 150-53.
129. M. Bussagli, op. cit., 1963, p. 45.
130. *Encyclopedia of World Art,* Vol. IX, 1964, p. 434.
131. M. Bussagli, op. cit., 1963, p. 36.
132. M. Bussagli, C. Sirvaramamurti, op. cit., p. 150.
133. G. Bazin, *A Concise History of Art,* Part II, 1964, p. 221.
134. M. Bussagli, op. cit., 1963, p. 43.
135. S.K. Saraswati, in discussions, *Proceedings of Workshop in History of Art,* 1977, p. 224.
136. M. Bussagli, op. cit., 1963, p. 51.
137. Ibid., p. 121. The ministers of Abbasid Calips known as Barmarks (Pramukha) 'were originally Buddhist and Heads (pramukha) of the Nava Vihara at Balkh' (Nicholson, R.A., *A Literary History of Arabs,* p. 259). Their temple later came to be known as the great Magian fire temple. Under them in 8th century A.D., Baghdad became the centre of Indian learning: D.P. Singhal, *India and World Civilization,* Vol. I, 1972, pp., 145, 395, Note.
138. Madaleine Hallade, op. cit., p. 33.
139. Ibid., p. 218.
140. M. Bussagli, op. cit., 1963, p. 74.
141. R.N. Misra, op. cit, 1978, p. 39.
142. Stella Kramrisch, op. cit., 1937, p. 25, 26.
143. Benjamin Rowland, op. cit., 1970, p. 187.
144. Andre Malraux, *The Metamorphosis of the Gods,* 1960, p. 140.
145. R.N. Misra, op. cit., 1978, p. 36.
146. M. Bussagli, C. Sivaramamurti, op. cit., 1963, p. 22.
147. Ibid., p. 85.
148. Andre Malraux, *The Voices of Silence,* 1956, p. 153.
149. Ratan Parimoo, op. cit., 1976, p. 289.
150. D.T. Rice, *The Appreciation of Byzantine Art,* 1972, p. 59.
151. André Malraux, op. cit., 1960, p. 44.
152. *Encyclopedia of World Art,* Vol. XIV, 1967, Col. 61.
153. David L. Snellgrove, op. cit., 1978, p. 131.
154. A. Ghosh (ed.,) op. cit., 1967, p. 38.
155. Ramesh Shanker Gupte and B.D. Mahajan, op. cit., p. 267.
156. David L. Snellgrove, op. cit., p. 438.
157. Madeleine Hallade, op. cit., p. 165.
158. David L. Snellgrove, op. cit., pp. 76-79. R.N. Misra, op. cit., p. 118. Everard M. Upjohn, Paul S. Wingert, Mahler Jane Gaston, *History of World Art,* 1958, p. 69. R. Sengupta, 'The Augustan Age in India,' *The Hindustan Times Weekly,* Sunday 18-11-1979, p. 1.
159. M. Bussagli and Sivaramamurti, op. cit., p. 23.
160. Madanjeet Singh, op. cit., pl. 71, p. 155.
161. M. Bussagli and Sivaramamurti, op. cit., p. 91.
162. Madeleine Hallade, op. cit., p. 151.
163. D.T. Rice, op. cit., 1972, p. 67.
164. Stella Kramrisch, op. cit., p. 93.
165. André Malraux, *The Metamorphosis of the Gods,* 1960, p. 161.
166. Ibid., p. 162.

167. A.K. Bhattacharya, *Citralakṣaṇa*, 1974, pp. 17-25.
168. Karl Khandalavala, op. cit., p. 56.
169. *Pictorial Space*, Catalogue, (Com.) Geeta Kapur, 1977, pp. 10, 11.
170. 'The Problem of the Popular Mughal Style: Some fresh Considerations in the context of Kankroli Paintings,' in *Proceedings of Workshop in History of Art*, R. Parimoo (ed.), 1977, p. 165
171. 'Review of Research and Proposed New Areas of Research on the Pictorial Art of the Deccan and South India,' ibid., p. 171.
172. 'The Greek soul and the Buddhist of that period were not without a common language, for though Asiatic, Buddhist is not oriental.' André Malraux, *The Voices of Silence*, 1956, p. 149.
173. Philip Rawson, an interview by S.A. Krishnan, *Lalit Kala Contemporary 26*, Sept., 1978, p. 9.
174. Ibid., p. 7.
175. Chairman Von Wiegand in 'The Oriental Tradition and Abstract Art' has stressed that 'Zen and various oriental aesthetics, no matter how poorly grasped, played a part in the postwar American consciousness.' Quoted by J. Burnham, *Beyond Modern Sculpture*, 1968, p. 102.
176. M. Sullivan, *The Meeting of Eastern and Western Art*, 1973, p. 235.
177. Georges Bondaille, *Gauguin*, 1964, p. 119.
178. Ibid., p. 265.
179. K.G. Subramanyan, *Moving Focus*, 1978, p. 115.
180. Mulk Raj Anand, *Marg*, Vol. XXV, No. 4, Sept. 1972, p. 57.
181. Geeta Kapur, *Contemporary Indian Artists*, 1978, p. 143.
182. W. G. Archer, *India and Modern Art*, 1959, p. 22.
183. Geeta Kapur, op. cit., p. 129.
184. Ratan Parimoo, *Studies in Modern Indian Art*, 1975, p. 20.
185. Geeta Kapur, op. cit., p. 38.
186. i.e., in use of sharp convergences by him (pl. 552a).
187. Ratan Parimoo, op. cit., p. 20.
188. Philip Rawson in his interview with S. R. Krishnan summed up the contemporary trend in India as 'eclecticism' primarily based 'on visions of Rajput Painting of the 18th century, modified by certain 'Picassism' ...'; *Lalit Kala Contemporary*, 26 Sept., 1978, p. 11.
189. *Pictorial Space*, op. cit., 1978, p. 8. Ratan Parimoo, op. cit., p. 29.
190. Ratan Parimoo, op. cit., p. 26.
191. Geeta Kapur, *Pictorial Space*, 1978, p. 8.
192. *Lalit Kala Contemporary*, 26, op. cit., p. 9.
193. Ratan Parimoo, op. cit., p. 24.
194. Ibid., p. 97.
195. Ibid., p. 100.
196. D.T. Rice, op. cit., p. 21.
197. Lionel Trilling, *The Experience of Literature*, 1967, p. 108.
198. P.A. Michelis, *An Aesthetic Approach to Byzantine Art*, 1964, p. viii.
199. D.T. Rice, op. cit., p. 41.
200. Ernst Kitzinger, *Byzantine Art in the Making*, 1977, p. 106.

201. Gojko Subotić, 'Values and Evaluations' (on the occasion of the seven-hundredth anniversary of Sopoćani painting), in *Umetnost*, Vol. I, 1965, p. 123.
202. Vojislav J. Djurić, *Sopoćani*, 1963, p. 114.
203. N. Komnenović, *Yugoslav Medieval Frescoes and Plaster Casts*, Catalogue, 1978, p. 3.
204. Vojislav J. Djurić, *Sopoćani*, 1963, p. 114.
205. Germain Bazin, *A Concise History of Art*, Vol. I, 1964, p. 138.
206. Otto Demus, *Byzantine Art and the West*, 1970, p. 195
207. Ibid., p. 218.
208. D.T. Rice, op. cit., p. 50.
209. Mila Rajković, *Sopoćani*, 1963, p. 6.
210. Vojislav J. Djurić, *Sopoćani*, 1963, p. 113.
211. Ibid., p. 114.
212. Ibid.
213. Mila Rajković, *Sopoćani*, 1963, p. 1.
214. Ibid., p. 1.
215. *Encyclopedia of World Art*, Vol. XIV, 1967, column 927.
216. Jara Ribnikar, *Yugoslavia: One Long Summer*, 1964, p. xvii.
217. As it could 'easily be made to do for the death of a saint or a member of a princely family'—Otto Demus, op. cit., p. 13.
218. Ernst Kitzinger, op. cit., p. 82.
219. Ibid, pp. 20, 23.
220. Basil, Bishop of Zicha, 'The Importance of the Celebration of the 750th Anniversary of the Autocephalous Serbian Orthodix Church,' *Serbian Orthodox Church: Its Past and Present,* Vol. III, No. 3, p. 9.
221. Vojislav J. Djurić., *Sopoćani*, p. 113.
— Dr. Sreten Patković, *Arilje*, 1965, P.v.
222. Vojislav J. Djurić, *Sopoćani*, 1963, pp. 122 to 141.
223. Ibid., p. 114.
224. Ibid., p. 112.
225. Ibid., p. 112
226. Ibid., p. 113.
227. Ibid., p. 114.
228. Ibid., p. 119.
229. Ibid., p. 119.
230. Ibid., p. 120.
231. As the figure of the Virgin painted by him closely resembles the style of Hilandar: Vojislav J. Djurić, op. cit., p. 119.
232. Ibid., p. 113.
233. Nanda Komnenović, *Yugoslav Medieval Frescoes and Plaster Casts*, 1978, p. 4.
234. 'St. Sava had many other churches built, small and large, whilst he was an archimandrite at Studenica monastery, and not only those made of stone, but also those made of wood in order that God should be glorified in every part of his state.' —Monk Theodosius, quoted by Dr. D. St. Pavlović in 'The Clergy as Builders, Artists and Founders of Wooden Churches in Serbia,' *Serbian Orthodox Church*, 1972, Vol. III, No. 3, 1972, p. 23.
235. Dr. Sreten Petković, *Arilje*, 1965, p. IX.

236. Vojislav J. Djurić, *Sopočani,* 1963, p. 117.
237. Ibid., 117
238. Dimitar Cornakov, *The Frescoes of the Church of St. Clement at Ochrid,* 1961, p. 4.
239. Radivoje Ljubinković has already drawn such divisions in epic power etc., of the paintings done by Sava I's painter and archaic elements of the paintings done with the initiative of Archbishop Arsenije: *The Church of Apostles in the Patriarchate of Peć,* 1964, pp. ix, x.
240. Konstantine the Philosopher confirms the fact of despot's taking a great deal of trouble in finding a suitable and 'of choice' artist to decorate Resava, —Vojislav J. Djurić, *Rasava,* 1963, p. iii.
241. Gojko Subotić, *The Church of Demetrius in the Patriarchate of Peć,* 1964 p. xi.
— not only the typical architectural settings but the symbolic-decorative motives over them is a point of special reference. The astonishing similarity of stance and oblongation between the maid pouring hot water in 'Nativity'—(nave central square, north wall, Sopoćani, plate X, V.J. Djurić, op. cit, and plate 22, G. Subtotić, op. cit., further emphasises the link of iconographic and other details between the two places.
242. Vojislav J. Djurić, *Sopoćani,* 1963, p. 119.
243. Gojko Subotić, op. cit., p. XVII.
244. Otto Demus, *Byzantine Art and the West,* 1970, pp. 218, 226.
245. Mila Rajković, *Sopoćani,* 1963, p. 2.
246. R. M. Frye: *Milton's Imagery and the Visual Arts,* 1978, p. 225. Fredrich Hartt, *History of Italian Renaissance,* 1969, pp. 445, 449.
247. Dr. Miodrag Kolarić, *Later-day Yugoslav Sculpture,* 1961, pls. 2, 3, 53, 91, 116-119, 120-21 and 133; i.e., for Ribinkar's 'recumbent nudes' Kolarić writes 'Her Arabasque is feverish, often abrupt, her development of form is full of vitality, gentle in movement, with clear surfaces.' p. 3.
248. Zoran Kržišnik, 'Yugoslavia', in *Art of Our Time,* (ed.,) Will Grohmann, 1966, p. 270.
249. Ibid, p. 270.
250. Ibid.
251. Germain Bazin, op. cit., Part 2, 1964, p. 431.
252. Zika Turinski, 'Sacral Creation of Bogdan Bogdanović,' - *Umetnost,* Januar, Februar, Mart 1965, p. 123.
253. Aleksa Čelebonović, *Modern Yugoslav Painting,* 1965, p. viii.
254. Ibid., p. viii.
255. Zoran Kržišnik, op. cit., p. 281.
256. Gojko Subotić, op. cit., p. viii.
257. Aleksa Čelebonović, op. cit., p. xxii.
258. Ibid, p. xix.
259. Ibid., p. xi.
260. Ibid., p. xii.
261. Zoran Kržišnik, op. cit., p. 288.
262. Aleksa Čelebonović, op. cit., p. xii.
263. Werner Haftsmann, *Painting in the Twentieth Century,* 1960, p. 371.
264. Aleksa Čelebonović, op. cit., p. xii.
265. Ibid., p. xii.

266. Werner Haftsmann, op. cit., p. 140.
267. Aleksa Čelebonović, op. cit., p. xiii.
268. Aleksa Čelebonović, op. cit., p. xiv.
269. Ibid, p. xxxiii.
270. Ibid., p. xxxvi.
271. Dr. Katarina Ambrozić, 'Mladen Srbinović,' *Umetnost*, 1 Januar, Februar, Mart, 1965, p. 124.
272. Benjamin Rowland, *The Art and Architecture of India*, 1970, Illus., 132.
273. Aleksa Čelebonović, op. cit., p. 192—'Study of head,'—plate 192.
274. Anand Das Gupta 'International Exhibitions; Thoughts and Counter Thoughts,' *Lalit Kala Contemporary*; No. 26, 1978, p. 42.
275. Nada Komnenović, *Yugoslav Medieval Frescoes and plaster casts*, 1979, catalogue.
276. *Serbian Orthodox Church*; Vol. III, No. 3, 1972, works printed on pp. 17, 48, 100; colour plates between p. 100 and 101.

CHAPTER II

FACTUAL CATEGORIES: Ajanta, Sopoćani, Comparative

Ajanta: Political Background

For the study in hand it is relevant to trace the political history from the time of Alexander's empire connecting the two ends of it, i.e., on the west, the region now called Yugoslavia and on the east, India. Alexander's successor, the Macedonian Seleukus Nikator, king of Syria, who had moved towards India in 305 B.C., had to cede to Chandragupta Maurya the territories then known as Asia, Arachosia and Paropanisoudal and a part of Gedrosia. Megasthenes, the permanent ambassador of Seleukus at Pāṭaliputra is believed to have brought artisans taking Hellenic art into the heart of India; and vice versa conveying Indian art forms to Syria, as there was a regular exchange of envoys and gifts.[1] Chandragupta's son, Bindusāra, extended Mauryan control to the south as far as Mysore. In the north he continued to maintain relationship with Antiochus-I. Bindusāra's son Aśoka too had very friendly relations with the Greek rulers, and he propagated his new ideology of peace and welfare of all beings in the Greek realms of Antiochus II, Theos of Syria, Ptolemy Philadelphus of Egypt, Antigonus Gonatus of Macedonia, Magas of Cyrene, and Alexander Epirus. Tradition has it that Aśoka had under him Kashmir and Khotan (Central Asia), he also married one of his daughters to a nobleman from Nepal. As his relations with the south as far as Ceylon were very close, his son went there as a Buddhist missionary. During his time Buddhism became an actively proselytizing religion.

The Maurya rulers after Aśoka, became weak and could not keep a strong hold over the far-flung Maurya empire, which began to break up, and became a prey to foreign invasion. Almost about the same time, far away in the west and north of India, the Selucid empire also began to break up. We have taken a brief note of these events as they have great bearing on the history of India for the next two centuries.

The governors of two of the provinces of the Selucid empire, namely Diodots of Bactria, the province in northern Afghanistan beyond the Hindu Kush now commonly called Balkh and known to Sanskrit writers as Vālthika, and Arsaces of Parthia (Khurasan and some adjoining territory), declared themselves independent in *c.* 250 B.C., during the rule of Antiochus II (266-46 B.C.); neither he nor his two successors did anything to recover these provinces. The next Selucidan emperor Antiochus III (223-187 B.C.) finding it difficult to assert his control, recognised their independence.

The Bactrian house of Diodots was displaced by Euthydemos whose son Demetrius invaded India in the second century B.C. and it were, probably his armies which overran Mathura, Mādhyamikā and Sāketa, and ultimately reached Kusumapura (modern Patna). As the Maurya King had proved too weak to defend his realm, he was deposed by his powerful commander-in-chief Puṣyamitra who founded his own dynasty known as the Śuṅgas in *c.* 184 B.C.

The Greek kings continued to rule over Bactria, but by *c.* 150 B.C. they were ousted from it partly by the Parthians and partly by another nomadic people, the Śakas, who forced the last of the Bactrian Greek rulers namely Heliocles to fall back on his dominions in the valley of the Kabul river and adjacent territory in India. After the loss of Bactria, the Greeks continued to rule in central and southern Afghanistan and in north-western India and gradually reached up to the river Rāvī. Amongst these Bactrian Greeks, the prominent names are those of Demetrius, Menander, Apollodotos and Antialkidas. Buddhist monk-philosopher Nagasena converted Menander (Milinda) and their dialogues, Milindapanha, written in Platonic style, are amongst the important Buddhistic documents.

Between 123–88 B.C., the Parthian emperor Mithrodatos II forced the Śakas out of their possessions in Bactria, and they moved towards the southern Indus valley. The Parthian viceroy of Arachosia, Gondophernes ousted the last Greek king Hermaeus even from the Kabul valley and ruled over the north-western Punjab including Taxila till the Parthian rule in India was supplanted by the Kuṣāṇa invaders under Kujūla Kadphises, in the first century after Christ. Around A.D. 25 Gondophernes was visited, as traditionally accepted, by St. Thomas. The other tradition believes that St. Thomas reached India through Malabar and died at Madras after establishing Orthodox Syrian Church.

Kujūla Kadphises or Kadphises I ruled between A.D. 15-65 over Gandhara, as well as the Kabul valley. He was succeeded by Wem Kadphises or Kadphise II who extended his kingdom further east in Punjab and who is noted for striking gold coins in imitation of the Roman *aureus*. He was succeeded by Kaniṣka, the most illustrious of the Kuṣāṇa kings and particularly famous for his patronage of art, literature and the Buddhist religion. Reigning from A.D. 375 to 414 he fought and defeated Śakas gaining access to trade with Mediterranean through western Indian ports.

Kaniṣka's rule ended in A.D. 101 or 102; the Kuṣāṇa empire continued to flourish up to A.D. 176, after which the process of its dismemberment commenced. In southern Punjab and adjacent Rajasthan, the warlike Yaudheyas wrested these parts from the successors of Vāsudeva I. In the Ganges valley, the Bhāraśiva Nāgas became independent and they claimed to have performed their consecration with the holy waters of the Ganges. Several small Nāga states arose at Mathura, Padmavati, Vidisha, and Ahichhatra. In Magadha, Chandragupta I laid the foundation of an independent kingdom in A.D. 318-19, which soon became a powerful empire under Chandragupta I's son and successor, Samudragupta, who was followed by his still more illustrious son Chandragupta II Vikramaditya who added not only more territory, but also great glory and prestige to the Gupta empire.

Taking the title of 'Vikramāditya' (Sun of Prowess), he became a great patron of arts and literature. In an alliance with Deccan, he married his daughter Prabhavati Gupta to Rudrasena II of the main branch of Vākāṭaka dynasty.

The Sātavāhanas, great patrons of art and literature since the time of Satakarni (after Mauryan disintegration *c.* 200 B.C.), were the rulers of Deccan and South. Lord of the west, Satakarnis ruled the region, now Maratha country, extending to its east and west. Nanaghat inscriptions suggest Yajnanagara (Junar) as their earlier capital which they changed to Pratisthana (Paithan) in the west and Dhanjakata in the east near the mouth of Krishna during the time of Gautamiputra Satakarni. Having regained the western regions from Śakas, he literally became 'the lord of the Deccan' (Daksiṇapatthapati). After his death the conflict again came up with the Sātavāhana's winning of the Upper Deccan and parts of Central India. Sātavāhanas were mentioned by Ptolemy and others. To Greeks the Sātavāhanas gave the name 'Yavana'— a significant derivation from Ionia. The great Buddhist teacher and the Madhyamika expositor and dialectician, Nāgārjuna, was a close friend of Gautamiputra. The Ikshvakus succeeded the Sātavāhanas in the Krishna valley—the eastern Vengi area—in the third century A.D. They were subsequently deposed by the Pallavas.

The Vākāṭakas are first mentioned in the Krishna valley inscriptions of the 4th period of Amaravati. They built their kingdom on the ruins of the Sātavāhanas in the first half of the third century, ruling for about three hundred years till around A.D. 510. The great ruler of this Vidarbha region was Pravarasena I.

Vākāṭaka genealogy is mentioned in the inscription of cave 16 of Ajanta. In it, the poet showers praises over Vindhyaśakti, the founder of the dynasty, saying that 'the dust thrown up by the hoofs of his horse would hide the sun himself.' Royal house of Vākāṭakas had been split up into two branches—the main for Gautamiputra, the eldest son of Pravarasena I and the other from Sarvesena and is named as Vatsagulma branch (Basim in Akola District). Pravarsena I, the real founder of Vākāṭaka glory was eulogized as *Dharma-Mahārāja* and *Hārītiputra.* He ruled for sixty years and brought Kosala, Kalinga and Andhra under his suzerainty. Gautamiputra was married to a daughter of Bhāraśiva dynasty of northern India. His son, Rudrasena, succeeded the throne in *c.* A.D. 331. His grandson was Rudrasena II to whom Chandragupta II married his daughter Prabhavati Gupta. She was a Viṣṇu devotee and became vice-regent of her two minor sons after she had lost her husband. To help her in her administration Chandragupta II sent reputed courtiers including the poet Kālidāsa who thus came to Nandivardhana, the capital, where he is supposed to have written his *Meghdūta.*[2] Later, her grandson Narendrasena (around A.D. 450) was married to a Rāṣṭrakūṭa princess. Prithvisena I was the last great king of the main branch of Vākāṭaka Dynasty (A.D. 300-490), which probably later merged with the Vatsagulma branch in the time of Hariṣeṇa (A.D. 475), the son of Devaṣeṇa.

In 'loveliness' Hariṣeṇa 'resembled Indra, Rama, Hara, Cupid and the moon. He was brave and spirited like a lion... He (conquered) Kuntala, Avanti, Kalinga, Kosala, Trikūṭa, Lāṭa, Āndhra...,'[3] thus reads the vital part of the rock inscription in cave 16 at Ajanta. This cave got excavated by Hariṣeṇa's minister Varāhadeva—an excellent administrator and a Buddhist (inscription of Gandhakuti—cave 19). Cave 19 and a few more were donated by Vākāṭaka feudatory of Risika—King Upendragupta. Along with the Vassal of Asmaka he dominated the area during the waning days of their overlords.

On the evidence of cave constructions, Walter M. Spink propounds that the whole group of Mahāyāna caves were dug during Hariṣeṇa's rule i.e., A.D. 460-*c.* 480.[4] The Vākāṭakas continued dominating in the Deccan but after the decline of the Guptas, their power also dwindled. The cultural channel was taken up by the builders of Badami (Vātāpī), the early Western Chalukyas (sixth-eighth century A.D.). Pulakeśin II was the greatest among them and his embassy was received by Khusro II, which is said to have been represented at Ajanta. The Chalukyas' contact with the Pallavas and their succession by the Rāṣṭrakūṭas brought about a beautiful synthesis of art in the Deccan and South India. A unique example of this is at Aihole where Buddhist *caitya* was turned into a structural temple (Durga temple, sixth century) like Western basilicas. In the later dynasties right from Pallavas to Pāṇḍyas (seventh-ninth century) and from Cholas to

Medieval Kerala (ninth to thirteenth century) the tradition was maintained and lasted beyond the Marathas (eighteenth-nineteenth century).

From eighth century onwards the Arab traders started settling on the coast of Malabar during the Chera dynasty. Earlier, Chalukyas had also given asylum to Zoroastrians of Persia who had fled Arab armies. They founded the Parsi community in India. Next important movement in the South is the advent of the *Bhakti* movement. In the sixth and seventh centuries Tamil devotionalism achieved the singular popularity of Śaivite and Vaiṣṇavite saints culminating in the conversion of Pallava king Mahendra Varman I (A.D. 600-630). The Buddhist concept of compassionate Bodhisattva together with the Paurāṇic, were to play a part there, although Tamil culture later rejected Buddhism. The highest example is that of Śaṅkarācārya, originally the disciple of a Buddhist teacher, turning a Vedāntist. R. Thapar is of the opinion that the Christians settled in Malabar, too, were an ingredient in it.[5] Perhaps, a political necessity again created a 'cultural compost,' covering the above three regions of India with religious currents flowing from every side.

Sopoćani: Political Background

The western end of Alexandrian Empire, Yugoslavia, had restarted a link with the east during medieval period. The earliest contact was established by Illyrians, people of Indo-European stock, (the race that gave to the world two great emperors—Diocletian and Constantine),[6] who settled in Yugoslavia during the beginning of the Bronze age. Yugoslavian contacts with Greeks and Etruscans are supported by fifth century B.C. pottery found on the Adriatic coast and helmet-like objects on the Glassinac Plateau. As the Greek colonies gradually started acquiring the status of Roman 'Municipia' by third century A.D., the road and river links across Yugoslavia gave it strategic importance. The Late Antique period saw the totalitarian government of Diocletian, a Dalmatian soldier, with royal residence at Split and court at Sirmium. Justinian, being of the Balkan peasant-stock must have played a special part in building valuable monuments in sixth century A.D. The progress of this cultural contact was interrupted by the Slavic occupation of Balkan area around A.D. 650. The same century saw the emergence of a Slovene state under Prince Samo, which marked the start of the formation of first Slav states. By the middle of eighth century A.D., Raška, became the political dominion of prince Viseslave, and Prince Tripmir formed the Croatian state. Prince Vladimir, in tenth century, made Zeta his political dominion. Chaslav's effort, the first of its kind to unite the Serbs, technically under Byzantine suzerainty, did not bear fruit owing to his death in A.D. 960.

The conflict of Eastern (Greek) and Western (Roman) Christianity gained political dimension by the end of the tenth century, as Serbia (the present-day area) and eastern Bosnia accepted the former and western Bosnia and Croatia the latter's Catholicism.

During the years between A.D. 1168 and 1196 the Grand Župan Stephen Nemanja founded the Nemanjid dynasty in Serbia proper (Raška). At an opportune juncture he united various clans, adopted Greek Orthodox faith, and after the decline of the Eastern Empire at the death of Manuel I Comnenus (A.D 1180), became independent of Constantinople. He conquered southern territories, and extirpated the Bogomil religious sect. Finally, after abdication, he retired to Hilandar, the monastery built by him and his son St. Sava at Mt. Athos, and died as a monk in A.D. 1200 and was canonized as St. Simeon the Myroblyte. His son, Stephen Nemanja-II, found the support of Bulgarians against his brother Vukan (who was backed by Hungarians) but meanwhile, with the mediation of St. Sava, Stephen was proclaimed as the First-Crowned in A.D. 1217 by the Papal Legate of Rome. And, for himself, St. Sava won the Arch-bishopric of the autocephalous Church of Serbia under mandate from Greek Patriarch of Nicaea to preclude Roman influence. Vladislav, the son of Stephen, ruled between A.D. 1234 and 1242. During his reign much of eastern Serbia was wrested by Bulgarians, political stability being established through his marriage to the daughter of the Tsar of Bulgaria.

King Uroš I, the founder of the monastery of Sopoćani with its church of the Holy Trinity, took up the reins from his brother King Vladislav in A.D. 1242. His ascent was in the turbulent times of Mongols on the west of Serbia and hostilities with Bulgarians in the east and Hungarians in the north. (By A.D. 1254, the Hungarians had established suzerainty over Bosnia and Hercgovina.) The situation was further aggravated by continued skirmishes with the people of Dubrovnik.[7] During his reign (A.D. 1242-76), Byzantium itself, already weakened by the onslaught of western crusades, was captured by Latins. It was, however, later revived as an empire by the Nicaean Greeks. By marrying Helen, a French lady of the House of Anjou[8] and 'heir of the Latin claims of Constantinople,'[9] and sharing political decisions with her, Uroš tried to consolidate his state by systematically tackling the conflicts. He was taken prisoner by Hungarians but by making an alliance with them, he established peace on the northern frontier. The marriage of his elder son Dragutin to Katelina, a Hungarian princess of the royal house, cemented the alliance. Being a clever statesman, he made peaceful settlements with Bulgarians, their warlike allies, the Kumans,[10] and with Byzantines in the south—where his attempted expedition ended in failure.

By the seventh decade of the thirteenth century, there evolved a strong clerical autocracy in Serbian states which controlled, to a larger extent, the more outstanding ruler. Rivalry of Eastern and Western Christianity persisted in West Balkan, and Bogamils, who had intruded into Bosnia during Stephen Nemanja's regime, continued tenaciously with heretical teachings.

Dragutin (A.D. 1276-1281), aided by Hungarians, seized the Serbian throne from his father but was ultimately defeated by Greeks and abdicated. His brother Milutin, taking advantage of the weakening Byzantine empire, extended the Serbian kingdom up to Macedonia, Adriatic Coast and towards Danube and Save in north. The Byzantine Emperor, Andronicus II Palaeologue, married his daughter to Milutin, presenting the conquered Byzantine territory of Serbia as her dowry. Stephen Dečanski, the illegitimate son of Milutin, annexed to the Serbian state most of Vardar valley. He was deposed by his son Tsar Stephen Dušan. He was the greatest of the Serbian rulers in the Middle ages. He was, proclaimed 'Emperor of the Serbs, Greeks, Bulgars and Albanians' on setting up his capital at Skoplje in A.D. 1364. He set up the Serbian Patriarchate at Peć for which he was anathematized by the Greek patriarch who recognized the Patriarchate only in A.D. 1375. In A.D. 1353, on defeating Louis of Hungary, Dušan acquired Belgrade. En route to Constantinople to conquer the Throne-Imperial, he died at the age of 46 in A.D. 1358. Specially during his reign, the landed nobility thrived on newly acquired conquests, estates and titles. Growing more powerful during his son Stephen Uroš V's rule, this nobility made its territories independent. A confederation of Serbian lords was defeated by the Turks in the battle of Marica in A.D. 1371. As vassal of the Turks, Marko, son of Vukasin, representing the remaining Serbian lords, held the title of King after the death of Uroš V.

Under the pressure of the Turks, the last independent Serbian state was pushed northward into the valley of the three Morava rivers.

The year A.D. 1371 saw the rise of Lazar I of the Herbelyanovich family as prince of Serbia. By then Zeta (Montenegro) had become independent. Tvrtko I, Lord of Bosnia, proclaimed himself king of Serbia and Bosnia, and was crowned by the monks of Mileśeva.

In A.D. 1389 (June 15) the Battle of Kosovo was won by the Turks making Serbia a vassal state recognizing Stephen Lazarević, son of Lazar I, as despot of Serbia. With the support of his nephew George Brankovich he tried to hold his own against the Turks; but finally, in A.D. 1439, the Turks conquered the country and by A.D. 1459 it was incorporated in the Turkish Empire, retaining, of course, Christian religion and way of life. The Eastern and central regions remained orthodox, whereas the Western part remained more or less Catholicized retaining 'Byzantine culture.'

Comparative

The political history right from the conquests of Alexander up to the fifteenth century obviously becomes the preface to the present comparative study since this incorporates 'his great dream of the marriage of Europe and Asia.'[11] It compasses the close exchange between the two areas of which Yugoslavia and India form two significant ends. The 'commonwealth' vision of Alexander found a universal dimension in the *Republic* written by Zeno, the Stoic.[12] The 'city-states' expanded into the dreams of 'Cakravartin' of Mauryas, into Harișeṇa's 'conquering Kuntala, Avanti, Kaliṅga, Kośala, Trikūṭa, Lāṭa, Āndhra...,' and after about a thousand years, into Serbian Tsar Stephen Dušan's proclamation—'Emperor of the Serbs, Greeks, Bulgers and Albanians.'

The political marriages, too, had a precedence in Alexander marrying the daughter of Darius. This was followed by matrimonial alliance like those of the Macedonian princess' with Chandragupta, Chandragupta II's daughter with the Vākāṭaka king; and in Yugoslavia king Dragutin's with Katelina, a Hungarian princess. All these marriages contributed to the exchange and synthesis of art and ideas.

To build cultural-sanctuaries during the turbulent, war engaging times, too, was one of Alexander's traits.[13] It became the passion of the Mauryans and culminated into 'Jaustinian' enthusiasm of Upendragupta ('in donation and creation of stūpas and vihāras,' inscription cave 19, Ajanta)[14] and in St. Sava's 'will', concretized by his brother's dynasty, to get churches built 'that God should be glorified in every part of his State.'[15] This 'King's divine will,'[16] had potency, means, religiosity by public sanction, and the sanctity of not becoming self-commendatory.[17] Getting this 'potential missionary spirit' with a universal vision or Oikoumene required something more than the science of politics imparted to Alexander by his tutor Aristotle.[18] Alexander required the concept of the 'Cakravartin,' the universal ruler, which Benjamin Rowland treats as the ancient Babylonian[19] and also Vedic nearing a temporal complement to the spiritual idea of the Buddha.[20] This concept stretched to ethereality becomes the *Buddhahood* and remaining temporal it is *Dharma Mahārāja*, 'Vice Regent of God,' or 'Sacred King'—what Fisher thinks in Alexander assuming 'the state of an oriental monarch.'[21] This concept within the 'Exemplary Wisdom'[22] made the Gupta and Vākāṭaka kings give full support to Buddhism, which since the time of Aśoka and Kaniṣka was still the prestige of the ruling class, although following Brahmanic orthodoxy both practised traditional sacrifice of horse, the *aśvamedha*. On the other hand, the 'Emissary Wisdom' of Christianity brought the concept of Holy-state looking after the spiritual and physical welfare of the people. Thus the 'Sacred Kings' or 'Vice-regents' of Nemanjid dynasty had entirely a different attitude from that of Sātavāhanas and Vākāṭakas. For the Nemanjans the national and religious interests were one whereas the Guptas and Vākāṭakas had the different end, namely that of the overwhelming prestige.

The revival of Hellenic culture gave to the Nemanjans the aroma of becoming 'oriental monarch.' There is the parallel between the Nemanjan King's kiths and Aśoka's son being religious missionaries. The courtly intrigues including 'royal eye gouging' (e.g., Mauryan's in Kunal and Byzantines' in Constantine VI),[23] substantiate this aroma.

Mauryan King's treaties and exchange of missions with the Syrian and Macedonian kings in the early part of third century B.C. were maintained during the most fermenting period, Justinian era of Byzantine art. The Berberini ivory of late fifth century A.D. (e.g., of Anastasius) shows the embassy from India. Ajanta also has foreign embassies painted in cave 2. During the Nemanjid dynasty the 'broad-mindedness' of Serbian Orthodox Church is exemplified by St. Sava's meeting with the Sultan of Egypt. These monarchs and kings also had the tradition of sending emissaries in order to bring back alien expressive art motifs.

Ajanta: Social and Cultural Background

The Buddhist idea of contemplation before a mirror or before still water, both reflecting all things perfectly,[24] became the leitmotif of Ajanta giving what Mulk Raj Anand noticed, viz: 'the early Ajanta masters had painted the illusion of life to develop the powers of the spirit by the confrontation with truth in the earthly phase of life.'[25]

It is one of the great characteristics of the Ajanta artist to have looked around him to find propositions for his painterly syntax. In this connection, Bird rightly observes: 'In the remains of these paintings we see women, with dark complexion, and features similar to those now observable among the natives of the south India.'[26] One needs only to look into the Ajanta works in order to relate them to factuals found out by other investigations.

Madanjeet Singh points out that 'the dancers in the Hīnayāna frieze, 'the Rājā with his Retinue' (cave 10) (plate 121) and what is possibly the latest Mahāyāna painting, 'the Dancing Girl with Musician,' (cave 1) (figure p. 57) reflect a true standard of the state of society of their time.[27] The cultural gap inherent therein would be felt somewhat more or less like the contrast between the archaic-smile of Greek art and the smile of French Gothic. The former expresses the *joie de vivre*; Madanjeet Singh finds this 'uninhibited joy'[28] resounding in whole of the painting, from gestures and stances to the placement and grouping of figures. The Hīnayāna *zeitgeist* is also expressed in the dressing and ornaments. With regard to the later panel of cave 1, which expresses Mahāyāna spirit, Hallade observes as having obviously a native dancer, 'combining abundant ornament and the taste for pearl necklaces typical of the period with a long-sleeved fitted tunic.'[29] In cave 10, the 'hieratic' figures are painted with open eyes as if encountering Gautama the Buddha, although not represented. They are like those whose 'eyes are wet, and whose behaviour filial'[30] as the inscription of cave 17 in gist says (Vs. 17. 18)[31] but it could have also applied to Satakarni painted in the said cave. One has only to look at these 'portraits'[32] closely, comparing them with Amrita Sher-Gil's in order to apprehend the reticently used supple brushing yielding width and monumentality of form—something quite comparable to queen Hatshepsut's classicism in Egyptian art. On the contrary, the dancer of Hariṣeṇa period becomes a rhythm of courtly poetry suggested through the stare transfixed in Tantra and a ritual lurking behind the dance.

Along with these earliest caves of Ajanta, the other artistic monuments of Sātavāhanas like Bhaja, Bedsa, stūpa of Sanchi and rails of Amaravati testify to their equal zest for all arts. One of their kings, Hāla, compiled poetry in Prakrit. His *Gāthāsaptaśati* was emulated in Sanskrit by Govardhana and in Hindi by Bihari in his *Satsai.* Bāṇa praised it as an immortal classic.[33] Chaitanya Krishna calls this work 'sophisticated' in preference to 'archaic,' the influence of which distilled down to Rajput miniatures. To him these lyrics appear 'exquisitely pastoral' comparing with the Sicilian songs of Theocritus. Gaṇāḍhya was a contemporary of one of these kings; his *Bṛhatakathā* appealed to masses giving their imagination 'freedom to roam and soar' and reflecting 'wish-fulfilment in fantasy.'[34]

The configurations of the two panels of votaries approaching stūpas in caves 9 and 10 conform to the 'majesty,' and 'lotus-like feet' (inscription in cave 16)—a reverence paid to the hierarchy. Importance of rituals is also signified by these panels painted during the Sātavāhana times. Their sacrificial rites are confirmed by the inscription of queen Nayanika in Nanaghat caves. The grove enhancing 'the feeling of freedom'[35] was actually a reality of administrative system of Sātavāhanas where the power, instead of being concentrated at the centre, was distributed throughout the hierarchy of officials consisting of a minister (*amātya*) and the chief military officer (*mahāsenāpati*). They were allowed even to mint their coins.[36] *Avadāna Śataka* speaks of 'rule of gaṇas' in the north as it was conveyed to the southern king by a group of merchants.[37] This ultimately brings us to the school of thought supported by Rhys Davids and boldly accepted by Jayaswal that the Buddha consciously took the model of *gaṇas* or *saṁghas* for his own monastic order.[38] In conformity with canons laid down in *Aggannsutta* regarding the Buddhist theory of the origin of state and democratic government, the Buddhist republics were based on democratic tradition of *saṁghas* right from sixth century B.C. The title of *Dharma-Mahārāja* of Vākāṭaka kings is in line with this thinking. Marriage within the royal family was encouraged to ensure loyalty. The village became the smaller administrative unit as was the case in the north. The matrimonial alliances were entered into for political strategy, as is confirmed by the marriage of a Śaka king's daughter to one of the Sātavāhana kings, although the latter were strict adherents of *varṇas*.[39]

The fact of presenting *Jātakas* with stories mostly centring at Banaras (e.g., *Syama* and *Chadanta Jātaka*) is evidence of the connection with the north especially with the places associated with the Buddha's life. Another noteworthy point was that Ajanta was near to an old trade route connecting the capital (*Pratiṣṭhāna*) with the north through Ujjain and to the south-eastern coast. This was a part of the grid of trade routes connecting the whole of India with Central and Western Asia, following the highway (Taxila to Pāṭaliputra which is today's Grand Trunk Road) and the river valleys. Coastal shipping, being cheap, was common and the merchants, being aware of trade-winds, intensified trade with Red Sea ports. Indian traders took advantage of the Roman luxury trade with China and South-East Asia. There were trading posts of merchants coming from Western Asia and the Mediterranean. These merchants were called *Yavanas* in the Sātavāhana kingdom and in the south.[40] Most of the urban centres of the south were ports such as Kāverīppattinam. The impact of Roman trade was more evident in the south, whereas in the north it was Romano-Hellenic. Barygaza (Broach) became the most active port. Since Rome was in conflict with Parthia during this period, the Silk Route goods were directed through this route. It is also an accepted fact that girls were brought by Greeks for the harems of Indian kings. Excavations since 1945 at Arikamedu near Pondicherry, Pumpuhar, and subsequently at Brahmagiri and Chandravalli on the coast to the north of Arikamedu have yielded Roman antiquities. The list has gone up with the names of Kolhapur, Nasik, Nevasa (Gujarat), Ujjain, and Bhilsa (Madhya Pradesh), Śiśupālgarh (Orissa) and Kondapur (Andhra Pradesh), proving trade since Augustus when Rome was having Indian goldsmiths and India their gem-cutters and muslin dyers. Augustus received Indian embassies in 21 and 25 B.C.

The opening was made by the Mauryan Empire in building roads and unified administrative system which ensured protection to traders and mercantile community. Romila Thapar categorizes the period from 200 B.C. to A.D. 300 as a period when this community gave impetus to urban life. Being in competition with this section, the guilds, existing since the Mauryans, were left with hardly any option but to secure protection, organize production and shape public opinion in securing high caste position. It may be borne in mind that the artisans were mostly from the 'shudras.' They became very important and their riches are reflected in their donations, e.g., the Sanchi gate was donated by the ivory carvers of Vidisha. The guilds started having a greater say in community life on account of their hereditary crafts and by becoming centres of technical education.[41] The kings started having financial interests in the guilds, as the Nasik cave inscription suggests, but the guilds themselves never showed political interest. The school of thought led by Oldenberg believes that the high caste, high ranks and merchants were the protectors of the Buddhist church. This view, though partial, does have its support in merchants (Tapussa and Bhallika) being among the first converts and by the motif of Kubera, usually placed on the facade of *caityas* having a pouch of money from which the coins spread and decorate the *caitya*-windows (cave 19 Ajanta). It was a popular decorative detail derived from the *Āgama* story of the gift of Jetavana park which was covered with gold coins by the merchant Anāthapiṇḍika who had purchased it for the Buddha's resort.

It was the time of emergence of Tamil culture with nucleus around the present-day Madras. This culture arose out of the confederacy of 'three crowned kings,' Chola, Pāṇdyas and Cheras, although they were continually at war with each other. Through the Sātavāhanas' intermediacy South India had already been absorbed in the total commercial development of India. Theoretical knowledge was imparted by the Brahmans. The Buddhist monastic colleges and universities were open to all and attracted foreign pupils also which served as a successful channel for popularising Buddhism. The monks and nuns had more rigorous training for ascetic Buddhism. The Buddhist drama of Aśvaghoṣa was influenced by Bharata's *Nāṭya-śāstra*, a treatise on dramaturgy. The Buddhist doctrines were also revised. It is believed that the Mahāyāna doctrine originated in Andhra around first century B.C. Nāgārjuna, a close friend of the Sātavāhanas, was the great expounder of the doctrine. It was also the time when Christianity came to India through St. Thomas.

Coming back to 'the Dancer' in *Mahājanaka Jātaka*, cave 1, we find here a picture of the royal courts and of the poetry of the great Kālidāsa. The exotic became a part of the pageantry as is also depicted in various panels containing people from far-off lands. It was not only that the lapis-lazuli was added to the lotus in the hand of 'Sidhārtha' or 'Padmapāṇi' (plate 157), it was a time when 'Hārīti' was made benefactory goddess and was established inside the *caitya*-cum-*vihāra*, turning these caves into 'temples of graces.' Matriarchal system prevailed in Kerala and among tribal people. Women maintained modesty but participated in political and intellectual life. Prabhavati Gupta's example, however, proves also their dependency—one may note the help given by

Chandragupta II during her widowhood. *Devadāsīs* of temples and courtesans were specially trained and brought up. Marriages for political adjustments as those among the Sātavāhanas, and inter-caste marriages alongwith other types were in vogue. By the fifth century A.D., mother-worship-rites of the cults of primitive societies and village agricultural communities were becoming magic-rites of Tantricism and Mother goddesses.[42]

Kālidāsa praises the life of a householder (*Raghuvanśa* V, 10) which confirms the belief in four *varṇas* and *āśramas* (stages of life). In the patriarchal social framework, man lead the life starting from *Brahmacarya* (celibacy) to *Sannyāsa* (reclusion). Hence *Manusmṛti*'s definite influence is seen on the social structure, although during Gupta time caste-system had not achieved that rigidity. Following different pursuits people enjoyed flourishing economy—the result of colonisation in South-Eastern Asia and the Pacific Ocean, foreign trade, efficient administrative system, evolution of land survey and taxation policies, well-knit organizations of guilds and merchants. The Guptas provided royal patronage to Vaiṣṇavism, but were tolerant to other religions as well. Temple constructions were taken up extensively. Court life pageantry on festival occasions, merry-making in games, dice-playing, hunting and elephant riding were all conspicuous. Dance and drama performances formed the common feature of civil life. Music, painting and poetry were looked upon as high-standard achievements. The common man wore a three-piece dress—loin-cloth, turban and scarf. Ladies wore bodice, loin-cloth and shawl; they paid special attention to their hairdos. Jewellery was commonly worn by both. In addition, one also finds in Ajanta paintings special dresses of silk with designs of woven flowers. Western India was one of the centres of silk weaving and Indian textile was in great demand in foreign lands. Most of the principal ladies can be seen wearing very transparent clothings and are usually with open body above the waist. There are clothed servants and workmen, which indicates the class structure of the society. The marvellous feature of Ajanta paintings lies in its embracing the panorama of monasteries, palaces, markets, mansions of lords with all their luxuries of wine, women and gold, kitchen scenes, mythological pantheon including flying *gandharvas*, furious elephants scaring the shopkeeper and several other facets of social life.

There are sufficient epigraphic records to substantiate the aforesaid mode of living of the Guptas and Vākāṭakas. The Vākāṭakas' artistic taste is embodied in Ajanta caves. C. Sivaramamurti ascribes to them also the earlier caves of Ellora and the later one of Elephanta,[43] although this attribution is refuted by R.N. Misra.[44] All the same, their being great patrons of art and literature remains undisputed. The glory of Pravarasena I and Hariṣeṇa is eulogized in Ajanta inscriptions which also throw light on the knowledge of various *śāstras* being essential part of the training and build-up of important personages. The Buddha's boyhood scenes (cave 2) are an excellent example to corroborate this. It was the time of great Buddhist Universities, like Nalanda, where strides were taken in all the sides of man's knowledge ranging from astronomy (Āryabhaṭa and Varāhamihira) to the study of law (*Kātyāyana*). The six systems of Indian philosophy were given a more clear exposition during this period. The Purāṇas were given their present forms. Kālidāsa, Bāṇa and Śūdraka—the great creative giants—nourished poetic imagination. Theories of poetics and aesthetics were put to standardized elaborations. In all respects it was the Golden Age of which Hariṣeṇa's reign, to recall W.M. Spink's words, was 'both the climax and the last luminous moment.'[45] India gained a common cultural pattern and emerged on the world plane. Even in Christian religious councils India came to be represented, e.g., in Christian conferences of Nicaea (A.D. 325) Johannes, Bishop of India maxima and Persia, participated.[46]

Deccan and South India made substantial contribution to Indian culture. With Deccan as bridge between the north and the south, the assimilation of the Aryan with the Dravidian gave birth to a synthesis in culture. The chain of cultural synthesis went ahead with the emergence of the Vākāṭakas, Chalukyas, Pallavas and Pandyas. Northern culture in the South acted, in the main, as a catalyst and produced new forms. The Tamil devotional cult was one of such forms. Śaṅkarācārya propagated *Advaita* (Monism) philosophy; Jainism and Buddhism gradually gave way to the new wave of religious worship and devotional cult, leaving their impact in the form of rituals, music and dance achieving the highest levels in great temple complexes.

Sopoćani: Social and Cultural Background

A comparison brought out by Theodor Metohit, the distinguished imperial officer of the Byzantine emperor Andronicus II Paleologue, is worth-recalling to vivify the cultural scene during king Milutin's reign (A.D. 1281-1321). That was the period of the transition of the style of works in the nave to that of exo-narthex at Sopoćani. Metohit wrote: 'The king himself was beautifully ornamented with jewellery. His body was covered with many precious stones and pearls as much as there was room for and he sparkled with gold. His whole home also glittered with furniture decorated in silk and gold.' They served 'various dishes and sweets on gold and silver plates and dishes—in a word, everything was arranged according to Byzantine taste and according to the ceremonial of the imperial court.'[47] The same 'Imperial grandeur' is testified with the setting vividly provided in the background of the frescoes of Sopoćani completed just a decade back during his father Uroš I's period. Long elaborate coats of brocade and turban-like and fur-trimmed hats for nobility revealed class consciousness. Alike were the attires given to Uroš I and growing Milutin and Queen Helena. This was all a part of the policy of 'ostentatious effects in order to stimulate popular imagination,'[48] maintaining the image of king as 'Vice-regent of Christ on earth,' the prototype of which was found in David, 'a king chosen by divine decree becoming a symbol for Byzantium's theocratic emperors.'[49]

The king's standard political philosophy was the outcome of the faith in his receiving divine visions. Such beliefs were inculcated in the rulers by Constantine's closest ecclesiastical advisors. As such, presentation of ecumenical councils (in Narthex) supports Yugoslavian kings' such attempts in 'Zabonik', the famous law-codes of Tsar Dušan. The father-image is maintained in the philanthropy practised by the elite and the church in building hospitals and sanatoriums etc.; it is also upheld by emperors in controlling public works like buildings, constructions, roads, mining, mint, special ornaments, clothes, art works and the like[50] (e.g., Uroš I took help of Saxons for mining; likewise he increased trade with coastal region). The images of medical saints repeatedly painted in Sopoćani testify to such philanthropic gestures.[51] Artists' guilds were appointed by kings or archbishops, levy and taxes were charged from them. Queen Helena's participation in politics and public life testifies the legality favouring dowry, equal share, and women's control over family right from housewife to queen. All the same, the ladies did not refrain from doing face-lifts.

But, due to pro-urban policy, although the farmers remained as the backbone financing emperors' glitter and expenses on armies and monastic orders,[52] there developed an official aristocracy of rich landowners (even purchasing official titles), with strictly disciplined and conservative culture of materially satisfied class loyal to the emperor.[53] These landowners not only tried independence but became the endower of churches, for instance the monastery of Kalenić (A.D. 1407 and 1413) was endowed by nobleman, Bogdan. In the frescoes of Kalenić the representation of nobleman's banquet in the 'Marriage at Cana,'[54] and the inclusion of 'figure-eight' (decorative pattern of tenth century ivories)[55] are suggestive of the tastes of noblemen holding fast to the ancient traditions of the class of Nicomachi and Symmachi, the old senatorial families in Rome.[56] This implied pagan revival. Dionysian monastery at Mt. Athos is an example of such vein where 'Dionysus himself, the Greek god of wine, supposedly planted the monastery's vine yard.'[57] Besides, the domination of religion, too, resulted in people believing in the supernatural and taking recourse to astrology and necromancy.[58] Under such conditions, the cosmology of church building, revival of Eleusinian mysteries and folk and primitive traditions were bound to come to the fore. In the above-mentioned marriage scene (at Kalenić) itself, the primitive blood-myth and pagan rite was mixed with Christian rites.[59] The primitive and prehistoric cults of 'Mother goddess' and 'Terra' are also apparent in the miraculous symbols of discs of concentric circles (Uroboros) at Milešava[60] and in the folk symbolism (specially Mary with the wheel, plate 103) painted in the church of St. Katarine (A.D. 1409) at Lindar in Istria.[61] Thus, it seems that what Philip Sherrard considers as 'Byzantine's great passion for three aspects of life—spectacular popular circuses, courtly intrigue (including royal eye-gouging) and religious mysticism,'[62] had its fill in Yugoslavia also. Lessons of life as 'endless tribulations and suffering' did not negate the concept of making life 'an occasion of colourful pageantry of festive gaiety.'[63] Mysticism and asceticism proved by presentation of stylites (figure 28)—ascetics on pillars—at Sopoćani, had its share in common man's life. But behind these colourful pageants there always remained a sense of the tragic, as is clear from the tragic symbolism discernible in Kalenić's 'Wedding Scene,' it is also apparent in the Poem of Love by Despot Lazarević.[64]

Learning being a passion and 'high-cultivation' a virtue, giving life 'the texture of a self-conscious work of art,'[65] goes back to the efforts of king of Moravia whose efforts made the Byzantine monks Cyril and Methodius evolve Slavic alphabets which became their 'own language' and base of culture of the entire Slavic world.[66] Almost every important monastic complex, Sopoćani, Mileševa, Peć, Dečani, Resava, to name a few, were the schools of learning; a few with their own printing presses, and scribes. Sopoćani's affinities with the style of contemporary literature have been pointed out by the scholars like Djurić. The learning centres at the monasteries of Mount Athos remained as prototype; Hilandar was the 'first Serbian University.' Serbia attracted men of learning and arts from all around, especially due to weakening of frontier Byzantine lands: Djurić rightly observes—'the enrichment and consolidation of the independent church and state of the Serbs, the development of their culture and art, in general, made Serbia in the thirteenth century the legitimate heir of the art of Byzantine and in particular of Byzantine painting.'[67] Despot Stefan Lazarević, being a poet himself and one of the finest intellectuals of fifteenth century Serbia, testifies such environment's persistence.

Comparative

The paintings of Sopoćani do not give account of social and cultural background in the manner the narratives of Ajanta do encompassing the court-life and the genre. Although the court-life 'of great decorum and modesty' echoes throughout on the walls of Sopoćani, it is only in the exo-narthex that the silk, glitter and gold vivify what Theodor Metohit explained of the life of ceremonial imperial court. Ajanta fully vivifies the jewellery, silk, palaces, royal pageantry, market, music, dance, games, hunting, elephant riding and all that which spoke of Harișeṇa's age as the climax of the Golden Age. Its parallel can be found in the 'colourful pageantry of festive gaiety' of Byzantines, despite the lessons of life as 'endless tribulations and suffering' in which both the ages believed.

'High cultivation,' a virtue giving 'life the texture of a self-conscious work of art,' is proved by the monastic learning centres, universities, and materially satisfied urban life taking hold of both the periods. India had crystallized such efforts in the four stages of life. Similarly, interest in literature, painting and drama etc., became part of the life giving birth to these great centres of art, whose patrons were themselves poets and men of taste who enthusiastically built these 'cultural sanctuaries,' although 'politically' living in turbulent times. Maurizio Taddei also notes the 'refined urban society of the privileged' in the golden age of Guptas and Vākāṭakas, finding 'its most complete expression in painting.'[68] It was true of the thirteenth century Serbia as well. At both the places the literary figures like Kālidāsa, Bāṇa and Domentian inspired the popular imagination—the adoption of Sanskrit in South India brought about a countrywide cultural pattern; similarly the Slavic alphabet founded the cultural base of the entire Slavic world. The art treatises (e.g., *Herminy* and *Citrasūtra*) and law-codes (Dušan's and that of Kātyāyana's Study of Law) were written and the religious and philosophic thoughts were crystallized.

The flourishing economy and the consolidation of state found both the centres of art amidst the artist's guilds paying levies, landowners, traders, trades through coastal regions, mining, minting and donating 'welfare-state' comforts to traders and the laity. Monasteries were donated the lands and sustenance. The Buddhist as well as the Brahmanical monks had contacts with the royalty and the aristocrats. The rich landowners were gaining independence in Serbia of this time, a phenomenon already crystallized in the rules of *Gaṇas* since Sātavāhana's time. Agriculture was the backbone behind the 'glitter of the court' in Serbia, so was it in India despite urbanization. The rituals and magic rites attached with fertility cults had the way and flourished in the dominance of matriarchal principles. Ladies participated in all spheres of life from household to court-life,[69] and paid special attention to their face-lifts or hairdos. Their modesty was appreciated in India as well as in Yugoslavia.

The class consciousness is evident in both the ages, although in India the four classes of the society were crystallized. Artists were accorded the lower strata of the social structure. Marriages for political ends are also evident as are the marriages within royal family to ensure loyalty. Hierarchy of royalty and officials was observed during this time of Nemanjid dynasty as is obvious from the inscriptions of Ajanta. Ostentatious efforts to stimulate the popular imagination were the mode of life during these periods which were marked with mystics, ascetics and tantrics or Eleusinian mystery cults. We notice a change from uninhibited joy in life, submitted in a votary's zeal to the Buddha, in the Sātavāhana period to the exotic country pageantry and refined urban milieu expressed as transfixed in 'tantra,' in Vākāṭaka regime at Ajanta. Similar change is represented to the glory of God in the frescoes of the nave at Sopoćani during Uroš's period and the later frescoes of exo-narthex etc., suggesting the change of more courtly-urban society, which later culminated into the comforts of easy life and aristocratic elegance expressed in Morava School almost becoming 'Oriental fairy tale atmosphere' of Kalenić.[70]

Considering the presence of giant literary figures like Kālidāsa in the Deccan during this Golden period it can safely be said that Ajanta attracted the best of artistic talent from far and near. Similarly Sopoćani, too, became the 'legitimate heir' worthy of the monumental art tradition of Byzantine.

Ajanta: Religious Background

The paintings of Ajanta represent Buddhism with almost all of its schools admitting Realism, Idealism and Absolutism. During the course of about one thousand years of its active life in India, Buddhism grew with its central theme—'Be ye to yourselves, Ananda, your own light,' which Ganeshwaranand Swami interprets as being 'on the rock of one's own exprience of life.'[71] This central theme when converted into the historical time and space was 'nourishing and getting nourished, speaking with the tongues of many Nations,'[72] thus observes Gladstone Solomon on the basis of its plastic representation at Ajanta. To these remarks may be added the view of Radhakrishnan and Moore, that 'the Buddha is not so much formulating a new scheme of metaphysics and morals as rediscovering an old norm and adopting it to the new conditions of thought and life.'[73] Thus Śākya Muni's metamorphosis into 'the thousand Buddhas' speaks of many fruitful interlinkings to become the world religion. On a wider perspective Buddhism not only brings out essential Vedic and Upaniṣadic thought finding Brahma and Paramātmā,[74] but also links the psychic-satisfaction of Jewish 'Saviour' and the Hellenic-Persian concept of 'emperor, the illuminator.'[75] Its flux gives a type of syntax to Ajanta Painting which, conceived on a mythic ground, parallels the conceptions of 'rhythmos' in an abstract-abstractionist painting.[76] Similarly, V.V. Ivanov finds the conceptions of language in Buddhist logic to be parallel to that of the modern structural linguistics. He observes it on comparing the works of Dharmakīrti and Sartre.[77] The parallelism is also in the blank canvases of modern artists and the blank papers of Zen-Buddhist masters, achieved through active 'Śūnya' (the principle of perpetual change occurring at every step in this phenomenal world).

The Buddhist philosophy is 'verbs' not 'noun.' It is a mysticism of *mārga*, a 'way,' not 'goal' (*artha*).[78] The Master's last words to Ānanda were '... such will henceforth, Ānanda, be my true disciple, who walks in the right path.'[79] The path is threefold—of *Śīla* (ethico-moral discipline of mind, body and senses), *Samādhi* (meditation) and *Prajñā* (insight into the nature of reality). R.C. Dwivedi elaborates the defence of 'the way' thus: Mysticism ought to concern itself with a way of life than with a way of thought... The crucial point will be whether he has pursued relentlessly the spiritual path and attained a life of awakening, of larger awareness, of cosmic consciousness.'[80]

The Ajanta artist pursued the 'way' 'relentlessly' right from the beginning. He steadfastly devoted himself to the change from the aniconic *uddeśika* stūpa for circumambulation (possibly a manifestation of early Buddhist doctrine of perceptual flux) to the discarding of circumambulation in cave 3, which echoes *Advaitic* thought that Reality is one and unchanging. He presents the 'portraits' of the Sātavāhanas in Hīnayāna caves in a sense conveying their absolute belief in historical Śākyamuni Buddha but of a mythical nature (presented since Aśoka's time). The anthropomorphic image, due to the cult of *Bhakti* (devotional movement), sprang up around the end of first century A.D.[81] and by the time the 'Wheel of Life' was painted in cave 17, the Tantra influence had penetrated with magic rites and mother-goddesses. Thus, this 'negative-element' was presented there as it is described in the legends of Padmasambhava.[82] With this, the Buddhist dialectical relationship is expressed in the incised inscriptions in this cave of Hariṣeṇa's period (last quarter of fifth century A.D.), eulogizing the beauty of Aticandrā, the wife of King Kṛṣṇadāsa, clad in garments as white as the rays of the moon, whose face resembled the full-moon, and whose ornaments were modesty and virtuous conduct.[83] Fa'hien (A.D. 394-414) also saw the Indian images of *Prajñā-pāramitā* (the goddess personifying 'transcendent' knowledge), which conforms to the presentation of Buddhist pantheon as described in *Guhyasamāja-Tantra* (A.D. 300) evolved under Vajrayāna-Tantrayāna Buddhism.[84] To pursue the path of *prajña* (wisdom) was the early school's ideal of Arhat (*Dhammapada*: 28, 90, 98),[85] the echo of which ('a wise strong man on the holy mountain might behold the many unwise far down below on the plain') is also found in the inscriptions of caves 16 and 26.[86] The Mahāyāna cave inscriptions also eulogize 'supreme-knowledge' confirming *Prajñā-pāramitā's* popularity since Nāgārjuna restored it to mankind from Nāgas where it had been kept in the custody of the Buddha till mankind became enlightened to receive it.[87] It was mixed with the popularity of Bhāgawat-cult (e.g., cave 2, the word 'Sarasvati' is written, over a painted cow, and the name of Kṛṣṇa is mentioned in the rock inscription over cave 26)[88] proving that the Mahāyāna was accepted mixed with popular beliefs, elements of mantra and mythic cosmology in cyclic concept of time.

It is not only the popular Indian beliefs which were accommodated in Buddhism in its second phase, but while getting adjusted as a 'world religion' it also accepted other concepts in the framework of its own logic.[89] Its *Majjhima Nikāya*, developing into activistic mysticism of Mahāyāna turned into Doctrine of *Karuṇā* as is expressed in Nāgārjuna's stress on there being no difference between *saṁsāra* and *nirvāṇa.*[90] On the other hand, this spirit of 'middle way' on reaching the land of Oxus-Jaxartes basin's 'cultural compost,' got oriented into the spirit of 'saviour' in stressing 'Maitreya'—a linear concept of time—as a future Buddha 'saviour' awaiting in Tushita heaven.

The concept of the Bodhisattva implies suffering for the good of others as the compassionate one who refuses to become Arhat[91] till every sentient being has achieved *nirvāṇa.* Sarvāstivādin's Bodhisattva who 'ceaselessly' strives for individual perfection through the path of *prajñā* becomes the 'compassionate one' because in the attainment of Bodhi-mind of activistic Mahāyānist, both are the 'unified state of *Śūnyatā* and universal compassion.'[92] At Ajanta the inscription of the cave 26 reads thus:

> (Buddha) . . . whose pure splendour is mercy, who (with) . . . final emancipation (yet) does good to the world. . . whose hearts are soft through mercy and who are greatly popular people by their well known virtues. . . . The results of the actions of sages who are exalted by virtue tend to the enjoyment of happiness by the people.[93]

During the course of time the positive concepts of *Śūnyatā* and *Nirvāṇa* of Sarvāstivādin, the former suggesting 'flux' (i.e., perpetual change—a logical concept), and the latter suggesting 'not yet state' (an ethical concept) got united. An ontological status was given to them rendering them 'almost identical with Brahman of the *advaitins.*'[94] According to Mahāyāna there are three aspects of bodies—*Dharmakāyā*, i.e., primordial body or Thatness of all existence, *Saṁbhogakāyā*, i.e., body of bliss and *Nirmāṇakāyā*, i.e., body of transformation (cave 9 has six such Buddhas and eight are painted in cave 2). The multiplication grows and becomes thousand Buddhas, the miracle of Srāvasti, in which, as

Bosch points out, individual becoming a chain of incarnations as 'the picture of the founder of the religion is reduplicated till infinity' (and so) 'loses its individuality'[95]—again the principle of non-egoity equating with all beings asserted, the moment the cyclic concept of Time of Hindu mythology was accepted.

The evidence of the above is not difficult to find. Reduced back to *Śūnya* ultimately, the Zen-Buddhist masters leave blank papers, and Ajanta's *sthaviras* carve space sculptures (of caves).

This dialectical movement brings us to Buddha's proclaiming *mārga* or the way, 'which starts by recognizing *suffering*, finding *Taṇha* (*Tṛṣṇa*) as *cause of suffering*, holds the hope of *rooting out the cause* and finally prescribes *the way*.'[96] Having given the above four noble truths, he prescribes the Eightfold Path: Right Outlook, Right Resolves, Right Speech, Right Acts, Right Rapture of concentration. With 'experiencing things as they are' explained as *anatta* (egoless), suchness (*tathatā*) and *śūnyatā* (vacuity), proceeds the motion of particulars which the Buddha avoids. And as well avoiding speculative metaphysics, the conception of soul etc., Buddha points to the Middle Path. 'The intermediary path alone, which the Buddha found, avoids these two extremes, opens the eyes, enlightens the mind and leads to peace, wisdom, light, *nirvāṇa*.'[97] Taking the path of *prajñā*, the Hīnayāna added rigorous asceticism whereas the Tantra added 'the path of gratification of passion and the enjoyment of senses.'[98]

Buddhism, proclaimed as world's first 'protestant reformism in Indian philosophical schools'[99] belongs to heterodox or unorthodox systems. To people like Weber, Buddhism presented the perfection of the soteriology of cultivated intellectuals especially in opposing the *ātman* doctrine.[100] But to S.S. Barlingay, it is the confusion of identifying metaphysical and logical, and metaphysical and ethical categories which caused the somersault of Buddhism from 'change alone is real to the changing alone is real.'[101]

Tracing the development of Buddhism it must be pointed out that since the beginning it was a twofold movement, one of nuns and monks, the other of laity representing popular Buddhism. These were organised into *Tri-ratna* (the Buddha, the Dharma and the Saṅgha).

The first council of Buddhism was held at Rajagriha soon after the Master's passing away (544 B.C.). The second was held at Vaishali after a hundred years. Here the schism appeared and the Mahāsāṅghika (later formed as Mahāyāna) seceded from the main order. The third council was held during Aśoka's time with *Kathāvatthu* and the *Abhidharma* treatise propounding earliest doctrinal differences. The despatch of missionaries also got recognized in this council.

The fourth was held about A.D. 100 at Jalandhar, during Kaniṣka's rule, making Sanskrit the language of the text commentaries. The main order, Hīnayāna (Theravāda and Sarvāstivāda schools), was followed by Mādhyamika with the phases of Yogācāra and Vijñānavāda and further divisions of the order followed with a number of denominations. Mahāsāṅghika sect migrated from Magadha into two streams—north and south. The northern stream split into five sub-sects one of which was the Lokottaravādins; Dr. Dutt[102] informs that they prepared the ground for the advent of the Mahāyāna school. The Andhaka, another of the sub-sects, moved down and settled in Krishna valley. Nāgārjuna, the Mādhyamika expositor, lived in Śri Parvata near Dhanya-Kaṭaka (*c.* A.D. 150); he advocated absolutism (*Śūnyavāda*) and wrote six treatises on the subject. In South India, by A.D. 520 Bodhidharma, a prince of Kanchi, founded the school of Buddhism known as Ch'an in China and the Zen Buddhism in Japan.[103] In Sri Lanka and South-East Asia Theravādin doctrine persisted. Mahāyāna accepted popular beliefs and Mantra-Pāramitā-naya or 'the discipline of supreme virtue' and Mantranaya introduced all sorts of esoteric principles and practices giving form to Tantric Buddhism of Vajrayāna, Kālacakrayāna and Sahajayāna propagating mantra, mudrā and maṇḍala to which elements of yoga were added.[104]

The Buddha had been aware of the dissensions taking place in the Saṅgha during his life-time itself; so rules were formed and these were recorded. The very fact of gradual divisions into the various forms of Buddhism[105] proved the apprehension of the Master. Of Śākyamuni's life, the earliest record is in *Lalitavistāra*, a Sanskrit work, in which his life is given up to the First Sermon. The later part of his life right up to the conversion of three Brahman (Kāṣyapa) brothers is contained in *Mahāvastu.* It was during the time of Kaniṣka that Aśvaghoṣa's *Buddhacarita* was produced giving the life of the Śākyamuni from his birth to the Relic-distribution.

The whole life of the Buddha with its historicity and mythical overtures has been disputed. Coomaraswami finds Upaniṣadic background in it, Rhys Davids questions family circumstances including his wife's name (Yaśodharā).[106] Snellgrove and others finding little history of Śākayamuni's life in the earlier works, regard the details of his life as 'spurious.' They stress the tradition that Śākyamuni's life has been set up according to the tradition of the Buddha's passage on earth with appointed places and four main acts, 'leaving his doctrine to replace him until it finally comes to nothing which stands as the time for the next Buddha.'[107] Through *Āgamas*, the Buddhists have given the life-story of Śākyamuni which would be taken up in brief in the portion on subject matter because *Āgama* stories have been quite frequently presented at Ajanta stressing important events of Gautama's life.

Sopoćani: Religious Background

The origin of Eastern Orthodox Church is found in the accounts of St. John (*John* 12:30-24). During the Pass-over in Jerusalem a few Greeks approached apostles Philip and Andrew with yearning to see the Christ. Discovering their 'unknown' God, in him, they found 'the way and the truth, and the life' (*John* 14:6). The basic foundations were laid and reaffirmed in the seven ecumenical councils held from A.D. 325 to 787 with the Sacred and Heritage traditions founded by them.[108] Serbia received Christian doctrine in ninth century A.D. The Serbian orthodoxy was founded at a ceremony at Nicea by St. Sava in A.D. 1219 within the religious traditions and by getting true understanding from Byzantine emperor Theodor I Laskanes and the Patriarch Manual Saranteen.[109] Its organizational principles were set up at the monastery of Žiča. Accordingly, in synodic system, a deacon serves a bishop in his diocese, the priest being the centre of spiritual authority (receiving from Bishop) over his parish. The Bishop is the head of Church in a given diocese over whom Synod supervises—Jesus Christ being the head of Synod and Church. By the end of sixteenth century the whole of Yugoslavia was divided into three dioceses, viz., Karlovac, the Dabro-Bosnian and Dalmatian.[110]

Embodying and proclaiming ortho-doxa, i.e., the right faith in Christ, the church makes no compromises in Sacred tradition. The church ensures tranquillity and internal balance, thereby preserving the faith from any extreme—'Lord himself being the regulator of this harmony and continuity to his own promise'[111] (Matt 28:29, Mark 16:20). The Holy Spirit is with the Church and guides it to the truth.[112] Succinctly putting the faith, Constantelos observes that it presents God revealed in Jesus Christ and man redeemed by Jesus Christ. God appeared among men in time and space to redeem man and reconcile him with himself. 'God was made man that man may become God' as St. Athanasios asserted.[113]

Preserving in the church's painting the assertion that 'Orthodoxy is Greek in form but divine in content and origin; the spirit is of God but the body in which it appears to man is Greek,'[114] the Yugoslavian artists, on their part, gave it a body of independent Serbian church by bowing and feeling deep piety towards their own saints, martyrs and the 'innumerable legions of their holy and righteous ancestors from emperors to shepherds.'[115] Such adherence to tradition, as Luke (5:39) said 'No one after drinking old wine desires new; for the old is better,' is best exemplified at the monasteries of Mt. Athos—'Arc of Byzantium.' There the Orthodox Monks, immune to the change, still paint icons, display imperial flag, remember Byzantine emperors in their prayers and tell time in true Roman fashion by the elevation of sun[116] 'in the belief that the disillusioned will return to the simple virtues of their holy faith.'[117] Preserving relics of the saints has, thus, been a passion of the Serbian orthodox church.[118]

This church of prayer and profound spirituality has Christ centred ethics: love and charity, justice and humanity,[119] implying orthe-praxe, i.e., right faith and right life.[120] Accordingly, social assistance is a part of church life since 'God... desires all men to be saved and to come to the knowledge of the truth' (1 *Tim.* 2:6) and Christ 'gave himself as a ransom for all' (1 *Tim.* 2:6). The Serbian Church accepted the knowledge and faith both influencing not only intellect but also the fine creative sensibility which brought about a renaissance in literature and art.

Thus, the vision built up was that of man being the microcosm of the whole creation and the centre of things having a key to his own fate; since his body has capacity for spiritual experiences, he can aspire union with God. This vision was reflected in Divine Liturgy in which man was assisted in the reliving of Christian mysteries serving as a remainder of his commitment to God.[121]

In mysteries 'the anthropic, the divine, and the human nature of Christ is extended to both his Church and to her means of grace as well,'[122] thus proving that everything had point of contact with spiritual world. The basic mysteries are as follows:

> *Baptism*: 'Be Baptized for the forgiveness of your sins' commands the Holy Spirit (Acts 2:28, 22 16). Men through this sacrament enter threshold of earthly Kingdom of God and become members of Church—Body of Christ. The mystery is completed with Holy Chrismation with oil.[123]
>
> *Holy Eucharist* is the central religious idea given shape in the Church of Holy Trinity of Sopoćani. As a proof of His love, faithfulness and providence, Christ explained that ancient-manna and bread are not eternal, instead, he offered that 'he who eats my flesh and drinks my blood abides in me and I in him' (*John* 6:46-58), which was the transubstantiation of the actual bread offering, a year after, at the Last Supper. 'It is remembering and reminding through the re-enactment of the life, the teaching, the death, the resurrection of our Lord.'[124] It implies communion and Eucharist—the writing of biographies, erecting monuments of art, painting pictures, since through Holy Communion a corporeal unity of man with Christ is achie-

ved.[125] Holy Eucharist is ultimately connected with Divine Liturgy which is a public service being a testimony of the Revelation of God. 'Through symbolic utterances, gestures, signs and symbols, the whole redemption plan of God is set before the congregation; the central theme being the life of Christ. It is done in three acts: (1) Offertory prayers—this act consists of preparing gifts to be transformed in 'body and blood' of Christ; giving redeeming plan manifested through prophets reaching Christ, reciting prayers and verses; commemorating old and new Saints, Church Militant (on earth), and Church Triumphant (in heaven), united as living organism of God;[126] invoking of Prophets, Apostles, Fathers, Mary, Martyrs, in brotherhood. (2) The second Act—Liturgy of Cathechumens is instructive for the members of Church. (3) Liturgy of Faithful—the third act, being most important, is done with recital of creed, putting gifts on altar, proclaiming faith with choir's singing—'The earthy and material are transubstantiated into Godly elements, the body and blood of Christ,' in mystic union through Holy Communion.[127] The liturgy finishes with depicting ascension, and expectations of church. In panegyric message of Easter Sunday, (and every Sunday), from total darkness, for some time, reminiscent of death of Church and plunging of followers into fear and despair, the Church is lighted, 'Christ is Risen,' with lamentation of Mary Magdalene and others—'O ye faithful, come forward and receive light from the light that never wares.'[128] Other sacraments are such as confession, for 'if you forgive the sins of any they are forgiven' (*John* 20:23). Ordination of Holy orders, which for the preservation and continuation, has the 'Marriage' as spiritual union (that is why marriage dances are shown in many of the monasteries, e.g., Dečani, Kalenić, etc.) and Holy Unction reminding holy miracles of curing symbolized by putting oil.[129]

The monastery of Hilandar played a great part in being 'the first Serbian University which provided no less than eight of the first ten Archbishops of Serbia.'[130] Besides, it imparted the training of painting to monks and artists. It always received donations since the First Crown, King Stefan, recommended, thus: 'I beg you sires and brothers, to whom God will give this throne and this state after me not to insult the Holy Virgin (whose property is the monastery of Hilandar) in all these rights as written down here, not to alter my words or my gifts.' Accordingly, Uroš, Dragutin and Milutin built defensive towers and Milutin constructed Church on the site of the old and decorated it with various objects of great beauty.[131]

Although rigorous monasticism had been prevalent in Egypt and Capadocia[132] much earlier, St. Basil is considered to be the father of Byzantine Monasticism: 'Think much and talk little' used to be his advice to the monks. In Sopoćani there are painted scenes of (Syrian) stylites sitting on pillars (plate 28) as St. Simeon did for thirty years to escape the distraction.[133] The monks follow three vows, poverty, chastity and obedience; they cultivate a rigorous daily routine of fasting, meditating and praying throughout night except a few hours of sleep.[134] Such life of the monks was a common sort at Mt. Athos. In the first half of the fourteenth century the Hesychast monks at Mt. Athos gave momentum to the ideas of true monastic life. And by the second half of the same century the movement was being spread in Serbia in full intensity by a whole group of monks from Mt. Athos, having the scholar Gregory the Sinaite amongst them.[135]

Comparative

Although both belong to the category of world religions, the basic difference of the Christian Church and the Buddhist Saṅgha lies in what Max Weber points that the former is 'a universalistic establishment for the salvation of masses' and the latter 'an exclusive association of religious virtuosos or of especially qualified religious persons.'[136] The Buddhist monks being *parivrājakas*, had no church-like organization nor hierarchy of clerics or head; 'they were essentially identical to the order of Brahmanical Sannyasins etc.'[137] Weber assigns such state of sect to early Christiandom's heroic-sects.[138] Similarly, Buddhist Saṅghas also became different outside India by 'having social relationship and trade activities.'[139]

Born out of what Weber calls the exemplary prophecy or wisdom of Indian mysticism, the Buddhism did not tender the ethic of daily life, while, it was rationally framed by the Christianity conceived out of emissary type prophecy.[140] This results in the difference of the basic premise of settling the images of the God-heads—Buddhists' of the Supreme and static being, and Christianity's of the active Lord of Creation. Thus pure Buddhism dispensed with gods in the 'Trans-worldly field of formless.'[141] Similarly, although in the Revelation Christ is the first and the last creation of God as his emanation but, as it is rightly observed by the Marxist critics, the monotheism had to make concession to polytheism to become a religion;[142] Christianity had heavenly court and Buddhism the Ādi Buddha with Four Buddhas, Dharmakāyā, Nirmāṇakāyā, Sambhogakāyā and Bodhisattvas denying any absolute difference between *saṃsāra* (phenomenal existence) and *nirvāṇa* (its extinction).[143] Additions of relics, charms and rituals are part of the same process of the development of these religions. The Trinity was affirmed at the Nicaean councils owing to this universalizing as there is no mention of it in the Revelation.[144] Trinity doctrine emerging with Mahāyāna also met the lay interest in the holy.[145] The Buddha being man is analogous to the second figure of Christian trinity. He being transient, has *nirvāṇa* as goal and saves man with example 'not as the representative sacrifice for their sin. For it is not sin, but transitoriness which is evil.'[146]

Nirvāṇa or salvation in Arhathood was attained in an extreme form of 'genuine mysticism' as an absolute individual affair. Such asceticism of true monastic life was propagated by Hescychast monks who were represented on the walls of Yugoslavian churches as 'ideal of Christianity.'[147] In *Majjhima* or Middle way doctrine the conservativeness of Hīnayānists gave way to compassionate catholocity. The ethic codes of the eightfold path became the 'Mahāyāna' or 'Mahāsaṁghika' which incorporated laity—with full acceptance of Heaven and Hell and Maitrīya Boddhisattva as a Messiah. Sahajayāna incorporated the individual's traits within the way. Thus Buddhism 'admitted a variety of followers—realists, idealists and absolutists in their fold;'[148] the inward contemplation remaining at the base there couldn't have come out the affinities of the 'Holy' state as it was with that of the active asceticism of Christianity with its weighty civic strata. Thus, contrarily, the Serbian Orthodox Church came out with the aim of 'happiness, spiritual rise and cultural progress of the whole Serbian people.'[149] It is only in the 'Cakravartin' aspects of Buddhahood as taken by the Mauryans, Guptas and Vākāṭakas in this respect, that claims similarity with Byzantine's in having monarch being the patrons of church or religious establishments and welfare state.[150]

But, in contemplative-monasticism, the similarity between the Christian and the Buddhist is that of the 'way,' the *via Mystica* starting from *śīla*, *via purgativa*, to *samādhi* , *via Illuminativa.* The *prajñā* or path of wisdom leads to active compassion since 'the actor is the acting and the acting is the actor and of this unification or identification Prajñā is awakened:' it is the same 'with which he (God) loves himself' in Christianity.[151] Mahāyāna's removing 'even the slightest difference between *saṃsāra* and *nirvāṇa*' echoes in Christ's teaching drawing no distinction between the life here and in Heaven, while saying 'I must work the works of Him who sent me.'[152] Yet there remains a difference between these conceptions of the enlightenment or bliss 'now-here' for the Orthodox Church, in "Transubstantiation,' the form remains but the spirit is elevated whereas in the Buddhistic 'Transfiguration,' the ethereality of the form is incorporated. Such a 'glimpse' is part of Christian miracles as these were of Buddhist's too.

Ajanta: Subject Matter

Ajanta's pictorial space is a complex perspective interwoven like a discourse on, or a vivification of, the *Jātakas*. It consists of the historical circumstances (the *Avadānas*—Śākyamuni's life with punctuations of religious, mythic and narrative importance), the story of the past (*Jātakas* of Bodhisattvas—identifying with him all the creatures before being born as Śākyamuni) and the mythic identification in a circular conception of time (—as the Master used to do at the end of narration of *Jātakas* in identifying past characters with the present). Thus, we find aniconic symbols together with the image of the Buddha who is being looked after by gods and demigods of Brahmanical pantheon, with a Tantric presentation and the realism like that of ants eating the sweet left-overs. All are 'edited' so to speak, in an epic of Buddhistic mythology. The murals of Ajanta seem to embody Bhāmah's dictum in *Kāvyālaṃkāra* (V40) that there is nothing in nature, thought and imagination which cannot be the subject matter of art. It has certainly cared for the start of narrative from the right as per Buddhistic circumambulation rites. Left-tilts of the heads of Bodhisattvas provide a strong lateral force which is aided by 'visual lines' of the glances of the majority of the figures. Although the liberty of random juxtapositions is perceptible in the narrative details, there is the strong evidence of the due care taken of the onlooker's psychology associated with narrative dominances.[153] To read the meaning and the sequence of narration it requires initiation and acquaintance.

Historically, it has taken a long time to identify the presentations of all the surviving pieces of paintings. Fergusson and Burgess made great efforts in identifying some in 1871, Oldenberg made some advance in 1895 and in 1902 Luders added to the list. It was in 1919 when Foucher decoded a large number of themes.[154] Now, with the efforts of all these scholars and a few subsequent ones like Waddell and Dikshit, the paintings of Ajanta have been fully identified except a very few disputed pieces and some others which have hardly any recognizable portions. Major portions of the surface in the caves of Ajanta were given to the story of *Jātakas*. These 546 stories are of Bodhisattvas—Buddha in previous lives. Identifying himself with all sentient beings, he upholds the life of truth and thus, progresses towards his emancipation of *Karma* cycles before born as the Buddha. These stories, while enhancing in good and pious deeds, stress upon the sacrifices done by the protagonist of the plot. A natural piety with the non-humans with one of a naive and candid wonder at the world and its inhabitants pervades all the *Jātakas*. *Jātaka* used to be the part of the discourses originally given by Buddha and later by the second or the third century they became an integral part of Buddhist tradition and were included in the nine-*aṅgas*, sacred books of Buddhists. Originally transmitted orally, they were written in Pāli and were modified from pure stanzas to verses. These were translated in Sinhalese, then to Pāli, again titling *Jātakaṭṭhavannanā* which Rhys Davids notices as the oldest, most complete and most important folk lore extant. Their sequence starts with enumerating the situation in *Avadāna* because of which the Buddha told the *Jātaka* (2nd part), with short commentary and the *gāthās* in the 3rd part, it ended with the Buddha's identification of characters in both the stories.[155] Their narrations at Ajanta are presented in varied ways. For example in cave 10, the *Chadanta Jātaka* is presented in a pictorial narrative idiom. The presentation is condensed in a decorative motif as can be seen in the lion-throne of Buddha (pointed out by Grünwedel) where *Sabbadatha-Jātaka* has taken this form.[156] Later, on metaphysical ground, these vegetal and animal forms giving importance to human beings, 'seem to have bequeathed their rhythm and ceaseless flow to the human figure itself,' as Snellgrove and others rightly observe.[157]

The *Jātakas* that have most fascinated the artists of Ajanta are—*Śibi Jātaka, Mṛga Jātaka, Mahājanaka Jātaka, Kśāntivādi Jātaka, Compeyya Jātaka, Syāma Jātaka, Vaissantra Jātaka, Sutasoma Jātaka, Vidhurapaṇḍita Jātaka, Mahā Umagga Jātaka, Nigrodhamiga Jātaka, Mahisha Jātaka, Samkhapala Jātaka, Mahāhaṃsa Jātaka, Chadanta Jātaka, Mahākapi Jātaka, Matripoṣaka Jātaka, Hasti Jātaka* etc.

Life of Śākyamuni through *Āgama* literature of Buddhist sacred books revolves around four principal towns: Kapilvastu, Bodhagayā, Vārāṇasi and Kushinagara. These four towns are also connected with the four major events of the Buddha's life respectively—the Annunciation (dream of Māyā) and Nativity, Enlightenment, the First Sermon and the Parinirvāṇa. The other principal events related to Śākyamuni's life in these towns are:

Kapilvastu—Seven steps, Presentation in the temple of Tutelary deity of Śākyas (*Divyāvadāna*), Sage Asita's visit, Schooling, First meditation, Four journeys, Departure from and Return to Kapilvastu.

Bodhgayā—Asceticism, Sujātā's food, 'Māra's assault and temptation, Buddhacakra, Grass presentation, Svāstika, Episode of Nāgarāja Muchalinda, Gift of the food by merchants, Tapussa and Bhallika, Presentation of stone-bowl by the four gods of the four quarters.

Kushinagara—Relic distribution. The other four lesser towns with principal events are:

Rājgṛha—Meeting with Ajātaśatru, Bimbisāra and Indra, Gift of Jetavana park.
Vaiśāli—Subjugation of the elephant Nalagiri.
Śrāvastī—Miracles and Transfiguration.

Samkāsya—The place of the assembly after Buddha's descent (on ladder) from Tushita Heavens, where he had gone to preach to his mother.

Divyāvadāna, Lalitavistara and *Nidānas* give detailed accounts of Buddha visiting different places in eastern India during his life-time.[158]

The Buddha's ancestry has been traced by Buddhaghoṣa to his very distant forefather Mahāsāmmata. The family had the tradition of marrying sisters in order to keep the purity of blood. The Buddha's grandfather was King Sihahanu. His father, King Śuddhodana of Kapilvastu, had two wives, Māyā and Mahāprajāpati. Māyā was the mother of the Buddha. Most of the scholars agree on putting the Buddha's date of birth in the middle of sixth century B.C. Nepalese tradition places it in 624 B.C. He was born on the full-moon day of the month of Vaiśākh (April-May) in the Lumbini Gardens near the city of Devadaha in Nepal Terai. According to *Nidānkathā* Māyā dreamt of a white elephant entering her womb. On asking the wise Brahmanas to decode the dream, the king was told that either a *Cakravartin*, universal monarch, or a Buddha was to be born to Māyā. Nearing her time she proceeded to her father's house at Devadaha. Near the city in a pleasure grove of *Sāla* tree in Lumbini, holding the branch of a flowering tree, she delivered the child from the lateral right of her body. Four wise Brahmanas came with a golden net to receive the Bodhisattva. From them four great kings received him on a ceremonial robe and then he was received by human beings. The Bodhisattva stood and walked seven steps. That day saw the birth of seven other beings: Rahul's mother Yaśodharā, the tree of enlightenment, the four vases of treasure, his elephant, his horse, Kanthaka, his charioteer Channa and the Minister's son Kaludāyin.

The child was named Siddhārtha and was mothered by his step-mother, as Māyā died on the seventh day of his birth. Sage Asita visited the infant and regretted that he (Asita) would not remain alive to listen to his great discourses. As a prince of a royal race, Kṣatriya, he was schooled and trained well. On four occasions, while on journeys, he saw an old man, a sick man, a dead man and on the fourth occasion a mendicant with peace of deliverance. These caused the Great Departure. Although Gautama was married to Yaśodharā and had a son, Rāhula by her, they could not bind him to worldly pleasures against the final *nirvāṇa* which he now sought to achieve. Channa, his charioteer, prepared the chariot with the horse Kanthaka over which Siddhārtha left the city gates leaving his family asleep. It was the full-moon day of Uttarāsādha (June-July). His desire to look back was sustained by the Earth herself turning around so as not to allow him to look back. As the other obstacle in the way to *nirvāṇa* was the sound of horse-hoofs, the earth had borne them on her palms to prevent it. In this 'homelessness' (*Mahā-sacchako Sūtta*), the *āśramas* of ascetics, he learnt *dhyāna* (meditation) and met the five ascetics who were later to become his first disciples. He tried Jina's methods also and came to Uruvela where he practised the severe penances and asceticism. Thus emaciated, he was still sensing the echo of desires remembering his first spiritual-trance which he experienced only due to the ceasing of desire. He decided his way, took Sujātā's food and sat under a *pipal* tree. Enlightenment came to him. Māra with his army tried to dissuade him. The Buddha won over him and touched the ground to make earth his witness (*Bhūmisparśa mudrā*). With his realization of the four Great Truths and The Eightfold Path of achieving *nirvāṇa*, he preached in the Deer Park of Vārāṇasi to his first disciples and set in motion the 'wheel of the law' (*Dharmacakra mudrā*). Here, a merchant, the first lay disciple, was taken into the order and the first lady disciple was also consecrated. With increasing numbers of disciples the Buddha came to Rajagṛha where king Bimbisāra adopted the order. *Dīgha-Nikāya* gives the number of Bhikkhus of Buddhist order as 500. The first Buddhist Council, meeting after the *Parinirvāṇa*, too, claimed to have 500 Bhikkhus. From there he went to Kapilvastu where he met Yaśodharā and Rāhula—claiming 'Give me my inheritance, ascetic'—the Buddha asked Śāriputta to admit Rāhula to the order. The Conversion of Nanda took place here. The order of Nuns was also sanctioned on asking by widow Mahāprajāpati, the foster-mother of the Buddha.

During the next forty years of his life the Buddha travelled extensively preaching the Doctrine. His most eminent disciples were Śāriputta and Moggallāna, and most loved one was Ānanda. Upāli, a Śākya barber, attained great importance and is said to have been the first propounder of the Buddhist Church. Among the other royal supporters of Buddha was King Prasenajit of Kośala. Devadatta tried to bring schism in the Saṅgha and attempted at assassinating the Buddha. The threefold formula of new converts taking refuge in the Buddha, the Dharma and the Saṅgha was evolved in which the Buddha himself gave importance to the Saṅgha.

The account of *Mahāparinirvāṇa* of the Buddha is given in three *suttas:* The *Mahāparinibbāna Sutta*, the *Mahāsuddassana Sutta*, and the *Janavasabha Sutta*. At the age of eighty, while on way to Kushinagara from Vaiśāli, Chanda, a smith of Pāvā, served him Sūkaramaddava in a mango grove. It made Buddha very sick. At Kushinagara, Ānanda prepared the bed of the Master between the two *sāla* trees. '... Strive without ceasing'—with these last words the Perfect-One entered *Nirvāṇa* (*c.* 544 B.C.) in the presence of his disciples and Mallas of Kushinagara. The Brahman welcomed the Buddha to Heaven. The mortal remains were burnt and relics distributed over which the *stūpas* were built.

Like *Jātakas*, the narrative elements of *Avadānas* also became iconic, their symbols, myths and narratives were arranged as subsidiaries around the image of Buddha—the protagonist. With the passage of time a full scheme of iconography was evolved and utilized in conformity with subsequent transformations in Buddhism, i.e., from Hīnayāna to Tantric Buddhism.

The previous Mānuṣī Buddhas as per *Mahāpadama Sutta* are 6, *Lalitavistara* mentions 54 and *Mahāvasthu* takes them up to 100. In the caves these are presented with varying numbers consummating in the 'image' of 'the thousand Buddhas' (miracle of Śrāvasti), wherby 'de-individualizing' the imagery in the Buddhistic dialectics got converted into the graphic dialectics.

Thus, significantly, the oldest painting at Ajanta is of *stūpa*-worship.

Sopoćani: Subject Matter

The whole theme of the decoration represents the church as a 'microcosm of the actual world,'[159] giving the order of hierarchy of church doctrine. The highest and most celestial point—dome for representing the Church Triumphant starting from Son of God,[160] the lower zones are occupied by the Church Militant. As an organic whole and as a part of the Divine Liturgy the paintings of Sopoćani present a programmatic exposition of the whole religious gamut. Martyrs, apostles, Archangel, prophets and Virgin are presented on the upper zone of pilasters (nave); the lower part has the paintings representing priests and Christ Enthroned. They all stand as 'pillars of faith' (Eph. 2 and Gal 2:9) to be invoked during the Communion. The lower zone is given to liturgical figures of saints and archbishops, in ceremonial attitude with sacred laws in their hands. On the middle zone the 'Communion of the Apostles'—'Eucharist', the giving of 'bread and wine'—is presented in the apse of the sanctuary. There, topped by the Pentecost (i.e., the celebration of descent of the Holy Spirit upon the Apostles on the seventh Sunday after Easter), the re-enactment of Ressurection, the culmination of the three acts of Divine Liturgy, is fully illustrated starting from Entombment of Christ and ending with the 'Incredulity of Thomas' on the north and the south walls.

Christ's life being the central theme of this Apostolic-Church, the pendentives have the Four Evangelists—St. Matthew, St. Mark, St. Luke and St. John—represented as writing Gospels. The visions of these Apostles seem to have been carried over by the Prophets and Patriarchs painted on the arches of the central square.

In the nave itself, on the north and south transepts, the upper zone has Martyrs from Subastia—the ancient city of Asia Minor. South transepts' upper zone has three angels of the Holy Trinity of the Old Testament having God personified in three aspects—Maker of Heaven and Earth, Redeemer or Saviour and Enlightener and Sanctifier.[161] The next is Baptism, the first of the mysteries representing Jesus being baptized of John in Jordon (*Mark* 1:9).

The first Gospel was written by St. Matthew, (earlier a tax-gatherer in Roman Service, his disciples St. Mark and St. Luke called him Levi.) He was thus presented as the first on the pendentives of Sopoćani starting from the south-east; he starts the Gospel from the Prophets, giving the genealogy of Christ. The Prophets have positions below the Evangelists on the arches. The Tree of Jesse, presented in the narthex, on the south wall (upper zone), gives this genealogy starting from recumbent Jesse, the father of David—'And there shall come forth a rod out of the stem of Jesse and a branch shall grow out of his roots'—as Toynbee puts it, 'Isaiah's prophecy of the coming of Messiah was given a literal form in Christian Art.'[162] It also serves as a link between the Old and the New Testaments. The Sopoćani painters extended this link up to Nemanjan dynasty presenting it below (and probably above also which is obliterated) the Tree of Jesse.

St. Matthew, giving the genealogy further, writes, 'So all the generations from Abraham to David are fourteen generations and from David until the carrying away into Babylon are fourteen generations, and from the carrying into Babylon up to Christ are fourteen generations' (*Matt.* 1:17). To this house belongs Joseph, whose wife Virgin Mary was favoured by God and Archangel Gabriel announced to her—'And behold, thou shall conceive in thy womb, and bring forth a son, and shalt call his name Jesus' (*L.K.* 1:31). Joseph and Mary moved from Galilee in Nazareth as per tax decree of Caesar Augustus, and went to Bethlehem, 'the city of David's house' to pay the tax and to get enrolled there. Jesus was born in a natural cave where cattle were bedded, as there was no place in the inns owing to crowding of the travellers for the census. Mary wrapped the child in swaddling clothes and laid him in a manger. The birth of child was announced to the shepherd who came to see him like the three Magi from the East, bringing gifts. The nativity of Christ is presented in the nave (north wall above).

As mother of God, Virgin Mary had special veneration in the Serbian Orthodox Church. As such, her life is fully presented from her Nativity (prothesis, upper zones of east-south and west walls) and is well painted along with the most prominent painting of Sopoćani—'the Dormition of the Virgin' (on the west wall upper zone of the nave). Mary is the ornate, the praying church in the story of her death.[163] Christ in her prayer told her that in three days he shall take her to his heavenly city. Mary summoned the Apostles and the Virgins of the Church of Jerusalem. She then ordered her 'grave clothes, with spices and perfumes, asking virgins to light lamps as evening came, then prayed at some length and lay down to die. Christ came for her straightaway riding in the chariot of the Cherubim, and her soul leapt into his arms.'[164]

Christ's life is further narrated in the nave. The child was brought to Jerusalem to be presented to the Lord (*L.K.* 2:20). In the temple St. Simeon, taking the child in the arms, thanked God that he could depart in peace now that he had seen Jesus because of whom '... the thoughts of many hearts may be revealed' (*L.K.* 2:35). Prophetess Anna also thanked likewise (*L.K.* 2:38). The narration is presented on the south wall at the top. Below it the miracle of twelve-year old Christ is presented. This happened in Jerusalem when his parents found him in the temple discussing with doctors, '... all that heard him were astonished at his understanding and answers' (*L.K.* 2:47).

After Baptism, Jesus' Ministry to the sick is presented at Sopoćani in exonarthex. The intermittent chapter of Temptation of devil doesn't find place on the walls, but the Transfiguration is given a place below the Nativity. The Transfiguration occurred after his finding the twelve Apostles, Galilean ministry, the Sermon on the Mount (Hattin), and the ministry of Capernaum. Jesus took Peter James and John amid the wild grand solitudes of Mount Herman at Cesarea Philippi,[165] and prayed intensively getting alone. The Apostles, after little prayers, lay down to sleep in their cloaks but soon were awakened by a sense of strange happening. They saw Jesus and 'as he prayed the fashion of his countenance was altered, and his raiment was white and glistening. And, behold, there talked with him two men which were Moses and Elias, who appeared in glory, and spake of his decease which he should accomplish at Jerusalem' (*L.K.* 9:29, 30, 31). Jesus' way to Jerusalem (Eucharist, symbolically), and the entry is painted in the nave on north wall. It is followed by the Washing of the feet, the Last Supper and the Eucharist at the house of John Mark in Jerusalem. At the garden of Gathsemane, on the Mount of Olives near Jerusalem, Jesus submitted all his worries, agonies with trust to the Father, knowing his forthcoming crucifixion, betrayal and future of the Church. Judas betrayed him by identifying him with a kiss in front of the soldiers. It was followed by the trial by Caiaphas—the high priest, the Sanhedrin—the Jew council of chief priest and elders, and Pilate—the Governor of Judea. The charge was: '... this fellow perverting the nation, and forbidding to give tribute to Caesar, saying that he himself is Christ a King' (*L.K.* 2:3). The high priest and the Sanhedrin found Jesus guilty of death, Pilate could not find so. But the instigated crowd constrained upon him, and Pilate at last delivered Jesus to be crucified. The Crucifixion is presented on the side of 'Dormition' on the south wall of the nave. At Golgotha Jesus was crucified with two robbers. Crying 'My God, why has thou forsaken me' (*Matt.* 46:28), Jesus 'yielded up the ghost' (*Matt.* 28:50). Mary Magdalene, Mary the mother of James and Joseph followed Jesus till the end, the Apostles fled in fear. He was laid in tomb and watched by Angels. The two Marys came to see the sepulchre[166] and met the resurrected Christ. Also, Christ appeared to the Apostles at Galilee. St. Thomas could not believe till he touched the wound on his side. These are all painted on the sanctuary walls in the nave along with the Pentecost, where the Church was born. Christ's descent into Limbo was to bring light for those long awaiting life after death[167] before His 'Ascension.'

Along with many parables and the Last Judgment, the artists of Sopoćani painted important events of the lives of contemporary kings and saints, specially in chapels devoted to them, i.e., St. Nicola, St. George and St. Simeon Nemanja. Near the Last Judgment on the west wall of the narthex, the Old Testament story of Joseph, son of Jacob (plate 69), runs in tiers starting from the upper left. Joseph was the most beloved of Jacob out of his twelve sons. On receiving a beautiful coat from his father he aroused the envy of the rest. They threw him in a pit while tending sheep and then sold him to the passing-by Ishmelites who took him to Egypt where he was auctioned to Potiphar. His wife wanted to entice Joseph, now full-grown, but the latter ran away leaving his garment, caught by the lady (second panel right extreme); Joseph was charged and imprisoned on this evidence. Winning the hearts of prisoners by his good behaviour and by his faculty of reading dreams, he became known to Pharos whose dream of famine he decoded and thus won the Governorship and Prime-ministership (second left scene on third tier). He stored abundant grain during the next seven years and used it for the great famine that followed. He even fed starving people coming from other countries to Egypt. Thus Jacob heard of 'the Magician' in his famine distress and sent his ten sons riding on asses. They were recognised by Joseph but he kept Simeon as hostage and sent the rest nine to bring the youngest brother also. The brothers found in the sack of grain the cost in money returned and tied up in the mouth of sacks. After persuasion Jacob allowed the youngest, Benjamin to go with all, taking back the returned cost of grains with gifts. Again Joseph favoured them this time with a gift of silver cup to Benjamin, and bid them a most courteous farewell. They were, however caught by guards, as designed, and sent back to Egypt. This time Joseph could not hide emotions and sent them all with riches to bring his father. For seventeen years the father lived with the sons. Later, on Jacob's death bed the two sons of Joseph received the benediction. And at the time of his death his twelve sons (the twelve tribes of Israel as nation) stood by the side of Jacob; the embalmed body of the Patriarch was sent back but that of Joseph, dying at the age of one hundred and ten, remained in Egypt.

Comparative

Sopoćani's function as a royal mausoleum and the cathedral church together, points to its enlarged function of decoration from being liturgical to the didactic, which widened the range of the painted subject matter. Thus subjects from the Old and the New Testaments were taken up along with the ecumenical councils combining national saints, martyrs, God's Vice-regents (kings) and their family as donors. All this gets juxtaposed like the mythic identification of the past and the present in the circular conception as was the subject matter presented at Ajanta, similar to the Master's identification of the past characters with the present at the end of his discourse. The scenes of Ajanta included subjects from *Avadānas* and *Jātakas* showing every sentient being, and a world of myriad forms. Thus, Sopoćani, although presents the 'microcosm of the actual world,' forms only a small fragment of the epic of Life depicted at Ajanta.

It is not only that the Bodhisattva Kundakumāra's story in the *Kśantivādi Jātaka* (of which only the inscription remains on the outside wall of cave 2 at Ajanta) bears resemblance to the 'passion' cycle of Christ's life, but also that St. Jerome (A.D. 340) narrates the Buddha's life and his virgin birth.[168] St. John of Damascus, (eighth century A.D.) wrote the story of Hermit Barlaam and prince Josaphat, virtually the story of the great Renunciation of the Buddha, which became the ideal of Christian monasticism and asceticism. By the sixteenth century Josaphat was made a saint in the Greek Orthodox Church.[169] It is significant to point out here that only by the fourteenth century, as Millet observes, the narratives and liturgical cycles were fully developed for the Church decoration. The other important factor connected with Josaphat story is that the major theme is interwoven with Indian fables and parables. The animal fables painted at Beram (1474 A.D.), Yugoslavia,[170] conform to such influences having deeply penetrated Yugoslavian land also.

Coming to the scenes concerning the protagonists of painted narratives at Ajanta and Sopoćani, there is a 'striking resemblance' between the life and teaching of Gautama the Buddha and the Gospel Story. Dr. S. Radhakrishnan points out that both were 'miraculously conceived and wondrously born.'[171] Gautama's father was informed by angels and *Lalitavistāra* informs of a virgin's life led by the Queen for thirty-two months.[172] The birth was announced to her as well. Erich Neumann speaks of primordial Mother Goddess symbolism of child bearing virgin, the Great Mother, with ear of grain—the earth gold corresponding to heavenly gold or luminous son. Supernatural conception and birth also belong to the archetypal sphere of the virgin. Neumann mentions

Akkadian basalt seal from the middle of the third millenium, showing the adoration of kings and shows its similarity with a Christian stone ring of fourth century A.D.[173] Four great kings also receive the new born Gautama. Although the Patriarchal spirit is obvious in the protagonist, the matriarchal concern of the subject matter is accentuated by the prominence given to the 'Dormition' at Sopoćani and Good and Evil aspects of Great-mother presented at Ajanta in the 'Wheel of Life' and by the excessive number of women presented in almost all aspects. Both Christ and Gautama were descendants in royal houses. Similarity in the names of Māyā and Mary has also been traced to archetypal symbolism.[174]

Future greatness is predicted on the day of birth. Radhakrishnan notes that "Asita is the Buddhist Simeon. He comes through air to visit the infant Gautama. Simeon came by the spirit into the temple."[175] Both Jesus and Siddhārtha revealed their unusual wisdom at about the same age, although the difference is that Jesus does through learned discourses and Siddhārtha through meditation.[176] Osborne also points to the similarity of 'Word' or 'Logos' as the 'fundamental' behind them, the Buddha being the incarnation of *buddhi*, the intermediary between the Absolute truth and man's mind.[177]

The 'Great renunciation' of the Buddha has similar implications in Jesus' 'missing' years. Likewise both are confronted with 'Temptation.' The Buddha's enlightenment is marked by thirty-two great miracles including healing and the blind receiving sight. He also begins mission with twelve disciples and sets forth 'to establish the kingdom of righteousness, to give light to those enshrouded in darkness and open the gate of immortality to men.'[178] Caring for the sick is again similar in their missionary lives (*Mahāvagga*, viii, 26, *Mat.* 24:40).[179] Condemning ascetic practices, both insist less on sacrament and more on the 'opening of oneself in faith.'[180] The similarity between their ways of discourse and use of parables has been pointedly marked. The Buddha's triumphal entry into his native city of Kapilvastu is marked by his 'Transfiguration' lighting up the city like the 'New Jerusalem illuminated by the lamb.'[181] On the last day before his death his body was again 'transfigured' (*Mahāparinibbāna Sutta* p. 46) and 'a tremendous earthquake was felt throughout the world' on his death (*ibid.*, p. 62). Three months after his death he was again 'transfigured' and identified with self-existent Supreme.[182]

The Buddha's cousin, Devadatt, 'was the Judas among his followers whose attempts of killing him and killers falling down to his feet, awed by his majesty is like the soldiers in the garden of Gethsemane. The edifying purpose of the story of Jacob presented in the narthex at Sopoćani, too, is akin to that of *Jātakas* presented at Ajanta. S. Radhakrishnan finds many of the parables being common: 'Buddha is a sower of the word, he feeds his five hundred brethren at once with a small cake.' Proving chronologically anteriority of Buddhist parables Radhakrishnan also finds analogy of 'walking on water with faith' (*Jātaka* 190 and as given in the Gospel of St. Luke).[183] He further adds that 'in the spirit of *Upaniṣads*' both Buddha and Christ 'demand the death or the sacrifice of the immediate natural existence as the condition of the new richer life.' He as well points to the dissimilarities in their personalities writing that 'while Jesus is angry with the world which will not hear him, the Buddha meets opposition with calm and confidence. He thought of the world as ignorant rather than wicked, as unsatisfactory rather than rebellious.'[184]

D.P. Singhal points out that 'a number of scholars from different countries such as Rudolf Seydel, A.J. Edmonds, and Richard Garbe have insisted on the Christian indebtedness to Buddhism.' He quotes Nicholas Notovitch's nineteenth century study supporting Christ's having visited India and studied here.[185] S. Radhakrishnan, too, confirms to such postulations that the Gospel study being the work of the Evangelists might have got influenced by the cult of the Buddha.[186]

Similarity of many of the practices of worship between Buddhists and Christians[187] led not only to the narrations starting from the left but also to the manner of presentation the identification which required initiation. The identification of saints, prophets and Bodhisattvas with iconic presentations of persons, places, relics and symbols etc., must have become clearer during such rites and services. This also entails a difference in the presentation. At Sopoćani the 'Divine Liturgy' being the overall purpose, the subjects are chosen accordingly with greater stress on each of the narrative's presentation in conformity to the liturgical rites.[188] At Ajanta, such punctuation is very liberal except that the 'divine-images' of the Buddhas and Bodhisattvas are placed in and around the sanctuaries.

REFERENCES

1. Romila Thapar, *A History of India*, 1974, p. 71.
2. Ramesh Shanker Gupte and B.D. Mahajan, *Ajanta, Ellora and Aurangabad Caves*, 1962, p. 40.
   Kālidāsa is said to have visited Ajanta while associated with the court of Chandragupta II. Madanjeet Singh, *The Cave Paintings of Ajanta*, 1965, p. 107.
3. Ibid., p. 256.
4. 'Ajanta's Chronology : Politics and Patronage,' in *Kalādarśāna* (ed.,) Joanna G. Williams, 1981, p. 109.
5. Ibid., p. 188.
   All times, the overlapping of religious myth-making was also due to ignorance, e.g., Bird finds Ajanta's 'Parinirvana' image being called 'Bhīma' by the natives. J. Bird, *Historical*

Researches on the Origin and Principles of the Buddha and Jain Religions, 1847, p. 16.
6. H.A.L. Fisher, *A History of Europe*, Vol. 1, 1970, p. 111.
7. Vojislav J. Djurić, *Sopoćani*, 1963, p. 111.
8. Ibid., p. 112.
9. It is also said that Uroš I married a daughter of the deposed Latin emperor, Baldwin II, and established an alliance with Charles of Anju, heir of the Latin claims to Constantinople—*The New Illustrated Encyclopedia of World History*, (ed.,) W.L. Langer, 1975, p. 267. Further reference pp. 266, 267, 335 to 337.
10. Vojislav J. Djurić, op. cit., 1963, p. 111.
11. S. Radhakrishnan, *Eastern Religions and Western Thought*, 1975, p. 153.
12. Ibid., 154.
13. As a 'missionary of Hellas' and 'untouched by fanaticism' he crowned the statues of Achilles and found temples of Zeus. H.A.L. Fisher, op. cit., p. 53.
14. Walter M. Spink, *Kalādarśāna*, 1981, p. 119.
15. Dr. D. Sť. Pavlović,'The clergy as Builders, Artists and Founder among founders of wooden churches in Serbia,' in *Serbian Orthodox Church*, 1972, Vol. III, No. 3, p. 23.
16. The founder among founders, who has built and restored many temples in Serbia and Macedonia, in the centres of Christianity, Salonika, Constantinople and Mount Athos, Palestine and Mount Sinai and lavished gifts on them "as countless as the sand of the sea". Thus, King Milutin was proclaimed as 'sacred King.' Mila Rajković, *The King's Church in Studenica*, 1964, p.i.
17. S.P.Gupta locates such 'Kings will' in Aśoka, *The Roots of Indian Art*, 1980, p. 13; and locating a corollary of such wills' deep root in the culture of the people, he says that 'the art of the Greeks and the art of the Indians, therefore, represent the kind of King's will,' p. 12.
18. 'The wise Aristotle... writes of the science of politics as if it were contained in the experience of cities small enough to hear the voice of one herald and based on the distinction of slave and free:' H.A.L. Fisher, *A History of Europe*, p. 55.
19. S.P. Gupta sounds objecting to the inclusion of West Asian Monarch.
20. Benjamin Rowland, *The Art and Architecture of India*, 1970, p. 60.
21. H.A.L. Fisher, op. cit., p. 53.
22. Max Weber, *The Religions of India*, 1967, p. 6.
23. Philip Sherrard, *Byzantium*, 1966, p. 76.
24. Anil De Silva, *Chinese Landscape Painting in the Caves of Tun-Huang*, 1967, p. 192.
25. *Marg*, Vol. XXV, No. 4, Sept., 1972, p. 57.
26. J. Bird, op. cit., p. 15.
27. Madanjeet Singh, op. cit., p. 141.
28. Ibid., p. 141.
29. Madeleine Hallade, *The Gandhara Style and the Evolution of Buddhist Art*, 1968, p. 180.
30. Gupte and B.D. Mahajan, op. cit., p. 258.
31. (V.17) ... whose eyes were suffused through fear, as though they were his (own) dear ones. (V. 18) Even he who had been treated affectionately like a son repeated, like a knowing human being, the excellent and pure thoughts in his heart. Vasudev Vishnu Mirashi (ed.), *Corpus Inscriptionum Indicarum*, Vol. V, *Inscriptions of the Vākāṭakas*, 1965, p. 129.
32. C. Sivaramamurti, *South Indian Paintings*, 1968, fig. 3.

33. Ibid., p. 39.
34. Chaitanya Krishna, *A History of Indian Painting: The Mural Tradition*, 1976, pp. 33, 34.
35. Madanjeet Singh, op. cit., p. 141.
36. Romila Thapar, op. cit., p. 102.
37. D. Chattopadhyaya, *Lokāyata*, 1968, p. 468.
38. Ibid., p. 468.
39. Romila Thapar, op. cit., p. 102.
40. Ibid., p. 114.
41. Ibid., p. 111.
42. D. Chattopadhyaya, op. cit., p. 322. Romila Thapar, op. cit., p. 160.
43. C. Sivaramamurti, *The Art of India*, 1977, p. 175.
44. R.N. Misra, *Bhārtīya Murtikala*, 1978, p. 136.
45. Walter M. Spink, 'Ajanta's Chronology: Politics and Partonage,' in *Kalādarśāna* (ed.,) Joanna G. Williams, 1981, p. 109.
46. J.F. Hurst, *Indika*, 1891, p. 309.
47. Nada Komnenović, *Yugoslav Medieval Frescoes and Plaster Casts*, 1979, p. 7. 'The very way of life of these people may be traced to Byzantine origin.' Philip Sherrard, *Byzantium*, 1966, p. 119.
48. Arnold Houser; *The Social History of Art*, Vol. I, 1968, p. 119.
49. Philip Sherard, op. cit., p. 81.
50. Ibid., p. 124.
51. Vojislav Djurić, *Sopoćani*, 1963, p. 111.
52. Philip Sherrard, op. cit., p. 122. 'Byzantine peasant and small landowners had the life what it is today for the Turkish and Balkan peasant,' p. 113.
53. Arnold Houser, op cit., p. 118.
54. Nada Komnenović, op. cit., p. 13; and related scene of dance with 'conversation' motif at Dečani (north aisle, A.D. 1335 to 1350), plates 18 and 19. Pavle Mijović, *Dečani*, 1963. Painted by group of masters, 'pictres graeci,' from coastal region. Šakota, Mirjana, *Decani*, 1960, p. 13. Earlier representations of such scenes are at St. Nikita and Gračanića—early 14th cent.
55. Svetozar Radojčić, *Kalenić*, 1964, p. x.
56. Ernst Kitzinger, *Byzantine Art in the Making*, 1977, pp. 34, 38.
57. Philip Sherrard, op. cit., pp. 178-79.
58. Ibid., p. 118.
59. Svetozar Radojčić; op. cit., pp. xiii, xiv. Such revivals are of the type of silver plate in Madrid 'silver Missorium of the Emperor Theodosius' with personification of Terra which 'evoke the memories of Attic art of the fifth century B.C., in recumbent female figure with cornocupia and three little nude putti surrounding her and playfully offering the gifts of her abundance to the monarch': Earnst Kitzinger, op. cit., pp. 31, 32, plates 37 and 39.
60. Mila Radojčić, *Milešva*; 1963, p. 69.
61. Branko Fučić, *Istarske Freske*, 1963, p. 19, (plate 103). The ultimate source of such folk symbolism are those like the clay figurines of Mother Goddesses (plate 109) of Yugoslavia's Bronze age found at Kaličevać, Hermaphroditic idol (plate 110) and female torso found in a sanctuary at Istria (*c.* 700-300 B.C): Erich Neumann, *The Great Mother*, 1955, pp.

103, 108, 110, figs. 6, 137.

Belonging to such traditions are also the miraculous Hilandar icon of the three-handed Virgin (*Serbian Orthodox Church*, Vol. III, No. 3, 1972, p. 31,) and the three-headed saint Trinity C. XIII century (plate 101) found in a village church at Sremu, whose predecessors were delineated by Radoslav M. Grujić in St. Clement Ohrid, Monastery of Matejca, Monastery of Studenica, church of St. Klement, and other places, including Sopoćani—'Ikonografski Motiv Slican Induskom Trimurti U Staroj Srpskoj Likovnoj Umetnosti,' *Tkalčićev Zbornik*, I, Zagrab; 1955, 101, Sl. 12.

62. Philip Sherrard, op. cit., p. 12.v
63. Ibid., p. 113.
64. Radojčić, op. cit., pp. XVI, XXIV.
65. Philip Sherrard, op. cit., p. 113.
66. Now scholars opine that Cyrillic alphabet was in fact composed by the end of ninth century by Constentine the priest and earlier Cyril invented Glagolitic—the older Slavonic alphabet: Partridge, *Serbo-Crotian*, 1964, p. 14.
67. Vojislav Djurić, op. cit., 1963 p. 111.
68. Maurizio Taddei, *Monuments of Civilization, India*, 1977, p. 132.
69. King Stephen Nemanja's first son king Radoslav (1227-33), while being 'driven crazy by his beautiful wife' was dethroned by his younger brother king Vladislav: Svetozar Radojčić, *Mileševa*, 1963, p. 67.
70. Svetozar Radojčić, *Kalenić*, 1964, p. xxii.
71. Review, 'Buddhism and Vedāntā' in *Prāci-Jyoti*, Vol. V, Part 2, December 1967, p. 512.
72. S. Gladstone, *Jottings at Ajanta*, 1923, p. 46.
73. S. Radhakrishnan and C.A. Moore, (eds.,) *A Source Book of Indian Philosophy*, 1967, p. 272.
74. Two realities are believed (1) of ceaseless changing and (2) of beyond it, eternal. Thus conditional existence having place in 'cause-effect-chain alone is in flux, beyond is *nirvāṇa*, (*śūnya*) or Mahatma-like Brahman of Vedantin is eternal or absolute.' Dr. S.S. Barlingay, 'Buddhism and Change,' *Buddhist Studies in India* (ed.,) R.C. Pandeya, 1975, p. 80.
75. Arnold Toynbee, *A Study of History*, 1972, p. 80.
76. "They started a school called 'The Subjects of Artists.' The whole movement is involved with mythology. Jackson Pollock is, and Newmann is... They're all involved with mythology. The great movement in American art is a mythological projection by the artists into a totally new imagery." Harold Rosenberg in an interview, *Lalit Kala Contemporary*, 26, Sept. 1978, p. 23.
77. V.V. Ivanov, 'About Conceptions of Buddhist Logic and Contemporary European Science, in *Prāci-Jyoti*, Vol. V, Part 2, Dec. 1967, p. 514.
78. W.S. Karunaratne, 'The meaning of the Buddhist Culture,' review in *Prāci-Jyoti*, Vol. V, Part 2, Dec. 1967, p. 516. A.K. Commaraswamy, *Elements of Buddhist Iconography* 1972, p. 58.
79. Ramesh Shanker Gupte and B.D. Mahajan, op. cit., p. 18.
80. R.C. Dwivedi, 'Buddhist Mysticism,' in R.C. Pandeya (ed.,) *Buddhist Studies in India*, 1975, pp. 108-09.
81. Nihararanjan Ray, *Idea and Image in Indian Art*, 1973, p. 18.
82. Erich Neumann, *The Great Mother*, 1955, pp. 232-38.

83. V.V. Mirashi (ed.,) *Corpus Inscriptionum Indicarum,* Vol. V, *Inscriptions of the Vākāṭakas,* 1963, p, 128.
84. D.C. Bhattacharya, *Studies in Buddhist Iconography,* 1978, pp. 8, 34.
85. Juan Mascaro, (Trans.) *The Dhammapada,* 1973, pp. 38, 48.
86. Ramesh Shanker Gupte and B.D. Mahajan, op. cit., pp. 257-60.
87. D.C. Bhattacharya, op. cit., p. 29.
88. Ramesh Shanker Gupte and B.D. Mahajan, op. cit., pp. 263, 260.
89. Max Weber, *The Religions of India,* 1967, p. 253.
90. R.C. Dwivedi, op. cit., p. 116.
91. The concept of individualistic perfectionism in Hīnayāna.
92. R.C. Dwivedi, op. cit., p. 116.
93. Ramesh Shanker Gupte and B.D. Mahajan, op. cit., pp. 260-61.
94. Dr. S.S. Barlingay, op. cit., 1975, p. 79.
95. F.D.K. Bosch, *The Golden Germ,* 1960, pp. 197-98. Berger John: 'Individuality can no longer be contained within the terms of manifest personality traits... an already established social stereotype. Every mode of individuality now relates to the whole world'—(This seems to be pleading for Buddhist painters). 'No More Portraits,' in *Arts in the Society,* (ed.,) Paul Barker, 1977, pp. 50, 51.
96. R.C. Dwivedi, op. cit., p. 103 (*Italics added by the researcher*).
97. Ibid., p. 103.
98. Ibid., p. 105.
99. Ganeswarananda Swami, 'Buddhism and Vedānta,' review in *Prāci-Jyoti,* Vol. V, Part 2, Dec. 1967, p. 512.
100. Max Weber, op. cit., pp. 205, 233.
101. Dr. S.S. Barlingay, op. cit., p. 81.
102. N. Dutt, *Buddhist Sects in India,* 1978.
103. David L. Snellgrove, (Gen. ed.,) *The Image of Buddha,* 1978, p. 9.
104. R.C. Dwivedi, op. cit., p. 118.
105. Ramesh Shanker Gupte and B.D. Mahajan, op. cit., p. 15.
106. Albert Grünwedel, *Buddhist Art in India,* 1972, p. 13.
107. David L. Snellgrove (Gen. ed.,) op. cit., p. 10
108. Ist (in 325) dealt with the Holy trinity, 2nd (381), 3rd (431) and 4th (451) discussed and passed decrees on issues over the person of Jesus Christ. 7th's (787) decisions were reaffirmed by the council in A.D. 843 proclaiming legitimate place of *heritage tradition,* i.e., icons, cross, symbols, representations etc., the Ecumenical decisions were *sacred traditions.* D.J. Constantelos, *The Greek Orthodox Church,* 1967, pp. 91, 95.
109. Basil Bishop of Zicha, 'The Importance of the Celebration of the 750th Anniversary of the Autocephalous Serbian Orthodox Church', in *Serbian Orthodox Church,* Vol. III, No. 3, 1972, p. 2.
110. Dr. Dusan Lj. Kašić 'The Serbian Orthodox Church and its Administrative Units,' in *Serbian Orthodox Church,* Vol. III, 1972, pp. 50, 56.
111. J. Contantelos, op. cit., p. 22.
112. Ibid., p. 23.
113. Ibid., p. 65.
114. Ibid., p. 19. Patriarch of Serbia, German, expresses after about 750 years on the celebration

of the anniversary of the Autocephalous Serbian Orthodox Church.
115. Basil Bishop of Zicha, op. cit., p. 6.
116. Philip Sherrard, op. cit., pp. 171-72.
117. Ibid., p. 180.
118. Basil Bishop of Zića, op. cit., p. 9.
119. D. J. Constantelos, op. cit., pp. 56-66.
120. Ibid., p. 24.
121. Philip Sherrard, op. cit., p. 99.
122. D. J. Constantelos, op. cit., p. 67.
123. Ibid., p. 68.
124. Ibid., p. 74.
125. Ibid., p. 75.
126. Ibid., p. 79.
127. Ibid., pp. 79-82.
128. Ibid., p. 83.
129. Ibid., pp. 84-89.
130. Dr. Dušan Lj. Kasic, *Hilandar and Serbia, Serbian Orthodox Church*, 1972, Vol. III, No. 3, p. 27.
131. Ibid., p. 27.
132. D.T. Rice, *The Appreciation of Byzantine Art*, 1972, pp. 119-20.
133. Philip Sherrard, op. cit., p. 29.
134. Ibid., p. 177.
135. Dr. Mirjana Ljubinković, *Ravanica*, 1966, p. v. D.T. Rice, op. cit, p. 9.
136. Max Weber, op. cit., p. 6.
137. Y. Krishna, 'The Transformation of the Buddhist Sangha', review in *Prāci-Jyoti*, Vol. XII, 1976, p. 170.
138. Max Weber, op. cit., p. 8.
139. Y. Krishna, op. cit., p. 170.
140. Max Weber, 'Major Features of World Religion' in *Sociology of Religion*, R. Robertson, (ed.,) 1969, p. 40. Max Waber, *The Religions of India*, 1967, pp. 342-43.
141. R.S. Lee, *Freud and Christianity*, 1962, p. 113. Max Waber, op. cit., p. 342.
142. *K. Marks and F. Engels on Religion*, p. 344.
143. David L. Snellgrove and Tadeuz Skorupski, *The Cultural Heritage of Ladakh*, 1977, p. 12.
144. *K. Marks and F. Engels on Religion*, pp. 329-30.
145. Max Weber, op. cit., 1967, p. 249.
146. Ibid., p. 249
147. Dr. Mirjana Ljubinković, op. cit., 1966, p. ix.
148. Dr. R.C. Dwivedi, 'Buddhist Mysticism,' in R.C. Pandeya (ed.,) *Buddhist Studies in India*, 1975, p. 107.
149. Dr. Dušan, L. Kasić, 'Hilandar and Serbia', *Serbian Orthodox Church*, Vol. III, No. 3, 1972, p. 26.
150. Max Weber, op. cit., pp. 238, 241.
151. D.T. Suzuki quoted by Dr. R.C. Dwivedi, in R.C. Pandeya (ed.,) op. cit., 1975, p. 111.
152. R.S. Lee, op. cit., 1962, p. 97.

153. This aspect of the onlooker's psychology is given importance in the school of experimental psychology. In support of this Rudolf Arnheim (*Art and Visual Perception*, 1960, p. 18) quotes an experiment done by Wölfflin on Raphael's 'Sistine Madonna' by explaining the loosening, the balance and the content in its image in the mirror. The effects are found to be parallel in the invert print of 'the Dying Princess' accidentally done in Madanjeet Singh's *The Cave Paintings of Ajanta*, 1965, plate 53. In this inverted right to left depiction (plate 71) the whole conception and balance is lost. The crown-bearer becomes the epilogue of the narration instead of being its prologue resulting in havoc to the narrative.
154. A. Ghosh, (ed.,) *Ajanta Murals*, 1967, p. 4.
155. Dr. Kumudini Mehta, 'The Jatakas,' in *The Times of India Annual*, 1972, pp. 61-66.
156. Albert Grünwedel, op. cit., pp. 53-57.
157. David L. Snellgrove, (Gen. ed.,) op. cit., p. 97.
158. R.N. Mishra, op. cit., p. 94. In depicting the life of Gautama the researcher has extensively used R.S. Gupte and B.D. Mahajan, op. cit., pp. 1-19.
159. D.T. Rice, op. cit., 1972, p. 120.
160. Paintings on the dome are completely lost.
161. Friedrich Rest, *Our Christian Symbols*, 1956, p. 15.
162. Arnold Toynbee, op. cit., p. 455.
163. George Every, *Christian Mythology*, 1972, p. 84.
164. Ibid., p. 83-84.
165. 'The Gospels do not tell us where the mount of Transfiguration was. The traditional site is Tabor but it was probably some height near Caesarea Philippi instead,' H.F. Rall, *The Life of Jesus*, 1928, p. 114.
166. It is as such painted in Sopoćani but the Gospel stories do not agree on whether they were Marys or with Salome or Mary Magdalene alone. H.F. Rall, op. cit., p. 190.
167. J.P. Smyth, *A People's Life of Christ*, 1926, p. 398.
168. S. Radhakrishnan, *Eastern Religions and Western Thought*, 1975, p. 118.
169. D.P. Singhal, *India and World Civilization*, Vol. I, 1972, p. 208.
170. Branko Fučić, *Istarske Freske*, 1963, Pl. 56.
171. Dr. S. Radhakrishnan, op. cit., p. 177.
172. *Ibid.*, p. 177.
173. Erich Newmann, op. cit., pp. 312—17.
174. D.P. Singhal, op. cit., p. 390.
175. Ibid., p. 177.
176. Ibid., p. 390.
177. Ibid., 110.
178. Quoted from *Mahāvagga* I. 6.8 by S. Radhakrishnan, op. cit., p. 178. He observes that 'Buddhism was in its very nature a missionary religion. In the second century B.C. Buddhist ascetics (*ṣamanas*) were found in Western Persia and in the first century B.C. in Bactria:' pp. 181-82, note 6.
179. Ibid., p. 179.
180. Ibid., p. 180.
181. Ibid.
182. Ibid., pp. 181, 183.
183. Ibid., p. 181.

184. Ibid., pp. 183, 184.
185. Ibid., p. 112.
186. Ibid., 187.
187. S. Radhakrishnan points to many practices common to Indian and Christian worships, such as the tonsure and the altar ritual including incense, flowers, lights and singing, which he postulates to have 'grown independently' but he finds 'some, such as celibacy, relics, and confessions, which are old and established institutions in Buddhism and seem to have no parallels in Jewish, Syrian, or Egyptian antiquity.' S. Radhakrishnan, op. cit., pp. 185-86, note 1.
188. 'About the middle of the fourteenth century the narrative tendency was dominant in Serbian wall painting, numerous cycles jostled each other on the church walls in a rather arbitrary way. But towards the end of the century the artists suddenly became more restrained; the subjects were carefully selected, and great sensibility was displayed in bringing their arrangement into harmony with the interior architecture:' Svetozar Radojčić, *Kalenić*, 1964, p. v.
Special reference should be made to the fruitful efforts of Dieter Schlingloff in correctly identifying and interpreting many of the paintings in Ajanta caves, which was first published in 1987. *Studies in the Ajanta Paintings Identifications and Interpretations*, Ajanta Publications (INDIA), Delhi.

CHAPTER III

INTERPRETATIVE CATEGORIES
Ajanta, Sopoćani, Comparative

Ajanta: Philosophy

The inscription in cave 17 of Ajanta, in gist, reads '.... They were glorious as the sun and the moon... of those, the creepers of whose glory and friendship have spread and who conduct themselves always in happiness and mutual agreement....'[1] (VS. 10, 11). These words, used as eulogy to kings, also point to a source-philosophy of the tradition well-established much before the advent of the Buddha. These were the traditions of Vedic philosophy[2] and popular cult worship.[3] Of the second tradition, D. Chattopadhyaya speaks as the ancient materialism (*Lokāyata*) of India ever prevalent in the form of Tantra.[4] This, being non-Vedic, always remained as survival of the tribal-past. But as a source working upon the aesthetics of the era, they were tremendously potent and provided that zest by which the great activity of art of Ajanta was accelerated and in the later phase, it was accomplished, to quote W.M. Spink in a 'bare quarter of a century.' The Buddhists accepted both as the key source to provide a 'prescriptive' philosophy of the 'flux'[5] and the 'forthcoming' to create the works of art.[6] It gave the anabolic signification[7] to the 'Law of Dynamic Direction'[8] (Köhler), in space relativity and in time relativity, a 'being' of ever presence in 'eternal-continuum.' Both the forces, quoted above in Ajanta inscription, reflect the 'theory of light' as the glories of sun (luminosity), and moon (illumination), the first symbolising *purūśa* or *prajñā* (male-principle) and the second representing *prakṛti* or *upāya* (female-principle).[9] Together they became the creative force as 'creeper' being the symbol of life-principle, *prāṇa*. It is what *Taittirīya Upaniṣad* propounds and Tantra literature speaks.[10] The wealth of *upāyas* in the Mahāyāna range from the sophisticated dialectic of Nāgārjuna 'freeing the mind,' to doctrine of liberation, *sukhavati*, through faith in 'Boundless light' of Amitābha, including all the variations of Tantric Buddhism.[11]

The source of Vedic literature forms part of the pastoral-patriarchal ideas and agricultural matriarchal ideas form part of *Lokāyata* tradition.[12] The Buddhist dialectical approach makes use of both. However, in course of time, the earlier patriarchal stratum was annulled or relativized with 'fundamental matriarchal structure proving so strong in orient.'[13] For example, *Udarmukh* motif, included during Vākāṭaka period at Ajanta,[14] indicates what Neumann points out as 'the positive elementary characters of the great vessel of the female body. . . emphasizing 'belly' zone connecting it with mouth and womb—the Great Mother,' while commenting on similar terracotta Baubo figures of fifth century B.C. from Asia Minor.[15] Dominance of matriarchal structure is also clearly exemplified in the prevalence of Mother Goddess images.[16] The womanhood painted in almost all of its aspects at Ajanta is in concrete conformity to the said principle. The pastoral-patriarchal could be traced back to the prehistoric art. The holes, circles and dashes of brush-strokes by these artists are abstract symbols of the universal male-female principles. These are also conveyed in the relationship of the painted animals containing the magic reality as well, presenting the ecological and seasonal stories. These concepts were later transformed into mother-goddess cults representing agricultural-matriarchal ideas. Further archaeological evidences prove that by the time of protohistory, (Mohanjodaro seals, plate 107)[17] and later (ring-stones with yogic implications continuing till late Sunga period, plate 108), the concepts of mother goddess were intermingled with the ideas of 'Tree of Life.'[18] In these, patriarchal and matriarchal bases were given different levels of symbolism and conceptions implying the coming to terms with the enigma of life and death. Gupta pertinently points to the *śavamudrā* of mother-goddess on ring-stones giving the philosophy of life-cycle in which Death and Birth are two stages of continuous process depicted as winding rhizomes of the lotus in some of the ring-stones from Taxila.[19]

The cult of mother-goddess with its archetypal imagery throughout the world has been thoroughly investigated by E. Neumann. With the support of Jung's theory of archetypes of the collective-unconscious manifested in the mythological motifs, he has arrived at a cohesive archetypal group of Good Mother and Terrible Mother.[20] Their elementary and transformative characters encompass the images at Ajanta—from 'Wheel of Life' (plate 105, in the verandah of cave 17) to the Buddhas with Bodhi-trees (cave 9) and from the imagery of *Prajñāpāramitā* (cave 1) to Hariti (cave 1). The 'Tree of Life' motif, being the basic element of Buddhistic iconography and Indian symbolism, was fully expounded by F.D.K.

Bosch.[21] He sums up the primordial duality of male and female, as Agni and Soma elements becoming the creative breath into the primary element 'water' in 'Hiraṇyagarbha'[22]—(the Golden germ, *Ṛg Veda* X, 121, 129). Based on this he further develops the philosophy of 'tree of life' with Padmamūla and Brahamamūla variations (plate 22) in their two-dimensional and three-dimensional images giving clue to the images from Cakra to Sun-pillar and the creeper (endless surge of form emerging from cosmic matter).

These basic ideas forming the essentials of Indian art, were elaborated in the paintings of Ajanta. Referring to Kālidāsa's *Vikramorvaśi* S.N. Dasgupta writes:

> Urvashi transformed herself into a creeper and the creeper was again transformed into the nymph. The unity between plant life and human life is so well illustrated in the paintings of Ajanta that even when a man and a woman are depicted as embracing and kissing each other, there is such a purity and innocence, such an absence of voluptuousness that it appeared as if a creeper was entwining a tree. It is this innocence that can justify such paintings in a Buddhist monastery.[23]

It is of vital importance here, to recall again the opinions of Snellgrove and others that plant and animal life 'bequeathed their rhythm and ceaseless flow to the human figure itself.'[24] This *cetanā* or 'force of life' or what *Citrasūtra* describes of painting 'as if breathing' (43:22),[25] in pure graphic terms is the flow of line and plastic quality of modelling (Stella Kramrisch)[26] and *chanda* or canons of art and architecture (Niharranjan Ray).[27] The presentation of this *cetanā* or *citta* is the cause of calling painting and sculptures as *citra* in Sanskrit.[28] Similarly, Yogācāra philosophy asserts that there is no material substance underlying *rūpa* unless it be *citta* itself.[29]

In Yogācāra, formal world arises spontaneously from the 'store-consciousness' (*ālaya-vijñāna*), flowing to *manas* for primordial differentiations, thence to six sense-consciousness (*manovijñāna*) producing sense organs or 'gates' (*āyatana*) through which projects the classified external world. The Buddhist yoga reverses the process by 'stilling the discriminative activity of the mind and letting the categories of *māyā* fall back into potentiality so that the world may be seen in its unclassified 'suchness.'[30]

The *śunya* or 'void' is relatedness or causality of things, which Nāgārjuna proves by showing the dichotomy everywhere. Max Weber looks upon this as a 'systematic dialecticism of Buddha like the dialogue of Socrates'[31] through which a psychic state of tranquillity and security was sought[32] which is 'cool... stoic... equanimity of the knowing man.'[33] But at this 'absolute calm,' the *karuṇā* (compassion) awakens due to the *prajñā* of 'suchness' and 'Bodhisattva lets the projection arise again, having become consciously identified with the playful and purposeless character of the void.'[34] Thus, this 'calm' was defined with the acceptance of everyday reality as 'void is form.'[35] Watts elaborates that 'by *karuṇā* it is seen that the dissolution of forms into the void is in no way different from the particular characteristics of the forms themselves. The life of things is only conventionally separable from their death; in reality the dying is the living.'[36]

The existence of external world was actually taken for granted by all the systems of Indian philosophy; hence there is no word for realism in Sanskrit (D.N. Shastri).[37] For the Buddha the external world existed with all its miseries, thus, as tension reduction process he used psychological means,[38] the essence of which he had put in the 'Noble Eightfold path,' and the formation of Saṁgha in the *Tri-ratna* in which the final authority was ultimately placed in the Buddha.[39] The co-existence and interdependence of various aggregates[40] were formed, (out of Buddha's saying), as philosophy of seeing the external world—that sight consciousness results from the contact of the sight faculty with the sight objects.[41] According to Barua, this explains all mental activities concerning mind and other senses.[42] Thus this 'sight consciousness' taken into the plastic-creativity as per the experiments done in Gestalt theory, proves validity of 'the tension reduction process' as 'the tendency towards simplicity, symmetry, regularity.' Quoting Köhler in naming this tendency as the 'Law of Dynamic Direction,' Arnheim explains it as 'a genuine cosmic principle directed towards the maximum of orderliness obtainable under the given condition of a system.'[43] The orderliness of Saṁgha did provide the corollary with such creative-psychology which is exemplified in Sārnath-Buddha. Its symmetrical and simplified posture expressing relaxed quietude as 'eternal continuum' is also the 'ever-presence' or 'being'[44] and in space relativity, the dominance of the principal figure of the Buddha is portrayed as unaffected by the surrounding activities reduced in size and symbols of iconography—a prescriptive aesthetics amply used in the paintings of Ajanta.

This orderliness points out a factor towards which the Buddha's 'dialectical materialism'[45] was conscious and which his doctrine of Impermanence and Change seems to imply.[46] As it was the outcome of the theory of dependent origin (*Pratītysamutpāda*), the 'orderliness' of visual perception, in creative psychology, seems to have undergone a systematic implication of reaching its structural decay. It is exemplified in the later formal metamorphoses at Ajanta where the individual artist was left to strive, according to his own personality (plate 143), to resolve the dichotomy of 'inner light' (luminosity) and illumination (plate 146). Parallel stress on the acceptance of all natural traits of the person, leading to the goal by themselves, came out in Buddhistic Sahajayāna.[47] Decorative and aniconic presentations of Hīnayāna and later during Mahāyāna, the liberal brushing, 'abstraction by inbrading'[48] and the spatial organization adopting grading system all speak of a felt-logic of 'reductivism' which the formal tendency of modernism has made clear.[49] It is also applied by condensing of narrative details in icons, leading finally to the Zen master's 'abstract' experiments on 'marvellous void.'[50] Thus, since the value of structural theme is constantly diminishing in creativity of visual perception, the second law of thermodynamics—'Entropy'—that in the material universe disorder increases, could be implied verifying such 'structural decay.' R. Arnheim, explaining the implication of this law on art in its metaphorical sense,[51] explains that the 'constancy principle' of Freud (namely, the dominant tendency of psychophysical existence is striving to keep tension at a minimum or eliminate it—'*Nirvāṇa* principle') has within it a negative concept of catabolic dissolution whereby 'instincts are drives of the live organism to return to the inorganic state[52] ... stimulation from the outside and impulses from the inside are viewed as producing disturbing tension, and the strategy of the ego endeavours to steer in mind toward desirable quiescence.' As such, David Riesmann has observed —'It seems clear that Freud, when he looked at love or work, understood man's physical and psychic behaviour in the light of the physics of entropy and the economics of scarcity.'[53] Arnheim puts both, the disorderly destruction (including metamorphosis played by seasons and time), and lowering of the level of order (which is the cause of promoting orderliness because of striving towards simplicity), as the factors to increase the entropy while losing the structural theme.[54] (Parallel to it is the decreasing influence of Buddhism and the 'decline' of the style of Ajanta.) The elemental matriarchal principle of 'terrible-mother' had the reign—as the 'Wheel of Life' painted in cave 17 also proves this aspect of mother-goddess. The lurking sadness in the scenes presented at Ajanta also conforms to this 'decay.' Thus the 'creative' philosophy of this Indian 'Temple of Graces'—Ajanta, starting from Hīnayāna's patriarchal stratum gave way to matriarchal in Mahāyāna along with a co-existence of both, with Good-mother transcendentally abstracting herself into *Prajñā* (male principle 'luminosity' and highest wisdom) and the elementary form of the Terrible-mother as 'she is whirling wheel of life birth-bringing' and death-bringing totality.'[55] And the 'birth-bringing' was provided within this 'catabolic dissolution' or 'death-bringing' as the two stages of continuous process in the creeper growth, the *prāṇa*, the 'forthcoming' surge of forms: the only creative possibility of eternal 'flux' of 'powerful biological creativeness... (with) indefinite transition of its modelling (thereby) it suits. . . (the) outlook which refuses, or fails to see anything at all definite in the world.'[56] The flux of life, the Buddhist metaphysics alongwith the Indian metaphysical truth of 'Life Surging out of Primeval-matter' reach its culminating visual-corollary in this 'forthcoming' 'flux' of form. Gestaltist's tension-reduction principle adjusting multiplicity and confusion of form in 'depth-dimension'[57]—ultimately implying the visual aesthetics of reductivism (till entropy)—was naturally sensed in 'suchness' of sight consciousness by the artist of Ajanta; hence to overcome this catabolic reductivism he gave the ultimate visual expression to the anabolic 'forthcoming' or *prāṇa* (propounded as aesthetics in *Citrasūtra* 43: 21, 22); and on the 'border-land' the 'flux' of visual rhythms conform to the *ākāśa-dhātu* or *śūnya*: the space sculptures—the caves—also become 'breathing' as is the pictorial space in interstices, which bulges out becoming dense and cohesive in being bordered by linear forms. The artist of Ajanta, thus, makes the catabolic dissolution into anabolic creativity in this 'flux' philosophy. This anabolic establishment of a structural theme 'introducing and maintaining theme' was further carried over again by creating a myth—the myth of 'Māyā' propounded by Śaṅkarācārya. By then, it was not necessary to give the abstractions of Patriarchal-pastoral mysticism in cave dwellings, since India created Meru 'Primordial-mountain' (worshipped as the Great Mother)[58] in the forms of temples.

Sopoćani: Philosophy

Out of the Nicene (Athanasian) creed of 'dominant faith,'[59] apostolic Serbian Orthodox Church was born between the Orthodox Byzantium and 'crusading' Europe, then full of political aspirations and intrigues, although it kept itself open to the influences both from the East and the West.[60] Thus, accepting both knowledge and faith, the orthodoxy of St. Sava, an autocephalous Church spelling national interests, accepted the Logos theology of Alexandrian circle later represented by Arius with its dichotomy with Faith-Creed of Athanasius.[61] To resolve this dichotomy it accepted Logos—the word of God—as well as naturally inherited the Nicean creed of Virgin as intercessor,[62] whereby king Stefan the First-crowned besought the forthcoming kings of Serbia 'not to insult the Holy Virgin' whose property was the Hilandar, the first Serbian University, where eight of the first ten Archbishops of Serbia were educated in the vein of Middle Age scholastics,[63] and, with Hesychast[64] contemplation.

Giving the history of Serbian Orthodox Church, Bishop Simeon observed its basic tenets as 'the coming down of the Holy Spirit into the soul of Man and into his history regulated by this three-dimensional world which is governed by natural law.' The ethical truth in the 'unadorned preaching of God's word' renews the world throughout the history with 'the infusion of new qualities and spiritual powers first in Man's soul, and then, spontaneously in his behaviours of everyday life.'[65] Thus, with Trinity, the Christian Theories of Historícity, New creation, Spiritual-rebirth and Resurrection, and the theories with ethical implications—Purgatory, Last Judgment and Kingdom of Heaven were given a cohesive unit.

Christian dogmas, being recurrently defined in terms of current beliefs, first found its momentum with 'The hour has come that the son of man should be glorified' (*John* 12:23), and the Greeks found in Jesus the image of their 'unknown' God. St. Sava's 'dialogue' with the Sultan of Egypt[66] was thus a confirmation of universalizing spirit inherited by Serbian Orthodox Church since 'The hour,' and in this vein was the adoption of 'Jovian' image of Christ, a prototype of father image, handed down through Justinian II coins to the artists of Sopoćani blending 'the divine and the human, the solemn and the personal.'[67]

The school of Form criticism argues that the oral traditions were brought together and given a shape suitable to the early Christian communities,[68] thereby, Christianity in the process of proselytizing 'anxiety to spread absorbed the language of every race and class and country,' whereby, as Radhakrishnan sums up, 'it seemed to be all things to all men.'[69]

Starting from a simple 'mystery religion,'[70] Christian theology, becoming Logos theology adopted Graeco-Roman and Graeco-Oriental forms of expression. The Apologists or the liberals both claim to have 'Hellas' as the source,[71]—'the universal church will continue to speak Greek.'[72] The Alexandrian circle with its Jewish Platonism, Gnosticism, Neo-platonism, and Christian Platonism gave great martyrs and profound thinkers, e.g., Clement of Alexandria, Origen, Gregoris,[73] Justin, and Dionysius, to mention a few. Added to it were Judaic forms and rituals from pagan religions, as evident in Serbian orthodoxy picturized in the fresco of Cana's wedding at Kalenić.[74] Almost all the forms of religious philosophy born in Alexandrian circle had the common basis of, as Radhakrishnan points out, 'an abstract of intermediary powers to bridge the chasm between the Absolute and the world, the connexion of matter with the principle of evil, and the recognition of ascetic self-discipline as a means to the clearer vision of absolute vision.'[75] Under the Logos theology Arius defined 'that word was as God—the creator, but as begotten Son was less than God and subjected to pain and change but remained good by his will. The spirit is related to Son as the Son to the Father.'[76] The Nicean resolution in Athanasian Creed brought out the 'dominant Faith' and weaned the tradition of tolerance and scholarship, and resulted in Justinian's closure of the Athenian Schools and codification of Law,[77] to which, the Sacramental doctrine added charms and relics.[78]

To St. James, faith was acceptance of dogma; to St. Paul, it was surrender of heart and mind to Christ, the Epistle to the Hebrews defined it 'as that outreaching of the mind by which we become aware of the invisible world.'[79] The last concept can be regarded as parallel to the Neoplatonic transcendence of the 'will' and 'knowledge.' Representing Christianity as the fulfilment of the aspirations of the Platonic and Stoic systems, the Apologists had the conviction that human philosophy is not complete and Christian revelation, being complete, is the 'cause.'[80] Since it is the 'Revelation' in which the whole tradition of old and new is accepted as the ultimate revelation, it became the Church dogma added with historicity—'... these things saith the first and the last, which was dead and is alive' (*Rev.* 2:8). The tendency chiefly represented by Justin[81] takes Revelation presupposing 'a divine person, one who makes himself known on earth. The Logos is often identified with the prophetic spirit. God cannot be without reason, and so he had always Logos in himself.' As an emanation Logos is the visible God produced for the sake of creation from himself. God being the first principle—'Absolute, self-existing, unchangeable and eternal exalted above every name and distinction.' Justin maintains that 'Christ was and is the Logos who dwells in every man.' He is the principle of vitality and form of everything that is to receive being.[82] 'Later, Irenaeus, agreeing with Gnostics' deification of human nature as highest blessing, affirmed that the creator and God are one and the same. God intends man, in whom exists the only possibility, to realize his immortality. Thus 'by his birth as man the eternal word of God guarantees the inheritance of life of those who in their natural birth have inherited death.'[83] The basic speculation of coming in terms with Life and Death was thus spelt, as its enigma would be in the old Latin hymn saying, 'In the very midst of life we live in the face of death.'[84]

Deification, (theory of spiritual rebirth, fulfilling Medieval Christianity's desire for eternal life),[85] was also recognised by Clement of Alexandria with an approach to God by ecstasy. Salvation to him was through gnosis attained by 'the purifying of the cognitive powers of the soul.'[86] Origon, adopting Platonists, Stoics and The Orientals,[87] too, confirmed 'rising above senses, figures and shadows to the mystical and unspeakable vision,'[88] and advocated prayer as a part of contemplative life.[89] This tradition of Alexandrian school continued in the Cappadocians—Basil and two Gregories 'asserting mystery of the divine being.'[90] For Basil, 'The Kingdom of Heaven is the contemplation of realities.'[91] Augustine with 'Thou has made us for thyself, and our hearts are restless until they rest in thee,' is 'the Christian Plotinus'—as Radhakrishnan remarks.[92] The mystic union for Plotinus was 'with the one beyond Nous' but for Augustine 'the world is itself the absolute.'[93] Dionysius the Areopagitea, the father of Christian mysticism, decisively influenced medieval church with his advice—'Seek therefore silently and mystically that perfect and primitive union with the Archgood.'[94] He distinguished three stages of mystic life—purification, illumination and consummation.[95] Dionysius' concept of a Divine Eros, 'an overflowing love which moves God to create reflections and participants of his bliss and freedom,'[96] is reconciliation between the Absolute (solemn) and the personal; as in art it was found in the father image of the all-ruler *par excellence.*[97]

We may now turn to the popular cults' mysticism as is found in the 'Revelation.' The ancient myth of Adonis[98] echoing in chapter 13, religio-magic rites like '...give him a white stone...' (2:17), image like dragons and negative aspects of the Great Mother (17:3.5), positive and good aspects of the Great Mother (19:7 and 8), Water of life (22:1) and 'Tree of life' (22:14)—all these conform to the sources of a philosophy of the folk traditions. This tradition was based upon the matriarchal principles of peasant-stocks who were and who remained the backbone of the Byzantine nations (the culture of the city dwellers, of course, found the patriarchal principles in the image of the Father-God). It is as well significant for proving the domination of the matriarchal principle that by the middle of the thirteenth century, the motif of 'the Death of Virgin'[99]—Dormition—entered the Byzantine Art.[100] Above all, Constantine's dedicating the new capital to St. Sophia itself proves the reinvigoration of popular matriarchal philosophies, popular since Eleusinian mysteries and confirmed by the clay-statuettes of the Bronze Age of Yugoslavia. These statuettes give the idea of the Balkan civilisation's[101] basic attempts to come to terms with the mystery of life and death—in being extrovertly 'sensuous' in naturalistic form expressing abundance and fertility, and 'introvert' in her aspect as ruler over the spirit and the dead 'favouring and stressing abstract.'[102] Moreover, the clay figurine of Hermaphroditic idol of Yugoslavian Bronze Age[103] (Plate 110) gives sample evidence to the philosophy having a resolution achieved between primeval 'male' and 'female' powers: the dialectical process, contained therein, restarted with the breakdown of classical art in the late second century A.D. and ran in the dichotomy of classical and abstract in art,[104] manifesting itself in the philosophy as exhibited in great striving for blending a 'personal' God with that of the absolute ruler.

From the ninth century onwards, the scholastic of middle age found Plato and Aristotle revived and the University of Byzantium, especially Psellus had a definite contribution in it.[105] Thomas Aquinas, by accepting the transcendence from sensible to pure being through the knowledge of truth (in analogical reasoning), took over the Aristotelian system—whence 'by a consideration of the implications of things we can reach the conception of God... but it is only revelation that gives us his triune nature.'[106] For him a 'beatified consciousness (*lumen gloriae*) distinct from ordinary consciousness (*lumen naturale*) and prophetic consciousness (*lumen gratiae*) is required for a beatific vision.'[107] Thus, in 'beatified consciousness' —'innerlight'—the dichotomy of 'faith' and 'reason' was finally resolved with the latter becoming not the 'competitor' but earlier's 'extension and crowning completion in which it is carried back to God.'[108]

The Arab works introduced a 'curious blend' of Greek, Jewish and oriental philosophy into the Church by the beginning of the tenth century.[109] Bogomils, with their Oriental orientation, the so-called heretical philosophies, influenced the primitive-strata, (i.e., serchophagi-stelae art), as did Berbers with their heretical Manichean belief, 'in a land where the sophisticated forms of Byzantine Art were flourishing.'[110] By the fourteenth century Hesychasts with their theory of 'inner light' and 'contemplation of an almost Buddhist character' had the sway over Mt. Athos and Serbia;[111] earlier, the ground was prepared by the works of Domentian giving 'inner light' as a content matter to the murals at Sopoćani.[112]

Comparative

The Buddha and Christ shunned delving into metaphysics and concerned themselves with 'spiritual-rebirth'.[113] Their teachings were expounded subsequently in the light of older philosophical insights. The Buddha's formulations were *Upaniṣadic* thoughts given 'new orientations.'[114] As for Christian theological implications, classical theories were handled by the Byzantians with 'imaginative tact'.[115] In their process of becoming universal religions, both adapted the philosophical insights ranging from the ancient wisdom to the living traditions of the folks and primitives. There is perceptible over-all transformation from the patriarchal dominance to the agricultural-matriarchal. It is corroborated by the females abounding in the presentations at Ajanta and by the largest space given to the 'Dormition' of Mary at Sopoćani.

The contemplation of realities or the 'inner light' of the orthodox Christians starts with the comprehension of the 'three-dimensional world governed by the natural law' or the *lumen naturale*. For the Buddhists, too, the 'sight consciousness' or the *pravṛtti vijñāna* is the first stage for the consciousness of the unclassified 'Suchness' or *tathatā*. With the stages of comprehensions in these doctrines of deification of human nature or transcendence, the recognition of the existence of suffering or the matter's connection with the evil becomes a prerequisite.[116] To attain the 'unspeakable vision' (Origen) or what is defined by Thomas Aquinas as 'Beatific vision' or the 'Enlightenment experience' of the Buddhistic *Nirvāṇa*, the volitional efforts ('*Orthe-praxe*' or 'the way') of human (only) are deemed to be capable enough in Plotinian-Christianity whereas Bodhisattva vows for the enlightenment of all till 'the last blade of grass.' But there exists cross currents of theories. In the light of medieval realization that 'Christ's birth is eternal' substantiated by such Biblical 'truths' as 'Before Abraham I am,' the conceiving of Him, as A.K. Coomaraswamy argues, 'as a living Tree' or as a 'lamb or Dove,' becomes a 'no less sound theology than to conceive him as Man,' thereby a theological development towards the First Principle, Godhead, parallels that of *Nirvāṇa* to *Parinirvāṇa*[117] and results in 'fulfilling the desires of all sentient beings.' On the other hand in Asaṅga we find the particularity with men in possessing Buddhahood in embryo.[118] Thus result the efforts (*Orthe-praxe* of Orthodox church and the Way of Buddhists) connected with the cessation of the conflicts between volitional faculty and the faculty of contemplation—the faith creeds and the reason adherents.

Buddhists with the aid of Yogācāra devised the contemplation method of stilling the discriminative activity. Knowing that world of form is *cittamātra*—mind only—(A.W. Watts puts it as slightly parallel to Western subjective realism),[119] they allow that the 'categories of Māyā fall back into potentiality'[120] to become conscious of the 'suchness,' which, finding the interdependence—*Servam Kṣanikam* of different stages of consciousness, results in the doctrine of 'flux'—*Servam Santānam.* The *Tanha* or selfish craving/thirst, too, is comprehended as a part of this *Servam Santānam* resulting in *vijñāna*—wisdom of formless-consciousness—which is egoless (*anattā*). This concentration results from the 'Noble Eightfold Path' of *Sammadassana* all inclusive of 'right' life—the varied concepts of which divide the various stages of Buddhistic philosophy from ascetic Hīnayāna to the middle-path of Mahāyāna culminating into Sahajayāna and Tantric thoughts.

The Christian, absorbing the Logos-philosophy, tried to solve the conflict of volitional and contemplative man keeping, as such, the triune nature—mind, form and matter—as the base of development with camping into subjective and objective propoundings. Plotinian distinction of calm mystic ecstasy led them to resolve the conflict of the faith and reason in a mystic experience with intense mental concentration, in solitude. The will in this volitional effort becomes passive but repressing imagination makes effort to recognize the First Principle. This unity with its like occurs when soul ceases as being and thus spirit gains spiritual perception of seeing within and spiritual intuition for apprehending above it. The individuality of soul becoming extinguished, Plotinus retains the individuality of spirit by his theory of compenetration owing to which the ethereal spirits don't have physical barrier as souls have and they are related to their potentiality—the Universal spirit. The synoptic vision of universal ideas at this stage removes the distinction of object and subject.[121] Dionysius puts these stages as purification, illumination and consummation for the 'primitive union with Archetype.' The purification through ethical and moral discipline is *śīla* of Buddhist Bhikkhu as it is 'via purgative' or monks asceticism in Christianity. Stages of *Dhyāna* or contemplation (*samādhi*) in Buddhism corresponds to 'via mystica' of Christianity, its consummation in 'via illuminative' matches *Lokottara-magga.* Finally the *prajñā* of Buddhist is the consummation in *lumen gratiae*, the prophetic consciousness of the Christians. In this 'inner-light' the faith, not remaining as a competitor of reason becomes its 'crowning completion' in which it is carried back to God, who overflowing with 'Divine Eros,' creates 'reflections and participants of his bliss and freedom.' Thus, Christ is the 'Fountain of Life' at Sopoćani. The Bodhisattva also, with the positive attainment of *nirvāṇa* and conscious identification with 'the playful and purposeless character of the Void' where the 'projection arises again,' becomes *Saṁbhoga Kāyā* (enjoyment body). He transforms individual freedom and the peace of Arhat into the consciousness of sacrificing for the universal freedom and peace. What St. Paul acclaims as 'Now the lord of peace himself give you peace always by all means' (II *Thessalonians* 3:16) is similar to what the *Dhammapada* speaks of Buddha whose 'thoughts are peace' (7:93). In Mahāyāna it becomes the doctrine of Liberation—*sukhavati*—and faith in the bondless light— *Amitābha*—similar to 'Kingdom of God' in Revelation where 'The Lord God giveth them light: and they shall reign for ever and ever' (22:5). A.K. Coomaraswamy in fact informs that 'a majority of Buddhists like the majority of Christians, looked forward to a resurrection in "Heaven" *sukhavati*, beholding God or Buddha face to face.'[122]

In *Sahajayāna*, individual traits became 'path' within themselves like the Christian 'glory in infirmities that power of Christ may rest upon him' (*Cor.* 12:9). The conception of spiritual-birth was given a basic matriarchal principle of dissolution or 'death-bringing' becoming the 'birth bringing', i.e., 'He understands that destroyed is rebirth' (*Samyutta-Nikāya* iii: 66).[123] In Buddhism and in Orthodox Christianity it was 'after destroying death by death, he gives life to all.'[124] Myths of Adonis ('true son of the deep water'), Ishtar (reproductive energies of nature) with annual-cycle of vegetable life[125] and the Eleusinian cult of 'peace' to initiates[126] got incorporated with Indian metaphors of the 'Cosmic egg' and the 'wheel of birth' becoming 'purification of soul' and 'cycle of births' for transcendental growth through Orphists and Pythagorians.[127] The *Upaniṣadic* growth of man's higher nature (*Tamas, Rajas* and *Sattva*) finds analogy in Plato's *Logistikan, Epithumia, Thumos,*[128] it gets transformed into Apostolic tradition—'Jesus advanced in wisdom and stature' (*LK* 2:52), with the 'wheel of birth' finding its place in epistle attributed to St. James.[129]

Thus, imbibed in *Hiraṇyagarbha* (Golden germ or Golden egg) are not only the conceptions of 'World soul,' 'Golden-*stūpa*,' *Vāc* or the 'word,'[130] but also of the 'New Jerusalem' with 'Tree of Life' and 'Water of Life' as there are *agni* and *soma* (their equivalents) in it (*Ṛg Veda* X.121).[131]

Ajanta: Aesthetics

The Buddhist *Pañca-skandhas*, i.e., the successive states of stream of consciousness start from recognising the world of form and name. Then relatively, and in the aggregate, the process continues turning into feeling, perception and comprehension, till in the end it becomes formless consciousness.[132] Accordingly, aesthetic object starting from the sight-object is successively given to the state which in Indian Poetics is called suggestiveness (*vyaṅgya* or *dhvani*). This is substantiated by the observation of Ānand Vardhana in his *Dhvanyāloka* that, 'we will only say that our definition of *dhvani* will be at least on a par with the definitions of perception, etc., proposed by the Buddhist philosophers themselves.'[133] The idea of *dhvani* is derived from the principles of Sanskrit grammarians. Patañjali (second century B.C.) had explained that the sum total on the word is the sense of the last syllable containing the comprehension (*saṁskāra*) of the earlier syllables—it is the *sphoṭa* (manifestation) of the word the quality of which is the suggestiveness (*dhvani*).[134] Sivaramamurti, speaking of the relatedness of this suggestiveness to painting, points out that 'poetry is enhanced by skilful verbal suggestions, which evokes the fragrant ideas associated with words, and this quality is equally powerful in the plastic arts.'[135] *Dhvani* is, 'unseen'—*adṛṣṭam*—in *Citrasūtram* (42:47).[136] Nihararanjan Ray supports it there in the sense of *rasadhvani*, with his contention that there is a remarkable similarity between *alaṃkāra* treatises and *śilpa* treatises.[137]

The conception of *dhvani* is the grammarian's *sphoṭa* or the power of the word, which according to *Śabda-Brahmavādins* is the seed of the world and is *nāda* or spoken word. As such, its symbol, the conch over the lotus (the symbol of the earth, plate 11) is presented in Ajanta (Yazdani, *Ajanta*, Pl. II, p. 53 and Pls. XLVIIa, XLIIXd).[138] Thus, it is not difficult to deduce that the formless consciousness—*vijñāna*—was known to the Ajanta artist as *nāda*; like *śūnyatā* (logical category), *Nirvāṇa* (ethical category), the *dhvani* or *nāda* was accepted as the aesthetic category.[139] As *nirvāṇa* was bliss, the highest in aesthetic enjoyment was also the bliss (the theory of *Raso Brahmavāda*), which was also considered as the highest truth in the metaphysical sphere of emotive experience.

Since this is considered singular in the categories of *rasas*, Abhinavagupta calls it as *Mahārasa* and parallels it with the *sphoṭa* considering as the highest ideal, self-content and undivided; he finds it as a thread running in a dramatic composition (*rūpaka*). This he designates as *Śānta-Rasa*[140] (the *rasa* which *Citrasūtra* also propounds as a *citrarasa* suggested in painting 43:1[141].) According to the indications of Bharat, it is *Prakṛti-Rasa*, the emotive experience of Nature from which other categories of *rasas* take their individual abstractions and get manifested in new denotations (B.D. Upadhyaya, who also proves that *śānta-rasa* has been a part of dramatic performances as in *Nāgānanda* where Bodhisattva has been characterised as *Jīmūtvāhana.*[142] Further, influences of theatre on Ajanta paintings are recorded by Ph. Stern and Ratan Parimoo).[143] This *Prakṛti-Rasa*, as discerned through the *prajñā* and explained in Buddhist mysticism, is *anattā* (egoless), *tathatā* (suchness) and *śūnyatā* (vacuity, zeroness). Along with this, Asaṅga's fourth century A.D. assertion that Buddhahood in embryo is present in all living beings and particularly in men[144] must have given impetus to present the image of Buddha. What Nihararanjan Ray calls 'being' or 'ever presence' of nature of 'eternal continuum,' is exemplified in Sārnath Buddha's relaxed attitude suggesting *śānta rasa* of transcendental bliss.[145] It is the registration of compassion of *karuṇā* and the illumination of *prajñā* as 'Water-lily in full bloom,' which, according to Snellgrove and others, is reflected in the Buddhas painted in Ajanta (caves 1 and 2).[146] As such on the images of Buddha, C. Wentinck comments:

> Of all the images of the divine that man has created, these are among the most perfect in their expression of a theological belief. They incarnate the state of Perfection, of the Supreme self, the depersonalized being who has extinguished his will to exist and has therefore realized himself fully. Nowhere else has art invented a formula that so adequately expresses a conception of what lies beyond life.[147]

These images of Buddha turning again into the symbol of 'spoken word' or 'seed of the world' become active space, *śūnyatā* of Zen master's blank canvases.[148] This materialistic dialecticism, in no way differing from spiritual one, is embodied again in the scientific fiction of Arthur C. Clarke, *2001 A Space Odyssey*, in which the whole galaxial-civilization becomes an active space.

In Kantian category of aesthetic experience this is one of 'Sublime' (mathematical and dynamical), which he accepts as an ethical aid as well.[149] 'A priori' of this can be explained in terms of 'ever presence' or 'eternal continuum' along with the concept of *cetanā* or vital rhythm derived out of nature. To quote Kant himself in this regard is worthwhile—'Nature is beautiful because it looks like Art, and Art can only be called beautiful if we are conscious of it as Art while yet it looks like Nature.'[150] P.A. Michalis puts such experience as 'spiritual expression of serene sublimity.'[151]

The emotive suggestiveness (*Citrasūtram* 42:81, 84) or *rasadhvani* is taken to be what is experienced by the appreciator.[152] Ānandavardhana accepts that the aesthetic originality (*camatkāra*) of suggestive meaning and not of assertive meaning, is poetic *dhvani.* Besides, he propounds that in the absence of the above it becomes the suggestiveness of aesthetic quality of style *Guṇībhūta-vyaṅgya.* K.S. Ramaswamishastri, explaining Ānandavardhana, suggests that '*Rasadhvani* (emotional suggestiveness) is thus the soul of poetry and is far more important than *vāstudhvani* (suggesting a fact) or *alaṃkāradhvani* (imaginative suggestion).[153] *Atthaśālinī* and *Samyutta Nikāya* report Buddha saying about painting, 'thus, Brethren that masterpiece of art is designed by the mind. Indeed, Brethren, the mind is even more artistic than that masterpiece.'[154] This is considered by the authors right from S.N. Dasgupta to Krishna Chaitanya as parallel to Croce's concept.[155] Dasgupta not only found, thus, Buddhaghosha (*Atthaśālinī* p. 64) anticipating the theory of art as expression (as intuition) but connecting it with the theory of 'flux' he says that the 'aesthetic state created by the flow of a moment becomes integrally associated with the successive aesthetic states created by the continuance of the same flow so that the aesthetic states of the different moments, being conceived and carried forth and entirely related together as a concrete whole, serve to produce the entire picture as a whole.'[156] Further, considering Buddhaghosa's view that 'internal picture could alone be called the true art while the external picture made in imitation of it is only the external translation,' Dasgupta says that to externalize the Hindu view was required which believed that 'the inner representation must be transported outside,' while quoting treatises on art such as *Śukranītisāra*, *Śilparatna* and *Pañcarata* works.[157]

Thus, the plastic factors and the formalistic tendencies were given a definite importance in the treatises of Indian art. *Citrasūtra* speaks of the art of painting as the act of 'decoration creating beauty'—*citrakarmaiva bhūṣaṇā.*[158] It propounds a complete aesthetics, specially that of Ajanta painter, as follows:

> The surface is as if glistening and embracing as if coming out to meet the spectator, the sweetness is as if smiling, it looks as if endowed with life... that is (beautiful) painting, which looks as if breathing (43:21, 22).[159]

Dasgupta informs that *Samarāngaṇa-sūtradhāra* describes a type of *rasa* as *prem-rasa* which is particularly applicable to plastic art. Calling it a 'joy of art' he categorizes it with the beholder's participating 'in the emotions of the artist through the language of art by which the artist has spoken of his sentiments.' Dasgupta parallels it with the 'significant-form' of Roger Fry, and supports it with Gestalt theories. Later on, this 'significant-form' is given clearer exposition, according to Dasgupta, in *Camatkāra* of the aesthetician Jagannātha in sixteenth century A.D.[160]

Abanindranath Tagore, explaining *Ṣadaṅga*,[161] says that each of them is arranged in a logical succession like a *chanda* (meter). The first *rūpabheda* he establishes as the knowledge of the essence (*marma*) of appearances. He elaborates that this knowledge desires structure of form (*pramāṇa*), and no sooner correct perception and measure is given, the action of feeling starts on the forms (*bhāva*). It is then infused with grace, artistic representation (*lāvaṇyayojnam*); while getting the embrace of similitude (*sādṛśam*) the amazing colour modulations (artistic manner of using the brush and colours—*varṇika bhaṇga*) appear. And this *chanda* starting from the knowledge (*bheda*) and ending in indulation (*bhaṇga*) has the key stone with yoking (*yojanā*). Through this Abanindranath Tagore hints at the rigorous training and *aucitya* (aesthetic appropriateness) mentioned in the art treatises which (with their prescriptive and descriptive approaches) were prevalent, and the artist had to undergo it before becoming a master like Ajanta's *sthavira* Achala Muni. Nihararanjan Ray has related *ṣadaṅgas* to expoundings in *Citrasūtra*.[162] As the Indian art treatises have close kinship with Poetics the whole aesthetic environment of Ajanta resembles that of the plays of Kālidāsa, the famous master of *upamā* (simile), which are replete with *alaṃkāra* (aesthetic ornamentation), *guṇa* (aesthetic quality of style), *rasa* (aesthetic emotion), *dhvani* (aesthetic suggestiveness), *aucitya* (aesthetic appropriateness) and *camatkāra* (aesthetic originality).[163]

In Ajanta inscriptions, the beauty has been designated in three ways: For decoration of pillars etc., the word *manohara*—captivating to the heart—has been used; and *suvīthi* connotes a picture gallery (*vīthi*, with prefix *su* suggests Truth, Beauty and Goodness as being part of Indian tradition because all the treatises on art give specific attention to the images which were 'for the attainment of supreme knowledge by all sentient creatures:' inscription in cave 27, Ajanta.) The third category is pointed out while describing the architecture of the cave as 'clothed in the brilliance'—*prabhā*—'of Indra's crown' (crown of the celestials: an inscription on cave 16).[164] This account confirms that beauty or aesthetic pleasure was taken to be of three types. The first is what *Samarāngaṇa-sūtradhāra* describes as *Prem-rasa* the 'significant-form' (Dasgupta), the second 'the art with Truth, Beauty and Goodness' and the third is a part of the second one described in Kantian term as 'sublime', or the 'luminance.'

The theoreticians in Indian aesthetics have always accepted a dominating *rasa* out of which others become derivative. Bhoja thinks of *Śṛṅgāra* as primary *rasa* and Viśvanātha attributes this position to *Adbhuta.* Accordingly, the practice and theory of art 'led to amplification of the content and application of each *rasa.*' For example, *Vīra Rasa* (heroism) was extended from *yuddhavīra* (heroism in battle) to *dharmavīra* (ethical heroism), *dānvīra* (heroism of munificence) and *dayāvīra* (heroism of compassion). Its further amplifications were in *satyavīra* (heroism in truth), *vidyāvīra* (heroism of knowledge), *tapovīra* (heroism of austerity), *yogavīra* (heroism of Yoga), *kṣamāvīra* (heroism of forgiveness).[165] Such amplifications became the dominant theme also of a particular epoch. Thus it is pertinent to think of *Śānta rasa* as the dominant theme of Ajanta art. In theory of dramatics *bibhatsa* (ghastly) is included as cause of aversion, *jugupsa,* hence feeling of emotion for the dominant flavour, *sthāyībhāva* of *śānta* (abiding peace).[166] The above varieties of *vīra-rasa* are also included among the causes for abiding *Śānta rasa.* All the *Jātakas* and the four causes of Gautamas to seek the *nirvāṇa,* are excellent examples of affecting the dominance of 'one *rasa*'—*śānta*—in the art of Ajanta. Later, *Śṛṅgāra* (love) was amplified into *bhakti* (love of God). The period dominated by this *rasa* is Rajasthani and Pahari miniatures. This may also be borne in mind that the theorists have always kept the *rasa* conditioned with *aucitya* (aesthetic appropriateness).[167] In the *Ṣadaṅgas* Abanindranath finds *yojnā* comparable in essence to *aucitya.* This implies, among other things, the preparation of the proper mental frame of the beholder. It is not for nothing that Ajanta murals have been painted inside the dark caves, providing thus ample introspection to the beholder while his eyes get adjusted to the darkness.

The art treatises of India belong to two traditions. The Northern tradition is known as *vāstu-śāstras* and the Southern tradition the *śilpa-śāstras.* The first has *Viśvakarma-prakāśkum-Śilpa, Samrāngaṇa Sūtradhāra, Aparājita-Pracchā* and *Rūpa-maṇḍaṇa* etc. The Southern tradition has *Mayamata, Manasāra, Kāśyapīya-Amśumadbheda, Agasty-Sakalādhikāra,* Srikumara's *Śilpa-ratna,* etc.[168] *Śilpa-ratna* has a chapter named '*Citralakṣaṇa*' written in the sixteenth century taking all the traditions and experiences of Indian classical paintings and sustaining, as A.K. Bhattacharya has shown, the earlier trend in subsequent centuries.[169] Of *Purāṇas, Viṣṇudharmottara* has the chapters on painting named as '*Citrasūtra*' and *Matsya* and *Agnipurāṇa* have chapters on iconography and *Śilpa-śāstra. Bṛhat Saṁhitā* and *Āgamas,* too, deal with these topics. The later treatises on iconography are *Mantras* and *Tantras. Āgamas*' contribution to *śilpa-śāstra* is valuable and as '*Purāṇas* excel in Iconology, *Āgamas* surpass them in Iconography, their iconographical prescriptions are common property of the artisans of the South as hand books or guidebooks of Art' (D.N. Shukla).[170]

The tradition of art in India is taken to hoary sources. Two *śilpācāryas* were supposed to govern two trends of art. The *Deva* tradition was established by Vishvakarma and the *Asura* by Śukrācārya.[171] Ancient Indian universities, as those of Nālandā, Taxilā and Sridhanya Kataka had courses in painting. By the way, Shastri Ramaswamy is of the opinion that these were 'the real sources of the wonderful Ajanta frescoes.'[172]

Sopoćani: Aesthetics

In *Herminy* (*Hermeneia*), the tradition of which goes back to the twelfth century, the monk-painter Dionysius of Furna[173] gives the aesthetics and theology of icons in the final chapter. He sums it up as follows:

> We do not venerate the colours or even the art, as the enemies of our Church allege, but our Lord Jesus Christ himself who is in Heaven. The veneration due to the icon, says St. Basil, passes to its proto-type.[174]

Dionysius of Furna's declaration not only indicates the Orthodox Church's antipathy towards the body, the flesh (as colour and art) but also that as medium of 'heritage-tradition' they become a part of Divine Liturgy, a testimony of the Revelation of God in which the earthy and material are transubstantiated into Godly elements, into the 'sacred-tradition'—the 'Word,' the prototype. Thus from St. Basil's 'contemplation of realities,' the Kingdom of Heaven is reached.[175] This vision of 'uncreated beauty' is either reached through the means of asceticism,[176] a way of self-discipline, or through what in the Plotinus' aesthetics is, 'detaching the soul from body and elevating it to spiritual level'[177] during the ecstasy of identification achieved in mystic catharsis. The dynamic conception of a divine 'Eros' (Dionysius the Areopagite)[178] in creating reflections has a similarity with the 'logoi' of spirit becoming the creative energy of the World-Soul or Logos (Word) in the process of emanation. It becomes the creative power of Nature from which the whole phenomenal world proceeds.[179]

The artist of Sopoćani gave the most prominent place to the most pathetic—The Death of Virgin—to bring about an oratorical sublime so that 'the grief which is before us is transmuted into spiritual strength.'[180] This spiritual strength is (the theory of) 'spiritual-rebirth' also, as it is said that 'except a man be born again, he cannot see the kingdom of God' (*John* 3:3), for which Jesus himself says '... be born of water and of the Spirit' (*John* 3:5): thereto they 'Be afflicted, and mourn, and weep ...' (*James* 5:9) and through doing 'his commandments, that they may have right to the tree of life and may enter in through the gates into the City' (*Rev.* 22:14). This is the final stage of aesthetic contemplation in Plotinus where the aesthete's soul identifies itself with the formative activity of its own higher principle.[181]

In adopting the theory of emanation, the work of art was to be beautiful, according to the manifestation of Idea, thereby the parts as well the whole of the work is beautiful, not the beauty of symmetry and harmony (because then only the whole would be beautiful) but a beauty of the mystic-contemplation in which the differences are merged into each other.[182] This calm mystic-ecstasy, for Plotinus, is experienced in solitude and is of mental concentration. The Apostles of Sopoćani, thus painted in their 'internal-solitude,' speak of this mystic contemplation confined to man since this 'recognitive experience' demands 'a higher kind of volitional and rational activity than memory.'[183] In terms of this strong contemplation, Plotinus' theory 'accounts for the product of the symbolic art'[184] by which the whole of the Church becomes a microcosm of the actual world. The decorative symbols and formal abstractions are also achieved by the artist of Sopoćani under this aesthetics where the dematerialization is beauty and predominance of matter is ugliness,[185] implying what Ernst Kitzinger deduces as "a preponderant interest in the timeless and ceremonial in subject matter 'corresponding' a full triumph of formal abstraction."[186]

This dematerialization is also verified in grid-module taken by the artist of Sopoćani[187] not only for the decoration spaces, but also for the growth pattern of form of 'characteristic beauty,' as the arboreal-growth in its modulation is a kind of continuous articulated network;[188] it is exemplified in the East Mediterranean Mosaic floors' growth of pictorial space, ultimately turning into diaper-grid and rinceaux rhythms, which influenced Byzantine conception of pictorial space.[189] This arboreal growth supports the postulation of P.A. Michelis that Byzantine art reflects 'characteristic beauty' by 'irregularity and departure from precision, presenting a transitional form, guiding as it strives towards the ideal.'[190] He calls it 'the unity of a tree, say, in which the proportions are not as important as the character of the tree. Type presupposes a canon of proportion.'[191] It is the way in which the expressive oblongation of the figure of maid with hot-water pot in the 'Nativity' at Sopoćani is achieved (plate 139). This 'unity of a tree' becoming a creeper-growth or the 'rhythmos' of compositions turns 'horror Vacui' into the 'movement and luxuriant growth everywhere and becomes a veneer beneath which the wall is perceived cohesive and solid.' Thus an organic relationship is achieved with this, 'reconciling the abstract and the real,'[192] parallel to the 'impulsive rhythm expressing individual exaltation in the free verses of the testament.'[193]

A vision of the 'contemplation of realities' starts with resemblance—a quality through which 'the divine grace of the subject represented is transmitted.'[194] This reality logically gives to Dionysius of Furna the insight into 'colours or even the art' with 'full triumph of formal abstraction' to promote 'orderliness.' It is a conception which also conveys the impact of the Iconoclastic period of Byzantine art giving reign to formal and geometric designs. Thus, these 'extroverted motivations'[195] get subjected to the 'felt-logic of reductivism.' Golden background, liberal brushing, abstraction by inbreeding, spatial organization adopting grading system, and the signitive system of narrative art—all these lead to the dematerialization or loosening the structural theme, the catabolic dissolution in 'entropy' as Arnheim puts it.[196] But since the 'Tree of Life' and 'Fountain of Water of Life' had already become the inspirations in the ambient of 'inner-light' of Domentian[197] and 'Buddhistic' contemplation of Hesychasts, the spiritual-rebirth, resurrection, was bound to be presented not in the recession of depth-dimension (to recede into zero), but in the 'forthcoming' or the upsurge of life. The 'creeper' motif was thus decoded by the artist of Sopoćani; and the spiritual upsurge of life, especially the resurrected Christ was presented in a 'forthcoming' motion,[198] (plate 62) of which Djurić speaks as 'projected composition.'[199] This forthcoming supplants the 'creeper' rhythm or the 'breathing-rhythm' of life. The space of the Church too 'breathes' freely in limitless depth and in the vertical infinity of the height, and returning to the dominance of the nave it gives our first intimation of sublimity in this 'play of infinite and finite.'[200] And with the rhythmos the tactile flatness of walls also dematerializes becoming a part of this 'breathing.'[201]

This Sprouting of Life, 'as if breathing,' was coded by the artist of Sopoćani in the chapel of St. Simeon Nemanja, below (lower zone) the band of the diaper-grid module, in the 'module' of the decorative pattern of sprouting palmette,[202] (plate 18) as it is used in the Leaf-Cross, to substantiate 'I am the true vine' (*John* 15:1) and that 'falling on good ground . . . did yield fruit that sprang up and increased . . . ' (*Mark* 4:8). And in graphic ingredients, the aesthetics of 'life-breathing' or *prāṇa* was creatively adopted in the principle of 'luminosity' by winning over the dichotomy of 'luminosity' and 'illumination,' for example, the bluish-green and the golden colour of the background which make the space as the 'form' of colour and light, the spontaneity of line and projected volumes of the shapes and interstices.

The feeling of 'a gentle, all-embracing sadness'[203] engulfing the walls painted with figures in rhetoric grace of 'the solemn beauty of antique form'[204] is an influence of the Greek dramatic theory and ancient theatre.[205] This fact is also confirmed by the scholastics of middle ages starting in the ninth century, expounding the Christian doctrine of Trinity on the basis of Platonian Triad.[206] In this connection Radhakrishnan opines that 'the theism of Aristotle was used as a preparation for Christian faith.'[207] The greatest of the Byzantine scholars, Psellus revived Platonic philosophy. Moreover, the heroic life of the frontier soldiers was made epic in the Digenis Akritas,[208] and the thirteenth century Serbian literature, works of Domentian and Theodosius speak of the same solemnity.[209] Hence, in Sopoćani are found, in epic and noble grandeur, the Aristotelian rhetorics and his concept of tragedy concretized as 'Oratorical sublime.' Spirito, too, concludes that art attains universality through rhetoric which, since the canons of Polykleitos, has influenced the artist's actively.[210] It is the artist's 'free will' which, with the balance of a golden mean, has presented this 'spectacle' in the 'universal statement,' bringing 'the contrasts of vitality and anguish to a logical conclusion.'[211] The acceptance of the Neoplatonic theory of 'emanation,' on the other hand, brought out the 'objective holiness' of the icon and relics with reference to their miraculousness, though this fact is accepted only with their consecration by the Church.[212]

Comparative

The evangelist looking skyward and expecting the 'word of God' or 'Logos' is a motif repeatedly painted on the rim of the dome of Sopoćani (plate 12). It speaks of the divine inspiration awaited by the artist on the one hand and on the other, the aesthetic preoccupation with the 'word' as literary charm and style. Similarly, the motif of 'conch over lotus,' painted on the ceiling of Ajanta (plate 11), symbolically represents the manifestations—*sphoṭa* or *nāda*—of *vāc* or *śabda,* the word, in addition, the conch symbolises the *ākāśa,*[213] the sky.

The artist's prayers and purification rites for divine inspiration are confirmed both by *Herminy* and *Citrasūtra.* Just as in *Herminy* the monk painter, Dionysius, quotes St. Basil saying that 'the veneration due to the icon passes to its prototype, in the same way the author of *Divyāvadāna* (XXVI) affirms: 'those who venerate earthen images of the Immortals do not revere the clay, but the immortals thereby designated.'[214]

The charm of rhetoric is accepted in *Herminy* as it says that 'we paint the eternal Father like the Ancient of days;'[215] besides, the artist of Sopoćani proves his skill in drama. The 'word' as aesthetic configuration received Aristotelian clarity and propriety, Theophrastus' correctness and ornateness and Quintilian's force and compactness. The agreeability or disagreeability of single syllables or even single letters was stressed by Dionysius.[216] The analysis of poetic qualities starting from Bharat and going up to the exponents of the suggested meaning (*Dhvani*) also embraced the comprehension of the single syllables as well as the manifestation of the total *vāc.* The Ajanta artist's required proficiency in dance and dramaturgy automatically connects him with rhetorics and poetics.

These analyses added to the aesthetic appropriateness or *aucitya* not only of significant form—the *alaṃkāra* (aesthetic ornaments)—but also of *guṇa* (aesthetic quality of style) in the 'modes' or *vṛttis.* The *aucitya* consummated in the suggestiveness of *rasa* (aesthetic emotion and its *dhvani*)—this is Ajanta's forte.

Out of the first century rhetorical treatises, the Byzantians derived the conception of oratorical sublime. It was the cathartic effect of presenting the aesthetic configurations with a rationalistic and demonstrative ideal filled with the pathetic element.[217] To express this 'idealism and the awareness of the tragic' together (this echoes at Ajanta also), the master of Sopoćani adopted the duality of 'symmetria' and 'rhythmos.' To H.W. Janson such a configuration has the aesthetic suggestiveness of the classical style of Greece.[218] Thus, mixed with the medieval mysticism nearly similar aesthetic suggestiveness is echoed in the noble and vital world of Sopoćani: Mila Rajković calls it 'a grief which is before us, transmuted into spiritual strength.'[219] Appropriately painted in styles, 'modes,' Sopoćani's world of this 'mystical communion' has its base in the Hellenistic phantasia theory of spiritually uplifting qualities of the work of art.[220] In presenting it, the 'Dormition' motif seems to have been inspired by the conception of Plotinus' mystical catharsis along with the 'Divine Eros' of Dionysius the Areopagite added to the Eleusinian mysteries and the religious catharsis of primitives through the presentation of dead etc.,[221] giving a sacramental value to the presented.

Emotion was admitted as the principle of unity by Bharata; Dionysius of Areopagite, too, stood for the divine 'eros' as being the principle of creation. Comparable to the mystic ecstasy, reached through Plotinus' calm and living contemplation in stages is the Buddhist's concept of *pañca-skandhas* having a 'formless consciousness' as the end of stream of successive states of consciousness starting from the world of form and name (—the contemplation of realities of St. Basil.) The basic difference of the two culminative stages lies in the concepts of 'mystic catharsis' and the, *nirvāṇa* consciousness.

The former had the means reached in the emotive tendency leading to the mystic experience of Plotinus entwined with its ascetic implications. As for the latter, Ānandvardhana puts it at par with that of *dhvani* theorists which Abhinavagupta expounds as 'a state of total unaffectedness (*Asamprajñāta Samādhi*)'[222] equating it next only to *Brahmānanda.*[223] Thus in the Indian consciousness, the pleasure is not denied but 'it is only transformed into a discipline in awareness, a deepening of consciousness, a realization of things undreamt of before....' That is why K.R. Srinivasa Iyenger connects the *rasa-dhvani* theory to the main Vedāntic tradition.[224] S.N. Dasgupta too points out that Buddhaghoṣa's internal picture which could alone be called the 'true art' required Hindu view to be 'transported outside.' Thus, the '*prāṇa*-aesthetics'—the 'breathing' picture[225] (or pictured wall)—was to be created. These art traditions were adopted by the Buddhists although they were aniconic at the start. To the dialecticism of Buddhist's prescriptive aesthetics the anabolic life-rhythm or *prāṇa* was added and the forms were made to forthcome out of the elemental space, making the whole wall as cognitive structure of this 'flux' in which the 'pure-space' of the cave participated.

Similarly, the formal and geometric traditions of Iconoclastic period of the Byzantine art[226] stood for the banishing of the image. But, since the Old Testament laid down 'an explicit instruction and commandment from God that in the liturgical life of the chosen People pictures and statues should be used,'[227] accordingly, Dionysius in *Herminy* regarded this as the Byzantine Painter's right 'to paint holy icons and venerate them.'[228] The conception of 'inner light' became the prescriptive aesthetics of creeper-module or inner-growth in giving sculptural forms 'pressing forward against the frame.' Its 'potential endlessness' was aided by the gold-background in which the whole wall dematerializes in order to participate into the dynamism of the Church's space. Through hieratic images the ethics was perceptualized in orderliness. The Buddhists as well as the Christians reached its extreme in aniconic traditions. Since in this 'Law of Dynamic Direction' structural organization reached zero,[229] the anabolic aesthetics of *prāṇa* was adopted by the Christians under the concept of 'inner light.'

However, the dissimilarity lies in Sopoćani-artist's conviction in the dictum that 'outward man perishes' (*Cor* 4:16), dematerializing wall as to become the 'breath' of ascending space of the church. On the other hand at Ajanta walls are transfigured into *prāṇa* in a cosmic oneness with the spaces of the caves.

AJANTA: SYMBOLISM

The art of Ajanta presents Buddhist symbolism through perceptual categories assuming *ars imitatur naturam in sua operatione*—as Coomaraswamy conceived it to be true symbolism without becoming idolatory.[230] The artistic form with its pattern and subject matter gives body to the 'invisible universal' as 'the final content of the work of art,'[231] i.e., *rasa-dhvani*.

The beholder is invited to participate from any level in receiving visual tensions in order to reach a state where 'these dynamisms are understood as symbols of the powers that shape human destiny'[232]— where the work of art itself becomes the symbol, what Andre Malraux explains as the 'decor of serenity'.[233]

Be it the sensuous torso-dominated appeal of Sundari ('The Dying Princes,' cave 16), it loses the physicality of body-torsions in convergences and starts becoming 'copper cauldron' in the female body which is 'the cosmic wheel whose spokes the creatures suffer every conceivable torment under the pressure of their passions.'[234] No sooner does the onlooker start seeing the cave 16 with this torment and finishes the 'wheel of life' inside this cave, than he faces in the next cave 17 (plate 105,) right in the varandah, the 'wheel of life' held by the green female demon of death.[235] By the side of this is given 'large yellow spotted snake coiling'[236] and representing 'the Uroboros' biting its tail which is the symbol of the origin and of the opposites contained in it.[237] From here the anagogical[238] symbol presented in absolute plastic images of *Śūnyatā* as a circle—'totality and primordial non-duality and the symbol of enlightenment of wisdom'[239]—is not far-off to be sensed inside 'the marvellous void,' made concrete in the space sculptures of the caves.

The symbol *par excellence* of Buddhists—the *stūpa*—in the next *caitya* cave 19, becomes a *bīja*, i.e., 'divinity in formless realm of pure sound,'[240] as soon as one chants the mystic syllable from the choir's balcony. Outside, on the facade, the *caitya-gavākṣa* window, receives the negative of the 'dome' of *stūpa* in its semicircular opening echoing the *bīja* outside. The perceptual tensions of its completion are visually brought out in a flux by the ceiling-ribs ending on the inner rim of its border which suddenly, on the outer counter, takes rhythm of the lotus-rhizome. Supported by the stroboscopic movement of 'egg and dart' type motif (symbolic of spreading coins for 'Jetavana-Dāna' by the 'Kubera' on both the sides), the rhizome proceeds. Its first bands or festoons emerge on either side of the lower part of the horse-shoe and on their top end they become 'pillars of the rising and setting suns.' The *toraṇa* now proceeds with a widening rhythm[241] gradually, then again narrowing on the pointed top covered by a rectangular member like harmika. Issuing from the heavy lintel base and successively reducing horizontal rhythms support this growth of the light of 'formless realm' into a concrete rising to *nirvāṇa* (plate 14).[242] The 'tree' module has been perceptually concretized as a symbol of concentric growth in *stūpa*. This *cakra* or wheel is the *agni* or 'fire,' aspect of the 'Celestial Fig-Tree,' growing in space;[243] the *soma* or 'water' aspect of this 'Cosmic Tree' is the 'Lotus-growth.' Actually the 'Tri-Ratna' symbol is the perceptual configuration of the above concept[244] (plate 98).

The symbol of *stūpa*, as V.S. Agrawala notes, has a form which is like a *Sūtra*, thread, made out of the twisting of the strings of many religions.'[245] These religions, comprising the oldest speculations over the destiny of mankind, were called *Meh* like *Vṛkṣa-meh* or *Rukkha-meh*—tree-religion, *Yaksa-meh, Sri-meh*—Mother goddess religion etc., out of which there developed a growth of symbolism to give a *sanātana*—universal—religion based on the three categories of representation—*Sāriraka*, those of Buddha's body, *Uddeśika*, prescribed, and *Paribhogaka*, associative symbols. The laws governing the growth of Indian symbolism have been described by F.D.K. Bosch as being Substitution (on internal and external similarity), Integration (of both similarities by raising one's tendency), Identification (with the concealed third), Shifting of Emphasis and selection, Schematizing (decorative forms prescribing characteristics of basic symbolic form), Jungle formation (mixed tendency) and Hybridization. Thus are derived symbols like Lion-head *Kirtimukha* (substituting Sun and *Brahmamūla* sharing fiery nature), Lotus-stalk as the symbol of arrow and serpent out of identification and hybridization, Gordian knots out of jungle formation etc.[246]

Belhan-Buddha's marks on body like *śrivatsa, amṛta kalaśa* encircled with snake, Flaming pillar topped by the Solar-wheel and moon etc,[247] (plate 96) convey the condensation of Vedic symbolism into the body of Buddha.[248] Similarity, to endow him with universality, animal and vegetal vitality and characteristics were incorporated into the icon. Thus, the humanization of the icon of 'Buddha' again gave him the dimension of an abstract universal symbolism, later turning into *maṇḍala.*

From earlier aniconic presentation the *karuṇā* element of Mahāyāna brought out the adoption of 'human form' for symbolic expressions—a form which, in creative visual perceptions, 'is a challenge being not the easiest, but the most difficult vehicle of artistic expression.'[249] The artists of Ajanta met this challenge creating 'alphabets' out of older conventions, synthesizing new influences within their own torment of the duality of Buddhistic dialecticism and taking forms of the human, animal and vegetal worlds in order to suggest new symbols.[250] To use George Braque's phrase, it was finding 'the common in the dissimilar.' Through structural correlation they clarified differences by making them all comparable in establishing a style having virtues of 'similarity and defining individuality.'[251]

The flowers, symbolising renewed joy of the beauty beyond change, tacitly embrace the whole of the available space beyond the forms which they lift in grace and mystique. As lotus sprang up under the first seven steps of the master, Buddhism retained it as the symbol of 'miraculous birth.'

Sopoćani: Symbolism

In their 'four senses (of scriptures)' P. Schaff and J. Herzog have pointed out the significance in the levels of increasing abstraction of symbols, e.g., '*Jerusalam* is literally a city of Palestine, morally the believing soul, allegorically the church, anagogically the heavenly Jerusalam.'[252] It is the 'expanding form'[253] of the anagogic level by which the painter of Sopoćani turns the form of Greek-cross from over the vestments of patriarchs and archbishops (nave, sanctuary, plate 150) into the halo behind the enthroned Christ or Christ blessing (narthex, east wall)—'the Lamb is the Light thereof' (*Rev* 21:23) of the new Jerusalem. Thereupon the painter of these 'icons' would write: 'In these outlines, my son, I have drawn a likeness of God for you, as far as that is possible; and if you gaze upon this likeness with the eyes of your heart, the sight itself will guide you on your way' (Hermetica, Lib. IV IIb).[254]

To reach this anagogical interpretation requires a tradition where a proper preparation is done; it was so in the Orthodox society where the investment of the corporeal world with an incorporeal symbolic meaning took on sacramental depth. This 'making the finite an allegory of the infinite' (Schelling),[255] has in base the three Christian ideas, which are: theory of creation, by which matter is a living symbol of divinity; theory of Incarnation, symbol carrying divine truth; and theory of double set of divine text, allegorical method having to unite the Old and the New Testaments and giving deeper meaning to the scriptures. The highest meaning is attributed to 'word' as it is direct from God and is 'fleshy robe' of concealed meaning awaiting 'unwrapping.' This all leads to the theory of symbolic form and such an 'image' being representation acknowledging 'God not only as its cause but also as its object,' leads to iconographic rules.

Within these iconographic rules the stances become 'signitive' of symbolic movements taken as a process of development according to the Christian religious conception of history with past, present and future.[256] This 'expanding form' extending in horizontality and verticality, gives infinity to the physical space of the church, 'the body of Christ;' the symbol of Tree of Jesse (plate 30) unites within this growth the whole ancestry of Christ with the living patriarchs (painted on the south wall of narthex at Sopoćani). Thus, the cross also, as symbol of Divine love, was used by the painter of Sopoćani in various forms—as Greek Cross, Calvary Cross, Eastern Orthodox Cross and Patriarchal Cross etc.—to symbolise various patriarchs and kings within this unity. It became the base plan of the Church (plate 4). To symbolise the 'characteristic' or the 'living' growth, it assumed the form of Syrian Cross having at the base two creepers growing on either side of the vertical—the Leaf Cross (plate 99) symbolising 'I am the true vine' (*John* 15:1). At Arilja 'Leaf Cross' finds special importance[257] (plate 23), expressing the archetypal symbolism of the 'Tree'. Dalton traces the association of the feminine vine with masculine tree in the vine-scroll placed around the story of Adam and Eve in Byzantine ivories embodying Eve's going alone to tend her roses before the fall.[258] Throughout the middle ages the myth of Odin was popular,[259] the meaning of its essential lines being, 'thus tree of life, cross, and gallow tree are ambivalent forms of the maternal tree: what hangs on the tree, the child of the tree mother, suffers death but receives immortality from her, who causes him to rise to her immortal heaven, where he partakes in her essence as giver of wisdom of Sophia. Sacrifice and sufferings are the prerequisites of the transformation conferred by her.'[260] Thus, at the place where 'tree of knowledge' stood the cross was set up. Christ as the 'mystical fruit' of the redeeming tree of life replaced the fruit (sin) of the tree of knowledge.[261] A fresco of the fifteenth century done by Giovani de Modena at Bologna shows Christ hanging on the tree of life (not cross), towering over the old bifurcate tree of knowledge, "just as Christ 'the Serpent of salvation' rises over the old serpent of doom."[262] Thus, the presentation of cross with two horizontal arms—the patriarchal—(Sopoćani, north-west and south-west pilasters, middle zone, plate 15) symbolizes 'tree of life' winning over that of knowledge embodying complete faith. The third type is with slanted horizontal in the Eastern Orthodox Cross (Sopoćani, narthex west wall, lower zone, held by Emperor Constantine and Empress Helena) because 'our Lord's limbs were of unequal length'[263] (plate 69). St. Andrews cross—Crux Decussata—divided crosswise in the shape of the latter X [264] (plate 106) is presented in the halo of Christ in the incredulity of Thomas (sanctuary south wall).[265]

The whole of the decoration plan is divided into the zone of heaven, the intermediate space and the earth, like a 'carrier of an idea' as Strzygowski puts it.[266] Unadorned from outside and luxuriant inside, the church symbolizes Christian soul completely turned introspective.[267] Abstract symbols of 'cold majesty, chaste beauty, dematerialized faces, spirituality and the like are turned into moving divinities by the polychromy of decoration.'[268] Demus perceives symbolic pilgrimage in the church itself,[269] by which every object, every subject, every gesture and every detail of the iconography becomes symbolic in its ascending order to the anagogic level—New Jerusalem. And there, from colour to the door, from pillar to the dome—all participate and get illuminated in 'the glory of God' (*Rev* 21:23). The painter's guide instructs the painter to use white for Christ in transfiguration, blue before crucifixion scenes, and purple after resurrection. The Virgin's robe was dark green, dark blue or purple.[270] The decorative motifs painted over buildings and vases etc., were also symbolic. It was the characteristic of the school fully developed by John at St. Demetrious (at Peć), taking motifs from the decorations over Greek buildings and Roman potteries. John painted them, especially on the amphora held by the maid in the 'Birth of the Virgin' and over the buildings in the 'Communion of the Apostles;' the latter has images of lotus with saplings shooting from top and flanking a pyramidal mountain with sun (plate 111, very much akin to Buddhist *Garbha-kośa-dhātu maṇḍala*, plate 113); the amphora is decorated with a symbol having the lotus base with a pillar standing in it and the other motif presents a 'dumbell' piercing a ring[271] (plate 114). In Greek cosmic myths Agyieus pillar and Phoebos pillar and Omphalos, the grave mound as navel of earth, are presented as such and were commonly painted on the Greek pottery of the fifth century B.C. The mythic figures on the right side building in 'Dormition' in the nave of Sopoćani—now almost obliterated—present a clear example of the convention indicated above (plate 83). Significantly, Meyer Schapiro finds a relation between spiral shaped mantle lines on the abdomen of Christ (esp. in Glory) with the contemplative practice of the Byzantine 'Omphalopsychoi' at Mount Athos.[272] On the decorations of borders etc., the presentation of classical motifs (like palmette, ovolo moulding, and diaper-grid, alongwith the low relief mouldings of Corinthian acanthus leaves (plates 17, 18), i.e., on the plinths in the nave and on the pillars in the painted architectural details of the scenes, would have parallel liturgical meanings in the pagan mystery religions connected with the enigma of life and death, which turned into folk imagination and were thus preserved. It is evident in the primitive blood myth mixed with Christian symbolism presented at the 'Wedding at Cana' at Kalenić.[273] The fourteenth century ecclesiastical literature, especially the part connected with the services written by Byzantine writer Nicifor Kalist, presents Virgin as the source of life[274] (plate 103)—the whirling wheel of Great Goddess as Mother.[275] The parallel imagery is presented in 'the Madonna as ship' in a psalter from Yugoslavia.[276] It is a 'cradle' and 'crib' symbol preserving 'Ark of Noah.' This maternal significance echoes in the 'nave' of the 'Church' symbolizing man's defence against the deluge of temptation. The cross with Christ becomes male counterpart as the mast of the ship.[277] With the same token the 'Death of Virgin' (a myth revolving round the house church on Mount Sion where Last Supper took place and Holy Spirit came on disciples and where Christ received the soul of his mother)[278] is a symbol of the transformation of Great Goddess as mother into the supreme essence of 'whirling wheel,' i.e., Life in the form of the highest feminine wisdom-nurturing Sophia—symbolised also as flower.[279] The place and the scenes connected are the indicator of this ultimate self-unfolding of the feminine nature.[280] The Last Supper is the index of suffering and sacrifice of the 'fruit' of maternal tree, so that the 'son' ascends to her heaven and partakes of the essence as the giver of the wisdom of Sophia.[281] The Holy Spirit came as 'Divine Wisdom' on disciples and finally there was the "Great Mother's" transformation. The oft-repeated symbol of Christ on paten in the decoration of Sopoćani (plate 17) anagogically transubstantiates the whole church in the Eucharist.

And in making styles as the symbols of content the painters of Sopoćani have used them eclectically, what Ernst Kitzinger defines as 'modes.'[282] Only a comparison between the Angel of Trinity (Vault of the south transept, nave),[283] unidentified Martyr (nave, north-west pilaster, south side)[284] and the 'Adoration of the Sacrament' (sanctuary apse, south side)[285] would justify such 'symbolism' in style. This becomes all the more lucid in the words of Leo Stainburg: '... the means of rendering and the modes of experiencing become subjectified open choices... styles become subjects to paint. Only in the mind of the perceiver and nowhere else is their unity reached.'[286]

Comparative

Symbols as the 'formative mode of discourse' were plastic and visual dynamism shaping the human destiny. Thus, styles in 'modes' became symbols for the artists of Ajanta and Sopoćani. Anagogically, all the meanings, literal, moral and allegorical were contained in their making the cave a *Gandhakuṭi* and the church a New Jerusalem. In these they incorporated the entire hierarchy of the universe and the Heaven participating into the enlightenment or bliss. The ultimate anagogical symbol of the 'inner-light' became 'the marvellous void' of cave spaces or the 'forthcoming' at Ajanta; at Sopoćani, too, this 'forthcoming' symbol pervaded with dynamic and 'breathing' interior space. To this effect the 'Creepers' are symbolized at both the places. The highest zone at Sopoćani symbolized 'word'. Ajanta's dome of *stūpa* is 'pure-sound' symbolized as *vāc* in the motif of conch over the lotus (plate 11).

At Ajanta the *stūpa* as the *padmamūla* of archetypal 'Celestial Fig-Tree' grows a concentric growth, as the 'Tree of Jesse'[287] grows at Sopoćani, and at both the places the 'Tree' becomes the symbol of all the narratives painted.[288] Its *brahmamūla* becoming *cakra* with *agni* and *Soma* aspects, is symbolized in the '*Tri Ratna*' (plate 98) turning into the halo as a divine attribute at Ajanta as well as Sopoćani (plates 97 and 122). The artists of Sopoćani present this 'Tree of Knowledge' (counterpart to *brahmamūla*) along with the 'Tree of Life' (unitedly giving birth to Leafed Cross—plates 99, 15) in the patriarchal cross and the former finds its place as Greek Cross in the halo. The cross, in gyroscope, became the base-plan and the vertical plan of the church of Sopoćani turning into 'cakra;'[289] it symbolized the ascending celestial spheres, the conception of Cosmological plan of *Cosmos Indicopleaustes* (plate 112) which is similar to that given in Ajanta cave 2 ceiling (plate 116). In the same vein the Buddhist *Garbhakośadhātu maṇḍala* (plate 113) finds a striking similarity with the decorative details in Yugoslavian medieval frescoes (St. Demetrius at-Peć). The 'Tree' becomes the *paribhogaka* (associative) symbol (*Mahābodhi rukka*, Great Wisdom Tree) of the Buddha similar to Christ's becoming the vine.

The 'Wheel of Life' (plate 103) or *cakra* in Mary's hand by the side of 'Crucifixion' at Linder conforms to the Yugoslavian medieval symbolism connected with the ecclesiastical writings of Nicifor Kalist. It connects these frescoes with archetypal 'Mother-Goddess' symbolism which again has a verification at the uroboros symbol being presented at Mileševa in the spiral motif. This motif with the 'Wheel of Life' and 'Mother Goddess' symbolism (plate 109) is presented at Ajanta (cave 17). Contemplative spiral mantle lines on the abdomen of Christ and yogic-belly of the Buddha have similar symbolic significance. Thus, under such theory of archetypal symbolism the 'Dormition' becomes 'the Great Mother's' transformation into the 'highest wisdom,' Sophia.[290] The monogram of Christ as the basic layout of the composition here substitutes the 'copper cauldron' in the female body for suffering torments to become the 'Higher-wisdom'[291] (plate 80). The same composition-symbolism applies to the 'Dying Princess' (cave 16 Ajanta) who 'dies' in concern with the consecration of Nanda attaining 'Divine Wisdom.' The images of *Prajñā-pāramitā* thus symbolise the transformation of 'Wheel of Life' and link the matriarchal-principle symbolised in the abundant presentation of femininity at Ajanta, making it a 'Temple of graces.' King Milutin also found 'a temple of fair womanhood,' the King's Church in Studenica, symbolising this part of life 'like spring beautiful and transitory'[292] (plate 34.) In more or less the same way some immediate symbol of transitoriness of life always accompanies the otherwise 'erotic' palace-scenes at Ajanta.

All the divine attributes and universal qualities are manifested in the image of man at Ajanta. It is also the microcosm of the universe at Sopoćani similarly representing the nature abstracted in the rhetorics of the figures. Here it also has the 'Tree' module for its configuration. The 'Lion of Juda', the 'Lamb' of sacrifice, the 'Sun' and 'Fountain of Life' etc., are as manifested in the human-symbol of Christ at Sopoćani as the Belham Buddha's universal attributes are given iconologically in the Bodhisattvas at Ajanta. Both *Herminy* and *Citrasūtra* provide colour symbolism for narration. Christ in 'Transfiguration' is instructed to be painted in white, so is the moon-white (*candrika gauri*) complexion of *haṃsa puruṣa* given in *Citrasūtra* (36:2) and rendered in the body of Bodhisattva Padmapāṇi. Prajñāpāramitā's green and Virgin's green robe have the symbolism of calmness in 'Perfection of Wisdom.'

As Sophia is symbolized as flower, the highest wisdom is silently embodied by the lotus in the hands of Padmapāṇi.

To sum up, the 'Tree' symbolism embraces right from Christ's 'vine' up to the cross' association with the 'Trees of Knowledge and Life' growing like 'Tree of Jesse' in the compositional rhythmos and in the dynamism of the interior space of the church. The laws behind this expanded 'Tree' symbolism, as pointed out by F.D.K. Bosch, are substitution, integration, emphasis, selection, schematizing, jungle-formation, and hybridization. They govern the configurations both at Ajanta and Sopoćani. Of 'hybridization' a concrete proof is the *Kīrtimukha* at Ajanta (plate 100) and there is a similar symbol at Studenica in Yugoslavia (plate 102). Overwhelmed by such a wealth of similarities in the elements of symbolism one can only find the difference in their execution. For the artist of Sopoćani the symbolism is implicit in the overall heroic spectacle of mankind. He displays less preoccupation with aestheticism. At Ajanta, the symbolism is more explicit, alongwith all inclusiveness—from aestheticism to the concept of universal life. Besides, while all the symbols are contained within a single complex of Ajanta, the canvas in Yugoslavia has to be broadened from Sopoćani to include all its medieval art with a view to encompassing such a vast treasure of symbols. Lastly, these 'cultural-sanctuaries' grew on arboreal module, as did their Indian counterparts.

REFERENCES

1. Ramesh Shanker Gupte and B.D. Mahajan, *Ajanta, Ellora and Aurangabad Caves*, 1962, p. 258.
2. S. Radhakrishnan and Charles A. Moore, (eds.,) *A Sourcebook in Indian Philosophy*, 1967, p. 272.
3. A.W. Watts postulates that in Mahāyāna a Buddha is worshipped as God since it is seen as 'a personification of reality' on the basis of popular cult-worship; *The Way of Zen*, 1971, p. 88.
4. D. Chattopadhyaya, *Lokāyata*, 1968, pp. 266, 329.
5. *See* Glossary.
6. *See* glossary.
7. *See* p. 91.
8. Sec p. 89.
9. D. Chattopadhyaya, op. cit., p. 328.
10. 'I am the moving (or animating) spirit of the tree of life. Next O ye gods, I shall support (i.e., nourish) the whole world with the life-sustaining vegetables, which shall grow out of my own body...' D. Chattopadhyaya, op. cit., p. 293.

11. A.W. Watts, op. cit., p. 78.
12. D. Chattopadhyaya, op. cit., pp. 243-51.
13. Erich Neumann, *The Great Mother*, 1955, p. 232. D. Chattopadhyaya, op. cit., p. 15
14. Misra, *Bhartiya Murtikalā*, 1978, p. 136.
15. Erich Neumann, op. cit., p. 44, pl. 48.
16. Ratan Parimoo, *Studies in Modern Indian Art*, 1975, p. 93.
17. Irene N. Gajjar, *Ancient Indian Art and the West*, 1971, Fig. 115.
18. Ibid., Fig. 115: Mohanjodaro seal. '... the image of the lotus goddess on Basarh terracottas was transformed into the goddess Padmapriya "to whom the lotus is dear," as seen on Buddhist monuments.' Madanjeet Singh, *The Cave Paintings of Ajanta*, 1965, p. 44.
19. S.P. Gupta, *The Roots of Indian Art*, 1980, p. 71, pl. 21, Disc-stone from Murtaziganj.
20. Erich Neumann, op. cit., pp. 21-8.
21. F.D.K. Bosch, *The Golden Germ*, 1960, p. 14. Coomaraswamy's initiative in this respect is gratefully acknowledged by Bosch.
22. The totality of man's experience includes the three stages of working, dream, and dreamless sleep, (*Gauḍapāda*, 1.2) '... In the stage answering to the dream *Iśvara*, the personal God, becomes Hiraṇyagarbha the world-soul, which is said to be the first-born son of God, (*Śvetāśvatara Up.* iii, 4, iv.12, vi.18).' S. Radhakrishnan, *Eastern Religion and Western Thought*, 1975, p. 127 with note.
23. S.N. Das Gupta, *Fundamentals of Indian Art*, 1960, pp. 101-02.
24. David L. Snellgrove (Gen. Ed.,) *The Image of the Buddha*, 1978, p. 97.
25. *Chitrasūtram* (trans.) Tarnish Jha, in Sammelan Patrika, *Kalā-aṅka*, Śakabda 1880, p. 472.
26. Stella Kramrisch, *The Art of India*, 1955, pp. 15, 31.
27. Niháraranjan Ray, *Bhartiya Kalā ka Adhyayana*, 1978, pp. 175-77.
28. Ibid., p. 89.
29. A.W. Watts, op. cit., pp. 92, 93.
30. Ibid., p. 95.
31. Max Weber, *The Religions of India*, 1967, p. 205.
32. Ramesh Shanker Gupte and B.D. Mahajan, op. cit., p. 16.
33. Max Weber, op. cit., p. 222.
34. David L. Snellgrove (Gen. ed.,) op. cit., p. 17. A.W. Watts, op. cit., p. 96.
35. A.W. Watts, op. cit., p. 90.
36. Ibid., p. 90.
37. Quoted in review of K. Damodaran, 'Indian Thought: A Critical Survey,' in *Prāci-Jyoti*, Vol. V-2, Dec., 1967, p. 591.
38. Ganeshwarananda Svami, 'Buddhism and Vedanta', review, *Prāci-Jyoti*, Vol. V-2, Dec., 1967, p. 512: Buddha 'wanted to found religion and philosophy on the rock of one's own experience of life. Consequently, he based his teachings fundamentally on the laws of human psychology'— Karunaratne, 'The Meaning of the Buddhist Culture,' review, *Prāci-Jyoti*, Vol. V-2, Dec., 1967, pp. 516, 517: 'The Buddha's path to purity, known to history as the middle path or the Noble Eightfold Path is, in its essentials, the way to the resolution of conflict within ourselves.'

39. D.R. Channa, 'Social Implications of Reason and Authority in Buddhism,' review, *Prachi-Jyoti*, Vol. V-2, Dec., 1967, p. 511.
40. R.K. Rawal, 'Lord Buddha: His Life and Philosophy', in *Journal of the Oriental Institute*, Vol. 26, No. 1, Sept. 1976, pp. 21-30: *Nāma-rūpa* (mind-matter), *Vedanā* (feeling), *Samjñā* (perception), *Saṁskāra* (comprehension) and *Vijñāna* (formless-consciousness), these *pañca-skandhas* are five kinds of successive states of stream of consciousness. 'These are very close to personality of man in modern psychology... as 'ego.' The interdependence (*Servam Sanghālam*) of the successive states over each other (*Servam Kṣanikam*) implies doctrine of perpetual flux (*Serva Santānam*). The re-birth is not through some external unchanging 'soul' (*Servam Anatamam*) but through the thirst (*Tanha*) of ego joining the new one in inescapable *Karma* casuality.' S. Radhakrishnan and C. A. Moore, (eds.,). op. cit., p. 272: *Saṁskara* is translated as 'volitional disposition.'
41. K. Damodaran, op. cit., p. 590.
42. Nihararanjan Ray., op. cit., p. 46.
43. Rudolf Arnheim, *Entropy and Art*, 1971, p. 27. E.H. Gombrich elaborates the relationship between the Gestalt's simplicity hypothesis and the inevitable importance of a framework or schema—*Art and Illusion*, 1960, p. 272.
44. Nihararanjan Ray, op. cit., pp. 147-198.
45. K. Damodaran, op. cit., p. 590.
46. R.K. Rawal, op. cit., pp. 27-30.
47. V.S. Upadhyaya, 'Mantrayana,' *Hindi Sahitya Kosa*, Sam. 2015, p. 559.
48. H.W. Janson, *History of Art*, 1977, p. 43: 'Any gesture of shape that is endlessly repeated tends to lose its original character—it becomes ground down, simplified, more abstract.'
49. In 'After abstract expressionism' in *Art International*, Oct., 1962, Clement Greenburg points out that this self-critical and entirely empirical reductionism of modern artist has reduced plastic arts to two irreducible norms, flatness and delimitation of it. This tension reduction has been shown by Arnheim in blurring Poussin's painting (plates 6, 7) proving that 'with increasing catabolic blur, the usual pattern will become simpler, and although we may assume, for the argument's sake, that it will remain orderly at each level, the value of its order will constantly diminish, leaving us finally with a homogeneously filled and therefore empty rectangular field:' *Entropy and Art*, 1971, p. 31. It is important here to note that these reducivistic trends producing modern American works have been now termed as decorative trends (Phlip Rawson, in interview, *Lalit Kalā Contemporary*, 26 Sept., 1978, pp. 8-9). 'The absolutization of this experimentation and quest for innovation in the area of form which has become an end in itself... the fact that it is above all this art which fuels the semantic philosophy of art and forms, the object of its apologetics cannot be disputed:' Yevgeny Basin, *Semantic Philosophy of Art*, 1979, pp. 229-30.
50. A.W. Watts, op. cit., p. 198.
51. Rudolf Arnheim, 'On Order Simplicity and Entropy,' in *Leonardo*, Vol. VII-2, Spring, 1974, p. 139.
52. 'Buddhist sculpture was the art of stillness, 'exempt from movement' with which it achieved its logical climax that could only lead to stagnation as in some of the Buddhas on the Ajanta Cave facades.' Ratan Parimoo, 'Elephanta in the Context of Evolution and Significance of Śaiva Sculpture,' in *Journal of Oriental Institute*, Vol. XXVI, No. 3, March, 1977.
53. Arnheim, *Entropy and Art*, 1971, p. 45.

54. Ibid., pp. 52-6.
55. Erich Neumann, op. cit., p. 333.
56. Germain Bazin, *A Concise History of Art*, Part-II, 1964, pp. 430-31.
57. Rudolf Arnheim, *Art and Visual Perception*, 1960, pp. 199.
58. Erich Neumann, op. cit., p. 44.
59. S. Radhakrishnan, op. cit., 1975, p. 275.
    —Basil Bishop of Zića, 'The Importance of the Celebration of the 750th Anniversary of the Autocephalous Serbian Orthodox Church,' *Serbian Orthodox Church*, Vol. 3, No. 3, 1972, pp. 2, 3.
60. Bishop of Gornji Karlovac Simeon, 'Continuity of History,' in *Serbian Orthodox Church*, Vol. 3, No. 3, 1972, p. 12.
61. S. Radhakrishnan, op. cit., 1975, p. 275.
62. Ernst Kitzinger, *Byzantine Art in the Making*, 1977, p. 105.
63. Dr. Došan Lj Kašić, 'Hilandar and Serbia,' *Serbian Orthodox Church*, Vol. 3, No. 3, 1972, p. 27.
64. One of the fourteenth century quietist sect of the Greek Church.
65. Bishop of Gornji Karlovac Simeon, op. cit., p. 11.
66. Ibid., p. 17.
67. Ernst Kitzinger, op. cit., p. 127.
68. S. Radhakrishnan, op. cit., 1975, p. 164.
69. Ibid., p. 276.
70. Ibid., p. 219. P. A. Michelis, *An Aesthetic Apporach to Byzantine Art*, 1964, p. 200.
71. P.A. Michelis, ibid., pp. 213, 256.
72. Demetrios J. Constantelos, *The Greek Orthodox Church*, 1967, p. 21.
73. Ibid., pp. 38, 39.
74. Svetozar Radojćić, *Kalenić*, 1964, p. xv. Philip Sherard, *Byzantium*, 1966, p. 11.
75. S. Radhakrishnan, op. cit., 1975, p. 42.
76. Ibid., pp. 274-75.
77. Ibid., p. 275.
78. Ibid., p. 276.
79. S. Radhakrishnan and C.A. Moore, (eds.) op. cit., 1967, p. 617.
80. S. Radhakrishnan, op. cit., 1975, p. 228. P.A. Michelis, op. cit., 1964, p. 256.
81. S. Radhakrishnan, op. cit., 1975, p. 274.
82. Ibid., p. 228.
83. S. Radhakrishnan, op. cit., 1975, p. 229. He quotes M. Couchoud's affirmation that 'Jesus is misplaced when placed in the series of religious reforms but his true place is among the resurrection gods with the great hope of winning the victory over death,' ibid., p. 388.
84. John F.A. Taylor, 'Medieval Christianity', in *An Introduction to Literature and the Fine Art*, (eds.,) D. Thimme and W.W. Heist, 1952, p. 35.
85. Ibid., p. 35.
86. S. Radhakrishnan, op. cit., 1975, p. 230.
87. Ibid., p. 233.
88. Ibid., p. 231.
89. Ibid., p. 233.
90. Ibid., p. 234.

91. Ibid.
92. Ibid., p. 237.
93. Ibid.
94. Ibid., p. 240.
95. Ibid., p. 241.
96. Ibid., p. 242.
97. Ernst Kitzinger, op. cit., p. 127.
98. J.G. Frazer, *The Golden Bough*, Part IV, Vol. I, reprint 1976, pp. 8, 9.
99. Every George, *Christian Mythology*, 1970, p. 136, refers to André Grabar's delineating the pagan biographical cycles underlying the development of the story of the Virgin's life and death.
100. Philip Sherrard, op. cit., 1966, p. 114.
101. H.W. Janson, op. cit., p. 30.
102. Erich Neumann, *The Great Mother*, 1955, p. 108.
103. Ibid., p. 110, Fig. 6.
104. Ernst Kitzinger, op. cit., pp. 110, 24.
105. *The Illustrated Encyclopedia of World History*, Vol. I, (eds.,) W.L. Langer, 1975, p. 204.
106. S. Radhakrishnan, op. cit., 1975, p. 278.
107. Ibid.
108. John F.A. Taylor, op. cit., p. 36.
109. S. Radhakrishnan, op. cit., p. 243.
110. B. Bazin, *The Loom of Art*, 1962, pp. 103-105.
111. D.T. Rice, *The Appreciation of Byzantine Art*, 1972, pp. 8, 9. Dr. Mirzana Lubinković, *Ravanica*, 1966, p.v.
112. Vojislav J. Djurić, *Sopoćani*, 1963, p. 116.
113. Jesus' saying 'it is not yet made manifest what we shall be' is similar to *Upaniṣad's* dynamic concept of negative description which is parallel to the Buddha's negative attitude. S. Radhakrishnan, op. cit., p. 170.
114. S. Radhakrishnan and Charles A. Moore (eds.,) op. cit., 1967, p. 272.
115. R.R. Bolgar 'The Greek Legacy,' in M.I. Finley (ed.,) *The Legacy of Greece*, 1981, p. 442.
116. A.W. Watts aptly points to the difference of approach being that 'Western idealists have begun to philosophize from a world consisting of mind (or spirit) from the matter, whereas the Buddhists have begun to philosophize from a world of mind and form:' *The Way of Zen*, 1971, p. 92.
117. Ananda K. Coomarswamy, *Elements of Buddhist Iconography*, 1972, pp. 3, 40, 73 note 53. 'The history of the Christian Church is the record of the gradual adaptation of an Eastern religion to the western spirit'—S. Radhakrishnan, op. cit., 1975, p. 271.
—He further quotes Fausset (A Modern Prelude) as to how he has travelled from orthodox Christianity to find in 'the inspired pantheism in which the vision and teaching of the Vedānta culminated, there the personal God was completed in the 'impersonal God,' there also the Christos or the divine self was known and expressed long before the birth of Jesus,' p. 250 note.

118. David L. Snellgrove (Gen. ed.,) op. cit., p. 360. 'For him who is strong and wise and only for him, Buddha repeatedly explains in his teachings,' Max Weber, op. cit., p. 208.
119. A.W. Watts, op. cit., p. 92.
120. A.W. Watts, op. cit., p. 96.
121. Dr. Kanti Chandra Pandey, *Comparative Aesthetics*, Vol. II, 1956, pp. 124-30.
122. Anand K. Coomaraswamy, op. cit., 1972, p. 13.
123. S. Radhakrishnan and Charles A. Moore (eds.,) op. cit., 1967, p. 280.
124. Demetrios J. Constantelos, *The Greek Orthodox Church*, 1967, p. 112.
125. J.K. Frazer, *Golden Bough*, part IV, Vol. I, 1976, pp-6-8 and 263-77.
126. S. Radhakrishnan, op. cit., p. 139.
127. Ibid., p. 140.
128. Ibid., p. 147.
129. Ibid., p. 227.
130. S. Radhakrishnan and Charles A. Moore (eds.,) op. cit., pp. 15-16.
131. Ibid., p. 24.
132. Review of K. Damodaran, 'Indian Thought: A Critical Survey,' in *Prāci-Jyoti*, Vol. V, part 2, Dec. 1961, p. 590.
133. K. Krishnamoorthy, *Dhvanyāloka of Ānandavardhana*, 1974 p. 263.
134. Krishna Kumar, *Alamkara Shastra Ka Itihas*, 1975, p. 128. Ānandavardhana writes '...the very expression 'suggestion' has been borrowed (into the field of poetics) from the grammarians who maintain that sound in its eternal form of *Sphoṭa* (Lit. Burst) is identical with ultimate Reality itself (and that it is only suggested and never expressed)' (III-337). K. Krishnamoorthy, op cit., p. 215. Dr. Kanti Chandra Pandey, *Comparative Aesthetics*, Vol. 1., 1959, pp. 6, 612-14:

    'Absolute in the context of philosophy of grammar, gave the principle of integration of different schools on the ground of this Absolute... Bharata propounded in philosophy of dramatic art—the *Raso-Brahma-vāda*, and since drama was recognised as form of poetry it was adapted in poetics. Subsequently under this influence the philosophy of music, *Nāda-Brahma-vāda*, and philosophy of architecture (containing painting and sculpture), *Vāstu-Brahma-vāda* (conceived by King Bhoja author of *Samrāngaṇa Sūtra-dhāra*) was asserted.'
135. C. Sivaramamurti, *The Art of India*, 1977, p. 128.
136. *Citrasūtram*, op. cit., p. 464.
137. NiharaRanjan Ray, *Bhartiya Kalā Ka Adhayayana*, 1978, p. viii.
138. Ananda K. Coomaraswamy, op. cit., 1972, p. 78, fig. I.
139. Classified pertaining (1) to the embellishable (*Vāstu Dhvani*), (2) to the embellishment (*Alaṇkāra Dhvani*), (3) to the transient emotion (*Bhāva Dhvani*), (4) to the aesthetic configuration (*Rasa Dhvani*) (*Dhvanyāloka* 86.7). Dr. Kanti Chandra Pandey, op. cit., p. 304. '*Nāda*' through Yogacārya was incorporated by Asaṅga, as is seen in Madame Blavatski's translation of 'The Book of the Golden Precepts:' A. Besant and C.W. Leadbeater, *Talks on the Path of Occultism*, 1930, p. 352.
140. Nirmala Jain, *Rasa-Sidhanta aur Saundarya Śāstra*, 1967, p. 128—ततश्च मुख्यभूतात् महारसात् स्फोट सदृशीव! 'It is just because *Śānta* is involved in all *rasas* that it is mentioned by the sage first of all:' Dr. K.C. Pandey, op. cit., p. 249.

K. Krishnamoorthi, op. cit., p. 249. p. 375 note: Udbhata, before Karikakara, was the first author to mention *Śanta* as ninth *rasa.* Further, as already noted by Raghvan, '*Śāntarasa* is known under the name of *Praśānta* to an early canonical work of the Jains viz. *Anuyogadvāra-sūtra,* whose date is very much earlier than Udbhata's (*Loc. cit.* p. 66).'

—Ānandavardhana: 'we state emphatically that there is a sentiment of Quietude (शान्त) and its nature is delineation of the joy due to the decline of desire...

Even granting that this joy is above the experience of many individuals, one will not be justified at all in dissenting to its constituting a unique experience of some extraordinary personages.'

—(*Dhvanyāloka,* commentary III:27) op. cit., 1974, p. 183.

141. Priyabala Shah, *Viṣṇudharmottara-Purāṇa,* third *Khaṇḍa,* Vol. II, 1961, p. 135.

142. Acharya Baldev Upadhyaya, 'Nātya-kalā men Śānta-Rasa,' in *Sammelan-Patrikā,* Kalā-aṇka, Sakabada, 1880, pp. 321-25.

143. Madeleine Hallade, *The Gandhara Style and the Evolution of Buddhist Art,* 1968, p. 206.

—Ratan Parimoo, 'Elephanta in the Context of Evolution and Significance of Śaiva Sculpture,' in *Journal of Oriental Institute,* Vol. XXVI, No. 3, p. 297.

144. David L. Snellgrove, (Gen. ed.,) op. cit., 1978, p. 360.

145. Nihararanjan Ray, op. cit., 1978, pp. 147-48.

—'The aesthetic experience of *Śānta* consists in the experience of the self as free from the entire set of painful experiences, which are due to the external expectations, and therefore, is blissful state of identity with the universal. It is the experience of self in one of the stages on the way to perfect self realization. Such state of self, when presented either on the stage or in poetry and, therefore universalized, is responsible for the arousal of a mental condition which brings the transcendental bliss:' K.C. Pandey, op. cit., pp. 249-50.

—Nihararanjan Ray, op. cit., pp. 147-48.

146. David L. Snellgrove, (Gen. ed.,) op. cit., pp. 101, 109.

—Dr. K.C. Pandey, op. cit., p. 115.

—Abhinavagupta also calls it 'a strange flower', *Dhvanyāloka locan* p. 165.

—A.W. Watts, *The Way of Zen,* 1971: In its own (probably rather late) tradition, Zen maintains that the Buddha transmitted awakening to his chief disciple, Mahākaśyapa, by holding up a flower and remaining silent,' p. 65.

Doctrine of net of Jewels 'of Hua-Yen (Kegon)' in which every jewel contains the reflection of all the others evoking 'vividly clear that in concrete fact I have no other self than the totality of things of which I am aware'... this reality is the 'suchness' (*Tathatā*) of our rational, non-verbal world: (pp. 140, 147), which is expressed in Ajanta painting on decoration over the doors (i.e., cave 17), as ornaments on human figures, and in the ceiling of cave 2.

147. C. Wentinck, *The Human Figure,* p. 22.

148. A.W. Watts, op. cit., p. 198.

149. Dr. K.C. Pandey, *Comparative Aesthetics,* Vol. II, 1956, pp. 342, 347.

150. Ibid., p. 348.

S.N. Dasgupta comments: 'The art of painting or sculpture can only abstract a particular moment of the creative flow for its representation. It is perhaps for supplementing this abstraction that the Indian artist always associated his human creations or the deities with plant life or animal life to indicate the uniformity of life that flows through nature and that throbs through spiritual appreciation.' He also refers to *Citrasūtra* (35:7)—dance is the supreme painting [नृत्तं चित्रं परं मतम्] since in dance the essence of the artistic impulse—'the rhythmic flow of the creative joy'—is best presented, *Fundamentals of Indian Art*, 1960, p. 51.

—Stella Kramrisch opines that "the ultimate unit of measurement for the organizing lines in the plan of a building is also called 'breath' (*prāṇa*). The rhythmic breathing quality of form is the test of a work of art, for it contains the life-movement (*cetanā*) of the subject. It was found that by the concentrated practice of controlling breathing, an inner lightness and warmth absorbed the heaviness of the physical body and dissolved it in the weightless 'subtle body' which was given concrete shape by art, in planes and lines of balanced stresses and continuous movement. This shape, inwardly realized by yoga, was made concrete in art." *The Art of India*, 1955, pp. 15, 27.

151. P.A. Michelis, *An Aesthetic Approach to Byzantine Art*, 1964, p. 201.

152. 'An abiding flavour or *rasa*, is the soul of an artistic or literary theme... Emotions (*bhāvas*)... are also used in artistic compositions. *Anubhāvas* and *Sātvikabhāvas* (being physical manifestations) suggest fleeting feelings of grief and sorrow. *Vyabhicāri bhāvas* are most fleeting and include momentary reactions like despair, fatigue, doubt and jealousy (complementing) the *rasa*... And the abiding and dominant flavour, the *sthāyibhāva*, allows the observer to recognize the *rasa* at once. The *Uddīpana vibhavas* which inflame the emotions, are aids like moon-light spring...:'C. Sivaramamurti, *The Art of India*, 1977, p. 134.

—For paintings are nine *rasas—Śṛngāra, Hāsya, Karuṇā, Raudra, Vīra, Bhayānaka, Bibhatsa, Adbhuta* and *Śānta*' (*Cittrasūtra* 43, 1).

153. Shastri K.S. Ramaswami, *The Indian Concept of the Beautiful*, 1947, p. 153.

154. Krishna Chaitanya, *A Ḥistory of Indian Painting: the Mural Tradition*, 1976, p. 15.

155. S.N. Dasgupta, op. cit., 1960, p. 107.

156. Ibid., p. 111.

157. Ibid., pp, 115-16.

158. Dr. Priyabala Shah, *Viṣṇudharmottara-Purāṇa*, third Khaṇḍa, Vol. II, 1961, p. 130.

—The relationship between the *bhūṣana* of *Citrasūtra* and *alaṃkāra* of poetics is also established by the author, note, p. 130.

159. Ibid., p. 136. C. Sivaramamurti, *Citrasūtra of the Viṣṇudharmottra*, 1978, p. 164:
लसतीव च भूलम्भो श्लिष्यतीव तथा नृप। हसतीव च माधुर्य सजीव इव दृश्यते ॥२१॥ सश्वास इव यच्चित्रं तच्चित्रं शुभलक्षणम्।

160. S.N. Dasgupta, op. cit., pp. 59, 122, 124, 133-34.

161. Abanindranath Tagore, 'Bhartiya Śilpa ke Ṣadaṅga' (tr.) Dr. Mahadev Saha, *Sammelan Patrika*, op. cit., Śakabda 1880, pp. 400-32.

—'Six limbs of Painting' in India were first written out from the popular tradition by Vātsyāyana—the writer of *Kāmasūtra.* Since their application in Ajanta works is almost accepted by the authors, they are safely presumed to have been atleast not of the later date. But commentary, *Jaimangala*, by Yashodhar Pandit, was written later on (*c.* 1246-61).

—A.B. Keith, *Sanskrit Sahitya Ka Itihas* (Trans.), M.D. Shastri, 1967, p. 592.

162. Nihararnjan Ray, op. cit., 1978, pp. 122-26.

163. Shastri K.S. Ramaswami, op. cit., 1947, p. 48.
164. Ramesh Shanker Gupte and B.D. Mahajan, op. cit., pp. 255-56.
—(Vs. 24, 25, 29) V.V. Mirashi (eds.,) *Corpus Inscriptionum Indicarum*, Vol. V, *Inscriptions of The Vākāṭakas*, 1963, pp. 109, 111.
—'For Bharata not only recognises wonder (*vismaya*) to be the basic mental state of *Adbhuta Rasa* but also mentions temple (*Devakula*) and assembly hall (*sabhā*) amongst the objects which are responsible for its arousal. And Bhoja also in his *Samarāngaṇa Sūtradhāra* admits the causality of work of architecture to arousal of the feeling of wonder.... A temple with Buddha in contemplation produces calmness in mind. And rising from the emotive and cathartic levels to the transcendental, the aesthete has the experience of the *vāstu brahmā* from a work of architecture exactly as the lover of music has the experience of the *Nāda Brahamā* from vocal or instrumental music or as the lover of poetry has that of *Rasa-Brahmā* from reading or hearing poetry:' Dr. K.C. Pandey, op. cit., Vol. I, 1959, pp. 610-11.
165. Shastri K.S. Ramaswami, op. cit., 1967, pp. 48-9.
166. Ibid., pp. 321-25.
167. Nirmala Jain op. cit., 1967, p. 446.
168. D.N. Sukla, *Vāstu Śāstra*, Vol. II, 1967, p. 84.
169. A.K. Bhattacharya, *Citralakṣana*, 1974.
170. D.N. Shukla, *Vāstu Śāstra*, Vol. II, 1958, pp. 52-57.
171. According to Dr. K.C. Pandey the tradition of Vishvakarma is Brahmā tradition and Samarāngaṇa Sūtradhāra and Viṣṇudharmottara (*Citrasūtra*) etc., belong to this tradition. A few of the treatises of this tradition represent Śaiva tradition also. He puts the other tradition as Māyā tradition represented in *Matsya Purāṇa*, and *Mānasāra* etc., and postulates that the *Māyā*-art of Central America and Mexico represent this tradition of superb draftsmanship, op. cit., 1959, Vol. I, pp. 587-93.
—K.C. Pandey as well points out the principles of harmony related to different conceptions of pillars.
172. Shastri K.S. Ramaswami, op. cit., 1967, p. 197.
173. He wrote the Painter's Manual of Mount Athos—*Hermeneia* or *Herminy, Encyclopedia of World Art*, Vol. XIV, 1967, Columns 280-81.
174. Dr. Lazar Milin, 'The Theology of Icons,' in *Serbian Orthodox Church*, Vol. III, 1972, p. 45.
175. S. Radhakrishnan, op. cit., 1975, p. 234.
176. Since 'a purified heart aids us in enjoying the vision of uncreated beauty' as St. Gregory of Nazianzen in his Neoplatonic ideas expressed: Ibid., 1975, p. 234.
177. K.C. Pandey, op. cit., pp. 121-23.
178. S. Radhakrishnan, op. cit., 1975, p. 242.
179. K.C. Pandey, op. cit., pp. 137, 138.
180. Mila Rajković, *Sopoćani*, 1963, p. 6.
—Assunto has delineated such 'oratorical sublime' by means of noble expression elevating beholders' soul, 'not only to a state of persuasion but of feeling of ecstasy, joy and pride' from 'rhetorical treatises of first century A.D. made out of the dispute of Appollodorians, (rationalistic and demonstrative ideal and rhetoric art) and Theodorians (giving importance to pathetic element; to suggestion and to fantasy). He adds that 'it has many implications

in Byzantine art. Those after the tenth century are attributed to Dionysius of Halicarnasus or to Cassiusdanginus.'

—*Encyclopedia of World Art*, Vol. XIV, columns 269-70.

—J.J. Pollitt traces the relevance of Plato's oral implications to Aristotle's ennobling effect. 'This, given more positive and reverent view of art in Hellenistic phantasia theory in spiritually uplifting qualities was ultimately viewed as a kind of mystical communion by Dio Chrysostom (*c.* 40-112 A.D.):'

—*The Art of Greece* 1400-31 B.C., 1965, p. xvii.

181. K.C. Pandey, op. cit., 1956, pp. 158, 162.

—'The first stage being that of distinterested love of sensuous beauty, the second is the true understanding of it in effort to rise to the archetype, the third step is to rise, with concentration, from rational to spiritual level with calm and living contemplation and recollection.'

182. K.C. Pandey, op. cit., 1956, pp. 155, 157, 163.
183. Ibid., p. 146.
184. Ibid., p. 115.
185. Ibid.
186. Ernst Kitzinger, op. cit., 1977, p. 75.
187. Vojislasv J. Djurić, *Sopoćani,* 1963, p. 136, Chapel of St. Simeon Nemanja, upper zone south wall.
188. Lawrence B. Anderson, 'Module: Measure, Structure, Growth and Function,' in *Module Symmetry and Proportion* (ed.,) Gyorgy Kepes, 1966, pp. 114, 116.
189. Ernst Kitzinger, op. cit., pp. 89, 90, 92.
190. P.A. Michelis, op. cit., 1964, p. 58.
191. Ibid., p. 52.
192. Ernst Kitzinger, op. cit., p. 85.
193. P.A. Michelis; op. cit., p. 58.
194. M. Chatzidakis, A. Graber, *Byzantine and Early Medieval Painting,* 1965, p. 4.

—In fact, D.T. Rice finds this love of realism as one of the principal factors which distinguishes Serbian school from the general stream of Byzantine art. He acclaims the founder's portraits, and shepherds in the Nativity at Sopoćani, as 'going further in realism, than other centres. . . for the artist treated them with complete realism,' *Yugoslavia-Mediaval Frescoes,* UNESCO, 1956, pp. 9, 11. In this respect the hot-water jug held in the hands with cloth in the Nativity (plate 139), is Cezannesque by any standards.

195. Securing abstract quality of structure.
196. Rudolf Arnheim, 'On Order, Simplicity and Entropy,' in *Leonardo,* Vol. VII-2, Spring, 1974, p. 139.
197. Domention spake—'that is not light which in east originates and on west sets, which with time concludes and divides dawn, night, which in common with animals we shall see', that what he calls light 'which with soul angel we shall be able to see, of heavens and transcendental.' Vojislav J. Djurić, op. cit., 1963, p. 71, translation by the researcher.
198. Vojislav J. Djurić, op. cit., 1963, pl. XX, 'The Appearance of Christ to the Holy Women'.
199. Ibid., p. 64.
200. P.A. Michelis, op. cit., p. 40.
201. Ibid., p. 112.

202. Vojislav J. Djurić, op. cit., 1963, p. 136.
203. Mila Rajković, op. cit., 1963, p. 6.
204. Svetozar Radojčić, *Yugoslavia Medieval Frescoes*, UNESCO, 1956, p. 20.
205. 'Like actors in the ancient theatre, the figures express here intense inner life in calm poses and measured gestures:' Vojislav J. Djurić., op. cit., 1963, p. 116.
206. Radhakrishnan, op. cit., 1975, p. 245.
207. Ibid., p. 243.
208. Langer, *The New Illustrated Encyclopedia of World History*, 1975, p. 204.
209. Svetozar Radojčić; op. cit., 1956, p. 20.
210. *Encyclopedia of Word Art*, Vol. V, 1961, column 35.
211. Mila Rajković; op. cit., 1963, p. 6.
212. Dr. Lazar Milin, op. cit., 1972, p. 46.
—D.T. Rice, op. cit., 1972, p. 188.
—P.A. Michelis, op. cit., 1964, pp. 104-05.
213. Dr. Priyabala Shah, *Viṣṇudharmottra-Purāṇa*, Third Khaṇḍa, Vol. II, 1961, p. 185.
214. Anand K. Coomarswamy, op. cit., 1970, p. 40.
215. Dr. Lazar Milin, 'The Theology of Icons', *Serbian Orthodox Church*, Vol. III, No. 3, 1972, p. 44.
216. Kanti Chandra Pandey, *Comparative Aesthetics*, Vol. II, 1956, pp. 112-13.
217. Assunto, *Encyclopedia of World Art*, Vol. XIV, Col. 269-70.
218. H.W. Janson, *History of Art*, 2nd ed., 1977, p. 55.
219. Mila Rajković, op. cit., 1963, p. 6.
220. J.J. Pollitt, *The Art of Greece 1400-31* B.C., 1965, p. xvii.
221. Kanti Chandra Pandey, op. cit., 1956, p. 87.
222. Kanti Chandra Pandey, op. cit., 1959, p. 240.
223. Kanti Chandra Pandey, op. cit., Vol. II, 1956, p. 114.
224. K. Krishnamurti, *Dhvanyāloka of Ānandavardhan*, 1974, p. vii.
225. Dr. Priyabala Shah, op. cit., (*Citrasūtra* 43:21, 22) p. 136.
226. A corollary between hedonistic evasion of Hīnayāna conventions and Iconolastic controversy has been also pointed out by Madanjeet Singh: op. cit., 1965, p. 44.
227. Dr. Lazar Milin, op. cit., 1972, p. 43.
228. Ibid., p. 45.
229. Rudolf Arnheim Metaphorically calls it 'entropy'—'On Order, Simplicity and Entropy,' *Leonardo*, Vol. VII-2, Spring, 1974, p. 139.
230. A.K. Coomaraswamy, op. cit., 1972, p. 3.
—Nihararanjan Ray, too, supports that these works were created to give concrete form to individual's emotions and in formal terms, to convey collectively emotions about material and idea. *Bhartiya Kalā Ka Adhyayana*, 1978, p. 21.
231. Rudolf Arnheim, op. cit., 1960, p. 372.
232. Ibid., p. 376.
233. *Voices of Silence*, 1956, p. 162.
234. (*Legends of Padmasambhava*), Erich Neumann, op. cit., p. 236.
—'The awareness of pain in the poignant compositions of Ajanta where the erotic palace scenes are always overshadowed by some immediate symbol of the passing away of life'—Mulkraj Anand, *Marg*, Vol. XXV-4, p. 66.

235. The negative feminine 'Wheel of Life' which is redeemed by contrary wheel of Buddha's presence. This, in Tibetan Buddhism, presents twelve *niddānas*—foundation causes embodying astrologically the woeful causality of birth, old age, death and rebirth with illustrative symbols as blind women representing ignorance, potter shaping a vessel—formless getting form in flux etc.: Erich Neumann, op. cit., pp. 232-38.
236. J. Fergusson and J. Burgess, *The Cave Temples of India*, p. 310.
237. Erich Neumann bases his theory of 'Great Mother' on Jung's theory of archetypes namely, the structural dominants of the psyche in general 'as a nuclear phenomenon transcending consciousness;' these are the 'mythological motifs' recurring without any conscious knowledge. He clarifies that the 'Urboros' is a prehistoric spiral motif representing male and female consciousness. It is the circular snake biting its tail symbolizing 'a state in which chaos, the unconscious, and the psyche as a whole were undifferentiated and which is experienced by the ego as a border line state.' It is 'The Great Round'—'elementary character of Great Mother' in which Good Mother and Terrible Mother form a cohesive archetypal group. In its transformative character it is Material Feminine. *The Great Mother*, 1955, pp. 19, 6-28.

— Adaptation of elementary and transformative character is clearly shown in the Hariti goddess in Buddhism. Other Prehistoric symbols like Bull for female genetic principle and Horse for male as the inducer have been taken up as the leitmotifs of the Buddha's life, the bull representing his birth and the horse the renunciation. Bull entwined with vegetative life force of 'Creeper-motif' is an important and integral part of the decoration in Ajanta, as it becomes the zodiacal emblem of Gautama's birthday—Full moon day of *Vaisākha*. A very significant adaptation is of the 'ring-stones' with their motifs adapted to represent the 'Great round' of Mother Goddess. The adaptation is clearly exemplified in 'the Dying Princess' where the peacock, (as the symbol of Amitabha Buddha also), on the upper rim of the visual circle (with palm tree on the right,) at once reminds of the ring-stone of Murtaziganj, Patna and Kausambi Group in which the Mother Goddess is flanked by peacock and palm trees (plate 108). The posture of these Mother Goddesses has similarity with the Mother Goddess on the gold plaque found in the stūpa at Lauria-Nandangarh. Both show preoccupation with life and death or the two stages of life-cycle in *śavamudrā* of yogic practices. It is a pose of extreme relaxation of death, as S.P. Gupta points out. *The Roots of Indian Art*, 1980, pp. 56-68 and 71, 72.

— Continuing 'preoccupation with death.' P. Fingesten has argued that Buddha's smile, earlier even forbidden, is not a sign of love or communication and human relationship, nor of psychological sickness, but is of 'the last possibility.' He explains it, through exemplifications, as 'the apparent smile of the dead'— the *risus sardonicus* of the one who has 'overcome life' and is 'dead to life.' It is apparently taken over by the artists from 'blissful smile of corpse' as an easily grasped and compelling symbol. It was known in Etruscan art too. Its development in stages from hidden implicit to sublime (which was never achieved in India, Fingesten notes, as only inward and ecstatic smile; later stereotypes were developed here, but sublime was developed in Wei and Cambodian Art), from deepening of the angulioris to increasing upward curvature of the *rima oris* until it becomes U or V shaped. He argues that otherwise Buddha having discovered that life is suffering should have serious mein: 'The Smile of Buddha,' in *Oriental Art*, New series, Vol. XIV, 3, 1968, pp. 176-83.

— It may be pointed out that Fingesten seems to have forgotten the basic necessity of Indian icons namely, that they should look 'breathing' and full of vitality. 'Sap' of life and not the lifeless dead. Hence, 'life within death' could have been the 'motif' behind taking over such 'suggestive' details even of a corpse.

238. A.L. Herman has pointed out four levels of meanings in Indian religious art—Literal, Moral, Allegorical and the last, Anagogical, which is mystic level of meaning by which ultimate truth is obtained 'Indian Art and Levels of Meaning,' in *Philosophy East and West*, Vol. XV, No. 1 1965, pp. 22-23.

He further argues quoting Morris (Signs, Language and Behaviour) that anagogic symbols in a highly developed tradition and culture, are post-language symbols as 'substitute for original signs and are dependent on language for their appearance and yet they allow the organism a measure of autonomy and self-stimulation independent of the environment, giving it a signification it could not otherwise have.' In highly developed fine arts 'marks on paper may also be the occasion for such symbols and the signs' (p. 25); these are 'formative mode of discourse' as Morris calls, 'applied to the absolute direction of one's life towards *Nirvāṇa* or *Mokṣa*:' p. 29, *see* Glossary.

239. David L. Snellgrove, (ed.,) op. cit., 1978, pp. 429-30.
240. Ibid., p. 429 30.
241. Looma Rishi cave has the *toraṇa* border emerging out of *Makara* the symbol of the Mūla of the 'Cosmic Tree' connected with 'soma aspect' (as in Ajanta this motif has been sufficiently used with River deities). The mountains of rising and the setting sun, Udaya and Astagari (*Atharva Veda* XII 3, 1, 4, 47) are represented as Yupas or 'sacrificial pillars' over which the sun's orbit has been presented as *toraṇa*.

— F.D.K. Bosch, *The Golden Germ*, 1960, pp. 145-46.

242. The top mountains over the caves are also of semicircular shapes. It is worthwhile comparing Wölfflin's appreciation of Micelangelo's St. Peter's dome's synthesis of 'massive heaviness and free-rising' in which, he says, 'the symbolic image of weight is maintained, yet dominated by the expression of spiritual liberation.' This is explained as an expression reached through a synthesis between cupola's circular curves possessing firmness with the circle of hemisphere 'making them look like a part of the one and the same curve appearing as deviation stretching upward,' Rudolf Arnheim, op. cit., 1960, p. 365.
243. *Padmamūla* as dome (*aṇda* or *garbha*), stem corresponding central part (Yupa), central branch as pinnacle (*Yasti*) and the roof of the tree's foliage corresponding with the sun-shade (*chatra*): F.D.K. Bosch, op. cit., pp. 169-70.
244. *Tri-Ratna* (The three Jewels—Buddha, Dhamma, the Doctrine, Saṁgha, the order). The wheel topped by a trident—the main three branches—wheel as Lotus-rosette-brahmamūla, the third element being bending festoons on either side of the lower part of the wheel: Ibid., pp. 162-63.
245. *Bhartiya Kalā*, p. 178.
246. F.D. K. Bosch, op. cit., pp. 100-04.

—Thus almost the whole array of symbols in Indian art was more or less adapted on this pattern.

247. C. Sivaramamurti, *The Art of India*, 1977, pl. 82.
248. Ibid., p. 130.
249. Rudolf Arnheim, op. cit., 1960, p. 368.

250. These were cononized in iconographic traditions, i.e., *Citrasūtra* in ch. 35 (*Āyāmocchrāya-māna*), ch. 36 (*Pramāṇādhyāya*), ch. 37 (*Sāmānyamāna*), ch. 38 (*Pratimālakṣaṇam*) and ch. 42 (*Rūpanirmāṇam*) gives exhaustive instructions for such details.
251. Arnheim, op. cit., 1960, p. 374.
252. *Webster's New International Dictionary of the English Language*, 1960, p. 998, quoted by A.L. Herman, 'Meaning in Indian Art,' in, *Philosophy East and West*, Vol. XV, No. 11, 1966, p. 23, *see* Glossary.
253. Ibid., pp. 24, 26: A term used by Heinrich Zimmer which to Herman denotes 'anagogic level:' *see* Glossary.
254. Ananda K. Coomaraswamy, *Christian and Oriental Philosophy of Art*, 1974, p. 50.
255. P.A. Michelis; op. cit., p. 19.
256. Ibid., p. 9.
257. Dr. Sreten Petković, *Arilje*, 1965, plate 24.
258. R.M. Frye, *Milton's Imagery and the Visual Arts*, p. 1978, p. 247.
259. Erich Neumann, op. cit., p. 252.
260. Ibid.
261. Ibid., p. 253.
262. Ibid., p. 256, plate 116.
263. Friedrich Rest; *Our Christian Symbols*, 1956, p. 25.
264. Ibid., p. 21.
265. Vojislav J. Djurić, op. cit., 1963, Pl. XXVI.
266. P.A. Michelis, op. cit., p. 35.
267. Germain Bazin, *A Concise History of Art*, Pt. I, 1958, p. 129.
268. P.A. Michelis; op. cit., pp. 120-21.
269. Ibid., p. 129.
270. D.T. Rice, op. cit., 1972, p. 202.
271. Gojko Subotić, *The Church of St. Demetrius in the Patriarchate of Peć*, 1964, p. ix. plates 17, 35.
272. It may be because the Sopoćani artists had affinities with Salonika; V.J. Djurić, op. cit., 1963, p. 117; in the late twelfth century Bishop Eustathios of Salonika wrote commentaries on the Homeric epics: Pollitt, *The Art of Greece, 1400-31 BC*, 1965, p. 238. Meyer Schapiro, *Romanesque Art*, 1977, pp. 291-92, 302 notes, 42, 43.
273. Svetozar Radojčić, op. cit., 1964, pp. ixv, xv.
274. Dr. Mirjana Ljubinković, *Ravanica*; 1966, p. ix.
275. Erich Neumann, op. cit., p. 325.
276. Ibid., plate 118.
277. Ibid., pp. 256, 258, plate 120.
278. George Every, op. cit., 1970, p. 83.
279. Erich Neumann, op. cit., pp. 325-26.
280. Ibid., 336.
281. Ibid., p. 252.
282. "This is the phenomenon of the so-called 'modes'—the conventional use of different stylistic manners to denote different kinds of subject-matters of different levels of existence." *Byzantine Art in the Making*, 1977, p. 19.
283. Vojislav J. Djurić, op. cit., 1963, plate LI.

284. Ibid., plate LII.
285. Ibid., plate I.
286. 'The Philosophical Brothel,' in *Art News*, October, 1972, p. 45.
287. Ananda K. Coomaraswamy, op. cit., 1972, p. 18.
288. Ibid., p. 11, this view is applicable to both the centres.
289. Ibid., p. 74, note 56.
290. Fresco of the 'Dormition' presented in the Narthex, of *Bodjani* (*c.* 1478) vivify such imagery: Olga Mikić, 1964, plate 3.
291. Erich Neumann, op. cit., p. 236.
292. Mila Rajković, op. cit., 1964, P. ii, plate 26.

CHAPTER IV

ARTIST AND PATRON:
Ajanta, Sopoćani, Comparative

Ajanta

Rock inscriptions, in general, at Ajanta substantiate the accounts of artists and patrons as given in the art-treatises. For example, the inscription on cave 26 speaks of *sthavira* Achala Muni who himself had reached almost a monk's status, has recourse to Bhikshu Dharanadatta and his disciple Bhadrabandhu and had constructed 'this temple through them.'[1] Apart from echoing the theory of transcendence through art, this testifies to the guild system as well. A guild's head, being a *sthavira*, looked after the complete job of 'temple' and was also guided by the 'enlightened' advice and patronage. Besides, it indicates the validity of an oral system, being the only system with the potential of a constantly changing adoption without losing the basic stance or *pramāṇa*, given in the art-treatises as 'headings.'[2] Sage Mārkaṇḍeya quenching King Vajra's thirst of knowledge for arts, says in *Viṣṇudharmottara-Purāṇa*:

> To build a temple is meritorious, so is the making of an image of a deity. Meritorious is the worship of a divine image and so its adoration.[3]

It almost echoes Ajanta inscriptions.[4] Similar echoes can also be traced showing parallels between the two. For example expounding the basic principle, Sage Mārkaṇḍeya instructs the 'wise man' to 'create proportions by his own genius.'[5] This freedom is discernible in the artists of Ajanta too. We may note this freedom exemplified in 'the Buddha in Kapilvastu' (cave 17, plate 122). David Riesman sums up this attitude in the intuitive principle of 'inner direction.'[6] Individual's endeavours can also be detected as 'different hands' in a single mural. These 'different hands' and the prevalent styles were properly utilized by the *sthavira* who had the full vision of the complex. In the said painting different levels of existence have harmoniously been expressed in such an application of different styles called 'modes.'[7]

According to guild hierarchy, the services of creative talents start with the *sthavira*, the chief of artisans, under whom the *sūtradhārin* would coordinate the whole scheme of the complex. The *vigyānin*, the art experts, would devise the entire iconography and iconology to be worked out by the *takśaki* (sculptor) and the *vardhaki*, i.e., the builder and carver and the painter. There was further work division coming down to the *rūpakāras* and *karmakāras* as technical assistants.[8] Such a pattern was inevitable in the type of 'social art' like murals and temple carving. It was a combined effort of all the experts to create an environment which could re-create the deepest aesthetic, emotive and spiritual vision which they 'experienced' before commencing the work.[9]

This was nurtured by constant practice, aided by oral *śāstric* tradition prevalent in the guild itself or by systematic instructions imparted in *gurukuls*, universities or schools attached to royal courts.[10] These instructions included the knowledge of various subjects especially of the treatises on dance and dramaturgy.

Another notable aspect to this gigantic art-activity was what S.P. Gupta calls the 'King's will.' This was not arbitrary but denoting 'social conscience,' which, to use Marx's terminology, resulted in 'Asiatic mode of production'.[11] King Upendragupta's unabated donations (inscription, cave 19) for building *vihāras* etc., in 'dire financial straits,'[12] give a glimpse of 'king's will' in the 'contest of piety.'[13] Prime Minister Varahadeva also 'acted as he liked' (ins. of cave 16) in building or engaging the architects of Ajanta,[14] so were Bhikkhu Buddhabhadra and wealthy nobleman Mathuradasa (inscriptions of caves 4 and 6).

As a liturgical craftsman settled in the temple-towns or artist villages near palaces, the artisan often had tussle with the 'priest' (regarded as king's representative) in the economic field as well in social status. Artisans' guilds were placed in low-caste; as such they realized their betterment in becoming 'secular' or favouring heterodox religions. This trend was responsible also for the rise of the journeyman-artisans. They not only assimilated various influences (Ajanta style has been termed eclectic)[15] but also wove a countrywide system by applying the 'modes.' These journeyman-artists (artisans)[16] must have devoted generations in serving the Buddhist community, ultimately by settling again in guild villages. Thus, a three-point tradition illuminates the working processes of Ajanta—the monks to set the 'standards,'[17] the artisans or court-artists[18] to give concrete form to their visions, and, the craftsmen to embellish them. As it was customary to have foreigners also among the Bauddh-Bhikkus, and donors (as Karli inscriptions mention), it is also very probable that there were foreigner-artists also working at Ajanta.[19] Karl Khandalavala infers it from the 'Persian embassy scene.' There have been instances of ladies surpassing males in the records of art-activities preserved in literature.[20] *Citrasūtra* also categorises the expert artists as having command over the *hairikajā* linear modulations, or over giving sketch *hasto-chāyā*, delineating fine nuances of *vartanā* in *Satya Citra*. These artists, when able to convey *prāṇa* and the 'force of wind,' were respected as great artists deviating from canons through their genius. The second category was of those having command of clarifying the iconographic details according to *citrarasa* and suggestiveness. They were *vigyānins-rūpkāras* delineating depth in *patraja* while having the knowledge of oblique and cubic spatial delineations (of *vaiṇik* and *nāgaracitras*). These 'smiters of the crowd of titled sculptors' were aided in the beautification (*śobhā*) by the painters who would be proficient in delineation of depth with the resonances of colours brought out by *binduja* methods. The ground, colour and griding—*maṇibhūmi*—preparations would be the work of apprentices and assistants.[21] After having attained proficiency and experience, these apprentices were gradually rising in their position, in the guild as well as in the society, since *sthavira* Achala Muni, too, had access to religious heads of the *saṁgha* at Ajanta. It is relevant to point out that Indian literature is full of examples of kings' friendship with creative artists. The examples of sending the artists as emissaries or *mahāmatras* to collect the novel motifs to augment the royal grandeur are also found since the time of Aśoka.[22]

The Ajanta complex, created through different political situations from Sātavāhanas to Vākāṭakas, had the 'King's will' as the modulator of its aesthetic configurations. It flourished under the patronage of not only the kings (among whom were the creators of *Gāthāsaptaśati* and *Bṛhat-Kathā*), but also under monks and different *śreṇis* of traders, and merchants, who were the donors of art works and were eulogized in the inscriptions. Thus, there arises the conception of secular patronage of Ajanta as was of other Buddhist monuments.[23] Since foreign patronage is also recorded for Buddhist monuments, it supports the theory that 'Persian Embassy' was also got painted as a part of winning foreign patronage.[24] There is a fairly good possibility of donor's portraits having been painted in the scenes. The title like *Dharma-Mahārāj*, the *Sūrya*, and the *Cakravartin* subscribe to the theory of king being the counterpart of gods on earth. As such, the kings got their portraits painted along with the Buddha or his symbol; Sātakarṇi's portraits in caves 9 and 10 serve as an example. Along with the popular practice of portraiture in India, the depiction of the life of court and aristocracy also supports the theory of personal portraits of donor-kings and his retinue. The kings presumably got their portraits transformed as protagonists; this is strengthened by Mulk Raj Anand's reading the face of Bhil chieftain in that of a Bodhisattva at Bagh (contemporary to cave 1 of Ajanta).[25]

Sometimes, these royal donors and patrons were also the canon-makers through art-treatises; e.g., *Samarāṅgaṇa sūtradhāra* was composed by Bhoja of Dhārā and *Mānasollāsa* by Someśvara. Proficiency of patrons in arts and their expertise in appreciation is confirmed in *Citrasūtram* (41:11).[26]

Sopoćani

Since there is no name and class of the artists handed down in texts or inscribed on the walls of Sopoćani, (as it is in its present state) it is only conjectural[27] but substantiated with concrete evidences that journey-craftsmen, royal-artists from guild villages or king's-villages, and monk-artists existed. The journey-craftsman, like *pictores graeci* [28] could have been the same who later settled in king's villages, as in the Dečani itself the inscription cut above the south portal of the narthex mentions 'the master-craftsman Vita from Kotor, city of kings.'[29] Artist-families were as much in existence as the tradition is still maintained in Osačani builders, the immigrants crossing Drina from Eastern Bosnia and settling in Serbia.[30]

The tradition of a master painter aided by a group of fellow workers, as Djurić points out in Sopoćani's decoration,[31] is well supported by the workshop of John the Metropolitan and the tradition of the family of painters by his brother Makarios who painted the frescoes in the monastery of Lubostinya (A.D. 1402-5).[32] Abbreviated instructions left by the master artist at Mileševa,[33] too testify this tradition. *De Diversis Artibus*, an eleventh century compilation by the Latin Monk Theophilus, informs that there was no problem of subsistence for an artist owing to his being attached to a workshop or a monastery.[34] Nevertheless, the very fact that Despot Stephen had to send emissaries 'as far as the islands,' for bringing expert painters[35] speaks of the difficulty of the patrons.

The contract signed by the head of the guild or master-craftsman and the patron was written record. One such record has been discovered in the archives of Dubrovnik; it is the contract of master-builder Desina and his son Blaz from Risan in Boka Kotorska to build the church of the monastery Davidovica[36] for 150 soldi (A.D. 1284). A text written with a dye on fresco-mortar is found in the Church of Our Lady of Levich in Prizeren built by Bishop Damian for king Milutin in A.D. 1307. Giving an account of the wages and obligations of church, it informs that the church 'was built and painted by the master-craftsmen Nikola and Astrap.' Astrap means 'lightning-like' (he had great influence in the early fourteenth century).[37] Such a self-commendation of the master-craftsman George and his brothers Dobroslav and Nikola is evident from the inscription in the church of Decani which reads: 'built and decorated many churches all over Serbia.'[38]

The above document also confirms that the total job of construction and decoration of the church used to be given to the workshop of a family or a guild. This practice is carried on even today by the wooden church builders from Osačani families.[39]

The patron, say, a king like Uroš, an archbishop like St. Sava, an intellectual and poet like Despot Stephen Lazarević, or a nobleman like Bogdan, was the sole arbiter in the selection of the artist and the programme to be carried out. This substantiates the conception of 'king's divine will' and the 'other-directed' efforts influencing the work of art.[40] In this connection, St. Sava's advice to the carvers deserves serious attention: 'Study well the wood which you will need, take care of your tools, and have confidence in your eyes and your hands.'[41] In the same fashion the fresco in the monastery church of Moracha shows a construction site with the king-founder consulting the master-builder and the line written thereupon 'the king at the counsel with the master-builder.'[42] At Sopoćani on the other hand, the 'inner-directed'[43] spirit is conspicuous in the works. It is evident in the nave where the artist seems to have won a synthesis over the dialectics of the 'inner' and 'outer' directions.[44] Rajković labels it as 'free perfection of intelligent and inspired command.'[45] Carrying his work with missionary zeal, though humble in his vocation, the artist was nowhere far from the apostles. Inscriptions like: 'God's gift by the hand of John'[46] or 'sinful priest Simeon the painter'[47] testify not only the humility of the painters but also supports the theory of 'anonymous painter' obliquely. Rice opines that since the work of art was an 'expression of collective outlook,' the personal or individual ideas were not essential. He attributes the system of giving the names of patrons and artists alongwith the portraits of donors etc., (plate 30) to the Macedonian style in the thirteenth century.[48] The metropolitan group certainly paid more attention to personal and intimate character of painting.[49] Further, 'built and decorated many churches' and such other self-commendatory inscriptions speak of the competitive spirit and the individual propaganda. According to Rice, this was the natural impact of the increase in the number of patrons adopting 'acts of piety' in the fourteenth century.[50] The signatures of Metropolitan Jovan and Monk Grigori of Prilep[51] on the frescoes in the fourteenth century confirm the practice of craving for popularity. All the same, the known numbers of celebrated painters is negligible owing to the transcendental attitude developed through religion which submerges individuality. The training of painting imparted in the monasteries promoted such an attitude. As for the names of the monk painters, Houser believes that their mention was designed 'to give pride and place to monks' own professional brothers'[52]—'a romantic exaggeration with patron's name added as predicate.'[53] In certain cases the monks did the decoration themselves avoiding costly professionals[54] giving rise to the genuine names of the monk-painters. The artist's innovations in the medieval atmosphere of strict regulations mostly implied sacrilege and risked punishment. His talent's use was 'a kind of Liturgy—sacramental and not didactic,'[55] hence his personality was suppressed, a part of which was his own 'temerity' as he belonged to the lower orders of social hierarchy.[56] Artisans' and slaves' dresses were the same—undyed, woollen, long-sleeved tunic of knee-length, girdled at the waist, and topped with a hood against cold.[57] This image is confirmed in the fresco of the monastery church of Moracha (the exception is, of course, in the lord-type dress of the master-builder). However, the patrons were sometimes eager for more influence and prestige; they thought that the rigidity of stand might undermine or stifle their national culture. Thus politically motivated, they employed expert immigrant painters and sent their own artists abroad with a view to bringing a repertory of more current and useful motifs. It was just the reverse at the Byzantine capital.[58]

Finally, the work of art was based on 'an immediate personal experience of the transcendental.'[59] Thus, as is evident in the Dionisius' *Herminy*, a prospective painter or a monk wishing to become a religious painter had to undergo a specific spiritual preparation. He was brought 'in front of the Icon of the Saviour and the Holy Virgin in the church and for the success of work special prayers were conducted.'[60] Didron described painter Joseph at Mt. Athos working with ease and quoting scriptures for inscriptions, which clearly proves religious involvement of the painter.[61]

Comparative

The great artist of Sopoćani, with his vision and quest for originality of the decoration, has a parallel in the *sthavira* of Ajanta. Both guided and adopted the stylistic variances applying them as 'modes;' they also utilized individual artist's capacity in solving the dichotomy of 'inner-light' or luminosity and illumination. In both the guiding spirit is the 'will' of the patron, as the arbiter in the selection of painters. However, his will was that of a 'divine arbiter' having potency and means to get such monuments of art conceived and created with the faith and conscience of the people.

At Ajanta, so also at Sopoćani, the basic patron or 'donor' was the king—the *Dharmarāj* or the 'Vice-regent of God.' The individual merchants or traders like

Mathuradasa, their *śreṇis* or the artists' guilds, Bhikkhus and religious *sthaviras* too would donate at Ajanta in the 'contest of piety;' this supports the concept of secular-patronage of such Buddhist monuments. Sopoćani, being the royal monastery, the 'pious patronage' got stuck to the Nemanjan dynasty, although in Serbia the noble 'Bogdans' did donate the monasteries. At Ajanta King Upendragupta's enthusiasm in donation has been compared to that 'of a Justinian.'[62] This was widened to incorporate 'a Serbian-King' who, although in difficult times encountering hostility from all the four sides, would still saturate the whole land with these sanctuary-monuments. These royal donors had abundant culture-consciousness and would imprint their presence in these cultural-cum-religious sanctuaries donating their portraits, too. In fact, at Sopoćani their 'family-tree' is given in visuals. This could only be compared with Ajanta's inscriptions and the speculated portraits of Satakarni in the want of further identifications. As the portraits were in vogue and the royal grace transcended, it would not be inappropriate to conclude that the eulogies to kings and queens inscribed at Ajanta were presented as visuals in the form of protagonists of the narratives—'Bodhisattvas' and their consorts. The history of Byzantine art also leads to a similar conclusion about Sopoćani's presentations of the 'divine personages.' This becomes evident especially with reference to sensual rendering of a religious image and excessive image-cult widespread before the iconoclastic crisis.

These culture-conscious patrons bestowed their prudence in matters of art upon their prime ministers and religious heads, the archbishops or the *sthavira* Bhikkus, who in turn, would put constraints of 'other-directed' stream into the stylistic manifestations in the art of Ajanta and Sopoćani. Prabhāvatī Gupta,[63] Anna, Helen and Katelina's[64] influences have also given an impetus to such streams.

Nurtured in the above environment, the artists had their rigorous training at the ateliers or the workshops of guilds in case of their having settled in king's or temple-town. Those who were trained at the monasteries or universities were either sought after by the patrons or became journeyman-artists seeking patronage by commending their talents. In turn, these journeymen got settled in king's or temple-town devoting generations in creating the art complexes like Ajanta and those of Serbia including Sopoćani. It has been specially noted that these artists were fully conversant with dance and dramaturgy as well.

The theory of the refugee artists holds good both in the case of Sopoćani and Ajanta. Djurić finds 'best artists of the great Byzantine centres being suddenly placed at the disposal of the Serbs.'[65] Karl Khandalavala discerns the presence of foreign artists working with those of Vākāṭakas in the paintings like 'Persian Embassy Scene' at Ajanta, too.[66]

At both the centres we find a three-tier art activity doing the total job of the sanctuary from building or carving to painting. The first was that of the visionary artists and guides who drew inspiration from the examples like St. Sava or Sage Mārkaṇḍeya. The second comprised the accomplishers and 'inner-directed' royal or monastic artists (or artisans)[67] and the third of apprentices and assistants, who, in course of time acquired higher responsibilities with experience and family succession. The swollen egos of successful masters are conspicuously recorded in Serbian and Vākāṭaka inscriptions in sharp contrast to the anonymity of the humble creator, creating masterpieces like the Padmapāṇi or the Dormition. Because of interaction with royal and religious patrons the head-builder or the *sthavira* had, of course, a higher social status than the artist in general who belonged to the lower orders of social hierarchy. However, even the ordinary artists could rise to the position of king's emissaries, *mahāmātras*, they collected new motifs from alien lands in order to enrich the repertory of their royal patrons.

The testimonies of *Herminy* and *Citrasūtra* sufficiently indicate the religious character of the vocation of these artists. A degree of differences, however, prevailed between the two. For the artist of Sopoćani it was a kind of sacramental liturgy followed by strict regulations. But the innovations did emerge owing to the 'inner-directed' capacity of the visionary artist. At Ajanta, on the other hand, even the didactic character of the narrative paintings did not suppress the creative freedom of its artist, though it did have imprint of the 'other-directed' stream. The artists at both the places were instructed to paint only after attaining a certain level of purification and aptitude through prayers and rituals. It was prescribed so that the experience of the transcendental could vividly be painted with an immediate personal experience.

This comparative survey brings to light a few other differences as well. At Ajanta we find the artisans' guilds making donations, thus participating in the 'contest of piety' in order to secure a position in the social echelon. Another difference is that although the artisans at Ajanta were at the lower level of social hierarchy, they have not been shown dressed like slaves as are their counterparts at Sopoćani. At Ajanta, as in the rest of India, the artists saw their betterment in remaining unattached to any religion or favoured heterodox religions, which gave 'secular' character to their art. This enabled them to assimilate various influences and work for all the religions—this gave rise to a countrywide style. The position was different in Serbia where the artists mostly remained attached to a workshop or a monastery. Women artists are also mentioned in Indian inscriptions and texts, it is not so in Serbia.

REFERENCES

1. Ramesh Shanker Gupte and B.D. Mahajan, *Ajanta, Ellora and Aurangabad Caves*, 1962, p. 260.
2. S.P. Gupta, *The Roots of Indian Art*, 1980, pp. 17, 18. A.W. Watts, *The Way of Zen*, 1971, p. 100.
3. Dr. Priyabala Shah, *Viṣṇudharmottara-Purāṇa*, third Khanda, Vol. II, 1961, p. 2.
4. For example, the painted inscription in cave 27 reads: The meritorious gift of the Sakya Bhikshu Masharsala... mother and father... for the attainment of Supreme knowledge by all sentient creatures. Whoever makes an image of Jīna (Buddha) becomes complete in beatitude, is brilliant through virtues and physical organs and is delightsome to the eyes.' Ramesh Shanker Gupte and B.D. Mahajan, op. cit., p. 267.
5. Dr. Priyabala Shah (*Citrasūtra* 39) 1961, p. 115.
6. Ernst Kitzinger, *Byzantine Art in the Making*, 1977, p. 13, *see* Glossary.
7. Ibid., p. 19, *see* Glossary. Cf. pp. 160-61.
8. Kanheri inscriptions and the information in *Mahāvaṁśa* relates to such division of work. Post Gupta period was marked by such a structure of the artist-guilds. R.N. Misra, *Bhārtīya Mūrtikalā*, 1979, pp. 72, 76, 271. C. Sivaramamurti, The Painters in Ancient India, 1978, pp. 2, 9.
9. Art-treatises instruct in *dhyāna* and concentration processes: *Citrasūtram* (40:11-14), *Citralakṣaṇa* (A.K. Bhattacharya, 1974, p. 45). Sankara, too, described, *śilpa* as *pūjā-vidhāna*—process of devotion. C. Sivaramamurti, op. cit., 1978, p. 25. The concentration through yoga in creating art inspired the modern artist-designers of Bauhaus, who were given such practices. I. Johannes, 'The Foundation Course of Bauhaus' in (ed.,) Gyorgy Kepes, *Education of Vision*, 1965, pp. 105, 115.
   —'To sound the depth one must become, as it were, a 'diviner' and this role is perhaps peculiarly suited to the Indian artists. In his own tradition it is the emotive-intuition which is considered the artist's most cherished and most developed quality of consciousness.'
   —Geeta Kapur, *Contemporary Indian Artist*, 1978, p. x.
10. Hemchandra, A.D. 1088-1172, confirms that *Śilpa-Śālās* were owned by Sātavāhanas.
   — R.N. Misra, op. cit., p. 271.
   —The southern-*toraṇa* of the Great Stūpa of Sanchi has inscription of donation as 'Vasishthi-putra Ananda, the head of King Satakarni's artisans.'
   —Maurizio Taddei, *Monuments of Civilization, India*, 1977, p. 64.
   —Max Weber, *The Religions of India*, 1967, p. 99
   —Karl Khandalavala, *The Development of Style in Indian Paintings*, 1974, pp. 14, 18.
11. As explained by Chesneaux it 'is characterized by the combination of the productive activities of the village communities with the economic intervention of a state authority that exploits them at the same time directs them' and which M. Taddei thinks as the contributing factor in the building of monuments of Art in India; *supra.*, p. 20.

12. Walter M. Spink, 'Ajanta's Chronology: Politics and Patronage, in *Kalādarśana* (eds.,) Joanna G. Williams, 1981, p. 119.
13. Ibid., p. 112.
14. Ibid., pp. 114, 116.
15. Karl Khandalavala, op. cit., p. 22.
16. 'Artisans,' explain their position better than the term 'artist'—which is getting various connotations now.
17. Monk painter theory for Ajanta, though refuted by Karl Khandalavala (op. cit., p. 18), gets a support from the inscriptions already cited. It is verified even by the Buddhas painted later in caves 9 & 10 which show the signs of abstract canons of Pāla palmleaf miniatures, the painters of which are accepted to be Buddhist monks by K. Khandalavala himself (ibid. p. 55).

    Recently K.D. Bajpai has further supported the theory by the evidences of Pangudari (Madhya Pradesh and located on crossraods towards Ajanta) rock shelters being painted by Boddh Bhikkus during Maurayan Period. He has also illustrated two images of Buddha (now in Mathura museum) carved by Bhikku Yasadinna (in A.D. 454) and some other bihikku artist, as the inscription reads.

    'Inscriptions and coins as a source of Art History and consideration of some allied problems,' in, (ed.,) Ratan Parimoo, *Proceedings of Workshop in History of Art*, 1977, p. 126.

    Art canons set by monks and sages is proved in *Citrasūtra.* The Cyclonese monk-artist was 'painting figures of the Buddha in a grave and dignified manner in Chiang-an in China during T'ang Dynasty in the seventh and eighth centuries, informs Anil de Silva, *Chinese Landscape Painting*, 1964, p. 133.
18. These journeyman-artists were responsible for standardization of the style of eclectic-synthesis (applying 'modes'), and the so-called court-style. These were the painters of 'rebellion class (as M. Taddei points about the Sanchi ones, op. cit., p. 37) donating in the 'contest of piety' and whose self-aggrandizement exclaimed like 'Lion among the painters' and who were always ready for competition to procure better market of patronage. Extreme humility, modesty and anonymity is recorded of those masters who would otherwise 'be overjoyed in achieving excellence in a picture' notes C. Sivaramamurti, op. cit., pp. 2, 23.
19. Already cited example of the Cylonese artist substantiated such postulations.
20. R.N. Misra, *op. cit.*, p. 273. Artist's lassitude noted and banned in creating Buddha images in *Divyāvadān.* Manohar Kaul, *Trends in Indian Painting*, 1961, p. 6.
21. The best combination of all such characteristics is found in a painting which is liked by all. *Citrasūtra* (41:12).
22. Concept based on S.P. Gupta's postulation of Asokan *Dhamma-mahāmātras* bringing back such motifs. *op. cit.*, pp. 299-300. *See* Glossary.
23. R.N. Misra, op. cit., p. 9.
24. Krishna Chaitanya, *A History of Indian Painting, The Mural Tradition*, 1976, p. 27.
25. *Marg*, Vol. XXV, No. 4, Sept. 1972, p. 57.
26. Masters appreciate linear values, knowers the emotions of *vartanā* depth dimension, others the colours and ladies the ornamentation.

27. Mila Rajković and Vojislav J. Djurić, in monographs over Sopoćani (1963), give their postulations only.
28. Artists from coastal region and interior of country. Vojislav J. Drurić ascribes, especially, the exo-narthex frescoes to them. op. cit., 1963, p. 119.
—Nada Komnenović, *Yugoslav Medieval Frescoes and Plaster Casts*, 1979, p. 10.
29. Al. Deroko, 'The Master-Builders of the Medieval Serbian Church' in *Serbian Orthodox Church,*, Vol. III, No. 3, 1972, p. 19.
30. Dr. D. St. Pavlović 'The Clergy as Builders, Artists and Founders of Wooden Churches in Serbia', in *Serbian Orth. Chuch,* Vol. III, No. 3, 1972, p. 24.
31. Vojislav J. Djurić, op. cit., 1963, p. 115.
32. Nada Komnenovic, op. cit., p. 13.
33. Svetozar Radojčić, *Mileševa*, 1963, p. 69.
34. D.T. Rice, *The Appreciation of Byzantine Art*, 1972, pp. 62, 197.
35. Vojislav J. Djurić, *Resava*, 1963, p. iii.
36. Al. Derko, op. cit., p. 18.
37. Ibid., p. 19 *Yugoslavia Medieval Frescoes*, UNESCO (introduction) Svetozar Radojčić, 1956, p. 22.
38. Al. Derko, op. cit., p. 19.
39. Dr. D. St. Pavlovic, op. cit., p. 24.
40. For the terms 'King's divine will' and 'other-directed,' *see* Glossary.
41. Dr. D. St. Pavlović, op. cit., pp. 23, 24.
42. Al. Derko, op. cit., pp. 20, 21.
43. Ernst Kitzinger, op. cit., pp. 12, 124, see glossary.
44. Ibid.
45. Mila Rajković, op. cit., 1963, p. 5.
46. Gajko Subotić, *The Church of St. Demetrius in the Patriarchate of Peć*, 1964, p. vi.
47. Nada Komnenović, op. cit., p. 25.
48. D.T. Rice, op. cit., p. 156.
49. Ibid., p. 152.
50. Ibid., p. 159.
51. Zdravko Blazić, *The Frescoes in the Church of St. Klement of Ohrid, in Makadonia*, 1957, p. 52.
52. Arnold Houser, *The Social History of Art*, Vol. I, 1968, p. 157.
53. Ibid., p. 158.
54. *The Book of Art*, Vol. I, p. 69.
55. Harald Osborne, (ed.,) *Oxford Companion to Art*, 1970, p. 179.
56. *Encyclopedia of World Art*, Vol. II, 1961, Col. 752.
57. Philip Sherrard, *Byzantium*, 1966, p. 115.
58. *Encyclopedia of World Art*, Vol. II, Col. 757.
59. P.A. Michelis, *An Aesthetic Approach to Byzantine Art*, 1964, p. 170.
60. Dr. Lazar Milin, 'The Theology of Icons,' in *Serbian Orthodox Church*, Vol. III, No. 3, 1972, pp. 37, 38.
61. D.T. Rice, op. cit., p. 199.
62. Walter M. Spink, 'Ajanta's Chronology; Politics and Patronage,' in Kalādarśana (eds.,) Joanna G. Williams, 1981, p. 119.

63. Karl Khandalavala, op. cit., p. 27.
64. Vojislav J. Djuric, *Sopoćani*, 1963, p. 112.
65. Ibid., p. 111.
66. Ibid., p. 46.
67. 'Artisans' is a better term to express their standing as a creator of these works of art in contrast with the modern connotations added to the meaning of the term—'artist.'

CHAPTER V

STYLE AND TECHNIQUE
Ajanta, Sopoćani, Comparative

Ajanta: Iconography

According to Snellgrove and others, the Bodhisattvas painted in cave 1 and 2 are the 'final expression' given to the contemporary ideological vision[1] (plates 122, 141, 157). These Mahāyāna Buddhas are actually a synthesis of the 'luminous' and the 'illuminating' aspects of *Sūrya*, the Sun; the paternal aspect finds its culmination in their images expressing the *Cakravartin* (the ruler of the universe) and the *Mahāpuruṣa* (the universal man.) Their iconography not only resembles those indicated in the inscription of cave 16,[2] but also conforms to those propounded in *Citrasūtra.*[3] Similarly the iconography of *Prajñāpāramitā/Tārā* (cave 1, plate 122)[4] partially answers to *Citrasūtra*'s 'Mahī' (the Earth-goddess); besides, it is in line with the inscribed description of the queen in cave 16.[5]

This confirms that iconographic developments of Ajanta were based on what had been inherited from the earlier *Meh* religions and later confirmed as parts of the Brahmanical texts. Starting from *vṛkha-meh* (the tree-religion), these iconographic delineations were subsequently given cosmological dimensions and Yoga-Tantric overtones in reducing the formative principle to *prāṇa*—the life-force or 'sap' of life.[6]

Ajanta-iconography starts with a perfect form given to the centrifugal force (*prāṇa*) in the *stūpa* which is worshipped in the earlier murals.[7] As soon as the 'niche' was carved on the *stūpa* to represent the externalized 'content' (the form of Buddha appearing on *stūpa* of cave 19,) the speculations over planery and dimensional aspects were brought in. The 'tree' symbol began to abound as verified by the 'creeper' motif which were presented everywhere (plate 46). On planery aspect, it was the 'Hom' motif (plate 21) dividing male and female attributes.[8] It was further developed into three basic configurations (plates 29 and 35) which are pointed out by Stella Kramrisch.[9] The first woman and tree '*Śālbhanjikā* motif' used for representing *Mahāmāyā* giving birth to Buddha.[10] The next comes the composite man and animal (plate 35)—the *yakṣas* and *kinnaras* presented in Ajanta (ultimately endowing their characteristics to the human body); the third is *Mithuna* (plate 125) especially presented on the lintel of the inner chamber of cave 17, ultimately becoming *edā* and *pingalā* (in Buddhist yoga system these are called *lulanā* and *rasanā* respectively) in human-cosmos of Tantra giving life sap *prāṇa*, the living 'breath', to the figures in the paintings of Ajanta. *Tri-ratna* (plate 98) is based on three main branches, (planery): top is *triśūla*, joint is *brahmamūla* or *cakra* or rosette, the third is festoons emerging on either sides.[11] The Celestial Fig-Tree (Ficus-species) was taken to represent two forms, *Nigrodha* (*aśvathā* etc., of male-fiery-nature whose branches go up in the sky) and *Nyagrodha* (banyan etc., of female-water-nature, whose branches go down). Those on root centre become *brahmamūla* and *padmamūla* respectively (plate 22) representing lotus of the sky (Sun) and lotus of the earth (plate 113) between which stands the axis or stem with regal function of a ruler—*Cakravartin*[12] (Hiraṇyagarbha iconographic scheme.) Iconography of *Cakravartin* Buddhas with lotus as the Sun behind the head, and lotus of the earth below the feet, were accordingly adapted at Ajanta. The Buddhas were painted in *Samapada* on pillars, specially with rosettes on lower sides of the beams in caves 9 and 10. The pillars and their decorative details with respective symbolisms of *Pūrṇa-Ghaṭa* (plate 47), 'Makara' and creepers give ample evidence of such metamorphoses in Ajanta. The Buddha as the first *deva* or '*yati*' was given constructional module, 'cubic', of a tree, already reached in *yakṣa* sculptures, (confirmed in the structural plasticity of the birth symbol of Buddha as elephant,) finding its manifestation in the construction modules of earliest figures in cave 9 (plate 121). The variations of cosmological dimensions in Buddhist pantheon were based on 'tree' significations as the eight Buddhas with their respective Bodhi-trees are presented in cave 17. Circumambulation rite gave a dimensional module in which the 'tree' growth as a centrifugal force gave the 'wheel,' its hub as 'axis' of the world and the pyramidal cosmology in five eternal Buddhas describing the relationship of absolute beings with phenomenal world.[13] The hub is Vairocana giving all the four compass points to *Akṣōbhya, Amitābha, Amōghsiddha,* and *Ratnasaṁbhava* with east, west, north and south sides respectively. Their signs (like *ūrṇā, ušṇīṣa), mudrās,* attributes, symbols and their relationships with female powers, *śaktis* were decided as well as their relation with historical and future Buddha were iconographically settled in the conceptions of *Dharmakāya, Saṁbhogkāya* and *Nirmāṇakāya.* Though *Guhyasamāja-Tantra* (by A.D. 300) described these iconographies but in their complete and clear forms these were adopted by seventh century, although Avalokiteśvara and Padmapāṇi, flanking the side-walls of the inner chamber (with Dharmacakra-pravartan Buddha made as historical-Buddha, Gautama, because of the Deer-park symbol) present the fully developed iconography.

The idea of future Buddha, Maitreya, giving a linear concept of time, and the conceptions of the 'saviour', the 'emperor' and the 'illuminator' (of Jewish and Hellenic-Persian origin) were in conflict with the circular (Vedic) concept of 'Luminaries.' This conflict was resolved in the iconography of softening of the contours and lustre of the surface, i.e. illumination and the realistic concept of space which gave Ajanta the walking 'Buddhas.'[14] Aśvaghoṣa's *Buddhacarita* gave narrative iconography to the incidences of the life of Gautama, the Buddha.[15] Compassion and 'salvation' (plate 122) added 'luminosity' principles in the plastic factors which were turned to tactile rhythms and oblique space formation and summed up in lotus-rhizome—the female generative principle. The miracle of Śrāvastī (plate 27) with thousand Buddhas (plate 124) was conceived as growing out of lotus-creeper (right hand wall of antechamber cave 2): Bodhisattva dreamt of lotus rising from his navel up to the heaven of *Akaniśtha* gods.[16] With the Yogācāras inclusion the icon of the Buddha was conceived on a universal plane as *Virāṭa-Puruṣa* with all the attributes and *lakṣaṇas* of monumentality, conquest of immobility and universality (plate 96). A preceptual form of it is exemplified in cave 17 ('Buddha in Kapilvastu' Plate 122.)

With the conception of life as suffering, the pathos lingering on every carnal desire was to be suggested; iconographically it was presented with the symbols of sirens and composite *kinnars* (plate 35). In the rhetoric understatements and Sundari's death-torments ('Dying Princess') were the echo of matriarchal principle solving the mystery of life into death. The 'Mother Goddess' with good, bad and transcendental aspects, was given by Tantra: its culminating conception was the 'Wheel of Life' painted in the vestibule of cave 17 (plate 105).

The general scheme of decoration of *vihāra* has the 'circle of transmigration' (Wheel of Life) to be painted in the vestibule along with the great miracle and the five divisions of the being; *The Dulva* (XI-Fol. 34b) gives this account as prescribed by the Buddha. It further instructs to paint (or to sculpt) outside the door a *yakṣa* with club in his hands. On the door of the inner chamber (of Buddha) *yakṣa* holding wreath and in the courtyards *Jātakas* are to be depicted. It adds that the congregating *bhikṣus* and *sthaviras* are to be painted on the cells of attendants. 'On the kitchen must be represented a *yakṣa* holding food in his hand, on the door of the store house a *takṣa* with an iron hook in his hand, on the water house, *nāgas* with various ornamented vases in their hands, on the wash house foul spirits or the different hells, on the medicine house the *Tathāgata* tending the sick, on the privy all that is dreadful in a cemetery, on the door of the lodging house a skeleton, bones and a skull.'[17]

The decoration scheme of *stūpa*, as given in *Mahāvaṃśa*, starts giving rows of motifs. Starting from eight auspicious signs, it includes creeper, foot-mark row, golden bull row, garland, sun-moon-stars, lotus, *pūrnaghaṭa* row, *dharmacakra* row, row of gods with cups in hand and various guardian gods. The module of such decoration in concentric bands is given in the centre of the ceiling decorations of *vihāras*[18] (plate 116)—giving the perception of the dome of the *stūpa* made of *ākāṣa* or 'lotus'.

Beginning with the arboreal growth rhythm (creeper, plate 116) and gradually becoming the rhythm of the water waves and ascendingly manifesting itself into the light of 'the Diamonds,' it transforms into a full-blown *padma*, the glory of the *prajñā*, in the centre. Reversingly, as the central circles have lighter tones, giving thus a radiating effect which maintains the 'flatness' of the surface, the whole cosmos grows out of *prajñā* in radiating circles. This whole cosmological decoration is guarded on the four corners by the flying *gandharvas* in the motif of 'conversation,' the embodiment of love.

Elaborating Buddhist iconography D.C. Bhattacharya observes that 'in fact the concept of several Buddhist divinities and even many of their iconographic formulations are to be found, sometimes in nascent form, in the art and thought of other faiths.[19] He rightly traces iconic forms of Buddhist deities like *Parnaśabani* (a form of Tārā) to those of tribal groups such as *Śabras* and *Kiratas.* As such, the whole galaxy of the images presented in Ajanta is simply the iconographic presentation of a *Sanātana* (Universal) faith. A phenomenal world is painted only to represent its residual, the 'flux' of life emerging out of the primeval *ākāśa-dhātu*, only to return to this 'active space' again. In this flux the primeval motivation is the matriarchal principle giving the iconography of Prajñāpāramitā as mother of the Buddhas as well as the wife of Gautama, the Buddha.[20] The principle is applied to the transformation of orgress Hāritī also who not only became a deity in Buddhism but was exalted as a mother of the king in the inscriptions of Ajanta.

A frequently occurring iconographic motif is the curtained space (plate 41) which is as enigmatic as the use of *kinnaras*, sirens and composite man-animal-bird images (plate 35). Bust portraits also abound (plate 44). Just as the 'wishing-tree' becomes Bejewelled Bodhisattvas (particularly in Central Asia), it also becomes creeping rhythms of 'bejewelled-ladies;' the iconographic details of which are the marvel of Ajanta in conveying their social status and psychological build-up (as propounded in *Citrasūtra* etc.).

SOPOĆANI: ICONOGRAPHY

Evidences have proved three tenets for deciding the determinants of Byzantine iconography. The first, which Kitzinger, Klauser and Brandenburg support,[21] is that before A.D. 200 there was no Christian Art as such and that by A.D. fifth century its content and function became clear.[22] The next tenet concerns the artists' and patrons' attitudes. Since Charlemagne's time the artist's subjective visualization (what Kitzinger terms as 'Inner-directed') has been accepted as having played a revolutionary part in transforming popular motifs into the Christian iconography, by what Backwith exemplifies by 'painting Venus without its purpose as Mary,'[23] or Frye exemplification of angelic wings added without 'Biblical warrant' which made a graceful addition to the biblical account supplied by art.[24] Added to it are the 'other-directed' elements as catalysts, and as referents which accentuate, reinforce and bring into focus the existing trends.[25] This 'other-directed' was the Nemanjid dynasty, their patriarchs, and the noble men who kept alive the Hellenism as 'modal convention' persistently but, of course, with zeitgeist's permutations, to which Kitzinger refers as 'model differentiations.'[26] The third tenet being the complex dialectics, having Hellenistic and Syrian,[27] impressionistic and abstract respectively, aesthetic ideals.

By the fourteenth century, as Millet distinguishes,[28] narrative and liturgical cycles got decided. The first usually contained twelve and the addition of the 'Dormition of Virgin,' and that too of such a size and magnitude, proves Sopoćani to be a church giving a matriarchal ideology[29] in 'the spirit of the performance' or iconography,[30] although it was dedicated to the Trinity. With regard to this 'spirit of the performance,' Andre Grabar points to the pagan origins of the iconography and development of Virgin's life and death.[31]

The whole of the church of Sopoćani, following the iconography of Basil I, is a microcosm of the actual world[32] (plate 112). The decoration plan of this 'Jerusalem'[33] was influenced by the conception of 'rectangular box' with water underneath and heaven above from where Almighty looks down, as it is presented in the illustration of the book compiled by Cosmas Indicopleustes[34] (plate 112). Quite similar is also the Apocalyptic imagery of cubical shape of 'New Jerusalem' (*Rev.* 21:16). Scriptural square compactness and classical circular compactness (eternity and time),[35] their interaction and solution of relationship were solved by Sopoćani painters in the Corinthian capital (plate 83) where this conflict is resolved with the growth-rhythm of accenthus leaves giving a resemblance of organic growth:[36] (plate 14) motif of palmette (chapel of St. Simeon Nemanja) symbolizes the 'righteous shall flourish like the palm tree' (*Psalm* 92:12). Thus the iconography of Tree of Jesse becomes the leitmotif—the Tree of Life (plate

30) (*Rev* 22:2, 14) being its basic form; and motif of 'hom'[37] becomes the basis of iconographic details: as Bosch has formulated the theory,[38] the divine attributes of 'male' nature are given on the right-hand side, and of 'female' on the left. Apocalyptic imagery of 'son of man sitting on the right hand of power and coming in the clouds of heaven' (*Mark* 15:62), conforms to such postulations. Accordingly, in the left hand are 'female' attributes like books, scriptures, baptismal bowl (Prophet on base of cupola, nave, north-west, plate 67,) flowers (Virgin in the annunciation at *Mileševa*,)[39] and above all Virgin's soul received by Christ on the left arm in the 'Dormition' of Sopoćani (plate 161). The 'male' attributes on the right hand, given in the Christian iconography, are sword (Archangel Michael, St. Demetrius, plate 115,) spear (St. George,) and cross and luminous (righteous) souls taken on right of Christ in 'Descent into Limbo.'

In deriving the conception of different forms of the cross, Bosch's three-dimensional system[40] gives not only the Greek cross, but as well decodes the 'space' conception in the church with its apex as the place of Almighty: the dome, painted with 'starry heaven at night' in many of the Byzantine churches (e.g., Mausoleum of Galla Placidia, Ravenna)[41] seems to be the outcome of such conceptions. The 'Mount of Paradise' of typical mesa formation[42] is again one of such concepts. The leitmotif of triangle (apart from its being the motif symbolizing Trinity,) in the compositions of Sopoćani[43] could also be attributed to this point of view.

As for circle used in the iconography, like a classic, the Byzantine artists had 'formal view of head proportioned by three circles having a common centre at the root of nose.' Radius of one nose (a norm), gave tip of nose and top of the forehead, two lengths gave hair area and the radius of three nose-length made halo (plate 36.) Artists of Sopoćani adopting this module as a practical routine suggested in the Painter's Manual of Mt. Athos, further multiplied the unit of head for the figure.[44] Panofsky, suggesting that this clue to proportion was taken from Roman system, as first outline by Vitruvius, says that length of body was given as seven heads or 28 norms.[45] Church's depth ending in semicircular apse, (plate 4,) a variation over circle, suggests 'a welcome embrace.'[46] The canopy, the simplest form of Apocalyptic architecture of heaven, became, as Mâl points out simple arcade being door to heaven[47] (Narthex, north wall, upper zone, plate 33.) The circle of 'celestial cupola repeats itself in the sun of 'Transfiguration' (plate 37) and in the medallion, containing portraits of saints and patriarchs (plate 45,) inserted here and there in the golden background conceived as the light materialized. Related to this is the concept of Heaven in terms of precious metal and stone as stated in *Revelation* 21:18-21. So, Backwith considers that 'gold and light provided the firmament beneath which the divine and imperial liturgies could be enacted like a sacred drama.'[48]

Light as 'principal metaphor for the Kingdom of Heaven'[49] provided halo; becoming inner 'luminosity' it gave 'Transfiguration' motif; and turning into inner-contemplation,[50] it inspired the iconography of stylite (plate 28) sitting on pillars and remaining undisturbed. The subdued light in the Church 'produced the atmosphere of recondite mystery which compels inward-dwelling in the worshipper.'[51] The inner conflicts, and triumph of light over darkness, found iconography of full armour, for example, in Archangel Michael (plate 115) which embodied Triumph of God.[52] The divine throne (*Rev* 4:3) or empty throne 'Etimasija' (having Bible on it) suggested the Byzantine kings ruling as its vicegerents: Christ enthroned (plate 16) is a part of this representation (Narthex, east wall, lower zone).

At Studenića (plate 102) there is one curious representation, in relief, of a lion's face out of the mouth of which is issuing the creeper motif.[53] Christ has been called 'the lion of the tribe of Juda' (*Rev.* 5:5), the 'vine' and light/glory are also Christ's attributes; the lion's face thus becomes the icon of 'glory' analogous to *kirtimukha* of the Indian symbolism which, with *brahma-mūla*, becomes the lion face issuing creepers out of the mouth.

The great concentration and spiritual attainment is symbolized by the mark between the eyebrows, especially in the faces of patriarchs, saints, St. John the Baptist and apostles painted in the nave. It becomes absolutely like a circular *ūrṇā* (of Buddhist-images) in St. John the Divine, painted on the east wall of diaconion[54] (plate 97).

Nude presentation, apart from being indicator of 'poverty, or shamelessness,' as Panofsky points out, 'specially when contrasted with its opposite, came to be understood as a symbol of truth.'[55] The nude figures with serpent (devil) coiled around in the 'Last Judgment' is iconographically presenting the truth of their state (Narthex, north wall plate 129). There are sirens and sea monsters painted in 'Hell' (Narthex plate 33): 'And the sea gave up the dead which were in it...' (*Rev.* 20:30). The Gate of hell is a combined motif of gate and the pit-opening, as Delton remarks[56] (Nave, north wall). The ideal beauty of the first parents is maintained in angelic faces and classical figures though ugliness is not hidden; still it is 'used as a repoussoir to turn over attention to the inner beauty.'[57] The portraits, as motif *par excellence* at Sopoćani, though present standardization with biblical attributes as those of St. Peter with rounded white beard, St. John—a scraggy one—and St. Paul—bald—yet are very sensitively rendered expressing spiritual qualities. Colours and attires, specially the Attic, were prescribed. Gestures, features, vivacity and animation of glance, all contributing to 'characteristic beauty' and individual expression, were condensed into the 'fertile moment' and presented. Christ is represented in Attic dress with 'Jovian' image.[58] The graven and time-less image of Christ with benedictory hands, 'frozen' face and with frontality, is represented in the 'Appearances' after Resurrection (plate 64) although his image at 'Dormition' looks suggesting dignified pathos full of compassion. 'Time-less images' were made through paradox of 'Life-in-death' by 'frozen immobility' of the whole body yielding to flatness of the wall and faces 'staggeringly life like.'[59] It is significant, as Michelis suggests, 'that a fixed immobility is of the very fabric of holy meditation, is eloquent, as nothing else could be, of complete self-withdrawal'[60] (plate 150). Such paradox is also a part of presentation of the 'dead' and relics ('Dormition' of Virgin—nave, Nemanja's relics and death—in his Chapel, plate 142, 'Death of Queen Anna' and that of Jacob—Narthex.) Motifs of door, varied perspectives and horizon, architectural and natural backdrops, placement of the scene at a particular place—all these contribute to the 'represented spirit' of the anecdote becoming a part of the liturgy, to which the motif of 'Christ on paten' repeatedly presented, gives the symbolic 'Eucharist' (plate 17). Motif of curtain, too, has special significance (plate 12)—the upturned ones over the buildings convey the liberal spirit of the Orthodox Church; the one turned aside in the 'Dormition' be-speaks endless space (plate 161). The space is made 'mysterious' with covered curtains, as behind the palmette motifs in St. Simeon's Chapel (plate 18). Quadrilateral baptistry (in the 'presentation of Christ,' plate 60.) Nave, south wall represents people coming from all the four directions 'who will sit down in the Kingdom of God' (*Luke* 13:29).

Raised-hand saints and Virgin make the popular iconographic motifs of intercessor called 'Deesis.' The fluttering and dropping of cloth-ends[61] (plate 38) are as suggestively and expressively used by the Sopoćani's artists as the poses of the body, gestures of hands and tilt of the heads. Djurić is of the opinion that since in ancient theatre the possibilities and scope of such poses and postures were tested, the painters of Sopoćani took them from there not insisting very much on the expression of the faces and choosing 'two-three most expressive masks which expressed some intense feeling. This was like a director of the ancient theatre consciously adapting certain set expressions for easy communication from a distance.'[62] To such faces were added the characteristic 'deep triangular'[63] shadows under the eyes (plate 138). Even flying ribbons are significant in as much as they convey the gentle breeze and the ethereality of the bodies.

Comparative

It looks pertinent to start this comparison with reference to what Michelis finds in Byzantine art, namely, 'a fixed immobility,' which is 'the very fabric of holy meditation,' fully eloquent of a 'complete self-withdrawal.' This also holds good of Buddhist art being the conquest of stillness. Out of these backgrounds, both Sopoćani and Ajanta, turned out the icons such as that of Christ in the 'Appearance to the Holy Women' (plate 62) and that of 'the Buddha visiting Yaśodharā in Kapilvastu' (plate 122). The frontality of such icons, as Coomaraswamy notes, expresses 'actually the position where the Great Person stands, where void looks into void ... his light directed towards the world, not that aspect which faces the unknown darkness of the altogether inexpressible with respect to which he is from the beginning silent.'[64] Thus, the Buddha's and Christ's demurring from metaphysical speculations has been made eloquent in such an iconography.

Though in such presentations the artists have abided by the 'modal conventions' or the *pramāṇas* as set by the art treatises etc., to represent these super-human figurative syntax, the subjective visualization of the inner content (utilizing the zeitgeist or 'modal differentiation') or 'inner-directed' attitudes of the artists have brought about a difference. The said image of Christ also expresses the conflict of Syrian stream of abstraction and the Hellenism's 'modal convention.' For the artist of Ajanta the image of the Buddha was a total abstract conception, though with the *Mahāpuruṣa*'s or *Virāṭpuruṣa*'s proportions as 'other-directed' modal conventions.

Prominent among these prescribed 'conventions' is the Buddha's aspect of *Cakravartin* which the Bodhisattvas of Ajanta manifest through the *Mahāpuruṣa* iconography and the expression of compassion (plate 157). The compassionate image in 'Jovian' iconography (plate 159) adopted for Christ at Sopoćani brings out a striking similarity of approach. The help of theatre to the artists of both the places is recorded along with the selection of a few major gestures condensed to a signitive or 'fertile movement.' Here, in the figures of Christ of the 'Dormition' and the 'Bodhisattva Padmapāṇi,' the difference in the reticence and subtlety is apparent. The reason is that in Padmapāṇi the signitive curve of the eyebrow is executed parallel to the spontaneous monumentality of the figure, but in the said figure and the face of Christ, this abstract homogeneity couldn't comparingly be brought out owing to the 'individual characteristic' sought to be accommodated along with the rhetoric grace of the figure.

Putting 'bust portraits' in the medallions (plate 45) and painting them at many places is the special trait of the artists of Sopoćani. This matches the *gavakṣa*-window 'busts' (plate 44) and other presentations of the faces at Ajanta.

The signification of the 'characteristic' approach was given to the arboreal growth of the figures in Sopoćani, for which module of Corinthian capital was adopted harmonizing the basic forms to express the monumentality. At Ajanta, too, the significance of lotus-growth and tree-growth is noted. This turned into the rhythmos of the body. Ajanta's noted various torsions or *bhaṅgas* and postures, *sthānas*, conveying rhetorics of the figure-expression (plate 128), find a similarity of approach at Sopoćani, specially in the figures of the Apostles in the 'Dormition' (plate 161). The *dvi-bhaṅgas* (twice twisted), *tri-bhaṅgas* (three times twisted) and *atibhaṅga* (more than three times twisted) are accomplished at both the places, exception being that of characteristic Indian bi-positional (centrifugal and lateral) *tri-bhaṅga* at Ajanta. Adherence to the presentation of the three-fourths of the face has a much stricter following at Ajanta. While at Sopoćani, most of the worldly personages (kings, donors etc.,) and some 'guardian' divinities (e.g., Archangel Michael, plate 115) are presented with front faces. Just as these guardians are usually painted flanking the entrance in Serbian Orthodox Churches, in the same way, Bodhisattvas flank the sanctuary doors at Ajanta. 'Reading' the narratives from left to right is adhered to at both places.

The iconography of the whole decoration plan of the church expressing the lower zones of mundane existence reaching higher up into celestial sphere of 'light,' has similar approach presented in the ceiling decoration of cave 2 at Ajanta (plate 116): *Cosmas Indicopleustes* plan (plate 112) matches in such transcendental plan with this unit of decorative symbolism.

Such a system of presenting 'all possible states of being' has been noted by Coomaraswamy as a gyroscopic presentation,[65] giving the three-dimensional system of viewing the basic iconographic modules.[66] The cross 'must be thought of from this point of view as constituted of three arms, mutually at right angles, intersecting at the one common point which is also the centre of the sphere in which the cross stands.'[67] The artist of Sopoćani has painted such presentations of the cross on the haloes of Christ (e.g., 'the Incredulity of Thomas')[68] substantiating such conception of seeing the cross as 'wheel' (plate 106) in presenting the celestial sphere in halo. Coomaraswamy calls it the 'revolving well-wheel.'[69] It becomes a part of the 'twin-wheel,' i.e. 'wheel of the sky' (Sun or lotus of yonder sky) or 'wheel of the earth' (the lotus in Buddhistic iconography).[70] There are such conceptions already prevalent in the Byzantine ivories done in the 'eastern formalism,'[71] or what Kitzinger calls 'abstract aesthetics' (plate 104). For example, in the 'consular diptychs' the solemnity of the king as an 'Axle-tree' between the nimbus-flower and the flower beneath the feet, parallels the Buddhistic iconography of this conception.[72] With reference to the lotus of *prajñā* presented as the centre of ceiling decoration of Ajanta cave 2 (plate 116) and the sphere of the 'light' kept on the 'dome' of Sopoćani, the haloed 'wheel's' significance becomes clearer.[73]

Thus, the Mary with 'wheel' at Linder (plates 103 and 105) and the 'Uroboros' symbol at Mileševa[74] (in Yugoslavia) significantly get connected with the iconography of the 'Wheel of Life' presented at Ajanta (cave 17) embodying the earth aspect of the 'twin wheel.'

The pagan origin of the iconographic development behind Virgin's life and death culminates ultimately in the 'Dormition' where the matriarchal principle or the 'Mother' 'dies to partake into the wisdom of her son,' thus becoming Sophia. At Ajanta, similar implications of the death-throes of Sundarī for the transcendence of Nanda are noticeable. Apart from the iconographic presentation of the 'Dying' or *Mahāparinirvāṇa* (plate 162, its iconography quite resembling that of the 'Dormition,' plate 161), the motifs like peacock and palmette substantiate the overcoming of the enigma of life and death (plate 108). The motif of palmcttc is also painted at Sopoćani (plate 18) with similar scriptural support. The presentation of composite images (of human and animal) enhances such enigma at Sopoćani as well as Ajanta (plates 33, 35).

The iconography of the 'Tree of Jesse' (plate 30) at Sopoćani is related to the 'thousand Buddhas' (plate 27) adopting the growth of a 'Tree' or a 'rinceau' or 'creeper' pattern in the three-dimensional and planery aspects. Both show the conception of 'navel-born' (*nābhija*, plate 31) or 'lotus-born' (*abja-yoni*) together becoming (as recumbent Nārāyaṇa) 'lotus-navelled' (*padmanābha*). Coomaraswamy relates this to *Lalitavistara's* narration of lotus, rising from the Buddha's navel. This conforms to 'the equivalence of western rose and eastern lotus, who is the central flower on the stem that rises from the navel of the recumbent Jesse.'[75]

The aspects of Christ like Lion, Root, Light, Water of life and Tree of Life[76] or Vine, get a cohesive unit in the aniconic iconography of the Leafed Cross of the Orthodox Church (plate 23). The meaning becomes clearer in the light of the Tree of Life and the Tree of Knowledge getting united in the said image of the cross.[77] Significantly, Ajanta's (in the wider sense Indian) motif of *Kīrtimukha*, i.e., 'Creeper' (plate 100) issuing out of a 'Lion's mouth' suggesting the unity of 'Growth' and 'Light' symbols, is found in Yugoslavia (plate 102) though not at Sopoćani itself. Iconography of *Tri-ratna* (plate 98) born out of 'tree' symbolism (denoting *padmamūla* and *brahmamūla* birth in *Hiraṇyagarbha*,[78] plate 22) has a striking similarity with the above conception.

The attributes distributed on the planery aspects of the tree combined with the motif of 'Hom,' (plate 21) and having the male element on the right and the female on the left, are generally applicable to the iconographic development at Sopoćani (plate 67) as well as at Ajanta (plate 13). Thus, 'conversation' motif, to concretise this unity, is in abundance at Ajanta and finds a place at Dećani. Gold as the metaphor of the 'kingdom of Heaven' has its counterpart in the 'Yellow' of *Ratnasaṁbhava* Buddha and the colour of *stūpa*, said to have been presented at Ajanta. The golden background of Sopoćani is also lost. The 'jewels' representing the relevant Buddhist doctrine, are painted near the highest zone of the ceiling decoration (Ajanta, cave 2, plate 116) likewise, the 'jasper' (*Rev.* 21:18) and other precious stones are painted on the celestial dress of the Archangel Michael (plate 115); such celestial attire also adorns the Bodhisattvas of Ajanta (plate 141).

The aniconic presentation of the Buddha as a pillared wheel (and empty throne) (plates 28, 29) has similarity to those stylites painted as contemplating on pillars (and, in 'Etimasija,') although the latter has iconic overtones. This quietist contemplation of Hesychast also brought out the 'concentration' mark between the eyebrows of St. John the Divine (plate 97) similar to the 'Ūrṇā' as a divine attribute of Buddha the Enlightened (plate 96).

Similarities of the iconographic details such as ribbons, curtains, rock-cliffs, cubical rock formation (of course, not the cubes as rocks), quadrilateral baptistry and *sarvatobhadrika* consecration-halls are also striking.

At Sopoćani the 'truth' embodied in the 'nude'[79] along with coiling snakes (devil) is more or less analogous to the 'truth' of misery lurking behind the uncovered feminine curves at Ajanta (plates 128, 129); in the latter the femininity representing 'growth' is, of course, given prominence.

Formal and Plastic Ingredients and Subjective Visualization of Inner Essence

Enumerating the formal and plastic qualities of painting, *Citrasūtra*[80] includes *kṣyavṛddhi* (i.e., diminution and augmentation) as one of them. Since the term *kṣyavṛddhi* follows *Sādṛśya* (semblance) in the relevant couplet, it denotes the modification on the dimensions of the plastic elements to coordinate with the content. This concept can perhaps be better understood with the help of K.G. Subramanyan's opinion:

> Few artists will talk today about the physical qualities of work of art without reference to their main purpose, whether their position be aesthetic (like those of Op, Systemic and Abstract Expressionist groups) or commentative (like those of Pop or post-Pop figurative artists) or configurational (like those of the designers of Environments and Happening).[81]

Thus, the modifications on the dimensions (*kṣayavṛddhi*) of the plastic ingredients were the artist's 'intentions' or his subjective visualization of the inner essence (content or main purpose). As such, both, *Citrasūtra* and *Herminy*, extol the 'immediate personal experience of the artist.'

Consequently, the following divisions of the formal and plastic ingredients have been studied separately (they include tools or language of design, plastic elements or attributes and the principles of design):

1. Space, perspective and styles defined on the basis of spatial dimensions.
2. Light, shape and form.
3. Line.
4. Colour and value.
5. Quality of surface.
6. Composition/balance, rhythm/movement, tension.

The following are the categories of inner-essence studied in relation to the foregoing formal and plastic ingredients:

(*a*) Emotion.
(*b*) Mystical.
(*c*) Mythical.
(*d*) Subconscious.
(*e*) Abstract.
(*f*) Transcendence and distortion.

It needs further to explain that the stylistic definitions based on spatial dimensions are taken up on the basis of Indian treatise on art, Byzantine aesthetics and today's need to define the style in this way.

The tectonic[82] structure of the pictorial surface or 'irreducible flatness' is reached through the process of the reductivistic logic of modern art,[83] which could also be described as *kṣaya* or diminution law of creativity as it is mentioned in *Citrasūtra.* The paintings of Agnes Martin exemplify this 'single undifferentiated tremor of form'[84] reached through this law as well as through the other, the additive law (*vṛddhi*). The latter law with 'a meaningful and logical connection' between 'horizontal and vertical standard elementary elements' re-defines the canvas by extending up to the edges.[85] This 'field' with its module (an extendible grid[86]) becomes that 'aesthetic' position from where, Ernst Kitzinger elaborates,[87] 'the Eastern Mediterranean floor mosaicists reinterpreted geometric patterns in organic terms.' They adopted the rinceau pattern spreading in 'potential endlessness.' Making it as a foil these mosaicists, by fifth and early sixth centuries, counteracted this 'field' by making it 'finite and centralized with primary and secondary structures.' This brought out the basic aesthetic premises of Byzantine art, as Kitzinger sums up:

> ... a desire to re-establish a natural view of things showing organic relationship and confine them in clear and reasonable limits; to tame infinity as it were, but without abandoning the premise of potentially limitless foil that cannot

be fully assimilated and mastered in terms of earthly experience.[88]

This was fully achieved at Sopoćani in what Djurić terms as the 'Projected structure of the composition from the wall.'[89]

The space in the paintings of Ajanta, Stella Kramrisch explains, 'is not conceived in terms of depth' or 'in terms of surface' but,

> It comes forward... deposits from a level at bottom of its visible expanse and from there it opens up and shows its contents... (in) the direction of forthcoming... such a bodily experience of space actually or potentially within ourselves underlies the vision of space in paintings in the Deccan of the type of Ajanta.[90]

Significantly the basis of George Kubler's study of formal solutions as 'chain' describing figure and space relationships, and Robert Rosenblum's thesis on cubism being an 'unstable structure of dismembered planes in indeterminate spatial position describing nature of reality in multiple and even contradictory ways, brings to the fore the original intention in artistic expression' (in Rosenblum's words).[91] John F. Moffitt has defined this 'intention' in 'visual terms' using 'tectonic (from the Greek *tektōn*—builder)' to 'refer to the use of a horizontal and vertical compositional structure joined together at about right angles....' Such 'tectonic and a-tectonic structures (with corresponding content) are also discernible in nonfigurative or abstract pictures.'[92] He explains proposing four syndromes of relevant styles from the archaic to the contemporary art. These 'permit,' Moffitt says, 'one to interpret usefully a pictorial work in terms of its artist's likely intentions, even if they are not consciously realized.' To these syndromes he gives the following visual terms with their related categories:

1. Planer-Tectonic (Archaic, Neoclassic, Contemporary Minimal art),
2. Tectonic Spatial (Classical),
3. A-tectonic Spatial (Baroque, Abstract-expressionism),
4. Synthetic a-tectonic Planer-Spatial (Mannerism, cubism).[93]

The position of Moffitt pertaining to the 'original intention of the artist,' suits the various spatial attitudes taken up by the artists of Ajanta and Sopoćani, with reference to their basic premises towards the pictorial space. Accordingly, the researcher has used the terms of Moffitt to describe the stylistic variations on spatial dimensions.

Clement Greenburg has aptly summed up the Indian 'obsession with three-dimensionality,' adding that:

> Whatever he did not suppress or exclude (he) did suppress flat surfaces or planes. And it seems to flow from this obsession with three-dimensionality that the Indian painting that got started in the Buddhist period should be the only kind out-side Greco-Roman and Western European to shade or model representations of the human form in a consistent way in order to achieve an illusion of relief and volume.[94]

This planer-spatial dichotomy *nimnonnata-vibhāga*[95] or 'relievo' (varying depth of projection) was aptly given credence also in Indian art-treatises in giving the stylistic variance while recognizing the best painting as that the surface of which is 'as if coming out to meet the spectator.'[96] It is the *satya*-style[97] in which volumes are fully presented.[98] This definition of '*satya-citra*' would be a-tectonic spatial[99] in visual terms considering what Germain Bazin defines as 'immanent baroque instinct, with its reserve in the East and not its resultant meeting with west (resulting in ultra-Baroque—Flamboyant Rococo etc.),'[100] and also keeping in view Heinrich Wolfflin's definition which is partly symptomatic of that 'instinct' of the East,[101] and the definition of P.A. Michelis characterizing Byzantine Baroque as different from 'Italian Baroque' with its classically Greek inheritance of plastic elements turning 'from the pictorial to the plastic.'[102]

Vaiṇika style, as explained in *Citrasūtra,*[103] and the definition of classical style as 'harmonic cadence' by Wolfflin,[104] is Tectonic-Spatial[105] and is *ardhacitra* owing to its balance between the dichotomy.

Nāgara style,[106] with its 'firmset' and circular rhythms is Planer-Tectonic[107] and is *citrābhāsa.*

Miśra is mixture of all the three styles.[108] Its visual term is Synthetic-a-tectonic Planer-Spatial. Its manneristic tendencies, which, as Moffitt counts, are: stressed originality, ambiguity in content, rhythms running across the picture, artificial autonomy of beauty, departure from nature and distortion of planes and scale of depth dimension etc.[109]

In the context of Byzantine art and Ajanta, *Miśra* also represents the 'modes' of proper selection of a suitable style for the required expression of the content. The artist who suitably delineates the *Nimnonnata-vibhāga* is *citrāvit*—the knower and a great painter.[110] Such an aesthetic sense was expected of a royal painter of Ajanta or Sopoćani though excess of manneristic attitude made them either 'cultural-aristocrats'[111] or degenerated them to the level of what C. Sivaramamurti describes as 'Dindins,' the dilettante employed only for repair works.[112]

Ajanta: Space, Perspective and Styles Defined on Spatial Dimensions

Explaining the space in the murals of Ajanta, Kramrisch calls it the 'elemental space,' *ākāśadhātu*, as 'the internal space of consciousness,' led from within the picture onward because of bones and sinews, flesh or skin, that a space is enclosed which is called a visible shape' (*Viśuddhimagga*, Part III).[113] Making it more explicit Maurizio Taddei, while calling it a Gupta synthesis, terms it as the canon of 'the characteristic way of conceiving the very quality of forms and volumes and their relationships, a refusal to consider the image as if immersed in space, an insistence on seeing the image as container of space itself, pressing towards the outside.'[114]

Such a tactile 'forthcoming' of space at Ajanta, and the foregoing categories as the artist's intentions of *kṣyavṛddhi* devices, can be summed up in two basic groups. These are also true for Sopoćani:

(1) The planer or two-dimensional structuring which consists of Planer-Tectonic or *Nāgara* style.

(2) Spatial structuring consisting of various spatial orientation devices including perspective. It includes the Tectonic-Spatial, A-Tectonic Spatial and Synthetic A-Tectonic Planer-Spatial, which are, as already noted, analogous to *Vaiṇika, Satya* and *Miśra* styles respectively.[115]

Planer or Two Dimensional Structuring of Space

On the ceiling of cave 2 the following basic perceptual devices have been coded in the decorative patterns (plate 39). (These give an insight into the use of pictorial space as 'a heraldic vision permitting the spectator a maximum of empathy.')[116]

(a) In pattern 1 the total area of the frame becomes the perceptual concern by uniting the upper and lower edges with verticals.[117] The pillars of the pavilions painted in the frescoes of Ajanta exemplify such concern. In windows (or *gavākṣa* windows) the head or the bust of the figure becomes such a referent uniting the frame with the framed surface (plates 43, 44). The curtained openings and backgrounds especially with the vertical strips (cave 17, plate 41) are also a variant of such devices. Besides, the broad borders painted around doors and windows (e.g., in cave 16) make them merge with the wall.[118] Numbers 3 and 5 providing two-dimensional referents, are evident in the grid patterns of the ceilings and in the visual axes connecting the figures and the cubical-rocks of the background. The diaper-grid pattern (No. 5) becomes a grid-pattern on the borders of serial imagery on the entrance to the monastery in cave 17 (plate 125). This serial-imagery is in alignment with the grid-pattern of the ceiling.

(b) No. 4, concentric circle and the repetitive or serial imagery (as an extendible grid-system, plate 124) give perceptual concern to the total frame. Haloes[119] and concentric circles on ceilings (cave 2, plate 116) exemplify this device.

(c) In No. 2, because of the sharp contours the narrow interstices get density and positive character and preserve the tactility of surface in figure-ground relationship[120] (plate 120). Their consistent shape is affirmed by the flowers which are incorporated almost everywhere in the background of Ajanta paintings (plate 120). Density of textural surfaces within the rectangles of grid on the ceiling-decorations, (plate 46), too, gives tactonic flatness to these rectangles. Inscriptions, written on interstices at a few places in Ajanta paintings, also vivify such a concern. Horizontal extension of the planer-surface (plate 75), with long bands of murals, was adapted in the earliest works (caves 9 and 10) and remained the basic attitude throughout the later works, which were extendible vertically as well.

Wainscoating figures (e.g., in *Sankhpāla Jātaka* cave 1, plate 50), rock-cliff edges (ibid.) and above all, the tactile-rhythms on the planer surface substantiate the two-dimensional concern of the surface or the 'border land,' as Kramrisch[121] defines the wall surface. Three dimensionality produced by overlapping of figures has been mostly negated by the disturbed alignment of feet on ground line, which produces its own planer rhythm (e.g., in *Vidhurpaṇḍita Jātaka*, cave 2 plate 51).

Spatial Structuring

(a) Overlapping gives spatial perception,[122] e.g., in *Chaddanta Jātaka* (cave 10, plate 53), since in these simple forms the consistency of biological rhythm connects the interrupted contours.[123] The vertical perspective is a variant of overlapping as exemplified in *Mahājanaka Jātaka* (cave 1, plate 56). Crowded scenes have been given prominence to produce greater dimensional effect (plate 53).

(b) Oblique orientation or *kṣyavṛddhi* of figures with bi-positional *tribhaṅga* of various stances (*sthānas*) and of other forms,[124] provide circular or screw-spatiality e.g., in the dance and music scene of *Mahājanaka Jātaka* (cave 1, plate 57). Three-fourth angles of the faces, used almost as a principle, show a concern for the dimensionality of space.

(c) In *Mahājanaka Jātaka* (cave 17), the artist of Ajanta decodes a visual solution in reaching a hexagonal (plate 59) form while demonstrating the three dimensionality of a cube. Such visual solutions are amply utilized in cave pillars showing a transition from square abacus to the octagonal column (e.g., in cave 17).

(d) *Perspective*:

1. Sharp convergence issuing from a centre cause asymmetrical spatial environment between the preaching Buddha in the centre and the congregators of almost

the same size (cave 17), resulting in the Buddha perceptually looking enlarged and 'forthcoming'[125] (plate 61). These convergences are subtly used inversely in the same mural to denote the background converging up to the centre (the Buddha). This device dynamically connects the narrative sequence of the Buddha's descent from Tūṣita heaven and his preaching to the congregation. The use of actual wall for producing the effects of sharp-convergence is shown in 'the Buddha in Kapilvastu' (cave 17, plate 122). By inverted perspective the protagonist figure in the narration is enlarged actualizing the forthcoming flux of space. Keeping such figures into sharp convergence helps the artist to create the *satya* or the 'multi-oriented' spatial experience for the beholder, e.g., in Padmapāṇi (cave 1).

2. Perspective in relative distance, central perspective, is used in the throne of the Buddha in the above-mentioned mural (plate 61).

3. Frontal-isometric perspective[126] is best exemplified in the 'forthcoming' blocks used, for example, in the background of 'Bodhisattva Avalokiteśvara' (cave 1, plate 141). Because of the gamma-motion[127] of the greater axis towards the smaller apex these blocks look projected from the base which is slightly enlarged[128] (see page 199, n. 426).

4. Different eye level renderings of the background and the figures (e.g., 'A group of votaries approaching a *stūpa*, cave 9) give multidirectional spatial orientation to the narration (plates 65, 66).

By such definition of multispatial reality in tectonic terms, the artists of Ajanta have vivified the rhythm of 'flux.' These rhythms ultimately preserve the tactility of the flat wall or the 'border land,'[129] defining the real space of the caves, what Bussagli expresses as 'pure space carved out of rocks.'[130]

Within the two broader and basic spatial categories of Ajanta murals, as defined above, the ultimate growth module is realized. The 'Tree' or 'Creeper' being this module, the murals of Ajanta extend in all directions. To this 'continuously articulated network' of arboreal growth, the artists of Ajanta gave tectonic modulization, as exemplified in the cubistic rock constructions painted in the backgrounds (e.g., 'the Bodhisattva Avalokiteśvara', plate 141).

The style of Ajanta defined largely as 'eclectic' (K. Khandalavala, 1974), or *Miśra*, uses the above-mentioned *Nāgara, Vaiṇika*, and *Satya* styles. The best example of this *Miśra* style is 'the Buddha in Kapilvastu' (cave 17).[131] Judging comparatively one finds the 'modes' of the three styles therein. The architectural unit in its 'firm set' value implies the *Nāgara* style or the planer-tectonic tendency. Such tendency in the Buddha gives it a 'heraldic vision' in which the proper measurement (*pramāṇam*), rich attainment of posture (*sthānalambhādhyam*) and 'four sided' (*caturaṣram*) rendering add to the classicism of *Vaiṇika* style expressing the mellowness of *karuṇā* (compassion) of the *Virāṭapuruṣa*—the 'Cosmic

Man.' The spatial-tectonic illusion giving sculptural sense (*caturaṣram*) accords *Vaiṇka* style to the figures of Rāhul and Yaśodharā. Their humanism is also stressed. The multidirectional spatiality is enhanced in the presentation of the magnified figure of the Buddha by the sharp convergence. Starting from the forthcomingly flying put to these are drawn further on right with the division lines of the painted architectural unit (plate 122), and on left with projection of the actual side wall. The figure of the Buddha, thus, is configurated in A-Tectonic Spatiality or the *satya* style producing the semblance of reality.[132] The actual relief work on the upper side of the architectural unit not only adds to this 'Baroque' attitude but also makes the 'flatness' of the 'border land' apparent.

SOPOĆANI: SPACE AND STYLE DEFINED ON SPATIAL DIMENSIONS

In the planer-tectonic or two-dimensional structuring to create 'the premise of a potentially limitless foil'[133] the artist of Sopoćani used the following perceptual devices:

(a) Extendible grid-system was adopted in dividing the narrative scenes (e.g., narthex, east wall, plate 69). Its module in the diaper-grid was painted on the wall of the chapel of St. Simeon Nemanja (plate 18). This surface-extending system is also evident in isocephalic array of saints and patriarchs and figures (e.g., over the nave pilasters, plates 70, 15). Such conception is supported by the use of gold foil in the background in the tesserae imitation giving the cube as a 'germ' module extendible all over the wall, as in the mosaics.

(b) Horizontal extension in the full-breadth of wall was adopted almost everywhere else in the narrative bands becoming a speciality of the decoration of Sopoćani (plate 69).

(c) Head or bust of the figure becoming referent for uniting the frame with the framed,[134] is evident in the chapel of St. Simeon Nemanja (south and west wall, plate 17.) Medallions with the busts, thus exemplifying planer-tactility, are painted nearly everywhere on the walls of Sopoćani (plate 45). Standing figures of the saints, and patriarchs (plate 42) and the pillars shown in the architectural units (plate 42) add to such perceptual devices.

(d) Borders on narrative bands, and on the doors and windows give them the value of a form in planer relation with the surface of the wall (e.g., in the chapels of St. George, St. Nicholas, St. Simeon Nemanja and the exo-narthex, plate 17). Curtain as a device for this end is used in prothesis (plate 40). A module for making a flat-surface perception through hanging the curtain in the background is given in the border design in the chapel of St. Simeon Nemanja (base of all the walls, plate 18).

(e) Angular interstices become consistent forms[135] as is demonstrated in the glory-halo of 'Christ in Transfiguration' (nave, north wall, plate 37). Inscriptions, profusely written on the walls of Sopoćani, add to such a concern (plate 17).

(f) Wainscoating figures (e.g, exo-narthex west wall—'Parable of the Rich man,' plate 49) rock-cliff edges (Chapel of St. Nichola, north wall—'Saving Three Dukes,' plate 48) and above all, tactile rhythms bring out the two-dimensional concern of the wall surface. Non-alignment of feet in overlapping of figures also produces such planer rhythms (plate 54).

The tactility of the wall, thus achieved, defines the real space of the church. For building the space of the church, 'the protomaster worked like potter 'outward' from within.'[136] The space dynamism was secured as 'breathing,'[137] since attracted by the verticality of barrel dome and recochetted by its semicircularity towards the dominant rectangular nave, the space receded into the tectonic-planerity of walls.

Spatial Structuring

(a) Overlapping: The hands overlapping the bodies in the 'Communion of the Apostles' (apse, sanctuary, nave, plate 70) bring out the perception of three-dimensionality in the semicircular apse (plate 70). The arrangement of overlapping goats and sheep in the vertical-perspective has also been used for such perception (Nativity, nave, plate 55). The crowd scene of the 'Dormition' produces greater dimensionality (plate 161).

(b) Oblique presentation for the figures (in various stances) and shapes gives circular spatial arrangements (e.g., in the 'Dormition' nave, west wall) or screw spatiality as in the 'Crucifixion' (nave, south wall, plate 58). The principle of using three-fourth faces almost everywhere shows a concern for the dimensionality of space.

(c) Bay-window type presentation of the quadrilateral baptistry adds to the orientation of cubic forms in the three-dimensional space[138] (plate 60).

(d) *Perspective*:

1. Sharp convergence 'project forth' the Resurrected Christ, e.g., in 'Appearance to the Women'[139] (nave, sanctuary, south wall, plates 62/64). The use of actual architectural unit, barrel-dome, for the effect of sharp convergences is evident at Sopoćani too. Inversely, the sharp convergences are used for presenting projection of Christ descending in glory in the 'Dormition' (plate 77).

2. Perspective in relative distance is exemplified, e.g., in the throne in 'Christ Enthroned' (nave, south-west pilaster, lower zone, plate 16).

3. Frontal-isometric perspective projects forth the smaller front from the slightly bigger back side of the block stone lid of the tomb in 'the Holy Women at the Tomb' (nave, sanctuary, south wall, plate 166).

4. Different eye level renderings of the background and the figures, e.g., the Evangelists on the rim of the dome (plate 67), give multispatial perception. Upturned curtains add to such a conception.

Such multidirectional spatiality perceptually vivifies the dynamism of the space.[140] Its tactility in spatial-rhythms ultimately preserves the surface of the walls, defining the interior space of the church.

This 'continuously articulated network' of multispatiality has the basic module of 'tree' (Tree of Jesse, narthex, south wall, plate 30) growing in all directions. Within this spatiality the style of Sopoćani consists of the 'modes' in which the appropriate variants of spatial-configurations have been used (as symbols). For example, the Synthetic A-tectonic Planer-Spatiality in the 'Dormition' (nave, west wall, plate 161) embodies all the three variants.

The groups of overlapping apostles, instead of retaining a perception of three-dimensionality betray Planer-Tectonic Spatiality due to the disturbed alignment of the feet on the ground line (plate 54), the sharp linearity of folds and angular interstices. The heads painted in three-fourth angles and Tectonic-Spatial style betray dimensionality. It is further enhanced by circular spatiality around Christ (plate 78) and by the architectural units painted in the frontal-isometric perspective in the middle ground. Thus, the group of angels with candle-stands in their hands, presented in sharp convergences, get A-Tectonic Spatiality.

The inverted convergences projecting forth the Christ in the Glory (plate 77) give a dynamic relationship to the Christ standing with the soul of Mary set in a sharp convergence made by the arrangements of the Apostles and the Angels. The inverted convergences given by the roofs of the buildings too, project forth the Christ near the bed enlarging it visually (plate 77).

Thus, the grace of the balanced and relaxed postures, axial symmetry, principle of idealization and sculptural sense of heads—all these give a classical style or Tectonic-Spatial illusion to the figures of the Apostles and Christ. The humanism expressed by the figures and the stress over the foreground enhances this classicism.[141] Through the sharp linearity of folds and angular interstices the bodies of these figures become 'heraldic' and turn as Planer-Tectonic as is the presentation of the architectural units. Thus, these figures while they 'reach out into space and envelop space;'[142] 'elastically' become, to use Stella Kramrisch expression, 'replete with its antagonistic tendency.' The multi-directional spatiality adds to the A-tectonic Spatial style of 'Baroque' rhetorics and illusions, overwhelming and convincing the viewer of the 'truth' of the artist's vision and message.[143]

Comparative

The artists of both Ajanta and Sopoćani ultimately conform to the 'Tree' growth module of the 'continuously articulated network.' The modules of such spatiality are inserted by them in the decorative details (for example the diaper-grid and the growing creeper or the Tree of Jesse). This multidirectional spatial approach also testifies to the practice of 'modes' or mixed, i.e., *Miśra*, style of spatial configurations. The similarities of their approach in the spatial variants are as follows:

1. Planer-Tectonic structures were developed using similar perceptive factors (i.e., making the total planer surface as the perceptual concern with the relationship of verticals and horizontal or the grid's continuously articulated network or with circular radiation or with making interstices confirming the surface). The second factor to which both the artists conform was to maintain the continuity of the planer surface. To this end they resorted to horizontal bands of structuring planerity. They also resorted to vertical structuring for achieving extendibility in all the directions (plates 119-24, 37, 68, 70, 75).

It is found that pictorial syntax, like the busts of the figures (plates 44-45) border-designs on the openings, curtains, non-alignment of feet on the ground line (plates 40, 41, 51, 54), wainscoating figures, and rock-cliff edges (plates 48-50) are commonly used for confirming the planer-spatiality. Above all, the tactility of pictorial rhythms preserved the integrity of surface of the wall; the recession of the 'bulging' out (of the forms) also added to the perception of the flatness. This acceptance of surface was used by the artists of Sopoćani and Ajanta to define the real space of the church or the cave which also dynamically 'breathed.'[144]

All said, still the difference of the planer tectonic mastery of Ajanta lies in its consummation of making the whole wall 'pressing towards outside,' the wall itself becoming the organic 'flux' of space.

Thus at Ajanta, to quote Clement Greenberg, 'space volume, mass are as though summoned from some inner centre of space.'[145] On the other hand, at Sopoćani such an endeavour was made by giving the gold-background which simulated the projection of 'inner-light' as well as maintained the tactile flatness of the surface. The figures left in 'fresco,' though given a-Tectonic spatiality, became silhouette and participated in the above spatial direction.

2. Spatial-Tectonic: Overlapping (specially through crowding), oblique

orientation of figures and three-fourth faces were the common methods used by the artists of Sopoćani and Ajanta. They arrived at circular or screw-spatial definitions by the above means (plates 57-58), difference being that Ajanta figures are of bi-positional *tribhaṅga.*

In perspective, similarity is evident in the spatiality achieved through sharp convergences (plates 61, 64), inverted perspective, perspective of relative distance, frontal-isometric perspective, and the different eye-level renderings of the background and figures. 'Tri-murti' plasticity of the volume of head achieved in India and medieval Yugoslavia is the logical outcome of such endeavours (cf. pp. 224 & 26, plates 65-67, 166, 141, and 101.)

3. A-Tectonic spatial: Thus in such multi-directionality the space is dynamically presented as 'flux.' And wherever this spatial dynamism describes the volumes as fully realised, the style becomes a-Tectonic Spatial. The artists of Ajanta and Sopoćani represented this 'flux' of 'reaching out into space' or 'forthcoming' particularly with sharp convergences, so that the experience becomes a reality to the beholder (plates 61, 62). The use of actual space of architectural units for sharp-convergences producing 'forthcoming' effects is evident at Ajanta as well as at Sopoćani (plates 122, 123).

It is found at both the places that the multispatial 'flux' conforms to the surface of the wall in tactile rhythms. Then, while defining the actual space of the church or the cave, it gets the dynamism therein through the subtle proportions of the interior (plates 1, 4). While the space sculptures of Ajanta caves breathe this dynamism between aisles and the dominant squarish naves through the spaces condensed between the heavy pillars, the total wall surfaces are also made to live this *prāṇa.* In *caityas,* the horizontal ribs of semicircular roof end on the frame of the *gavākṣa*-window (plate 14) and carry over the space of the narrow nave out of the window, where, becoming the creeper growth over the frame, it reaches the summit of the mountain. At Sopoćani, the interior space flows branching in transepts and is drawn back by the dominant nave; then the verticality of the central barrel dome attracts it with sudden elevation to the vast openness above (plate 5). There is also the effort echoing the 'breathing' of wall surface by giving a golden foil to it and maintaining its balance with the spatial projection of figures. Ricochetted, the 'flux' of space returns by the semicircularity of the dome at Sopoćani and by the apex of the *gavākśa* window at Ajanta, giving the 'breathing' of real space.

The basic difference between the space woven at Ajanta and Sopoćani remains that of the domination of spatial-flux. At Sopoćani, there is a conflict between the assertion of the 'object' represented and the spatial modularities defining it. As this conflict is not fully resolved, the discordance is reflected in the angularities of the configurations (plate 62). The angularly defined interstices and folds on the figures, although they 'bulge' them out in space, conversely become the surface rhythms[146] 'dematerializing' the bodies in skeletal-flatness surrounded by the glistening gold-background—the promise of 'Heaven.'

At Ajanta, on the other hand, either the cubistic spatiality defines similar objects (e.g., in caves 9 and 10, plate 65) or the growing dynamism of the spatial rhythm harmonises with the 'vegetal' rhythm (Lotus-style) resorting to the human forms (plate 57). The carrying back of these forms by the metaphysical movement of 'forthcoming' leaves the glistening and 'living' surface—as if breathing—of *Sukhavati.*

Another dissimilarity in the spatial weaving consists in that the space factor at Sopoćani is governed by greater stress on historicity and tangibility which is not so at Ajanta since the transcendence of these factors itself is accepted as the tangible reality. At Sopoćani, the 'characteristic growth' of spatial-structuring leads to the supremacy of Euclidian polygonal module of space, which always remains in conflict with the concept of 'forthcoming' inherent in the growth-module of the 'Tree.' The best example of this conflict is found in the figures of apostles and angels with difference of treatment in the body and the face, resulting only in a partial harmony achieved between 'modes' (plate 130).

At Ajanta, however, the space is encompassed with the total acceptance of its dynamic 'flux' (plate 134). Hence the inner growth-module for structuring the space is fully accepted. The basic shape of this 'creeper' module remains *stūpa*—the arch example of 'centrifugal pressure.'[147]

Ajanta: Line

Solomon Gladstone, while regarding line as the 'golden clue,' speaks of Ajanta tradition as having maintained the golden rule of 'what cannot be well expressed in line or silhouette should not be attempted by the Mural Painter.' The latter being the basis of such painting, he adds that 'Ajanta tradition maintains it with line through its forceful independence and power of continuity. It worthily encloses Bodhisattvas, undulates over the bosoms of women, flickers over flowers and plants and twists and models a thousand incomparable items of decoration.'[148]

Such differentiated elements get fused by the line—a common contour given to 'chaotic profusion of imagery.'[149] It becomes the *prāṇa* of the style of Ajanta because of being 'a tremendous abstraction as it is the one-dimensional trace ... eminently concrete and direct rendering of perceived shape.'[150] With the knowledge that the contour has its own self-contained 'physiological factors underlying the perceptual process itself,'[151] a fact adhered to by them in cave 2 (plate 127),[152] the masters of Ajanta made the area within the boundary extremely compact by brightness (as in Avalokiteśvara), contour shading (plate 128), subtle lines of Hairika vartanā[153] (plate 128) and by giving biological consistency of form to suggest its monumentality, e.g., in Padmapāṇi (cave 1, plate 157). By using contour line around pearls and diamonds etc., the artists of Ajanta have made clear their conception of making the spaces compact. That is why the forms and interstices presented by them gain consistency in becoming dense. The linearity becomes essential in view of the above turning into the *prāṇa* aesthetics. Paintings like 'the Buddha in Kapilvastu' (cave 17, plate 155) give various dimensions, physical and psychological, achieved by the artists of Ajanta in their 'one-dimensional trace.' It traces the grossness of buildings in the grossest of lines having mechanical mode. Graces of femininity and innocence of the child are defined by flickering hair and undulating contours. It encloses the sublime monumentality of the Buddha in 'as laconic a manner as the *sūtrakāras*' conveying 'maximum of form with a minimum of line.'[154]

The lighter lines, used along with the darker ones, as in votaries bringing offerings' (cave 2, plate 148)[155] present the phase when light (periphery light and high light) is transformed as line. It becomes descriptive line also and starts 'sharpening' the form by subdivisions. These lines, used with the dark ones, add to the skeletal value substantiating the silhouette.

Sopoćani: Line

By virtue of being the derivation of the mosaic technique and also by nature of the medium and handling, the linearity is the life of the forms in the murals of Sopoćani. The linear values, embodying the form and the content cohesively, are verifiable in the grand conception of the 'Dormition.' To take a closer view, in the portrait of the Pope below the spirit of Mary (plate 126),[156] one finds the masterly drawn laconic contour on the right of the face. It delineates the depths and heights of the form as successfully as it speaks of the hardness of forehead, undulates the softness of cheek and defines the flowing hair of the beard. On its one side the thick line modulates the heaviness of Christ's attire and on the other, the mechanical lines configurate the buildings.

The lines, as contours and as means of subdividing the form, give a cohesive unity to the figures and bring them out as a unified field. The interstices, too, governed by such contours, get density and cohesiveness.[157] Brushing for modulating the forms while applying colours is a part of such an endeavour.[158]

The individual value given to linear work is thus subordinated to the consistency of form. The examples of the paintings in the chapel of St. Simeon Nemanja (plate 142) show such concern in bringing out the monumentality of form by giving extreme brightness to the area within contoured lines.

Lines defining light became also the subdividing factors of form 'sharpening' it to achieve monumentality, e.g., in the figures of the Archangels.[159] The use of such lines with the darker ones adds a skeletal-relief value to the form flattening it and enhancing the silhouette.

Comparative

The masters of Ajanta and Sopoćani have used the qualities of line for physical and psychological dimensions presenting these in the most abstract and 'one-dimensional trace.' A close examination reveals that the linearity expressing grossness of architecture, undulation of flesh, flickering of hair and sublimity and monumentality in its laconic vein are similar in the 'Dormition' and 'the Buddha in Kapilvastu' (plates 161 and 122). Nevertheless, there is a difference. It can, perhaps, be described as linearity being of an intimate nature in the works of Ajanta which gives them rather an approach of a miniaturist's intimate lines. On the other hand, the master of Sopoćani undulates the linearity in a grand mural monumentality while being overwhelmed by his own excellence. The lines here betray a vision, which, to quote Mila Rajković's words, is 'constantly alternated between the contrast of vitality and anguish.'[160] Contrarily, a composure of having become 'grateful at accomplished desires and virtuous,'[161] as that of *sthavira* Achala Muni, bestows substance on the lines delineating the monumentality of Ajanta.

Both the artists, knowing the self-contained status of linear work, used it for achieving organic quality (through linear brushing for modulating forms—*Hairika vartanā*), cohesiveness and density (through contours) and silhouette, the basis of mural painting (through 'sharpening' and skeletal value). They suppressed the contours and made the bound area bright to achieve the monumentality of form, e.g., in Avalokiteśvara (cave 1, plate 141) and in the paintings of chapel of St. Simeon Nemanja (plate 142). At Ajanta, line became autonomous in leaving alignment with the mass of colour and value (cave 2, 'the Bodhisattva,' plate 127). At Sopoćani, application of the colours remaining linear, did not allow this abstraction.

Both the centres having made the line as the transcription of light (periphery light and high light), modulated the tint-lines alongwith the dark ones achieving a monumental transparency of form for conveying ethereality in an effect almost like solarization of photo-negative (plates 130, 131). The difference is that at Sopoćani it became a vogue and at Ajanta, it was experimented upon. Besides, Ajanta has the distinction of using high-light lines as ornaments. However, as patterns they also adorn the attires of angels at Sopoćani. Further, Ajanta excels in showing transparent attires of its elite ladies by the lines of periphery light (plate 120).

The linear style became the life of the content for the artists of both the places owing to their desire to give impact by 'projected composition' or 'forthcoming.' It was so because the contours provided density to the interstices and projected them forth with the forms to speak the tactile monumentality of the walls and also because with their lines only these artists brought out the harmony amidst myriad forms.

Ajanta: Light, Shape and Form: Light

As the artists of Ajanta have utilized the principles of linear perspective to their ends they have also successfully used the principles of orientation of the object through illumination.[162] A portion of the mural depicting 'a monastery' in cave 17[163] (plate 136) is an example of such a virtuosity. It not only explains the principles of creating space and desired emphasis of the forms through visual perception of the illumination, but also tells as to how these principles were rejected for the depiction of the illumination itself and were used for the enhancement of the volumes of form and the space. In short, the illumination was turned into the principle of the luminosity[164]—'inner light.'

The chiaroscuro presented in the wooden structure of the monastery doesn't give the perception of being illuminated through a single source (plate 136). It is the use of light as a factor treating the space through emphasis of form in graded brightness. Such sensitivity shown towards the illumination and its resultant graded density in describing the depth dimension has a parallel experience in the lighting of *vihāra* caves. The windows and doors of these *vihāras* become the brightest light sources separately extending gradients of brightness to the darkness of the corners. This uneven illumination 'is not perceived primarily in itself but as an aspect of distance'[165] enhancing the depth dimension.

The treatment of figures in the above referred illustration also conforms to such 'abstract' use of the brightness contrasts serving to enhance the overlapping without the need of justifying the result as an effect of illumination.[166] Such 'traditions of the past' in the arbitrary use of chiaroscuro in separating planes are confirmed by the experiments of Cézanne.[167] This 'Cézannesque' use of chiaroscuro by the artists of Ajanta also finds an appropriate example in the rendering of the 'Gate in King Brahmadatta's Palace,' in *Mahāhaṁsa Jātaka*, cave 2[168] (plate 137).

These principles of *vibhaktatā*—distinctness—and *kṣayavṛddhi*[169]—diminution and augmentation—of the light perceived as a factor of brightness, are also apparent in introducing the highlight as the form of the lightest ornaments suggesting the planes of the limbs,[170] although the highlight explaining illumination is also preserved in the works, e.g., the figures in the 'wheel of life' (cave 17, plate 105)[171] and in the eyes of 'the Lady under the parasol' (plate 135), *Vessantara-Jātaka*, cave 17.[172] The principle of highlight as the highest point of the raised volume in bright gradient, without suggesting source of light, is generally adhered to. The tints and highlights are 'actually at times laid on with thick white colour.'[173] The cast-shadows are avoided since they would darken the area that should remain bright otherwise and would interfere with the spatial orientation. In the same way the bright reflections of highlight 'that light up the dark places'[174] are also avoided. Highlights turning into the linear factor and becoming the drawing of the form is quite evident in the figures like those in the scene of votaries bringing offerings in cave 2 (plate 148).[175] This is what Benjamin Rowland defines as the 'II Indian Manner,' while realizing its effect of aesthetics of light on Central Asian paintings.[176]

The luminosity or the principles of 'inner light' are best exemplified in showing the glowing objects presented as the abrupt spots of tint-values, e.g., the garlands of bright pearls and flowers spread over the ground (plates 120, 122). The 'halo' presented as the luminous form testifies the principles of inner source of light. In the figure of Bodhisattva Avalokiteśvara (cave 1)[177] the bright gradients have been marvellously used for modelling the form as well as for creating the effect of 'luminosity' (plate 141). One understands these 'luminous' images all the more with reference to what Van Gogh saw as 'the flaming face of Halios glowing in the orange of a sun flower' since he found in it the eternity 'which the halo used to symbolize and which we seek to bestow by the actual radiance and vibration of our colouring.'[178] In this respect it is important to recall the undeniable fact of Buddhists preoccupation with the 'aesthetics of light' which S. Taki finds in their sacred books like the *Saddharmapuṇḍarīka Sūtra* and the *Suvarṇa Prabhāsa*, through which 'hypostasis of the Śākyamuni'[179] (presented in left) is shown as the Buddha's essence of light in the 'Avalokiteśvara' (on right in cave 1, plate 141). Such lighting is physically experienced while reaching the back of *stūpa* during the circumambulation around it in the *caitya* caves. It is graphically presented in periphery lighting given to many forms. The best example of the light gradient starting as brightest on the contours of silhouetted form is evident in the flying *apsarā* painted in the verandah of cave 17 (plate

145).[180]

The 'painterly'[181] style is presented in cave 1 (e.g., 'the woman with the lotus' in a palace scene, plate 146).[182] It represents the 'battle between light effect and form in painting.'[183] In other words, it shows the conflict of the principles of the illumination and luminosity: a faintcast shadow over the neck confirms the conflict.

Shape and Form

Formal elements, illuminated for the grasping of their integral features, remain shape or pattern[184] in their abstract structures.[185] The 'human' shape is, thus, created by the artist of Ajanta on the basis of *nṛtta* or choreography assimilating the principle of rhythm, *tāla* and *laya*, conceived as measurement units and rhythm in a painting,[186] in order to create the various postures or *sthānas*. When these postures are coordinated with *nṛtya* or dance expressing emotions, *bhāvas* (which is equated with *āṅgikābhinaya*—acting with parts of body),[187] they become 'form.' As such the mere presentation of 'human shape,' *mānavākāratā*, is taken to be a major defect in a painting[188] until it has semblance—*sādṛśya*—with the form of invisible entities—*adṛśṭam*.[189] Withal, Rudolf Arnheim holds that:

> In dancing—and the same holds true for acting—the artist, his tools, and his work are fused into one physical thing, of human body. One curious consequence is that the dance is created essentially in a different medium than the one in which it appears to the audience. The spectator receives a strictly visual work of art... as far as his own body is concerned, he creates mainly in the medium of the kinesthetic sensations in his muscles, tendons, and joints....[190]

That is why the artist of Ajanta created 'movements' seemingly 'essential to the phenomenal existence of the body.' And since 'posture is probably experienced as the terminal phase of motion'[191] this 'situation'[192] is best utilized in the paintings of Ajanta. The portraiture (as proved by the *Purnaka*'s being repeated in *Vidhurpaṇḍita Jātaka* in cave 2) and type characters presented in the murals of Ajanta also conform to the *sādṛśya* principles.

The artists of Ajanta were governed by the *tāla* or measuring unit consisting of the width equivalent to twelve times to that of the finger (*aṅgula*), a principle of 'Symmetria,'[193] for creating the shapes of different kinds of human bodies. As such the measurements given for the *haṁsa* type male figure in *Citrasūtra*[194] conform to those of the Padmapāṇi painted in cave 1 of Ajanta (plate 19). These figures are drawn with their height equal to their breadth—'across the chest along the outstretched arms from the tip of the right middle finger to that of the left' as Kramrisch explains the proportions given in *Citrasūtra.*[195] This also testifies to the round *maṇḍala* as the basic structure of the 'frontal' posture of the body or *Ṛjvāgata Sthāna.*[196]

The conception of *tāla* as the module of development gives a harmony of the proportion, symmetria, to the shapes as they were made over the grid system drawn of *tāla* measure (*Citrasūtra* 39:34, 35, plate 19).[197] The rectangular grids drawn all over the ceilings of Ajanta also prove such preliminary grid drawn over walls (plate 19). It is further confirmed in the '*tāla*' roughly repeated in the cubistic rocks interconnecting, in an invisible grid system, the axes and contours of figures and forms[198]—what *Citrasūtra* (37:17) propounds as '... with *sthānas* having many beam-like lines and with steady *bhūmi-lambhas.*'[199]

The harmony based on modular units of shapes, specially the cube and circle, had also been the basis of the stylistic divisions. The Early Veṅgi style has been based on cubic and later, the Deccan-Gupta, on globular or circular—*vṛttul*—forms[200] (plate 57). Mulk Raj Anand interprets the texts speaking of Buddha's image as 'round, round, seven times round' saying the roundness here was supposed to suggest coherence, harmony and poise (plate 157).[201] The earlier tradition of *yakṣa* sculptures is evident in the early works of cave 9 and 10, the *vṛttuls* is in the later caves. Here, it is pertinent to point out the harmony achieved between the cubic or rectangular and the circular forms through the luxuriant growth of a creeper. This is evident in the rectangular impost (between the architrave and the round capital of the pillar) harmonised by such a growth of the *pūrṇa-ghaṭa* motif (plate 47) given to the capital (hall, cave 23).[202] The modular units also provide a 'continuously articulated network' of the growth of form which is akin to arboreal growth.[203] Accordingly, to Gombrich also, the biological growth of form attunes itself to the recognition becoming tolerant to the 'standards of formal correspondence.'[204] Hence, Snellgrove and others, too, perceive in the human figure of Ajanta vegetal and animal forms bequeathing 'their rhythms and ceaseless flow' as the artists of Ajanta adopted this structural clue. The module of such growth of form has been left by them everywhere in the form of 'creeper' of abundance painted in the grids of the ceiling-painting (plate 46). Bosch has classified the styles of Indian art, in general, to be those of *vanaspati* and 'Lotus' styles from this structural clue and bases the former on *agni* or fire (male) and the latter on water (female) conceptions of Indian philosophy.[205]

Thus the tree or 'creeper' module not only provides the growth of shape but also gives them consistency of 'form' by giving a living rhythm of *prāṇa* or 'life as if breathing.'[206] To understand and create such living-rhythms, *Citrasūtra* (43:37) extols the intimate relationship between *nṛtta* and *citra.*[207] This, in painting, is to create 'an illusion of volumes from within which space presses outward' as 'the movements of dance start from within the body,' as Clement Greenberg observes about the paintings of Ajanta.[208] To create such forms, the artists of Ajanta resorted to the principle of *vartanā* or the manner of applying paint through brush[209] creating a sense of modelling and harmony of the form. The linear-brushing according to the structure, '*hairkajā*, is evident in the modelling of the drapery over the body of the Buddha in 'The Buddha and the one-eyed Monk' (cave 10, plate 153),[210] and dotted application, *Bindujā*, is evident in most of the later works of Ajanta. These efforts in plasticity are substantiated by the experiments of Seurat, partially, and Cézanne.[211] A logical conclusion of assimilation of such solidly conceived form in the total structure of the painting by unifying them with the spatial tensions of the plane, was that the broken contours got separated from the defined areas, of colour, e.g., in 'the Bodhisattva' in cave 2 (plate 127).[212] Such results are confirmed by Cézanne's later experiments.[213]

Arnheim calls the plasticity of form 'created from within' as an 'introverted' theory of the growth of form. In this introvertly motivated growth he acknowledges Gustof Britsh's principle of growth of form as 'a self-contained mental process of unfolding, similar to the growth of plant growing from the simplest to more and more complex patterns in a process of gradual differentiation.'[214] With reference to such complexities 'looking human,' Arnheim further elaborates that "the more complex the pattern of forces that manifests itself in motor behaviour, the more 'human' the performance looks." This justifies the stress of the artist of Ajanta on the gestures of hands and the movements of fingers including the pupils and the eyebrows etc. By effecting movements to these periphery lighter and flexible forms the seemingly 'heavy' form of the body gets imparted with 'a strikingly organic quality.'[215]

To overcome the ambiguities arising out of the above-mentioned complexities of patterns, the two basic complementary principles of clear-cut structures were adopted by the artists of Ajanta. *Citrasūtra* (43:19) speaks of them as *madhuratva,* sweetness and *vibhaktatā*, distinctness.[216] Such endeavour befits the 'extroverted' theory based on external motivations of differentiation, in which Arnheim includes 'levelling' and 'sharpening,' the two complementary principles to achieve clear-cut structures.[217] The 'sweetness' or 'levelling' consists of such factors as *bhūlamba*[218]—'enhancement of symmetry'[219]—*kṣaya*—diminution —*vṛddhi*—augmentation'[220]—'dropping of non-fitting details and elimination of obliqueness'[221]—and unification[222]—'*svadehasādṛśya.*'[223] 'Levelling' is best achieved, e.g., in the figure of Buddha in cave 17 (The Buddha in Kapilvastu, plate 122)[224] and in the hieratic figures of Buddha painted in caves 9 and 10. In the figures of 'the wailing women' (cave 1, plate 143)[225] 'levelling' efforts are very much apparent. Sharpening or *vibhaktatā* involves simplification to help eliminate the ambiguity. It is to achieve the dimensional quality or *nimnonnatavibhāga* (heights and depths)[226], through subdivisions, enhancement of differences and stressing obliqueness;[227] it is best exemplified, e.g., in 'Buddha and the one-eyed Monk' (cave 10, plate 153).[228] Benjamin Rowland refers to such conception of the body 'in terms of a collection of interlocking rounded surfaces' being the 'device to suggest the expanding inner breath or *prāṇa*.'[229] It is clearly exemplified in such works as 'The votaries with offerings' in the side chapel of cave 2 (plate 128).[230] The monumentality achieved in a form through the unification and removal of ambiguities at its best is exemplified in such figures as those of Padmapāṇi (cave 1, plate 157) and 'the Buddha in Kapilvastu' (cave 17, plate 122).

Being a part of the 'introverted' growth, figures become the exponents of the impact of 'forthcoming' flux of space. Besides, they also remain within the 'rhythmos' of the tactile flat surface.[231] This annihilates their 'gross' weight. Therefore, the figures are rendered 'ethereal.' To achieve this, the middle tone of illumination gradients is given as the body tone[232] and the highlight as white ornaments leaving the body tone and shaded depths in unity with the darker background. This generates the 'simpler total figure' striving for completion of form in the suggestion of volume.[233] The postures also suggest the inner-volume's weightage being brought on the chest by making them like 'breathing.' The feet are painted with a 'just touching the ground' feeling so that there is none 'who would tread upon the flowers with his gross weight'[234] (plate 120). The image of Avalokiteśvara (cave 1), too, in its 'hypostasis' etherealizes the gross weight (plate 141).

Sopoćani: Light, Shape and Form: Light

In the scene of the 'Dormition' the cast shadows, falling on the necks, below the noses and on the lower lips of the angels and Christ, tolerably conform to the illumination effect produced by the burning candles held by the angels[235] (plate 138). But as one carefully scans such effect on the group of the Apostles on the left side of Mary's death-bed (plate 161), it is found that the convention of brightening the larger side of the three-fourths face is followed and the source of light does not become clear, though, the cast shadows are adhered to. In the same way, there is the adherence to triangular shadows below the eyes in the face. There are no cast shadows on the ground anywhere, which proves the non-conformity to illumination (plate 139). The light effect on the garments of the Apostles is, again, treated with the Byzantine system of schematic illumination and compartmentalization[236] becoming light striations alongwith a dark line and culminating into comb-pattern on the figure of Archangel Gabriel (nave, north-east pilaster, west side plate 131).[237] The comb pattern not only concretizes the light as such but it also produces an effect of emitted light-rays. Thus the illumination effect is 'transubstantiated' into that of the 'luminosity' or 'inner light' to represent divinity, although the cast shadows etc., are also maintained on the limbs and faces to retain the 'characteristic-beauty' and historicity. The golden background, now lost, was a parallel endeavour in 'materializing' the light in this respect; it was a final synthesis done by the artist of Sopoćani since the 'frame of his art of painting that way existed complete.'[238] The halo, painted behind the heads, also justifies such concerns with 'luminosity.'

On observing the interior of the church of Sopoćani one finds what P.A. Michelis has noted to be true that in Byzantine churches 'the light plays its part progressively increasing in its upward ascent.'[239] This part played by the light is plasticized in gradual use of brighter gradients in the paintings, culminating into white high-light[240] (plate 154). These gradients are applied over the dark colours, one above the other while they do not blend on the surface. Rice calls such an application of colour as 'pursuing rather the glory of light itself.'[241] This accords with Byzantian's preoccupation with the aesthetics of light. And in Yugoslavia, especially the heavenly light described by Domentian and the 'inner light' of Hesychasts had its hold. The raised volumes with tints leave the darkness over the receding planes towards the contours, to which is further added the convention of one-fourth part of attached shadow on the limbs by the artists of Sopoćani (plate 139). Such a preservation of the dichotomy of the 'characteristic' illumination and the 'divine' luminosity produces an overall tension of the efforts in reconciling the abstract and the real. This gives a sense of 'strange light' in the paintings. Given to their own space creation, the cast shadows and the projection of form (by subsequent laying of brighter gradients) produce a highly charged spatial rhythm of modulation of depth and forth-projection which reconcile the real and the abstract or the illumination and the luminosity. A superb artistic example of concretizing the 'illumination' into the modelling of form irrespective of the cast shadow or illumination effects, can be seen in 'the transference of the relics of St. Simeon Nemanja' (Chapel of St. Simeon, vault, north side, plate 142).[242]

In the paintings of the Diaconicon this reconciliation of the effects of the natural and abstract light has reached a perfect blending. Here the artists, without caring for the new experimentations done in the paintings of nave in producing volume and plasticity of figures through illumination, adhered to the concretizing of illumination effects into abstract light striations giving rise to the luminosity effects, e.g., the lines of highlights simultaneously produce the forms of the wrinkles on the forehead of St. John the Divine (east wall, plate 97).[243] Djurić calls these works belonging to the traditional school,[244] in contrast with the new experimentation by the artist of nave in producing monumental effects, whereas the fact seems to be that in these works the truly painterly values secure the same dignity of heavenly light. To such effect belongs also 'the Virgin' from the 'Presentation of the Donor' (nave, south wall, plate 140).[245]

Shape and Form

On the faces of Apostles in the 'Dormition,' 'traditional' use of the cast shadows and light and shade suggests that they were to gain the modelling and not to show the effect of illumination (plate 126). This is corroborated by the arbitrary use of light and shade in bringing out the modulations of the clothes of Apostles. It is what Chatzidakis and Grabar call 'free plasticity in the figures based on the methods and visual perceptions of antiquity' at Sopoćani.[246] An excellent example of such modelling over the faces etc., without cast shadows, is as has already been noted in the Chapel of St. Simon Nemanja.[247] The linear brushing over the faces, too, suggests the building up of the form. The 'autonomous pictorial organism'—to use Werner Haftsmann's term for Cézanne's work[248] —was thus achieved by the artists of Sopoćani (plate 154). Logically in this pursuit of realizing the form for the expression of the monumentality, the griding, as the base module, was adopted as a further logical end for systematically devising the proportions and harmonious relationships over the pictorial surface (plate 36). The neutral-foil background (golden colour) itself substitutes, by silhouetting, the acceptance of flat surface[249] over which the imitation of tesserae forms[250] gives the final support to the grid proportion system.

The module or 'norm' of the relationship and proportion of the figures' symmetria was 'nose' as given in *Herminy* (plate 36). After having achieved the structural modulations and the symmetria in the human shape it was necessary to invest it with the consistency of the form of 'prototype' having 'intense inner life in calm poses and measured gestures.'[251] Here the ancient theatre[252] came to the rescue of the painters of Sopoćani. Gestures of the body, hands, fingers, pupil and eye brows etc., like those of 'actors,' kinesthetically render even the most hieratic of images 'organic.' In striving for a more 'characteristic' form the artist of Sopoćani resorted to the 'introverted' theory of arboreal growth and plasticity of form. This has been pointed out as the base of the Byzantine art in general by P.A. Michelis[253] and is applicable to the figural work of Sopoćani too, although portraits and type characters abound on the walls (plate 154). A very revealing reference of this module to achieve the harmony between the different shapes is aptly presented in the 'Corinthian' capitals over the pillars painted in the frescoes (plate 83). In these the harmonious relationship is brought out 'with a semblance of organic growth:'[254] the bell-shaped capital is covered with acanthus foliage which turns it into a foliate calyx, the abacus rests over it and on the volutes growing out of inner core. Similarly over the figures, the rhythmic lines of the folds play the part of the 'foliage' in harmonizing the cubes, cones, cylinders and spheres—being the basic forms seen and combined in them; it is parallel to the construction of plastic modulations through brush-strokes (plate 138).

The figures meant to represent the hieratic attitude, e.g., the liturgical figures (plate 150) in 'Adoration of the Sacrament' (nave, sanctuary apse)[255] were subjected to the 'extroverted' theory of formal configuration. Through the principles of 'levelling' the figures are shaped to enhance the symmetries and simplification—by means of giving them particular types of gestures and by dropping the non-fitting details. Obliqueness is reduced to the minimum and the repetition of cross motif over the vestments adds to the unification principle applied to these figures.

The monumentality in the figure of Joseph ('the Nativity,'[256] nave, central square, north wall, plate 156) is achieved by the addition of the principle of 'sharpening' to that of levelling. Here, the ambiguity is eliminated with the simplification, dimensional quality is gained through subdivisions; the differences are also enhanced with contrasts and there is the stress over obliqueness, e.g., the halo becoming ellipse. All these give 'ponderous weight' to the thoughtfulness of Joseph. Such structural simplicity is also achieved in the sharpening principles applied in the painting of the jug of hot water held on cloth by the maid in the Nativity (nave, central square, north wall, plate 139).[257] The figures of the Apostles and Christ in the 'Dormition' (plate 161) are sufficient examples of such structures of simplicity (plate 159).

The figures, though looking modelled, are subjected to the flatness of the wall in their formal relationships. This enhances the 'rhythmos' of the composition. Their 'gross' weight is annihilated by their ground plan position in relation with each other, particularly the placement of feet in the manner which Kitzinger terms as 'highly charged Bach fugue,'[258] (plates 139, 54) and which enhances these spatial modulations; the 'projection' of the figures, too, adds to it. In the figure of 'St. John the Divine' (plate 97) the 'transparency' is achieved through the highlights given on the body tones. Moreover, the modelling through the 'inner light' or 'luminosity' as evident in the figures of the Chapel of Nemanja (plate 142) or 'the Virgin in the Presentation of the Donor' (plate 140) transubstantiates the 'gross' flesh.

Comparative: Light

On studying the factors producing the effect of illumination it is found that the artists of both the centres resorted to the arbitrary use of light and shade gradients for shaping the form (plates 128, 129). This 'cubistic-aesthetics,' in general, made them reject the 'illumination' effects, except wherever these were required, e.g., over the faces of the angels etc., in the 'Dormition' (plate 138) at Sopoćani suggested with the cast shadows and over the face of 'Lady under parasol' (plate 135) in *Vessantara-Jātaka* at Ajanta suggested through the highlights in the eyes.

Thus, the chief concern of the artists at both the centres was to give the 'luminosity' effects. The use of haloes behind the luminaries becomes the standard example left by them in this regard. The concretizing of the effects of 'illumination' in the linearity of form is quite evident in the comb-patterns over the clothes and angles (plate 130), the wrinkles over the face of St. John the Divine (plate 131) at Sopoćani and over the faces of the votaries at Ajanta (plate 148). The use of gold to 'concretize' the luminosity effect was resorted to by the artists of both the places—but unfortunately hardly any trace of it is left. The light gradients put over the dark background (to effect the modelling of form), highlights gaining concrete form for suggesting muscles or the ornaments, and the middle tone of the 'illumination' effects used for the body colour (plates 154, 97 and 157)—all these are a few parallel plastic efforts of the artists of both the centres. These artists, with a superb mastery in building up the forms with the light gradients, achieved 'luminous' form in 'Bodhisattva Avalokiteśvara' (cave 1, plate 141) at Ajanta and in the 'Transference of the relics of St. Simeon Nemanja' (Chapel, plate 142) at Sopoćani.

The conflict of the 'illumination' effects and the 'luminosity' is evident at Ajanta in the paintings like that of 'the Woman with lotus' (cave 1, plate 146). At Sopoćani this conflict or dichotomy is accepted and is perceptible in the 'strange-light' gained on the figures rendered in 'modes' of light-effects of one kind on head and other limbs and different on the garments (plate 62).

At Sopoćani the use of cast-shadows on the neck and below the nose only, is characteristically different from that of Ajanta where these are absent except in the 'painterly' style presented in cave 1 (plate 146), where the cast-shadow below the neck seems only to have been suggested.

Shape and Form

The artists of Ajanta and Sopoćani rejected the aspect of human shape as being sufficient within itself; both of them aspired to give it the consistency of form by achieving semblance, *sādṛśya*, of the 'invisible'—*adṛṣṭam* or the 'proto-type.' They resorted to the dramatics in order to bring in human poses, gestures and glances and synoptically presented them in the 'most fertile moment' (plates 57, 62). Indian treatises on art support such use of dance (*nṛtya*) and drama by the artist and Ph. Stern discerns it in the paintings of Ajanta. Djurić, too, confirms such concerns of the artists of Sopoćani.

The growth of form was a 'continuously articulated network' as is proved by the artists' acceptance of a norm (as 'nose' or *tāla*) for achieving this symmetria. Ultimately it shows that they were conscious about the elementary shapes of things and their inter-relations. Thus by tradition they started building upon the grid-module as a device for proportions and figure-ground relationship in trajectories and axes which were made visible or left invisible. We have already noted that both of them have left such modules in the decorative patterns (plates 39, 46, 18).

This sense of 'primary' structure, as is evident by their brushing as well as by the arbitrary use of chiaroscuro, consequently made them attempt the mutual relationship of the objects along with the consideration of the ground (plates 153, 154). Such a perception is confirmed by the experiments of Cézanne in achieving 'a surface with spatial vibrations.'[259] Both the artists of Ajanta and Sopoćani, adopted the 'introverted' process of 'biological' growth and the 'extroverted' motivation of achieving the 'clear-cut' and visually satisfying structures. The former was revealed in the motif of the 'creeper' having a plant-growth, which also encompasses the 'symmetria.' The best examples of achieving such harmony within the diverse basic-structures are found in the pillars' capitals painted by these artists in their paintings (plate 43). The roundness of the pillar is visually harmonized with the squarish shape of the abacus by the rhythms of vegetative growth given over the head of the pillar. This solution was usually a 'Corinthian capital' (plate 83) at Sopoćani, and a *pūrṇaghaṭa* motif (plate 47) or a bud etc., at Ajanta. P.A. Michelis, thus finds a 'characteristic growth' in the Byzantine works, a similar attitude is exhibited in Buddhist aesthetics by providing a characteristically different 'tree' as a symbol for different Buddhas (Ajanta, cave 17).[260] 'Type' and 'characteristic' faces as one finds for the Apostles etc., at Sopoćani can be seen at Ajanta, too. Repetition of the face of Purnaka in *Vidhurapaṇḍita Jātaka* (cave 2) conforms to the prevalent practice of portraiture, as does the portraits of Satakarni's in caves 9 and 10. At Sopoćani also the portraits of the king and his family, archbishops and popes etc., abound. To endow more 'human' semblance to such forms, the periphery units such as hands, fingers, head and pupils etc., (plate 57) are given 'motor behaviour' in contrast with the 'calm poses' of the bodies (plates, 155, 156, 161). The use of ornaments and clothes, bespeaking of the zeitgeist of the age, add to the 'live' atmosphere of the presentations and the 'historicity' of the narrative.

Such 'fully modelled' forms were achieved through 'sharpening,' *vibhaktatā*, under the 'extroverted' motivation. It invested monumentality and grace to the figures of the Buddha, Christ and the Apostles. With this stress on obliqueness and dimensionality the ambiguity of form was eliminated and the simplicity achieved. This graphic achievement can, for example be noted on images like that of 'the Buddha with one eyed monk,' cave 10 Ajanta (plate 153), and Christ in the 'Dormition' (plate 161).

When these 'sharpening' principles are applied with the conceptions of *madhuratva* or levelling, we get the monumental images like those of Padmapāṇi (cave 1, Ajanta, plate 157) and 'Joseph in the Nativity' (nave, Sopoćani, plate 156.)

The application of levelling principles (i.e., those of enhancement of symmetry, simplification with removing nonessential details and obliqueness) brings about a unity of form which is best utilized in the monumentality of hieratic images like those of the popes and bishops in the sanctuary (nave) at Sopoćani (plate 70) and of the 'Buddha at Kapilvastu,' cave 17 at Ajanta (plate 122).

The ethereality of form and the transformation of their gross weight is achieved by the artists of both the places with the help of almost similar techniques. One of them is modelling with light gradients (plates 141, 142). Another is the highlight rendered as ornaments, comb-patterns and forms of muscles (plates 130, 157) leaving the body or figures into a simpler totality (plate 97) which though compelling the suggestion of volume, makes it as if of translucent form. Added to these are suggestive elements like flying ribbons and clothes' edges (plates 144, 62) sharp convergences and placement of feet etc., (plates 51, 52) providing ethereality to the figures. Moreover, since the figures are subjected to the 'rhythmos' of the total surface, they gradually tend to lose their 'gross weight' into these rhythms of the compositions (plates 76, 161).

With the cast-shadows over the face, neck, and the triangular shadow below the eyes, not giving their hint anywhere else on the body, the artists of Sopoćani wanted to add to the 'historicity' of the narrative. Besides, in most of the figures, especially those of the nave, the adjustment of the 'characteristic head' with that of the 'type' body, an endeavour in the 'modes' technique of uniting the different styles in a single figure also resulted in a tension of the harmony (plate 130). On the other hand, no such tension of 'modes' within a figure is apparent at Ajanta (plate 134).

Ajanta : Colour and Values

With the help of the principle of *kṣyavṛddhi* the artist of Ajanta delineated *vartanā* or sense of depth[261] by the modulatories of colour and values. He used *vibhaktatā*,[262] i.e., contrast and distinction, resulting in the perceptual clash of various colour areas; by adaptation he enhanced differences and similarities in hues, values and saturation.[263] For him colour was to become intrinsic form, *rūpa*, and active space, he did not regard it merely as an 'aesthetic etiquette' since the form appearing in colour was meant to produce an impact.[264] This impact was created by the spatial tensions aroused by the so-called 'earthy-tones' which, to quote Rudolf Arnheim, could be called 'deviations from the dominant fundamental' and which exhibited 'a tension towards the purity of that fundamental.'[265] This is supported well by the structural module of cube or square inserted as a germ-module giving a spatial dynamism to the surrounding rectangular blocks of rocks etc.,[266] (plate 157), in the same way, the germ-module of fundamental colours in smaller colour units or as accents of contours and hair is maintained in the build-up of these areas of 'earthy-tones'[267] (plates 157, 120). These modules simultaneously become referents for adapting or enhancing the value-key.

Citrasūtra speaks of mixing green with blue (40:18, 19) in proportion as required by the form. When these fundamentals are placed side by side, they produce a visual 'structural inversion' giving harmonious relationship. Such a balance is reinforced by their being separate and silent in pure value; this quality in a harmonious crescendo of values[268] is aptly used by the painters of Ajanta in expressing the serene contemplation of the Buddha in cave 10[269] (plate, 134). The 'structural-inversion' with bluish-yellow and yellowish-blue are used stepwise to create a 'planer-spatial' or *vaiṇika* style (with classical balance) in the background on the left side of the Bodhisattva Padmapāṇi (cave 1, plate 157). Starting from the background of dark yellowish-green, the wisker-bearer clothed in greenish-blue makes the lateral middle plane. The Prajñāpāramitā with almost the same green and its value[270] as the background, becomes the forward-middle plane projecting forth the warmer complementary light tone of bluish-red arm of the Bodhisattva ('structural contradiction').

On the other hand, more mutually exclusive pairs of colours are used to bring out the *satya* or *vaiṇika* spatial dimensions in conformity with the aesthetics of *prāṇa*—the 'forthcoming.' Such a treatment of colours is noticeable in the two Bodhisattvas—'Avalokiteśvara' (plate 141) and 'Padmapāṇi' (plate 157 in cave 1). In the former the intensity of brightness values is secured as that of inner-light and the complementaries are employed (yellow reds and their complementaries green blues, the mixture of green and yellow and their complementaries around violet and purple) in order to enhance the 'forthcoming' of form as if built of 'inner-light.' In the latter the tendency of the complementaries to group together as a single whole[271] has been fully exploited in creating volume and a monumental form. For creating volume by dark recessions on the edges, the artist has used purple violet as against the light yellow-greenish-white body,[272] the pairing together of which gives the desired effect. Cézanne treated his still-life paintings in this manner with a view to achieving volume as well as preserving the tectonic flatness of the canvas.[273]

The whole of the scene of 'the Votaries with Offerings' (side chapel, cave 2) is almost entirely based on burnt-sienna and is deliberately painted so exhibiting a technical skill of the maestro (plate 128). This colour scheme, showing one-sidedness by looking 'thin and in need of blue'[274] is used for creating a powerful tension of aloofness—a tension of quest towards the object of worship. This need for completing the colour is satisfied in the plantain tree, a sacred symbol, placed on the edges.

The general harmony of Ajanta paintings, particularly of yellowish-reds and bluish-reds, seems to be based on 'similarity of dominant' producing 'identical colours, distinguished by different admixtures.' Arnheim regards them as creating 'jarring'[275] effect with the 'vital force,' but by showing the 'totalness' of complementaries a rich effect is produced in such schemes.

The yellow colours used in the halo of Bodhisattvas[276] speak of the proper understanding of the spreading movement of long wave colours (warm colours). This is supported by Kandinski who says that such 'movement outward from the centre... almost markedly approaches spectator.'[277] The concentric movement of short wave (cool)[278] colours is given in the halo of the Buddhas in cave 10 (plate 134).[279]

The understanding of the principle of *vibhaktatā* in colours enabled the artists of Ajanta to create the distinction of form even in the identical values of saturation and hues. A characteristic example is 'the Raja with his retinue' in cave 10[280] (plate 121). Though a single dominant colour is mixed in different hues, the structural quality is brought out here with the use of the colours of different wave lengths (warm and cool). It is to create, as Kramrisch expresses, the feeling of being 'aloof the one from the other even where they are placed closely together.'[281]

Sopoćani: Colour and Value

In Byzantine art, colour's perceptive values for discrimination of form and as essence of the composition were supported by St. John of Damascus,[282] and Dionysius expounded its significance as symbol[283] in *Herminy*. Rice distinguishes Serbian school for its colours in comparison with Greek and Constantinople centres and accepts the supremacy of the artists of Sopoćani for their 'abilities in this distinction subtly displayed.'[284] Colour, specially gold, was used to convey dematerialization while emphatically proclaiming unity and integrity of surface,[285] giving visions of 'the sphere of the transcendental.'[286]

Since the main trend of Sopoćani's art was structural monumentality dematerializing into the final metamorphosis of the dynamic space, the factor of colour was used to convey this sublimating process. Colours in fundamentals, admixtures and their various juxtapositions of values were applied to convey the dimension in spatial planes—'the projected composition'—and recessions. They have their module in cubistic tesserae dividing golden background[287] and the dynamism secured through this germ-unit changing into the rectangular grid spread throughout the walls of Sopoćani. Consequently, the bright fundamentals, given as germ-modules in smaller units[288] (plate 115) always enhance the scheme as it would in an 'Impressionist' work and in Greek mosaics.[289] Fundamental colours were known to the artist of Sopoćani as clearly separating and remaining silent in pure value[290] without serving transition, for which they used the admixtures. Thus, the Archangels were painted in green blue and white clothes.[291] The Apostles, painted in transpets, were also mostly with blue and green clothes.[292] The calm 'spirit' of Mary in the hands of Christ is thus vestured in light bluish green[293] to express the calm serenity through these proper colours (plate 161).

Green, violet, blue, yellow, red, black, gold and white as basic colours along with white as a stringent and for making tints, were used by the artists of Sopoćani.[294] The same colour basics were more or less handed down to Morava school.[295] Again, by accepting green as one of the fundamentals, the pairing of complementaries containing more common fundamentals[296] could give as rich a colour scheme as is evident in the Archangel Michael (Chapel of St. Stephen, plate 115).[297] Pairing of complementaries, with stabilized contrasts producing an effect of 'completeness achieved,'[298] has been remarkably used in Mary's figure (blue) and the spread-over death-bed (orange) in the 'Dormition'[299] (plate 161). A remarkable use of complementaries in attached shadows giving a segregation along with a unified sense of volume[300] is seen in 'portraits' with greenish-blue shadows used for orangish-pinks on the lighted area. The portrait of apostle John[301] in the north transept is the best example of such volume-building for the monumentality of form.

The artists of Sopoćani achieved their desired aesthetic appeal through juxtaposition of various colours and values which can be explained in terms of the module of Arnheim's admixture-theory.[302] The application of this module is valid all the more since violet and green and blue and yellow or ochre has been basically used as alternate colours[303] which prove to be supporting Arnheim's 'landing-tone' systems. A deeper understanding of the dynamism of admixtures is evident in using orange cloth spread over the death-bed of Mary in the 'Dormition' (plate 161), which as a colour of 'relatively high stability and self-containedness,'[304] becomes a balance between two fundamentals (red and yellow). In the same fresco, the pale-gamboge of thc attire of Christ (getting a clearer definition through the adaptation[305] given by the orange of the death-bed and whitish tints of gamboge for the three surrounding patriarchs and complemented by the violet of the clothes of the flanking angels) gives the 'animated repose.'[306]

In 'the transfer of the relics of St. Simeon Nemanja'[307] (plate 142), the yellowish-blue of the background gets a recession on account of blue-red of the cloth on the bier having almost the same tone. This blue-red is simultaneously contradicted by reddish-yellow (ochre) of the halo. The depth between the halo and the yellowish-blue background is superseded by the darker tone of the yellowish-blue contour-stroke-lines given to the dark ultramarine—the colour of the cloth around the face of St. Simeon (similarity of dominant).[308] This ultimately has structural contradiction with yellowish-red of the face of the saint. Before grasping of lively depth projection of these colour juxtapositions, it is worth-while to notice the structure of the face created by colour-modelling. In the three-fourths face of St. Simeon the dark raw-umber on the side of the cheek-bone gives (because of 'structural-inversion'[309] of brown) projection to the dark burnt sienna given in the frontal depth of the cheek-bone. The cheek-bone with its yellow and warm highlights, gives a depth to a more orangish-brown given in the area of the closed eye (which, due to this colour, also gets a projection from the side of the cheek-bone). Maintaining thus a harmonious relationship with the dark areas (i.e., the dark and lesser side of the face which had the lighter tone of raw-umber with further juxtapositions of relative reddish-browns giving structural modelling up to the eyebrow), the structure of the face is further modelled by an almost light orangish-brown in projection with light yellow on the lightened cheek and umberish light on the side of the nose. These tones also work as adaptive, enhancing the differences of the other colours in structural syntax. The upper portion of the nose with light orangish-brown continuing from the forehead, thus, gets a high elevation especially with its warm highlights. The tip of the nose gets 'structural contradiction'[310] with light yellowish blue (with relative whites) of the moustaches. Similarly the highlights, tuned to the repelling of landing tones on structural basics, create a solidly modelled face with the tip of the nose becoming the highest point of the projection which started from the yellowish-blue of the clothes of the disciple carrying the bier. Thus the 'blowing' or the 'projection' of form is secured in structures made through colours. Above all, the yellows, ochres, orangish-browns and raw siennas in their lighter gradients become the brightness value and structure the bodies as if made of 'inner-light.'

Brought out on the tactile plane are the general dynamic rhythms given by the connecting repetition of colours. The 'Dormition'[311] (plate 161) has almost a formal division of rhythms of violets and green-blues on the garments of saints and apostles. The rhythms starting from the sides of the equilateral-triangle of the main ensemble spiral up to the apex and interconnect the shapes and forms (plate 79). The aplomb of this colouring rhythm is the pale-gamboge of Christ's attire. The gamboge with repetition on the horizontal border of the hangings on the death-bed makes the base of the aplomb. The centralization of the whole ensemble is given to the isolated unit of saturated greenish-blue of the lower garment of Mary. The module of such rhythms is again given in the decorative motif of palmette on the lower zone border design in the Chapel of St. Nemanja (plate 18). The monumentality and the 'individual' forms of the apostles and saint, showing their 'spiritual isolation,' are achieved by treating the whole mass of their clothes in almost a single colour (plate 161), suggesting those who were the same 'in singleness and wisdom shed no tears.'[312] Though like 'characteristic portraits,' these holy figures 'tangible and human' become generalized in structural colour rhythms of composition 'to be beyond day-to-day experience.'[313] The very material 'suchness' of bright and saturated colours given to the death-bed and the dress of Mary starts vanishing in the tints of 'infinity'[314] transforming itself into the white of the glory which is brought back 'forthcomingly' with the stroboscopic rhythm and becomes the glory[315]-ellipse behind Christ holding the spirit of his mother.

Comparative

It is seen that the perceptual and symbolic values of colours were so used by the painters of Ajanta and Sopoćani that their structuring and distinguishing qualities pour forth the 'essence' (the 'intrinsic form') as the rhythms of space of 'flux' and transcend themselves. Colour becomes the dynamic 'character' ultimately to be beyond day-to-day experience,[316] to get sublimated to a living sacred symbol; thus gold and blue turn into 'active space' showing dimension as well as tactile surface. A rich and subtle colour experience has been left by these artists utilizing almost the same palette by adding green as one of the basics (plates 157 and 115).[317] Their technique of colour handling juxtaposes lending tones in various admixtures, subordinating, dominating, inversing and complementing in almost identical syntax. Apparently the paintings at Ajanta conform to the 'earthy-tones' and those at Sopoćani to the 'powdery and suffused light'[318] only to submit to the unity and integrity of the wall surface. No sooner the germ-modules of fundamental colours start stirring the perceptive values, the beholder finds on a closer examination the flatness of the wall giving a series of space impressions. These are created by colour dimensions, modelling and vision, which make the tactile surface recede and bring forth the rhythms, resulting in a sense of 'active space' while becoming one with the sublimity of the real space of 'Gandhakuṭī' or 'New Jerusalem.'

Colour as bright-gradient illuminates the structural monumentality and turns the 'animated repose' of complementaries into intrinsic luminosity (plates 141, 142). The principles of separation of fundamentals, unity of complementaries, spreading and concentric movement of long wave colours and short wave colours, mutual repellings of 'landing tones' etc., were utilized to create great images like 'Padmapāṇi Bodhisattva' (cave 1, plate 157)[319] and Christ with Mary's spirit (nave)[320] (plate 161), and portraits with superb modelling in colour like those of Sātvāhana King (cave 10)[321] and apostle John (in north transept)[322] and ethereal figures like 'Gautama, the Buddha' (cave 10)[323] and the 'Archangel Gabriel' (nave).[324]

To sum up, basic similarities lie in maintaining the spatial and the luminous, tectonic monumentality and rhythms, in addition to making green as one of the fundamentals which renders the palette rich. However, the basic differences are also apparent.

The 'similarity of Dominant' (plate 120) is the principle generally followed at Ajanta producing 'essentially identical colours,' distinguished by different 'admixtures.' Since the same colour is torn into two different scales, the effects, as Arnheim aptly points out, becomes 'jarring'[325] and produces the required 'forthcoming' spatiality. The complementaries having this dominant colour, i.e., of one of the fundamentals but leaving the basic white, produce the general effect of 'earthy-colours' or the colour scheme in tertiaries (plate 120). The general resonance thus becomes a 'coloured-light' owing to the dominance of a colour other than white. Such an approach indicates the concretization of the lively warmth of 'colourfulness' to put it in Stella Kramrisch's words, 'it burdens, while it dilates the figures.'[326] To Kurt Badt it is extinguishing of 'every particularity.'[327] Arnheim explains that 'instead of being divided in large opposing camps' in such pairings of complementaries, the 'variety of vital force is displayed in many gentle steps and richness rather than contrast results ... the colours show their total range in each spot of the picture (and) add up to completeness everywhere; the result is a kind of overall greyness, loaded with life but serene.'[328] At Sopoćani the dominance of white is seen may be owing to its being mixed in colours as astringent. Here, generally the admixtures are gained with the 'similarity of subordinate' producing essentially different colours connected by the same admixture'[329] (plate 161). The effect produced is that every colour remains quite near to its hue and produces an undisturbed presence which adds to the content of 'individuality' sought by the artists of Sopoćani. The general resonance becomes the 'white-light' which, lacking the variety of vital forces, echoes 'completeness and nothingness.'[330] Significantly the artist of Sopoćani paints the face of the Resurrected Christ ('Appearance to the Holy Women', plate 62)[331] in the admixture of 'similarity of Dominant' producing the colourful and live-warmth of the 'inner light.' For that reason almost all the 'portraits' are painted with admixtures or 'landing-tones.' In the chapel of St. Simeon Nemanja such 'inner light' is realized in colours (plate 142).

Quality of Surface

The technical aspect of this factor is separately treated in the relevant portion of this study. It is being taken here because it is important for its impact as a plastic ingredient.

Ajanta

The *maṇibhūmi* at Ajanta was a burnished crystal-like wall surface which endowed the final 'shine' to the paintings. It also served as a proper background for the picture,[332] indicating the appropriate technical quality of the surface as well as the grid etc., drawn for proportions and placements of the axes of figures. The shine of the surface, now lost leaving a matte smoothness,[333] must have once added to the reflection of the lights helping the beholder's sight to get adjusted with the darkness of the caves. The lustre and the glistening must have enhanced the sense of the flatness of wall and its transparency. Withal, it served as a part of the inner-light—the principle of 'luminosity' like that of sages or *munis* of great lustre'[334]—or, express the live-lustre of a newly-born bursting forth with the life-force. The mosaic-like shining and glistening of *maṇibhūmi* is a tradition descending down from Bārābar and Nāgārjuni hill caves.[335]

Sopoćani

At Sopoćani, the gilded background imitating gold tesserae, now lost, gave an 'aesthetic expression' of catching and reflecting the light.[335] Amidst this glistening the matte surfaces of the 'fresco' would have given a silhouette quality to the figures, though its 'powdery and suffused light shining at various points among the dark tones'[337] tried to cope with the lustrous-dematerialization of surface.

Comparative

The golden background of Sopoćani and the glistening surface (*maṇibhūmi*) of Ajanta both equally submitted to the aesthetics of 'inner light,' the difference being that at Ajanta, the unity of the whole surface was maintained with lustre all over, while at Sopoćani, the matte surfaces of the figures in 'fresco' added to the effect like those of silhouettes peeping out of the 'magic' golden background.

At present, the glistening surface of Ajanta and the golden background of Sopoćani are lost and matteness reigns over both with hardly any apparent difference. A thin calcite layer over the works of Sopoćani and a residual astringent of Ajanta further bring a similarity of lustrous matte surface. The thickness of colour layers is perceptible at Sopoćani but at Ajanta the flat marks of brushing are left as the thickness had been levelled by burnishing.

Ajanta: Composition/Balance Bhūlamba[338]

The mistake of inversely printing 'The Dying Princess' (plate 71) or 'the Renunciation of Nanda' (cave 16)[339] has proved to be a defence of the psychological and physical balance secured by the artists of Ajanta in the whole mural giving it 'the character of necessity in all its parts.'[340]

As Wolfflin has pointed out 'pictures change appearance and lose meaning when turned into the mirror image,'[341] the inverted 'Dying Princess' is not only imbalanced but even the narration is made ludicrous with the change of the direction of 'reading' the picture, i.e., instead of being left to right it is inversed. The crown, brought by the messenger on the left at the subjective centre,[342] (plate 72, in original painting) as the cause of this catastrophy, becomes now, the goal, the catalyst for remedy in the inverted print. Moving to right, the crown turns heavy and conspicuous becoming the centre where everybody in the picture wants to turn instead of turning away from it. This endows the half-cut figure of the messenger with the action of 'going away with the crown' instead of entering with the crown of Nanda to announce his renunciation.[343] The right-hand pair of maids, now in inverse position, becomes the message conveyer (instead of showing anxiety adding to the gravity of the scene in the original).

The figure of 'the Princess,' Sundarī, was made heavy with tone, size and the striking feature of torso centred nudity stressing vegetative function, in order to balance the almost symmetrical recession around it.[344] The optically-centred position of this figure was related to the entry of the crown, in its directional axis and glance direction (plate 72), i.e. visual lines. But in the inverted version it becomes imbalanced with its axis attraction towards the legs gaining much more weight and importance due to their position on the right side now. This picture, owing to this pivot, focuses importance on the lady attendant standing in front of Sundarī. This lady, owing to her distance from the tectonic plane as well as the space around her, was already having weight[345] enough to balance the right side occupied by the heaviness of Sundarī's figure (in the original).

Actually, 'the Dying Princess' is a very unique example of balance in dimension and on tectonic plane. The upper part has been made heavier as all the faces are arranged in almost an equilateral triangle making base with the lintel (plate 73). As there is overlapping of figures, the depth is perceived instantaneously making lintel as representing the broader base on the background from which the gamma direction of the axis of the triangle (in oblique presentation) centres on the head of Sundarī. This head as the radiating centre projects forth these sides making again an equilateral triangle with the base line of the pillars. Thus, the head of Sundarī becomes the hub of convergences and the gamma directions of a sphere put in space, or in two dimensions it is the 'World-Wheel' (plate 73). Her pathos radiates on all the sides[346] in a perfectly balanced sphere. The neck stretching movement of peacock and the bending leaf of palm tree (heaviness given to them by placing on top), add to the oblique circular rhythm in depth plus the circular tectonic rhythm (plate 73).

The three-fourth faces, profusely used in Ajanta, convey a whirling movement because every face suggests spatial depth.[347] These as well suggest nodal centres connected by rhythms throughout the surface. Having their own axes (*bhūlamba* —balances), like sculptures,[348] the nodal centres add to the mural quality of the surface expressing a mode of existence. When given in a frame, as in the 'Thousand Buddhas' (plate 124) they convey a 'mood' of themes in 'atonal' structural map.[349] The nodal centres as units within the total surface have all the characteristics of 'compositions scandées' as Rudrauf classifies, i.e. axial, centred, and polarized.'[350] These have been utilized with the hierarchy of accents in the theme. The examples of the first is 'the Dancing Girl with Musicians' (*Mahājanaka Jātaka* in cave 1, plate 57) and 'Padmapāṇi' (cave 1, plate 157). The best example of the second type is the 'Dying Princess.' The third type is represented by 'the Preaching of the Buddha' (cave 17). Here, the preaching in Tūśita heaven (plate 61) is dynamically related in reversed perspective, with the preaching of the Buddha in the world; as such the subject matter becomes an 'integral part of the conception.'[351] In the first type the sequence is 'organized around the pivot' of the principal figures of the Dancing Girl and Bodhisattva (plates 57, 157). 'The Dying Princess' has the organizational lines radiating from her head made as the 'point of gravitation' (plate 73). In the 'preaching Buddha' a dynamic relationship with the other principal event in the background, i.e., preaching in the Tūśita heaven, is secured making it a polarized composition plate 61). The composition *par excellence* above mentioned three types of compositions of Ajanta is Simhala Avadāna[352] (cave 17, plate 74). It has units comprising the above mentioned three types of compositions scandées homogeneously distributed (as nodal points) and with arbitrarily arranged sequences of the narrative. The latter quality is the spirit of arranging Ajanta narratives making the whole of the wall as a unit to be scanned repeatedly to grasp the subject.[353] The horizontal narrative sequences started with caves 9 and 10 (plate 75).[355] In cave 17 the verticality of the narrative is stressed, e.g., in 'the capture of the sacred Deer' (plate 76).[354] In the chapels, flanking the main shrine of cave 2 (plate 54), there is a definite sense of framed composition, though the organizing rhythm remains that of a mural decoration. 'Dying Princess' is the superb example of the subject treated in the framed space (plate 72).

The principles of grouping, of formal organization, are governed by *madhurattva* (levelling) and *vibhaktatā* (distinctness) summing up in the principle of extrovert-motivation. The structural skeletons, as described in the major trends mentioned above were 'cubic' in earlier works (plate 75) and *vṛttula* (circular) (plate 57) in the later giving the visual axes accordingly. Unity and proximity (*sādṛśya*) are achieved by directional glances and gestures in these compositions. The natural intrinsic similarity (*sādṛśya*) is brought out in the works of Ajanta owing to their biological growth module governing each of the form (introvert-motivation, plate 53). Like a creeper-growth are maintained the rhythms of the border land—the tectonic surface of the walls (plates 46, 75). In the 'forthcoming' movement also they unite in the way Kramrisch defines. She observes that 'though they are staid and yield themselves to the connections that bind them as inmates of the border land, still, in the way in which the figures are modelled, the impact is felt; they are bodied forth.'[356]

Sopoćani: Composition/Balance

The grand compositional scheme of the 'Dormition'[357] has conception of 'spatial rhythms and a hierarchy of accents,' as Rudrauf's category of 'composition scandées' defines[358] it with the inclusion of axial, central and polarized organizations contained in one (plate 161). Its axial characteristic springs from the principal figure of Christ holding the spirit of Mary, around whom the circular and almost symmetrical pictorial factors have been laid out. His radiating central position in the lower half has been weightily secured by colours, by location (a little to the right of the centre),[359] by the background of white halo, and above all by the weightiness of death-bed with which it is attached. Thus, a dynamic relationship between the 'heavy' death-bed, 'weighty' Christ, and the 'brightest and biggest' elliptical halo of descending (and ascending—due to axial force of ellipse)[360] Christ is maintained in a polarized composition (plate 77). Further, the upper half of the composition contains roundish forms of clouds (containing celestial hierarchy escorted by angels) which are of equal size and are distributed symmetrically all over, giving the picture a quality of an 'atonal structural map'[361] (composition diffuses as classified by Rudrauf). Although there is an accent of centralization on 'descending Christ,' a little tilt of the elliptical halo 'displaces' the centre giving full rein to the evenly distributed element, and giving expression to an 'over-all character of a mood'[362] of 'grief' (plate 77).

Creating a dynamic spatial balance within this symmetrical-looking fresco, the circular ring of the angels in the depth dimension has also been balanced with the heaviness of the frontal plane, since the depth has created weight on the distant row of the angels.[363] The 'heavy' buildings on both the sides together with the same 'eye-view' stress the pressure to maintain the balance with the weightage of the front (plate 78). The flatness is reinforced by the forward thrust of the semicircle. The staring glance of the central angel adds to it with the upturn of the ring in the frontal plane as halo. The 'ring' behind Christ gets the upturning perception due to more weightage on the base; the farthest edge of this ring is tightly secured by the semicircular line of busts, the latter simultaneously causes the contour of the halo to dominate with frontality (plate 78). As such, though the perception of depth dominates, it is gradually made 'flat' in sequence, giving importance to the horizontal lines, which uninterruptedly connect both the sides. Thus, the whole of the composition is clearly perceived to have been built on horizontal bands (plate 78). These bands as pictorial schemes of the church, divide the spheres gradually ascending to the higher divinity. Stressing the axial centre to reinforce the verticality, the artist makes the wall surface 'a single undifferentiated tremor of form.'[364] The central axis grows in a contrapuntal rhythm balanced by the gravity pull on the base, otherwise the whole of the composition would have upturned with the perceptual weight carried by the ensemble on the top,[365] the 'atonality' of which, too, helps in securing the ground of gravity on the base. The death-bed is the heaviest due to the 'visual lines' of glances, complementary colours, and above all, due to the frontal isometric projection giving it a 'projection-value.' Its force with the greater axis[366] (starting from the head-side as a heavy base) towards smaller side (feet side) gives a projected perception which is countered by the line of Mary's body, placed parallel to the horizontal base line and cutting the axis of the death-bed near the pelvic-region like X. Above it, the axis of the whole composition (the figure of Christ) shoots up making a Chi-Rho symbol[367] with the Greek 'P' made by the circular rhythm carried over by the hands of christ, the beginning—angel and heads of the angels up to the tilted head of Christ. The halo of the 'spirit' becomes the visual centre of this round. The small dark grey cross over the white stole of the bending patriarch becomes the 'key' stone of the balance of this configuration (plate 80). The cross too, aided by stroboscopic images on the left and directional edge of the death-bed, continues the rhythm on the left, further taken over by the array of the heads of the angels, arranged in a semicircle, to return the eyes to the dominant centre—the 'spirit' of Mary. The 'spirit' is now on the directional axes of the candle stands,[368] ready to be connected with the 'forthcoming' Christ above. Flanking the 'ring' of angels there are two triangles with their bases attached to the buildings and their directional axes pointing towards Christ. These work as wedges to combine the ring with the rectangles of the buildings (plate 80). As the left one has 'grief' in the facial expression, the right one shows the mastery of the artist turning a piece of space and an architectural motif into expressive symbols of 'grief.' Its comparatively blank space or the emptiness caused by the death of the Virgin, is enhanced by the curtain pulled aside and tied to the round pillar. The pillar itself acts as a fulcrum through which the angle of the curtain pushes forth the emptiness reigning the building, stroboscopically brought out by the row of square pillars. Thus, the 'bereavement' engulfs the whole back space of the mural. The repetition of the colour of the death-bed on this curtain not only relates but also suggests multidimensional symbolism. The tied fold of the hanging curtain has direction pointing to the eager hands of the flying angel above—this continues the creeper-rhythm starting from the bending apostle below. The creeper has shoots and tendrils flanking the central axis and coiling both sides of the lower corners—the Leafed Cross is manifested thus (plates 81, 99).

A lively and contrapuntal balancing embodied in single figures becomes the modus-operandi of this grand scheme of composition.[369] It is a 'module' of arboreal growth in which the whole composition is mutually determining 'necessity'[370] grown in all directions and becoming an integral part of the conception[371] (plate 18). The inversion of the whole picture would not only imbalance the physical and psychological forces but would cause havoc in reversing the subject by giving the impression of Christ bringing the spirit to revive Mary.

Coming to the organization of groups (composition) the basic principles of similarity of size, shape, brightness of colour, location, proximity, spatial orientation, consistent shape[372] as 'levelling' factors have been solved in taking a tree-module of characteristic growth.[373] There is a natural intrinsic similarity expressed even in modes,[374] in adjusting different stylistic manners whereby the walls become pictorial units like icons, utilizing all the openings and mouldings.[375] Structural-skeletons are mostly guided by basic geometric units—triangles, squares, circles, rectangles[375] and their solids in spatial configuration, e.g., in the 'Dormition of Virgin' equilateral triangular configuration is apparent, and around Christ the figures are arranged in a circular base (plate 78). The crucifixion (nave, south wall, plate 58)[377] has circular movement of figures with cubistic format of figures in the group around the lamenting Mary. Long rectangular bands are the basic units of repetitive images of saints, patriarchs and apostles (sanctuary and pilasters in the nave, (plate 15). Oblique orientation, angular isometric presentation of buildings and 'screw' orientation of figural movement are parts of such scheme. The last type is best represented in the flying angels of 'Crucifixion' (nave, plate 58). Location in basic geometric configuration becomes proximity or nearness principle aided by rhythms of tectonic-plane, and dynamism of spatial movements, glances, directional movements, gestures and 'synoptic' narrative elements etc.

Comparative

Artistic excellence in the composition and balance has been achieved by the painters of Sopoćani and Ajanta with contrapuntal rhythms and tensions giving a visual corollary to the theme or content of the picture.[378]

By giving visual emphasis to the protagonist with his location on a bit right of the centre and maintaining other 'hierarchy of accents,' it is evident that the artists of both the places emphasised the reading of the picture (in case of Ajanta the unit of the wall) from left to right (plates 161, 72). They create a web of stresses of visual forces and counters, contrapuntal 'weights' and rhythms in spatial dimension and on tactile plane (plates 78 and 73). The artists of Ajanta and Sopoćani have used the composition scandées (in axial, centred and polarized conceptions) in order to represent the identical themes, e.g., the 'Dormition'[379] (plate 161) and 'the Dying Princess'[380] (plate 72) both epitomize matriarchal principle in their deaths 'giving birth to Highest Wisdom.' The artists at both the places make the protagonists centres of radial axes and dissolve their 'gross-material' aspect. This 'transformation' takes place in an environment of pathos where even empty spaces also express the grief and the figural arrangement of basic shapes melts into rhythms.

The axial counter-balancing of tensions in a single figure or in composition, on spatial depth and on tactile plane has been used to give monumentality in enriching and forthcoming rhythms. Three-fourth faces, used by both the artists, facilitate the vision of dimension secured by overlappings. Thus, the oblique 'rings' of rhythms creep and counter-balance,[381] giving the character of 'necessity' to all the parts of the composition (plates 161, 57).

The dynamic relationship between the two groups in reversed perspectives and sharp convergence is achieved in Buddha coming down from Tūśita heaven to preach the congregation (cave 17)[382] (plate 61) and Christ coming down from heaven to take the 'spirit' of Mary[383] (plate 161). Above all, the 'composition diffuses' in homogeneous distribution of forces and balances has been used by both of the artists to convey the 'mode' and 'mood' as in upper half of the 'Dormition' and in the 'Thousand Buddhas' or 'Miracle of Srāvasti' (cave 2 plate 124).[384]

For grouping, the artists of both the places reached unity and similarity by making tree-module as the principle of orientation. Levelling and proximity in location (specially 'forthcoming' or 'projected composition') helped them in achieving the unity. Directional glances and gestures were an extra support to them in this regard. The general trend in composing at Sopoćani is to provide frames or a wall's edge-to-edge surface for a single narrative as in the 'Dormition' (plate 119) whereas, at Ajanta, a full wall comprises many narratives with arbitrary sequences (plate 118). At Sopoćani, the left to right sequence is also maintained in the bands of narrative, e.g., in the story of Joseph (narthex, west wall, plate 68). Although a concern for wall as a frame is shown in the chapels of cave 2 (plate 54) and the bands of narratives are maintained in the earlier works (plate 53), the arbitrary arrangements of sequences remain the spirit of compositional attitude at Ajanta adding to a sense of total aesthetics of walls in the perception of the beholder. Thus, though possessing the qualities of 'composition scandées' in units, these compositions become a 'mood' of 'composition diffuses' and like 'Thousand Buddhas' add to the 'myth.' In the compositions of Sopoćani the individualized punctuations given to the 'myth' tend to claim the historical veracity.

All said, it is worthwhile quoting Arnheim that though 'compositional balance reflects a tendency that is probably the mainspring of all activity in the universe' but 'merely' balance is not art, as 'living is on directed activity and not on empty response,' art 'is not balance, unity, harmony, but on a pattern of directed forces that are being balanced, ordered, unified.'[385]

Hence, follows the discussion on patterns of forces as rhythm/movement, and tension as unified by the art of Ajanta and Sopoćani.

Ajanta: Rhythm/Movement

Rhythm or movement in the paintings of Ajanta can be denoted by the structure of space which has its juxtaposition with the peacefully 'active' space of the cave. Hence, the movement is a whisper only and not a rattling of wind on the mountain as at Tung-Huang.[386] The space defined by modulations of multi-perspectives and circular definitions of postures has been made living by the *prāṇa*, as if the figures were 'breathing.' The flux of life is animated by such pictorial structures having a kinesthetic relationship in the perception of the onlooker. Associative factors have worked in subordination, e.g., 'the flying Apsaras and Gandharvas adoring Buddha' (cave 17, plate 144)[387] has the motifs of 'effortless flight'[388] with flying ribbons, the associative directional counter-action with going-ahead clouds[389] checks it and gives a balance of directional movement to which the frontal-flying *apsarā* (on right) gives a sense of turning. These 'walkers of the sky' of *sukhāvaṭi*, who tread the winds above the waves, 'whose step touch not the water,'[390] are made vivid by below the eye-level rendering of scenes of the architectural units (plate 65.)

The 'levitating' figures, conforming to the anagogical meaning of the paintings, have been logically brought out with a full exploitation of the viewers' frame of reference and in a framework of plastic-vocabulary. The 'enclosedness' of dimensional rocks,' vertical and horizontal spatial movement of the visual axes, contours dialectics with interstices, film colour ground with flowers[391] (plate 120) spread over it associatively giving ethereal meaning to the figures—all these submit to the perception of the beholder rendering the beings who are physical but still become a part of the flux.

The observer may start by 'fixating object' anywhere, be it size, tone, or in associative reference of head or hands, he is at once transported into the rhythms, into the sequences of the activity of the whole body and into the presentation of the 'Life,' for which the end has the beginning as the beginning has the end.

Thus, the sequence of the narration is hardly maintained in the paintings of Ajanta.[392]

In the famous 'the Dancing Girl with Musicians' in *Mahājanaka Jātaka* (cave 1, plate 57),[393] the dancer with torso torsion dominance (through her legs hidden in the dominant horizontal rhythm of the design over loin-cloth and her own head being neutralized in the rhythm with others) expresses the 'vegetative function' of a 'child of nature.'[394] Below the eye-level-roof with almost horizontal orthogonals conform to such speaking.[395] The posture, being 'terminal phase of motion,'[396] the dynamism of kinesthetic experience ushers the tension experience of the onlooker to the head as centre of nervous system[397]—the verticality of the drooping corner of *kurta* as well supports this movement. The movement of rhythms, then reversed through that of arm connects the heads of the musicians in a serpentine curve and reaches the ascending vertical in the pillar[398] on the left approaching the conversation of Mahājaṇaka, with Śivālī[399] (plate 57). The surprising element here one perceives is that Śivāli is completely nude (in contrast with the almost covered dancer,) she bespeaks only the mental and emotional reactions as she participates a-sitting in the conversation through the gestures of hands and head—as do the other participants (with usual attires) enlivening the whole conversation.[400] Thus, with connecting rhythms and movements a 'scale of complexity triggers off motion imparting an inner flexibility producing a strikingly organic quality which give a more complex pattern of forces manifesting motor behaviour looking human.'[401] This holds true even in the whole sequence and within the kinesthetic body of the dancer.[402]

The vertical stress of the Aśokan pillars has been translated visually by a very subtle juxtaposition of eye-level figures within the changing levels of horizons contrived through below/above-the-eye-level views, glances and gestures. With such 'flux' of space definition the figures without obstruction, soar high or low, defining perpendicularity. This gives an aplomb to the rhythms all around growing kinesthetically in a 'tree-module.' The beholder senses the same vertical ascent and descent, perceiving what Michelis puts as 'first intimation of sublimity.'[403]

With rhythmic 'scale of complexity,' movement of visual rhythms touching the nodal points, movements of the visual axes changing eye-level perspectives, the forthcoming and receding—all act on the 'borderland,' the surface, and the creeper motif becomes alive.

Sopoćani: Rhythm/Movement

There is a typical movement apparent in the figures combining the time in 'historicity' with the dynamic 'flux' of the space. The faces seem to have been defined by the rigour of the suffering 'borne individually.' Though 'generalised,' there is still the individual repenting, which the sorrowful faces testify. The rest of the body has 'solemn dignity... tranquil and silent,'[404] (plate 161) alongwith 'the power of man and his claim to heroic stature'[405] to remain 'unwavering in faith' (*James* 1:6). This juxtaposition represents 'the vision constantly alternated between the contrast of vitality and anguish.'[406] But when repentance and prayer has 'transubstantiated,' the heroic becomes sublime; one has only to see the feet in the groups of the apostles and saints, with a view to sensing the 'levitating' rhythms of dematerialization attuned to the outgrowing 'tree growth' module[407] (plates 52, 81).

And within this solemn silence even a flutter of the dropping of the mantle-corner causes movement and surprise[408] (plate 38). The spiral of this flutter when straightening at the edge gives a frontal-push or 'forthcoming' to the Resurrected and 'levitating' Christ (plate 62).[409] Floating ends of the fillets tying the hair of thc angels reveal angels to have just descended (as Christ would with stroboscopic imagery), encircling Christ to proffer help[410] (plate 161)—a perception which the wings of the angels also convey, by being just secured on the back, or by remaining aloft[411] (plate 166). The artists of Sopoćani added to the liveliness with body movements, gestures, (the most 'fertile' ones or what Arnheim puts as 'the terminal phase of motion')[412] and glance-directions. The shifts of the horizon add ascending or descending movements to the figures presented (plate 67). Seeing them from the eye-levels (the 'mode' in which they are presented), the beholder, too, kinesthetically gets a levitating feeling— 'the first intimation of sublimity'[413] whence the Divine liturgy is made alive.

In the 'Dormition' the passivity of the complementaries seizes the beholder's glance; the central position of the death-bed makes it a 'fixating object' from where the eye movements start. Christ's central figure, almost staring into the eyes of the beholder, becomes the aplomb of the movement. This verticality is supported by the apex of the equilateral triangle shape given to the composition (plate 77). Eyes caught up by the direct staring of the central angel just above Christ, move further up to the stroboscopic image of the descending Christ, aided by the radiating angles of candle-stands held by the angels. To this aplomb movement is added the lateral one on the left of Christ holding the spirit. A flying angel is seen bending to proffer help and the other (nearby) bending and pushing forward for the same. This movement catches the whirl of the heads of angels and growing like a tendril into the circular arrangement of the group of apostles on the right side punctuates at the frontality of the apostles. On the left, the lateral movement also, almost in a symmetrical rhythm, ends at the frontal posture of the apostle (plates 81, 161). This complex pattern of forces generates 'a striking organic quality.'[414] It is also manifested in the human figures. This organic rhythm starting from the head (which as the centre of the nerve system receives the sole importance for 'individuality' and 'pathos') gets supported by the gestures of the hands, stances of the body, and the wavy folds of tunics and mantles, as such, a 'kinesthetic body' (called 'human') is created to act vividly in the 'kinesthetic field'[415] of the 'Dormition.'

Thus the 'Dormition' becomes rhythmically the 'Tree of Jesse' (plates 30, 81) having its aplomb in Christ's stroboscopic images. It shoots its growing branches of rhythms pervading all dimensions and becoming groups of apostles and rings of angels, further ascends heavenward. The tree sprouts from 'The Mother' as 'dying she will give birth.'[416]

Comparative

The faithful was given to experience the presented icons or themes like the narrations of *Jātakas* and parables as a living and palpable 'organism' with which the kinesthetic rapport was achieved. To this end, the artists of Ajanta and Sopoćani made the connected movements in a figure or in the whole of the fresco, gradually increasing in the 'scale of complexity' (plates 161, 57). Thus, the mere 'shape' gets a start of motion and giving 'inner flexibility' produces the tensions of living organism. Further complexity (reaching the nerve-centre, with expressions on face) manifested in the motor behaviour of such living forms give the perception of a 'human'[417] enacting the narrative. Thus movement and rhythm reign supreme. Though to both (the artist of Sopoćani and Ajanta) the movement arrested in 'fertile' pose is dignified and still[418] yet it contains the past and future movements; these with surrounding 'plastic-tensions' become 'organic' getting into the forthcoming and receding (plates 62 and 61).

The 'breathing' space of the church or the cave, embracing the walls and its content, grows and flows to become an experience of the sublime and comes back establishing the holy communion, the enlightenment to illuminate and to proffer help to the whole of the ensemble, the beholder included. A movement in 'tree-growth' module—of 'Jesse' or 'Asvaṭha'—characterizes and generalizes the basic intuitive forces from Christ or the Bodhisattva to the faithful or the shepherd who are all typified, as such kinesthetic forces are created from thoughts and emotions on the faces to the gestures and stances of the body. In accordance with these, connected movement—stroboscopic or of actualized rhythms in lines and colours—are produced (plates 78, 61, 157, 161).

The identical process of 'projective images' while giving (invisible) elevations and levitations in all directions, (plates 65, 67, 66), impart kinesthetially a sense of required tension manifesting the 'growing' pattern (plates 161, 73, 81). The movements are made to enliven the Divine Liturgy in the church and the turning of the Wheel of Life throughout the caves' walls. They evoke sublimity coming on terms with the basic cosmic principles of Death and Life. The 'Dormition' (plate 81) becomes the abstract rhythms of the 'Tree of Jesse' and 'Dying Princess' in her demise finds the 'male principlc,' Nanda—receiving 'the divine wisdom'—Sophia or *prajñā* (plates 73, 43).

The difference lies in the sensitivity of the artists in devising the rhythms and movements; the Ajanta artist actualizes this virtuosity in a composure and intimacy; on the other hand, the rhythms and movements in the Sopoćani murals bear testimony to the conflict of 'vitality and anguish' overwhelming the viewer.

Ajanta: Tension

Tension as the 'movement in immobile patterns' organizing the perceptual stimuli'[419] has been well defined in *Citrasūtra*. In its chapter on *kṣayavṛddhi* (39) the form of a figure has been directed to be balanced through this principle applied by the genius in the artist. It has been denoted as 'structural skeleton' along the 'line of force' (gamma motion) in *maṇḍalas*, and through 'studies in locomotion' by 'directional orientation' or what Kandinsky calls 'directed tensions,' as *sama-asama-viṣama*,[420]—the artist is asked to organize it.

The 'tree' module, with its base of directed growth and tension creating forms in space dimension was also adapted for the form of the growing pictorial space. This, as a key formula was coded in the barrel-vault of *caityas* with its horseshoe window (plate 14) conveying a tension for completion, made perceptually felt[421] in 'a growing of space in the upward direction.'[422] As a conception of Mount Merū[423] actualised in choosing the actual mountain, its *prāṇa* was realized in carrying the 'heart'—the caves—with the 'breathing' dimensions of expansion and reduction *kṣyavṛddhi*.[424] It was the *tāla* module which gave proportion to the space of the cave[425] as well as to the pictorial space in cubic and rectangular block arranged in a grid system.

Tension in the proportions was created by these blocks being made along with heavy base (on wall) creating directed tension ('gamma motion along with the greater axis') towards the smaller apex (plate 141).[425] Three dimensionality of 'the forthcoming' automatically arises because of the tension inherent in two-dimensional patterns and also because of the direction of the movement towards simpler and fully grasped pattern. 'Crescendo of breath' (as Wolfflin has shown in Baroque architecture) in central perspective, gives a movement towards the 'free ends' in the open area around the observer[427]—as in 'the preaching Buddha' (cave 17, plate 61)[428]—especially made dynamic since the right-hand upper convergence has been utilized to invert the space becoming a side of the forward-moving rectangular block in '*Tūśita* Heaven.'

As *Citrasūtra* speaks of *nimnonnatta*[429] heights and depths, shown distinctly as being the quality of the painting made by great painters; it is the quality very much needed by the forms of lively contours, (based on 'organic[430] effect'.) Effect of being compellingly intent or eager is secured, thus, in profiles as on the face of the monk watching the 'Conversion of Nanda' (cave XVI.)[431] The profusion of such forms is created only to show the space dimension for the 'flux' of life (plate 61); such space dimension could be created by 'oblique' tension or by the 'pyramidal' projection of *patraja vartanā* and overlapping (plate 53).

'Gamma motion' of a pattern was well studied by the artist of Ajanta as round or its oblique, i.e. ellipse, is properly utilized as an aid to levitating perception[432] in the form of seats and offering trays (Hārīti-shrine votaries cave 2, plate 54)[433] and 'Queen in a Palace Scene' cave 1).[433] These ellipses give a forthcoming dimension, specially in central perspective as could be verified by oblique plates in Cézanne's still-lifes. The halo behind the heads also 'projects forth' the head (plates 122, 134).

The *pramāṇa*, proportion modules, give balance[434] (plate 122) to the tensions (inherent in the *kṣyavṛddhi*) given to *sthāna*, postures, and is utilised in the paintings of Ajanta. Here the principle of tension is given a kinesthetic coordinate with *sādṛśya*, the similitude to be felt by the onlooker as being the tensions of his own body.[436]

The posture given to princess Irandati (on a swing)[437] (plate 82) has the distortion governed by the *kṣyavṛddhi* principles (in directed tensions). The vertically placed rectangle between two poles has a broad and heavy rectangular feature on top, lintel, giving a downward thrust of gamma motion to the rectangle between the posts. This motion is taken up by the strings of the swing which carry it in a convergence inside the space. Shape convergence in the structure of upper body and lower limbs of Irandati also give this depth direction. The space in vertical rectangle, placed by the side of an open door, gets the spatial depth psychologically also—owing to the repetition of units. The right-side pole of this rectangle is overlapped by the princess (in a repetitive image) who has the left arm resting on hip with the fore-arm projecting forward. This orients the depth recession of the gamma direction inherent in the sharp isosceles-triangular formation of the lower body of the princess on swing, the left edge base of which is overlapped by the left post. This point is also the apex of the triangle with its base on the right pole reinforcing depth direction. To explain the forthcoming thrust, the fixating object to start with is the third (tilted) equilateral triangle which also starts from the same place—its left edge of the base is also hidden by the same vertical post—giving a connecting link. The direction of the forces in this tilted triangle is from centre to corners pushing them outwards[438] and giving it a stability of rotating circle. The vertical strings on either side of the triangle support its balance and placement. Besides, the decrescendo movements of scarves on these strings, too, confirm this stability. Aiding the rotation starting from the fixate centre of this triangle, is the point at the edge hidden by the pole. This point becomes the fulcrum-centre of the rotative semicircular formation of the body (half *maṇḍala*) thrusting forward the feet due to the gamma force of the sharp isoceles-triangular formation of the legs from knees onward. The 'distorted' figure of Irandati also gets a psychological 'forthcoming' movement for a full showing of the body towards its standing-image repetition on the right in a 'stroboscopic effect.' It is so, also, because of its own striving to pull apart from the hiding post, for completion.[439] The point where the body touches the pole becomes a radiating centre by getting convergences from the two figures on the right (opposite) side, thus, the forthcoming of the body is reinforced by the surroundings as well. Accordingly, the whole of the configuration gets tensions guiding the swinging crescendo and decrescendo movements of the body of Irandati inside the posts, and attains a plastic balance with the organization of perceptual stimuli. 'The Princess on swing' (plate 82) thus, becomes a 'dynamic composition in which the movement of each detail fits logically in the movement of the whole.'[440]

Sopoćani

The immobile patterns and shapes, as utilized in the basic compositional forms or in a pattern as such, conveying an inherent tension owing to their own 'gamma motion,'[441] have been the forte of the painters of Sopoćani. For example, the stress of verticality in the 'Dormition' has been made more compelling by a strong dominance in the centre of the triangle of compositional pattern on the base, which, giving psychologically a short-exposure to the full breadth of the triangle, conveys 'a violent upward thrust of the apex from the base'[442] (plate 77): the incomplete elliptical shape of the glory, behind Christ holding the spirit, produces a tension towards closure,[442] and its stroboscopic completed image above at once gives the glance a vertical motion (plate 78).

In the plan of the church (plate 4) the central 'square' of the nave was very well used for its 'gamma motion' directing tensions on all the four sides,[443] as were the semicircles used in apex and dome for a thrust towards them. The conception of Indicoplustes' cosmological plan was realized in the upward thrust gained by the suddenness of apex in drum of the dome. The inside space with thick walls was made 'palpitating' by choosing a dynamic proportion modified on the 'central-square' in rectangles used as the base of other members. The same dynamism is secured in modifying cubic tesserae shape into rectangular grid on the decoration of the walls. Such 'tension in the proportions' is properly used in the stone block on tomb in 'the Mary at the Tomb.'[445] The block, being oblongated and made heavy towards the wall, creates a directed tension ('gamma motion along the greater axis') towards the smaller apex (plate 166). Thus, the tension inherent in two-dimensionality would automatically direct the movement towards simpler and fully grasped pattern of three-dimensionality, giving the perception of the pulling forth of the stone which is aided by angular isometric-perspective and the obliqueness. The Mary's body up to the knee being painted behind the block, keeping the feet quite ahead gives a sort of liver-push throwing the block forward.[446] After seeing the tomb the Marys did not find the body of Christ and the angel told them about the Resurrection, which is confirmed by the motif of the sleeping soldiers. The 'crescendo of breath' pushes the Resurrected Christ (plates 38, 62) forward towards the 'free ends in the open area about the observer'[447] this crescendo is provided by the figures of Apostles and Holy Women.[448] Similarly, a compelling eagerness or intent is expressed well in the profiles of the Holy Women (plate 62) on the left of Christ, and in the shepherd in 'the Nativity'[449] (plate 165); the mere wedge shape of three-fourth face's contour, the 'crescendo or decrescendo' of profile contour makes it more compelling.[450] Such lively tensions of depressions and volumes are expressed in whole of the figures. The 'crescendo of breadth' has been also expressively utilized for the form of the central space in whole of the 'Dormition' (plate 77) scene. The central portion of this form, pressed by the lateral buildings, gives it a pillar's monumentality with the triangular base giving a gushing movement upwards and reversely, the heavy top again flows down settling on the base. The glory-ellipse of the descending Christ levitates due to its oblique form[451] and gets pushed up by the obtuse angles of the wings of the angles holding it. The movement is further projected forth by the sharp inverted convergences making the lower sides of the central space[452] (plate 77). The free end in front, with all other 'gamma forces' of 'projected composition' including the light tone, attracts the Christ in elliptical glory and brings 'Him' nearer to the beholder behind the death bed of Mary, which, of course, owing to its plastic-heaviness, remains in a direct visual context with the Christ who is shown 'partaking in her essence as giver of wisdom,' i.e., Sophia.[453] And she 'the Mother' becomes 'birth bringing and death bringing totality'[454]—the whirling wheel of life.

Comparative

Directed tensions as 'the happening' within the visual forms[455] were perceived, then patiently and perspicaciously used to their narrative ends. It is dynamically re-created in the beholder in whom the narrative is kinesthetically enlivened, making him participate in the Divine-Liturgy or the Wisdom-Congregations.

The squares, rectangles and triangles with their 'line of forces' or 'gamma movements' and their oblique forms and solids having spatial-dynamism, vivify the 'fertile forms' or 'pregnant moments.'[456] Thus, the postures or the *sthānas* of figures are enlivened first with their visual tension within (plate 82), then transmitting these arouse kinesthetic sensations in the beholder[457] (plate 77). The beholder is, thus, visually compelled to identify the levitating, growing, forth-coming and receding forms to enliven the content of 'the divine wisdom' in the parables and *Jātakas* (plates 65, 62, 61, 73 and 81). With intent gazes in profiles[458] and round haloes to project forth the glorious faces, the artists of Ajanta and Sopoćani manifest the Divine visions and 'conversions' reaching out to the beholder. Just by creating tensions in proportion the whole of the church or the cave becomes 'dynamic space' growing towards 'the light;' the perception of a tesserae or a 'nose' or *tāla* unit (of proportion) is made to breathe in the dimensions of space as well as on the 'flat-wall.'

It is in such directed tensions that Irandati swings (plate 82) and in her stroboscopic images[459] the narrative is made 'pregnant.' In the same way, the stroboscopic glory-circles transmit the spirit of Mary from the lap of Christ to the Christ in Glory who descends and takes it away making her the 'Highest Wisdom'[460] (plate 77). The 'glory to the divinity'[461] (plate 161) is created in such kinesthetic tensions so that the celestial visions become dynamic like the visions in the Revelation which 'cannot be meant to be stationary.'[462] On the other hand, the visual tensions inherent in the works of Ajanta convey the movement of a creeper silently assuming, to quote the words of Ingrid all, 'a poetic dynamism set in motion.'[463]

Subjective Visualization of Inner Essence

A comparative study of the subjective visualization of inner essence now follows as a corollary to its examination along with the formal and plastic ingredients:

'Thus a painting drawn with *karaṇas* (execution), *kānti* (beauty), *vilāsa* (ele-gance) and *rasa* (sentiments) executed by the genius of the well-versed artists becomes the real (new) eye (sight) for seeing and fulfils all desire', *Citrasūtram*

(42:84).[464] The humanism 'with real feeling for the story' is the verve of the artists of Sopoćani, transforming their observations in plastic terms.

Emotion

The *bhāvas* or mental states producing *citrarasas* were visualized in formal and plastic ingredients as noticed in the study. In brief they are as follows:

Citrarasa Sṛṅgāra or erotic, *madhura* or soft and sweet, is executed (arousing mental states) by showing illumination in the eyes of 'the Lady under parasol' (plate 135) suggesting scorching sun light from which the delicate lady of the elite is protected. The 'charm and sweetness of figure,' (plate 128)[465] of Ajanta woman achieved by levelling 'melt in the heart of the onlooker.'[466] Erotic (mundane) emotions are aroused by below-the-eye-level presentation of roof-top over the dancing girl in *Mahājanaka Jātaka* (cave 1). The half covered and half open verandah behind her signifies the eroticism inherent in her open waist portion in the dress (plate 57). The conversation motifs (e.g., on the lintel of the sanctuary door (cave 17, plate 125), add to *śṛṅgāra.* At Sopoćani (narthex, west wall) eroticism is suggested by below the eye-level bed and Potiphar's wife's enticement shown in the Story of Joseph (plate 32). The delicate colour values in 'Vidhurpaṇḍita and Princess Vimlā' (*Vidhurpaṇḍita Jātaka*, Ajanta, cave 2),[467] enhance the *śṛṅgāra* environment, on the other hand erotic motif of the Ogress in *Simhal Avadāna* (cave 17, plate 133)[468] prefaces and suggests the impending 'horrific' *rasa* which is presented in the adjacent ghastly sights.[469] The charm and sweetness of the nudes presented in the purgatory[470] (narthex, south wall, Sopoćani, plate 129) overtly combines *madhuratva* with 'horrific' (*bhayānaka*) for the abiding flavour of compassion for sublimation.

At Ajanta, *karuṇā* (compassion) is best suggested in the 'Dying Princess' (cave 16, plate 72) and its *ātmastha* or self-centred kind in the Padmapāṇi' (cave 1, plates 157, 160). *Ātmastha* compassion reigns over the 'calm poses and measured gestures' in the 'Dormition' at Sopoćani too. Here, the rhetorics of figures gives expressions to collective emotions of the 'suppressed' (due to isolated and tight grouping of human figures (plate 161), simultaneously each of the figures is reassured (resurrected) in a 'kind of Greek pathos transmuted into Roman nobility of character.'[471] The figure of Christ here in the 'Dormition' suggests 'compassionate heroism' (plates 158, 159) with his stature as a Saviour. At Ajanta in Padmapāṇi (cave 1) the *dayā-vīra* (heroism of compassion) is suggested in its *ātmastha* kind but the 'grouping' of the figures around does not have that 'isolated' tightness to express 'suppressed' state; instead, a 'divine serenity, detachment and mystic love,'[472] felt collectively, is suggested through such grouping of man, animal and nature (plate 157). The figure of Christ treated in a single fundamental colour is 'isolated' (as are the other figures) for individual reassurance (expressed through its plastic 'mass' endowing the individual with monumentality). In Bodhisattva's body the complementaries (light yellowish-green and violet) bring a compactness and monumentality signifying acceptance of the complementary nature of duality harmonized in a monumental form. Significantly, such a dynamic harmony pervades the face of Christ, too, in the 'Dormition' with bluish-green and reddish-brown shadows and reddish-yellows on the lighter sides (plate 161).[473]

The difference in rhetorics of the figures and expressions is apparent, for instance the reticence of eyebrow solitarily suggests pathos and compassion over the face of Bodhisattva (plate 160), whereas in Christ's face (plate 159) the intensity is exaggerated in pathos and compassion becoming an integral part of every member of the face. The linearity of the eyebrow of Padmapāṇi conveys the miniaturist's intimate composure (albeit in a monumental frame) while the artist of Sopoćani expresses the mural boldness alternating between anguish and vitality in the eyebrow of Christ. Withal, the 'calm figure, meditation, and concentration'[474] depicted on both of these figures suggest, in Indian terminology of aesthetics, the *śānta* or the 'tranquillity.'

Mystical

The inner-light (luminosity) building up the forms of 'Bodhisattva Avalokiteśvara' (cave 1, plate 141) and the similar conception of structuring the forms with light gradients in the chapel of St. Nemanja (plate 142) speak of these artists parallel approach in expressing the mystical content through proper plastic syntax. However, we may note the difference as well. A sense of particularity with the artist of Sopoćani gives his forms a realist-human context, while the form of 'Padmapāṇi' is secured through an ideal and motivational formal context (levelling and sharpening), although one may discern a realist-human context, too, because of its resemblance with Bagh cave Bodhisattva supposedly modelled on a Bhil-chieftain. Such formal *kṣayavṛddhi* in extreme simplicity and monumentality expresses ponderous contemplation in 'the Buddha in Kapilvastu' (cave 17, plate 155) and, similarly, in Joseph in the 'Nativity' (nave, plate 156). The artist of Ajanta, using a *miśra* or 'modes' of planer-spatiality in the vein of Planer-Tectonic styles adds the mellowness of *karuṇa* and 'inner-light' to the figure of the Buddha with 'soft, abstract and sensitive treatment of the plastic mass and the tender and light treatment of the plastic surface,'[475] as though such sculptural qualities were translated into pictoriality. In the figure of Joseph ponderous-mellowness is reinforced with folds made of inner-light streaks. But with such 'solarization'[476] effects to achieve the transparency or 'mellowness' the mass is dematerialized into a linear skeletal work owing to the consistency added to the contour angularities. On the other hand, with minimum lines in the figure of the Buddha the mass itself is made transparent and ethereal, although the 'solarization' effects also concern the artists of Ajanta (e.g., in cave 2, plate 148).

Sharp convergences are added to the mystic effect of forthcoming to the Buddhas and Bodhisattvas of Ajanta (plate 61) and in 'projected composition' to the Resurrected Christ at Sopoćani (plate 64). *Cetnā* or 'breath of life' in the plastic quality of modelling and the flow of line[477] is 'bequeathed' by plant and animal life in a mystic-union with the 'universal' at Ajanta. Its corollary is in the 'free plasticity'[478] of the figures of Sopoćani and in the 'creeper' rhythm modulating and knitting these forms in an ultimate dematerialization. This flatness is given a mystic dimension in the golden background which, in Indian terminology of *Citrasūtra* (43:21) would be the surface 'as if glistening and embracing, as if coming out to meet the spectator—it looks endowed with life.' The surface of Ajanta was also 'glistening and embracing;' above all, the planer tactility embracing the whole wall was also made to reach the consummation in the paradox of endowing the forthcoming to the whole of the wall itself as if it was also born out of the primeval matter.

Mythical

The levitating figures with flying ribbons, agitating folds, debased-feet presentation, figures on the horizon and projection through sharp convergences—all these are similar plastic and associational syntax of the artists of Sopoćani and Ajanta to express myth. The soft wind whispers around the graceful dignity of the figures on the walls of both the places. The 'elemental space' of Ajanta gained in the 'form of colour is the golden background of Sopoćani—the 'matrix of all things'[479] over which the 'Fountain of Life' is plasticized in transcendence and sublimity of Domentian's lauds. What Michelis speaks of 'characteristic' beauty growing in 'tree' module, [480] grows and strives, containing all (including the beholder),[481] towards verticality reaching the 'celestial sphere' of the dome of Sopoćani. Such a myth is created on the 'total canvas' of the caves by the artists of Ajanta. For example, the negative 'Great Wheel' with routine activities of life 'circumambulates' with the beholder inside cave 17. This flux, becoming the *Jātakas* and *Āgamas* in the pictoriality of Ajanta walls, transfigures into the flying-*gandharvas* of the *Gaṇdhakuṭī* or *Sukhāvatī*; rejuvenated by the contemporaneity[482] of the onlooker, it adorns the enlightened on the exit. The 'plant-like surrender to being alive and passing away' becomes the 'enchantment'[483] of the presented personages on the walls. This 'enchantment,' as the rhythm of 'creeper' on 'borderland,' submits to the 'flux' of space of the cave and is projected forth through the *caitya*-window towards the summit. All such expressions of flux are 'ordered in accordance with living myth' serving as its symbols and carrying out 'its rhythm.'[484]

The reversal of the sharp convergences in the 'Dormition' (plate 77) and in 'the Buddha Preaching' (plate 61) creates a myth in dynamically relating the celestials with the mundane world. Such A-tectonic spatial structures are the plastic means for myth creation of the artists of Ajanta and Sopoćani. The archaic delineation of Planer-Tectonic style in many of the 'hieratic figures' of Buddhas in caves 9 and 10 at Ajanta and the 'hieratic' figures of Popes and Saints in the sanctuary (nave) at Sopoćani are the 'immobility' reached in coming to terms with the duality of life and death. The 'Buddha in Kapilvastu' (plate 122) and the Resurrected Christ (appearing to the Holy Women, plate 62) are a part of such configurations utilizing Planer-Tectonic frontality. The artist of Sopoćani shows the 'fountain of life' on the face of Christ—through the dynamism of colouring whereas the frontality of the body is made alive with associative plasticity of 'flying' edge of the stole. On the contrary, the entire frontal body of the Buddha is projected forth in its monumentality[485] and in the forthcoming of the wall itself.

Subconscious

The artist of Ajanta, through humbly practising art and elevating from the stage of grinding colours to the creative directorship of the *sthavira*, achieved the ultimate simplicity of a plastic form in finding the 'joy of creation' even in a touch of brush. Here, nothing predominates in an 'ultimate simplicity of effect and counter effect.'[486] With the concentration and psychological preparation of yoga practices, as *Citrasūtra* informs,[487] these artists intuitively made the tradition or *pramāṇa* the rhythms of the creeper[488] and movement of wind (*Citrasūtra* 43:28), making the *karaṇas*' (execution) the movements 'in which beauty enters' (*Saundaryānupraveśena*—Abhinavaguptapādācārya).[489] Accordingly, Amrita Sher Gil found the works of Ajanta as 'vital vibrant, subtle and unutterably lovely.'[490] This 'transfiguration' was a part of deep-rooted arboreal 'flux' enjoyed as a living force in anabolic growth—the aesthetics of *prāṇa*. It was the inner-growth, as Kramrisch quoted, being discerned through *manodvāra-viññāṇam*, the gate of the mind, and never *cakhuviññānam*, discerned by the eye (*Kathāvattu*).[491] The Buddha, too, spake 'Brethren, that masterpiece of art is designed by the mind. Indeed, brethren, the mind is even more artistic than that masterpiece' (*Atthasālinī* and *Samyuttanikāya*).[492]

Similar rigorous training and purification through prayers (*Herminy*) made the subconscious of the artists of Sopoćani. He attempted to reveal 'I am the vine,' His 'Tree of Life' and 'Water of Life.' But, as we have noticed in the purest of graphic-equivalence, line, as the direct transcription of his perception, his excellence to overwhelm with monumentality betrayed anxiety caused because of his alternated vision between 'vitality and anguish.' Contrarily, the artist of Ajanta exhibits composure of 'plant like surrender.' The artist of Sopoćani although a visionary of 'inner light,' had a vision bound in thinking 'of the saint in person' and 'thanked God for having given him the strength to perform such heroic feats to establish orthodoxy beyond dispute' (Dionysius in *Herminy*).[493] Thus, he defined 'Existence' as 'an unresolved contradiction of opposites'[494] with an optimistic attitude 'serene, confident on victory.'[495] The humble artist painting the scenes of Ajanta, 'though with reverence to the Great one who preached a faith that once brought light and hope to millions in India, has a vision which is given only to few. Not a vision of God, but a vision of Life itself in its varied manifestation'[496] conjuring up the 'cosmic man' in 'the Buddha in Kapilvastu.'

Abstract[497]

The appreciation bestowed upon the strength of *Hastochāyā*—perfected preliminary sketch,[498] *śobhā* of colours, use of 'spreading' yellow (in haloes), interlocking of basic forms (in 'Votaries with Offering,' plate 128), transposition of light gradients into colour values reduced even to line (II Ajanta Manner, Votaries, cave 2, plate 148) and above all, the 'breathing flux' of space made bodily felt—all these are a few salient features of the Art of Ajanta strongly indicating the abstract preoccupation of these artists. The same preoccupation of spontaneous linearity (Pope's face in the 'Dormition,' plate 126), interlocking and modulation of basic forms etc., along with use of surface rhythms, use of movements, tensions and above all, 'breathing' space preserve the abstract quality of the works of Sopoćani (plate 129). Here again surfaces the dichotomy of 'existence' in its 'unresolved contradiction of opposites' in the work of Sopoćani whereby 'modes' become detectable, say, in the structural rendering of heads and the mass of body and light and shade along with 'luminosity' principles (plate 62). The consistent linearity transforms the mass into skeletal heraldic form. Although the linearity tends to get separated with form in the late works at Ajanta, too (plate 127), the dichotomy is resolved in the ultimate principles of harmony and rhythms 'where nothing predominates' in 'an ultimate simplicity of effects and counter-effects.' The 'flux' here transfigures the abstract ingredients into the 'life-force' in its full consummation (plate 122). But the 'breath' of Sopoćani 'transubstantiates'—substance changes but the appearance remains—giving only a glimpse of 'transfiguration.' The 'Baroque' or A-Tectonic Spatial variant of multidirectional spatial configuration of Ajanta is *Satya* style in giving semblance, *Sādṛśya*, to the ultimate Buddhist 'Truth' of 'flux' realized in the denizens of *Sukhāvaṭi* and in making the whole wall project forward. The 'Baroque' of Sopoćani, though having antique-classicism, develops the reality in the 'voluminous and organic figures'[499] of the Church Militant although participating into the hierarchy of the New Jerusalem. Both the artists used style of spatial-dimensions and Planer-Tectonic configurations in 'modes' as the abstract element. This range also includes the classical balance of Tectonic-Spatial configurations.

Transcendence and Distortion

The abstract or the non-referential function was given a transcendence by the 'exaltation in pure relation.'[500] Its crux was achieved in the extendibility of the vertical and horizontal in emphasising the 'thereness' of 'surface' as well as its surrender to the void in its accretion and seemingly infinite growth. This space is transformed into the 'breathing' of the actual space of the church and the cave. At Sopoćani, the 'thereness' of the wall surfaces defines this breathing of the interior which exalts in verticality whereas at Ajanta, the 'thereness' of the wall itself is also transformed into the living *Prāṇa* participating into the exaltation of the 'pure-space' of the caves. Amidst 'this metaphysical exaltation, this play of infinite and finite, the beholder feels alternatively subdued and uplifted, and gains his first intimation of sublimity,' as observed by P.A. Michelis.[501] And the reassurance of coming to terms with this 'total solitude' is given at Sopoćani by 'Christ as the King of Glory or Triumphant victor, bigger and stronger than the surrounding figures'[502] (plate 161) for which basically the exaggeration of massiveness, the free plasticity, sharp convergences and the sharp contrast of complementaries (or fundamentals) in the figure and ground relationship were employed. Simultaneously, the linearity was also exaggerated which resulted in the heraldic images of such figures endowing them the Planer-Tectonic spatiality.

At Ajanta, too, the reassurance came out with 'Heroism of compassion' of Padmapāṇi (plate 157) employing almost the same principles of *kṣaya* and *vṛddhi*, although with a difference of transfiguration of form into the 'living principle' or *prāṇa* with employing the complementaries within the form itself which gave a heraldic as well as monumental plasticity in Tectonic-Spatial attitude (plate 122). This distortion of form according to the vegetative module, although adopted also at Sopoćani, was specified there for the characteristic growth whereas at Ajanta, it became the characteristic of the cosmic relationship for achieving the total harmony.

The distortions in shape are employed as an expression of the 'respectful eagerness' of the maid with the water-jug (Nativity, plate 139) and with an angle in the plumb line of the figure of Mary ('Presentation in the temple' at Sopoćani, plate 123). Such distortions transcend the form in maintaining the dominance of the suggestiveness.[503] At Ajanta the 'compassion' of Padmapāṇi (plate 157) is given dominance not only by the form of the body in making its axis in a semicircular turn like the turn of hand in protective gesture, *abhaya-mudrā,* (or like the shading given by the spreading foliage of the tree), but also in its background the abstract shape is given this 'compassionate' axis. The abstract shape itself becomes the 'compassion' as the walls of Ajanta become *prāṇa.*

Ajanta: Technique

Since preservation of surface is regarded as one of the main requirements, the physical, the chemical as well as the insecticidal properties were carefully looked after in the preparation of the ground in Ajanta paintings. The ground surface, called *maṇibhūmi* (lit. surfaces having the crystal-like brightness)[504] in art-treatises, which seems to connote angular granulity, firmness and compactness of the plaster,[505] the shine and smoothness of the surface and it also indicates the modular grid pattern drawn as the preliminary proportion guide[506] (plates 19, 117, 157). This ground was not only to be applied for the mural surfaces but throughout on the sculptures and architectural units in varied thickness and layers.[507] Hence, obviously, the proper astringents and maturity time for the catalysis of raw material etc., were decisively admitted in the art-treatises and practice.[508] It is already noted that the process of carving out the caves started from the roof and was simultaneously followed by the painting work.[509] The speed (Spink's theory) of the work was also taken into consideration before arriving at a proper decision about the technique and surface preparation.

The three layers, as B. B. Lal has pointed out, are of varied thickness. The paint layer is of about 0.1 mm., the middle, intonaco layer is about 2 to 3 mm., the base of course, varies in thickness having two layers at many places. The researcher found in cave 16 (since the restoration work was in progress during his study there) that the total plaster put on the properly grooved carrier, was about one centimetre thick at many places, with absorption of colours almost into the total thickness of intonaco. The marks of the brushing left even after the fading of colour, the light ground colour being left while darkening the interstices, impesto for whites and highlights (plate 141), form modulations through brushing *vartanā* tints made on the surface purely by the medium, *kūrcakakṣālana*,[510] and above all, the various tones incorporated with the brush-modulations for drawing contour lines (plate 120)—all point to a technique in which wetness or dampness of the ground and liquidity of medium and colours were fully taken care of.[511] Further, lines were drawn on 'sacco' surface in order to give, in contrast, a hard and 'engraved' effect with negligible tone modulations. Also an effect of dry-brushing would often be incorporated.

To make the surface look 'wet' for excellent quality of work, the artisans of Ajanta used a technique which could not be given a name other than fresco, not the buon-fresco but a type out of which Āla-gīla[512] Mughal or Jaipur fresco, was derived.

The ground base, *lepa*,[513] was required to be neither too thick nor too thin and was to be applied in one to three layers on a cleaned smooth[514] or grooved[515] surface. The mixture was a preparation of brick-powder (*cītrākareṣṭakā*),[516] sand (especially to be procured),[517] lime made of conch (*sudhā*),[518] rice-husks, gum resin, saffron with oil, bee wax, molasses and liquorice; to this, pulp of banana or Betree (*Feronica elephantum*), or *vajra-lepa* (made out of boiling of buffalo skin) was added. The mixture was kept for about a month and then applied to the rock surface.[519] This inference is based on the preparation of ground-base given in art-treatises alongwith B.B. Lal's finding that it has fibrous material, vegetable-matter, ferruginous mud and gritty rock-powder, sand and angular grained silica.[520]

After the application of the plaster it was required to be kept wet or damp either by milk, juice or water till the thin layer of intonaco, consisting of thin layer of lime made of conch or oyster shell (*sudhā*) and mixed with coconut milk etc.,[521] was applied and kept moistened.

The lime of conch etc., was also used as the astringent in colours, and was mixed for tints. The pigments were mostly made as *Citrasūtra* also advises, from indigenous materials[522] of mineral origin such as glauconite, ochreous clays, lamp black, gypsum etc. Earlier records speak of 'gold' colours,[523] it can be inferred that the copper compounds must also have been in use. Imported lapis lazuli was used but indigo was prepared as vegetable colour.

Since the tools used at Ajanta were of simple type, the brushes etc., are also thought to have been simple and indigenously made for various effects.[524] Starting from grid giving *sūtrapātCrekhā,*[525] (at many places incised lines of tracing are visible) the painting process proceeded with *śubhavartirekhā*[526] (sketch-finishing giving all iconographic details etc., in red-ochre) to colour modulations from light to dark (underglazing of light) terreverte seems to have been used in some works (plate 157) and lastly the contour depths and forthcoming were modulated with *dvika-karma.* The use of crayon for preliminary sketch as suggested in art-treatises could not have been possible on 'wet' surface. Burnishing of the surface in the end was done to give a smooth and polished lustre.

Sopoćani

The *Painter's Guide* (*Herminy*) has given the technique of Byzantine fresco which tallies well with that given by Vitruvius, Theophilus, and Cennino-Cennini.[527] The latter's account of the techniques partly explains those adopted by the painters of Sopoćani. Rice also finds hardly any change in the working of Byzantine painters throughout ages.[528] Thus, it substantiates the scriptural verification of the technique.

According to The *Painter's Guide*, the first coating of plaster (arricciato) was prepared with the mixture of lime, with a little quantity of the powder of bricks,[529] and straw made to workable consistency and left for two or three days before application.[530] On it the design was drawn with charcoal, the main lines were incised and the contours and main shades indicated with sinopia.[531] Intonaco or the second layer called 'opsis,' was made of fine but slaked lime mixed with beaten tow (well-cleaned of bark), and kept some days for maturity.[532] Opsis was applied after some hours on the first-layer and left for three days before start of the painting.[533] The second layer was applied on the surface according to the requirement of the space area to be kept damp enough for the painting, obviously keeping the edges of the opsis along with the divisions of forms or grid-frames presented in the work in order to avoid the ensuing demarcation line. This system was sometimes not followed possibly because of the pressure of work or the artist's mood. For example, at Sopoćani, the division of opsis line over the architectural units in the 'Dormition'[534] (plate 161) indicates that the painter, in a frenzied mood of inspiration forgot to hide the division lines and went ahead with the completion of this large scale work. It is also recorded that 'a painter could cover six to seven square yards of walls space in a single day' in Serbia.[535] Moreover the dampness retained by the straw and tow persisted for quite a long period.[536] Figures were drawn in Verdaccio—mixture of black, lime white and cinabrese (sinopia and white lime) with water mixed with lime.[537]

The flesh-parts of the figure were given a dark undercoating of terreverte over which modelling in lighter tone was resumed till finally the white highlights were given in thick colour (plate 97).[538] Hatching was used to add further colour and tones.[539] The working of the light gradients starting from the darkest was adopted all over the surface. The background was done at first and the details were taken up at the end.[540] The practice seems to have been not to care much about the damp ground and build up the layers of colours.[541] The flaking of colours at many places gives evidence of this mode of *al secco* mixed with the undertones done in fresco buono. V.J. Djurić speaks of one of the best painters of Serbia painting against every rule of fresco painting as 'he applied his medium as thick and wet as required in oil painting.'[542] This was recorded of the painters painting murals up to the time of Resava monastery (A.D. 1406-18).

The fresco-Byzantine was inspired mainly by the mosaicist's technique of giving guidelines of design in the damp plaster laid for the tesserae work.[543] The linear technique of applying colours without half-tone mixing is an outcome of mosaic technique (plate 154); besides, the requirement of the damp background necessitated the brushing to be done in a linear *a la prima* way. Brushing over the quite damp ground especially with linear hatching (of Indian 'Hairikajā' type) has given elevated lines of structural modulation according to which the painter's brush ran (plate 138). But there are passages of colouring at Sopoćani which have a half-tone mixing on the surface itself,[544] which conforms to not-too-damp ground theory. Broad and bold application of colour (plate 126) suggests the painters' understanding that the natural pigments tend to become lighter on drying; consequently this adds to the purity, strength, and monumentality[545] of the form.

It was on the insistence of Uroš I that the frescoes in the Church and narthex were given an uplift in the background by sticking gold-sheet on the yellow ground in the form of tesserae. All the first-view-range sacred zones and places were given golden background leaving those which were out of sight (e.g., behind the eastern pilaster).[546]

Comparative

'Working over a damp ground was a common practice followed by the artist of Sopoćani and Ajanta. For this very purpose there existed the tradition of mixing fibrous vegetable material to retain the humidity in the plaster. Such a device also helped to strengthen the plaster basically made of lime mixed with sand and powder of brick. At Ajanta, however, the ferruginous mud was mixed in a sizeable quantity. Although mixing of vegetable material was more elaborate at Ajanta, the maturity time followed the mixing and the applying of plaster on the walls at both the places. On this first plaster of varied thickness the artists applied the intonaco layer, *lepa* or 'opsis' made of either slaked lime or *sudhā* properly matured and of a thin layer (Ajanta artists kept it specially moistened). Mixing of vegetable material in this intonaco was also similarly followed, at Ajanta in mixing coconut milk etc., and at Sopoćani, finely beaten tow. The requirement of this layer also being wet, its application can reasonably be presumed to have been at both the centres, i.e., applying as per required area. According to what D.T. Rice informs about the speed of the painter of Serbia along with Walter Spinks theory about the hectic spread of the artist working at Ajanta (plates 163, 164), it can safely be deduced that the required working area of the day should have been enormous.

The Byzantine fresco technique demanded working down from the highest zone; the same requirement constrained the working of the Ajanta artist too because the painting followed the carving of the cave from the top.

Preliminary grids helping the proportions were drawn (plates 19, 36). Indian treatises speak of the use of crayon drawing; the Serbian painter too, used it for such beginning. Either incised tracing lines or drawn *sūtrapātarekhā* was followed by *subhavartirekhā* in sinopia mixed with lime (as astringent) and water at Ajanta; the artist of Sopoćani, too, similarly came up to the basic light and shade and iconographic details. An undercoating of terreverte is not ruled out at Ajanta and is apparent at Sopoćani. Interstices were darkened and since neither was using the fresco buono they applied thick layers of the colours starting from dark to tint values up to the lightest of white highlight or ornaments (plates 146, 154). To bring out tints there are passages of colours being mixed with the medium on ground. The colours applied in *Hairika Vartanā* or in brush lines in order to modulate form are apparent both at Sopoćani and Ajanta (plates 153, 154). Although *bindujā* or the dot-technique for colour saturation was used at Ajanta; at Sopoćani, the brush lines or 'hatching' gave the same effect of darkening and saturation (plate 138). At both the places the 'secco' touches are also evident (plates 140, 163). The *dvika-karma* giving final lining work (plates 126, 127) was accomplished with dark or various values. Sopoćani had the gold foil applied usually on the yellow background. Ajanta's surface, too, glistened with burnishing. Ajanta had some singularly indigenous vegetal and animal astringents used in the ground preparation and colour mixing.[547] *Citrasūtra* speaks about the mixing of lime-white as astringent in colours (40:17-24). *Citralakṣaṇa* also confirms it adding the mixture of gum of elephant apple and neem.[548] As for Sopoćani, water mixed with lime was the medium and astringent. Generally, the colours applied at Sopoćani remain 'linear' with no half-tone used (plate

154). But since not-too-wet ground was at hand, the half-tone passages were also incorporated. These are found in the paintings of Ajanta, too, (plate 153) along with, 'line' work in *hairika* and *bindujā* application (with plain colours of *patrajā* application of colours) bringing out spatial dimensions.

AJANTA: INFLUENCE OF TECHNIQUE OVER STRUCTURE AND VICE VERSA

In ground preparation the use of herbal ingredients and crystalline granules indicates the same structural module as that of a 'Tree.' The pliantness acquired due to 'wet' technique is of the same spirit of which a creeper motif is conceived and painted to bring out the 'breathing' structure. The saturation and luminosity preserved in colours substantiate the theory of light as a 'luminous' source over which the highlights add to the creative use of the understanding of light as illumination. One has only to confirm this treatment in the details of the figures painted on the 'Great-wheel of Life,' (cave 17, plate 105).[549] This leads to the perception of having a very smooth and burnished surface, which was required to reflect 'the glistening' and 'the sweetness as if smiling'[550] of life—like a newly born. The dark spaces of the caves were also 'filled with an otherworldly light'[551] owing to the reflections over such surfaces. The light inside the caves was also reflected by such surfaces, which facilitated the adaptation of the eyes to the darkness.

A tree-like growth process of painting starts from *sūtrapātarekhā* (*bhūlamba*) or the grid (plate 19) and goes on gradually developing the structure through *pakśa-vṛddhi* giving depth, value and *pramāṇa* (the proportion) to each of the plastic ingredients. It further follows the rules of *kṣyavṛddhi*—subtraction and addition along with that of '*vibhaktatā* (distinctness.) Even when the purity of ingredients was desired and appreciated as of colour or line, the essential was reached through a proper process of elimination, *kṣya* (plate 122); thus the most appreciated *hastochāyā* (sketch endowed with life), and the depth of film-colours (to convey 'active space') were achieved (plate 141). On a *vajralepa* surface the touch of the brush filled with the lucid-stickiness of the fine-grained colour and the medium was bound to reflect the delicacy required for the spatial relationship (achieved through *patrajavartanā*) of overflowing forms (plate 127). *Hairkajā* and *bindujā* brushing were appropriately developed to give surface modulations like those of hair and luminosity resonance of colour on such a moist and hard surface (plate 153).

The mural technique itself required a permanent ground and material; it also needed a monumentality of structure to suit it as being the member of an architectural complex (plate 122).

'Forthcoming' dimension being the 'inhibition' and 'flux' being required expression, the most suitable ground for such theme could be the 'non-existent walls' (walls made dark by keeping aisles in front). Then with the opening through the 'false-pillars;' the space or the *ākāśadhātu*, becoming forms on the walls, is projected into the spaces of the caves and ricocheted back through these 'holes,' gliding over the reliefs.

The combination of architecture, sculpture and painting into a unit[552] suggests what was desired to achieve as *Vāstū-brahma* the ideal of *Vāstū-Śāstra*, by conveying a multidimensional emotive-experience, the *dhvani*, which makes Solomon Gladstone exclaim 'but is it strange that in the very temple of art, it seems to many better to dream than to paint?'[553]

Sopoćani: Influence of Technique Over Structure and Vice Versa

The practice of putting colours in a linear, broad and bold brushing added to the structural monumentality (plate 156) by giving two-dimensional silhouettes befitting the concept of mural.[554] Owing to the breadth of handling surfaces this monumentality was 'sharpened' (plate 126). The damp surface gave lucidity to the brushing movement and spontaneity and rapidity to the execution.

Again, it was the breadth of handling the surface required for the 'fresco' technique which brought about the marvel of Sopoćani's monumentality and concretised the vision of its great painter—'his optimism, vigour and nobility, and his sublime answer to man's destiny, eternity and death.'[555] The luminosity of inner light over which the Hesychasts made a creed, was achieved through the resonance of depth and transparency of colours which the technique of 'fresco' preserves; it was manifested as the thickness of white gradients reaching the highlight from the dark undertones pursuing 'rather the glory of light itself.'[556] The linear hatching process was to modulate the structure of the form and weave the interstices giving a 'rhythmos' to the figures done in the idealism of *symmetria*. This duality brought out 'the idealism and the awareness of the tragic.'[557]

Comparative

The 'thick' medium of the techniques of Ajanta fresco and the Byzantine-fresco of Sopoćani was significant in maintaining the unity of the technique with the consistency and permanency of the wall and the monumentality of the mural painting (plates 122, 156). Conversely, the total effect desired was the etherealization of the walls into the dynamism of the space of the Church at Sopoćani and at Ajanta, it was to 'transfigurate' into 'flux.' The thinness of colours achieved in the 'fresco' technique, the 'soaked-up' intensity of colours producing suffused light from the surface (of figures) left between the golden background—all these added to the flattening, silhouetting and dematerializing of walls at Sopoćani. At Ajanta the *patrajā* and *bindujā* application of plain and 'film colours' brought out the perception of 'colours as space' and the burnishing 'transfigured' the walls into 'smiling' and 'glistening, as if breathing' in tune with the desired 'flux.'

The 'wetness' added to the pliantness and sweeping of the brush lines along with the spontaneity of execution (plates 126, 157). This became an integral part of the tree-growth 'module' adapted at both the places. Although the spontaneity achieved at Sopoćani overwhelms the onlooker in 'heroic' stance, at Ajanta it sweeps the surface in natural pliancy of a creeper.

The hatching or *Hairika-vartanā* added to the linear application of colours modulating the forms in their basic shapes to achieve the monumentality (plates 153, 154). It also brought out surface modulations combining the 'bulging' of the interstices, whereby the flatness was achieved disintegrating the perception of form. The hatching, *bindujā* and *hairika vartanā* given on the under coating helped to achieve an effect similar to scrumbling'[558] providing the 'germ-module' of fundamental colours and enhancing the dynamism of landing tones. The linear technique gave consistency to the contours and angular divisions on the murals of Sopoćani which caused the forms to 'bulge' out 'into space' as well as to reduce back to a skeletal flatness, to which the addition of lighter values or white lines gave 'solarization' effects (plate 130). (Specially so with the highest-zone figures which were given severe linearity for visual clarity.) Adding such technique and effects to their repertoire the artists of Ajanta also gave 'periphery-light' lines to attain the 'bulging' and 'flattening' of heraldic forms (plates 145, 148).

The combination of architecture, sculpture/relief and wall paintings brought out the total 'aesthetic' complexes at both Ajanta and Sopoćani, giving the beholder his first 'intimation of sublimity.'

Ajanta: Influence and Originality

The originality of Ajanta lies in providing spiritual isolation amidst the bustling of life. It is the world as viewed by the Buddha before his *Parinirvāṇa*. The Lord seems to be in a 'rather blessing than enamoured spirit' while saying to Ānanda: 'colourful and rich resplendent and attractive is India, and lovable, charming is the life of men.'[559] As if to achieve this end, the artist of Ajanta unified a plethora of styles,[560] be it the Gupta synthesis of Mathurā and Sārnāth schools digesting foreign heraldic motifs,[561] the Deccan style of Sātavāhanas and Kistna valley overcoming the indulgence of Roman streams[562] or the ever-renewing vigour of folk traditions. Accordingly, the originality with which the artist of Ajanta came out was not the 'novelty for its own sake, but that it provides truly new insights, that it illuminates rather than merely dazzles,'[563] as Feldmann would say.

With the bases of 'luminosity' (perception of the inner-exuberance) and 'illumination' (perception of expression) Ajanta provided the experimentations which made her the Mother-school of the art of Asia.[564] The ecstatic-delight of devotion—*bhakti*—in inner-exuberances of Amarāvatī, configurations and the nature-module of 'Tree' exploited fully in the living-*prāṇa* (breath) of Bagh were united[565] at Ajanta in the best of what 'folk' spirit of India could bestow and the royal artisans could achieve under the benign art directorship of *sthavira* Bhikkhus. The result was that the 'spirit in static repose'[566] of the figures of Jaggayapeta were transformed into the tanslucent grace of Hārīti-shrine ladies (cave 2, plate 128) and the luminous-monkhood of the Buddha[567] in Kapilvastu (cave 17, plate 122). In these the vitality of Amarāvatī,[568] proportion of Sārnāth and figurative impetus of the terracottas of the East-Mediterranean, Myrina and Tanagra styles[569] got merged.

It was the artist of Ajanta who decoded the Aśokan Sārnāth pillar as the *Dharmacakra*—eternal aspect of Buddha's preaching carried over by 'the Chariot of Time which is moving constantly on its own axis,'[570]—and gave it a Life-breath, *prāṇa*, of mythic 'Wheel of Life' well along Buddha's presence by its side. In it not only the cosmic interpretations were fulfilled, but also the popular religious dialogue with the enigma of Life and Death found its 'picturesque illusionistic-visionary'[571] equivalence.

The dialogue started on the amulets of Mohanjodaro and Harappa[572] in the 'passivity of animals'[573] as well as in the symbol of tree generating out of the womb of a nude Mother-goddess presented in suspension like 'dried-up seed.' Added to it were symbols universally adopted and synthesised in the West Asia. Thus were created ring-stones having the Yogācāra in Śavāsana[574] of the Mother-Goddess and procreation and resurrection[575] symbolised by peacock and 'water-fecundity,' in *nāgapuṣpa* or honey-suckle with *padma* or lotus-rhizome. These mutations along the *Uttarāpaṭha*, connecting Taxila and Pāṭliputra, gave impetus to 'folk' religions with their adoption by the elite, i.e., Mother-goddess in terracotta earlier influencing stone-carving and later getting influenced by it and becoming full-fledged architectural decorations at Ahichatra etc.[576] Thus it also became the experimental motif of Sātavāhanas and 'The Dying Princess' motif was experimented upon also at Ajanta as C. Sivaramamurti points out. Its real mystic-cosmology was given *prāṇa*, 'living-breath,' at Ajanta (cave16, plate 71) where it is (alongwith peacock and palmette or plantain motifs) given a cause of 'dying' for the 'becoming' of a Bodhisattva—the eternal cause of human salvation—thus unifying the dichotomy of *Prajñāpāramitā* standing by the side of Bodhisattva Padmapāṇi (cave 1, plate 157)—the musings over the 'Hoṃ' motif. Thus, Hairīti as fostering, protecting and destroying life[577] became 'mother of Pravarsena' and was given special veneration in side chapels (cave 2).[578]

The moon stone from Kesanpalle, Andhra Pradesh, has the *tri-ratna* and *padma* emerging out of 'honey-suckle rhizome and it symbolizes the transformation of tree emerging out of womb.'[579] This again is concretized in Gandhakuṭī (as cave 19 of Ajanta was named)— the 'Jetavana'—where miracle of Buddha was performed by sprouting 'tree' out of mango-seed,[580] which in connotation equalizes with vegetative life-force 'laden with fruits and blossoms' (*kalpa-latā*) presented in ornate pillars, paintings and decorations. This 'Jetavana' covered by golden coins is synoptically symbolized as 'rosary with leaves' arranged in the bead-and-reel or egg and dart motif on the border of the *caitya*-window giving a stroboscopic movement to its transforming the semicircular opening into a *stūpa*. The same indigenous manner of utilizing 'ovolu' and curved fold hanging motifs of West Asian and Hellenic origin[581] is seen, along with the 'Hom' motifs on the pillar carvings and decorations.[582]

The Ajanta caves were a gradual improvement over those of Rājgīr to Bārābar, which had developed into Western-Ghāṭ caves.[583] Similarly, the transparency for 'luminosity' acquired in the carved lines of *Katra*-Buddha culminated into the 'wet-cloth' nudity of Ajanta figures suggested by subtle border lines of the garments and the shade condensing on contours along with the volume reinforced by the suggestion of ornaments as highlight. This is how Ajanta gave 'ethereality' to the figures participating into an epic, containing all the *rasas* subjected to the basic, i.e., *karuṇā* turning into the dignity of *śānta*—the culminating *nirvāṇa*.

Plastically, the Gestalt's 'principle of simplicity,' finding a 'depth perception' in orderliness with multiplicity and going up to the catabolic state, was successfully readjusted by the artists of Ajanta with the anabolic over-flowing projection of forms from the primeval matter *ākāśa*. The expression of 'forthcoming' was, thus, the originality of the artist of Ajanta imbibed with the solutions in 'visual' and 'metaphysical' enquiries.

And finally, with the integration of three spatial arts, Architecture, Sculpture, and Painting,[584] a living 'myth' was created in an 'environmental' aesthetics[585] in order to provide a 'spiritual isolation' to the onlooker by taking him inside the *vihāra* with 'illumination,' where he projects his perceptual consciousness into the receding dark interiors only to find 'luminosity,' which in 'flux' returns the light of 'Sukhāvaṭi' into himself.

Sopoćani: Influence and Originality

The broad-mindedness of Greek Orthodox Church in granting an independent Serbian Church, unsettled political situations on the periphery Byzantine states including the capital, consolidation of Serbian State attracting creative inflow and the self-consciousness of the young nation imbibing a sense of dignity, and above all, the enlightened patrons embodying 'King's divine will' with a deep root in the colour of the people—all these factors prepared the ground for sowing the seed of the as yet accumulated experience of Byzantine art[586] for the unique flowering of the art at Sopoćani. It was synthesis achieved in 'other' and 'inner' directed processes whereby the decoding of creeper motif became possible by the artist of Sopoćani.

Since the master-painter of Sopoćani is considered to have been directly emerging from the classical source,[587] namely, either Salonika or Constantinople itself, he had with him the synthesis of post-iconoclastic period, which was ultimately resumed and built upon the traditions established before that crisis.[588] Thus, the formal experience of the atelier producing the Sopoćani genius had those seven principal groups of influence which Rice has pointed out in the formation of Byzantine art,[589] and which could broadly be divided into two: Syrian and Helenic.[590] Kitzinger points them out as the 'complex dialectics' out of which the 'medieval form emerged.'[591] This dialectical process, having 'begun with the breakdown of classical art in the late second century,'[592] brought in the synthesis of Gupta-Sassanian art.

The master-painter of Sopoćani left the figural 'modal-conventions'[593] (plate 83) in the (saint's) attic-figure, a modulation on characteristic Kausia (The Greek colonial helmet) wearing figure and Corinthian capitals on architectural decoration over the right-hand side building painted in the 'Dormition' (plate 161). The ornamental designs of diaper-grid and palmette in the chapel of St. Simeon Nemanja (plate 18) become the 'modules' of his 'modal' differentiation.[594] The results were to be what developed in the St. Maria Magiore Antiqua out of 'Helenistic impressionism' brought by the artists from Greek East, [595] involving 'conscious and deliberate revival efforts' and having "every appearance of a gradual 'inner directed' change"—the change which the great painter of the nave at Sopoćani visioned in the ambiance provided in Hesychast's 'inner light' and Domentian's literature. Though the art historians like Rajković have categorically denied signs of local influence regarding them only as archaic or folk-loristic tendencies,[596] there are a few unavoidable signs which at once point to a past continuously surfacing from about seventh or sixth century B.C.. The archaeological findings confirm the prevalence of basic matriarchal principles in pre-historic Mother Goddesses found at Istra[597] (plate 110). The Greek frescoes (of sixth century B.C.) and Hellenic statues at Stobi including even Mycynian and Diplon influences, findings of Illyro-Thracean Cultural Traditions, Greek terracottas of Tanagra Type (near Bitolj)[598]—all these confirm a continuity of rhythmic volumes and monumental masses, specially achieved through draped figures. The Roman art and its Hellenic-Byzantine syntheses on the coastal area (from Diocleatian times to Ravenite-Justinianic mosaics in the basilica at Porech) also became a part of this unbroken cultural heritage which was naturally perpetuated by *pictores graci*—the artist from coastal regions and interior country working at Sopoćani. The whole account substantiates the view that there existed a definite 'elite' preserving and 'other-directing' the 'renaissance' of the cultural values. A clear example of such an elite was Bogdan, the nobleman, who endowed the Monastery of Kalenić (A.D. 1407-13).

Thus, it can be seen that the folk-loristic tradition of the Balkan civilisation is coming to terms with the opposites—male and female (plate 110), Life and Death, the naturalistic and the abstract, the extrovertly 'sensuous' and the introvertly 'ruling over the spirit' (plate 109) reasserted in the dichotomy of 'illumination and 'inner light'—'luminosity'—in the aesthetics of Hellenistic impressionism and that of eastern abstract. It was the 'complex dialectics' to be won over so that the artist could utilize the rhetoric lessons of 'the Ancient days' and 'sublimity of the visionary inspirations' of Domentian. The first was the 'modal-convention' to be found in the attic youth with Kausia, over which the modulations of saint's attic-figure were brought out (plate 83). The other, the zeitgeist, working as 'modal differentiation' was transformed through the 'inner-light' principles of the quietistic Hesychasts. The plastic equivalents of these 'inner-light' clues are the modules left by the artist of Sopoćani in the architectural decorations and decorative details (plate 18). In the process of finding these clues the Eastern Mediterranean littoral lands, with their 'Asiatic-solutions' gained in the Greek-colonial regions, must have come to the fore. D.T. Rice's finding a profound relationship between the paintings of Sopoćani the Church of Hagia Sophia at Trebizond,[599] further proves the synthesis. It was reached by the regions of Asiatic hinterlands of the Eastern Mediterranean, Antolian highlands, Syrian Desert, Parthian Mesopotamia and Iran, which were permeated thoroughly with Greeco-Roman forms along with their interaction with the Buddhist aesthetics of 'inner light.'[600] It did play a definitive role in the formation of styles of the 'ateliers' of the journeyman-artists, settling down in King's-town or Byzantine Monastery-villages. Successively, earlier Kuṣāṇa morphology with its Hellenic, Parthian and Indian interactions and later Gupta aesthetics[601] had given to the regions of Gandhāra style and Central Asian Art (from first or second century B.C. to seventh or eighth centuries A.D.) a synthesis which could almost be the 'anticipation' of the solution which the 'west was to adopt in the late antique and Byzantine phases' as Bussagli has rightly noted.[602]

The recent discoveries by some Soviet archaeologists and art historians near the town of Termez (Airtam and Shibarghan),[603] (plate 91) have, without doubt, proved such a synthesis by the Kuṣāṇa civilization (first century B.C. to first century A.D.).[604] A very interesting comparison between the faces of 'Annunciation' in the Church of St. Clement at Ochrid[605] (A.D. 1295, plate 92) and the musician in the central portion of the relief found at Airtam (*c.* first century B.C. to first century A.D.,[606] plate 91 shows prevalence of the 'Kushana' formal synthesis across centuries and lands.[607] The youthful 'inner growth' of this synthesis endowed to the Hellenic traditions by Michail and Eutichois (the disciples of the great founder of Serbian School, Astrapas—the 'lightning like')[608] in St. Clement became the starter of the monumental tradition of thirteenth-fourteenth century Yugoslavian Medieval painting.

To mark the channel it is important to note the manifestation of the Kuṣāṇic tradition in the works of 'Tita' of Miran School (late third-early fourth centuries A.D.). According to Mario Bussagli these Central Asian paintings 'unmistakably link the classical and Byzantine world.'[609] The isocephelic array of overlapping males and females found in the wall paintings of Kara-Tepe[610] (*c.* first century B.C), the monumental simplicity of the winged figure in shrine (3) at Miran[611] (*c.* second half of the third century A.D., plate 132) and the mystic ascetic Mahākaśyapa (Arhat) in the large cave of Qizil (A.D. 600-50, plate 149)[612]—all these anticipate the isocephelic array of patriarchs and saints in the sanctuary (nave,[613] plates 70, 150) and the Archangel Gabriel of the 'Annunciation' (north east pilaster, nave)[614] at Sopoćani (plate 131). The latter had its catalytic agent in the monumentality of the angel achieved over the Hellenistic impressionism in the St. Maria Antiqua at Rome.[615] The Gandhāra was the 'alone sphere where the illusionary forms of Hellenism fully survived' as Bussagli sees it in contrast with the Roman's turning away from it after the revitalization of the imperial mystics and the triumph of Christianity.'[616] Thus, this also substantiates that Gandhāra was the source area of 'model convention' of the Byzantine art besides being the radiating point of the 'spatial' synthesis done in the region and the adjoining areas. Mario Bussagli also points out the 'schematic perspective solutions' in the Miral School, specifically in the 'Royal figure praying'[617] (plate 152): this painting represents what Djurić explains as 'projected structure of the composition from the wall'[618] in the paintings of Sopoćani. The front side of the seat of the protagonist's figure in this painting has the black colour with grid-dot pattern. It gives a spatial resonance of the projection in addition to the grid's maintaining the surface quality. The figures are set to start getting projected from the wall surface giving the 'forthcoming' spatiality, which is the forte of the artists of Ajanta. In this way this painting becomes a kin of the 'Buddha with one-eyed Monk' (plate 153) at Ajanta (cave 10).[619] The adaptation of the Buddhist aesthetics of 'light' by the painters of Central Asia becomes the strong linking point in these works. Moreover, with regard to this aesthetics, Bussagli finds the most striking resemblance between these Central Asian works and those of Byzantine.[620] Further, as the wooden images of Pjandzikent seem to have been influenced by the Ajanta aesthetics, and there is also the evidence of an interchange of the Pjandzikent and the Byzantine works,[621] Sogdiana,[622] thus, also became a fermenting area for such a synthesis.

Ernst Kitzinger has traced the influence of the spatial synthesis of East Mediterranean mosaics over the works of Byzantine period, starting specially with the Justinian mosaics of St. Vitale at Ravenna. He calls it a 'reconciliation of the irreconcilable inasmuch as it adheres to the surface while bringing out 'movement and luxuriant growth everywhere.'[623] This he traces to the eastern influence reinterpreting the geometric patterns in organic terms with the result that the grid-patterns of the said mosaics (in the East Mediterranean) turned into the 'spread' and 'potential endlessness' of rinceaux growth. Further, the vogue of 'inhabited' rinceaux gave the aesthetics of surface modulations in primary and secondary structures according to the relative importance to the 'inhabiting' animals or birds. To this arboreal growth-module was added water -cosmological significance with inscriptions like—'The tree landscape stands for the earth, the aquatic band around it for the encircling ocean'—in the mosaic floor at St. Demetrius in Nikoplis in Epirus (A.D. 225-50). It has the basic similarity with the principles and ideals involved in the 'atelier of S. Vitale' as pointed out by Kitzinger.[624]

The water-cosmology with the 'Tree' growth is basic in Indian philosophy synthesised in art forms since the Mauryan period.[625] The artist of Ajanta had given full plastic signification to such origin from cosmic matter in the aesthetics of 'forthcoming' or *prāṇa* (breath).

Motifs like the aquatic birds flanking the flower vases in the dome mosaic of the church of St. George at Salonika (fifth century A.D.)[626] bear out the above mentioned significance added to this Eastern Orthodox Church.

With the conclusions already reached by Ernst Kitzinger namely, that Justinian aesthetics influenced the post-Iconoclastic works of Byzantine art and with Djurić's acceptance of a link between the works of Salonika and Sopoćani,[627] it is not surprising that the 'projected structure of the composition' arrived at Sopoćani had its base in Indian aesthetics of 'forthcoming.' This view is reinforced by the Buddhistic quietistic Hesychast contemplation providing the psychological make-up and the rhetorics of inner-light given by the works of Domentian.

Such 'forthcoming' is best expressed in 'The Appearance of Christ to the Holy Women'[628] (plate 62). The aesthetics of 'inner-light' gets its manifestation as light-gradients employed in building up the forms also. The best examples are 'the Virgin from the presentation of the Donor' (south-wall nave, plate 140) and 'the transition of the Relics of St Simeon Nemanja' (in the chapel of St. Simeon, vault, north side, plate 142). Such plasticity along with a mark between the eyebrows (*ūrṇā*), as a proof of inner contemplation, is perceptible in St. John the Divine (diaconicon, east wall,[629] plate 97).

Christ's 'divine power and the passing of earthly things'[630] manifested with dignified and monumental grace with most expressive and laconic poses and movements of figures, rhetorics of restrained emotional expression on faces,[631] suggestive space units and folds of cloth, mastery over the perspective and spatial implications giving the 'forthcoming' and dematerializing of form on the tactile surface of the whole wall—'the borderland'—turning into (rinceaux) rhythmos and grid for space division—all these constitute the originality of Sopoćani. Above all, these formal and plastic ingredients are presented, as if in an eager anxiety, to become the space within the church striving for vertical ascendance to the 'Heavenly dome' and coming back into the monumental dignity of the figures and in the space of the 'New Jerusalem' or 'Pure land.' This excellence is attained by the creatively ecclectic genius of the artist. He had the great vision of the 'inner-light' providing him with 'spiritual strength and sublimity to collectively endure with dignity the sorrows of human life.'[632] The duality of rhythmos and *symmetria*, resolved through the Gandhāra-Hellenic inspirations took the master of Sopoćani close to the aesthetics of classical style of Greece of fifth century B.C., (plate 85) its art being 'a fit vehicle to express both the idealism and the awareness of the tragic'[633]—the oratorical sublime of Byzantine. The aesthetic of surface, which Miljković Pepek calls 'the dogmatic principles of Byzantine aesthetics in finding the solutions for the composition,'[634] along with the maintenance of the logic of nature itself, transforms the entire units of the walls of Sopoćani into beautiful icons.

Comparative

Among the influences flowering into the art of Ajanta and Sopoćani, it is pronouncedly deduced from the foregoing study that similarities abound except for the factors concerning time and space. Their pictorial syntax ranged right from the Greek classicism to the Sassanian and Gupta art including Hellenism,

Roman East Mediterranean terracottas, Gandhāra and Kuṣāṇa synthesis with Central Asian heritage. Added to all this were the basic questions on existence and the almost universal answers provided by the primitive and folk traditions. All this sums up in fact as essence of 'an age, a whole period of civilized world history'—this observation of Rice suits Ajanta as aptly as it is said of Byzantine.

As Byzantium of Justinian era[635] produced works similar to the pictorial syntax synthesised in Central Asian Art and since Ajanta was the Mother-school of this art, it is not hard to deduce the relationship between the art of Ajanta and Byzantine (plates 131, 132, 148, 149, 150). Thus the inference is that motifs such as water birds used with creeper in the Byzantine churches, and the lotus having its triangular and mountain-like pericarp topped with the sun in Yugoslavian churches (plate 111) support Sopoćani master's 'modal convention' (plate 83) having been from Asiatic hinterlands. And the '*trimūrti* motif' (plate 101) and *ūrṇā* developed in Yugoslavia (plate 97) substantiate a relation with Indian plastic solutions. The 'projected composition' becomes the apex of such relations developed in the vein of Hasychast contemplation.

Over a thousand years of Byzantium's preoccupation with classical art and its refinement at Sopoćani 'in the true spirit of its inspiration in a Hellenic past,' came from their store-house of Gandhāra which remained the 'lone' survivor of such traditions. This store-house in its later phases included the synthesis of Ajanta. Thus the position of Kuṣāṇa, Sassanian and Gupta compost (first century B.C. to seventh or eighth century A.D.) becomes evident as a radiating point.

The prime synthesis or the originality of Sopoćani lies in adapting the canons of 'forthcoming' and inner light or luminosity. These are also the basics of the art of Ajanta. Comparatively speaking, while adapting the light gradients as colour values and lines, arbitrary use of light and shade and almost similar intentions of the artists in planer and spatial variances and schematic perspective solutions, the artists of Sopoćani gave, though apparently, the synthesis in 'sculptural' or 'reaching the space'[636] projections of monumental figures and architectural units. But in his vehemence to overwhelm, the rhythmos, in duality with *symmetria*, got upper hand in giving signification to the linearity. As such the contours got consistency bringing about the consistent interstices also (plate 130). This effect was reinforced by the angularities resulting from the acceptance of object and space relationship in an unresolved contradiction, e.g., sculptural faces and frontal massiveness of bodies, light and shade along with the modelling in colour and values, and fundamental colours used for separating the mass of the body and the background (plates 62, 161). The white lines (of luminosity—II Indian manner—plates 130, 148) given alongwith the dark-contours produced a solarization effect in a skeletal frame. The use of gold brought the background on tactile plane making the frescoed figures look silhouettes; thus, a dematerializing monumental wall was achieved. All this became a part of the classical aesthetics expressing both the 'idealism and the awareness of the tragic,' the oratorical sublime. In effect, the canons of 'forthcoming' and inner light were also utilized in the vein of the classical aesthetics by the artists of Sopoćani.

Transforming the fervent rhythms of Amarāvati with modularities of 'biological' or creeper growth of Bagh, massive volumes of Mathurā and mellow surfaces of Sārnāth school, the artists of Ajanta made the space, volume and mass participate in the movement of forthcoming[637] and caused the whole wall to turn into the organic flux of the creeper module. There was no acceptance of the contradiction of duality in this cosmic relationship.

On the contrary, the anabolic organic flux resolved all such contradictions and the whole wall breathed with the aesthetics of *prāṇa.* The intimate linearity did not over-rule the monumental form[638] achieved through the subtle use of complementaries and the dynamism of landing tones or admixtures. Incidentally, with a view to conveying such living forms the artists of Sopoćani also resorted to the use of such colour scheme in the faces. This brings to the fore the similar use of light gradients in building up luminous forms (plates 141, 142).

It is pertinent also to point out the similarities between the logical outcome of the aesthetics of *prāṇa*[639] (coded in creeper module with the *kṣyavṛddhi* and *nimnonnatavibhāga* plasticity) as arrived at in India as well as Yugoslavia. Dr. Ratan Parimoo (1976) has shown that the Elephanta sculptors were putting into high-relief what had been gained by the painters of Ajanta (cf., p. 17); thus, the plastic solutions of *tri-mūrti* also fall within *prāṇa* aesthetics. This logic conforms to Rudolf Arnheim's demonstration that the bay-window (types) and the small Sumerian bronzes showing divinities with four faces symmetrically arranged around the head, are the outcome of the plastic intensions of the artists to present the tactile volumes of the projected window and the head respectively.[640] The *tri-mūrti* plasticity was also achieved in Yugoslavian medieval art to represent the three headed Saint Trinity (plate 101) a concept which germinated at Sopoćani with the decoding of the creeper module within characteristic growth.

Lastly, both actualized the 'breathing' of inner space of the church or the cave. The church achieved it by dematerializing the stable massiveness of the wall while the space breathed the verticality and the returning movement. Such movements were accomplished at Ajanta with 'breathing' walls.

REFERENCES

1. David L. Snellgrove, (Gen. ed.,) *The Image of the Buddha,* 1978, p. 123.
2. Lotus like feet, broad and stout chest, lotus-eyes, arms resembled a scant-elephant, loveliness as Indra, Rāma etc., and the moon, brave and spirited like Lion: R. S. Gupte and B.D. Mahajan, *Ajanta, Ellora and Aurangabad Caves,* 1962, p. 256.
3. 'A Haṃsa has a beautiful face, nice waist, a gait like that of swan and is strong, has arms like the king of serpents, i.e., *Śeṣa,* moon-white complexion and eyes having the colour of honey.' The feet of *Cakravartin* should be shown with *jāla, ūrṇā* (tuft of hair) between eyebrows, hands charming 'red like the blood of hare and slenderly curved,' hair—'thin, wary, shiny' and 'like dark blue sapphire,' halo is proportionate to head and circle resembling god. Dr. Priyabala Shah, *Viṣṇudharamottara Purāṇa*, third Khaṇḍa, Vol. II, 1961, pp. 107-09.
4. '*Prajñā-pāramitā,* who, here as elsewhere at Alchi, is dark green in colour. Thus, both by colour and by membership of Amōghasiddhi's family, she is explicitly identified with Goddess Tārā.'—David L. Snellgrove and Tadeusz Skorupski, *The Cultural Heritage of Ladakh,* 1977, p. 56.
5. The earth goddess is of 'Parrot colour, garment white like the beams of moon.' (Dr. Priyabala Shah, op. cit., p. 153). The inscription also says of 'white dress as the beams of moon, face was like full moon, adorned by modesty and good behaviour', (R.S. Gupte and B.D. Mahajan, op. cit., p. 258).
6. As per pre-Buddhist and later references 'Tree of Life' 'synonymous with all existence, all the worlds, all life, it springs up, out, or drawn into space from its root in the navel centre of the Supreme Being, Varuna, Mahāyakṣa, Asura, Brahman, as he lies extended on the back of the waters, the possibilities of existence and the source of his abundance. That tree is his procession in a likeness, the emanation of his fiery-energy (*tejas*) as light, the expiration of his breath (*prāṇa*); he is its wise, indestructible mover:' A.K. Coomaraswamy, *Elements of Buddhist Iconography,* 1972, p. 8.

   From Vegetal Basic Form not only the naga-body developed but also a type of Buddha image characterized by the possession of a hood or cobra-hood 'Muchilinda-type:' F.D.K. Bosch, *The Golden Germ* 1960, p. 201. Bosch further explains that hand's 'protective and gift giving gestures are metamorphosis of a five-hooded cobra, a protective deity transformed from outspread shoots. Even in literature, the titles are based on Tree-motif, i.e., *Śabdakalpadruma Avadāna, Kalpalatā* etc., the narratives are also painted like lotus-scrolls carrying '*rasa*' dividing and separating different units like its 'fruits:' ibid., p. 216-28, 237. Thus a shaded tree, a fruitful tree or alike, are all symbolized as motifs.
7. The identity between *stūpa* and bodhi-tree leads to similar ways of worship and decoration: *Padmamūla's* 'golden colour transferred to *stūpa* is confirmed by Hiuen-Tsang:' F.D.K. Bosch, op. cit., 1960, pp. 171-72.
8. Planery with stem as axis and two-side branches (Bosch, op. cit., p. 70): 'Hom' motif, (plate 21) as used in Assyrian seals having animal or bird confronted on either side of a plant-motif: G. Bazin, *A Concise History of Art* I, 1958, Illus. 176, p. 152 adapted in Buddhist-iconography as adorned sun-pillar having male on the right and female on the left, e.g., at Sanchi (illus. 11—Stella Kramrisch, *The Art of India,* 1955, plate 29). As such, the left side of the female creative principle was given attributes (on an icon) having qualities like those

of hollow, bent, cool and dark objects, i.e., moon, plants, flowers, bow, *ghantā*, bowl, book etc., and to the right were attributes of the male creative principle, i.e., of pointed, straight sharp, hot or luminous—as arrow, *vajra*, sacrificial knife, sword, sun etc. (F.D.K. Bosch op. cit., p. 220).

—C.f. plate no. 13, 'Nāgarāja and his consort' (cave 19), conforming to the above-mentioned *Hiraṇyagarbha* inconographic scheme (cf. pp. 89, 118n., 22., 230n., 78) e.g., lifted index finger of the left hand of the wisk-bearer expresses female consciousness as does the lotus in the left hand of the *nāga* queen. Contrarily, lotus in the right hand of Bodhisattva Padmapāni (cave 1) symbolizes the male (*Agni—prajñā*) principle.

9. Irne Gajjar, *Ancient Indian Art and the West*, 1971, p. 130.
10. A.K. Coomaraswamy, op. cit., 1972, p. 77, note.
11. F.D.K. Bosch, op cit., 1960, p. 163.
12. Ibid., p. 163.
—A.K. Coomaraswamy, op. cit., 1972, p. 20, Fig. D, page 31.
—David L. Snellgrove, (Gen. ed.,) *The Image of the Buddha*, op. cit., p. 40.
13. F.D.K. Bosch, op. cit., p. 85.
14. The narrations like that of Buddha's image being made out of his projected image or shadow on a canvas done on the request of Udayana (*Divyāvadāna*) are probably outcome of such a situation.
—Manohar Kaul, *Trends in Indian Painting*, 1961, p. 6.
—Albert Grünwedel, *Buddhist Art in India*, 1972, pp. 67-68, refers to Bimbasāra's artists in this reference quoting from the *śāstras* that Buddha's image was made during his life time.
15. Narrative incidences were reduced to suggestive signs of the most expressive situations, e.g., in *Vidhurpaṇḍita Jātaka*, cave 1, the horses repeated in a decorative form not only connect the scenes but as well indicate Yakṣa Purnaka as a visitor.
—The cubic rocks with suggestion of tree or animal etc., are also in the category of such representations—palace facades, pavilions, balconies *sarvatobhadrika* type ceremonial pavilions for various suggestions, folds and ribbons for speed, action and airiness; *sthānas, mudrās* and eye gestures for suggesting conversations, conversation motifs for conjugal-intimacy, various suggestions (as propounded in *Citrasūtra*) for seasons (as flowers of the season) taste (as ants are shown to bespeak sweetness, cave 17), and environments.
—The motif par excellence seems to be *gavākṣa* window (plate 44) as enigmatic as sphinxes. It is similar to the insertion of portraits here and there especially as busts (either divided from body by some object, e.g., with plates of offerings as near *Avalokiteśvara* (cave 1, plates 44, 157) or just inserted with suggestive gestures and *mudrās*. C. Sivaramamurti finds it as the evolution of *caitya*-window (*The Art of India*, 1977, p. 547).
16. F.D.K. Bosch op. cit., 1960, (*Lalitvistara*, ed. Lefmann, I, p. 196) quoted on page 56:
—Buddha as Logos, *Dīgha Nikāya*, III, 84, as 'The Eye in the World' I, 158.
A.K. Coomaraswamy, op. cit., 1972, p. 77, note.
17. Albert Grünwedel, op. cit., 1972, p. 46.
—Mario Bussagli points out that the cupolas of the Bamiyan sanctuaries are covered with Buddha images arranged in continuous circles or hexagons, forming a mandorola, symbolically filling the sky, *Paintings of Central Asia*, 1963, p. 36.

—David L. Snellgrove and others cite Buddha in mandorola (Italian: almond), illus. 64: *The Image of The Buddha*, 1978, p. 100.

18. *Ajanta Paintings*, L.K.A., 1956, Pl. III, Decoration of the ceiling, cave 2.
19. D.C. Bhattacharya, *Studies in Buddhist Iconography*, 1978, p. 2.
20. Ibid., p. 31.
21. Ernst Kitzinger, *Byzantine Art in the Making*, 1977, p. 19.
22. Ibid., p. 5.
23. John Backwith, *Early Medieval Art*, 1964, p. 44.
24. R.M. Frye, *Milton's Imagery and the Visual Art*, 1978, p. 169.

    —Serious countenance of Christ is the other example being certainly not from gospel stories. Isaiah's prophecy of 'the man of sorrow and acquainted with grief' is an anti-thesis since living Christ enjoins his disciples, 'when ye fast be not of sad countenance':

    J.P. Smyth, *A People's Life of Christ*, 1926, pp. 103-4.
25. Ernst Kitzinger, op. cit., p. 124, *see* Glossary.

    —'Other directed' includes iconographic conventions as given by the fathers of the Church. The Decrees of the second Council of Nicaea clarifies thus 'the composition of figures is not the invention of painters but the law and tradition of the Catholic Church, and the ordination and dispensation of our father': *An Introduction to Literature and Fine Arts*, (eds.) D. Thimme and W.W. Heist., 1952, p. 38.
26. Ernst Kitzinger, op. cit., p. 123. *see* Glossary.
27. D. T. Rice, *Byzantine Art*, 1935, p. 122.
28. Ibid., p. 125.
29. Ibid.
30. A. K. Coomaraswamy, *Christian and Oriental Philosophy of Art*, 1974, p. 41.
31. G. Every, *Christian Mythology*, 1970, p. 136.
32. D.T. Rice, *The Appreciation of Byzantine Art*, 1972, p. 121.

    —P.A. Michelis, *An Aesthetic Approach to Byzantine Art*, 1964, p. 40.
33. i.e., the presentation of saints and patriarchs on plinths for 'him that over-cometh will I make a pillar in the temple of my God, and he shall go no more out: and I will write upon him the name of my God, and the name of the city of my God, which is new Jerusalem, which cometh down out of heaven from my God....' (*Rev.* 3:12). It is presented as a 'community city' and 'Garden' as was heaven presented since the early middle ages—R.M. Frye, op. cit., p. 192.
34. D.T. Rice, op. cit., 1972, pp. 121-22.

    —Asunto, 'Treatises on Byzantine Art,' in *Encyclopedia of World Art*, Vol. II, 1961, Column 280.
35. R.M. Frye, op. cit., p. 196.
36. Ernst Kitzinger, op. cit., p. 77.
37. D.T. Rice, op. cit., 1972, p. 134.

    —Dr. Mirjana Ljubinković, *Ravanica*, 1966, p. 1 (illus.). This motif as well became the royal insignia of Byzantines with adorsed-eagles. Philip Sherrad, *Byzantium*, 1966, pp. 120, illustration 187.

    —This motif with frontal birds is found in Yugoslavia: illustration on page 28, Laidoyer Pro Domo, 'Povodom Izlozbe-Jugoslovens kog Srendjevekovnog Slikarstve Plastike U Parizu, 1950 Godine,' in *Jugoslavija*, Zime, 1950.

38. F.D.K. Bosch, op. cit., pp. 14, 219-20; cf. pp. 89, 118n., 22, 230n., 78.
39. Svetozar Radojčić, *Mileševa*, 1963, plate 20.
40. F.D.K. Bosch, op. cit., p. 85. A clear conception of cross seen in three dimensions is given in the mosaics of *c.* 1315 at the Church of the Holy Apostles at Thessaloniki, i.e. in 'Descent into Limbo,' especially in the hands of Christ who frees Adam and Eve:
    Andre Graber, *Greek Mosaics*, 1964, plate 26.
41. Ernst Kitzinger, op. cit., Fig. 98.
42. R.M. Frye, op. cit., 1978, p. 231.
43. Vojislav J. Djuric, *Sopoćani*, 1963, p. 116.
44. *The Oxford Companion to Art*, (ed.,) Harold Osborne, 1970, pp. 334-35.
45. Philip Sherrard, op. cit., 1966, pp. 148-49.
    —D.T. Rice, op. cit., 1972, p. 13.
46. P.A. Michelis, op. cit., 1964, p. 39.
47. R.M. Frye, op. cit., p. 94.
48. Ibid., p. 201.
49. Ibid., p. 199.
50. D.T. Rice, op. cit., 1972, pp. 8, 9.
51. P.A. Michels, op. cit., p. 93.
52. R.M. Frye, op. cit., pp. 44-45 'Put on the whole armour of God...' (*Eph.* 6:11-18).
53. Laidoyer Pro Domo, op. cit., 1950, illustration 'detail on the southern portal at Studenića', p. 16.
54. Vojislav J. Djurić, *Sopoćani*, 1963, pl. LVIII.
55. R.M. Frye, op. cit., p. 139.
56. P.A. Michalis, op. cit., p. 177.
    —Vojislav J. Djurić, *Sopoćani*, 1963, Chapel of St. George, illus. p. 140.
57. Ernst Kitzinger, op. cit., p. 122.
58. H.A. Groenewegen-Frankfort and Bernard Ashmole, *The Ancient World*, 1967, p. 38.
59. Ibid., p. 38.
60. P.A. Michelis, op. cit., p. 119.
61. i.e., in 'Christ appearing to the Apostles' (Pl. XXIV—Vojislav J. Djurić, *Sopoćani*, the dropping and fluttering of the edges of the cloth suggests sudden appearance of Christ and the right side apostle, as if taken aback in surprise (plate 38).
    —The feeling otherwise is suggested in hands, gestures and body postures.
    —Djurić too speaks of dramatic movements, stress on dramatic happening together with structural support to total composition through the fluttering curves of clothes: *Sopoćani*, 1963, p. 58. The forthcoming of resurrected Christ is suggested by the flying of the corner of his stole in 'The Appearance of Christ to the Holy Women', *Sopoćani*, 1963, Plate XXII (plate 64.)
62. Vojislav J. Djurić, *Sopoćani*, 1963, p. 65.
63. Radivoje Ljubinković, *The Church of the Apostles in the Patriarchate of Peć*, 1964, p. VIII.
64. A. K. Coomaraswamy, op. cit., 1972, p. 83, note 108.
65. Ibid., p. 26.
66. F.D.K. Bosch, op. cit., 1960, p. 85.
67. A.K. Coomaraswamy, op. cit., 1972, p. 26.

68. Vojislav J. Djurić, *Sopoćani*, 1963, Pl. XXVI.
69. A.K. Coomaraswamy, op. cit., 1972, p. 74, note 56.
70. Ibid., p. 28.
71. D.T. Rice, op. cit., 1972 p. 69.
72. A.K. Coomaraswamy, op. cit., 1972, p. 28.
73. A.K. Coomaraswamy supported by the authority of R. Guenon, E. Rousselle and J. Strzygowski aptly points out that the 'Axle-Tree and Axis are the same, of course, as the trunk of Tree of Life, the stem of the Lotus of space and the vertical of the cross are with the Fiery Pillar and with the Sacrificial Post—when universally considered.' Ibid., p. 82, note 100.
74. Cf. pp. 114, 116.
75. A.K. Coomaraswamy, op. cit., 1972, pp. 18, 68 note 28.
76. *Rev.* 5:5, 21:23, 22:1, 22:2.
77. Mystically, Christ is the fruit of the Tree of Life replacing the fruit of the Tree of Knowledge in the 'Crucifixion.' Erich Neumann, *The Great Mother*, 1955, p. 252.
78. S. Radhakrishnan points out that '*Iśvara* the personal God becomes *Hiraṇyagarbha* the World-soul which is said to be the first-born son of God' (*Eastern Religions and Western Thought*, 1975, p. 127),

    — In this way the *Hiraṇyagarbha* or the 'Golden Germ' having the *agni* (light or fire element) and *soma* (water element,) is applicable to the basics of both Christian and Buddhist iconographies. The *Padmamūla* and *Brahmamūla*, (plate 22) as elaborated by F.D.K. Bosch (*The Golden Germ*, 1960) determine the common basics.
79. V.J. Djurić, *Sopoćani*, 1963, p. 23, (presented in the hell.)
80. स्थानप्रमाणं भूलम्भो मधुरत्वं विभक्तता।
    सादृश्यं क्षयवृद्धी च गुणाष्टकमिदं स्मृतम् 43:19.
    Chitrasūtram (Trans.) Tarinish Jha, in *Sammelan Patrika*, 'Kala aṅka' Śakabd 1880, p. 472.

    — *Sthāna*—position, *pramāṇa*—proportionate measurement, *bhūlamba*—perpendicular reaching to the ground, *madhuratva*—sweetness, *vibhaktatā*—distinctness, *sādṛśya*—semblance, *kṣaya*-diminution and *vṛddhi*—augmentation.

    Dr. Priyabala Shah, *Visṇudharmottara-Purāṇa*, third Khaṇḍa, Vol. II, 1961, p. 129.
81. *Moving Focus*, 1978, p. 35.
82. Tekton (LL, Gr., Greek) builder. Indian tradition also speaks of *Takṣka* as builder or sculptor (D.N. Shukla, *Samrangan-Sūtradhāra*, part. II, 1967, p. 7).
83. Clement Greenburg, 'After Abstract expressionism,' in *Art International*, op. cit., 1962.
84. Lawrence Allowey, 'Formless Breaking Down Form—The Paintings of Agnes Martin,' in *Studio International*, Feb. 1973, pp. 61, 62.
85. R.P. Lohse, 'Standard, Series, Module: New Problems and Task of Painting,' in (ed.,) Georgy Kepes, *Module Symmetry Proportion*, 1966, p. 145.
86. H.H. Arnason, *History of Modern Art*, 1977, p. 678.
87. Ernst Kitzinger, op. cit., 1977, pp. 89-90.
88. Ibid., p. 91.
89. V.J. Djurić, *Sopoćani*, 1963, p. 64.
90. Stella Karmrisch, *A Survey of Painting in the Deccan*, 1937, pp. 3-5.
91. Quoted by John M. Moffitt in 'An Historical Basis for Interpreting Styles of Late 18th to

late 20th century Pictorial Artworks,' in *Leonardo*, vol. XII4, 1979, pp. 296-97. Braque has stated that he and Picasso had been trying to paint 'not objects but the space they engender:' G.H. Hamilton, *19th and 20th Century Art*, p. 208.

92. Ibid., p. 298 note 6.
93. Ibid., pp. 298 note 6, 298-300.
94. Foreword for Maurizio Taddei, *Monuments of Civilization India*, 1977, p. 7.
95. *Citrasūtram*, (43:29), op. cit., Śakabd 1880, p. 473.
96. Dr. Priyabala Shah, (*Citrasūtra* 43:21, 22) *Viṣṇudharmottara-Purāṇa*, third *khaṇḍa*, Vol. II, 1961, p. 136.
97. *Citrasūtra* (41.1) (Satya, Vaiṇika, Nāgara and Miśra are the four styles enumerated). —'Whatever (*Yatkiñcid*) painting depicts semblance of the world (*lokasādṛśyam Citram*) is called *satya*. It is elongated (*dīrghāngam*), well proportioned (*sapramāṇaṃ*), delicate (*sukumāram*), and has a proper background (*subhūmikam*):' Dr. Priyabala Shah, op. cit., p. 120.
98. Dwelling on the unity of the plastic-arts A.K. Bhattacharya described the stylistic divisions given in *Citralakṣaṇa* (1974, p. 41) as that *Citra* is depiction 'by showing all parts of the body,' *Ardhacitra* 'the half that is shown in clinging to the wall,' and *Citrābhāsa* 'when painted.' These definitions suit sculpture as done in round in 'alto-relievo,' 'mezzo-rilievo' and 'basso-rilievo,' to transform these into the characteristics (*lakṣana*) of painting (*citra*) these are required to be translated into 'rilievo,' *nimnonnatavibhāga*, of painting.
99. A-Tectonic Spatial, John F. Moffitt defines it as illusionistic and visionary, 'real' as a scene from a didactic stage-drama. He further elaborates that to convince the 'truth' the objects are presented in a state of becoming or flux. It has principle of transcendent expression, concept of infinity and timelessness, and, open, spatial and painterly form with pictorial unity and narrative focus—arousing both the emotions and intellect, ecstasy of mystical belief—and contains allegory and myths. With genre subjects it has universal psychological characteristics and reactions, op. cit., 1979, p. 299.
100. Germain Bazin, *A Concise History of Art*, part II, 1964, pp. 528-29.
101. Such as that 'fragments of world rather than world in themselves, which overflow the limits of the frame. Baroque forms are imponderable... organic, living, comprehensive, resulting in a close dependence of the form one upon the other:' G. Bazin, op. cit., p. 524.
102. 'Whereas Italian Baroque, with its rich mediaeval legacy of pictorial elements, made of a plastic almost a pictorial art:' P.A. Michelis, *An Aesthetic Approach to Byzantine Art*, 1964, p. 200.
103. 'Which is four sided (*caturasram*), well finished (*susampūrṇam*), not long (*nadīrghāngam*) and having proper measurements (*pramāṇam*) and rich in the attainment of postures (*Sthānalambhāḍhyam*):' Dr. Priyabala Shah, *op.cit.*, 1961, p. 120.
104. '... strike a balance between form as it is conceived by the intellect on the one hand and the direct observation of nature on the other, express itself in centred compositions and through a strict arrangement of component parts, each of which retains its distinct unity; Classical forms are ponderable and static, and obey the laws of gravity, while movements are governed by rhythms and may be reduced to a harmonic cadence:' G. Bazin, op. cit., 1964, p. 524.
105. Tectonic Spatial has been defined by John F. Moffitt as having canons of idealization

with credence, organic rhythms (not rigid) mostly with axial composition, three quarter oblique views and bent axes, spatial and tactile approach with principal of three-dimensionality, rational subordination to the primary idea of beauty, generalized psychology, secularization and humanization, op. cit., *Leonardo*, vol. XII, 4, 1979, pp. 298-300.

106. 'All parts of which are firmly set (*dṛḍhopacitasarvāngam*), circular (*vartulaṃ*), not thickly bright (*na ghanolvaṇam*) and showing just a few (*svalpa*) garlands and ornaments:' Dr. Priyabala Shah, op. cit., p. 120.
107. John F. Moffitt defines it as having linear and relief type depiction, rigid postures, flat colours, schematic anatomy, tectonic principles and repetitive rhythm; op. cit., 1979, p. 298.
108. Dr. Priyabala Shah, op. cit., p. 120.
109. Ibid., pp. 299-300.
110. *Citrasūtram* (43:28, 29), *op. cit.*, Śakabd 1880, p. 473.
111. J.F. Moffitt, op. cit., 1979, p. 300.
112. C. Sivaramamurty, *The Painters in Ancient India*, 1978, p. 19.
113. Stella Kramrisch, op. cit., 1937, p. 6.
114. Maurizio Taddei, *Monuments of Civilization India*, 1977, p. 133.
115. Dr. Priyabala Shah explains that the *vṛttis* or poetic styles hold good for architecture and the styles of painting and that when their syntheses were utilized they produced Miśra. (Dr. Priyabala Shah, *Viṣṇudharmottara Purāṇa*, Third Khaṇḍa, Vol. II, 1961, pp. 121-22). Translating the *vṛttis* as 'modes,' Dr. K. Krishnamoorthy quotes Ānandavardhana that "once the *Dhvani* theory of the suggested-suggester relationship is grasped, the so called 'modes' relating to the nature of sound as well as to the nature of meanings will become intelligible:" (Dr. K. Krishnamoorthy, *Dhvanyāloka of Ānandavardhana*, 1974, pp. 260-61). Similar discrimination is alluded to by Ernst Kitzinger in explaining 'modes' (Ernst Kitzinger, op. cit., 1977, p. 19).
116. Robert Rosenblum quoted by John F. Moffitt, op. cit., 1979, p. 297.
117. Such a figure push 'into and over the ground:' (Rudolf Arnheim, *Art and Visual Perception*, 1960, p. 194). In the canvases of Barnett Newman such vertical line touching the edges of the canvas establishes "a tangible tension between the colour surface and the 'line' which seems to be a structural or spatial opening and closing especially with its deliberately fragmented edges:" (H.H. Arnason, *History of Modern Art*, 1977, p. 510).
118. The frame of the window 'confirms the figure character of the opening and provides a protrusion beneath which the ground surface of the wall can end.' Rudolf Arnheim, op. cit., 1960, p. 193.
119. Since its 'dynamic forces irradiate symmetrically in all directions:' ibid., p. 342.
120. Rudolf Arnheim has demonstrated that such interstices get a 'playful alternation' with figures and preserve the surface: op. cit., 1960, p. 190.
121. Stella Kramrisch, op. cit., 1937, p. 26.
122. (Arnheim, op. cit., p. 201). In an over-crowded view the perception receives gradual denominators of bulging rhythm. This has been verified by the film director of Josef Von Sternberg that 'space was most visible when crowded with objects' (Arnheim, op. cit., 1960, p. 386 Note p. 201).
123. Interrupted contour completes only the simple shape otherwise the point of intersection becomes consistent and dominates: (Arnheim, op. cit., 1960, pp.200-201). The famous

carving of four deers in cave 1, Ajanta, is an example of sharing of contours by the similarity of consistent shapes (Louis Frederic, *Indian Temples and Sculptures*, 1959, p. 106.)

124. '... the receding parts of the face are contracted the more visible parts enlarged ... the Indian terminology, as we see, applies perfectly to this treatment of foreshortening:' Mario Bussagli, *Painting of Central Asia*, 1963, p. 32.

—Compare Plates 126, 127/164, 163: latter would bespeak of such 'bi-positional *tribhaṅga* even in the faces in contrast with the anatomical structuring of the faces in plates 126 and 164.

125. 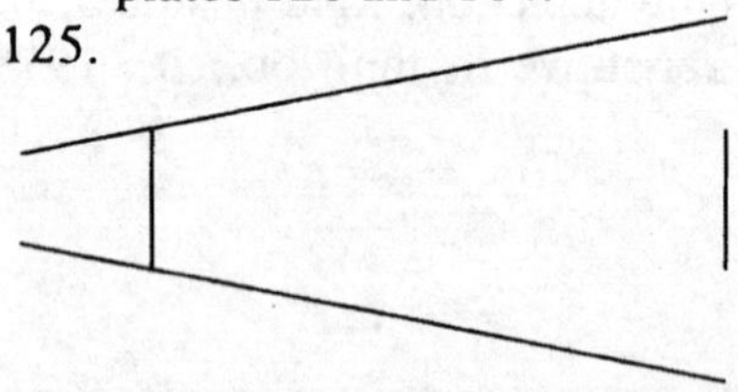

'Even in a flat plane of bundle of beams issuing from centre causes distortions similar to those observed in three-dimensional pyramidal space. It is hard to believe that the two verticals (in the figure accompanying) are of the equal size. The one closer to the 'vanishing point' appears much larger:' Arnheim, op. cit., 1960, p. 387. Note. p. 222.

126. It is a term used by Arnheim for orthographic projection or parallel perspective as its features are known in isometric method. Here 'all frontally oriented surface maintains their objective size relations regardless of their distances for the observer' (Arnheim, op. cit., 1960, 228).

In 'a gate in King Brahmdatta's Palace' (cave 2, plate 137) the frontal and side planes run diagonally giving 'angular-isometric' as Arnheim calls it adding that the object develops as an invented pattern which is given rhythmic ajdustments either by mirror image or repetitions to balance various obliquities rendering a multidirectional spatial system or 'multi-oriented' system as in Pompeian paintings (Arnheim, op. cit., 1966, 230.) Cubist's experiments with such spatial frame-work led to disintegration of object, as is verified from what Baroque stated that he and Picasso had been trying to paint 'not objects but the space they engender:' (G.H. Hamilton, *19th and 20th Century Art*, p. 208): the 'spatial obsession' of Ajanta painters made the space a tactile objectivity 'forthcoming' with all referents.

127. 'Gamma motion' is a kind of perceived locomotion in a visual pattern varying with the shape and orientation. 'It occurs essentially along the axes of what I have called the structural skeleton of the pattern... along the line of force.' The gamma motion permits observation of 'perceptual force at work in the creation of patterns' furnishing 'a kind of anatomy of the forces or tensions characterizing the dynamics of patterns when they are observed at rest under normal conditions:' Arnheim, op. cit., 1966, pp. 340-41).

128. Ibid., p. 342.

129. 'This however, extends only as far as the forward movement allows, now here, now there, a shiver across its impact, a tendency to sink back into its origin. It remains in that stage and does not go further back carried as it is by the metaphysical movement of forthcoming. Elastically it is replete with the antagonistic tendency:' Stella Kramrisch, op. cit., 1937, p. 11.

130. Mario Bussagli, 'Introduction,' M. Bussagli and Calembus Sivaramamurti, *5000 Years of the Art of India*, nd. p. 32.

131. Madanjeet Singh, *The Cave Paintings of Ajanta*, 1965, pl. 38, p. 80.

132. Dr. P. Shah, op. cit., 1961, p. 124.

133. Ernst Kitzinger, op. cit., 1977, p. 91.

134. R. Arnheim, op. cit., 1960, pp. 194-95.
135. 'Convexity makes for figure, concavity for ground.... The opposite effect is usual when he fixates the pointed angles between the bulges, because their narrowness makes for figure character:' R. Arnheim, ibid., p. 185.
136. P.A. Michelis, op. cit., 1964, p. 40.
137. Ibid., p. 40.
138. R. Arnheim, op. cit., 1966, p. 164.
139. The same dynamism is suggested in the decorative panels over the closed doors behind the Resurrected Christ ('Appearance to the Apostles'). The central square in these panels is put into sharp convergences and is shown beaming forward. (Cezanne's experiments are significant in this regard, e.g., Illus. 214, p. 132, H.H. Arnason, *History of Modern Art*, 1977, Fig. 63.)

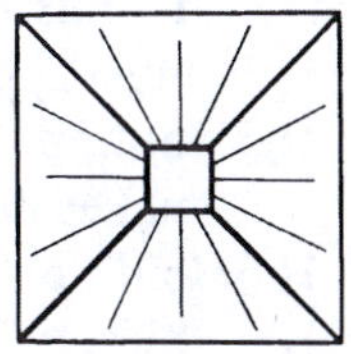

140. 'Heroes of the artist of Sopoćani feel that in that space they move freely and easily:' V.J. Djurić, *Sopoćani*, 1963, p. 68.
141. John F. Moffitt, op. cit., 1979, pp. 298-99.
142. Demus Otto, *Byzantine Art and the West*, 1970, p. 194.
143. John F. Moffitt, op. cit., p. 299.
144. P.A. Michelis, op. cit., p. 40.
—Stella Kramrisch, op. cit., 1937, p. 33.
145. C. Greenberg, 'Foreword' to Maurizio Taddei, op. cit., 1977, p. 7.
146. Since owing to the unsimplified shape of the figures the points of intersections become consistent and dominant (Arnheim, op. cit., 1960, pp. 181-82).
147. Clement Greenberg, 'Foreword' to Maurizio Taddei, op. cit., 1977, p. 7.
148. W.E. Gladstone Solomon, *The Bombay Revival of Indian Art*, 1924, p. 58.
149. To Roger Frey Indian works of art were 'chaotic profusion of imagery' but in Ajanta's later frescoes he found 'an extraordinarily accomplished and assured art:' *Last Lectures*, 1962, pp. 157, 158.
150. Rudolf Arnheim, *Art and Visual Perception*, 1960, p. 136.
—'The teachers or preceptors admire *rekha*-haromny of lines' (*Citrasūtra* 41:11). Dr. P. Shah, op. cit., 1961, p. 130.
151. Rudolf Arnheim, op. cit., 1960, p. 136.
152. Madanjeet Singh, op. cit., 1965, Pl. 67, p. 146 (The Bodhisattva).
153. Applying paint with thin bands (P. Shah, op. cit., 1961, p. 128) or application of colour in a shape leaving thin brushing lines showing modulations of depths and heights.
—Madanjeet Singh, op. cit., 1965 pl. 54, p. 118, ('The Buddha and the one-eyed Monk,' plate 153).
154. As the *viduśaka* appreciates lines in *Viddhasalabhanjika*. Quoted by C. Sivaramamurti, op. cit., 1978, p. 27.
155. A. Ghosh, (ed.,) *Ajanta Murals*, 1967, Pl. XLVI.
156. V.J. Djurić, *Sopoćani*, 1963, Pl. XL.
157. R. Arnheim, op. cit., 1960, p. 136.
158. V.J. Djurić, *Sopoćani*, 1963, Pl. XLIX.
—The Apostle Peter, north transept, east wall (plate 154).

159. V.J. Djurić, *Sopoćani*, pl. VII. (Plates 130, 131).
160. V.J. Djurić, *Sopoćani*, 1963, p. 6.
161. Inscription on cave 26. R. S. Gupte and B.D. Mahajan, op. cit., 1962, p. 260.
162. The best example of using the illumination for the orientation of object is popularly shown by the guides at Ajanta in cave 1. The stone image of Buddha in the sanctuary changes its facial expressions with the circulation of the spot-light around it.
163. Madanjeet Singh, op. cit., 1965, Pl. 30, 'A Monastery,' p. 63.
164. '.... luminosity results when brightness is not perceived as an effect of illumination. To this end shadows must be eliminated or kept at a minimum and the strongest light must appear within the limits of the object:' R. Arnheim, op. cit., 1960, pp. 264-65.
165. Ibid., p. 253, 'asymmetrical distribution produces a more disturbing distortion and thus makes its elimination more urgent' by producing a depth effect more readily.
166. Ibid., p. 261.
167. Ibid., p. 261-62.
168. Madanjeet Singh, op. cit., 1965, Pl. 44, p. 97.
169. Dr. P. Shah, op. cit., 1961, (*Citrasūtra* 41:9,) p. 129.
170. Khandalavala: *The Development of Style in Indian Painting*, 1974, p. 34.

—'The high light of beaded and twisted strings of jewellery accentuates the modelling of the smooth skinned bodies:'

—S. Kramrisch, op. cit., 1937 p. 20.
171. Maurizio Taddei, op. cit., 1977, Pl. 59, p. 106.
172. Ibid., Pl. 60, p. 107.

—It is interesting to note in this regard 'The transparency of the shadows' found by Lorenzo Cecconi in 'the Bodhisattva' (cave I) 'very like those of Corregio,' *Guide of Ajanta Frescoes*, 1927, p. 19.
173. S. Kramrisch, op. cit., 1937, p. 19.
174. R. Arnheim, op. cit., 1960, p. 254.
175. A. Ghosh, (ed.,) *Ajanta Murals*, Pl. XLVI.
176. B. Rowland, *The Art and Architecture of India*, 1970, p. 191.
177. Madanjeet Singh, op. cit., 1965, Pl. 26, p. 55.
178. Werner Haftsmann, *Painting in the Twentieth Century*, vol. I, 1960, p. 26.
179. Mario Bussagli, *Painting of Central Asia*, 1963, p. 35.
180. Madanjeet Singh, op. cit., 1965, Pl. 69, pp. 150-51.
181. Within Wolfflin's terms—'linear' and 'painterly,' Arnheim distinguishes painterly 'whereby the object is evoked by an outer principle, and the resulting appearance is a joint product of the shape of the object and the effect of light upon it:' op. cit., 1960, p. 266.
182. Madanjeet Singh, op. cit., 1965, Pl. 16, p. 34.
183. Arnheim, op. cit., 1960, p. 162.
184. Ibid., pp. 131-3.
185. Paul Klee's Jene Lectures quoted in '*60 Works from the Modern Art Museum Dusseldorf*,' 1979, p. 6.
186. Dr. P. Shah, op. cit., p. 38 note.
187. Dr. P. Shah, op. cit., refers to Dhananjaya's *Daśrūpa*, and *Abhinaya Darpaṇa*, and relates *nāṭya* or drama with it, p. 38 note.

—Madeline Hallade, in *Gandhāra Style and the Evolution of Buddhist Art*, 1968, refers to Stern Ph.'s recording the influence of the theatre on the paintings of Ajanta, p. 206.

—R. Parimoo in 'Elephanta in the Context of Evolution and Significance of Śaiva Sculpture,' (*Journal of Oriental Institute*, Vol. XXVI, March, 77 p. 296.), points out the relationship of Ajanta murals with theatre and dance.

188. Dr. P. Shah, op. cit., (*Citrasūtram* 41:7, 8) p. 128.
189. Ibid., (*Citrasūtram* 42:47, 48), p. 132.
190. Ibid., p. 332.
191. The observation of Michotte is quoted by Arnheim, op. cit., 1960, p. 332.
192. Arnheim quotes Merleau-Ponty that he points out: 'My body appears to me as posture,' adding 'and that, in contrast to visually observed objects, it does not have a spatiality of position but one of situation,' op. cit., 1960, p. 332.
193. 'Means the commensurability of part, selecting a module from the smallest parts which can be applied to the largest:' J. J. Pollitt, *The Art of Greece, 1400-31B.C.*, 1965, p. 20 and note.
194. Dr. Priyabala Shah, op. cit., 1961, pp. 106-7.
195. Ibid., p. 105.
196. Ibid., p. 115.
197. Ibid., p. 114.

—Grid system of proportion 'is a discipline imposed by a designer freeing him from the time-consuming burden of making certain decisions (dimension, proportion) without which fruitful and creative work is extremely difficult. He can move directly to those aspects of the problem in which individual expression, novel ideas, and freedom of choice are essential ... In brief, the intelligent designer will recognize that the grid can help him achieve harmony and order, but also that it may, when and if necessary, be abandoned:' Paul Rand, 'Design and Play Instinct,' in *Education of Vision*, (ed.,) Gyorgy Kepes, 1965, pp. 162, 164.

198. Inter-connection of axes through a grid system (plate 117) is clearly drawn on an unfinished painting of the Buddha in Kanheri caves.

—Louis Frederic, *Indian Temples and Sculptures*, 1959, pl. 136, p. 167.

—Grid system as observed in the carving of the facade of Loma Rishi cave is found out by S. Ganesh Rao, in S.P. Gupta, *The Roots of Indian Art*, 1980, pp. 220-21.

199. Dr. Priyabala Shah, op. cit., 1961, p. 109.
200. R.N. Misra, *Bhārtiya Mūrtikalā*, 1978, p. 136.
201. *Marg*, Vol. XXV, No. 4, Sept., 1972, p. 38.
202. A. Ghosh, (ed.,) *Ajanta Murals*, 1967, pl. P.
203. Lawrence B. Anderson: 'Module: Measure, Structure, Growth and Function,' in (eds) Gyorgy Kepes, *Module Symmetry Proportion*, 1966, pp. 114, 116.

—It is relevant to point out Mondrian's arrival on verticals and horizontals through abstract meditations on tree shapes (abandoning gravity): W. Haftsmann, *Painting in the Twentieth Century*, vol. I, 1960, p. 128.

204. Quoted by Arnheim, op. cit., 1960, p. 34.
205. F.D.K. Bosch, op. cit., 1960, pp. 220-23.
206. Dr. P. Shah, op. cit., 1961, (*Citrasūtra* 43:21, 22) p. 136.
207. Ibid., p. 137.
208. Maurizio Taddei, op. cit., 1977, p. 7.

209. P. Shah, op. cit., 1961, p. 127.
210. Madanjeet Singh, op. cit., 1965, pl. 54, p. 118.
211. Werner Haftsmann, op. cit., Vol. I, 1960, p. 33.
212. Madanjeet Singh, op. cit., 1965, Pl. 67, p. 146.
213. H.H. Arnason, *History of Modern Art*, 1977, p. 52.
214. R. Arnheim, op. cit., 1960, pp. 135, 150.
215. Ibid., pp. 325-26, 329.
216. Dr. P. Shah, op. cit., 1961, p. 129.
217. R. Arnheim, op. cit., 1980, pp. 47, 48, 379.
218. *Citrasūtram* (43:21,) op. cit., Śakabd 1880, p. 472.
219. Arnheim, op. cit., 1960, pp. 47, 48.
220. Dr. P. Shah, op. cit., 1961, p. 129.
221. Arnheim, op. cit., 1960, pp. 47, 48.
222. Ibid.
223. *Citrasūtram* (42:56,) op. cit., Śakabd 1880, p. 446.
224. Madanjeet Singh, op. cit., 1965, pl. 38, p. 80.
225. Ibid., pl. 24, p. 51.
226. *Citrasūtram* (43:29,) op. cit., Śakabd 1880, p. 473.
—Dr. P. Shah, op. cit., 1960, p. 137.
227. Arnheim, op. cit., 1960, pp. 47, 48.
228. M. Singh, op. cit., 1965, pl. 54, p. 118.
229. *The Art and Architecture of India, Buddhist, Hindu, Jain*, 1970, p. 82.
230. Stella Kramrisch, *The Art of India*, 1957, pl. III.
231. Stella Kramrisch, *Survey of Painting in Deccan*, 1937, p. 17.
232. 'Delacroix, January 13, 1857, notes that the true tone of the object is always found next to the luminous point because that area is hit by the full light:' Roudolf Arnheim, op. cit., 1960, p. 388 n. p. 251.
233. Ibid., p. 251.
234. Stella Kramrisch, op. cit., 1937, p. 23.
235. Vojislav J. Djuric, *Sopoćani*, 1963, Pl. XXXII.
236. Frederich Hartt, *History of Italian Renaissance*, 1969, p. 36.
237. Vojislav J. Djurić, *Sopoćani*, 1963, Pl. VIII.
238. Ibid., p. 71.
239. P.A. Michelis, op. cit., 1964, p. 83.
240. Vojislav J. Djurić, *Sopoćani*, p. 68.
241. D. T. Rice, op. cit., 1972, p. 203.
242. Vojislav J. Djurić, *Sopoćani*, 1963, Pl. LV.
243. Ibid., pl. LVIII.
244. Ibid., p. 87.
245. Vojislav J. Djurić, *Sopoćani*, 1963, Pl. LIV.
246. M. Chatzidakis, A. Grabar, *Byzantine and Early Medieval Painting*, 1965, p. 23.
247. V.J. Djurić, *Sopoćani*, 1963, Pl. XXXV.
—'*The Death of the Virgin*' detail, nave, west wall.
248. Ibid., p. 33.
249. Ernst Kitzinger, op. cit., 1977, p. 106.

250. Vojislav J. Djurić, *Sopoćani*, p. 116.
251. Ibid.
252. Ibid.
253. 'The Christian work recalls the unity of a tree, say, in which the proportions are not as important as the character of the tree. Type presupposes a 'canon of proportions.'
—P. A. Michelis, op. cit., 1964, p. 52.
254. Ernst Kitzinger, op. cit., 1977, p. 77.
255. Vojislav J. Djurić, *Sopoćani*, Pl. I.
256. Ibid., Pl. IX.
257. Ibid., Pl. X.
258. Ernst Kitzinger, op. cit., 1977, p. 80.
259. Werner Haftsmann, op. cit., Vol.I, 1960, p. 33.
260. A. Gosh, (ed.,) *Ajanta Murals*, 1967, Pl. LXII.
261. Chapter 41 of *Citrasūtra* is devoted to the explanation of *vartanā*. In verse 11 it is noted that *vartanā* is liked by experts and *rekhā* by preceptors; couplet 29 of chapter 43 speaks of the delineation of heights and depths being the quality added by experts. This implies that the spatial dimension is the sense behind *vartanā*. Further, as Rāghavabhaṭṭa takes *vartanā* as *lepaviśeṣaḥ* and Ajay treats it as *paṭalepah* (Dr. Priyabala Shah, *Viṣṇudharmottara-Purāṇa*, third *khanda*, Vol. II, 1961, pp. 127, 130), the colour smearing is meant by the term *rangavartanā*. Moreover, *Bindujā* (a type of *vartanā* mentioned in *Citrasūtra* 41:5, 6) implies achieving the colour-saturation or intensity by applying colours in dots (N.S. Bendre in a recent interview has supported such a tradition of colour application followed up in Indian miniatures (*Dinmān*, Vol. 17-1, 4/10-1-1981, p. 39). The reference of *Patrajavartanā* should mean the spatial dimensions created by the layers (*patra*) of colours having different wavelengths (i.e., warm and cool colours.) It is significant in this context that *Citrasūtra* speaks of '*patravinyāsa*,' thinned into leaves, for preparing colours from metals. (Dr. P. Shah, ibid., p. 118).
262. *Citrasūtram* (41:9). Tarnish Jha, op. cit., Śakabd 1880, p. 458.
263. *Viṣṇudharmottara Purāṇa* gives basic colours twice. In chapter 27 verse 8 they are given as '*Śveta*—white, *Rākta*—crimson, *Pīta*—yellow, *Kṛṣṇa*—black and *Harita*—green (P. Shah, *Viṣṇudharmottara Purāṇa* Khanda Vol. II, 1961, p. 117), and in chapter 40 verse 16 they are white, yellow, violet, red, black and blue.

In the same chapter shade (*śyāma*) and tints (*gaura*) tonalities are mentioned (verse 15). *Citrasūtra* further adds that the painting looking 'wet' (*ārdrameva*) is excellent (since it has proper saturation, through stippling *bindujā* application, and colour-technique). Those which fail to maintain proper saturation and technique look 'dry' (*śuṣka*) and are medium quality paintings, while those which have 'dry and wet' (*śuṣkārdra*) are worst.
—Chapter 42 verse 18.

—A.K. Bhattacharya (*Citralakṣaṇa*, 1974) speaks of Ajanta and classical tradition and gives five basic colours—white (*sita*), yellow (*pīta*), red (*rakta*), black (*kajjala*) and terreverte for deep green shade (*śyāma*) and adds 'golden' gilding also, pp. 33, 54.

—Ample evidences have been given by the earliest visitors to Ajanta on having seen golden Buddhas (J. Bird, *Historical Researches on the Origin and Principles of the Buddha and Jain Religions*, 1847, pp. 14, 15, 16.)

—This also brings us to the controversy of taking 'green' as one of the basic colours.

In art-treatises of India and the verification of paintings at Ajanta prove that 'green' was taken to be one of the elementary colours owing to its 'stability' (as Gestaltists' investigations speak and an artist like Kandinsky also calls it 'most restful colour in existence' (Rudolf Arnheim, op. cit., 1960, p. 281). Cosmic set of five Buddhas is also identified by *Citralakṣaṇa's* five basic colours including Green for Amōghasiddhi and goddess Tārā (Saviouress) linked with him (D.L. Snellgrove and T. Skorupski, *The Cultural Heritage of Ladakh*, Vol. I, 1977, pp. 10, 12). *Citrasūtra* also pays special attention to the making and modifications of blue, green and red colours (Chapter 40). Arnheim proving green as a turning point of scale from blue to yellow (while orange is not in red to yellows) further elaborates that on taking green as elementary or fundamental the complementary pairs are rich and clearcut in combinations with a greater tendency for mutual completion since some pairs contain all four fundamentals, some three but none less than three. It leaves two mutually exclusive areas as none of the pair has either yellow or green in common but red and blue are contained in more than half of the colour circle: Arnheim, op. cit., 1960, pp. 296-97.

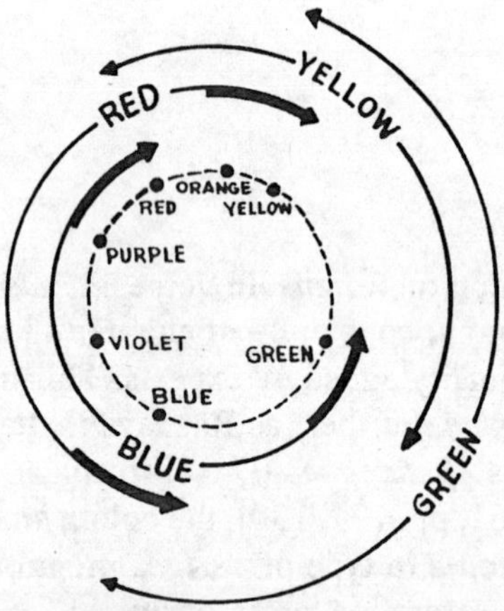

264. *Abhidharmakośa* (I. 28) speaks of colours as intrinsic form —*Rūpa*, quoted by S. Kramrisch, op. cit., 1937, p. 203 note 3.
—'The form which, derived from the great principle is visible under the appearance of colour and produces impact,' *Dhamma Saṅgani*, quoted by Stella Kramrisch, op. cit., 1937, p. 28.
265. Arnheim's 'Admixture theory' based on landing tones results in the folowing chart of the syntax of colour mixtures:

BLUE	violet	blue and red	purple	RED
RED	yellow red	orange	red yellow	YELLOW
YELLOW	green yellow	green	green blue	BLUE

It has principal mixtures as stages of transition with values in central column as evenly balancing the two fundamentals. Central values, too, thus resemble fundamentals having 'relatively high stability and self-containedness;' others having one fundamental dominating have dynamic properties of 'landing tones' because 'they appear as deviations from the dominant fundamental and exhibit a tension towards the purity of that fundamental.' This in the values of pattern is the perceptual theory of tension in which a 'rectangle of the ratio 2:1 may disturb us as against a simple and balanced sequence by pretending unity and rectangularity while threatening to break up into two squares.' The proportion of golden section with ratio of 8:5 'may successfully combine unity with lively tension:' (Arnheim, op. cit., 1960, p. 290.)

The following are the six basic variants of admixture theory:

(a) 'Structural Inversion' 'takes place when the two elements exchange positions, that is, when the colour that serves as subordinate in one mixture is the dominant of the other and vice versa.' 'Symmetry in the exchange of structural places' and mixtures lying in the same scale (analogous) produce harmonious relationship: Arnheim, op. cit., 1960, p. 292 Fig. 237.

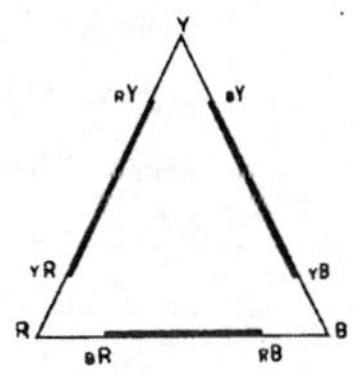

(b) 'Similarity of Dominant'... 'produces two essentially identical colours, distinguished by different admixtures. The same colour is torn into two different scales,' ibid., Fig. 236, p. 292.

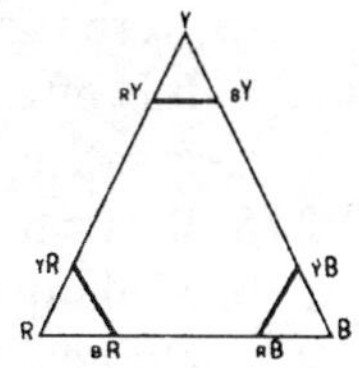

(c) 'Fundamental may appear as the dominant in the mixture' and colours looking 'essentially alike—one hue dominates the pair but disturbance arises because one being pure than the other —they become asymmetrical,' ibid., Fig. 238, p. 292. *Citrasūtra* (40:19, 20-21, 22-24) too suggests such syntax of admixture.

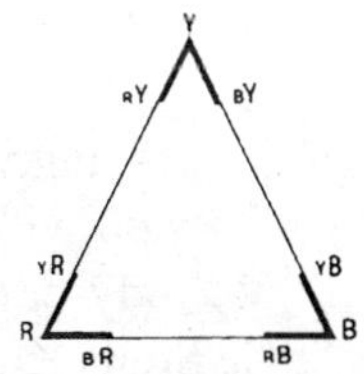

(d) 'Similarity of the subordinate,' 'produce two essentially different colours connected by the same admixture,' ibid., Fig. 234, pp. 291, 92.

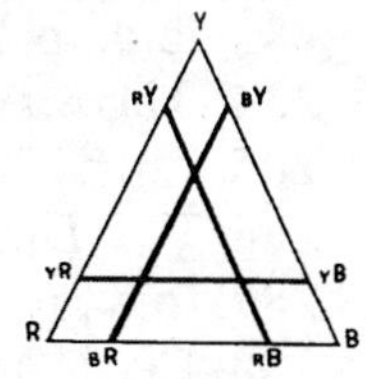

(e) 'Structural contradiction for one common element,' Fig. 235 p. 291; —'each pair of mixture is placed asymmetrically in relation to all three poles. The color each pair shares lies close to its pole in one mixture (dominant) and distant from it in the other (subordinate).' R. Arnheim, op. cit., 1966, p. 291.

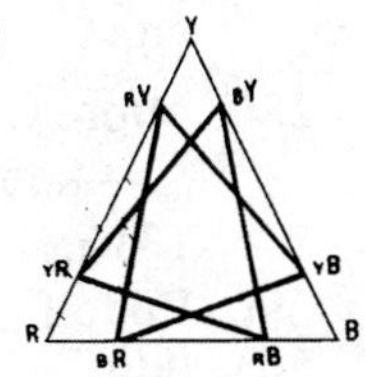

266. E.g., by the side of 'Bodhisattva Avalokiteśvara,' cave 1.

267. E.g., 'Bodhisattva Padmapāṇi,' cave 1.
—Illustrated here is the 'Toilet Scene' (cave 17, Plate 120).

268. 'Syntactic character of elementary colours is that they are unrelated to each other having no common dimension except being pure colours... not fitting into any common scale... their company produce little tension neither attraction nor repulsion;' Arnheim adds that the colour of the 'slight deviation' from the main colour 'determines the effect.' R. Arnheim, op. cit., 1960, pp. 289, 277.

269. Madanjeet Singh, op. cit., 1965, pl. 1.

270. Giving her a 'calmness' of the 'perfection of wisdom' as she is painted in Alchi frescoes at Ladakh: D.L. Snellgrove and T. Skorupski, op. cit., 1977, p. 56, pl. X.
271. Complementaries 'show completeness as the balance of opposites. They exhibit the particular force that constitutes the whole. The stillness of achievement appears as an integration of antagonistic tendencies. A painting built on a theme of complementaries may attain this animated repose,' R. Arnheim, op. cit., 1960, p. 297.
272. Madanjeet Singh, op. cit., pl. 25, reproduces quite near values.
273. R. Arnheim, op. cit., 1960, p. 298.
274. 'The eyes spontaneously seek out and connect complementary colours.' Other schemes 'show onesidedness, which seems to call for completion. Thus, a pattern based entirely on red and yellow looks thin in need of blue—an effect that is not necessarily undesirable. It is often used deliberately by the artist' to produce 'quest'; 'need for completing colour is satisfied in another area of the picture, or, in stage setting...'
275. R. Arnheim, op. cit., 1960, pp. 292, 297.
276. Madanjeet Singh, op. cit., 1965, Pl. 46.
277. Quoted by R. Arnheim, op. cit., 1960, p. 276.
278. Ibid., p. 280.
279. A. Gosh, (ed.,) *Ajanta Murals*, 1967, Pl. LXXXV.
280. Madanjeet Singh, op. cit., 1965, pl. 43.
—Ingrid Aall speaks of it as '...maintaining the same tonal level, as if nailed to the wall without highlighting the transgration of planes by shading or drawing marked body-contours... A. Gosh (ed.,) *Ajanta Murals*, 1967, p. 41.
281. Stella Kamrisch, op. cit., 1937, p. 45.
282. D.T. Rice, op. cit., 1972, p. 203.
283. Ibid., p. 202.
284. *Yugoslavia-Mediaeval Frescoes*, UNESCO, 1956, p. 9.
285. Ernst Kitzinger, op. cit., 1977, pp. 60, 62.
286. V. J. Djurić, *Sopoćani*, 1963, p. 116.
287. Ibid., p. 116.
288. Cf., plate LVI, 'The Archangel Michael' (Chapel of St. Stephen,) V.J. Djurić, *Sopoćani*, 1963.
289. André Graber, *Greek Mosaics of the Byzantine Period*, 1964, pl. 27.
—Apostle-detail, 'Dormition of the Virgin,' Chruch of Holy Apostles, Thessaloniki c. 1315.
290. Rudolf Arnheim, op. cit., 1960, p. 290.
291. Ibid., p. 289.
292. V.J. Djurić, *Sopoćani*, 1963, Pls. XVII, XXI, XLVIII, XLIX, L.
293. Ibid., Pl. XXVIII, p. 116.
294. Ibid., p. 116.
295. V.J. Djurić, *Resava*, 1963, pp. vii, viii. Mirjana Lubinković, *Ravanica*, 1966, p. xiv.
296. Rudolf Arnheim, op. cit., 1960, p. 296.
297. V.J. Djurić, *Sopoćani*, 1963, Pl. LVI.
298. Arnheim, op. cit., 1960, pp. 299, 93.
299. V.J. Djurić, *Sopoćani*, 1963, Pl. XXVIII.
300. R. Arnheim, op. cit., p. 298.

301. V.J. Djurić, *Sopoćani* pl. XLVIII.
302. R Arnheim, op. cit., p. 289-293.
303. V.J. Djurić, *Sopoćani*, 1963, p. 116.
304. R. Arnheim, op cit., 1960, p. 290.
305. Ibid., p. 299.
306. Ibid., p. 297.
307. V.J. Djurić, *Sopoćani*, 1963, Pl. LV.
308. R. Arnheim, op. cit., p. 292.
309. Ibid., 292.
—V.J. Djurić, *Sopoćani*, 1963, p. 64.
310. R. Arnheim, op. cit., 1960, p. 291.
311. V. J. Djurić, *Sopoćani*, 1963, pl. XXVII.
312. Anand K. Coomarswami, op. cit., 1972, p. 13.
313. Ernst Kitzinger, op cit., 1977, p. 121.
314. V.J. Djurić, *Sopoćani*, 1963, p. 69.
315. Mila Rajković, *Sopoćani*, 1963, p. 2.
316. Ernst Kitzinger, op. cit., p. 121.
317. Madanjeet Singh, op. cit., 1965, Plate 25, 'Bodhisattva Padmapāṇi,' Cave 1.
— V.J. Djurić, *Sopoćani*, 1963, Pl. LVI—'The Archangel Michale' as 'Guardian of the Holy Trinity,' Chapel of St. Stephen.
318. P.A. Michelis, op. cit., 1964, p. 135.
319. Madanjeet Singh, op. cit., 1965, Pl. 25.
320. V.J. Djuric, *Sopoćani*, 1963, pl. XXXIX.
321. Madanjeet Singh, op. cit., 1965, pl. 48.
322. V.J. Djurić, *Sopoćani*, pl. XLVIII.
323. Madanjeet Singh, op. cit., 1965, pl. 1.
324. V.J. Djurić, *Sopoćani*, 1963, pl. VII.
325. Rudolf Arnheim, op. cit., 1960, p. 292.
326. Stella Kramrisch, op. cit., 1937, p. 62.
327. Quoted by R. Arnheim, op. cit., 1960, p. 297.
328. Ibid., p. 297.
329. Ibid., p. 292.
330. Ibid., p. 297.
331. V.J. Djurić, *Sopoćani*, 1963, pl. XXII.
332. Dr. P. Shah, *Viṣṇudharmottara-Purāṇa*, Third Khaṇḍa, Vol. II, 1961, p. 116.
333. This is the condition after the restoration removing the varnish 'misguidedly applied by the earlier restorers.' Madanjeet Singh, op. cit., p. 11.
334. S.P. Gupta, *The Roots of Indian Art*, 1980, p. 202.
335. Ibid., p. 207.
336. D.J. Djurić, *Sopoćani*, 1963, p. 71.
—Andre Grabar, op. cit., 1964, p. 6.
337. P.A. Michelis, op. cit., 1964, p. 135.
338. 'Perpendicular reaching to the ground'—*Citrasūtram, op.cit.*, Śakabd 1880, Chapter 41 verse 9 and Ch. 43 verse 19.
339. Madanjeet Singh, op. cit., 1965, Pl. 53.

—A. Ghosh, (ed.,) *Ajanta Murals*, 1967 (without the mistake of inversion) Pl. III.

340. Rudolf Arnheim, op. cit., 1960, p. 9.
341. Ibid., p. 18.
342. In contrapuntal relationship with the centre of the picture the 'observer experiences, facing the left side a second and asymmetrically located centre' carrying more weight: R. Arnheim, ibid., p. 19.
343. Figures half cut by the frame on left show the anonymity and a sense of just entering from a distance, etc. This convention was very much used by Giotto:' Frederich Hartt, op. cit., p. 57.
344. 'Van Pelt has pointed out that in a symmetrical arrangement of three arches the central one should be larger. It would look too weak if it had merely the size of the other two:' R. Arnheim, op. cit., 1960, p. 12.
345. '... a distant object appears relatively large for reasons of perspective. By appearing larger, it may pull more weight than a picture area of its size would do otherwise' as exemplified in the girl picking flower in Manet's 'Dejeuner sur 1' herbe:' R. Arnheim, op. cit., 1960, p. 11.
346. Plus the gamma axes of the triangles around add to her misery by denoting that she is in agony from every corner of existence.
347. 'Unlike a strict profile or an en-face, which tends to be flush on the picture plane, the transitional three-quarter aspect implies spatial depth:' L. Steinberg, 'The Philosophical Brothel (part-2),' in *Art News*, Oct., 1972, Vol. 71, No. 6, p. 43.
348. '... *Sthānas* having many beam-like lines and with steady *bhūmi-lambhas*:' (*Citrasūtram* 37; 17).

   —Dr. P. Shah, *Viṣṇudharmottara-Purāṇa*, Third Khaṇḍa, Vol. II, 1961, p. 109.

349. R. Arnheim, op. cit., 1960, p. 15, or what Rudrauf classifies as composition diffuses: ibid., p 375.
350. Ibid., *see* Glossary.
351. 'Only because shapes are recognized as head, body, hand, chair, do they play their particular compositional role:' Ibid., p. 26.
352. 'Beyond such compositions painting in Ajanta does not go. They are complete and altogether exhaustive:' Stella Kramrisch, op. cit., 1937, p. 5.

   —J. Fergusson, J. Burgess, *The Cave Temples of India*, 1969, illus. 61, p. 314.

353. Madanjeet Singh, op. cit., 1965, pp. 186, 187.
354. Ibid., fig. 8, pp. 120, 103.
355. Ibid., fig. 11, p. 124.
356. Stella Kramrisch, op. cit., 1937, p. 116.
357. This is being put forth as a representative study.

   — (V.J. Djurić, Sopoćani, 1963, pl. XXVII.)

358. R. Arnheim, op.cit., 1960, p. 375.
359. Ibid., p. 12. The reading of picture from left to right, as adopted at Sopoćani, makes the objects look heavier at the right side.
360. Ibid., p. 15.
361. Ibid., p. 16.
362. Ibid., p. 16.
363. Ibid., p. 12.

364. Lawrence Allowey, 'Formless breaking down from the paintings of Agnes Martin,' in, *Studio International*, Feb. 1973, pp. 61-62.
365. R. Arnheim, op. cit., 1960, p. 12.
366. Ibid., p. 343.
367. 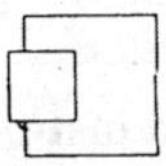 'The symbol P is derived from the first two letters of the Greek word XPICTOC (pronounced Christos). The letters abbreviate the name of Christ.' It is an ancient monogram of Christ: Fridrich Rest, *Our Christian Symbols*, 1956, p. 6.
368. The candle stands have the shapes of bead-and-real motifs escalating stroboscopic movement, hence directional axis.
369. Lawrance B. Anderson, 'Measure, Structure, Growth and Function,' in (ed.,) Gyorgy Kepes, *Module, Symmetry and Proportion*, 1966, pp. 114-16.
370. R. Arnheim, op. cit., 1960, p. 9.
371. Ibid., p. 26.
372. Ibid., pp. 54, 61.
373. What Djurić describes as 'towards the centre of composition and bound up with central compression of the body,' *Sopoćani*, p. 65.
374. Ernst Kitzinger, op. cit., 1977, pp. 124, 19.
375. D.T. Rice, op. cit., 1972, p. 150.
376. V.J. Djurić, *Sopoćani*, 1963, p. 116.
377. Ibid., Pl. XVII.
378. Rudolf Arnheim's view of 'artistic excellence' applies here, op. cit., 1960, p. 26.
379. V.J. Djurić, *Sopoćani*, 1963, p. 65, Pl. XXVII (The Dormition).
380. A. Ghosh, (ed.,) *Ajanta Murals*, 1967, Pl. III.
381. V.J. Djurić, *Sopoćani* 1963, Pl. XXVII.
—Madanjeet Singh, op. cit., Pl. 47, (The Dancing Girl with Musicians,' cave 1, Fig. 57.)
382. A. Ghosh, (ed.,) *Ajanta Murals*, fig. 20.
383. V.J. Djurić, *Sopoćani*, 1963, Pl. XXVII.
384. M. Singh, *INDIA Painting from Ajanta Caves, UNESCO*, 1954, Pl. XV.
385. R. Arnheim, op. cit., 1960, p. 21.
386. Anil de Silva, *Chinese Landscape Painting*, 1967, p. 47.
387. M. Singh, op. cit., 1965, Pl. 69.
388. Stella Kramrisch, quoted by Benjamin Rowland, for 'Gandharvas and apsaras from Sondani' (a motif in which steps have been used to take a plunge with a push from vertical ascending side) —*The Art and Architecture of India*, 1970, p. 240.
389. R. Arnheim, op. cit., 1960, p. 311.
390. M. Blavatski's translation of Asanga's *The Book of Golden Precepts*, quoted in A. Besant & C.W. Leadbeater, *Talks on the Path of Occultism*, 1930, p. 409.
391. 'Lightly are the figures born by it. None there is who would tread upon the flowers with his gross weight:' Kramrisch, op. cit., 1937, p. 23.
392. R. Arnheim quoting Buswell's experiment confirms that '... there was surprisingly little connection between the order and direction of fixations and the compositional structure of the picture. And even the order of the subject is largely irrelevant just as it makes little difference for the final structure of a spider web in what order the threads were woven:' op. cit., 1960, p. 308.

393. M. Singh, op. cit., 1965, pl. 47.
394. —'head and limbless, that is, despiritualized torso:' R. Arnheim, op. cit., 1960, p. 331.
395. Even the half of the verandah space in the background, covered with curtain, contains sex appeal parallel to the *kurtā* which uncovers half of the physical zones of abdomen and hip of the dancer.
396. R. Arnheim, op. cit., 1960, p. 332.
397. In Greek tradition French dance teacher Delsarte divides human body, as an instrument of expression, into three zones—head being mental, torso being spiritual emotional and physical zones as abdomen and hips and arms and legs as contact organs of respective zones: R. Arnheim, op. cit., 1960, pp. 330-31.
398. Pillar, being a consistent shape, gives impetus to movement. Lady between pillars is one of the most repeated motifs throughout the history of art. Thus both the pillars on the sides of the dancing girl are suggested even on the bodies of musicians covering hair's mass and continuing with faint lines. This motif gives a forthcoming perception to the dancing figure along with contrasting the body rhythms. The roof on the top as well acts as consistent shape giving variable rhythm to the dancer (and musicians) whose body twists like a snake on hanger against the roof. Brightness of this architectural piece gives a movement through 'displacement' to the dimmer toned bodies, (R. Arnheim, op. cit., 1960, p. 309.) Juxtaposition of violet (in the sleeves), against its complementary green in the background gives an 'animated repose' whereas the (red) yellow of the rest of the *kurtā* gives a dynamism in 'structural contradiction for one common element' to Green (yellow blue).
399. *Ajanta Paintings*, Lalit Kala Akademi, 1956, Pl. XVII, 'A Palace-Scene', cave 1.
400. 'The dancer can frankly exclude the body as in Hindu dances; these dances can be performed even when the person is seated, and consist of stories told by the hands while the head and face supply an accompaniment of emotional reactions. But if the whole body is to be involved, action must issue from its visible and motor centres in the torso rather than from the centres of the nervous system:' R. Arnheim, op. cit., 1960, p. 330.
401. Ibid., pp. 326-329.
402. Nature of kinesthetic experience being the dynamic quality that is 'the common element, which unites the two different media. When the dancer lifts his arm, he primarily experiences the tension of raising.' This is visually conveyed to the spectator through the image of the dancer's arm..., ibid., pp. 332-33.
403. P.A. Michelis, 1964, p. 40.
404. Svetozar Radojčić, *Yugoslavia-Mediaeval Frescoes*, UNESCO, 1956, p. 22.
405. Mila Rajković, *Sopoćani*, 1963, p. 2.
406. Ibid., p. 6.
407. P.A. Michelis, op. cit., 1964, pp. 35, 52.
408. V.J. Djurić, *Sopoćani,*, 1963, pl. XXIV—'The Appearance of Christ to the Apostles', Sanctuary.
409. Ibid., pl. XXII-'The Appearance of Christ to the Holy Women,' Sanctuary.
410. Ibid., pl. XXVII-'Dormition of Mary,' nave.
411. Ibid., pls. XXI—'The Marys at the tomb,' Sanctuary, LI—'The Holy Trinity,' VII—The Archangel Gabriel,' nave.
412. Radolf Arnheim, op. cit., 1960, p. 332.

413. P.A. Michelis, op. cit., p. 40.
414. R. Arnheim, op. cit., pp. 326-29.
415. Ibid.
416. Erich-Neumann, op. cit., 1955, p. 317.
417. R. Arnheim, op. cit., 1960, pp. 326-29.
418. V.J. Djurić, *Sopoćani*, 1963, p. 65.
419. R. Arnheim, op. cit., 1960, p. 359: 'Formalistic analysis talks about balance or unity but avoids the question without which the existence of the work remains incomprehensible: what is being balanced and unified ?'
420. R. Arnheim, op. cit., p. 339.
—*Citrasūtram* 39:44, 45, 46, 51.
421. 'The incompleteness of a well-structured pattern produces a tension towards closure.' Arnheim, op. cit., 1960, p. 348.
422. Ibid., p. 343-44.
423. The Mahāmeru is the macrocosmic replica of *Padmamūla*—the base module of 'Tree of Life.'
F.D.K. Bosch, op. cit., 1960, p. 93.
424. '... cave temples are pure space carved out by the rock.' Here, 'there is a complete reversal of the architectural approach. Space delimiting perimetrical walls are non-existent and the facade is unimportant; what counts is only the cutout inside space divided by the false ribs of the false vaults and the false pillars carved out of the rock to create spatial effects:' Mario Bussagli, 'Introduction,' in M. Bussagli, C. Sivaramamurti, *5000 Years of the Art of India*, p. 32.
425. Stella Kramrisch, op. cit., 1955, p. 15: (*Tālachanda*—metrical floor-measure. *Urdhva-cchanda* metrical height-measure.)
426. (Gamma-motion; *see* Glossary)
R. Arnheim, op. cit., 1960,
pp. 227-28, 341-42.

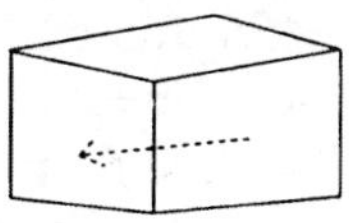

427. Ibid., p. 343.
428. A. Ghosh, (ed.,) *Ajanta Murals*, 1967, fig. 20.
429. *Citrasūtram* (43:29).
430. '...livelier dynamics and more complex formula of shape makes for a more organic effect'... as crescendo or decrescendo rate is added to mere wedge shape:' R. Arnheim, op. cit., 1960, p. 343.
431. M. Singh, op. cit., 1965, pl. 62.
432. Brown observed that 'disks seemed to move much faster in the upward than in the horizontal direction:' R. Arnheim, op. cit., 1960, p. 341.
433. Stella Kramrisch, op. cit., 1955, pl. III 'Votaries with offerings for *Hāriti* and *Pañcika*,' cave 2.
—'Round tray heaped with offerings, round seat of a Bodhisattva-like youth are rotating islands, spinning into steadiness with the load which they carry:' Foucher, *The Beginning of Buddhist Art and Other Essays*, 1972, p. 46.
434. M. Singh, op. cit., 1965, pl. 17:' 'A queen in a palace scene,' cave 1.
435. Sense of proportion is dynamic 'as the active equipoise of concentrated forces:' R. Arnheim, 'A review of Proportion,' in Gyorgy Kepes; *Module Symmetry Proportion*, 1966, p. 218.

436 ...Visual perception can be accompained by kinesthetic sensations. But these will be expected to occur only when and because visual tension is experienced in the first place:' op. cit., 1960, p. 340.
437. S. Kramrisch, op. cit., 1955, Pl. II, cave 2 (Fig. 82).
438. R. Arnheim, op. cit., 1960, pp. 340, 341.
439. As Michelangelo's unfinished statues called 'Slaves' '... the body remains partly embedded in the block of marble and this exhibits an impressive struggle for completeness, that is for liberty:' Arnheim, op. cit., 1960, p. 348.
440. Ibid., p. 352.
441. Ibid., p. 340. *see* Glossary.
442. Ibid., pp. 340-41.
443. Ibid., p. 348.
444. Ibid., p. 341.
445. V.J. Djurić, *Sopoćani*, 1963, Pl. XXI.
446. R. Arnheim, op. cit., 1960, p. 343.
447. Ibid., p. 348.
—Djurić, *Sopoćani*, 1963, Pl. XXII ('The Appearance of Christ to the Holy Women').
448. V. J. Djurić, *Sopoćani*, 1963, pl. XXIV ('Christ Appearing to the Apostles'), Pl. XXVI ('The Incredulity of Thomas').
449. Ibid., Pl. XI.
450. R. Arnheim, op. cit., 1960, p. 343.
451. Ibid., p. 15.
452. Ibid., p. 341.
453. Erich Neumann, op. cit., 1955, p. 252.
454. Ibid., p. 333.
455. Rudolf Arnheim, op. cit., 1960, p. 336.
456. Ibid., p. 346.
457. Ibid., p. 340.
458. M. Singh, op. cit., 1965, pl. 62.
('A monk watching the conversion of Nanda,' cave 16).
—V.J. Djurić, *Sopoćani*, 1963, Pl. XI (The Nativity).
459. Stella Kramrisch, op. cit., 1955, pl. II.
—Stroboscopic effect is similarly pronounced in 'the communion of the Apostles' (nave, sanctuary apse) at Sopoćani, V.J. Djurić, *Sopoćani*, 1963, pp. 126-27.
460. V.J. Djurić, *Sopoćani*, 1963, Pl. XXVII (The Dormition).
461. Mila Rajković, *Sopoćani*, 1963, p. 2.
462. Ernst Kitzinger, op. cit., 1977, p. 98.
463. Ingrid all, 'Ajanta, An Artistic Appreciation,' in *Ajanta Murals*, 1967, p. 11.
464. Dr. P. Shah, *Viṣṇudharmottara-Purāṇa*, Third Khaṇḍa, Vol. II, 1961, p. 134.
465. Ibid., (*Citrasūtram*, 43:2) p. 135.
— e.g., the votaries painted in the chapels of cave 2.
466. Dr. K. Krishnamoorthy, *Dhvanyāloka of Ānandavardhan*, 1974, p. xxxix.
467. Madanjeet Singh, op. cit., 1965, pl. 42, pp. 92-93.
468. C. Sivaramamurti, op. cit., 1970, Fig. 2, p. 35.
469. Madanjeet Singh, op. cit., 1965, pl. 75, p. 163.

470. V.J. Djurić, *Sopoćani*, 1963, p. 23.
471. H.W. Janson, *History of Art*, 1977, p. 174.
472. Germain Bazin, *A Concise History of Art*, Vol. II, 1964, p. 438.
473. V.J. Djurić, *Sopoćani*, 1963, Pl. XXIX.
474. Dr. P. Shah, op. cit., (*Citrasūtram* 43:10,) p. 135.
475. David, L. Snellgrove, (ed.,) *The Image of The Buddha*, 1978, p. 109.
476. *See* Glossary.
477. Stella Kramrisch, op. cit., 1955, p. 15.
478. M. Chatzidakis, A. Grabar, *Byzantine and Early Medieval Painting*, 1965, p. 23.
—Ernst Kitzinger explains this as 'strongly modelled' forms 'pressing forward against the frame-work' giving the example of the apse mosaic of S.S. Cosmos and Damian (Plate 93) Rome: op. cit., p. 93.
479. P.A. Michelis, op. cit., 1964, p. 149.
480. E. Kitzinger elaborates: 'a mystical dissolution into a green atmosphere' the spirit of which was found in the diaper grid floor carpet mosaics of Eastern Mediterranean influencing the aesthetics and Church-decoration of Justinan era: op. cit., 1977, pp. 88-90.
—'Leonardo's system of bowers in which branches were tied together as Lomazzo informs. These structures became a vogue and were simulated in ceiling painting:' R.M. Frye, *Milton's Imagery and the Visual Art*, 1978, p. 225.
—Frederich Hartt points to Michelangelo's Sistine ceiling in tree-growth patterning and also the module in 'swelling movements of the bodies of the figures:' *History of Italian Renaissance Art*, pp. 445-49.
481. P.A. Michelis, op. cit., 1964, pp. 40, 150.
482. G. Kubler and Levistrauss refer to rejuvenation of myth in analogous terms that 'when an ancient version becomes unintelligibly obsolete a new version, recast in contemporary terms, performs the old explanatory purpose:' Brodsky, 'Continunity and Discontinuity in Style: A Problem in Art Historical Methodology,' in *Journal of Aesthetics and Art Criticism*, Vol. XXXIV, Feb. 1981, p. 29.
483. Stella Kramrisch, op. cit., 1937, p. 11
484. Ibid., p. 10.
485. The mystic awe and the need for salvation are the two major sources to which Geeta Kapoor alludes as corresponding between the world's great mythologies and man's superabundant imagination: *Contemporary Indian Artist*, 1978, p. 28.
486. Kurt Badt quoted by R. Arnheim, op. cit., 1960, p. 298.
487. This fact is proved at Bauhaus as informed by Ittan Johannes already noted in the chapter 'Artist and Patron,' p. 139 n. 9.
488. R. Arnheim explains that the sense of proportion is dynamic 'as the active equipoise of concentrated forces:' 'A Review of Proportion,' in Gyorgy Kepes, *Module Symmetry Proportion*, 1966, p. 218.
489. Quoted by Dr. P. Shah, op. cit., 1961, p. 43.
490. Quoted by K.G. Subramanyan, *Moving Focus*, 1978, p. 85.
491. Stella Kramrisch, op. cit., 1937, p. 15.
492. Quoted by Krishna Chaitanya, *A History of Indian Painting, The Mural Tradition*, 1976, p. 15.
493. Quoted by Dr. Lazar Milin, 'The Theology of Icons,' in *The Serbian Orthodox Church*,

Vol. III, No. 3, 1972, p. 45.

494. Defining 'Unconsummated mixture' of 'illumination' and the object on G. Braque's still-life, Arnheim thus sums it up; op. cit., 1960, p. 270.

495. V.J. Djurić, op. cit., 1963, p. 71.

496. Karl Khandalavala, op. cit., 1974, p. 39.

497. 'But beauty due to an artistic arrangement of *śabda* or *artha* by the poet comes to be regarded as *guṇa*. This has been hinted at by Abhinavagupta in his *Locana* on the *Vṛtti* of *Karika*:' K. Krishnamoorthy, *Dhvanyāloka of Ānandavardhan*, 1974, p. 336 notes for p. 118-LI.

—'It follows that a transposition of nature, even when it is very far-fetched, remains figurative and is figuration; but it also follows that a transposition taken up to the point where nothing in the work suggests or evokes some basic naturalistic subject—a transposition, therefore, which to the naked eye does not even imply the act of transposition itself—will rightly be called abstract abstraction.' Michel Seuphor, *A Dictionary of Abstract Painting*, 1958, p. 3.

498. C. Sivaramamurti, op. cit., 1978, p. 24.

499. Otto Demus, *Byzantine Art and the West*, 1970, p. 194.

—It is what Wolfflin described of the spirit of Baroque in Michelangelo's St. Peter's dome where, 'the symbolic image of weight is maintained yet dominated by the expression of spiritual liberty'; quoted by R. Arnheim, op. cit., 1960, p. 365. Mila Rajković confirms to the similarity in the spirit of Michelangelo and the artist of Sopoćani, *Sopoćani*, 1963, p. 2.

500. Bernatt Newman as quoted by Charles Harrison, 'Abstract Expressionism II,' in *Studio International*, Vol. 185, No. 952, Feb., 1973, p. 59.

—'On this earth men are mostly void of proportions on account of the power of time and condition (state) therefore, understanding this, a wise man should in relation to *kṣaya* and *vṛddhi* create proportion by his own genius' (*Citrasūtra* 39:51): Dr. Priyabala Shah, op. cit., p. 115.

—'Thus like the artists of today the Byzantines often resorted to deliberate distortions of the figure.'

— D.T. Rice 'preface' to *Yugoslavia-Mediaeval Frescoes*, 1956, p. 9.

501. P.A. Michelis, op. cit., 1964, p. 40.

502. Svetozar Radojčić, 'Introduction' in *Yugoslavia-Mediaeval Frescoes*, 1956, p. 20.

503. '... (if critic) is convinced that the suggested beauty surpasses the beauty of the expressed, he will rate it as *dhvani-kāvya* or first-rate poetry. If the suggested element is almost negligible in appeal, it will be third-rate poetry (*Citra-Kāvya*):' Dr. K. Krishnamoorthy, op. cit., p. xxxii-iii.

—Mila Rajković significantly comments that at Sopoćani 'the content is a final synthesis stripped of all that would age it...' *Sopoćani*, 1963, p. 5.

504. Dr. Priyabala Shah, *Viṣṇudharmottara-Purāṇa*, Third Khaṇḍa, Vol. II, 1961, p. 116.

505. 'A study of the grain size of the particles constituting the plaster has shown that the mixture of ferruginous mud and gritty rock-powder and sand was very carefully gauged and that the grains of silica possessed marked angularity, which has considerably contributed to the firmness and compactness of the plaster:' Dr. B.B. Lal, 'The Murals, Their Composition and Technique,' in *Ajanta Murals* (ed.,) A. Gosh, 1967, p. 54.

506. Since *Maṇibhūmi* is called *citravapuṣā*, (instrumental singular) it would mean the *maṇibhūmis* should be accompanied by proper background for pictures: Dr. Priyabala Shah, op. cit., p. 116, p. 114, (*Citrasūtra* 39:34:35).
507. I.e. sculptures had only one layer of intonaco—*sudha lepa*.
508. I.e., *Citrasūtra*, Ch. 40.
509. I.e., in cave IV which has unfinished and partly painted ceiling and sculptures.
510. C. Sivaramamurti, op. cit., 1978, p. 36.
511. *Citrasūtra* (42:82), 'The theme or subject matter (*Vastu*) of painting becomes *uttama*, i.e., best done when the application of paint is wet (*ārdra*), of the middle (*madhyama*) type, when it is dry (*śuṣka*) but it is worst (*adhama*) when it is somewhat wet and somewhat dry:' Dr. Priyabala Shah, op. cit., p. 134.
— *Ārdra* should also denote the unified resonance of transparency, intensity and depth quality of a coloured surface.
512. Jaipur-fresco or the Fresco-technique of Mughal school; D.N. Shukla, *Silpa-śāstra*, 1967, p. 92.
513. V.S. Agrawala, quotes *Vinaya Pīṭaka* (3/36) where 'lepya citra' has been mentioned. He refers to *Mahaummaga Jātaka* for the Ajanta type paintings on *Sudha kamma*—white plaster etc. 'Sanskrit Sahitya main chitrakalā sambandhi shabdāvali,' in *Sammelan Patrika*, Śakābda 1880, p. 95.
514. I.e., in caves IX and X, and on sculptures.
515. I.e. deeply grooved chisel marks on ceiling for the firm grip of lepa.
516. Dr. P. Shah, op. cit., 1961, p. 116.
517. Varieties of sand given include those coming from the caves of the mountain, D.N. Shukla, op. cit., 1967, p. 89; Nand Lal Bose said to one of his students that Ajanta artists used the clay of termite-hill for protection against the white ants, *L.K. Contemporary (14)* confirms it (p. 46) by referring to demonstration chart at Santiniketan.
518. *Śilparatna*, quoted by D.N. Shukla, op. cit., p. 95.
519. These ingredients and processes are given in *Citrasūtra*, Ch. 40, verses 1 to 10.
—*Citralakṣaṇa*, A.K. Bhattacharya, op. cit., 1974, pp. 42-45.
520. Dr. B.B. Lal, op. cit., 1967, p. 54.
521. Dr. P. Shah, op. cit., 1961, (*Citrasūtra*) p. 118.
522. Ibid., p. 118.
523. D.N. Shukla, too, pleads on the basis of text like *Citrasūtra* that gold and other metallic substances were used, op. cit., pp. 120-22.
524. *Mānasollāsa* and *Śilparatna* give an account of three types of brushes—*Sthūla* for *lepa* application, *Madhya* for outline and *Sukṣma* for finishing. *Samarāngaṇa-Sūtradhāra* gives five types, D.N. Shukla, op. cit., pp. 122-23.
—'It is remarkable instance of how great works of art have been created by simple means:' Madanjeet Singh, op. cit., UNESCO, 1954, p. 10.
525. Bāṇa Bhaṭṭa indicates that 'these *sūtras* or lines like *Brahmasūtra, Pakasūtra* and *Bahissūtra* vary and fall at particular points on the canvas cutting particular parts of the form according as the *Sthāna* or pose in front, profile or three quarter-view and so forth:' D.N. Shukla, op. cit., p. 201.
526. C. Sivaramamurti, op. cit., 1978, pp. 33, 34.
527. D.T. Rice, op. cit., 1972, p. 199.

—*The Oxford Companion to Art,* (ed.,) Harold Osborne, 1970, p. 444.

528. D.T. Rice, op. cit., 1972, p. 200.
529. Prof. B. Prodanović, and Late Prof. Milo Milunović gave to understand in their classes.
530. K. Herberts, *The Complete Book of Artists' Technique,* 1963, p. 291.
531. D.T. Rice, op. cit., 1972, p. 201.
532. K. Herbert, op. cit., 1963, p. 291.
533. Ibid., p. 292.
534. Vojislav J. Djuric, *Sopoćani,* 1963, Pl. XLI.
535. D.T. Rice, op. cit., 1972, p. 200.
536. K. Herberts, op.cit., 1963, p. 291.
537. *The Oxford Companion to Art,* 1970, p. 444.
538. D.T. Rice, op. cit., 1972, p. 200.
    The Oxford Companion to Art, 1970, p. 444.
    Vojislav J. Djurić, *Sopoćani,* 1963, p. 68.
539. I.e., over apostle John's face in north transept West wall, Vojislav J. Djurić, *Sopoćani,* 1963, Pl. XLVIII.
540. D.T. Rice, op. cit., 1972, p. 201.
    Vojislav J. Djurić, *Sopoćani,* 1963, Pl. LVI.
541. D.T. Rice, op. cit., 1972, p. 200.
542. Vojislav J. Djurić, *Resava,* 1963, P. XV.
543. *The Oxford Campanion to Art,* 1970, p. 444.
544. Vojislav J. Djurić, *Sopoćani,* 1963, Pl. XXXI, XL.
545. *The Oxford Companion to Art,* 1970, op. cit, p. 444.
546. Vojislav J. Djurić, *Sopoćani,* 1963, p. 71.
547. B.B. Lal, op. cit., 1967, p. 55.
548. A.K. Bhattacharya, op. cit., 1974, pp. 34-35.
549. Maurizo Taddei, op. cit., 1977, pl. 59.
550. *Citrasūtra,* (43:21, 22).
551. Mario Bussagli, *Painting of Central Asia,* 1963, pp. 32, 35.
552. 'Very surely in the world's history,' writes Havell, 'has there come together that true symphony of the three arts: painting, sculpture and architectonic design, creating the most perfect architecture, which are so beautifully harmonized at Ajanta.'
    —quoted by Dr. S. Siddiqui, *The Charm of Aurangabad; A Pictorial Guide,* 1977, p. 30.
553. Solomon Gladstone, *Jottings at Ajanta,* 1923, p. 54.
554. P.A. Michelis, op. cit., 1964, p. 135.
555. V.J. Djurić, *Sopoćani,* 1963, p. 71.
556. D.T. Rice, op. cit., 1972, p. 203.
557. J.J. Pollitt, *The Art of Greece, 1400-31B.C.,* 1965, p. 55.
558. Madanjeet Singh has reproduced such effects of the paintings of Ajanta (cave 17), op. cit., 1965, pl. 12, p. 26.
559. Heinrich Zimmer, *The Art of Indian Asia,* vol. I, 1964, p. 190.
560. Karl Khandalavala, op. cit., 1974, p. 47.
561. S.P. Gupta comes out with the thesis that during Aśoka's times the heraldic-symbols were brought back in drawings by his *Dharma-mahāmātras,* emissaries to West Asia.

These were synthesised and made to suit the 'will of the people' hence digested on the Indian philosophic and aesthetic grounds. This he propounds against the refugee or journey-craftsmen theory. These were men behind the Mauryan art-motifs, believed to be from Persia (Wheeler, Boachhofer etc.), Bectria (Marshall) and Assyria (Irwin): S.P. Gupta, *The Roots of Indian Art*, 1980, pp. 273-300.

The relation of the Gupta-art with the north-west (Gandhāra) is seen in the terracottas of Mīrpurkhas (Sindh) and Devnimori (Gujarat). At both the places Corinthian type capitals could be noticed. U.P. Shah also found clear Gandhāran influence in some of Shamlaji sculptures—M. Taddei, op. cit., 1977, pp. 122-23. M. Taddei also quotes Philostratus (a neo Pythagorean philosopher living in 1st century A.D.) describing the Fire Temple at Jandial (Taxila) as a Zoroastrain temple, having the copper plaque-reliefs narrating events of Alexander and Porus and reminding one of 'production of Zeuxis, Polygnotus and Euphranor:' ibid., pp. 79-81.

—Appearance of 'Hunting-scenes' and theses related to other cults like Mazdaism from 1st century B.C. to 2nd and 3rd century A.D. (Madeleine Hallade, *The Gandhara Style and the Evolution of Buddhist Art*, 1968, p. 22). This is significant with reference to the 'animal frieze' along the stylobate in cave 9 at Ajanta.

562. At Nāgārjunakoṇḍa Śāka dresses and Dionysus's portrayal show the trade relations between Rome and South India, but its influence is negligible on Vengi-area.
—R.N. Misra, *Bhāratīya Mūrtikalā*, 1978, p. 114, 118, 122.

563. E.B. Feldmann, *Varieties of Visual Experience*, 2nd ed., p. 659.

564. 'Buddhist doctrine led to far-reaching speculations on the subject of light—and further developed under the influence of Iranian religious thought—to Amitabha Amitayus, the supreme Buddha of infinite Light and Life, hypostasis of the *Śākyamunī*'; S. Taki finds the theory of 'light' precisely worked out in *Saddharmapuṇḍarika Sūtra, Suvarṇaprabhāsa* and *Sukhāvativyuha*: Mario Bussagli, *Painting of Central Asia*, 1963, p. 35.

565. 'The principles of Amarāvatī art were executed and continued in the Gupta period... bustle and turmoil of human life—quietened down to a balance of equilibrium and peace...' S.N. Das Gupta, *Fundamentals of Indian Art*, 1960, pp. 96, 97.
—'The Gupta aesthetic put an end to this feverishness, and may be compared with early Gothic which shares the same moral and plastic significance:' Germin Bazin, *A Concise History of Art*, Pt. II, 1864, p. 445.
—'The Bagh Padmapāṇi is the major preceding source that influenced the painting of both the *Padmapāṇi* and *Vajrapāṇi* of Ajanta:' J. Anderson 'Bagh Caves, Historical and Descriptive Analysis, 3 paintings' part II, in *Marg*, Vol. XXV, No. 3, June 1972, p. 42.

566. Henrich Zimmer, op. cit., 1964, p. 349.

567. About the conception of the Buddha's figure there have always been divergent opinions. The synthesis is not denied by any of the historians of Indian art. The later scholarship supports that the technique and conception gave the ensuing visual perception as and when adapted. Snellgrove is also of the view that the new material (grantie rock of the Sahyadri hills) and the new cutting technique led to new language of form with regard to Buddha images formally and stylistically different from Mathura and Sarnath—*The Image of the Buddha*, 1978, p. 108.

568. Benjamin Rowland calls this 'attenuated indolent grace:' *The Art and Architecture of India*, 1970, p. 210.

569. Myrina terracottas of around 1st century B.C. of East Mediterranean school (late Hellenistic period) are of elongated figures (gen. women) of charming face and graceful poses having drapery clinging to body in looped folds up to legs. Stucco work of Afghanistan had its decisive influence. They are like elongation of figures in Amarāvatī and Nāgārjunakoṇḍa: S.P. Gupta, op. cit., 1980, p. 318 (though a direct influence on Mauryan art is denied by S.P. Gupta but a metamorphosis is also not denied). There were cycles of revival movement in Eastern Mediterranean which could be traced upto 4th century A.D. as Ernst Kitzinger has pointed out: *Byzantine Art in the Making*, 1977, p. 27. The probability of such artifacts reaching Deccan Roman settlements or ports cannot be ruled out. 'Dionysus' subjects presented at Nāgārjunakoṇḍa and at Ajanta should stand testimony to such influences. Threshold or step of cleft rocks in the foreground, a device to emphasise depth plus strengthen illusion of horizontal floor beneath the figure (e.g., 'Princess at her toilet,' cave 17, plate 120) has parallel representation in 5th century Roman mosaics. This tradition goes back to Late Hellenic and Roman Panel painters (Ernst Kitzinger, op. cit., 1977, p. 54), which also proves exchange of Roman pictorial devices.

—Such oblongation of figures becoming more of 'a sign in the silence of eternity than a reminder of earthly existence' is found in Etruscan 'ombara' bronzes—C. Wentinck, *The Human Figure*. Since Greeks influenced Etruscans, they played a decisive part in Roman painting. The Etruscan's 'Asian sensibility' in giving a 'live-vitality' (G. Bazin, *A Concise History of Art*, part I, 1964, p. 102), makes it logical to conclude that there was a certain relationship between 'ombara' and Myrina figures. Such formal hypothesis has a definite support in the works of Modegliani (1884-1920) and Giacometti (1901-66). Both fall in the line of spiritual restlessness of ElGreco for being tormented by the Illumination and Luminosity principles of light and space configurations.

—Thus it can also be logically said that in Myrina terracotta the synthesis made by East to balance the above 'restlessness in spiritual isolation' (as Feldmann, op cit., p. 19, puts for the figures of Giacometti) returned to its home-land to revitalize the Pitalkhora experiments in the 'attenuated indolent grace' of Amarāvatī.

—Not only religious but cultural aspect of Sātavāhanas was also in common with Hellenized Scythians. Mediterranean terracottas were leaving stylistic and technical influence on the productions from Pratishthanapura. M.N. Deshpande views the same. Port of Arikamedu—Virapatnam also had Roman ceramics due to southern maritime trade. (M. Taddei, *Monuments of Civilization, India*, 1977, p. 64.) The vases as presented in Ajanta paintings betray such influences. (Yazdani, *Ajanta*, part I, 1930, p. V, the Lady with Roman Amphora near the Royal seat on the right).

— The 'illumination' was used in late Hellenic and Pompeii's illusionistic effects, and behaviour of light in an 'unsystematic' and 'sensuously real in detail' style (H.W. Janson and Jane Dora, *History of Art*, 2nd edition, 1977, p. 187). It is evident in the small figures of the 'wheel of life' (cave 17, plate 105) which betrays assimilation but is used to describe physical world.

570. S.P. Gupta, op. cit., 1980, p. 127.

571. Heinrich Zimmer, op. cit., 1964, p. 224.

572. Irne Gajjar, *Ancient Indian Art and the West*, 1971, p. 29.

—'Most striking about these Harappan Sealing is their identification with later Indian traditions.'

573. Ibid., p. 32.
574. S.P. Gupta, op. cit., 1980, p. 72.
575. The vertical straight line expressing the joined and tightened legs indicates pre-*śavāsana* yoga exercises in pressing together the legs tc 'let the energy of your whole body fill your body below your navel, breathing centre and loins ... to gain the life-sap.' This exercise also gives the round abdomen indicated in Ajanta with the concave top-corners of *dhotis*. Such exercises are explained by the great Zen painter Hakuin Zenji.
— R.D.M. Shaw, (Trans.) *The Embossed Tea Kettle*, 1963, pp. 29-30.
576. S.P. Gupta, op. cit., pp. 173-82.
577. Heinrich Zimmer, op.cit., p. 137.
578. In this connection it is important to note the frontal nude figure of 'Mother goddess' between Hairiti and Pañcika having a lotus in the right hand, perching on the left is a composite bird having lizard's head and peacock's body behind which is painted a palmette-creeper—(The symbols used on ring-stones esp. of Kausambi Group, cf., S.P. Gupta, op. cit., p. 64).
579. Ibid., p. 325.
580. Heinrich Zimmer, op. cit., 1964, p. 335.
581. D.P. Singhal quoting S.K. Saraswati explains that Mathura being a converging point of ancient roots synthesised not only the Greek cult of image-worship but also adapted *Gandhāra's* motifs like drapery hanging in curved folds, women and acanthus: *India and World Civilization*, Vol. I, 1972, p. 56.
582. I.e. Left centre pillar in back aisles cave 4 (Plate 10).
583. S.P. Gupta, op. cit., 1980, pp. 105-203.
584. In Hariti temple (cave 2) the children carved in relief are carried over from the painting.
585. 'A mixed-media approach to architecture is almost inevitable when the designer feels that every part of the structure is magically alive:' E.B. Feldmann, *Varieties of Visual Experience*, 2nd ed., p. 420.
—It is what Allan Kaprow aims at in 'breaking down of the distinction between art and life,' *Dictionary of Art*, (ed.,) Eleanor S. Greenhill, 1974, p. 277.
586. Vojislav J. Djurić, *Sopoćani*, 1963, p. 58.
587. Mila Rajković, *Sopoćani*, 1963, p. 3.
588. Ernst Kitzinger, op. cit., 1977, p. 2.
589. David Talbot Rice, *Byzantine Art*, 1935, pp.29-35. They include Greece and Hellenic world; Asia Minor; Rome and Italy; "Syria and the Semitic East especially 'The mausoleum of Diacletian' at Spalato (early 4th century A.D.) where eastern ornament has to a great extent conquered the purely classical;" Palmera and Dura Eupopa; Northern Mesopotamia; Southern Mesopotamia and Southern Persia. He sums up "... so that it is in actual fact an age, a whole period of civilized world's history that must concern us. . . ." p. 208.
590. D.T. Rice, op. cit., 1972, p. 122.
591. Ernst Kitzinger; op. cit., p. 4.
592. Ibid., p. 124.
—Kitzinger has pointed out the morphological changes starting with the decomposition of classical form from Antonine and Severan periods and reaching in the Arch of Constantine (A.D. 315), a synthesis through 'the Eastern Mediterranean littoral and their Asiatic and African hinterlands' (p. 10), with 'spatial orientation of figures having pressed,

trapped as it were, between the imaginary planes and so lightly packed within' (p. 3.) Reassertion of Hellenic tendencies through 'Eastern Mediterranean' came in 4th century sarcophagi. Again, in 5th century, with the principles of affirmation of surface and shape as per the tendencies of *emblema* in Eastern Mediterranean mosaic floors in the Justinianic period and the use of Helenic-impressionism for dematerialization, came reductionism in painting of the late and post-Justinianic period. Hellenic tradition and transformations were brought out in 7th century. All such modularities in the formation of Byzantine Art have been pointed out as its greatest achievement lying 'not in their innovations—important as these are... but in having preserved, in the vast and cataclysmic changes, basic and essential elements of the 'Greco-Roman heritage' (p. 126): Kitzinger, op. cit.

593. 'It was primarily the habitual and natural use of a Hellenistic style for secular subjects and contents which kept that style alive at a critical stage:' Ibid., p. 123.
594. 'A slow and broadly based process of formal evolution with a powerful impetus of its non-involving conscious and deliberate revival efforts:' Ibid.
595. Ibid., p. 114.
596. Mila Rajković, *Sopoćani*, 1963, p. 3.
597. Erich Neumann, op. cit., p. 137, 1955, Fig. 22.
598. Djodje Mano-zisi, 'The Fascinating Land of Archaeology,' *Makedonija*, 1957, pp. 22-28.
599. D.T. Rice, op. cit., 1972, p. 152.
600. Mario Bussagli, 'The Art of Gandhāra,' in Bussagli and Sivaramamurti, *5000 Years of the Art of India*, p. 77.
601. Bussagli, 'Indian Influence in Central Asia', in ibid., p. 149.
602. M. Bussagli,' 'The Art of Gandhara' in ibid., p. 92.
603. 'New light on Kushan art,' *The Hindustan Times*, Vol. LVIII, No. 105, 17.4. 1981, p. 21, with photo of the central part of the relief 'Three musicans' found at Airtam.
—V.I. Sarianidi, 'More Sensational Discovery on the Archaeological Front,' 1980, Q-3, Archaeology, 18th Jan, 1980, Embassy of USSR, India.
604. M. Bussagli, 'The Indian Influence in Central Asia,' in op. cit., M. Bussagli and Sivaramamurti, p. 144.
605. D. Cornakov; *The Frescoes of the Church of St. Clement at Ohrid*, 1961, pl. 12, 'Annunciation,' detail.
606. *The Hindustan Times*, volume. LVIII, No. 105, 17.4.81, p. 21.
607. Mario Bussagli and Sivaramamurti, op. cit., Pl. 161.
—Fragment with Buddhist Monk's heads. Miran 2nd half A.D. 3rd cent., p. 145.
608. D. Cornakov, op. cit., pp. 4, 5, 7.
Svetozar Radojčić, *Yugoslavia, Mediaeval Frescoes*, UNESCO, 1957, p. 22. There is a curious detail of moustache-partition leaving the central part of the upper lip hairless on the face of St. Mercury and St. Nestor (Pl. 58 and 60, D. Cornakov, op. cit.,) and on the face of Christ (Nave, west wall, lunette of main doorway) at Sopoćani (Djurić, *Sopoćani*, pl. XLII) reminding one of Boddhisattvas of Gandhāra terracotta and the terracotta of Ushkar (Pl. 93 and 101, Bussagli and Sivaramamurti, op. cit., reminiscent of Gallic Hellenistic Roman types (Bussagli, 'The Art of Gaṇḍhara,' in ibid., p. 91).
609. Mario Bussagli, 'Indian Influence in Central Asia', in M. Bussagli, C. Sivaramamurti, op. cit., p. 147.
610. 'Boddha-Kala-ke-Srot,' Stebiski, in *Soviet Nari*, No. 12, 1974, p. 25.

611. M. Bussagli, C. Sivaramamurti, op. cit., Pl. 159.
612. Mario Bussagli, *Painting of Central Asia*, 1963, p. 71.
—Benjamin Rowland, *The Art and Architecture of India*, 1970, p. 192, pl. 132, p. 142.
613. V.J. Djuric, *Sopoćani*, 1963, Pl. I.
614. Ibid., pl. VII and also pl. LVI, The Archangel Michaelas Guardian of the Holy Trinity; Chapel of St. Stephen, South Wall.
615. Ernst Kitzinger, op. cit., 1977, p. 118-19 and Fig. 200.
616. Mario Bussagli, 'The Art of Gandhāra', in Bussagli, Sivaramamurti, op. cit., p. 77.
617. Mario Bussagli, 'Indian Influence in Central Asia', ibid., p. 142, pl. 158.
618. V.J. Djurić, *Sopoćani*, 1963, p. 64: 'Projektovanja compozicione structure na Pozadinu.'
619. Madanjeet Singh, op. cit., 1963, pl. 65.
620. Mario Bussagli, op. cit., p. 35.
621. Ibid., p. 48, 49.
622. Sogdiana, a province of the ancient Persian empire betwen the Oxus and Jaxartes rivers.
623. Ernst Kitzinger, op. cit., 1977, p. 88.
624. Ibid., p. 91.
625. S.P. Gupta, op. cit., 1980, p. 35.
626. Ernst Kitzinger, op. cit., Pl. II.
627. V.J. Djurić, *Sopoćani*, 1963, p. 117.
628. Ibid., Pl. XXII.
Such floating 'forthcoming' being the outcome of the 'inner-light' aesthetics is evident in Christ presented in the apse of SS Cosmo and Damian, Rome (A.D. 526-30) (plate 93.)
D.T. Rice, op. cit., 1972, p. 9.
629. V.J. Djurić, *Sopoćani*, 1963, pls. LIV, LV, LVIII.
630. Ibid., p. 119.
631. Ibid., p. 65.
632. Ibid., p. 71.
633. J.J. Pollitt., *The Art of Greece, 1400-31 B.C.*,, 1965, p. 55.
634. Petar Miljković-Pepek, *Nerezi*, 1966, p. III.
635. D.T. Rice finds in the apse mosaic of SS Cosmo and Damian (Rome A.D. 526-30) (plate 93) the influence of Eastern 'inner-light' principle later culminating into that of Hesychasts (op. cit., 1972 pp. 8, 65.) Ernst Kitzinger calls these forms 'strongly modelled' and 'pressing forward against the frame' (op. cit., 1977, p. 93). Thus the very synthesis of 'sculptural form' and 'projected structure of composition' reached at Sopoćani conforms to such Eastern principles of 'inner-light.' Miran school's 'schematic' perspective and 'forthcoming,' and II Indian style of white line used with black (Ajanta cave 2) are the concrete examples to prove further that the conception of inner growth of rinceaux-pattern or creeper-growth with potential endlessness and primary and secondary structures pointing to the projection of forms, as given to Justinianic mosaics (added with water-cosmology,) was of Indian origin.
636. Otto Demus, *Byzantine Art and the West*, 1970, p. 194.
637. Clement Greenberg, 'Foreword,' to Maurizio Taddei, op. cit., 1977, p. 7.
638. Except in later experiments (cave 2, plate 127) where the consistency of line separated

from the mass of colour and the conflict of illumination and luminosity brought out the 'painterly' form of *Vartanā*, cf. p. 170 (plates 127, 146).

639. *See* Glossary.

640. R. Arnheim, op. cit., 1960, pp. 164-72.

CHAPTER VI

SUMMARY

Since 1822, the year of Ajanta's introduction to the Bombay Literary Society, followed by the researches of about 150 years, Ajanta has become so well-known by now that it hardly requires any formal introduction. The murals in this art-complex of thirty caves are the surviving examples of India's panorama of a thousand years of creative activity starting around second century B.C. and giving a 'linguistic structure' to line, form, colour and value, spatial dimensions and the quality of surface.

On the other side, the modern research on Serbian painting, started in 1906 by Gabriel Millet, V.R. Petković and Josef Strzygowski, has acclaimed it among the finest creations of medieval Europe. It is rightly held that 'the best school of fresco-painters' of Greek-Byzantium created 'the most beautiful work of Serbian art' in the murals of Sopoćani (pronounced as Sopotchani). Sopoćani was also introduced to the world of letters in the middle of the nineteenth century by Gilferding. The painting started around A.D. 1263 in the church of the Holy Trinity of this monastery built amidst a fascinating landscape in the heart of Raška near the present capital of the socialist republic of Serbia in Yugoslavia. These precious works of art, comprising almost a century's creative endeavour, are regarded as a landmark in world-art, as is the art of Ajanta, both of them have been honoured by being published in the UNESCO World Art Series. Thus, the harm done by centuries of neglect and desecration has been compensated at least in part. The idea for the present research occurred while studying, first hand, the works of Byzantine art at almost all the centres in Yugoslavia including Mt. Athos. The study of Ajanta art before and after this period undertaken at the picturesque site gave strength to this idea. Astonished at the similarities suggested by the analogous aesthetic principles of inner-light and remaining conscious of the dissimilarities and constraints at the same time, the researcher decided to undertake *a comparative study of the art of Ajanta and Sopoćani.* As for the latter, it was found to be the most significant art centre representing the apex of similarities apparent in the broad canvas of the art of medieval Yugoslavia. The research was benefited by the insights of scholars like Grünwedel, Foucher, Coomaraswamy, Ray, Grabar, Rice, Rowland, Bazin, Kitzinger, Bussagli, Sivaramamurti, Grujić, Djurić, Radojčić, Rajković, Arnheim, Moffitt and Sakhalkar. Moreover, being a practising artist and a student of contemporary art, the researcher was also struck by the modern pictorial syntheses reaffirming a similarity between the inspirations given to it by the East and the Byzantine art. Withal, a form-meaning-expression model for the research process was taken up covering the following categories:

(A) General Categories: Comprising place and its environment, phases, scope, importance and relevance.

(B) Factual Categories: Political, social and cultural, and religious background and subject matter.

(C) Interpretative Categories: Philosophy, aesthetics and symbolism.

(D) Artist and patron.

(E) Style and technique: Iconography, subjective visualization of inner essence in formal and plastic ingredients, technique, influence of technique over structure and vice versa, originality and influence.

Following is the summary of the comparative studies presented according to the model of the research.

I. Formal Qualities

(a) Space and perspective and styles defined on the basis of spatial dimensions.
(b) Light, shape and form.
(c) Line.
(d) Colour and value.
(e) Quality of surface.
(f) Composition balance, rhythm movement, tension.

II. Expression

(a) Subjective visualization of inner essence; emotional, mystical, mythical, subconscious, abstract, transcendence and distortion.
(b) Subject matter, iconography, symbolism.
(c) Aesthetics.
(d) Religion.
(e) Philosophy.

III. Technique and influence of technique over structure and vice versa.
IV. Artist and patron, political, social and cultural background.
V. Influence and originality, importance, scope and further investigative possibilities.

(I) Formal Qualities

(a) *Space and perspective and styles defined on the basis of spatial dimensions:* The original intentions of the artists of Ajanta and Sopoćani were to re-establish their spatial modulations, harmonizing the continuously articulated network of the growth in the module of arboreal growth, on the total 'breathing surface' or the flat foil. To this effect they created a consecutive series of projections and depth dimensions to suit their signification and the content of the theme. In creating the most heraldic visions and the feeling of dimensional configurations these artists have used such original intentions which *Citrasūtra* appropriately terms as *nimnonnata vibhāga*, heights and depths, and classifies the artist using them properly as the knower and a great painter (*citravit*). In the use of 'modes,'[1] both the artists of Ajanta and Sopoćani have clearly suggested such concerns. These original intentions of artistic expressions, for a scientific study, can be explained in some basic syndromes whereby a comparative study can clearly be embarked upon. These syndromes are classified on the basis of visual terms of building ('tectonic') the dimensions of the surface of the picture encompassing horizontal and vertical structuring. These are as follows:

(i) Planer-Tectonic, (ii) Tectonic Spatial, (iii) A-Tectonic Spatial, (iv) Synthetic A-Tectonic Planer Spatial.

In fact, John F. Moffitt (1979) has defined these syndromes relating them to the art styles from Archaic periods to the contemporary art. As Indian art treatises also defined styles concerning *nimnonnata* and showing artistic intentions in its variances, the researcher found analogy between the classifications done by Moffitt and those of *Citrasūtra.* As such, the *satya-citra*, representing full volumes with its surface looking as if coming out to meet the spectator, relates to A-Tectonic Spatial intentions of the artists. The 'projected compositions from the wall' at Sopoćani relate to such a spatial experience. This immanent 'baroque' instinct is thus defined in the terms of Ajanta as well as Sopoćani turning pictorial into plastic experience (plates 155, 161). The balance of Tectonic Spatial is 'classical' and its harmonic cadence denotes the Vaiṇika style of Ajanta. Planer-Tectonic, with its 'firmest' forms having rhythmos, is Nāgara style in which the most heraldic of hieratic figures are conceived at Ajanta and Sopoćani (plates 122, 150 and 43). The synthetic A-Tectonic Planer-Spatial is the use of 'modes' to vivify various concerns of the themes. It is Miśra style of Ajanta shown in the 'Buddha in Kapilvastu' (cave 17, plate 155) and is also evident at Sopoćani in figures as well as in a grand-scheme like the 'Dormition' (nave, plate 160.) This 'manneristic trend' was found among the royal painters of both places. Comparison of their approach in other such syndromes is as follows:

(i) *Planer-Tectonic*: Similar perceptive factors in making the total planer surface as perceptual concern were adapted. The grid's continuity and articulated network was the basic denominator which the configurations followed (plates 19, 36). Planer concern is also achieved by means of circular radiation, consistency of interstices and horizontal bands. Pictorial syntax like busts (plates 44, 45), border designs, curtains, non-alignment of feet on ground line (plates 51, 52), wainscoating figures and rock-cliff edges (plates 48, 50) are commonly used in conforming the horizontal and vertical concerns to bring about the planer tactility. Pictorial rhythms and 'bulging' out of forms served the perception of the 'borderland' of the surface, which ultimately defined the dynamism of the inner spaces of the church or the caves.

The difference is that the total walls of Ajanta breathe and press towards outside whereas at Sopoćani the configurations are built to 'bulge, but the background adheres to the flat extendibility, although the gold background simulates the 'inner dimension.' The silhouetted figures, too, are flattened with the gold foil all around.

(ii) *Tectonic-Spatial*: Overlapping (especially crowding), oblique orientation of figures, (bi-positional *tribhaṇga* at Ajanta,) and three-fourth faces gave circular or screw-spatial dimensions, (plates 53, 70). Similar approaches in perspective are also evident, e.g., the use of sharp convergences, inverted perspective, perspective of related distance and frontal-isometric perspective, (plates 61, 62, 16, 141, 166). Different eye-levels of the background, too, build spatial feelings (plates 65, 66, 67). 'Tri-murti' plasticity of the volume of head achieved in India and medieval Yugoslavia is the logical outcome of such endeavours (plate 101) (cf. pp. 226).

(iii) *A-Tectonic Spatial*: In such multidirectional spatiality the space is dynamically made alive describing the volumes and its own 'flux' (plates 122, 123). This perception of the 'real' is aided by the actual use of the architectural units, e.g., by providing sharp convergences to achieve the 'projected' effect. Similarly, at both the places this multidimensionality is subjected to the rhythms of composition on the surface. At Ajanta these surfaces also breathe with the interior space of the caves which in *caityas* reach out through the *gavākṣa-*

windows to the summit of the mountain and is made to return through subtle curves and shape of the window (plate 14). At Sopoćani the walls act as periphery to define the dynamism of vertical ascendance of the interior space which, owing to subtle proportions, returns to define the tangibility of the objects presented in the murals. Since the objects have their own characteristic 'thingness' the integration of spatial rhythms are defined in Euclidian polygonal module which shows the conflict with the inner growth of the forms. The spatiality defined in 'modes' also does not conform to the movement of space resulting in discordance visually perceived.

In the full acceptance of the tree-module, there is harmony with spatial flux fully grasped at Ajanta—the arch example of such relationship is represented by the *stūpa*.

(b) *Light, Shape and Form*:

Light: The Buddhists' and Byzantians' preoccupation with 'inner-light' or 'heavenly light' is evident in their liberal use of a halo behind the head of the luminaries. This influenced their aesthetics of light in rejecting the principle of presenting 'illumination' through light gradients. Instead, the artists of Sopoćani and Ajanta, while accepting the 'luminosity' principles, made the arbitrary use of light and shade in building up of the forms. Thus, colours were used with their values like 'linguistic structure,' denoting the required expression in traditional art.

Thus, as was the case shown in the wooden structure of the monastery (cave 17) at Ajanta (plate 136), and faces painted at Sopoćani (plate 97), the virtuosity shown in the orientation of the 'objects' through the use of illumination principles also became 'linguistic.' But since such light gradients are also used in bringing out the effect of dimension in the real space of the cave or the church, they prove that such usages are being consciously and purposely done by the artists of Ajanta and Sopoćani. The analogy could be found in the use of the light gradients over the dark ground reaching up to the highlight or lightest ornaments. The superb mastery of these artists to build up the forms with such light values is evident at Ajanta in 'Bodhisattva Avalokiteśvara' (cave 1, plate 141) and the works in the chapel of St. Simeon Nemanja at Sopoćani (plate 142). The highlights in the eyes of the 'Lady under parasol' (cave 17) at Ajanta (plate 135) is comparable to the usages of illumination at Sopoćani (plate 138). It was not only halo shown as concretising the luminosity effects, but these artists also used luminous line effects, the II Indian manner (of Ajanta, plate 148) which became the standard of dark and light lines and even comb-patterns at Sopoćani (plate 130).

The conflict of the principles of illumination effects and those of luminosity are evident in the 'painterly style' of the 'woman with lotus' (cave 1) at Ajanta (plate 146) suggesting even the cast shadow on the neck. Such dichotomy is accepted by the painters of Sopoćani and is rendered as modes producing the effect of 'strange-light' (plate 161).

Shape and form: For the artists of Ajanta and Sopoćani the human shape was insufficient within itself unless it was given consistency with the ideal of *sādṛśya* with *adṛṣṭam* or prototype.' So the rhetorics of poses, gestures and synoptic presentation was adapted from the drama. These characteristic forms, including portraits, acquired growth, *vṛddhi*, in the introverted process of biological growth or arboreal growth over a system of proportion having *tāla* or nose as the germ unit or grid module. Such a module is perceptually evident in the paintings of Ajanta and Sopoćani in figure ground relationships, in trajectories and axes.

The sense of 'primary' structure is brought out in the brushing or *hairikajā-vartanā* and also in building form through the arbitrary use of chiaroscuro (plates 97, 138, 153). The visually satisfying clearcut forms were the outcome of the principle of *kṣaya* or *vibhaktatā*, extroverted motivation. A sense of *madhurattva* or levelling was added to the extroverted motivation to get the images like that of 'Bodhisattva Padmapāṇi' at Ajanta (plate 157) or of Joseph in the 'Nativity' at Sopoćani (plate 156). The unity of the principle of *vṛddhi* and *kṣaya* is moduled in the 'capitals' of the pillars painted in the paintings of Ajanta and Sopoćani. Both have harmonized 'primary' structure with arboreal growth (plates 47, 83)—a principle equally applicable in the unity achieved in the basic form of figures through rhythms. The 'living' semblance of human forms was achieved by the 'motor-behaviour' of periphery units in contrast to the calm poses painted by these artists. To all this was added the zeitgeist of the age with ornaments and clothes (plates 57, 58). Cast shadows below the eyes and face and over neck were 'type' at Sopoćani to enhance the 'historicity' (plate 138). But the tension in harmony is felt in these figures in comparison with those of Ajanta where total unity is apparent in the use of 'modes' in a figure (plate 122). To add to the myth and mystique, such forms were given ethereal look transforming their gross weight by modelling in light gradients, highlights as ornaments and comb-patterns leaving the body in simpler totality. Associative elements like flying ribbons and cloth-edges, horizon and use of steps gave them levitating effects. Figures subjected to rhythmos also made themselves 'ethereal' by submerging into these tactile rhythms.

(c) *Line:*

Transcription of form in this most abstract and one-dimensional trace reduced the contour shadows and made the linear bound form become bright (Avalokiteśvara, plate 141, and Chapel of St. Simeon Nemanja, plate 142,) organic—especially with modulations of brush lines (*hairikajā vartanā*)—and cohesive in bringing forth the interstices. Such a cohesive effect of form and interstices became the true mode of 'projected composition' at Sopoćani and of 'forthcoming' at Ajanta making the linear style the life of content and a means to bring harmony between the myriad forms at both the centres.

Self-contained status of line, though reached an autonomous state (plastically) in detaching from the mass of colour at Ajanta cave 2 ('the Boddhisattva', plate 127) delineated the material and the psychological states, e.g., in 'The Buddha in Kapilvastu' (plate 155) and the 'Dormition' (plate 161). Line, becoming the transcription of periphery light and highlights was resorted to give silhouette forms achieving monumentality and transparency effect similar to solarization of photo negative. The use of dark lines alongwith the light ones was experimented at Ajanta (cave 2, plate 148) but was in vogue at Sopoćani. The periphery-light-line defined the transparency of attire and the high-light-line as ornaments defined the transparency of volume at Ajanta. The effect of transparent and luminous volumes was achieved at Sopoćani by making these light lines as patterns (in angels, plate 130.) The basic difference of the linear work can be seen in composure at Ajanta (plate 155) and the constantly alternating mood between anguish and vitality at Sopoćani (plate 159).

(d) *Colour and Values*:
The artists of Ajanta and Sopoćani used the colours in perceptual and symbolic values for structuring and pouring forth the essence. Colours had a dynamic character for them to be rendered ultimately beyond day-to-day experience. Thus, gold and blue of the background turned into 'active space' showing dimension as well as the tactile surface. By using green as one of the basics both the artists have left a rich and subtle experience of colour. Used almost for identical syntax, their technique consisted of juxtaposing landing tones[2] in various admixtures, subordinating, dominating, inversing and complementing. Apparently, Ajanta colours conform to 'earthy' tones as do those of Sopoćani to the powdery and suffused light. Ultimately, both submit to the unity and integrity of the surface of the walls.

The germ-modules of fundamental colours left by them here and there stir the sight and create a lively harmony, dimension and modellings. Both of them have used the principles of separation of fundamentals, unity of complementaries, spreading and concentric movements of long and short wave colours and the mutual repellings of landing tones to create the images like Padmapāṇi, and Christ in the 'Dormition.' Colour as a bright-gradient illuminated the structural monumentality giving an 'animated repose' of intrinsic luminosity to Avalokiteśvara (plate 141) and to the paintings in the chapel of St. Simeon Nemanja (plate 142).

The dissimilarities become evident in the use of 'similarity of dominant colour' maintained at Ajanta in the admixtures. This, by giving essentially identical colours, still produces the dynamism, since the same colour is 'torn into two different scales' and provides the 'forthcoming' (plate 120). The use of complementaries, too, under this scheme produces tertiaries and 'earthy' colours giving a general resonance of coloured light giving a bodily or tactile sensation along with the extinguishing of particularity. On the other hand, at Sopoćani, the mixing of white (lime) as astringent is dominating with the principle of 'similarity of subordinate' colour producing essentially different colours connected by the same admixture. The colour produces undisturbed presence, the 'individuality,' (plate 161) giving a general resonance of white light. It lacks variety of vital forces and echoes 'completeness and nothingness.' The portraits painted in the admixtures of 'similarity of dominant' colour provide them a lively sense. Such a resonance of coloured light is realized also in the works of Chapel of St. Simeon (plate 142).

(e) *Quality of Surface:*

Although the glistening of the burnished surface at Ajanta and the gold foil in the background of Sopoćani paintings submit to the aesthetics of 'inner-light', the basic difference is that the surface of the former maintain the similar lustre all over but that of the latter has broken effect owing to the flattened silhouettes of figures painted in 'fresco' and peeping out of the golden glare.

Presently, this mystique of the surface is lost at both the places and a lustrous-matte surface is left with the disappearance of burnished shine and gold's glare. Calcite layer at Sopoćani and a residual film of astringents are noticeable at Ajanta. The thickness of brushing is perceptible at Sopoćani but at Ajanta only flat marks are left owing to the burnishing.

(f) *Composition/Balance, Bhūlamba*:

By treating similar themes of matriarchal principle in giving emphasis on centres of radial axes with basic shapes of figural arrangement, and melting them into a rhythmic web of visual stresses and contrapuntal weights, the artists of Ajanta and Sopoćani show artistic excellence in giving visual corollary to the theme.

Their such excellence of composition scandées is shown in 'the Dying Princess' (plate 72) and the 'Dormition' (plate 161).

The celestial myth conveyed in composition diffuses by homogeneously distributing forces and balance in the upper half of the 'Dormition' (plate 161) and in the 'Thousand Buddhas' (plate 124). This remains as spirit of the compositions of Ajanta alongwith the arbitrary sequences starting from left and distributing all over the wall and making the whole wall an aesthetic concern of a rhythmic-creeper added to the myth (plates 72, 76). Wall as a frame (cave 2, plate 54) and bands of narrative (caves 9 and 10, plates 53, 65 at Ajanta are noticed as individualized punctuations of Myth, but at Sopoćani (nave and narthex, plates 68, 69, 161), the artists tend to claim historical veracity through them. All the variants of compositional attitudes, i.e., composition *diffuses* and composition *scandées* (axial, centred and polarised,[3] e.g., in 'the Buddha preaching', plate 61) have been used at Ajanta as these are united for example in the 'Dormition' at Sopoćani (plate 161).

In grouping the similarity of basic module of orientation, i.e., tree-growth, has helped both the artists, 'forthcoming' and 'projected composition' have brought out proximity and parallel extrovert-motivations have given similar levelling processes. Directional glances and gestures are extra support in this unity achieved at Ajanta and Sopoćani.

Rhythm/Movement:

Rhythm, and movement reign supreme in the art of Ajanta and Sopoćani. Both used the connected movement in a figure, creating kinesthetic responses and reaching to the scale of complexity in hands, gestures and expressive units of the faces to give the form a palpable 'organism' as human participating in the narratives. Fertile movements arrested in stances and postures add to such a concern. With such rhythms/movements and the addition of 'projective' images creating verticality and horizontality in 'levitation' (plates 65, 66, 67) the artists create the Leafed-cross myth (plate 81) or actualize the 'Tree of Jesse' in the 'Dormition.' Similarly, these rhythms create the turning of the 'Wheel of Life' in 'The Dying Princess' (plate 73) inside the caves moving as the rhythmic creepers and actualizing the myth of *Hiraṇyagarbha*. The 'forthcoming' movement is evidently experienced in the 'Appearance to the Holy Women' at Sopoćani (plate 62), whereas it is the basic aesthetics of Ajanta. The spaces of the church and the caves also 'breathe' with such movements by which the walls of Sopoćani dematerialize but the walls of the caves of Ajanta participate as a unit.

The difference lies in the composure and intimacy of rhythm/movement at Ajanta and the conflict of vitality and anguish overwhelming the beholder at

Sopoćani.

Tension: Directed tensions, used as 'the happening' in the visual forms were applied to the narrative ends in the art of Ajanta and Sopoćani; with such 'happenings' the swinging of the figure of Irandati is created at Ajanta (plate 82). Similarly, 'the Christ in Glory' descends and returns in the 'Dormition' at Sopoćani (plate 161). Here the celestial vision is dynamic like the vision of 'Revelation' but at Ajanta it is 'a poetic dynamism set in motion.'

(II) Expression

(a) *Subjective Visualization of Inner Essence*:
The 'real (new) eye (sight)' of Ajanta paintings (as *Citrasūtra* propounds) and humanism with real feelings of Sopoćani paintings are created thus:

Emotion: *Bhāva* or mental state of *śṛngāra* or erotic, *madhura* or soft and sweet is made with highlight in the eye of 'the Lady' protected from sunlight under parasol at Ajanta (plate 135); similarly, illumination enhances the physicality of the *lāvaṇya* of angels at Sopoćani (plate 131). Below the eye-level roof behind the 'dancer' (plate 57) is as erotic as the bed behind the Potiphar's wife in the story of Joseph (plate 32). Erotic as preface to 'horrific' is presented in *Simhala Avadāna* (plate 133), as are the nudes in the purgatory at Sopoćani (plate 129). All submit to flavour of compassion for sublimation. *Ātmastha* or self-centred kind of compassionate heroism' overflows from Padmapāṇi (plate 157) in more or less in the same way as it does from the rhetorics of the figures of Apostles and Christ in the 'Dormition' (plate 159). The isolated groups of Apostles at Sopoćani express suppressed state binding them together in the emissary wisdom (plate 161). At Ajanta, groupings suggest detachment in serenity of mystic love (plate 157). Such dynamism of cosmic relationship is the *dhvani* of complementary colours making the mass of the body of Padmapāṇi. It is similarly expressed in the face of Christ but separated complementary colours in the figure ground relationship give isolation of re-assurance and man's individuality.

The difference in rhetorics of figures is exemplified in the eyebrow drawn with the miniaturist's intimate composure made monumental by giving contrast of the greater reticence of other members of the face of Padmapāṇi (plate 160) whereas in Christ (plate 159) its vitality is exaggerated by the participation of every other member, although the 'oratorical-sublime' is accentuated in the 'Dormition.' Serious countenance of Christ and smile of the Buddha are among popularly accepted differences (cf. pp. 110n. 237 on pp. 128-29, 147n. 24 on

p. 228).

Mystical: The light gradients structuring the 'luminous' bodies of Avalokiteśvara at Ajanta (plate 141) and the figures in the Chapel of St. Nemanja (plate 142) conform to the mystically glowing haloes used by the artists of both the centres. The difference is that of stress over individuality at Sopoćani. Ponderous contemplation in "The Buddha in Kapilvastu' (plates 122, 155) is similar to that of Joseph in the 'Nativity' (plate 156). Using the 'modes' of spatiality the artists of Ajanta create the mellowness of inner-light with tender and transparent treatment of mass which transfigures itself with minimum lines. The solarization effect of dark and light lines drawn together as folds in the figure of Joseph dematerializes itself in the consistency given to lines. Sharp convergences add to the 'forthcoming' of Bodhisattvas (plate 157) and Resurrected Christ (plate 62) done with 'breath of life' in plastic modelling and flow of line at Ajanta and free plasticity' and renceaux-rhythm at Sopoćani. The gold-background of the latter adds to mystic glow in which the figures left in fresco become silhouette and dematerialize, whereas the walls of Ajanta 'breathe' with glistening surface throughout.

Mythical: Plastic and associative syntax (flying ribbons, agitating folds, debased-feet, sharp-convergences, use of horizon and steps-syntax) showing 'levitation' have similarity of approach with the artists of Ajanta and Sopoćani. The 'elemental-space' gained through film-colour at the former and gold-background in the latter are similar in approach in making a mythic form of colour. The church and the cave spaces, by achieving verticality, form part of the myths rejuvenated. The reversals of sharp convergence dynamically relating the celestial with the world in the 'Dormition' (plate 77) and the 'Buddha preaching' (plate 61) are also such rejuvenations. Immobility of 'hieratic' figures treated in planer-tectonic frontality become a part of coming to terms with the duality of Life and Death (plates 122, 62). The myth of 'tree of life' is recreated in the creeper-rhythm and in the 'Tree' module adapted in *symmetria* and *rhythmos*[4] by the artists of Ajanta and Sopoćani. The former transfigures the whole-complex; in contrast, the latter transubstantiates preserving the material thing.

Subconscious: The concentration and rigorous study were an integral training for the artists of Ajanta and Sopoćani in order to present ultimate synthesis of their convictions born out of the inner-light aesthetics. The former, in a 'plant-like surrender,' humbly exhibits composure and resolution reached in the vision of life itself in its varied manifestations. The artist of Sopoćani, of course on a visionary plane, expresses unresolved contradiction of opposites in the vitality of confidence in the victory of man and anguish born out of the conflict with the opposite.

Abstract: Perception of the linear strength, sensibility towards the spread and concentration of colours (plates 122, 126, 127 and 142) interlocking of basic forms (plates 128, 129) and the use of style as 'modes' clearly indicate the preoccupation of the artists of Ajanta and Sopoćani with the abstract. The dissimilarity however, becomes apparent when 'modes' become detectable in the works of Sopoćani, i.e., using illumination principle in the head and the use of the luminosity principles in the body. The most abstract, 'breath,' transfigures at Ajanta but transubstantiates at Sopoćani.

Transcendence and Distortion: The crux of the exaltation of pure values is in the extension of verticality and horizontality emphasising the 'thereness' of wall. At Sopoćani these walls define the breathing of the inner space of the church; at Ajanta, 'thereness' also 'breathes' in living *prāṇa* participating in the exaltation of pure space of the caves. At Sopoćani, in the solitudes of these exaltations, the beholder is reassured by the 'Triumphant King of Glory' created in heroic image by exaggeration in the relationships of plastic factors (plate 161). At Ajanta, too, 'the heroism of compassion' is achieved in the reassuring Padmapāṇi (plate 157) by *kṣyavṛddhi* in the plastic syntax. Both the artists adapt vegetative module to their needs. At Ajanta, it becomes characteristic of cosmic relationships and at Sopoćani the 'characteristic' growth. The respectful eagerness is made dominant by the distortion of the shape and angle of plumb line transcending the figures of the maid in 'Nativity' (plate 139) and the Mary in 'Presentation in the temple' (plate 123). By similar methods the compassion surpasses in the figure of Padmapāṇi and suggests *abhayamudrā* even in the abstract shape in the background (plate 157).

(b) *Subject Matter*

As at the end of every discourse the Buddha would identify the characters of *Jātakas* with the present; in the same way the artists would paint the narratives on the walls of Ajanta juxtaposing events in this 'epic of Life.' By adding the function of cathedral church to that of the royal mausoleum, which Sopoćani originally was, the artists of Sopoćani also came to similar juxtaposing in the microcosm of the actual world. A circular conception of time overrides here as well. Such preoccupations suggest the story of Virgin's life being heavily indebted to the archetypal sphere of the Mother-Goddess, primordial symbolism of child bearing virgin, supernatural conception and birth of luminous son. Such conceptions of primordial matriarchal dominances are evident at Ajanta in the story of Gautama's birth, the presentation of 'Wheel of Life' and the excessive delineation of femininity, making it a 'temple of graces.' As such, not Sopoćani, but relevant medieval 'cultural sanctuaries' of Yugoslavia, too, have the 'temple of fair womanhood' (the King's church in Studenica, plate 34), the 'Wheel of Life' in the hands of the Virgin at Linder (plate 103) and *Jātaka* stories (presented at Beram).

Both the artists would present the narratives starting from left. The artist of Sopoćani gives stress on the subject in accordance with the Divine liturgy; for the artist of Ajanta, however, such punctuation is arbitrary except that the Buddhas and the Bodhisattvas are placed for ritual purposes usually in or around the sanctuary.

The similarities in the subject-matters of the lives of the Buddha and Christ are astonishing. Apart from 'miraculous conception and wondrous birth,' the names Mary and Māyā, too, suggest archetypal overtones. Future greatness is predicted on their days of birth. Asita is Buddhist Simeon visiting on air or by the spirit. At about the same age, both Siddhārtha and Jesus reveal their wisdom. Also, both have 'word' or 'logos' representing them (symbolically suggested) at Ajanta and Sopoćani (plates 11, 12). The 'Great Renunciation and Jesus' 'missing years of life' have similar implications as have the 'temptations' in both the cases. Both begin mission with twelve disciples to establish the Kingdom of righteousness caring for the sick, condemning asceticism and insisting on 'opening of oneself in faith.' Similarities between way of discourse, parables and miracles are pointedly noticeable: the blind receiving sight, walking on water with faith and feeding of hundred with small cake are but a few examples. 'Transfigurations' of both are presented. The Buddha gets transfigured after *nirvāṇa*, finally identified with self-existent Supreme; this matches with Christ's transfiguration and identification with the Supreme. Christ on Glory returns to help Mary become the 'highest wisdom.' The same is implied in the Buddha's return from Tūśita heaven where his mother participates in his divine wisdom and becomes *Prajñapārmitā* in the Buddhist cosmology.

The Buddha's cousin Devadatta is Judas and the soldiers' falling at Christ's feet in the garden of Gethsemane is similarly presented in Buddhism. The life of Bodhisattva Kundakumara's story in *Kśāntivādi Jātaka* matches with the 'passion' cycle of Christ's life. The presentation of the story of Jacob at Sopoćani is akin to the *Jātakas* in its edifying purpose.

Iconography: The frontality with 'immobility,' in 'Appearance to the Holy Women' (plate 62) and 'the Buddha in Kapilvastu' (plate 122) is eloquent of complete self withdrawal. In such images the *pramāṇa* or 'modal convention,' modified by 'modal differentiation'[5] or the zeitgeist is given the iconographical ideas; the 'other-directed'[6] one gets adjusted with what the artist of Ajanta and Sopoćani had visualized subjectively or 'inner-directedly.' The icon of Christ represents the conflict between the stream of Eastern abstraction and the Hellenic aesthetics. The Buddha's image presents a total abstraction of the 'Virāṭapuruṣa.' All the metaphysical signs of such imagery are perceptually or kinesthetically made alive like a cosmic reality (plate 122). Rhetorics of figure is theatre-influenced which brings about a similarity of approach with Christ in the 'Dormition' at Sopoćani (plate 159). This compassionate 'Jovian' image is parallel to the Bodhisattva Padmapāṇi (plate 160), although the reticence and subtlety of 'fertile' movements differentiate this image from the former's stress on 'individual traits' accommodated with the rhetorics of grace.

Bust-portraits have special charm for the artists of both the places (plates 44, 45), as is the stress on three-fourth faces. Likewise, the stances and torsions of body find similarity of arboreal module (plates 157, 161).

The narratives start from left and their arrangements speak of a process of transcendence from mundane to celestial sphere of light. The water cosmology has influenced the narrative cycles at Sopoćani (plate 112). Such a gyroscopic presentation of 'Twin-wheels,' the sun and the lotus, became the *Dharmacakra* and the wheel of Earth at Ajanta as the element of Buddhistic iconography.

Archetypal matriarchal principle through the popular religions has given the iconography of Mary's 'Dormition.' The enigma of life and death has been given the transcendental aspect in 'Mary becoming Sophia' (plate 161). Similar iconographic layout is found in the *Mahāpparinirvāṇa* (cave 17) at Ajanta (plate 162). In Sundari's death also the transcendence of Nanda is found (plate 72).

The Vedic conception of 'navel born' (plate 31) is the root of Tree of Jesse (plate 30), as it is of the iconography of the 'thousand Buddhas' (plates 124, 27). In *Hiraṇyagarbha*, the *Padmamūla* 'Tree of Life' and *Brahmamūla* (plate 22) 'Tree of Knowledge' overlap and become leafed-cross (plates 99, 23) as well as the iconographic base of other crosses (plates 15, 16), as it is also the base of *Tri-ratna* (plate 98). Lion and Root aspects of Christ (plate 102) find such base in the leafed-cross. The halo behind divinities is a part of such conception of both the places. 'Tree of Life' alongwith the ancient 'Hom' motif (plate 21) becomes the base of iconographic distribution of attributes (plates 13, 15, 21) i.e., the male attributes on right and the female on left (hence the concretization of idea in 'conversation' motif, a type of which is also found in Yugoslavia. Gold as celestial 'metaphor' and jewels expressive of eternity are made concrete at both the places (plates 115, 116, 141).

Buddhistic aniconic pillared-wheel (of inner-light) and 'empty throne' (plate

29) is similar to 'iconic' presentation of 'etimasija' and stylites on pillars (plate 28), in quietistic-meditation at Sopoćani. Thus, Buddha's *ūrṇa* (plate 96) also finds its place between the eyebrows of St. John the Divine (plate 97). Similarly, nudity as 'truth' is presented at Sopoćani (plate 129); it embodies ephemeral, phenomenal world at Ajanta (plate 128). Composite images are painted at both the centres (plates 33, 35). The similarities of iconographic details of ribbons, curtains, rock-cliffs, cubical rocks, quadrangular baptistry—consecration pavelion (*sarvato- bhadrika*)—are striking. All these are guarded by flanking deities at Ajanta as well as in Yugoslavian churches.

Symbolism:
The styles of various spatial dimensions were themselves the symbols used in 'modes.' They were anagogically enlarged to contain literal, moral and allegorical meanings for making the cave a Gandhakuṭi and the church a New Jerusalem. Their ultimate inner-light symbolism was breathing space which was symbolised in the creeper or the vine by the artists of Ajanta and Sopoćani.

Of this space the ultimate symbol was the *stūpa* or dome as *vāc* or 'word' (plates 11, 12). Their concentric growth as archetypal 'Celestial Fig-Tree' was symbolised in Tree of Jesse, or *Padmamūla* having the 'Sun' (*agni*) and 'Water of Life' (*soma*) aspects. This symbolism encompassed the presented symbolism from narratives to the halo and from *Tri-ratna* to Leafed Cross (plates 98, 99). The 'Tree of Life and of Knowledge' (plate 22) overlapping each other were symbolized in patriarchal cross; in gyroscopic presentation they became the base plan and the vertical plan of the church signifying the cycles of narrative from the mundane world born out of 'fountain' or 'water' to the celestial sphere of light (plate 112) and turned as a *cakra* (plate 106) in the halo of Christ at Sopoćani. All this is echoed in the symbolism presented on the ceiling of cave 2 at Ajanta (plate 116) and in Buddhist *Garbhakośā-dhātu maṇḍala* (plate 113), which has a striking similarity with the decorative details in Yugoslavian churches having a pillar paricarp (plate 114) topped with the sun born out of the lotus (plate 111). The 'Tree' symbolism finds its consummation in becoming the module of the growth of form at Ajanta and Sopoćani. Its basic laws governing the growth of symbol at Ajanta are also manifested in Yugoslavia. For example, the hybridization law has concrete proof in *Kīrtimukha* at Ajanta which also finds its place at Studenica (plate 102). The growth of these cultural sanctuaries is also arboreal in Yugoslavia as well as in India.

The 'Wheel of Life' in Mary's hand at Linder (plate 103) conforms to the symbolism in the ecclesiastical writings of Nicifor Kalist connecting archetypal Mother-Goddess symbolism. The spiral motif or uroboros, symbolising primeval male and female consciousness as an undifferentiated whole, finds its place at Mileševa, and significantly as mantle lines on the abdomen of Christ in Glory showing contemplative 'omphalopsychoi' practice. Similarly, it is presented by the side of the 'Wheel of Life' at Ajanta. By means of such symbolism Mary in the 'Dormition' and Sundari as the 'Dying Princess' become 'Copper-cauldron' in female body dying to give birth to the Highest Wisdom. Thus Sophia and images of *Prajñapāramitā* symbolize spiritual transformation of 'Wheel of Life' in the archetypal matriarchal symbolism. Their colour symbolism, too, finds striking similarity in Mary's green robe and *Prajñapāramitā*'s green colour. It is similar to the white for Christ in 'Transfiguration' at Sopoćani (as prescribed by *Herminy*) and moon-white given to Padmapāṇi at Ajanta (according to *Haṃsapuruṣa* concept in *Citrasūtra*).

Divine attributes and universal qualities are manifested in the images of man at Ajanta, so is he the 'microcosm of world' at Sopoćani. The difference is that at Sopoćani the symbolism is implicit in the overall heroic spectacle of mankind, having less preoccupation with aestheticism. It is more explicit in Ajanta's all-inclusive aestheticism, and the concept of universal life.

(c) *Aesthetics*

'Word' as literary charm, style and the divine inspiration presented in the motif of the evangelists looking skyward (plate 12) is similar to the motifs of conch over lotus painted at Ajanta symbolizing *sphoṭa* or *nāda* or *vāc* (plate 11). Conch symbolizing 'sky' implies also the divine inspiration for which *Citrasūtra* and *Herminy* both provide purification rites. As *Divyāvadāna* speaks of veneration to the designated in images, so does *Herminy*.

The word's aesthetic configuration was analyzed as rhetorics of figures influenced by dramaturgy at Sopoćani in the light of classical and medieval aesthetics. Similarly, the poetic qualities had found analysis from Bharata to the exponents of suggested meaning, *dhvani*, or *vāc*. Thus, the required proficiency in dance and dramaturgy automatically connected the artist of Ajanta with rhetorics and poetics. This was added with aesthetic appropriateness in 'modes' or *vṛttis* consummating in suggestiveness at both the places. The oratorical sublime at Sopoćani was suggested through rationalistic and demonstrative ideal filled with the pathetic element. For its configuration the idealism and the awareness of the tragic was adopted by the master of Sopoćani (this echoes at Ajanta too). This duality of *symmetria* and *rhythmos* woven together created, as H.W. Janson points out, the aesthetic suggestiveness of the classical style of Greece. The motifs such as the 'Dormition' also represent the Hellenistic phantasia theory of spiritually uplifting qualities of the work of art. Representing the 'mystical catharsis' and the 'religious catharsis' of primitives, this motif receives a sacramental value.

Emotion was also admitted as the principle of unity by the artist of Ajanta. In 'mystic-ecstasy,' through which the 'formless consciousness' of Buddhists was to become the *brahmānanda* of *dhvani* theorists in *rasa-dhvani* adapting the *prāṇa* aesthetics of the Vedantic tradition (*Citrasūtra*), thus, 'breathing pictures' were created. These were the cognitive structures of the Buddhist's 'flux' manifested in 'forthcoming.' Thus, the aniconic tradition based on the reductive (*kṣya*) principles of configuration (the extreme of which in the catabolic state reduces the formal organization to zero), was given the anabolic (*vṛddhi*) significance in the *prāṇa* aesthetics[7] or the aesthetics of 'inner light.' The creeper growth became its living symbol revitalizing the reductive grid on the ceilings of Ajanta.

This conception of 'inner light' brought out the creeper signification again in Justinianic Byzantine art through which the aniconic traditions of iconoclastic period were given the inner-growth of form. With such adaptation of 'forthcoming' aesthetics the artists of Sopoćani created images of the Resurrected Christ and 'projected composition.' But the concept of physical dematerialization before spiritual rebirth dominated and the creeper-*rhythmos* dematerialized the picture on the wall surface making it only an ingredient defining the dynamic space of the church. This was dissimilar to the making of the whole wall breathing and participating in the cave-space dynamism at Ajanta.

(d) *Religion*

The basic difference between Buddhist *saṁgha* and Christian church lies in the former's exclusive association in contrast with the universalistic establishment of the latter. As both gave concession from monotheism to polytheism in order to become religion, both also adapted common features to become world religions. The Hīṇayāna gave way to the catholicity of Mahāyāna, i.e., from 'exemplary prophecy' (wisdom) to 'emissary' type of wisdom. Similarly, the Serbian Orthodox Church adapted from 'emissary' type wisdom to the Hesychast's quietistic contemplation of 'exemplary prophecy.' Thus, the image of the Buddha from Supreme and static being gave way to multiplication in thousand Buddhas. Similarly, for the Revelation's Christ being first and the last creation of God, a full hierarchy of 'heavenly court' was added. There is a striking similarity between the Buddhist and Christian worships (both using incense, flowers, lights and singing, and having institutions like celibacy, relics and confessions). The charms were added later from the popular religions. Thus as Sahajayāna incorporated the individual traits within the 'way,' the individuals' 'infirmities' would also find Christ's grace.

In the universalizing concepts given to Christianity at the Nicaene councils, the Trinity was accepted. In the Mahāyānic Trinity, the Buddha being man is similar to the second 'being' in the Christian Trinity. The Buddha saves with example, not with the representative sacrifice for sin. The conception of Holy State of Serbian Orthodox Church is the outcome of emissary prophecy and active asceticism with its weighty civic strata. The inward contemplation of Buddhists did not result as such in the Holy state. Only the *Cakravartin* aspects of the Buddhahood resulted in a 'welfare state' and the conception of Maitrīya Buddha as the saviour awaiting in the Heaven. Analogously, Christ's second coming also became the major theme of many of the Byzantine churches. This brings out the similarity between the welfare aspect of Serbian monarch and the *Cakravartin* aspect taken up by the Guptas and the Vākāṭakas.

Similarity between the mystic-way or the consummation of mysticism is evident from *śīla* 'via purgativa' to *samādhi* 'via illuminativa' where active compassion of Buddhists and God's love both draw no distinction between the world here and heaven. But within themselves the distinction remains as that of 'Transubstantiation' in Christianity and 'Transfiguration' in Buddhism, the former giving a glimpse of the latter.

(e) *Philosophy*

Shunning metaphysical speculations and rejuvenating the ancient wisdom both, the Buddha and Christ, had the basic concern for spiritual rebirth. In universalization, the living traditions were added and a transformation from patriarchal to the dominance of matriarchal conceptions took place.

With the contemplation of 'inner-light' the stages of comprehension start from miseries of the matter going up to the enlightenment experience. The volitional effort is 'the way' *orthe-praxe*; the difference between faith and reason, thus, ceases. A theological development towards the first principle is evident starting from 'only for the human' in Christianity, the same all-embracing concept is meant 'for all sentient beings' in Buddhism. Absorbing the Logos philosophy, Dionysus' three stages are for the mystic experience—purification, illumination and consummation—attaining which the Divine eros creates reflections and Christ becomes the 'Fountain of Life.' Allowing the categories of *Māyā* to fall back into potentiality, the Buddhistic meditation, started with *śīla*, becomes conscious of interdependence resulting in the doctrine of flux, *Servam Santanam*; this brings the *vijñāna* or formless-consciousness as a positive attainment where the Buddha becomes identified with playful and purposeless character of the 'void' and the projection arises again. Peace of Arhat turns into the universal peace as it is in Christianity: 'Now the lord of peace himself give you peace always by all means.' The doctrine of Liberation, *Sukhavaṭī* with 'bondless light' is kingdom of God. Jesus 'advance in wisdom and stature' speaks of apostolic tradition transforming the Alexandrian philosophy heavily indebted to Indian metaphors of the 'birth' becoming 'purification of soul' and 'cycles of birth' for 'transcendental growth.'

Thus, the conception *Hiraṇyagarbha* imbibes 'world soul' Golden *Stūpa*, *vāc* or 'word' as the 'New Jerusalem' with 'Tree of Life' and 'Water of Life,' the *agni* and *soma* equivalents.

(III) Technique

With the indigenous modulations of proportion and maturity time, the mixture of sand (mud), lime, brick powder, vegetable and fibrous material was prepared by the artists of Ajanta and Sopoćani for the required thickness of the primary layer. Both started working from the top. The intonaco or *Suddha lepa* or 'opsis' consisted of fine slaked lime (with vegetable material) in thin layer and kept for not-too-wet technique of Ajanta fresco and the Byzantine-fresco at Sopoćani. Painting passages ranged from transparent to thick application and 'sacco' using linear brushing as well as the half-toning with medium on surface. The medium remained water with lime-white as astringent (with vegetable material at Ajanta). Colours were applied in plain patch (*patraja*) and hatching (*hairika* and *bindujā*) giving spatial and formal modulations. Starting with grid drawn for proportions and using charcoal (Indian treatises confirm) and sinopia for preliminary lining, (over incised tracing lines), light and shade areas and iconographic details were added after this *subhavarti rekhā*. The under-coating of terreverte is not ruled out before filling up the interstices with darks and bringing out the light gradients up to highlight or white ornament, while leaving at places the under-coating which render the effect similar to scrumbling. The artists of Sopoćani added foils of gold in tesserae form in the background and 'glistening' was achieved by burnishing at Ajanta (the use of gold is not ruled out).

Influence of Technique Over Structure and Vice versa:

Both chose heavy medium to bring out the unity of aesthetic complex combining sculpture/relief and architecture for the ultimate expression of dynamic space for 'Revelation' at Sopoćani and the 'flux' at Ajanta. The dematerializing was achieved by 'fresco transparency,' suffused light aided with golden background, and the consistency given to linearity at Sopoćani. The transfiguration of Ajanta walls was achieved through 'glistening' of burnishing and *bindujā*, and *patraja* application of (film) colours entailing 'space.' Linear application and hatching added to form modulations but also reduced them into the rhythmic planer-tectonic surface owing to the bulging interstices. Above all, the pliantness of wet surface added spontaneity to their lines.

(IV) Artist and Patron

The visionary master-artist of Sopoćani and the *sthavira* of Ajanta are comparable inasmuch as they harmonized different stylistic manners and also reconciled the directions of their patrons with the individual capacities of their assistants. By dint of their expertise and their leading role in art activity, both of them occupied high status in the society. They were at the top of three-tier system, the accomplishers, i.e., royal or monastic artists came next to them, and still below were the apprentices, evidently having the lowest social position. The higher positions in these artists' guild system were generally acquired by degrees; the experience and the family succession, too, played their parts. The master artists had direct access to the royal patrons. As such they could be sent as emissaries to alien lands where they collected novel and useful motifs and thus enriched the royal repertory of their native countries.

Indigenous artists, having had rigorous training in guild workshops and monasteries/universities including that of dance/drama, and expert foreign artists would be invited by the patrons, which would end their self-commending journeyman or refugee-artist status. Then onward would start the tradition of construction, carving and painting which continued for generations, and ultimately culminated in such cultural-sanctuaries as those of Ajanta and Sopoćani. The monk artists were also absorbed in this system. The general anonymity of these mature artists could be ascribed to their spiritual purification requirements prescribed both by *Herminy* and *Citrasūtra*.

In spite of striking similarities listed above there appears to be difference in vocational attitudes between the artists of Ajanta and Sopoćani. Although there was a general Buddhistic environment at Ajanta, it allowed sufficient scope for 'secularism' catering to the longing of the lower-strata artists who were sometimes in tussle with religious higher-ups. Becoming heterodox in their outlook they worked for all religions and, thus, contributed to the evolution of a countrywide style. The didactic character of narrative paintings at Ajanta did not fetter the freedom of the artist while his counterpart at Sopoćani seems to have been mostly impressed by the requirements of sacramental liturgy. Lastly, there are mentions of women artists working in India, it is not so in Serbia.

The royal patronage can be regarded as the manifestation of 'King's divine will'[8] at both the centres. It took concrete shape in the multiplication of cultural sanctuaries, speaking thus of their 'Justinian enthusiasm' and justifying the patron's titles like *Dharma-mahārāja* or 'Vice-regent of God.' The patrons were also the protectors of culture in as much as they assimilated the indigenous traditions while exercising their authority in the selection of the *sthaviras*/ master-artists.

The patrons' 'contest of piety' is perceptible through inscriptions and visuals. At Sopoćani we notice the family tree of Nemanjas, giving it a distinct character of dynastic patronages. However, at Ajanta, the non-royal and foreign donations give it a facet of secular patronage as well. Lastly, there is ample proof of ladies' patronage excercising its influence all along the graded male patronage including that of guilds, merchants, ministers, and religious heads.

Political, Social and Cultural Background:

With the 'commonwealth' vision of Alexander, the *city-states* expanded into the dreams of *Cakravartins*. It was the dream of Guptas and Vākāṭakas on this end of Alexander's conquered land and after a couple of centuries 'the vision' flowered at the other end into that of Tsar Dušan's proclamation as 'Emperor of the Serbs, Greeks, Bulgers and Albanians.' As an ancient Babylonian and Vedic concept, *Cakravartin* as 'a temporal complement to the spiritual idea of the Buddha' now turned into Vākāṭakas being 'Vice-regents of God' maintaining a 'welfare-state' and sending emissaries. The difference was that of the 'Holy state' status given by tzars (tsars) to the latter's territories.

With such backbone conceptions the 'Alexandrine module' also brought about political marriages, courtly intrigues, and 'royal eye gouging' in Byzantine-political philosophy, as was practised by the Mauryās (i.e., Gupta's ideals) too. The 'cultural sanctuaries' continued to be built in turbulent and war-engaging times.

The presence of giant literary figures like Kālidāsa in the Deccan speaks of Vākāṭaka age being the Golden period attracting the best of artistic talents and intellectuals making Ajanta the epitome of Indian art. Similarly, the Nemanjans attracted the best talents making them the legitimate heir and worthy of monumental tradition of Byzantine art, culminating into the most beautiful art of Sopoćani. Their literary figures like Domentian and Theodosius, and Dušan's law-codes plus the art treatises like *Herminy* speak of the similarity with that age of India which contained Kālidāsa and Bāṇa, the consolidated law-codes of Kātyāyana and art-treatises like *Citrasūtra*. The adoption of Sanskrit unified India, so were the Slavic regions with their own alphabet. Philosophies were crystallized, universities and monastic learning centres gave to the materially satisfied urban life the insights into literature, painting and drama to make life itself 'the texture of self-conscious work of art.' Parallel court pageantries and festive gaieties existed alongwith the lesson of life as 'endless tribulations and suffering.' Painting became the supreme expression of these refined urban societies whose backbone, of course, continued to be the agriculture. In this very age, Serbian landlords were establishing their independence, a phenomenon already got established during Sātavāhanas in India. Royal and social hierarchies were in vogue in both the ages and in India it was crystallized in caste system as were the four stages decided for the life of householder.

Owing to matriarchal dominance in thoughts, women participated from household to court-life and paid special attention to their physical presentation, not ignoring modesty. Mode of the general life in these two ages was marked with mystics, ascetics and tantrics or Eleusinian mystery cults. A liberal humanism existed alongwith the desire for erotic, aristocratic elegance and ceremonial imperial court. The finances were in a flourishing state due to coastal-trade, mining, internal trade and agriculture supporting the glamour of the court and monks. For Sātavāhanas and Vākāṭakas supporting Buddhism was a status symbol whereas for Nemanjids it was the task of the holy-state.

Started during the Sātavāhanas, Ajanta was completed during Gupta and Vākāṭaka period. Walter Spink's theory that most of its paintings were completed during the reign of Hariseṇa (last quarter of the fifth century) has started gaining serious attention. The monastery of Sopoćani was founded by King Uroš I and its major paintings were completed by about A.D. 1268. Exonarthex was painted during King Dušan's time (A.D. 1331-46) and side chapels were painted by seventh decade of the fourteenth century; the lower zone of the nave was repainted in the eighth decade. The works of these centres have been major sources of inspiration till today with their varying shades of art syntax.

(V) Influence and Originality, Scope, Importance and Further Suggestions

The influence maturing into the art of Ajanta and Sopoćani constitute 'a whole period of civilized world.' The artists of both the places synthesised their originalities from the pictorial syntax ranging right from the Greek classicism, Hellenism to the Sassanian and Gupta art including the Roman. The synthesis of the East Mediterranean, the Gandhārakuṣāṇa and the art of Central Asia added to their vigour. Above all, basic encounters with the existence and universal answers for coming to terms with Life and Death were provided by the folk and primitive traditions.

Sopoćani's flowering out of Byzantine's preoccupation with classical art, solely surviving in the Gandhāra and significantly synthesised by the Sassanian, Kuṣāṇa and Gupta compost (first century B.C. to seventh/eighth centuries A.D., especially by the art of Central Asia, the mother of whose art remains Ajanta) shows the intrinsic relationship between the arts of Ajanta and Sopoćani—for the latter the Byzantine art had become a vehicle ever since the Justinian era. The motifs such as water-birds used with creepers in Byzantine churches and lotus with triangular mountain like pericarp topped with sun (plate 111) in Yugoslavian churches support such conclusions. The Ūrṇā in Sopoćani (plate 97) and the *tri-mūrti* motif (plate 101) developed from there substantiate not only the 'modal convention'[9] of the artist of Sopoćani (plate 83) being from the Asiatic hinterland but also that the inner-light and 'forthcoming' conceptions (developed in Byzantine art since the time of Justinianic art, plate 93) belonged to it. It culminated into the 'projected composition' and Ajantasque forthcoming in the resurrected Christ manifested in the vein of Hesychast's contemplation (plate 62).

The plastic-code, creeper motif with water-cosmology, was provided to Byzantine art through East Mediterranean mosaics, as proposed by Ernst Kitzinger (1977), giving the forthcoming in the Christ of SS cosmo and Damian (plate 93, Rome A.D. 526-30). This is described by D.T. Rice (1972) as the influence of Eastern inner-light principle giving Buddhistic contemplation in Hesychast movement.

While synthesising fervent rhythm of Amarāvati, modules of creeper growth of Bagh, massive volumes of Mathurā and mellow surfaces of Sārnāth school, the grand originality of Ajanta lies in giving a tactile visuality to the 'forthcoming' and 'bodied-forth' of the primeval-matter *ākāśadhātu* as fully realised in the 'breathing' walls having cosmic relationship with the pure-space of the caves. These spaces, too, breathe in this *prāṇa* aesthetics giving an anabolic creative urge to the catabolic principles of formalistic activity—the latter being the *kṣaya* principle of *Citrasūtra* and the former the *Vṛddhi* principle which in its dichotomy with the earlier provides the *prāṇa* aesthetics or the aesthetics of 'living' and 'breathing-form' of primeval space—through which the Buddhist 'flux' is given a tactile form by means of calm and intimate 'transfiguring' brush in the hands of the artist of Ajanta.

The originality of the artist of Sopoćani lies in synthesising and decoding of the 'creeper motif,' transforming it into the zeitgeist of the Serbian Orthodox Church which came under the influence of Hesychast's inner-light concept. He too creates the variance of 'forthcoming' in what Djurić terms as the 'projected composition' and sculptural forms reaching the space. But in his vehemence to overwhelm, a trend born out of his overindulgence with the idea of man's victory, the *rhythmos* in duality with *symmetria* get exaggerated and the contours (a synthesis over dark lines and luminous lines of the IInd Indian manner) receiving consistency bring out the skeletal frame of the figures like the effect of 'solarization.' Such effects dematerialize the walls making them peripheries of the celestial-dynamism of the interior space in the church. Thus, through creeper-motif the artists of Sopoćani signifies 'transubstantiation'.

In short, the *prāṇa* aesthetics transfigures in the hands of the artist of Ajanta and 'transubstantiates' in those of the artist of Sopoćani.

The study of such aesthetic significance is of utmost importance for the present-day art environment in which the 'felt reductivism' is prevailing, cultivating the metaphor of 'entropy' in catabolic trends. Its scope as future study goes to the dawn of Western civilization—the Greeks, since its preoccupation with 'Tree' module in Art and Life is significantly borne out by such works as 'Man Between Two Trees' (plate 84) painted inside an East Greek cup of early Archaic period of Greek Art.[10] Maybe it symbolizes man's fate between the *Aśvattha* and Nyagrodha—(the celestial Tree with inverted position or the 'Bodhi Tree' of Buddhist Pali-literature.)[11]

REFERENCES

1. *See* Glossary.
2. Ibid.
3. Ibid.
4. Ibid.
5. Ibid.
6. Ibid.
7. Ibid.
8. Ibid.
9. Ibid.
10. M.A. Groenewegen Frankfort and Bernard Ashmole, *The Ancient World*, The Library of Art History, Vol. I, 1967, pl. 42, p. 143.
11. F.D.K. Bosch, *The Golden Germ*, 1960, pp. 70, 75.

—Scholars can discern 'Tree' motifs (plates 24, 25) in the Nestorian and the Manichean Budded crosses (Cross Botonée) at Valiya Palli, Kottayam and a similar cross at St. Thomas Mount Madras, India (plate 26) (plates given by P.V. Mathew, *A Reader in Early Christianity and Manichaeism in India*, 1977). These do prove a symbolic relationship with Leafed-cross (plate 23) (Patriarchal cross) at Arilje (Yugoslavia, Dr. Streten Petković, Arilje, 1965, pl. 24.) The Botonée cross at Madras also indicates a clear adaptation of '*Makara Torana*'—a symbolism which abounds at Ajanta.

—The scope of research of Ajanta's influence over Modern Art is substantiated by Dr. Laxmi P. Sihare's article on 'Indian Contribution to Expressionism and Its Impact on Modern

Indian Painting,' in *German Expressionist Painting*, catalogue, 1982, p. 153, showing a copy of Ajanta wall painting—'Hariti-Shrine', cave 2—by Ludwig Kirchner done from the copies published in John Griffiths' volumes). In the same vein Alex Von Jawlensky's portraits (e.g., self-portrait, illus. 329, p. 192—H.H. Arnason, *History of Modern Art*, 1977) could be compared with 'the woman with lotus in a palace scene' (cave 1, Ajanta, plates 146, 147) for its 'painterly style' and a 'battle between light effect and form in painting' (pp. 90, 170 and n. 181 on p. 236 of the present study); this comparison would ultimately illuminate the relationship between the aesthetics of Russo-Byzantine icons and the later 'inner-light' aesthetics developed in the Buddhist paintings.

BIBLIOGRAPHY

Agrawala, V.S., *Bhārtīya Kalā*, Prithvi Prakashan, Varanasi, 1966.

——., 'Gupta Art,' in Journal of the Uttar Pradesh Historical Society, Lucknow, 1948.

Anand, M.R., *Hindu View of Art*, Asia Publishing House, Bombay, 1957.

Archer, W.G., *India and Modern Art*, George Allen and Unwin Ltd., London, 1959.

Arnason, H.H., *History of Modern Art*, Prentice-Hall, Inc., Englewood, Cliffs, N.J. and H.N. Abrams, Inc., N.Y., 2nd ed., 1977.

Arnheim, R., *Entropy and Art*, an Essay on Disorder and Order, Univ. of California Press, 1971.

——., *Art and Visual Perception*, Univ. of California Press, 1960.

Ashton, L. (ed.,) *The Art of India and Pakistan*, Catalogue of the Exhibition at the Royal Academy of Arts, London, 1947-48.

Auboyer, J., 'Composition and Perspective at Ajantā, in Art and Letters, India and Pakistan, New Series, 22, 1, 1948.

Bajpai, K.D., in *Proceedings of Workshop in History of Art*, Baroda, 1977.

Baker, P. (ed.,) *Arts in Society*, Fontana/Collins, 1977.

Bank, A., *Byzantine Art*, in the collections of Soviet Museum, Aurora Art Pub., Leningrad, 1971.

Barrett, D., and Gray, B., *Wall Painting (2nd to 6th Century) Indian Painting*, Skira, 1978.

——., *Indian Painting*, Treasures of Asia, Skira, 1978.

Basin, Y., *Sementic Philosophy of Art*, Progress Publishers, Moscow, 1979.

Bazin, G., *A Concise History of Art*, The World of Art Library, T & H, London, (2nd. impression), 1964, Part I and II.

——., *The Loom of Art*, T & H, London, 1962.

Backwith J., *Early Medieval Art*, T & H, London, 1964.

Berger, J., in *Arts in the Society*, (ed.,) Paul Barker, Fontana, 1977.

Besant, A., and Leadbeater, C.W., *Talks on the Path of Occultism*, Vol. II *The Voice of the Silence*, Theosophical Publishing House, Madras, India 1930.

Bhargava, P.L., 'A Comparative Study of the Sanskrit and the Greek Dramatic Theory,' paper read at the Seminar on 'Principles of Literary Criticism in Sanskrit, Deptt. of Sanskrit, Univ. of Udaipur, Dec. 26-28, 1968.

Bhattacharya A.K., *Citralakṣaṇa*, A Treatise on Indian Painting: Saraswat Library,

Calcutta, 1974.

Bhattacharya, D.C., *Studies in Buddhist Iconography*, Manohar, N.D., 1978.

Bird, J., *Historical Researches* on the Origin and Principles of the Buddha and Jain Religions, Bombay, 1847.

Bondaille, G., *Gauguin*, The World of Art Library, Artists, T & H, London, 1964.

Bosch, F.D.K., *The Golden Germ: An Introduction to Indian Symbolism,* Mouton & Co., S-Gravenhage, 1960.

Brown, P., *Indian Painting*, Association Press, Calcutta, 1927.

Burgess, J., "Notes on the Buddhist Rock Temples of Ajanta and the Paintings of the Bagh Caves," Archaelogical Survey of India, 9, (1879), Bombay.

Burnham, J., *Beyond Modern Sculpture*, Allen Lane the Penguin Press, London, 1968.

Bussagli, M., Sivaramamurti, C., *5000 Years of the Art of India*, H.N. Abrams, Inc., New York–The T. Shah Enterprises, n.d., Bombay, India.

Bussagli, M., *Painting of Central Asia*, (Trans. S. Lothian), Skira, 1963.

Čelebonović, A., *Modern Yugoslav Painting*, Publishing House, 'Jugoslavija' 1965.

Chaitanya K., *A History of Indian Painting: The Mural Tradition*, Abhinav Pub., N. Delhi, 1976.

Chandra, M., *Studies in Early Indian Painting*, Asia Publishing House, New York, 1970.

Chattopadhyaya, D., *Lokayata*, Peoples Publishing House, N. Delhi, (Reprint, 1968).

Chatzidakis M. and Grabar, A., *Byzantine and Early Medieval Painting*, (Trans.) Taylor, S.W. Contact Books, London, 1965.

Christensen, E.O, *A Pictorial History of Western Art*, Mentor Book, 1964.

Constantelos, D.J., *Greek Orthodox Church*, The Seaburg Press, N.Y., 1967.

Coomaraswamy A.K., *Elements of Buddhist Iconography*, Munshiram Manoharlal, N. Delhi, 2nd Edition, 1972.

——, *Christian and Oriental Philosophy of Art*, Dover Publication Inc., N.Y., 1956.

——, *History of Indian & Indonesian Art*, Edward Goldsten, London, 1927.

Čornakov, D., *The Frescoes of the Church of St. Clement at Ochrid*, Izdavački Zavod, Jugoslavija, Beograd, 1961.

Cunningham, A., Archaeological Survey of India, Reports, 1872-73.

Dasgupta, S.N., *Fundamentals of Indian Art*, Bharatiya Vidya Bhawan, Bombay, 1960.

Davidov, D., *Krusedol*, Izdavački Zavod, Jugoslavija, Beograd, 1964.

——*Hopovo*, I.Z.J., Beograd, and Metica Srpska, Novisad, 1964.

Dey, M.C., *My Pilgrimages to Ajanta and Bagh*, London, 1925.

Dhavalikar, M.K., *Ajanta, A Cultural Study*, Poona, 1973.

Djurić, V.J., *Sopoćani*, Srpska Khnizevna Zadruga, Izdavačko Preduzeće, Procveta, Beograd, 1963.

——, *The Church of St. Sophia in Ohrid*, Izdavački Zavcd, Jugoslavija, Beograd, 1963.

——, *Resava*, Izdavački Zavod, Jugoslavija, Beograd, 1963.

Dutta, N., *Buddhist Sects in India*, Motilal Banarsidass, Delhi, 1978.

Dwivedi, H.P., *Sahitya Ka Marm*, Lucknow, Vishva Vidyalaya Vyakhyanmala-I.

Eliki, Z., 'A Realistic View of Gandhara Art': Interpretations', *The Hindustan Times*, Vol. LIV, No. 241, p. 7, Saturday, Sept., 3, 1977, N. Delhi.

Every, G., *Christian Mythology*, Hamlyn, London, 1970.

Feldmann, E.B., *Varieties of Visual Experience*, Prentice-Hall, Inc., Englewood Cliffs, N.J.H.N. Abrams, Inc., NY. 2nd. ed.

Fergusson, J. and Burgess, J., *The Cave Temples of India*, Oriental Books Reprint Corporation, Delhi, (First pub. 1880) 1969.

Finley, M.I. (ed.,) *The Legacy of Greece*, Clarendon Press, Oxford, 1981.

Fisher, H.A.L., *A History of Europe*, Vol. I, The Fontana Library, (7th ed) 1970.

Fisković, C., *Dalmatinska Freske*, 'Zora' Izadavačo Poduzeće, Zagreb Medieval Art in Yugoslavia Series, 1965.

Foucher, A., *The Beginnings of Buddhist Art* and other Essays in Indian and Oriental—Asian Archeology; Indological Book House, Varanasi, Delhi, (Trans.) Thomas L.A. and Thomas F.W., 1972. (1st Pub. 1917).

Frazer, J.G., *The Golden Bough*, A Study in Magic and Religion, Part IV, Adonis Attis Osiris, Vol. I, 3rd Edition, The Macmillan Press Ltd., London and Basing Stoke, reprint, 1976.

Frederic, L., *Indian Temples and Sculptures*, Thames and Hudson, London, 1959.

Fry, R., *Last Lectures*, Beacon Press, Boston, 1962.

Frye, R.M., *Milton's Imagery and the Visual Arts*, Iconographic Tradition in the Epic Poems, Princeton Univ. Press, N. Jersey, 1978.

Fučić, B., *Istarske Freske*, 'Zora' Izdavočko Poduzeće, Zagreb, 1963.

Gajjar, I.N., *Ancient Indian Art and the West*, A Study of Parallels, Continuity and Symbolism from Proto-historic to Early Buddhist Times, D.B. Taraporevala Sons & Co. Pvt. Ltd., Bombay, 1971.

Garcia, L.P., Galloway, J. Lommel A., *Prehistoric and Primitive Art*, Thames and Hudson, London.

Gardner, H., *Art Through the Ages*, G. Bell & Sons Ltd., 4th Ed., 1959.

Gerola V., *Bharatiya Chitrakalā*, Archaeological Survey of India, N. Delhi, 1967.

Ghosh, A. (ed.,) *Ajanta Murals*, Archaeological Survey of India, N. Delhi, 1967.

Gladstone S.W.E., *Jottings at Ajanta*, The Times Press, Bombay, 1923.—*The Bombay Revival of Indian Art*, Pub. Sir J.J. School of Art, 1924.

Goetz, H., *India, Five Thousand Years of Indian Art*, Methuen, London, 1924.

——, 'The Neglected Aspects of Ajanta Art,' in Mārg, 2, n.4, 1947.

Goswamy, B.N. and Dahmen-Dallapiccola, *An Early Document of Indian Art The Citralakṣaṇa of Nagnajit*, trans. of the *Citralakṣaṇa* based on the Tibetan Tanjur, edit. and trans. by Berthold Laufer, Manohar Book Service, New Delhi, 1976.

Gombrich, E.H., *Art and Illusion*, N.Y., Pantheon, 1951

Grabar, A., *Byzantine Painting*, The Great Centuries of Painting (Trans. Gilbert, S.) ——,SKIRA, NY.

Greek Mosaics of the Byzantine Period, (Mentor-UNESCO), The New American Library of World Literature, Inc., 1964.

Greenhill, E.S., *Dictionary of Art,* Dell Pub. Co., Inc., NY, 1974.

Griffith, J., *Painting in the Buddhist Cave Temple of Ajanta,* 2 vols., London, 1896-97.

Groenewegen, Frankfort M.A. and Ashmole B., *The Ancient World,* the library of Art History, Vol. 1, Mentor: The New American Library, Inc., NY, 1967.

Grohmann, W. (ed.,) *Art of Our Time,* Thames and Hudson, 1966.

Grünwedel, A., *Buddhist Art in India,* (Trans.) Gibson, A.C. and Burgess J., Revised and Enlarged, S.Chand & Co. Pvt. Ltd., N. Delhi, Reprint 1972 (first published 1901).

Gupta, S.P., *The Roots of Indian Art,* B.R. Publishing Corp., Delhi, 1980.

Gupte, R.S. and Mahajan, B.D., *Ajanta, Ellora and Aurangabad Caves,* D.B. Taraporevala Sons & Co. Pvt. Ltd., Bombay, 1962.

Haftsmann, W., *Painting in the Twentieth Century,* (2 Vols.) Lund Humpahries, London 1960.

Harold, M. (ed.,) *The Oxford Companion to Art,* Oxford, 1970.

Hartt, F., *History of Italian Renaissance Art,* Prentice-Hall, Inc, N.J. and H.N. Abrams, Inc., N.Y.

Havell, E.B., *Ideals of Indian Art,* John Murray, London, 1920.

Herberts, K., *The Complete Book of Artist's Techniques,* Thames & Hudson, London, 1963.

Herringham (Lady) C., *Ajanta Frescoes,* Indian Society, Oxford Univ. Press, 1915.

Hinnells, J.R., *Persian Mythology,* The Homlyn Publication Group Ltd., N.Y. 1973.

Houser, A., *The Social History of Art,* Vol. I (Trans. in collaboration with author-Sanley Godman), Routledge & Kegan Paul, reprint, 1968.

Hurst, J.F., *Indika,* Harper & Bros., N.Y., 1891.

Ivančević, R., *Beram,* Izdavački Zavod, Jugoslavija, Beograd, 1965.

Jain, Nirmala, *Rasa Siddhānta aur Saundarya Śāstra,* National Publishing House, Delhi, 1967.

Jairazbhoy, R.A., *Oriental Influence in Western Art,* Asia Publishing House, Bombay, 1965.

Janson H.W. and Dora, J., *History of Art,* H.N. Abrams and Prentice Hall, 2nd ed., 1977.

Janson, H.W., *History of Art,* 2nd edition, Prentice Hall Inc., E. Cliffs, N.J. & H.N. Abrams, Inc., N.Y. 1977.

Kapur, G., *Contemporary Indian Artists,* Vikas Publishing House Pvt. Ltd., N. Delhi, 1978.

Kaul, M., *Trends in Indian Painting, Ancient, Medieval, Modern,* Dhoomimal Ramchand, N. Delhi, 1961.

Keith, A.B., *Sanskrit Sahitya ka Itihas,* Trans. Shastri, M.D., Motilal Banarsidass, India, 1967.

Kepes, G. (ed.,) *Sign, Image and Symbol,* Studio Vista, London.

——, *Module, Symmetry Proportion,* Vision Value series, Studio Vista Ltd., London,

1966.

——, *Education of Vision*, Studio Vista, London, 1965.

Khandalavala, K., *The Development of Style in Indian Painting*, Heras Memorial Lectures, 1969, Mecmillan India, 1974.

Kitzinger, E., *Byzantine Art in the Making*, Main lines of stylistic development in Mediterranean Art, 3rd 7th century, Faber & Faber Ltd., London, 1977.

Kolaric, M., *Latter-day Yugoslav Sculpture*, Jugoslavija, Belgrade, 1961.

Kramrisch, S., *Survey of Painting in the Deccan*, Archaeological Deptt. H.E.H. The Nizam's Govt., 1937.

——, *The Art of India*, Tradition of Indian Sculpture Painting and Architecture, The Phaidan Press, London, 2nd Edition, 1955.

Krishna K., *Alamkara Shastra Ka Itihas*, Sahitya Bhandar, Meerut, 1975.

Krishnamoorthy, K., *Dhvanyāloka of Ānandavardhana*, Karnatak University, Dharwar, 1974.

Leach, E., *Lévi-Strauss*, Fontana Modern Masters, 4th impression, 1972.

Lee, R.S., *Freud and Christianity*, Penguin Books, 1962.

Levey, M., *A Concise History of Painting from Giotto to Cézanne*, Thames & Hudson, London, 1964.

Levi, *The Aquarian Gospel of Jesus the Christ*, Devors & Co. Calif, U.S.A.

Lévi-Strauss, C., *Structural Anthropology*, Trans Jacobson and Schoepf, Penguin University Books, 1972.

Ljubinković, M., *Ravanica*, Izdavački Zavod, Jugoslavija, Beograd, 1966.

——, *The Church of the Apostles in the Patriarchate of Peć*, Izdavački Zavod, Jugoslavija, Beograd, 1964.

MacIntyre, A., *Marxism and Christianity*, Pelican Books, 1971.

Maity S.K., *The Imperial Guptas and Their Times*, (Cir, A.D. 300-550) Munshiram Manoharlal Pub. Pvt. Ltd., N. Delhi, 1975.

Malraux, A., *The Metamorphosis of the Gods*, (Trans.) Gilbert S., Secker and Warburg, London, 1960.

——, *The Voices of Silence*, (Trans.) Gilbert S., Secker and Warburg, London, 1956.

Maranda, P. (ed), *Mythology*, Penguin Education, 1973.

Marx, K. and Engels, F., *On Religion*, 2nd impression, Foreign Languages Publishing House, Moscow.

Mascaro, J., *The Dhammapada*, The Path of Perfection, Trans. from Pali, Penguin Books, 1973.

Mathew, P.V., *A Reader in Early Christianity and Manichaeism in India*, Pub. the author, Cochin, Kerala, 1977.

Michelis, P.A., *An Aesthetic Approach to Byzantine Art*, B.T. Batsford Ltd., London, 1964.

Mijović, P., *Dečani*, Medieval Art in Yugoslavia Series, Izdavački Zavod, Beograd, 1963.

Mikić, O., *Bodjani*, Izdavački Zavod, Jugoslavija, Beograd, 1964.

Miljković-Pepek, P., *Nerezi*, Izdavački Zavod, Jugoslavija, Beograd, 1966.

Millet, G., Ibrovac, P.E., and Kašanin, M., *d'art byzantin chez les slaves*, II, Paris, 1930 (Orient et Byzance, IV).

——, *L'ancin art serbe*; *les églises*, Paris, 1919.

Mirashi, V.V., (ed.,) Corpus Inscriptionum Indicarum, Vol. V, Inscriptions of the Vākāṭakas, 1963, Hyderbad Archaeological Series, XIV.

Misra, R.N., *Bhārtīya Mūrtikalā*, The Macmillan Co. of India Ltd., N. Delhi, 1978.

Mitra, D., *Ajanta*, Pub. The Director General, Archaeological Survey of India, N. Delhi, 7th edition, 1974.

Mitra, R., 'On Representation of Foreigners in the Ajanta Frescoes, in *Journal of the Asiatic Society of Bengal*, 47, 1878.

Moffitt, J.M., in *Leonardo* Vol. XII4., 1979.

Morey, C.R. *Early Christian Art*, Princeton, 1942.

Murray, P. and Murray, L., *A Dictionary of Art and Artist*, Penguin, 1975.

Myres, B.S., *Understanding Art*, Holt Rinehart and Winston Inc., N.Y., 1958.

Ness, J.L. (ed.,), *Lyonel Feininger*, Documentary Monographs on Modern Art Series, Praeger Publisher, N.Y. 1974.

Neumann, E., *The Great Mother*, an analysis of the Archetype (Trans. Manheim P.), Routledge & Kegan Paul Ltd., London, 1955.

Nikolovski, A., *The Frescoes of Kurbinovo*, Medieval Art in Yugoslavia Series, Publicističko-Izdavački Zavod Jugoslavija, Beograd, 1961.

Okunev, L., *Monumenta artis Serbicae*, I-IV, Prague, 1928-32.

Otto, D., *Byzantine Art and the West*, Weidenfeld & Nicolson, London, 1970.

Oursler, F., *The Greatest Book Ever Written*, The World's Work, (1913) Ltd., Surrey G.B., 1952.

Ozenfant, *Foundations of Modern Art* (Trans. Rodker, J.), Dover Pub. Inc., N.Y. 1952.

Pandey, K.C., *Comparative Aesthetics*, Vol. I, 2nd Edition, The Chowkhamba Sanskrit Series Office, Varanasi, 1959.

——, *Comparative Aesthetics*, Vol. II, *Western Aesthetics*, Vol. IV, The Chowkhamba Sanskrit Series, Banaras, 1956.

Pandeya, R.C. (ed.,) *Buddhist Studies in India*, Motilal Banarsidass, Delhi, 1975.

Parimoo, R. (ed.,) *Proceedings of Workshop in History of Art, 1977*, Pub. R. Parimoo, Baroda, 1979.

——, *Studies in Modern Indian Art*, Kanak Publications, N. Delhi, 1975.

Partridge, M., *Serbo-Croatian*, Jugoslavija, Beograd, 1964.

Perkins, A., *The Art of Dura-Europos*, Oxford, 1973

Petković, S., *Arilje*, Izdavački Zavod, Jugoslavija, Beograd, 1965.

Petković, V., *La peinture Serbe du* moyen-âge, 2 vols., Belgrade, 1930-34.

Pierce, J.S., *From Abacus to Zeus*, Prentice Hall, Inc. Englewood Cliffs, N. Jersey, 1968.

Pollit, J.J., *The Art of Greece 1400-31B.C.*, Sources and Documents, Prentice Hall, Inc. Englewood, L., N. Jersey 1965.

Radhakrishnan, S. and Moore, C.A. (eds.,) *A Source Book in Indian Philosophy*, (Princeton, N., Jersey) Pub. Oxford Univ. Press, 6th printing, 1967.

Radhakrishnan, S., *Eastern Religions and Western Thought*, Oxford Univ. Press, (Indian 2nd Impression) 1975.

——, *Dharma Tulnātmak Dṛśti main*, (Trans. of East and West in Religion), Trans. Viraz, Rajpal & Sons, Delhi, 1966.

Radojčić, S., *Mileševa*, Srpska Khnizevna Zadruga, Izdavačko Preduzeće, 'Prosveta' Beograd, 1963.

——, Kalenić, Izdavačko Zavod, Jugoslavija, Beograd, 1964.

——, *IKONE*, Serbije, Mekedonije, Publishing House, Jugoslavija, Beograd, 1961.

——, *Yoguslavia-Mediaeval Frescoes*, UNESCO, 1956.

Rajoković, M., *Sopoćani*, Medieval Art in Yugoslavia Series, Jugoslavija, 1963.

——, *The Kings Church in Studenica*, Izdavacki Zavod, Jugoslavija, Beograd, 1964.

Rall, H.F., *The Life of Jesus*, The Methodist Book Concern, N.Y. 1928.

Randhawa, M.S., and Galbraith, J.K., *Indian Painting, the Scene Themes and Legends*, Oxford & I.B.H. Pub. Co., Calcutta, Bombay and N. Delhi, 1968.

Ray, N.R., *Idea and Images in Indian Art*, Munshiram Manoharlal Pub. Pvt. Ltd., 1973.

——, *Bhārtīya Kalā Kā Adhyayana*, The Macmillan Co. of India Ltd., N. Delhi, 1978.

Rawlinson, H.C., *Intercourse between Indian and the Western World*, Cambridge, 1916.

Read, H., *Art and Alienation*, Thames & Hudson, London, 1967.

Rest, F., *Our Christian Symbols*, The Christian Education Press, Philadelphia, Pennsylvania, 1956.

Ribnikar, J., *Yugoslavia-One-Long-Summer*, McGraw-Hill Book Co., N.Y., Toronto, London, 1964.

Rice, D.T., *The Appreciation of Byzantine Art*, The appreciation of the Art (Series) (General ed.,) Osborne Harold, Oxford Univ. Press, London, 1972.

——, *Byzantine Art*, Oxford, G.B., 1935.

Robertson, R. (ed.,), *Sociology of Religion*, Penguin Modern Sociology Readings, 1969.

Rowland, B., *The Art and Architecture of Indian Buddhist, Hindu, Jain*, Penguin Books, 1970.

——, *Art in East and West*, An Introduction Through Comparisons, Harvard Univ. Press, Cambridge, 1954.

Roy, Krishnadas, *Bhārat Kī Chitrakalā*, Bharti Bhandar, Leader Press, Allahabad, 2023 V.

Sakhalkar, R.V., *Ādhunik Chitrakalā Kā Itihās*, Rajasthan Hindi Granth Akademi, Jaipur, 1971.

Sakota, M., *Dečani*, Tourist Union and Touristička Štampa, Beograd, 1960.

Sarianidi, V. I., *More Sensational Discoveries on the Archaeological Front*, Q3,

Archaeology, issue of the Embassy of USSR, India, N. Delhi 18th Jan., 1980.
Schapiro, M., Romanesque Art (Selected Papers), George Braziller, N.Y. 1977.
——, Late Antique, Early Christian and Mediaeval Art, George Braziller, N.Y. 1979.
Seuphor, M., *A Dictionary of Abstract Painting Preceded by a History of Abstract Painting*, Methuen and Co. Ltd., London, 1958.
Shah, P., *Viṣṇudharmottara-Purāna*, Third Khanda, Vol. II, Gaekwad's Oriental Series, No. 137, Oriental Institute, Baroda, 1961.
Shastri, D.D., *Kamasutram*, The Chowkhamba Sanskrit Series, Banaras, 1964.
Shastri, R.K.S., *The Indian Concept of the Beautiful*, Univ. of Trawancore, 1947.
Shaw, R.D.M., *The Embossed Tea Kettle*, (Trans.) Orate Gama, and other works of Hakuin Zenji, George Allen & Unwin Ltd., London, 1963.
Sherrard, Ph., *Byzantium*, (Great Ages of Men, A History of the World's Cultures), Time Life Books, N.Y. 1966.
Shukla, D.N., *Vastu Śāstra*, Vol. II, Vastuvanmaya Prakashan, Lucknow, 1968.
——, *Śilpa-Śāstra*, Pub. Vastuvanmaya Prakashan, Lucknow, 1967.
——, *Vastu Śāstra*, Vol. II, Gorakhpur Univ., Gorakhpur, 1958.
——, *Royal Arts* (Six Fine Arts) Yantra and Citra, Vastuvanmaya Prakashan, Lucknow, 1967.
Siddiqui, S., *The Charm of Aurangabad*, A Pictorial Guide to Aurangabad, Daulatabad and Ellora and Ajanta, Mohamedbhoy Publications, Aurangabad, 1977.
Silva, D. Anil, *Chinese Landscape Painting in the Caves of Tun-Huang*, Art of the World Series, Methuen London, 1967.
Singh, M., *The Cave Paintings of AJANTA*, Thames & Hudson, London, 1965.
Singhal, D.P., *Indian and World Civilization*, Vol. I, Rupa & Co., Delhi, 1972.
Sivaramamurti, C., *The Art of India*, Pub. H.N. Abrams, Inc. N.Y. 1977.
——, *The Painter in Ancient India*, Abhinav Pub., N. Delhi, 1978.
——, *South Indian Paintings*, National Museum, N. Delhi, 1968.
——, *Indian Painting*, India the Land and People Series, National Book Trust, India, N. Delhi, 1970.
——, *Chitrasūtra of the Vishṇudharmottra*, 1978.
Smyth, J.P., *A People's Life of Christ*, Hodder & Stoughten Ltd., London, 1926.
Snellgrove, D.L. (G. ed.,) *The Image of the Buddha*, Vikas Pub. House Pvt. Ltd., UNESCO N. Delhi, etc., 1978.
Snellgrove, D.L. Skorupski, T., *The Cultural Heritage of Ladakh*, Vol. I, Vikas Pub. House, N. Delhi, etc., 1977.
Spink, Walter, M., 'Ajanta to Ellora' in *Prāchi-Jyoti*, Dec., 1967.
Stolnitz, J., *Aesthetics and Philosophy of Art Criticism*, Houghton Mifflin Co., Boston, 1960.
Subotić, G., *The Church of St. Demetrius in the Patriarchate of Peć*, Izdavački Zavod Jugoslavija, Beograd, 1964.
Subramanyan, K.G., *Moving Focus*, Lalitkala Akademi, N. Delhi, 1978.

Sullivan, M., *The Meeting of Eastern and Western Art*, Thames & Hudson, London, 1973.

Taddei, M., *Monuments of Civilization India*, Cassell & Co. Ltd., London, 1977.

Thaper, R., *A History of India*, Vols. I and II, Penguin Books, 1974.

Thimme, D. and Heist W.W. (eds.,) *An Introduction to Literature and the Fine Arts*, The Michigan State Univ. Press, 2nd Impression, 1952.

Toynbee, A., *A Study of History*, Weathervane Books, N.Y., 1972.

Trilling, L., *The Experience of Literature-Poetry*, Holt, Rinehart & Winston, N.Y. 1967.

Tripathi, R.P., *Sammelan Patrika*, (Kalā anka) (Chetra and Ashad Anka), Hindi Sahitya Sammelan Prayag, Śakabda, 1880.

Upjohn, E.M. and Wingert, P.S. and Mahler, J.G., *History of World Art*, 2nd Edition, Oxford Univ. Press, N.Y., 1958.

Watts, A.W., *The Way of Zen*, Penguin Books, Thames & Hudson, Reprint, 1971.

Weber, M., *The Religions of India*, The Sociology of Hinduism and Buddhism, The Free Press, N.Y. 1967.

Wentinck, C., *The Human Figure*, Trans. Eva Cooper, The Tulsi Shah Enterprises, Bombay.

Wheeler, M., *Roman Art and Architecture*, Thames & Hudson, London, 1964.

Williams, J.G. (ed), *Kalādarśana*, American Studies in the Art of India, Oxford & IBH Publishing Co., N. Delhi, in collaboration with American Institute of Indian Studies, 1981.

Yazdani, G., *Ajanta*, Oxford Univ. Press, London, Part I, 1930, Part II, 1933, Part III, 1941, Part IV, 1955.

Zimenko, V., *The Humanism of Art*, (Trans) Bean Brian, Progress Pub., Moscow, 1976.

Zimmer, H., *The Art of Indian Asia, its Mythology and Transformations*, Vol. I & II, Bollingen Foundation, N.Y. 1964.

Encyclopedias, Journals and Catalogues, etc.:

Ajanta Paintings, Lalit Kala Akademi, N. Delhi, 1956.

Art International, October, 1962.

Art News, March, 1976; October, 1972, Vol. 71, No. 6.

Binod Behari Mukherjee, Lalit Kala Akademi, N. Delhi, 1965.

Design, A Review of Architecture—Applied and Free Arts, Bombay, Nov., 1957.

Dinman, 9-15 December, 1979.

Eve's Weekly, Special issue, Indian Culture, Vol. XXXI, No. 33, Bombay.

Gazetteer of Bombay Presidency, Vol. XII, Bombay 1880.

German Expressionist Paintings (catalogue), An Exhibition from the Federal Republic of Germany, February 11 till March 14th 1982, National Gallery of Modern Art, New Delhi.

Guide to Ajanta Frescoes, The Archeological Department H.E.H. The Nizam's Govt., 1927.

GLOSSARY

'Anagogical' symbol: Heinrich Zimmer's term, i.e., Expanding form, suggests 'the phenomenon of the growing or expanding form,' an aesthetic effect encountered by him 'nowhere except in certain of the most remarkable and significant Hindu creations.' Related to this aesthetic effect is the 'anagogical symbol reached as the final signification in the levels of increasing abstraction in the senses of scriptures noted by P. Schoff and J. Herzog—quoted by A.L. Herman 'Meaning in Indian Art', in *Philosophy: East and West*, Vol. XV, No.1, 1965.

Composition diffuses,

Composition scandées: 'A systematic study of compositional patterns has been made by Rudrauf (summarised in J. of A. and A.C. 1949, Vol. 7, pp. 325-54). He distinguishes between Compositions diffuses, in which units are evenly and homogeneously distributed without centre of radiation or accent (Bosch, Brueghel, Persian miniatures), and Compositions scandées, which have spatial rhythm and a hierarchy of accents. He divides the latter into (1) axial compositions, organised around the pivot of a principal figure or group; (2) centred compositions radiating from a point of gravitation; and (3) polarized compositions, made up of two opposing figures or groups, between which there is a dynamic relation'—Rudolf Arnheim, *Art and Visual Perception*, 1960, p. 375 note for p. 16.

Gamma motion: 'is a kind of perceived locomotion in a visual pattern varying with the shape and orientation. It occurs essentially along the axes of what I have called the structural skeleton of the pattern... along the line of force.' The gamma motion permits observation of 'perceptual force at work in the creation of patterns' furnishing 'a kind of anatomy of the force of tensions—characterizing the dynamics of patterns when they are observed at rest under normal conditions'—R. Arnheim, *Art and Visual Perception*, 1960, pp. 340-41.

Hesychast: One of the thirteenth-fourteenth century quietist sects of the Greek Church. In the first half of the fourteenth century the Hesychast monks at Mt. Athos gave momentum to the ideas of true monastic life. And by the second half of the same century the movement had been spreading in Serbia in full intensity by a whole group of these monks. The contemplative practice of the Byzantine 'Omphalopsychoi', and the concept of Inner-Light were their important characteristics.

'King's divine will': A model term expressing the potency and means of the King in carrying out the 'Will of God' by building cultural sanctuaries. He conforms to the 'will of the people' as well owing to his own deep roots in their culture. The term is in line with the interaction of Greco-Roman and Indo-West Asian shades of 'King's will' as discussed by S.P. Gupta in *The Roots of Indian Art*, 1980, pp. 12-18. This model of 'King's divine will' gives the eclectic tradition combining court style, monastic art and folk traditions.

Landing Tones: In Rudolf Arnheim's Admixture Theory of colours the following chart is maintained:

BLUE	violet	blue and red	purple	RED
RED	yellow red	orange	red yellow	YELLOW
YELLOW	green yellow	green	green blue	BLUE

It has principal mixtures as stages of transition with values in central column as evenly balancing the two fundamentals. Central values, too, thus resemble the fundamentals having 'relatively high stability and self-containedness'; others having one dominating fundamental show dynamic properties of 'landing tones' because 'they appear as deviations from the dominant fundamentals and exhibit a tension towards the purity of that fundamental': *Art and Visual Perception*, 1960, p. 218.

Mahāmātras: A concept based on S.P. Gupta's postulation of Aśokan *Dhamma-mahāmātras* who, while returning home from their assignments in foreign countries brought with them novel and suitable motifs of art and architecture: *The Roots of Indian Art*, 1980, p. 299-300.

Modal convention: Habitual and natural use of the older style for the subjects related to them; this process keeps these styles alive at a critical stage.

Modal differentiation: 'It is a slow and broadly based process of formal evolution with a powerful impetus of its own' but also containing 'the revival efforts': Ernst Kitzinger, *Byzantine Art in the Making*, 1977, p. 123.

Modes: 'The phenomenon of the so-called 'modes'—the conventional use of different stylistic manners to denote different kinds of subject matters or different levels of existence.': Ernst Kitzinger, *Byzantine Art in the Making*, 1977, p. 19.

Other directed: David Riesman's term suggesting 'an open and insistent reference to a pre-existent style that is being quoted so to speak, for the sake of its mental associations' as catalysts, 'they do not revolutionize but rather accentuate, reinforce and bring into focus existing trends by introducing a clear reference to an earlier work.'

Inner directed: David Reisman's term suggesting 'an artist's intent and outlook essentially intuitive autonomous within aesthetic sphere': Ernst Kitzinger, *Byzantine Art in the Making*, pp. 13, 79, 124.

Prāṇa aesthetics: A *Paurāṇic* concept in prescriptive aesthetics by which the *nirvāṇa* principle, reached as 'flux' in Buddhistic dialectics, was given a form by 'an illusion of volumes from within which space presses outward. Space, volume, mass are as though summoned from some inner centre or source... *stūpa* is, of course, an arch-example of this centrifugal pressure' (Clement Greenberg, 'Foreword' in Maurizio Taddei, *Monuments of Civilization, India*, 1977, p. 7). M. Taddei explains it as one of the Gupta canons of art given to Ajanta as 'the characteristic way of conceiving the very quality of forms and volumes and their relationships, a refusal to consider the images as if immersed in space, an insistence on seeing the image as a container of space itself, pressing forward the outside' (*ibid.*, p. 133). Stella Kramrisch explains it as 'forthcoming' and adds that 'such a bodily experience of space actually or potentially within ourselves underlies the vision of space in paintings in the Deccan of the type of Ajanta' Differentiating it from the 'terms of surface' Kramrisch's sharp aesthetic vision doesn't fail to recognize that the 'forthcoming' 'is moreover relatively the least exploited in painting outside India' (*A Survey of Painting in the Deccan*, 1937, pp. 3-5). She connects 'breath' or *Prāṇa* containing *cetanā* with the *Tālchanda* (metrical floor-measure) and *Ūrdhvachanda* (metrical height-measure) of a temple and explains that 'the rhythmic breathing quality of form is the test of a work of art for it contains the life movement (*cetanā*) of the subject' (*The Art of India*, 1955, p. 15). It has the echo of what *Citrasūtra* (43: 20, 21) speaks of the auspicious painting:

लसतीव च भूलम्बो बिभ्यतीव तथा नृप॥
हसतीव च माधुर्यं सजीव इव दृश्यते॥ २१
सश्वास इव यच्चित्रं तच्चित्रं शुभ लक्षणम्॥

'The surface is as if glistening and embracing as if coming out to meet the spectator, the sweetness is as if smiling, it looks as if endowed with life... that is (beautiful) painting, which looks as if breathing' (Dr. Priyabala Shah, *Viṣṇudharmottara-Purāṇa*, third *Khaṇḍa*, Vol. II, 1961, p. 136). This aesthetics of *Nimnonnata* (heights and depths) and *Vāyugatya likhet* ('paints like the movement of the wind', *ibid*, p. 137) was left or coded into the 'creeper' motif by the painters of Ajanta in accordance with what A. K. Coomaraswamy cites from ancient wisdom of India becoming the elements of Buddhist iconography: 'That Tree is his procession in a likeness, the emanation of his fiery-energy (*tejas*) as light, the expiration of his breath (*prāṇa*); he is its wise, indestructible mover': *Elements of Buddhist Iconography*, 1972, p. 8.

In Such aesthetics there cannot remain the difference between the religious and the secular. Every aspect of this life is incorporated into a known hierarchy of values in the physical, psychological and metaphysical realms: S. Kramrisch, *The Art of India*, 1955, p. 10.

Rhythmos: Compositional patterns, especially of figures in movement: J.J. Pollitt, *The Art of Greece—1400-31 B.C.*, 1965, p. 57.

Symmetria: 'Commensurability of all the parts of a statue... Parrhasios was the first to introduce *symmetria* into painting': J.J. Pollitt, sup., 1965, pp. xii, 57.

Ūrṇā: 'The brow locks (*ūrṇā*) of the *Cakravartin*, which are placed between the brows, should be made of the size of one digit...

The forehead lock (*ūrṇā*), emanating light, has its place between the brows. (Chapter III, 576-618, 1011-56, *Citralakṣaṇa*): B.N. Goswamy and A.L. Dahmen-Dallapiccola, *An Early Document of Indian Art 'The Citralakṣaṇa of Nagnajit'*, 1976, pp. 83, 101.

ऊर्णेय च भ्रुवोर्मध्ये तेषां कार्यं तथा शुभम्।

(*Chitrasutra*, chap. 37:5)

Tarnish Jha translates as ...

उनकी भोंहो के बीच में मंगलमय भंवरी बनावें।

The underlined words translated in English are 'auspicious circle' marks between the eyebrows: *Sammelan Patrika*, 1880 Shadabd, p. 440.

Prin. V.S. Apte's *The Practical Sanskrit-English Dictionary*, Vol. II, 1957, p. 484, (ऊर्णा) (*ūrṇā*) as 'circle of hair between the eyebrows'—Dr. Priyabala Shah reads it as 'The *ūrṇā* or tuft of hair should be shown as an auspicious mark between their eyebrows': *Viṣṇudharmottara-Purāṇa*, third khaṇḍa, Vol. II, 1961, p. 108.

A systematic study of concentrating/meditating brows expressed in Byzantine art since Justinian period, reveals a progressive formation of *ūrṇā* symbol realized at Sopoćani in St. John The Divine.

INDEX

ILLUSTRATIONS

Plate 1. Ajanta: Ground Plan

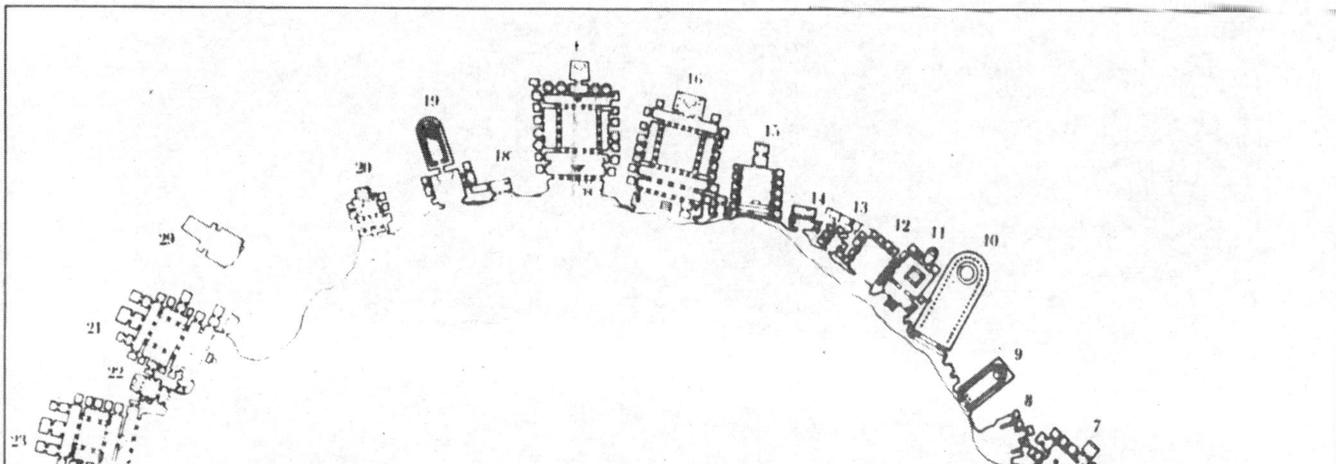

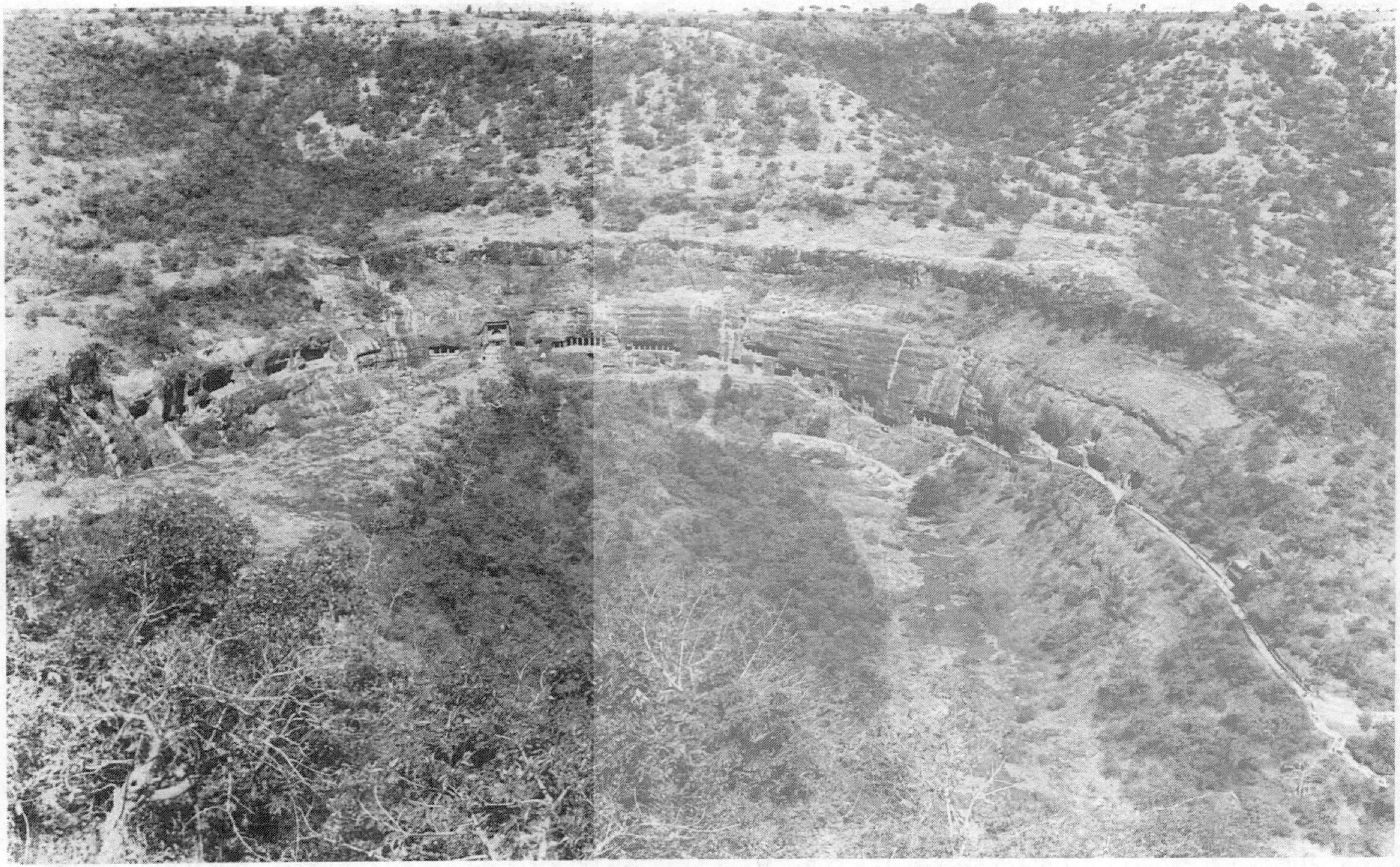

Plate 2. Panorama

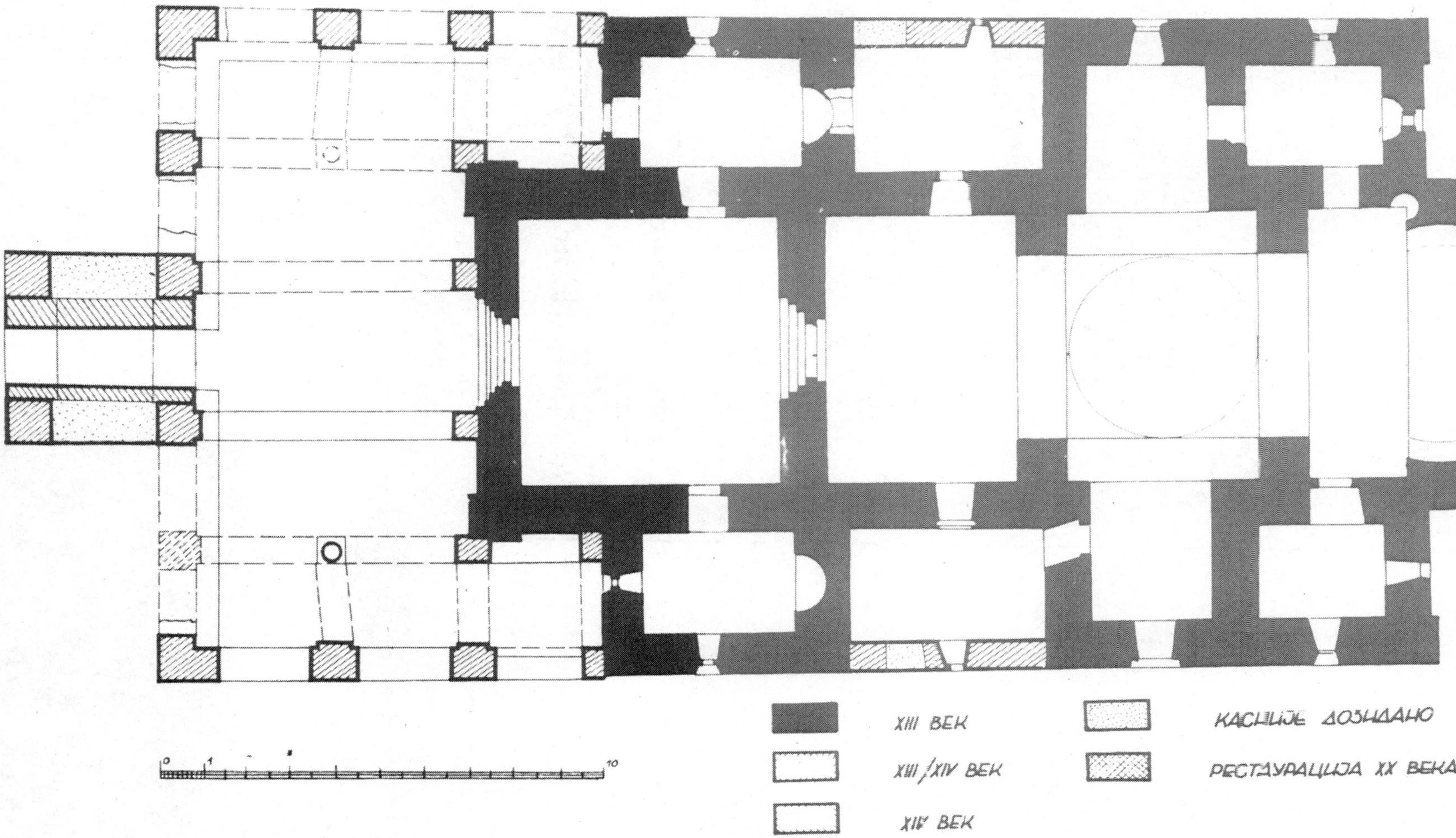

Plate 3. Sopoćani Ground Plan

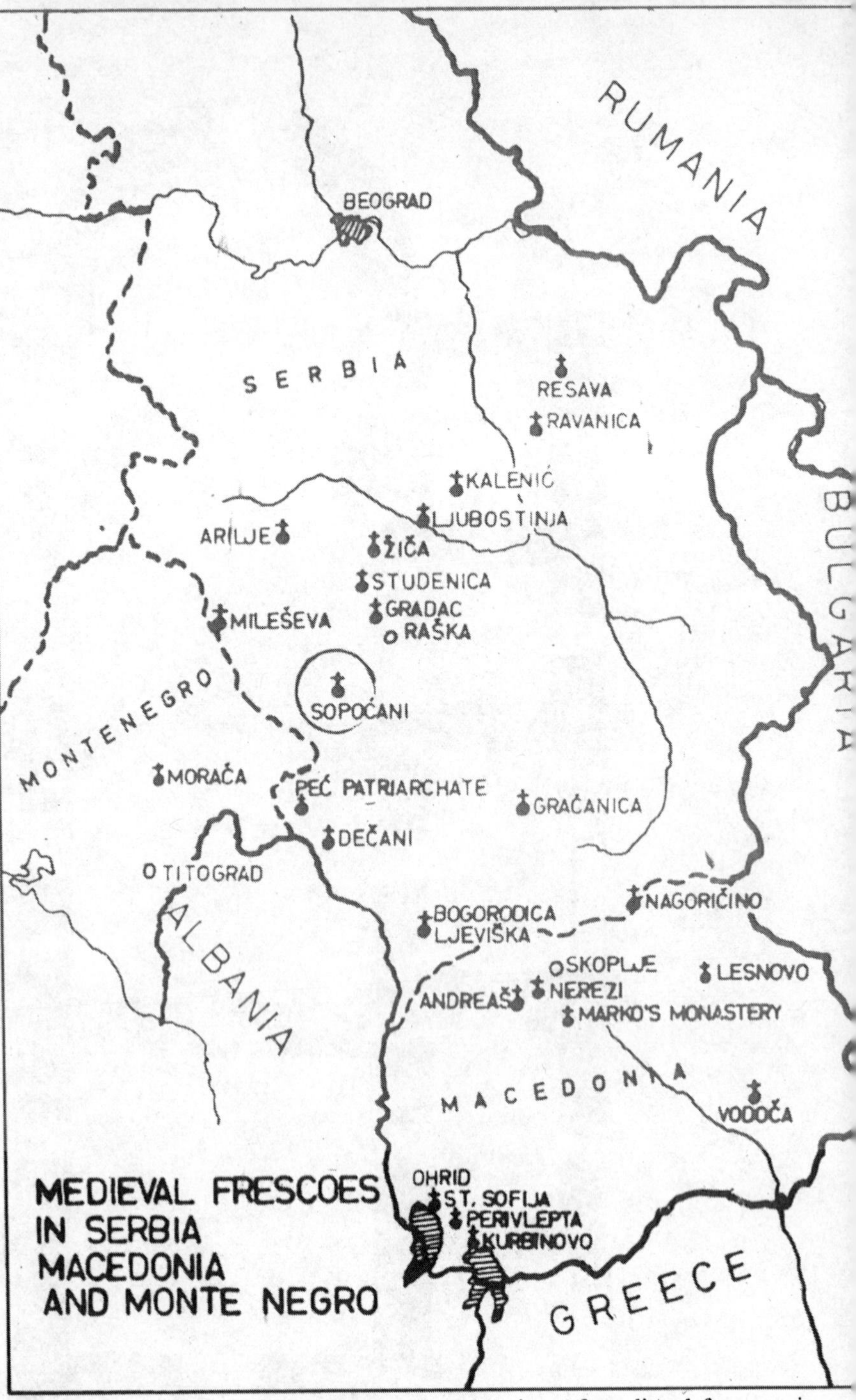

Plate 5. The map showing the sites of medieval frescoes in Yugoslavia.

Plate 4. Panorama

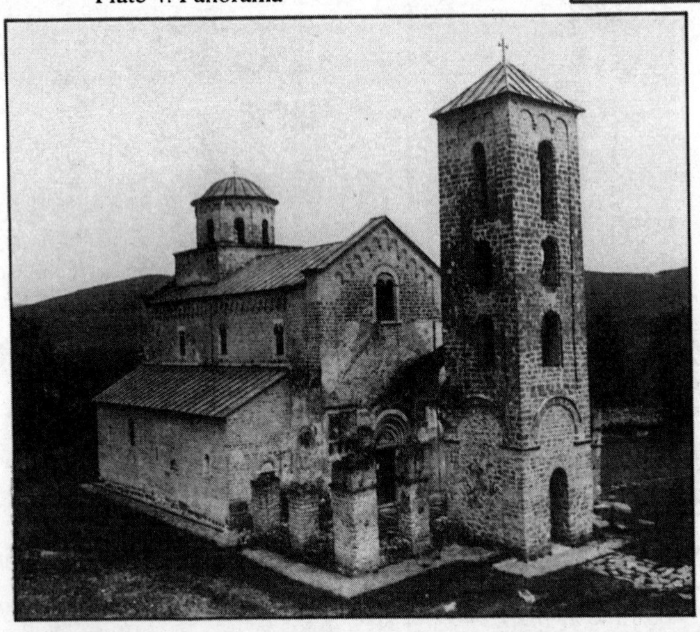

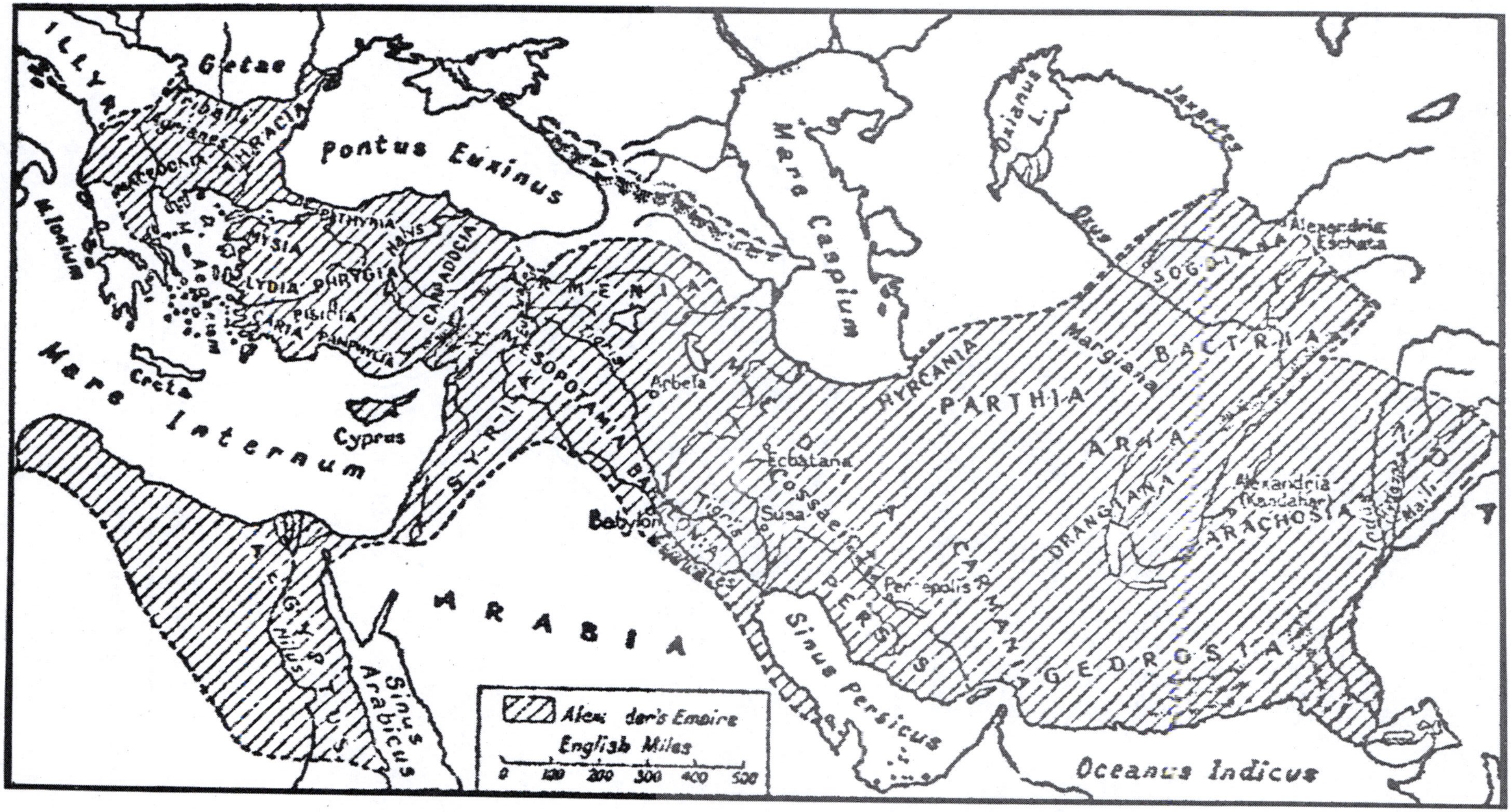

Plate 6. The Empire of Alexander the Great

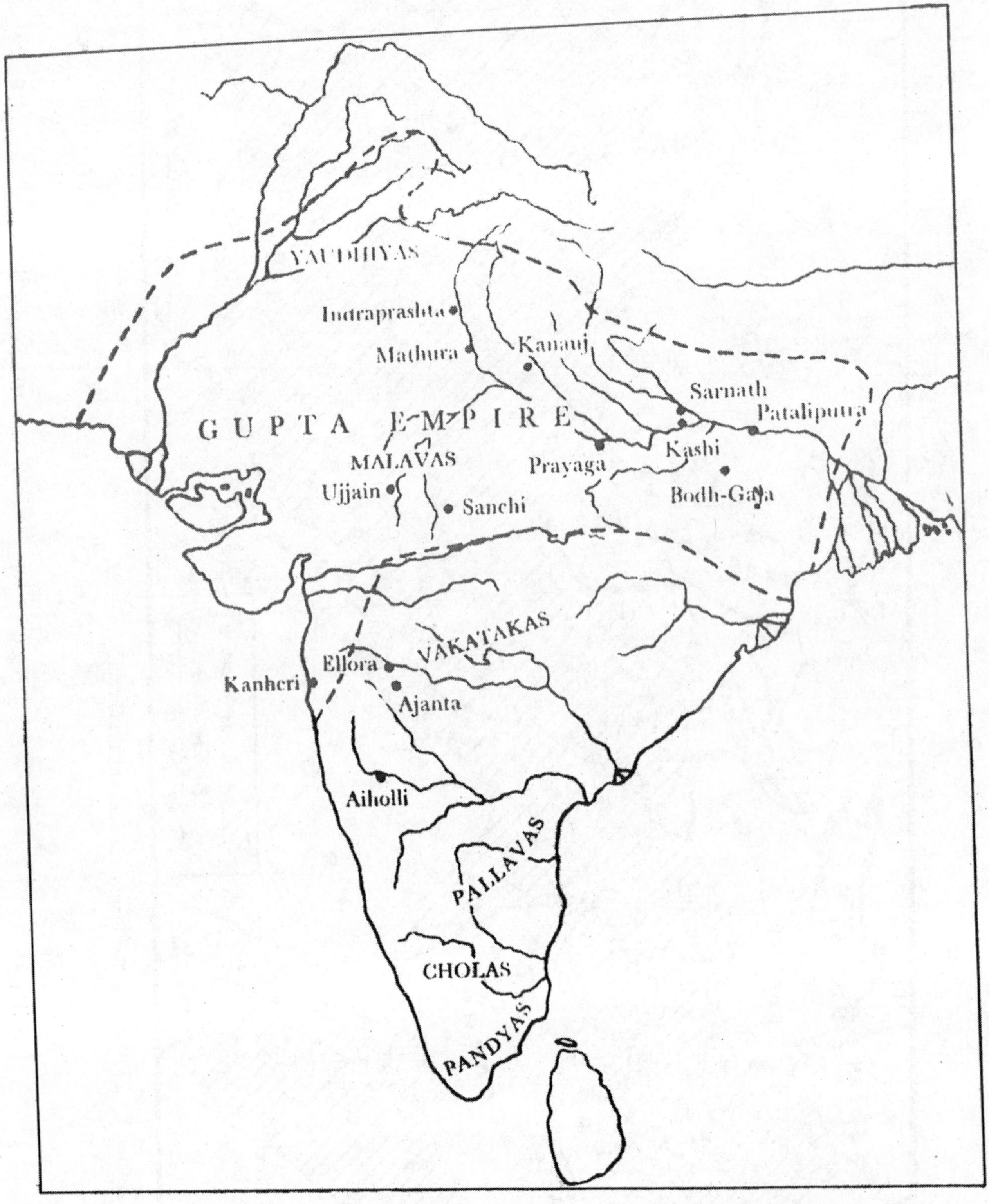

Plate 7. India at the time of the Gupta Empire

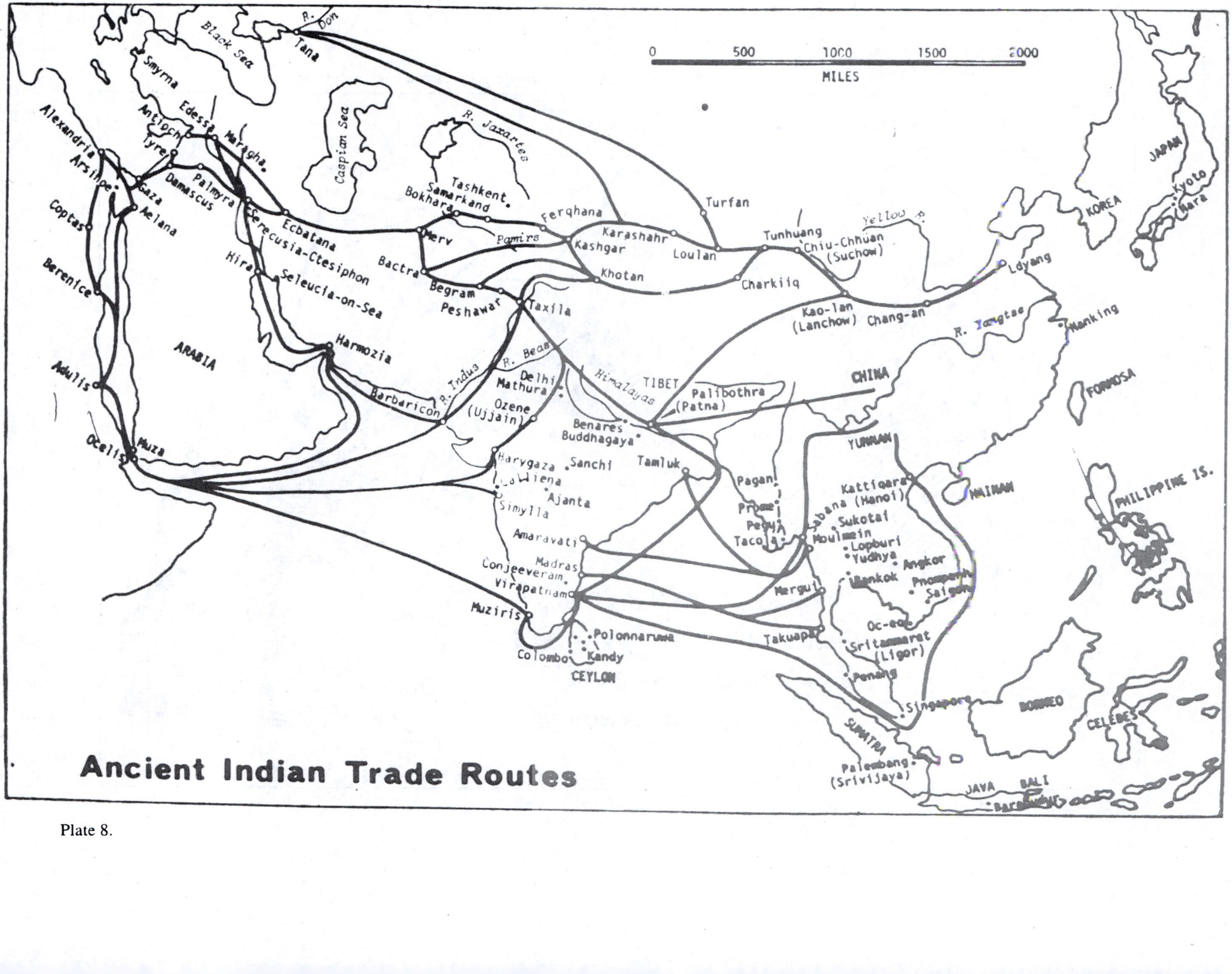
Ancient Indian Trade Routes
0 500 1000 1500 2000
MILES
Black Sea
R. Don
Tana
Smyrna
Alexandria
Antioch
Edessa
Maragha.
Tyre
Arsinoe
Gaza
Damascus
Palmyra
Aelana
Coptas
Berenice
Caspian Sea
R. Jaxartes
Tashkent.
Samarkand
Bokhara
Ecbatana
Serecusia-Ctesiphon
Hira
Seleucia-on-Sea
Merv
Bactra
Begram
Peshawar
Pamirs
Ferghana
Karashahr
Kashgar
Khotan
Turfan
Loulan
Charkiiq
Tunhuang
Chiu-Chhuan
(Suchow)
Yellow R.
Kao-lan
(Lanchow)
Chang-an
Loyang
R. Yangtse
Nanking
KOREA
JAPAN
Kyoto
Nara
FORMOSA
CHINA
YUNNAN
HAINAN
PHILIPPINE IS.
ARABIA
Harmozia
Taxila
R. Beas
R. Indus
Barbaricon
Adulis
Ocelis
Muza
Delhi
Mathura
Ozene
(Ujjain)
Himalayas
TIBET
Palibothra
(Patna)
Benares
Buddhagaya
Barygaza
Sanchi
Tamluk
Ajanta
Simylla
Amaravati
Madras
Conjeeveram
Virapatnam
Muziris
Polonnaruwa
Colombo
Kandy
CEYLON
Pagan
Prome
Pegu
Tacola
Moulmein
Kattigara
(Hanoi)
Sukotai
Lopburi
Yudhya
Angkor
Bankok
Saigon
Mergui
Takuapa
Oc-eo
Sritammarat
(Ligor)
Penang
Singapore
SUMATRA
Palembang
(Srivijaya)
BORNEO
CELEBES
JAVA
BALI

Plate 8.

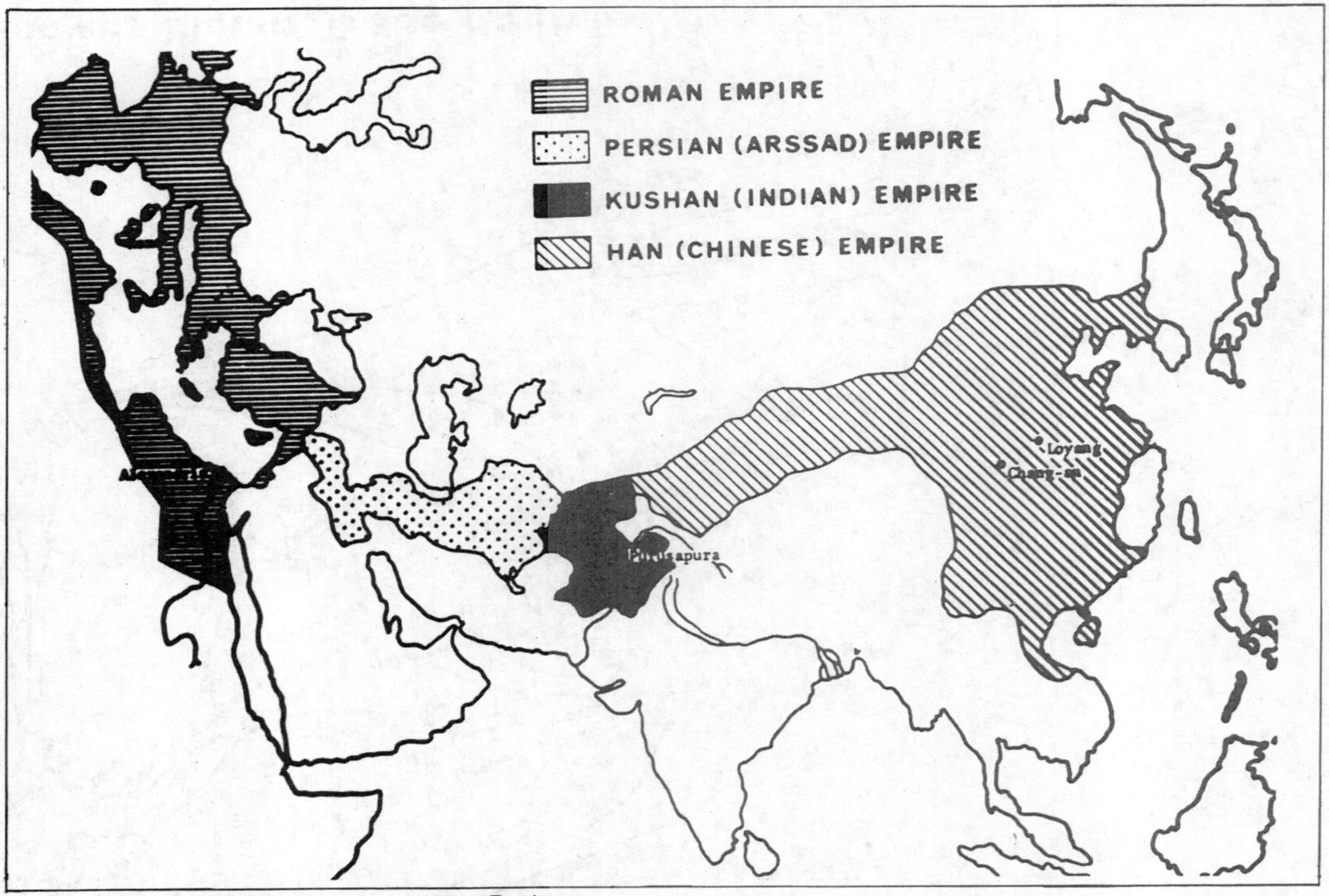

Plate 9. Roman, Persian, Kuṣāṇa and Hūṇa Empires

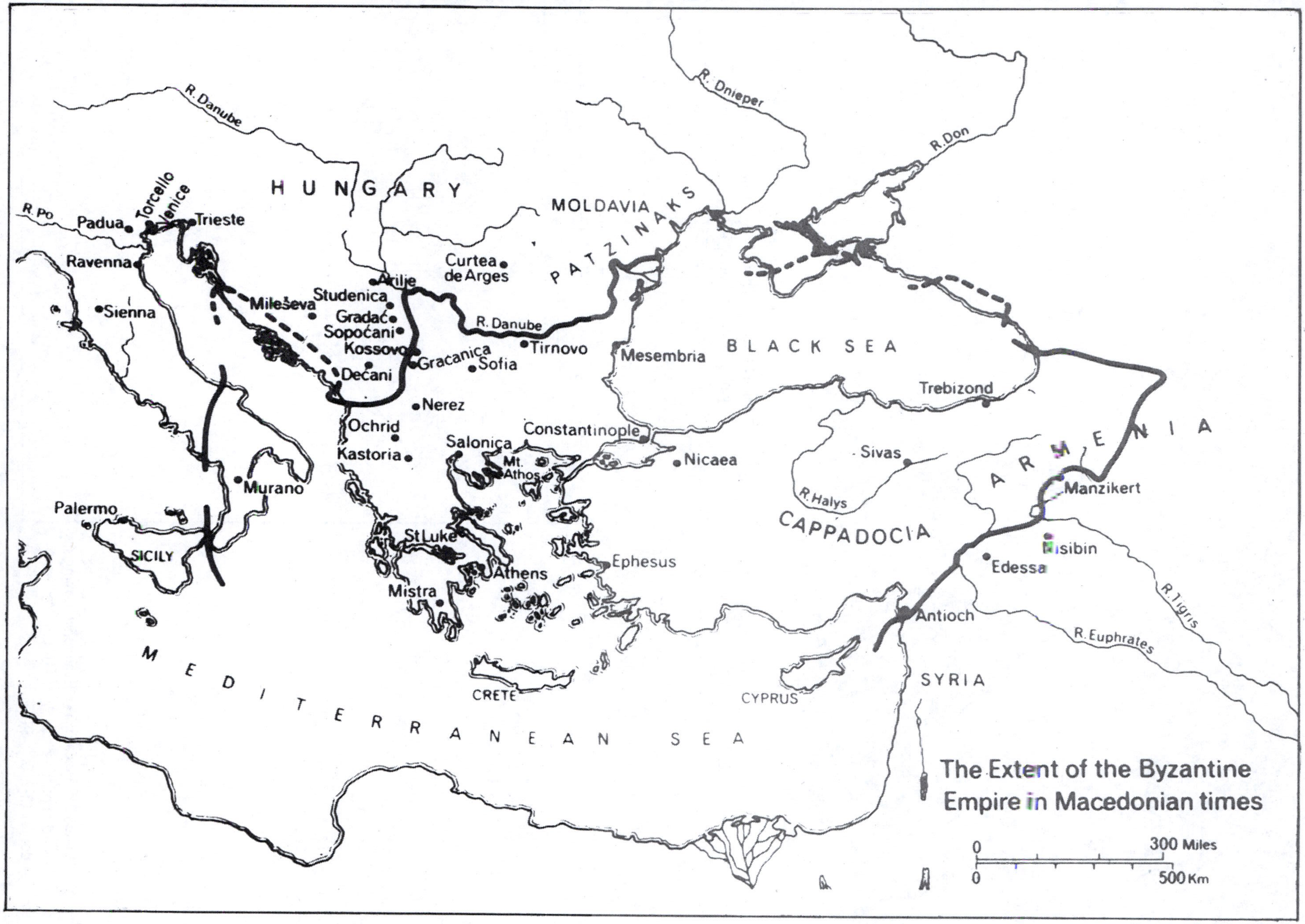
The Extent of the Byzantine Empire in Macedonian times
R. Danube
R. Dnieper
R. Don
R. Po
HUNGARY
MOLDAVIA
PATZINAKS
Padua
Torcello
Venice
Trieste
Ravenna
Sienna
Curtea de Arges
Arilje
Studenica
Mileševa
Gradać
Sopoćani
Kossovo
Gracanica
Dećani
Sofia
Tirnovo
Mesembria
BLACK SEA
Trebizond
Nerez
Ochrid
Kastoria
Salonica
Mt. Athos
Constantinople
Nicaea
Sivas
R. Halys
CAPPADOCIA
ARMENIA
Manzikert
Nisibin
Edessa
R. Tigris
R. Euphrates
Antioch
SYRIA
Murano
Palermo
SICILY
St Luke
Athens
Mistra
Ephesus
CRETE
CYPRUS
MEDITERRANEAN SEA
0
300 Miles
0
500 Km

Plate 10.

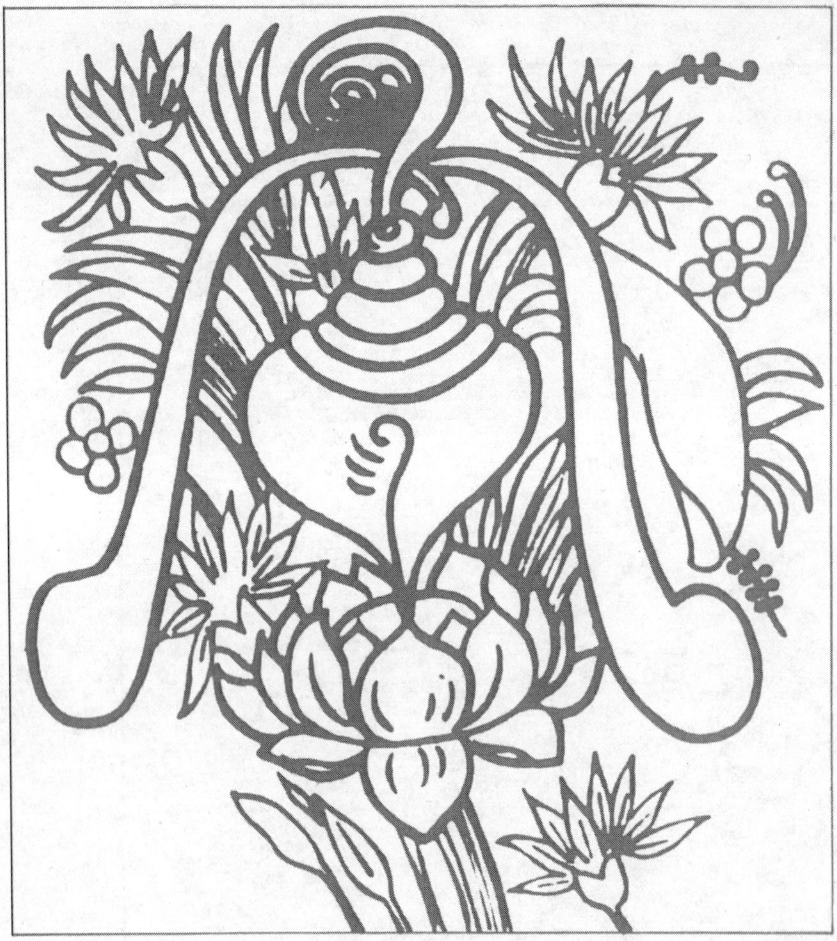

Plate 11. Ajanta: The Conch over the Lotus—symbol of 'Nāda' or 'Vāc'.

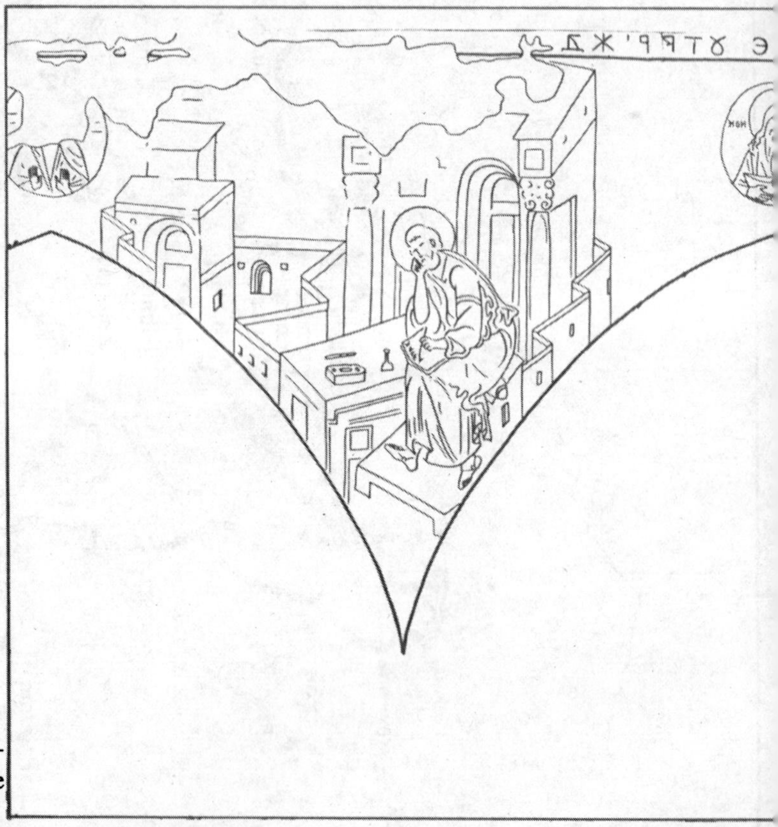

Plate 12. Sopoćani: The Evangelist looking skyward expecting the 'Word of God' (rim of the dome, A.D. 1263-68).

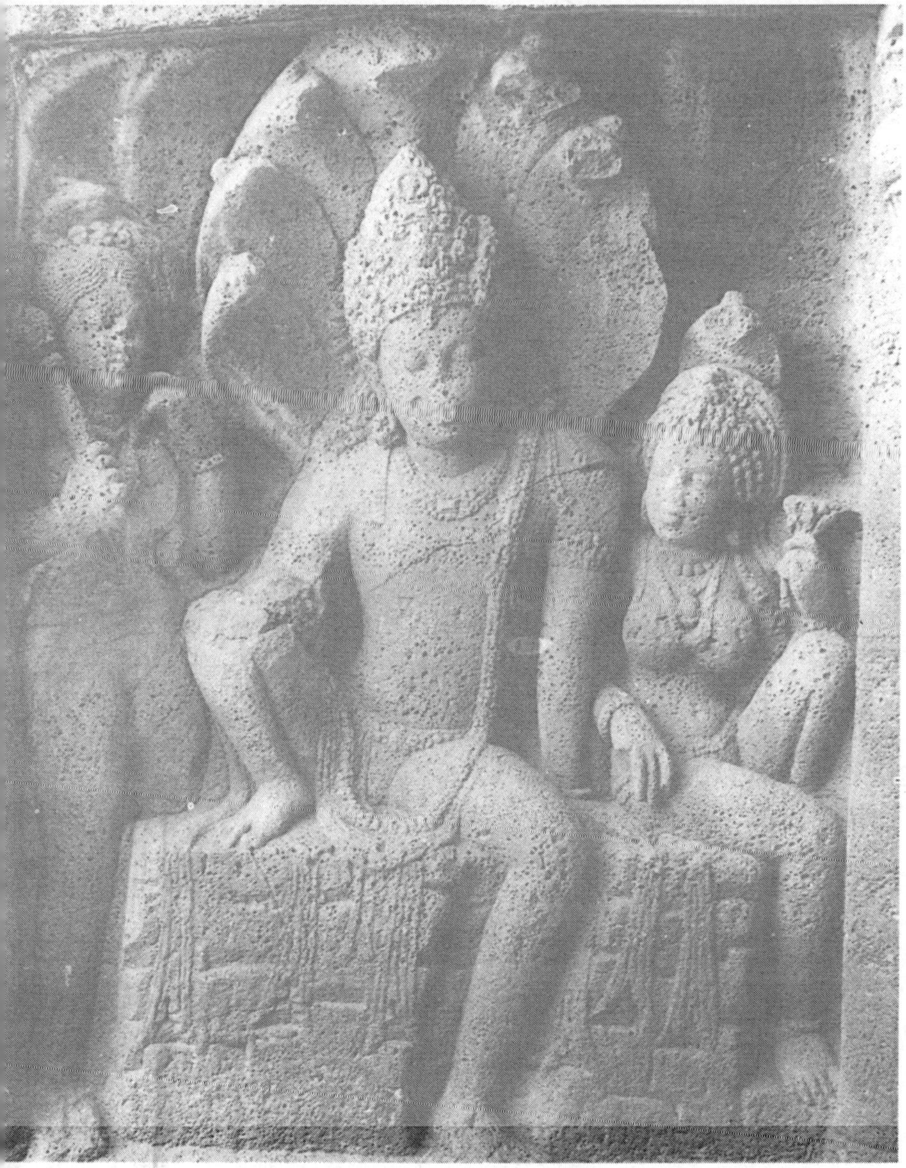

Plate 13. Ajanta: 'Nāgarāja and his consort' (cave 19) conforms to the 'Hiraṇyagarbha' iconographic scheme by placing female elements (Soma substances) on left and male (*Agni*) elements on right, e.g., lifted index finger of the left hand of the wisk-bearer expresses female consciousness as does the lotus in the left hand of the nāga queen. Contrarily, lotus in the right hand of Bodhisattva Padmapāṇi (cave 1) symbolizes the male (*Agni-prajñā*) principle.

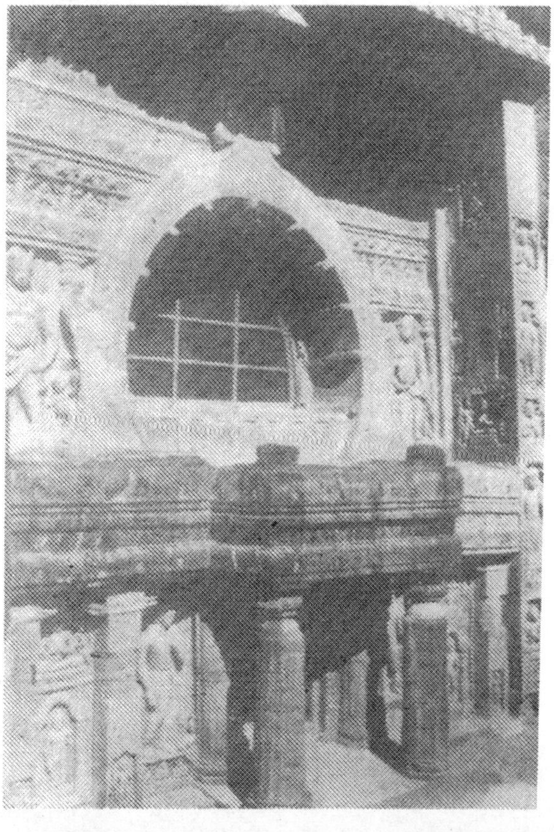

Plate 14. Ajanta: *Caitya*-window (cave 19).

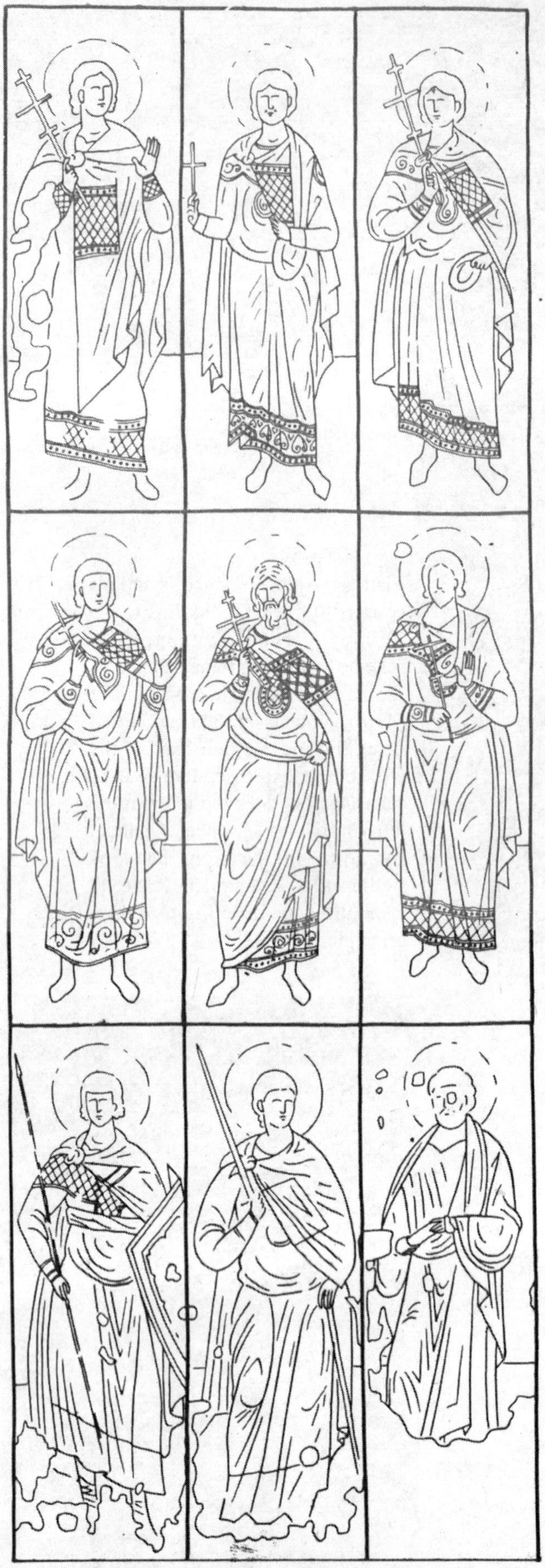

Plate 15. Sopoćani: Martyrs, saints, apostle, evangelist.

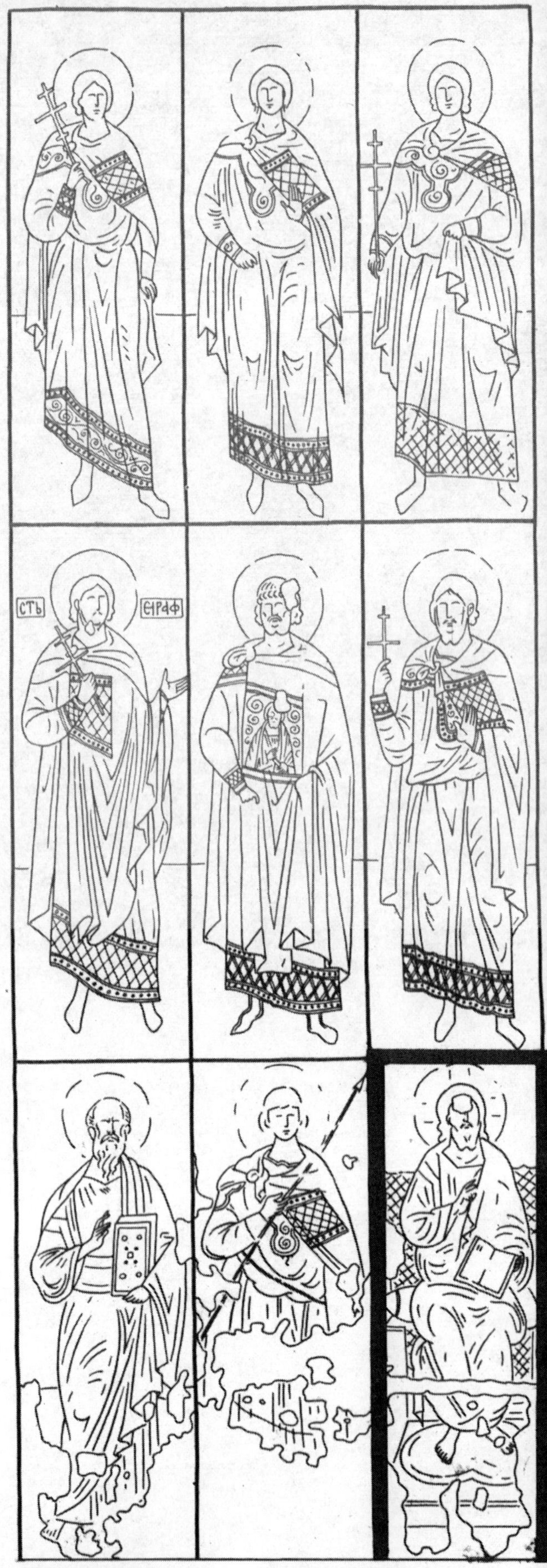

Plate 16., 'Christ Enthroned' (pilasters, nave, A.D. 1263-68).

Plates 17-18. Sopoćani: symbols and decorative motifs (Chapel of St. Simeon Nemanja, A.D. 1263-68).

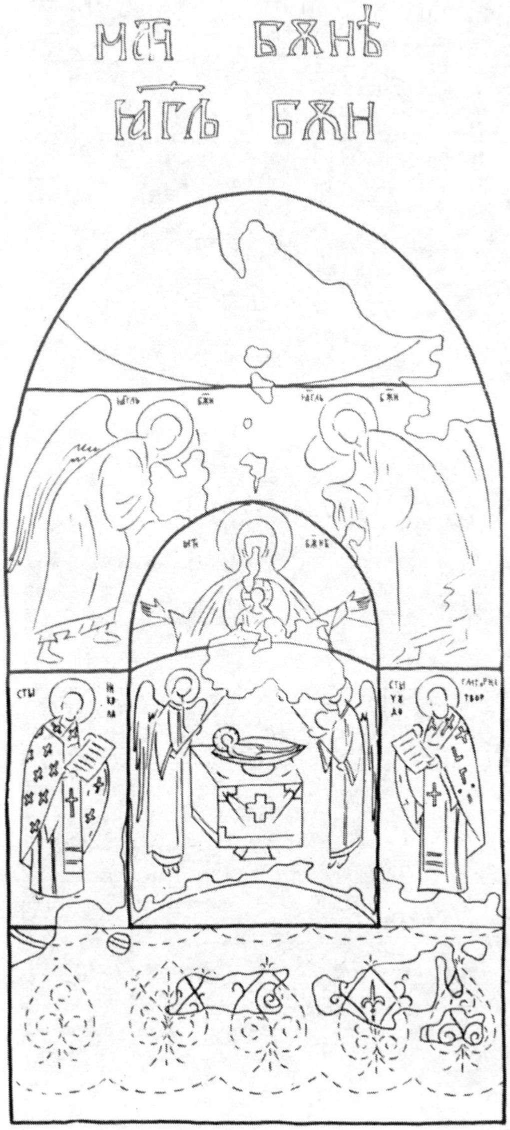

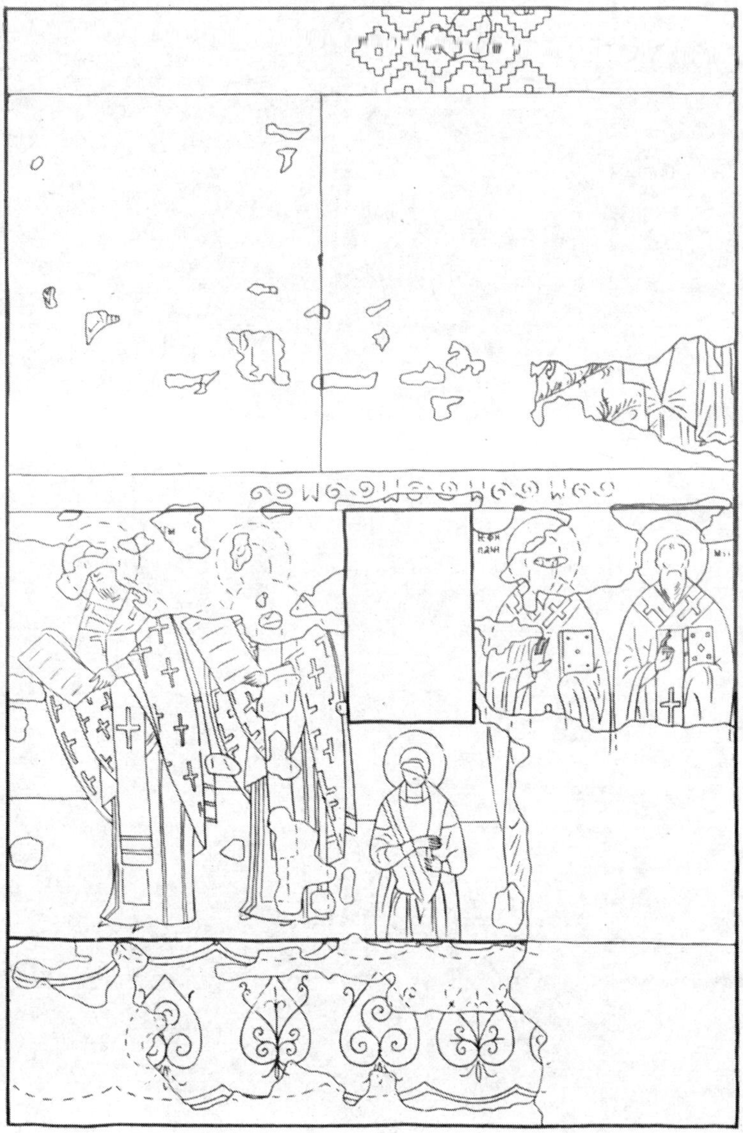

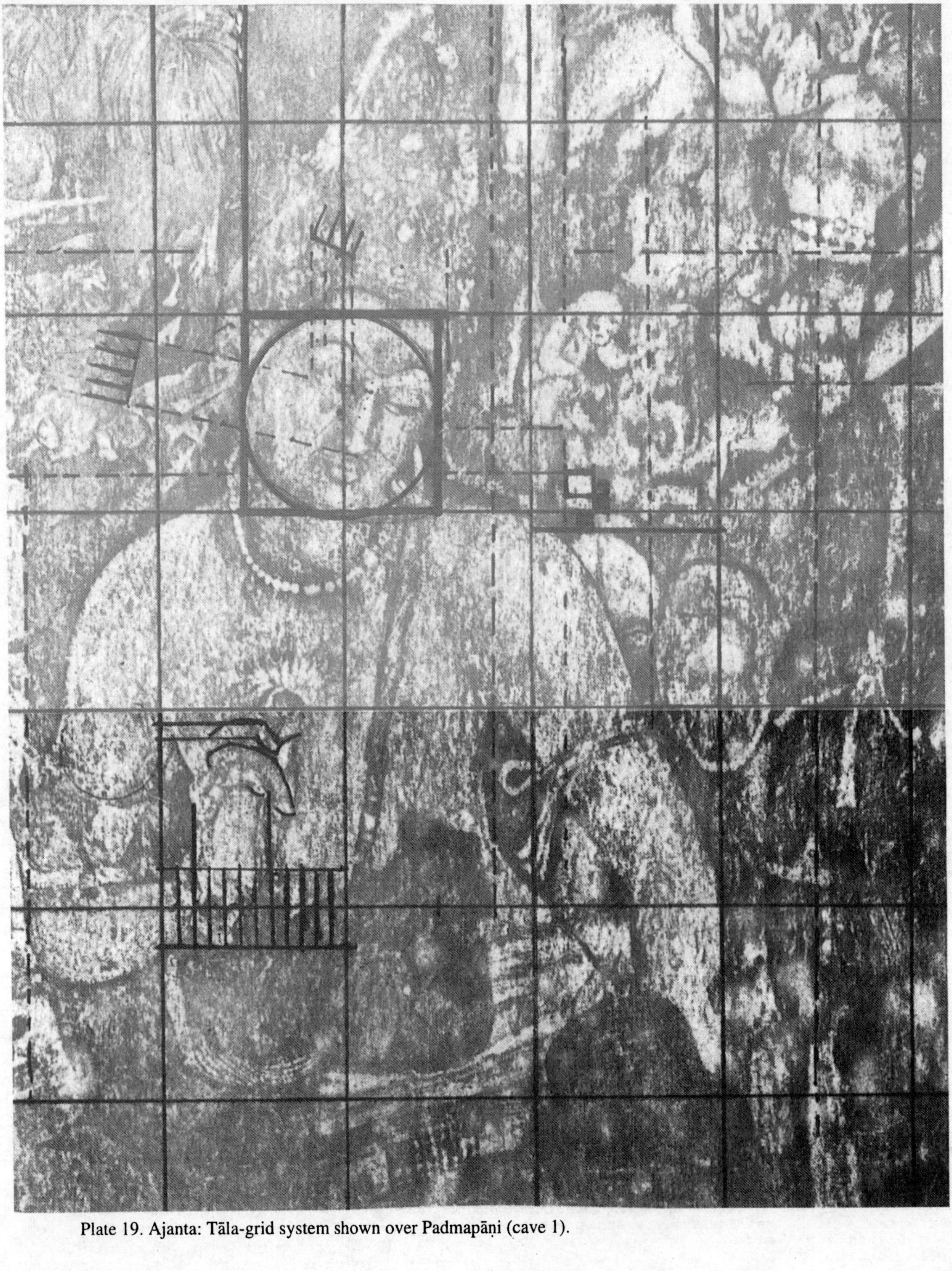

Plate 19. Ajanta: Tāla-grid system shown over Padmapāṇi (cave 1).

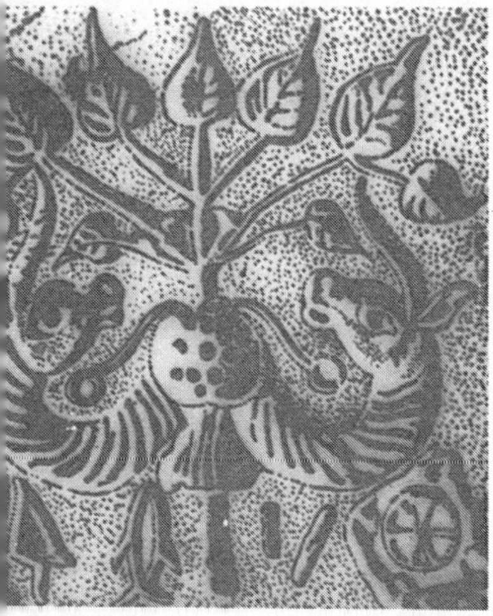

Plate 20. Mohenjo-Daro: Seal with 'Hom' motif—two animals around a tree (2500 B.C.).

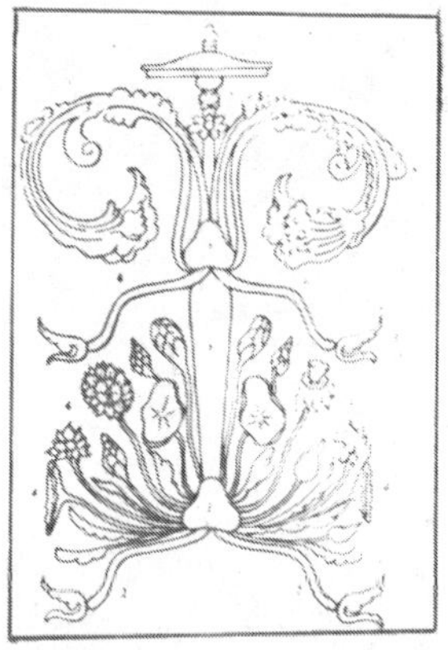

Plate 22. The basic form of the Cosmic Tree with the Padmamūla and the Brahmamūla concepts.

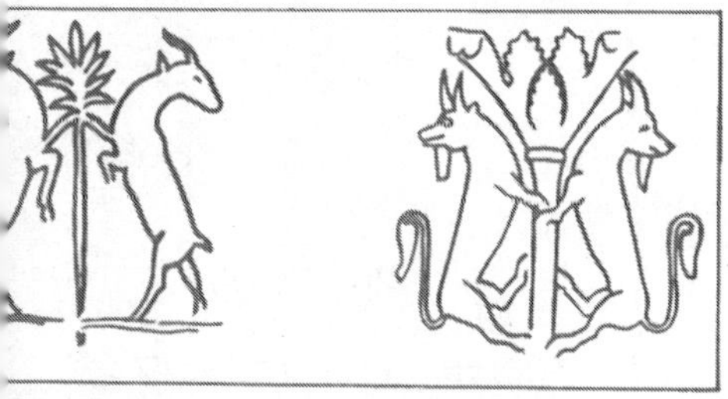

Plate 21. (Left) Assyrian Cylinder-seal with 'Hom' motif; (right) its adaptation in Christian art during Romanesque period (St. Martin-d' Ainay, Lyons).

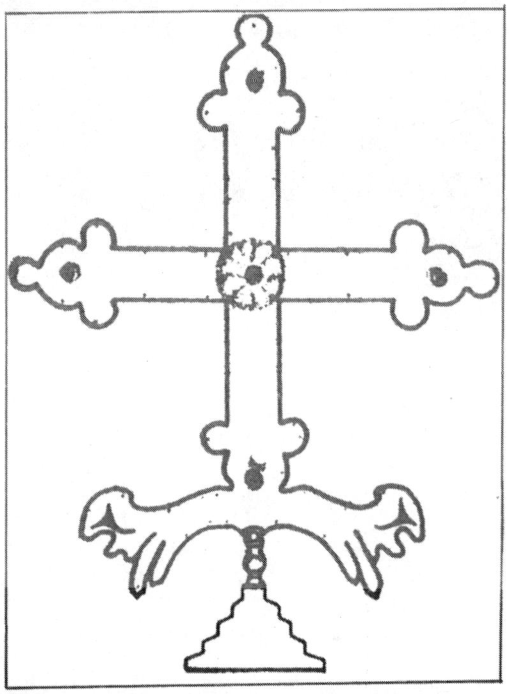

Plate 24. Kottayam, Valiya Palli (India): The Nestorian Cross (Cross Botonée).

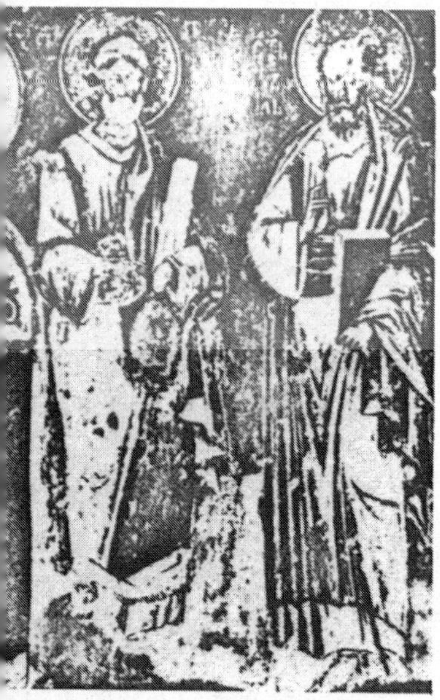

Plate 23. Arilje (Yugoslavia): Fresco showing a Leafed Cross in Serbian Orthodox Church (A.D. 1295-96).

Plate 25. Kottayam: The Manichean Cross (Cross Botonée) with the Dove.

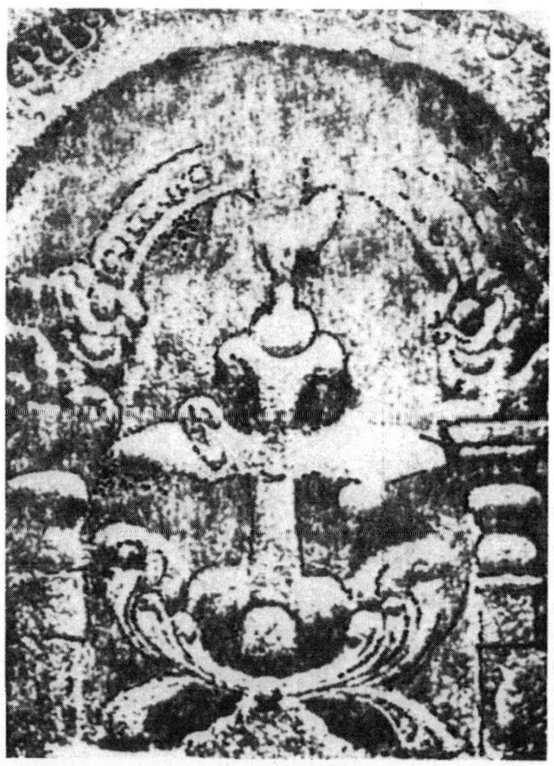

Plate 26. Madras (India): St. Thomas Mount; similar to the above cross with 'Makara-toran'.

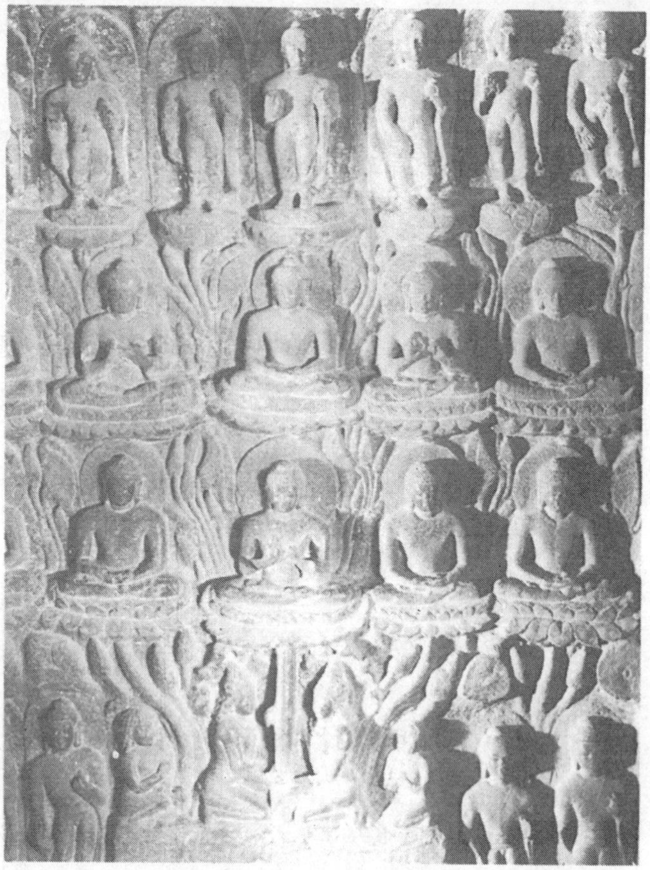

Plate 27. Ajanta: 'Miracle of Śrāvastī' (the Thousand Buddhas) (cave 7).

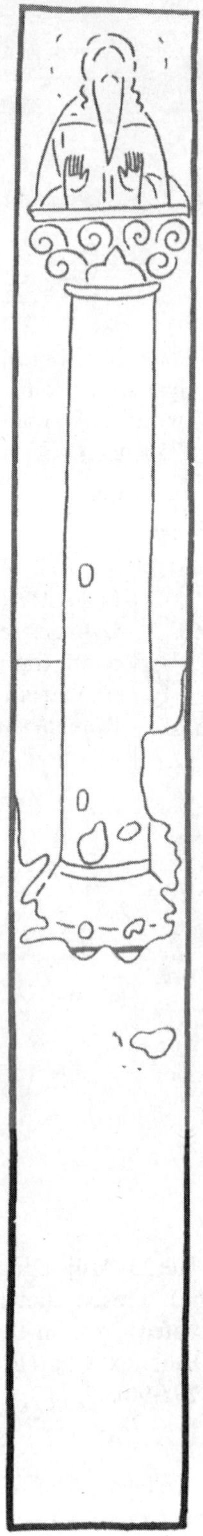

Plate 28. Sopoćani: Unidentified Stylite on pillar (nave).

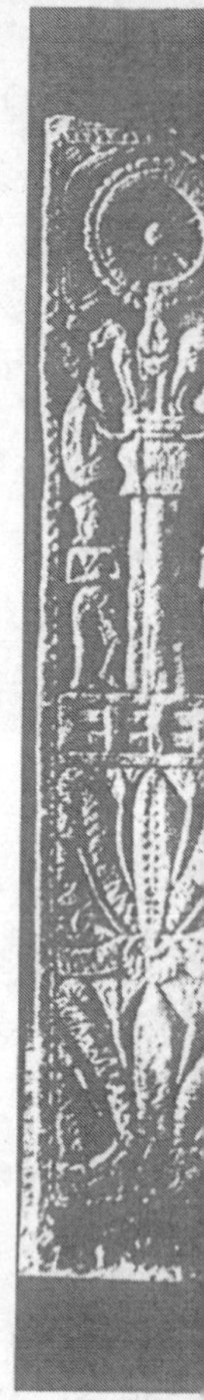

Plate 29. Sanchi: Adorned Sun-pillar having male figure on right and female on left (railing of Stūpa 2, early 1st cent. B.C.)

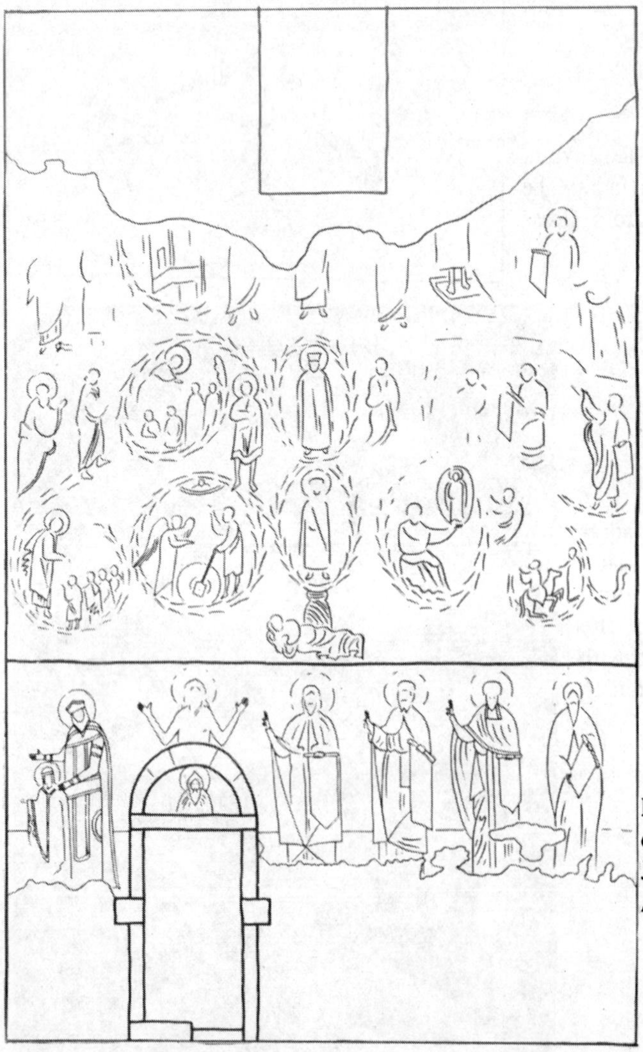

Plate 30. Sopoćani: 'Tree of Jesse' (Narthex A.D. 1263-68).

Plate 31. Sanchi: Creeper issuing from the navel of Yakṣa (railing of Stūpa 2, early 1st cent. B.C.)

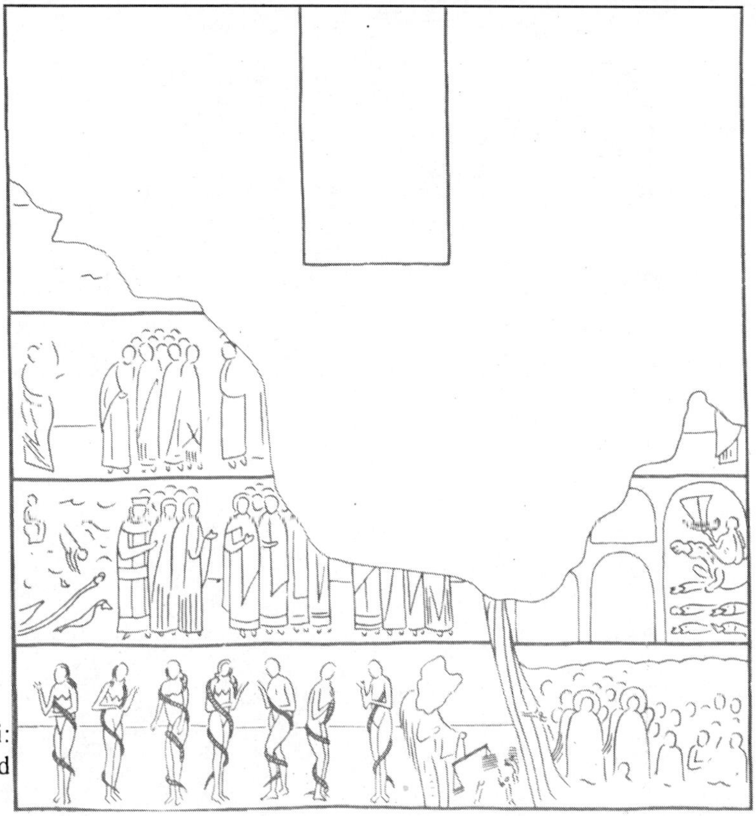

Plate 33. Sopoćani: The Last Judgment and the Hell (Narthex).

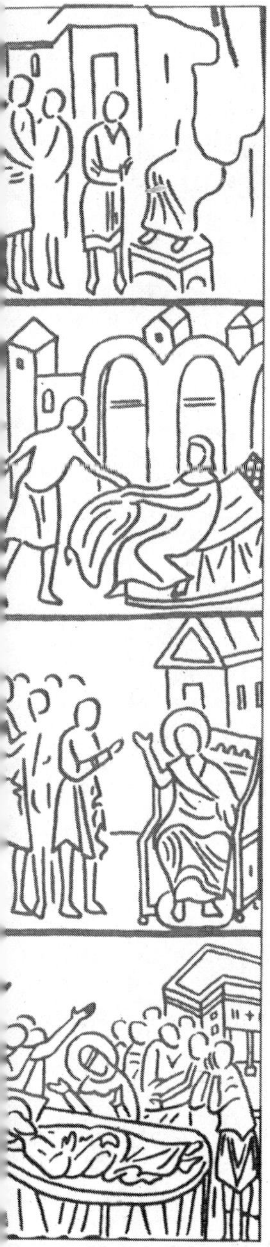

Plate 32. Sopoćani: Potipher's wife enticing Joseph in the 'Story of Joseph' (Narthex).

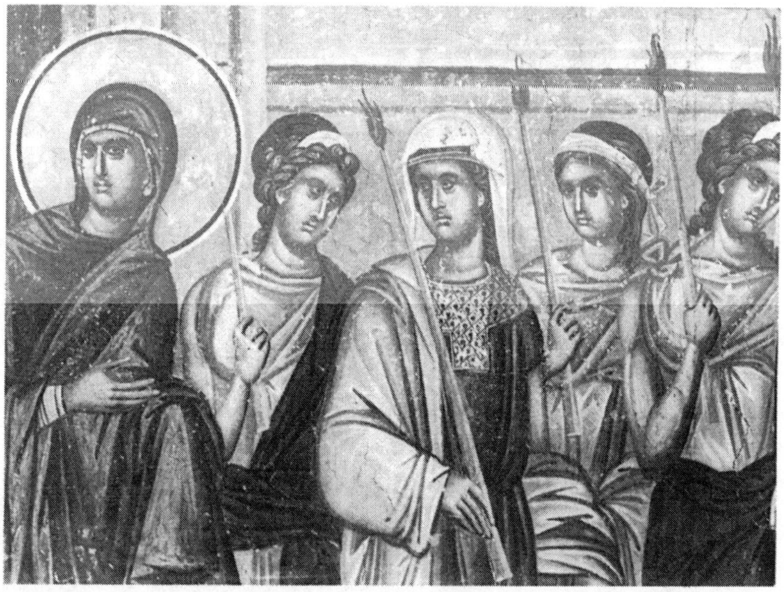

Plate 35. Studenica (Yugoslavia), The Kings Church: The presentation of the virgin in the Temple (detail, completed by A.D. 1314).

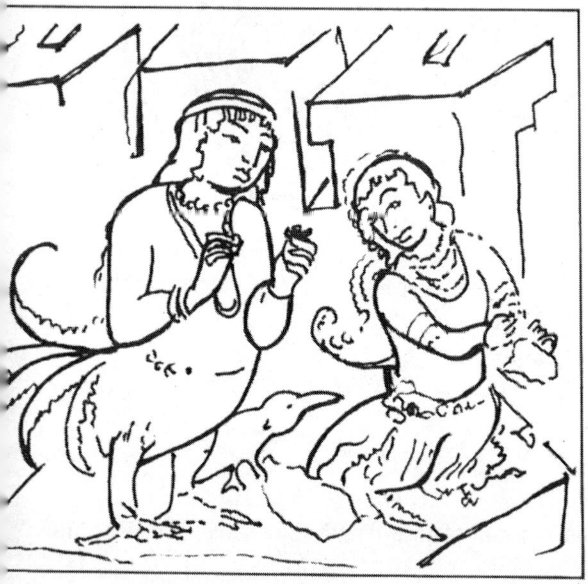

Plate 34. Ajanta: Composite man and animal, part of the scene of the worship of Buddha (cave 17).

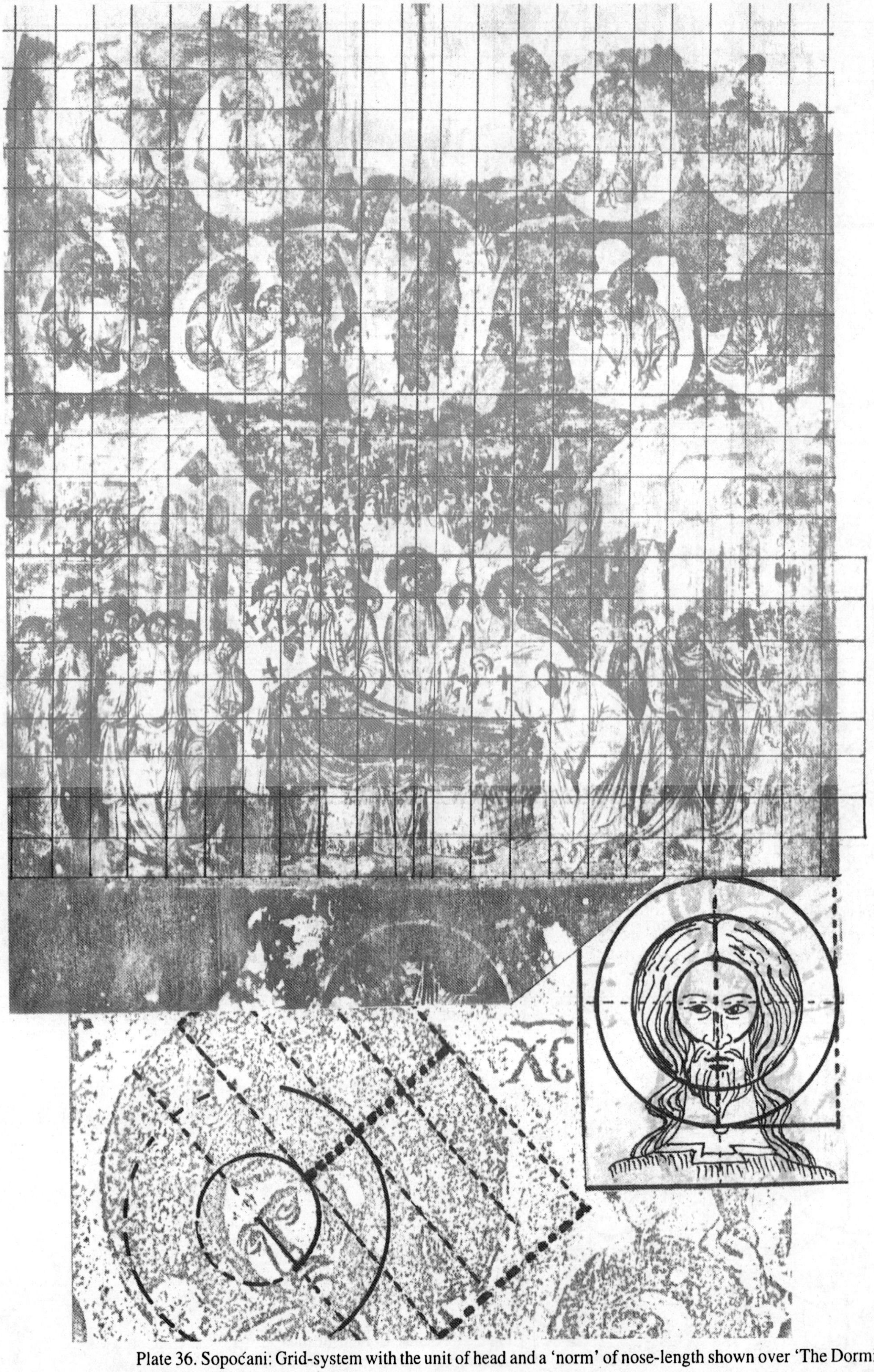

Plate 36. Sopoćani: Grid-system with the unit of head and a 'norm' of nose-length shown over 'The Dormition' (nave).

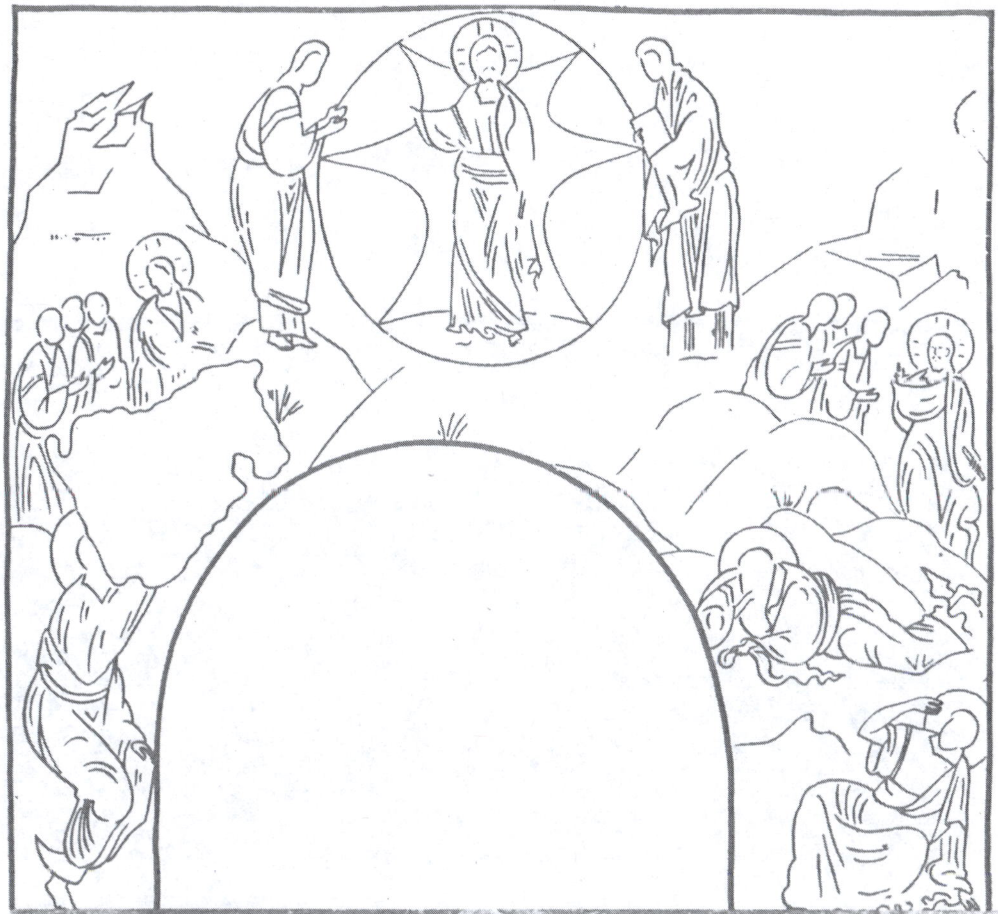

Plate 37. Sopoćani: Angular interstices becoming consistent form in the glory-halo in 'Transfiguration' (nave).

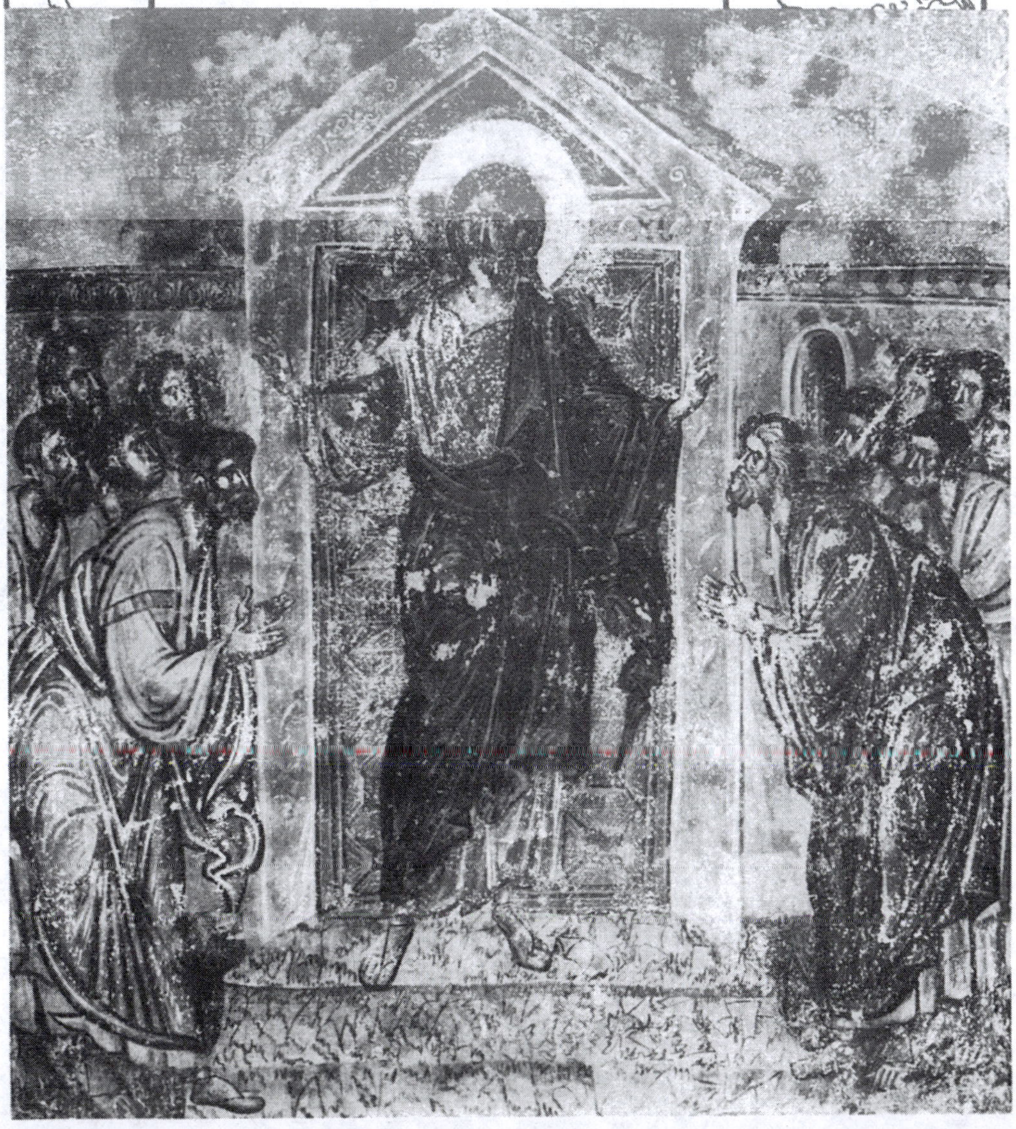

Plate 38. Sopoćani: Agitated folds in 'The Appearance of Christ to the Apostles after the Resurrection' (sanctuary, nave).

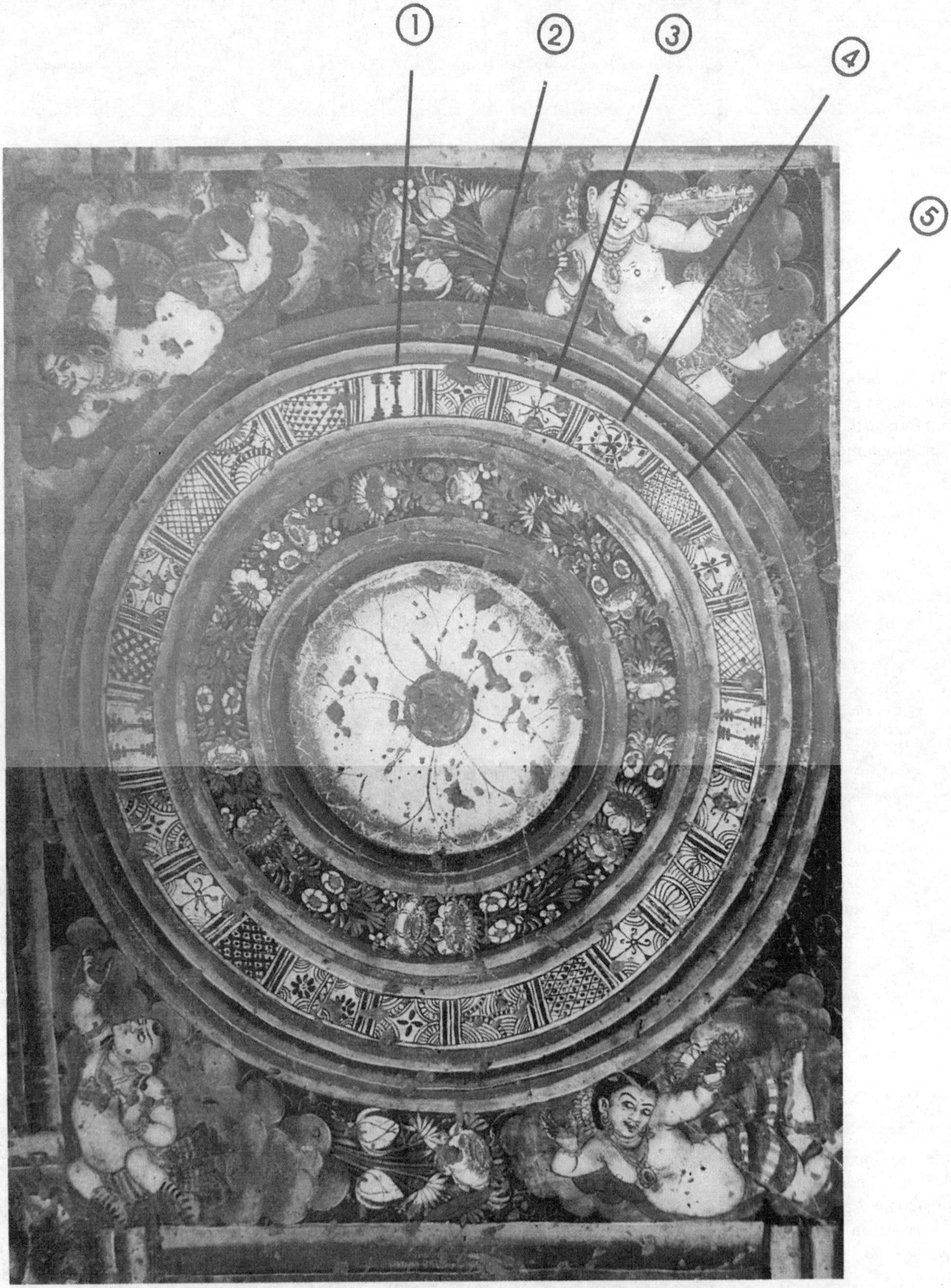

Plate 39. Ajanta: Five basic perceptual devices of planer structuring coded in the decorative patterns of the ceiling (cave 2). Curtained opening as a referent uniting the frame with the framed 'surface'.

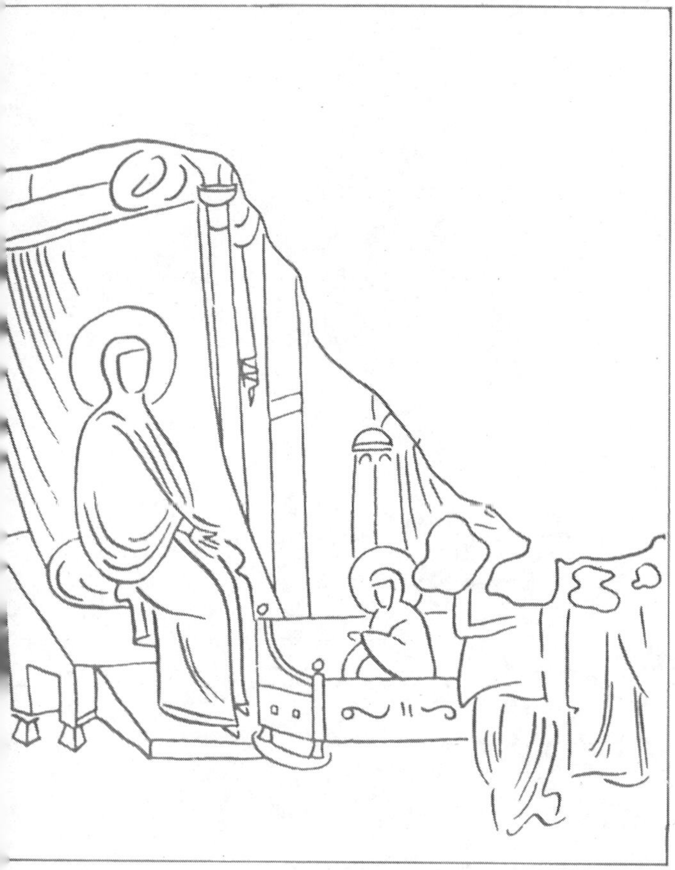

Plate 40. Sopoćani: 'The Nativity of the Virgin' (prothesis, A.D. 1263-68).

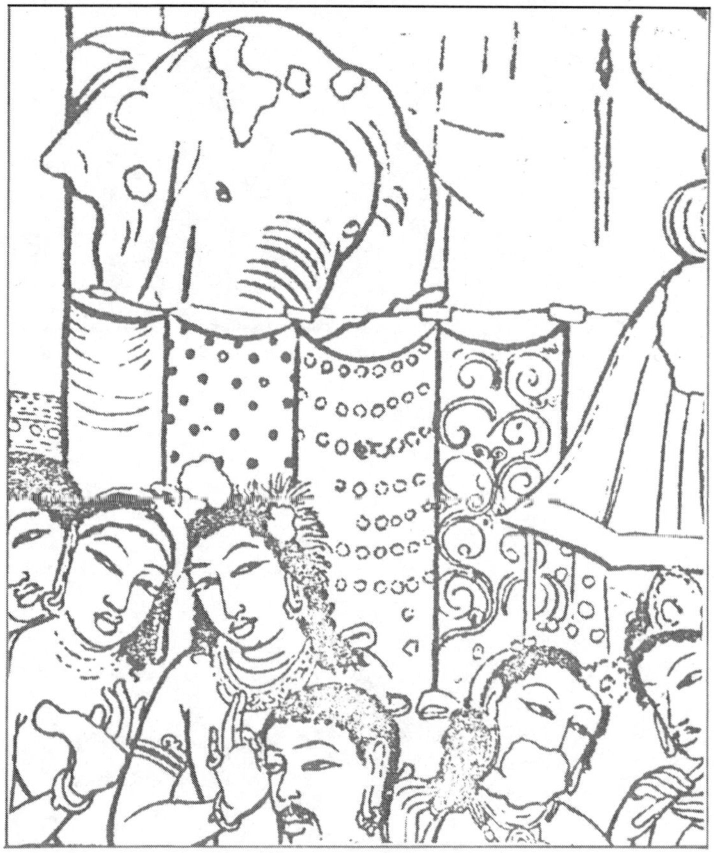

Plate 41. Ajanta: 'Mahāhaṁsa Jātaka' (cave 17). Pillars uniting upper and lower edges making total area of the frame as the perceptual concern.

Plate 42. Sopoćani: 'Christ among the doctors' (nave).

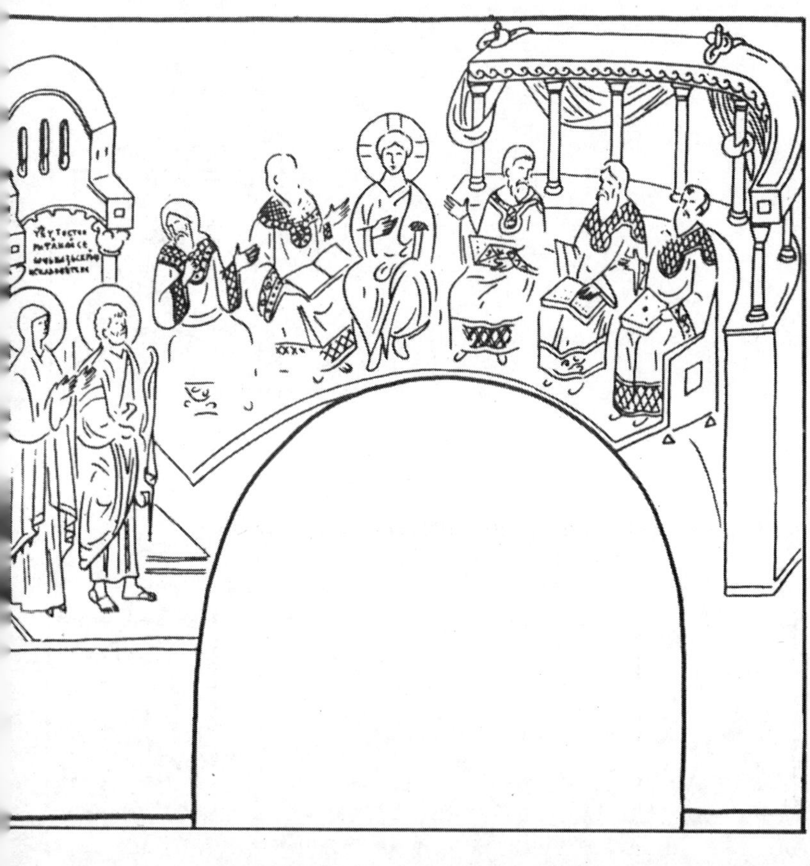

Plate 43. Ajanta: 'The Consecration of Nanda' (cave 1). 'Bust motif' and its use as a referent uniting the frame with the framed surface.

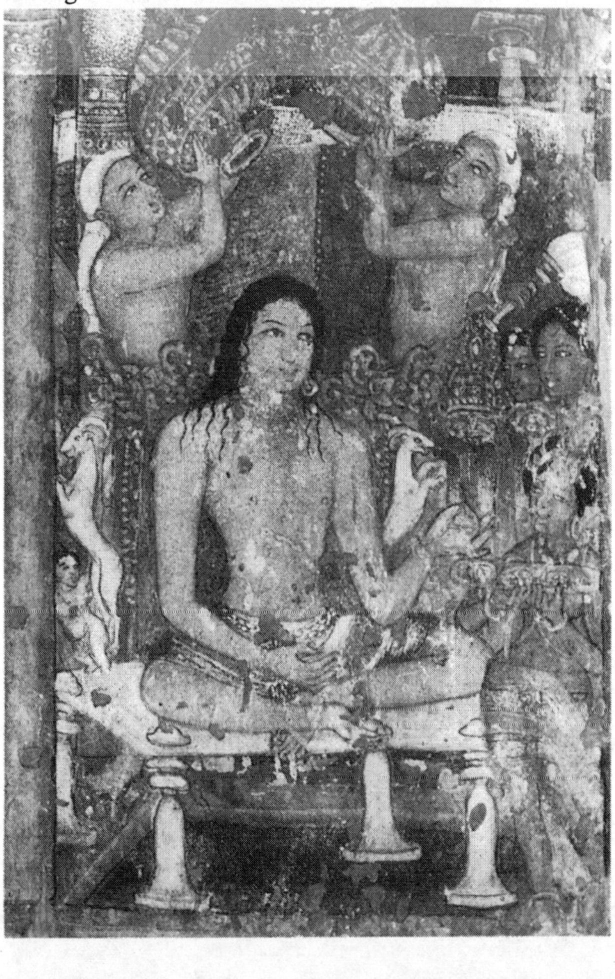

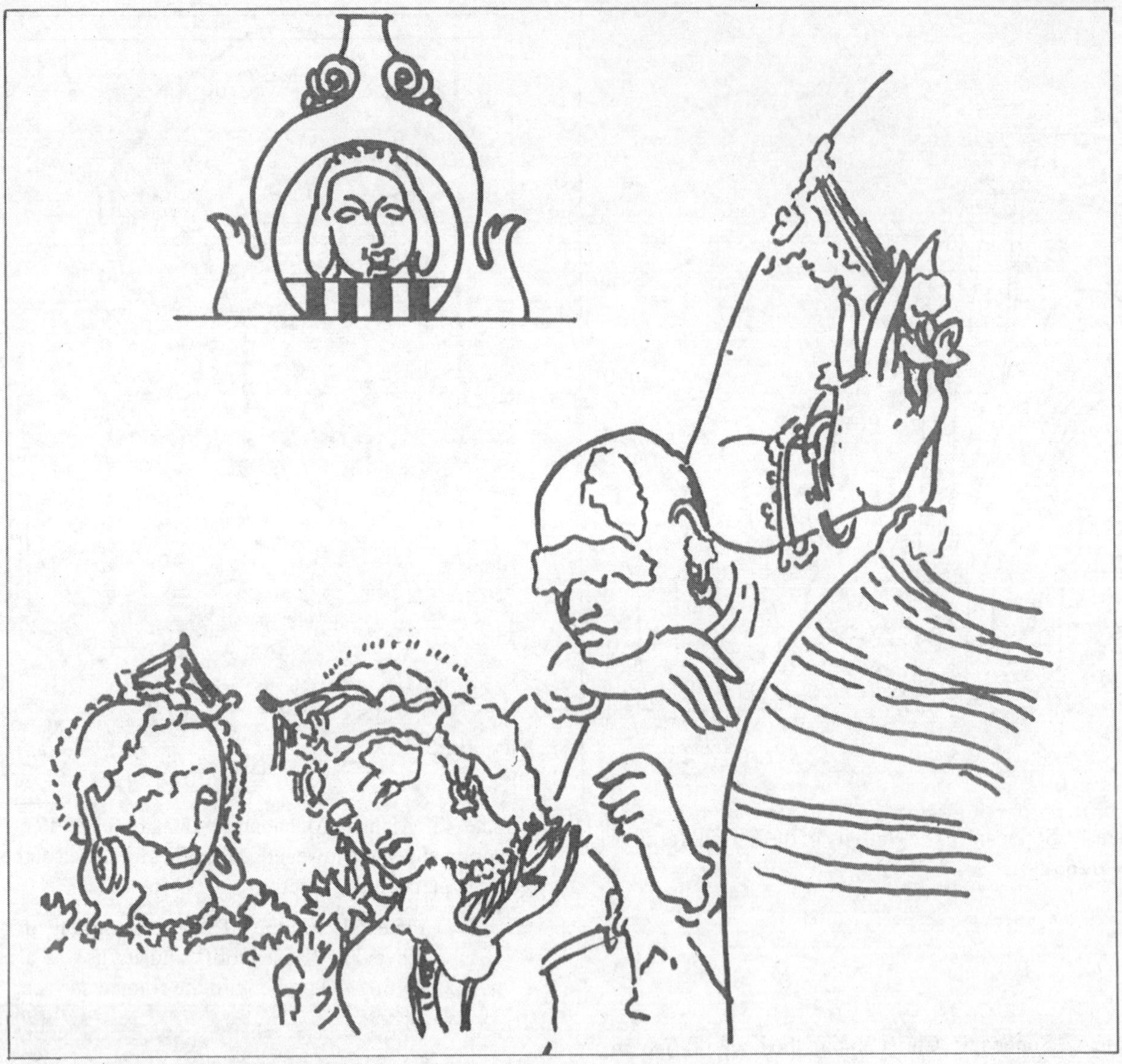

Plate 44. Ajanta: *Gavākṣa* window; Avalokiteśvara mural (cave 1).

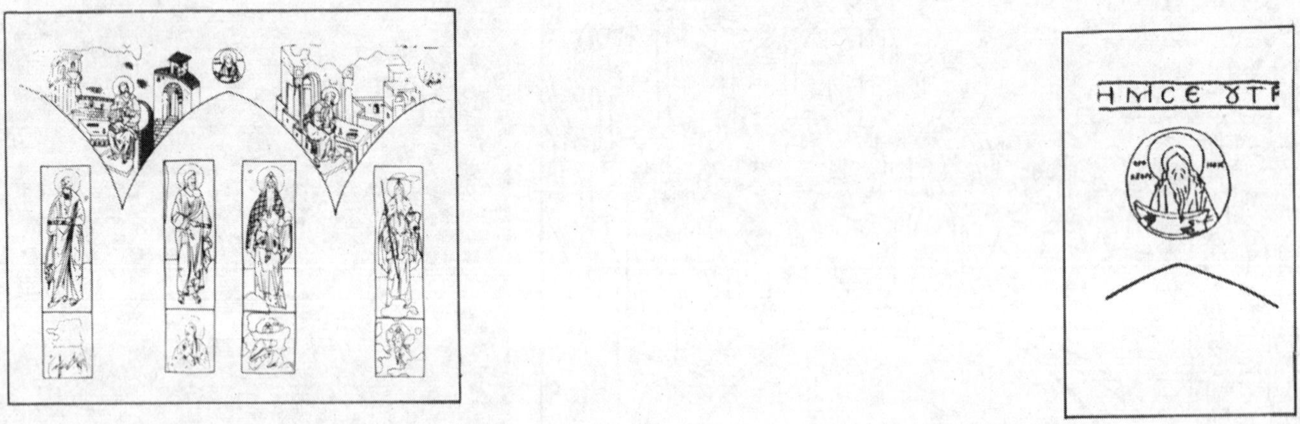

Plate 45. Sopoćani: Medallions and busts on the base of cupola, pendentives and below (nave).

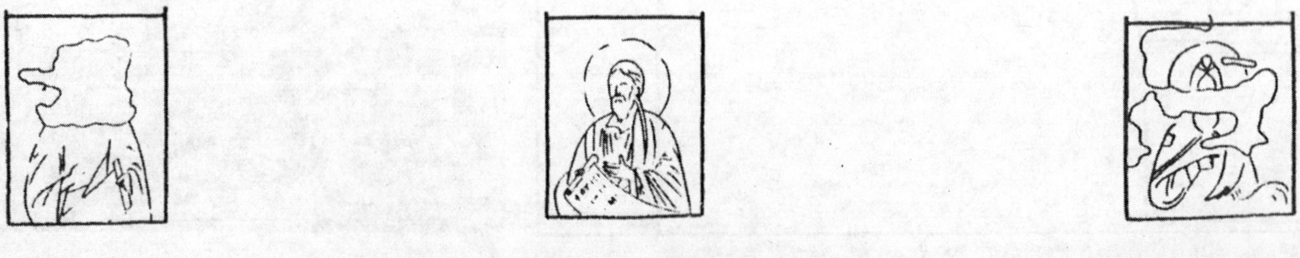

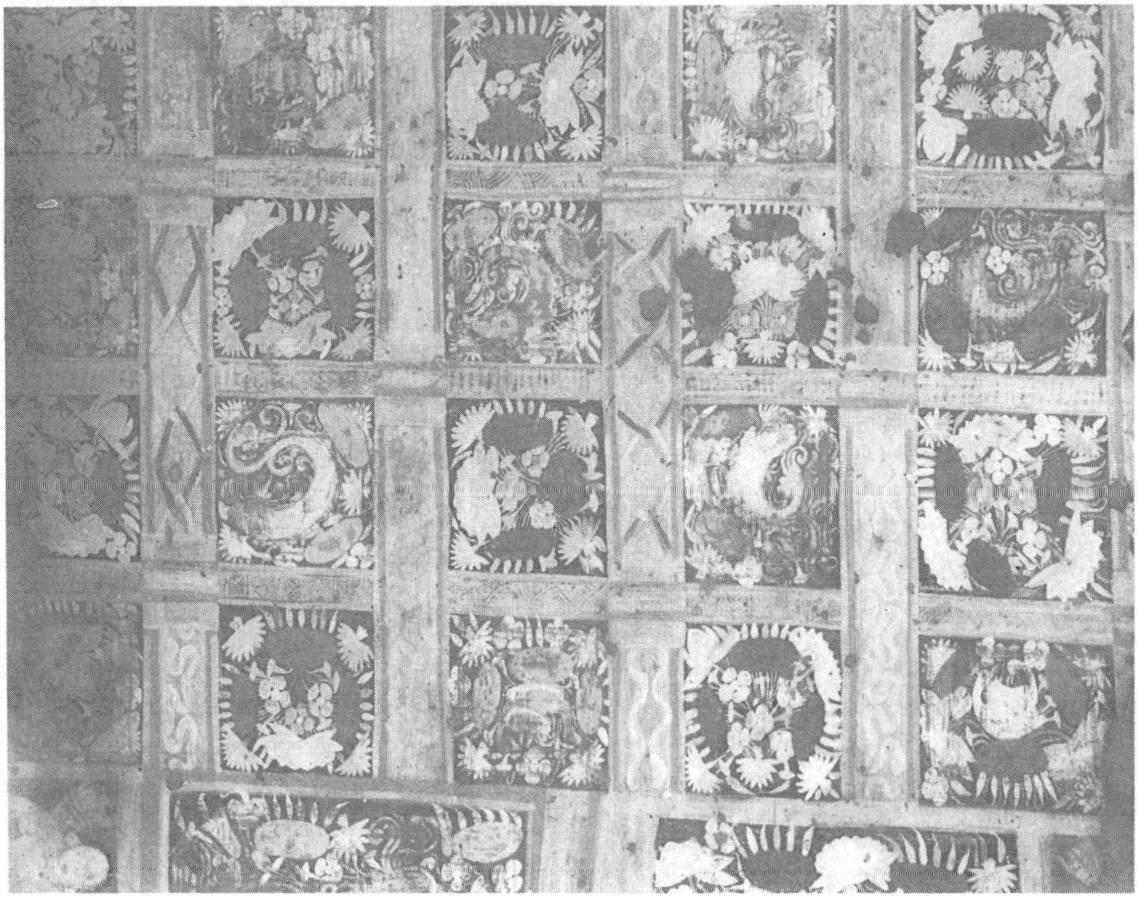

Plate 46. Ajanta: Grid-module on the ceiling decoration (cave 17).

Plate 47. Ajanta: Rectangular impost harmonised with the round capital of the pillar by the luxuriant growth of creeper of *pūrṇa-ghaṭa* (cave 23).

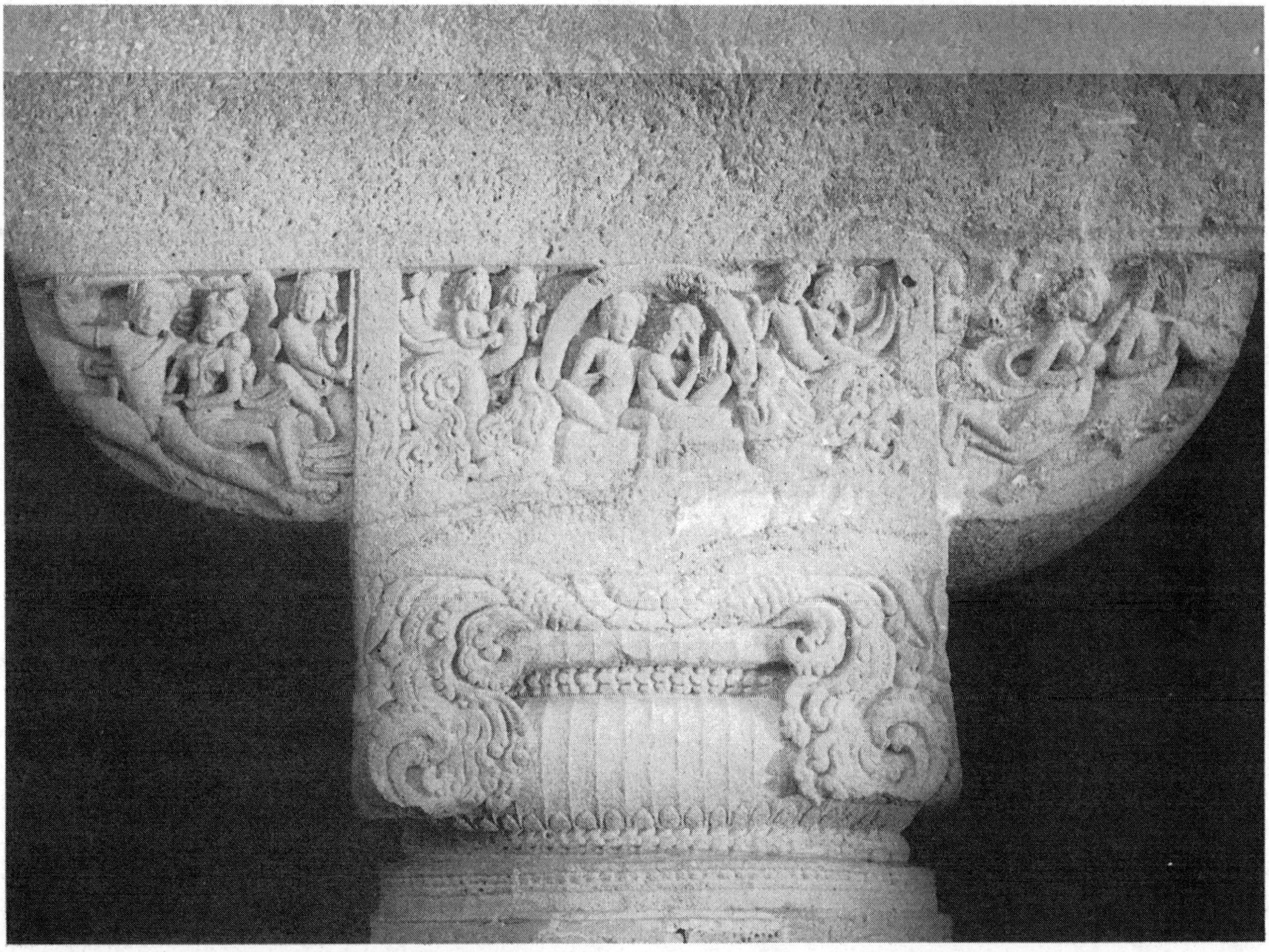

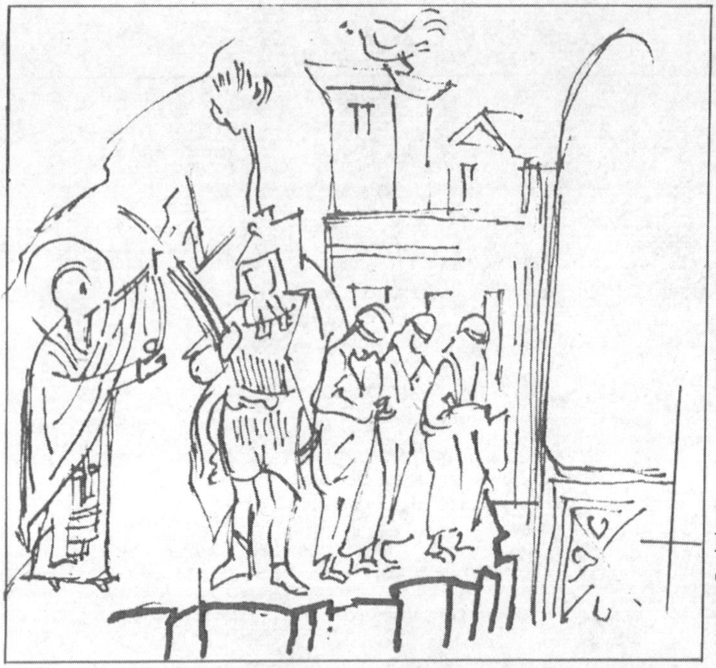

Plate 48. Sopoćani: Rock-cliff edges, 'Saving Three Dukes' chapel of St. Nichola, A.D. 6th or 7th decade of 14th cent.

Plate 49. Sopoćani: Wainscoating figures, 'Parable of the Richman' exo-narthex, (C.A.D. 1331-46).

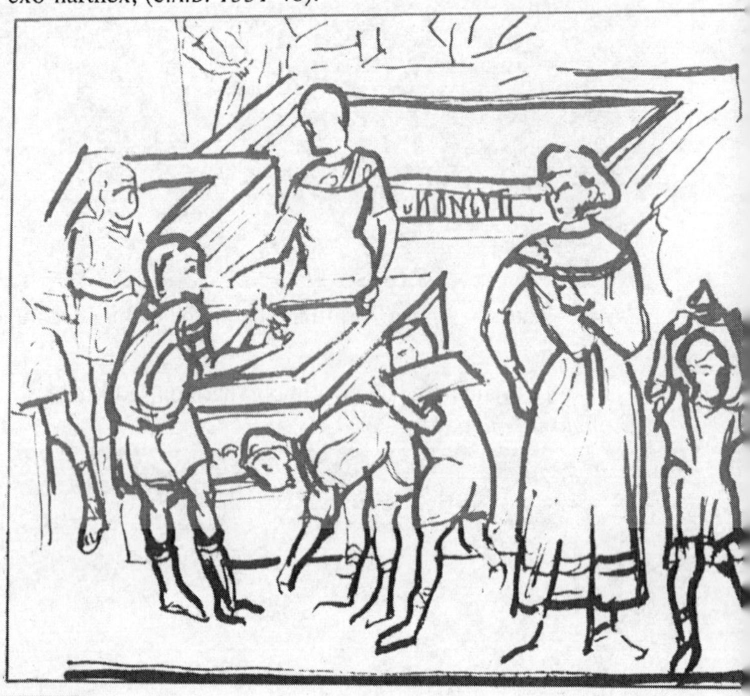

Plate 50. Ajanta: Rock-cliff edges and wainscoating figures, *Sankhpala Jātaka* (cave I) Disturbed alignment of feet.

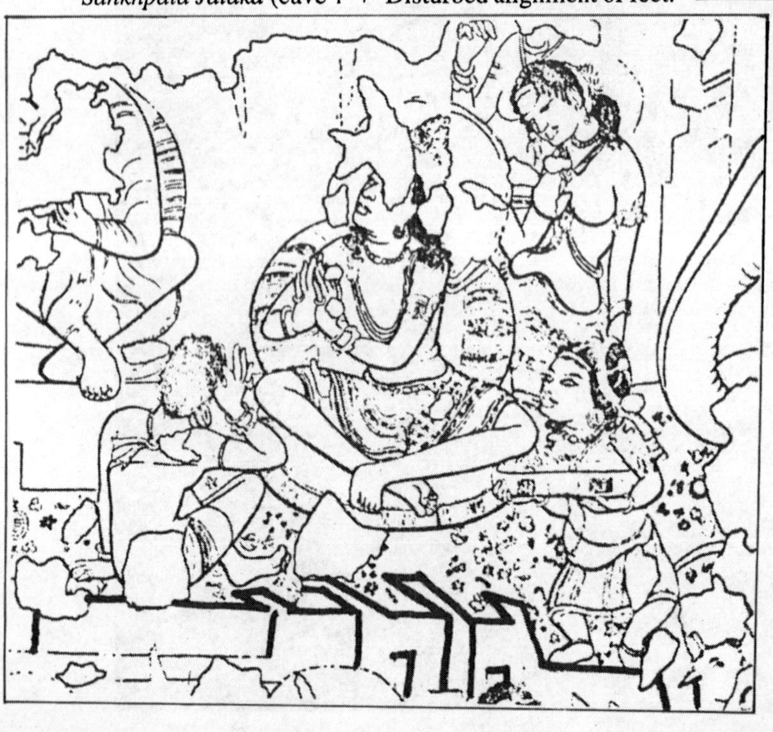

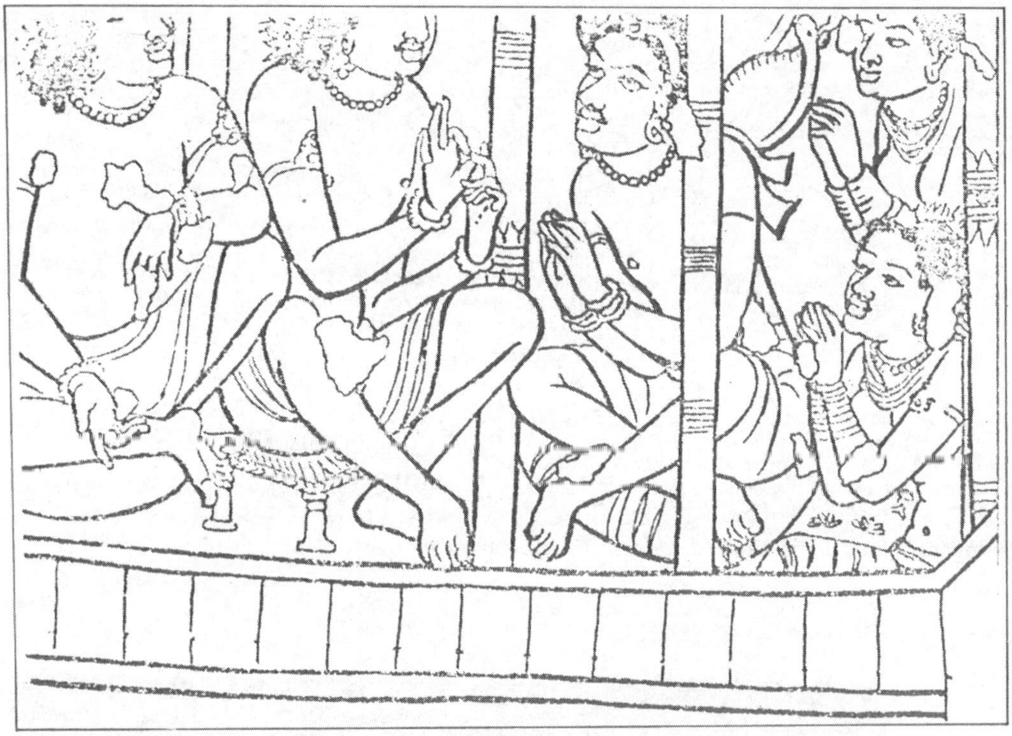

Plate 51. Ajanta: *Vidhurpandita Jātaka* (cave 2).

Plate 52. Sopocani: 'The Dormition' (nave).

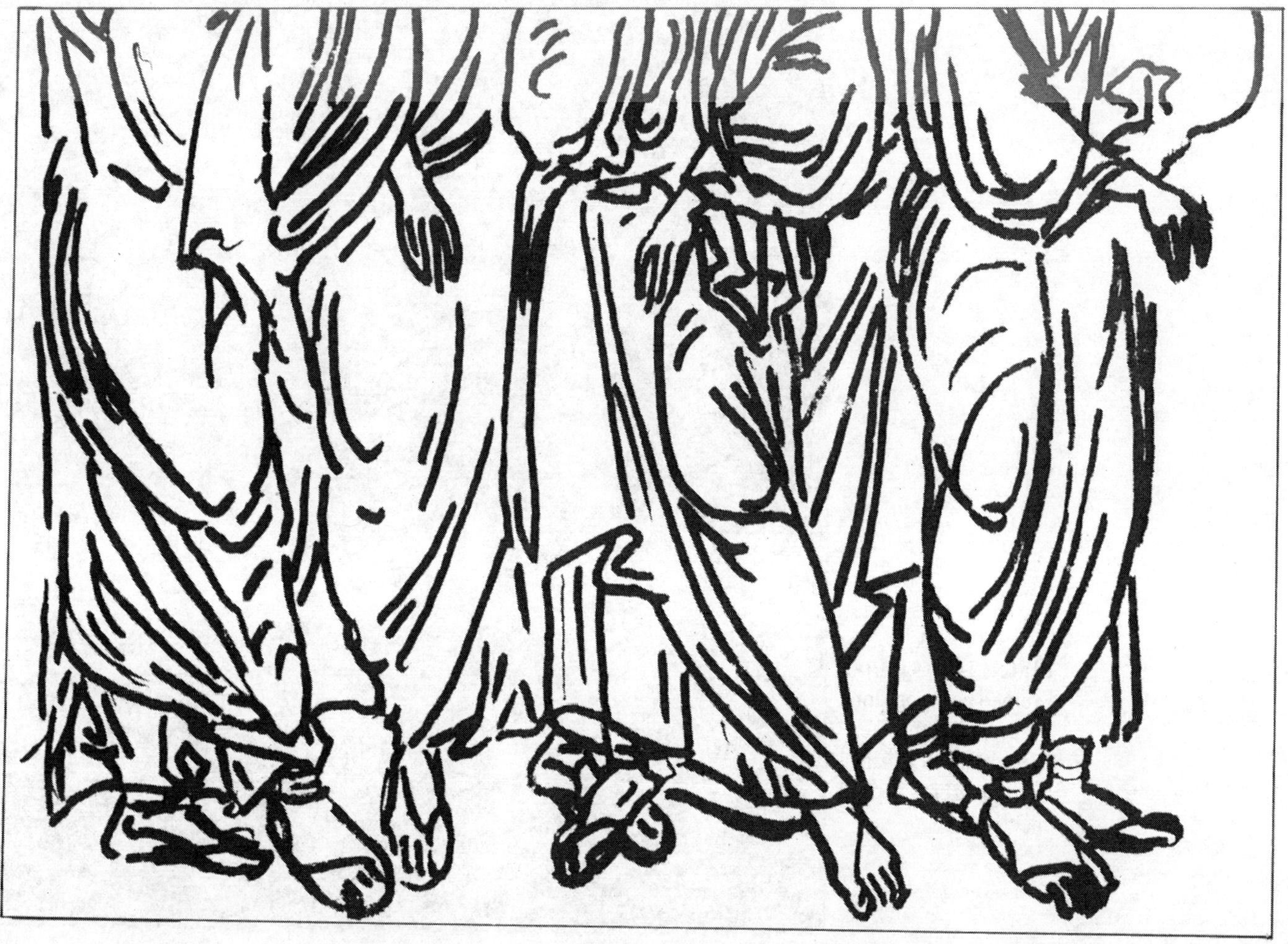

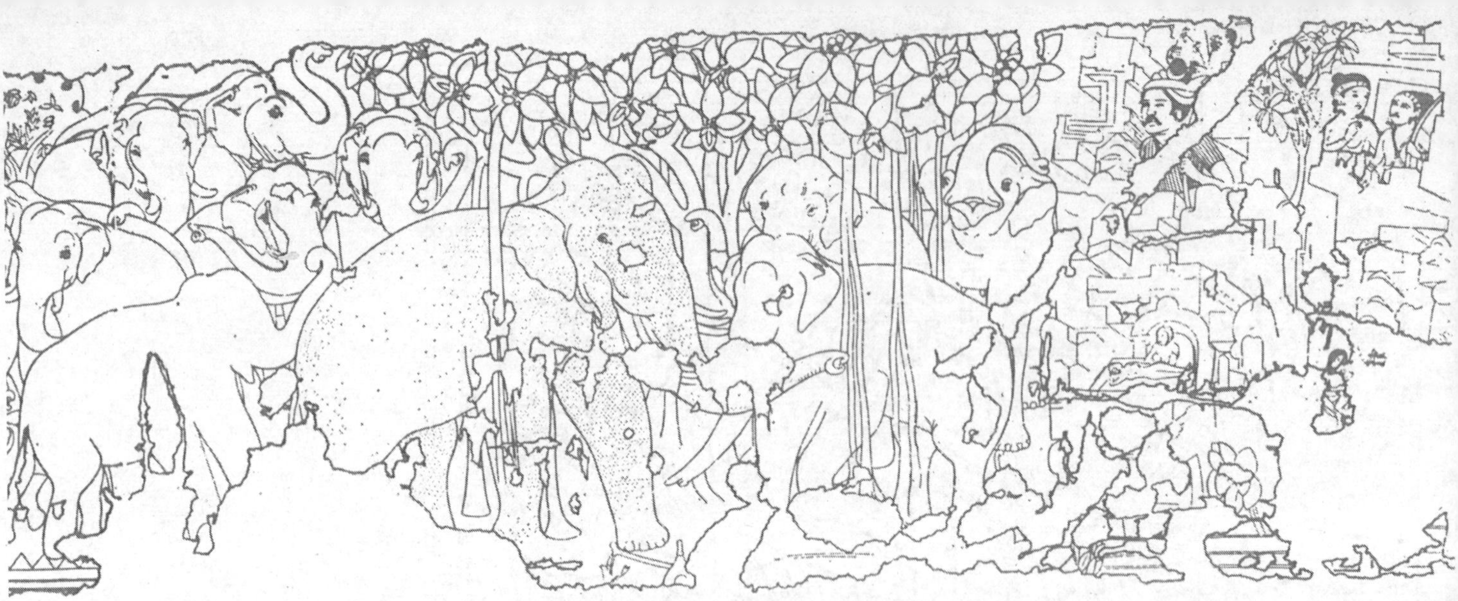

Plate 53. Ajanta: Overlapping for spatial perception, *Chaddanta Jātaka* (cave 10).

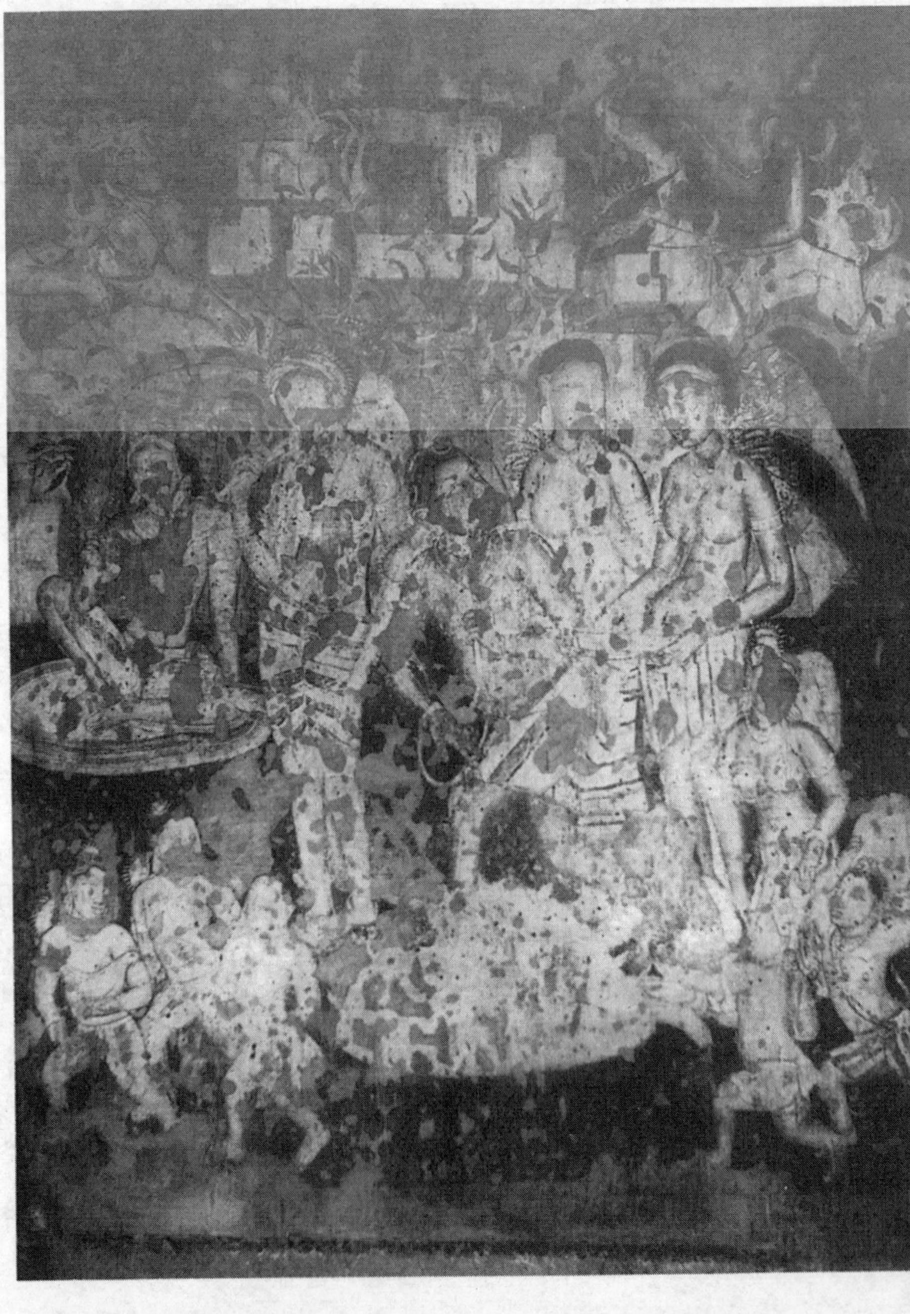

Plate 54. Ajanta: Framed composition, 'Votaries with offerings' (Hariti Shrine, cave 2). Vertical perspective.

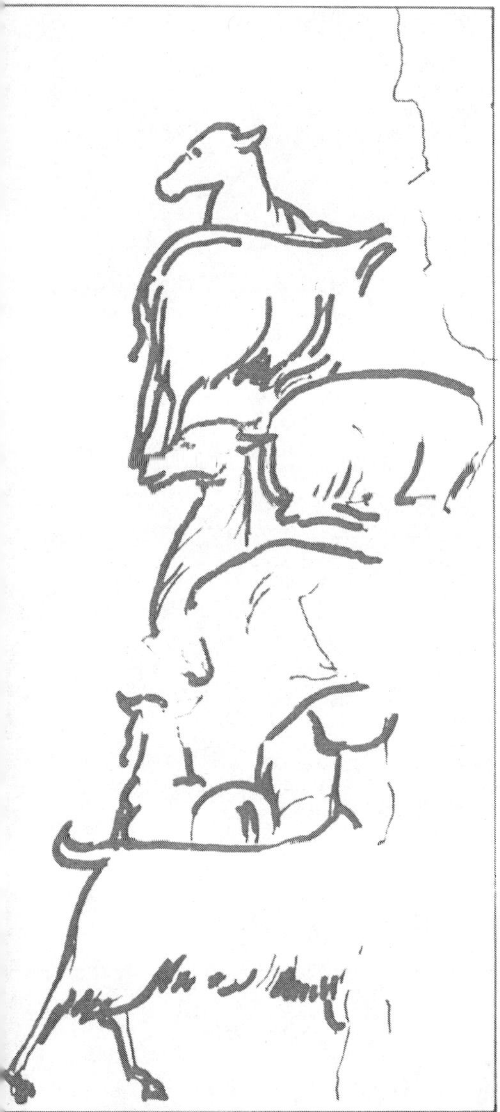

Plate 55. Sopoćani: 'The Nativity' (detail, nave).

Plate 56. Ajanta: *Mahājanaka Jātaka* (detail, cave 1) . Circular or screw-spatiality:

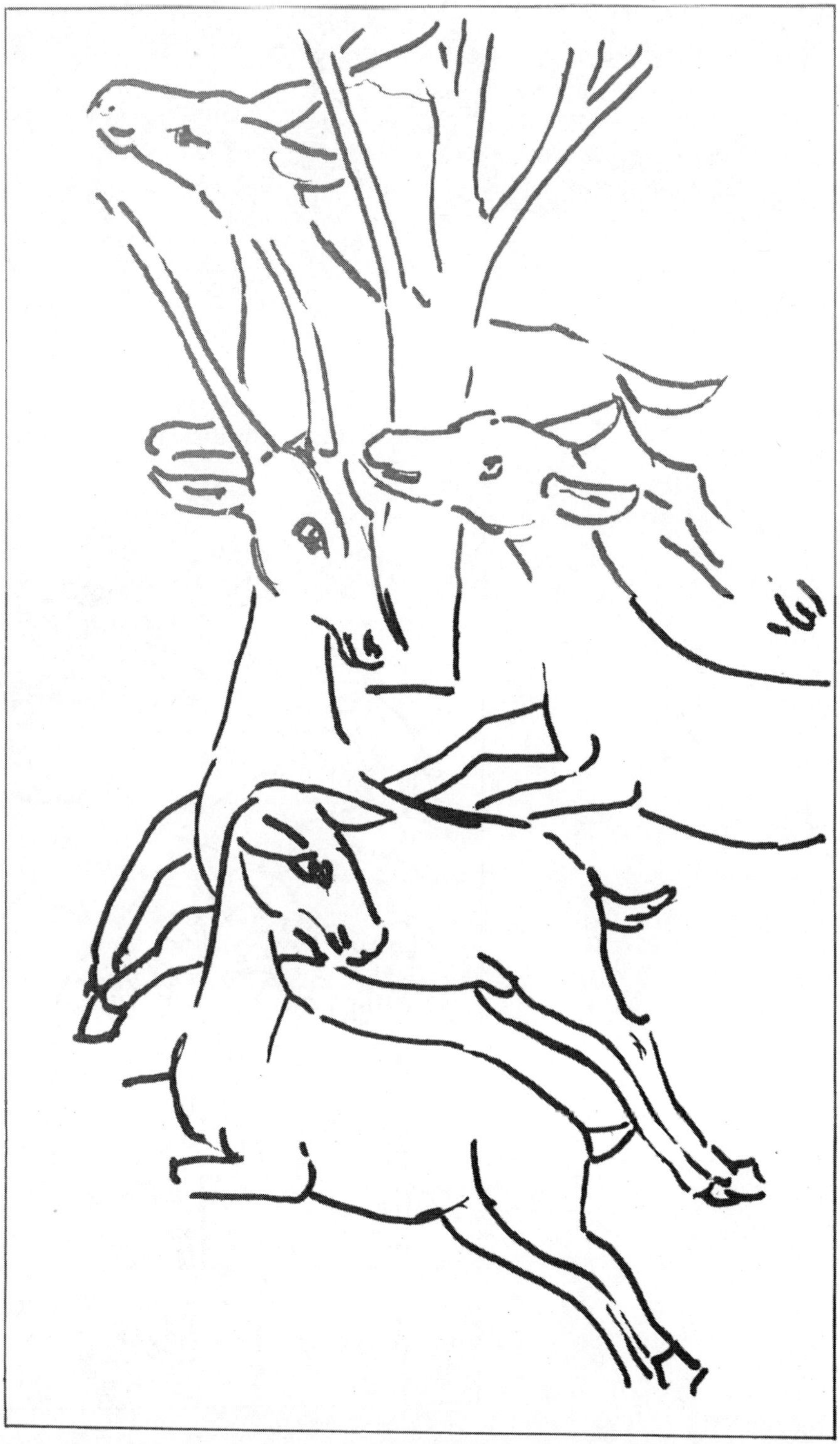

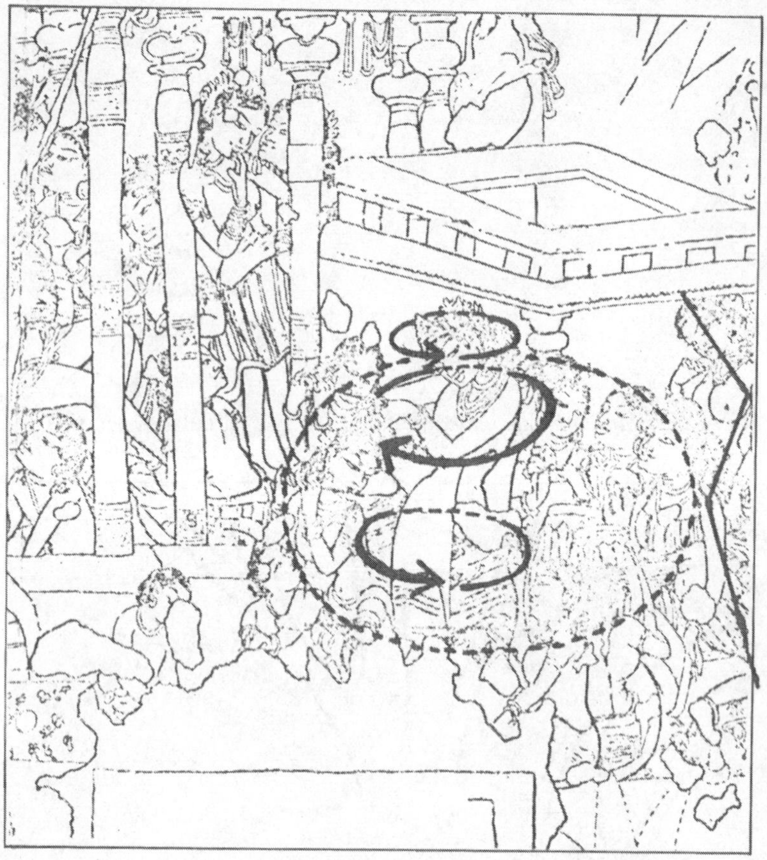

Plate 57. Ajanta: Mahājanaka Jātaka (detail cave 1).

Plate 58. Sopoćani: 'Crucifixion' (nave).

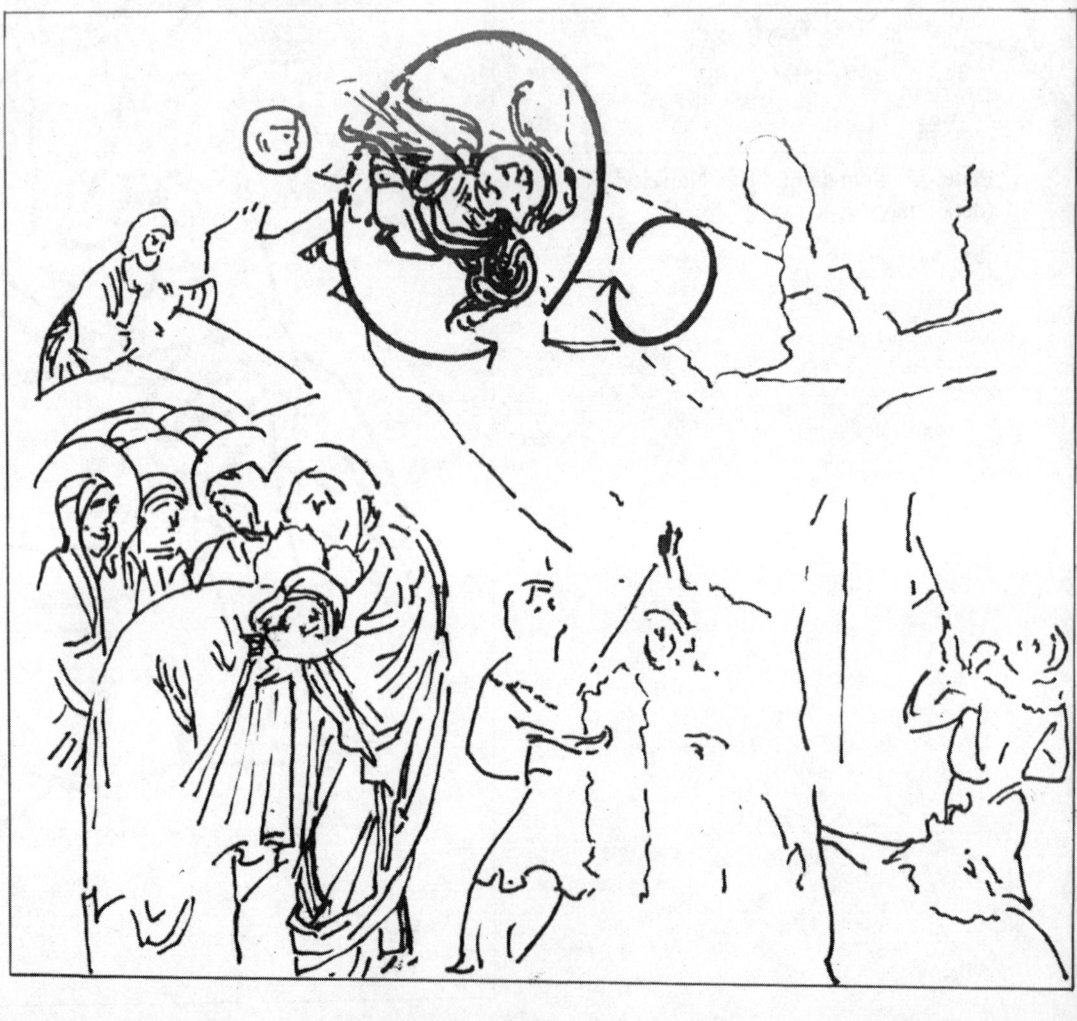

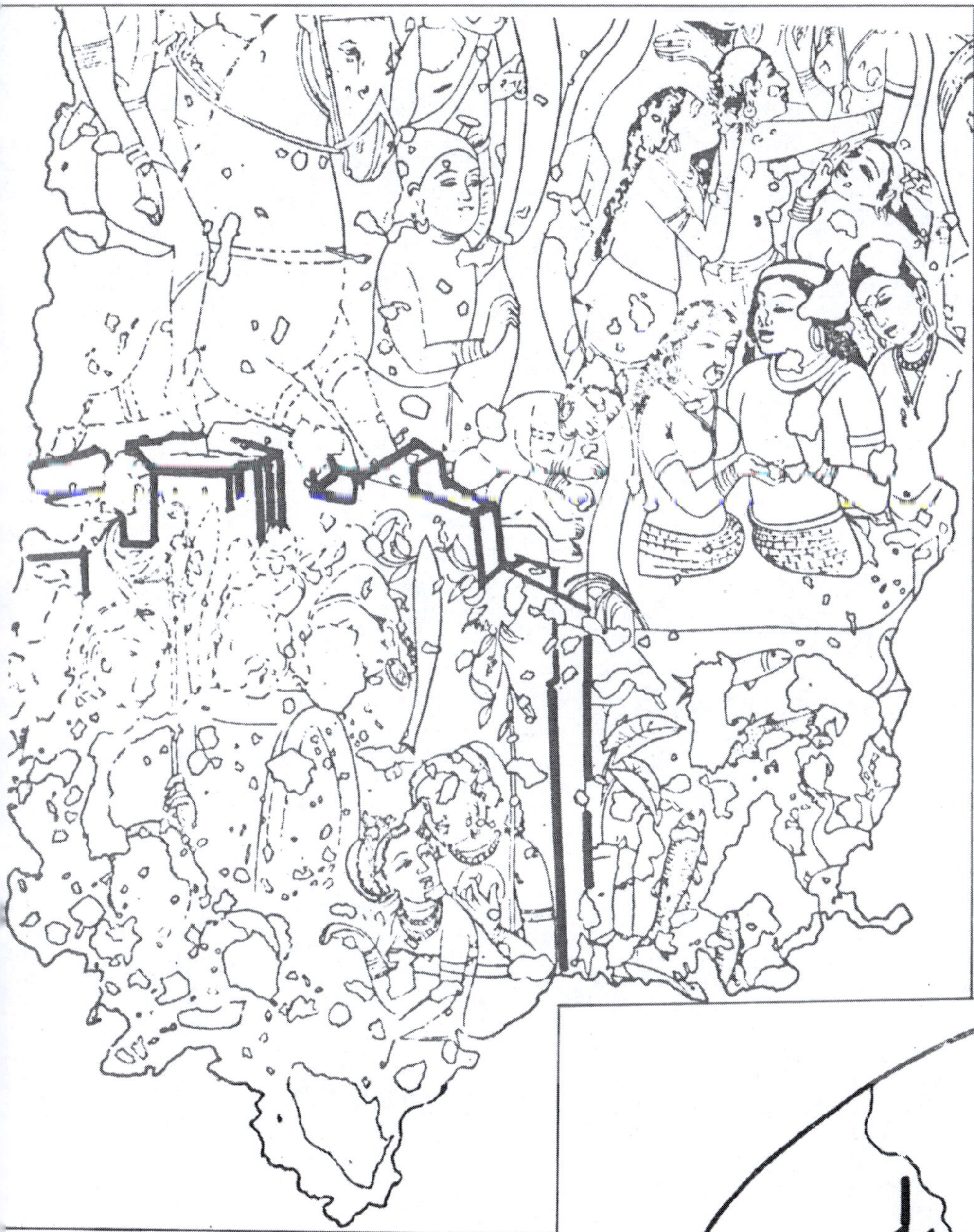

Plate 59. Ajanta: Visual solution in reaching a hexagonal form demonstrating the volume of a square corner, *Mahājanaka Jātaka* (cave 17).

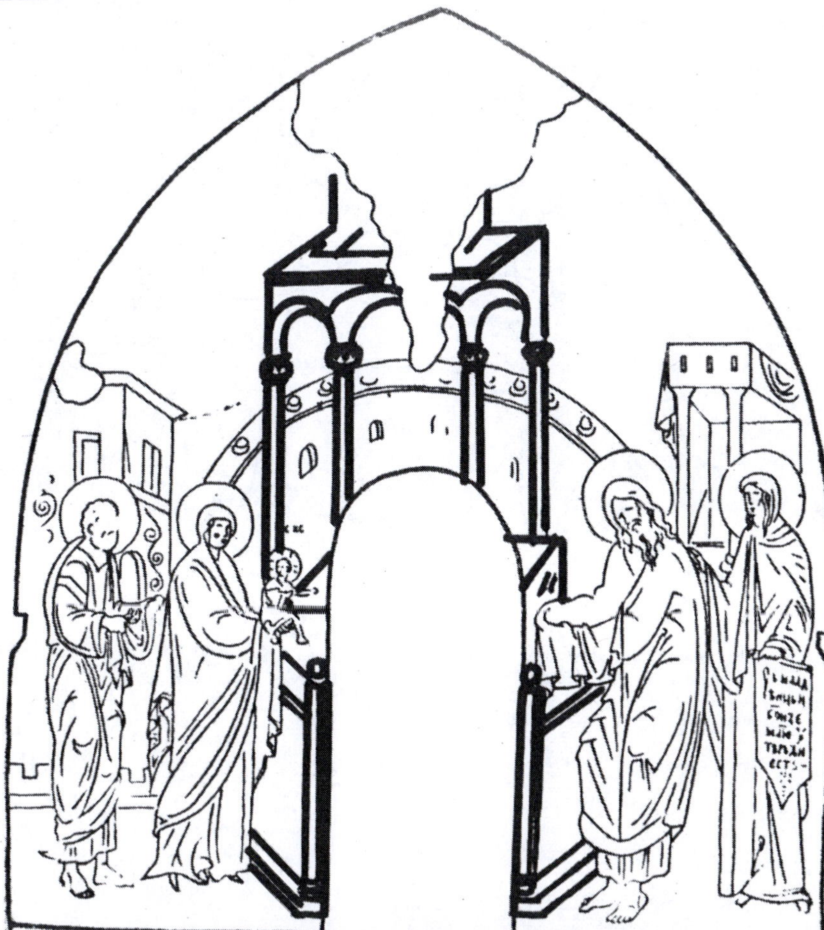

Plate 60. Sopoćani: Bay-window type solution of the above-mentioned visual problem, 'The Presentation in the Temple' (nave). Sharp convergences and their inverse use for expressing the 'forthcoming':

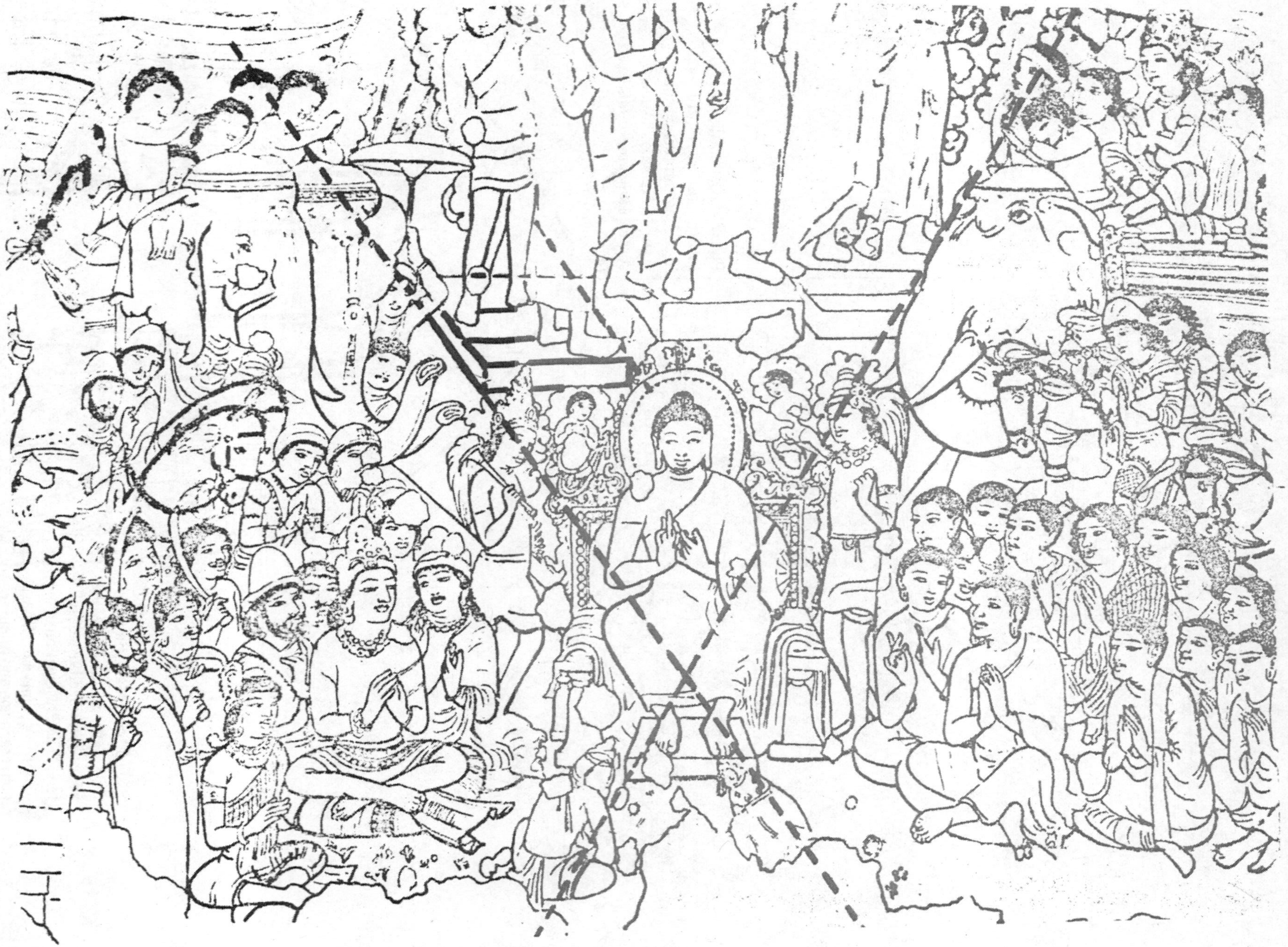

Plate 61. Ajanta: 'The Buddha's descent from Tushita Heaven and the Preaching' (cave 17).

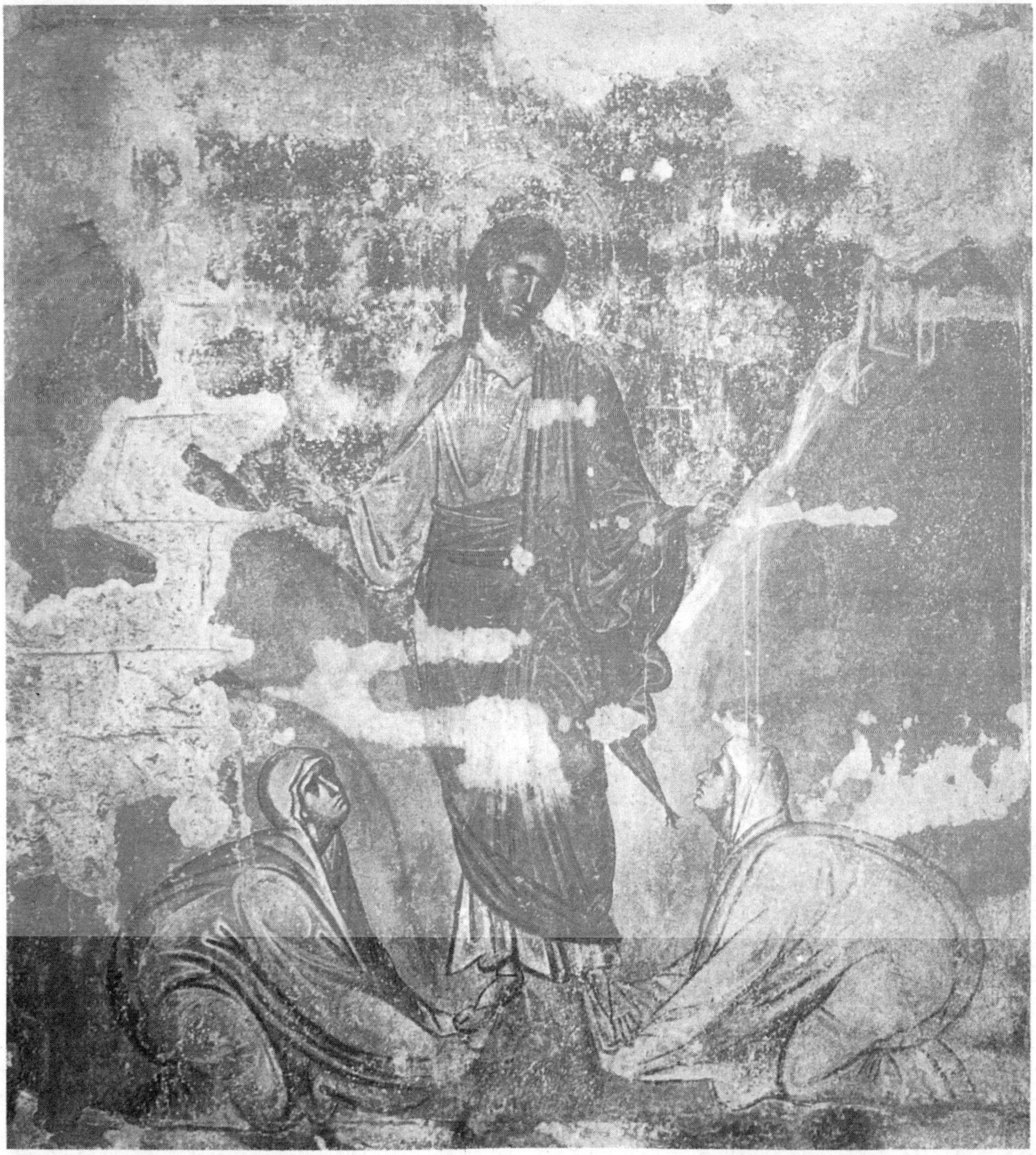

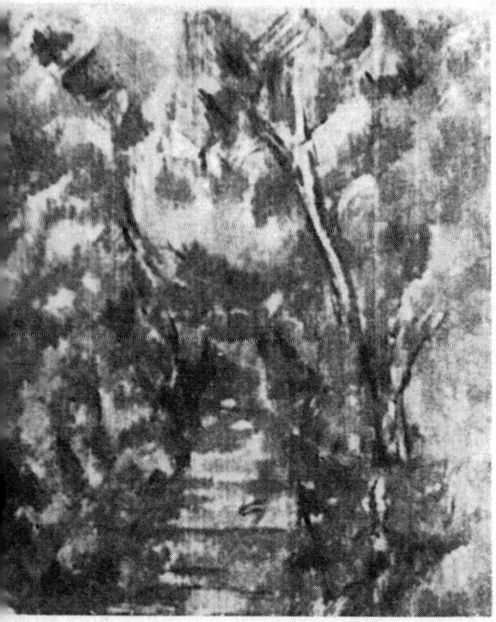

Plates 62-64. Sopoćani: 'The Appearance to the Holy Women' (Sanctuary, nave).

Plate 63. Paul Cezanne's experiments with sharp convergences, 'Forest Path' (c. A.D. 1900). Different eye-level renderings:

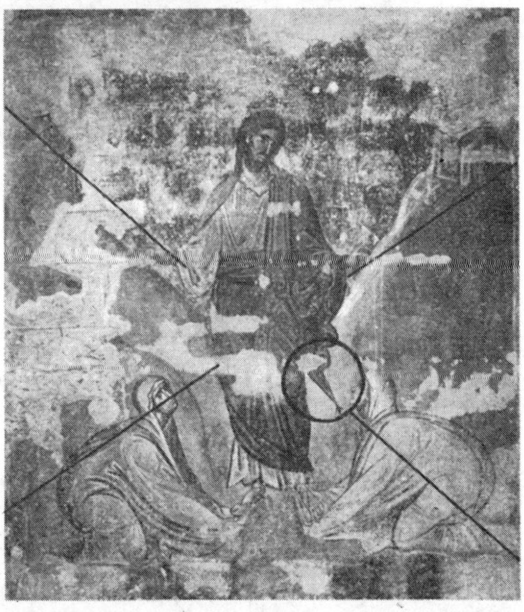

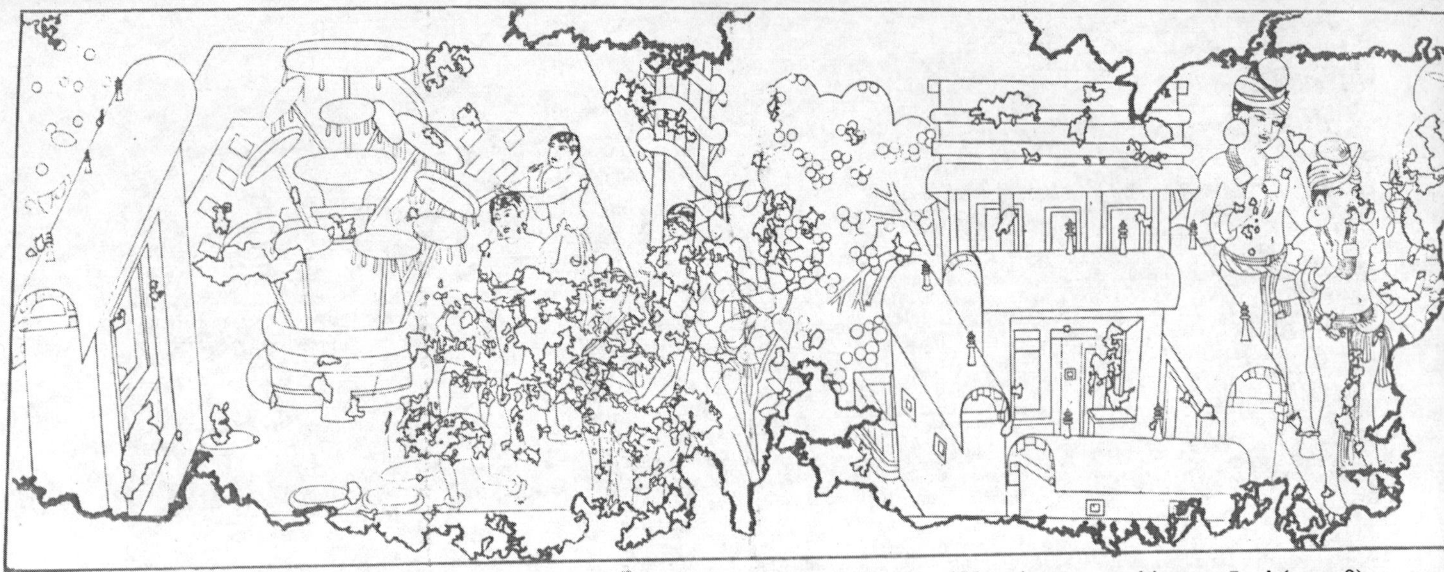

Plate 65. Ajanta: 'A group of Votaries approaching a stūpa' (cave 9).

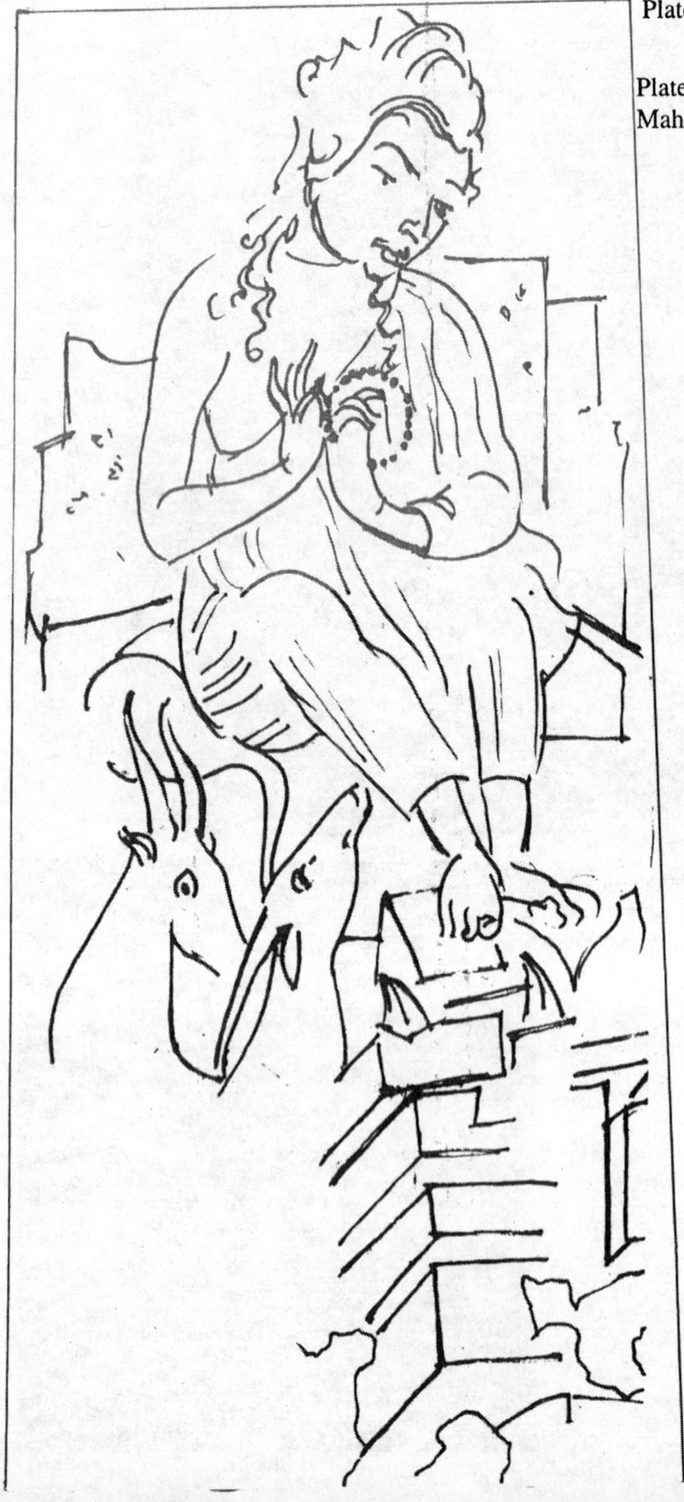

Plate 66. Ajanta: 'A prince listening to the discourse of a hermit'—Mahājanaka Jātaka (detail, cave 1).

Plate 67. Sopoćani: 'The Evangelist' on the rim of the dome (nave): Attributes, according to 'Hiraṇyagarbha' iconographic scheme, are verifiable in the patriarch presented below on the right side.

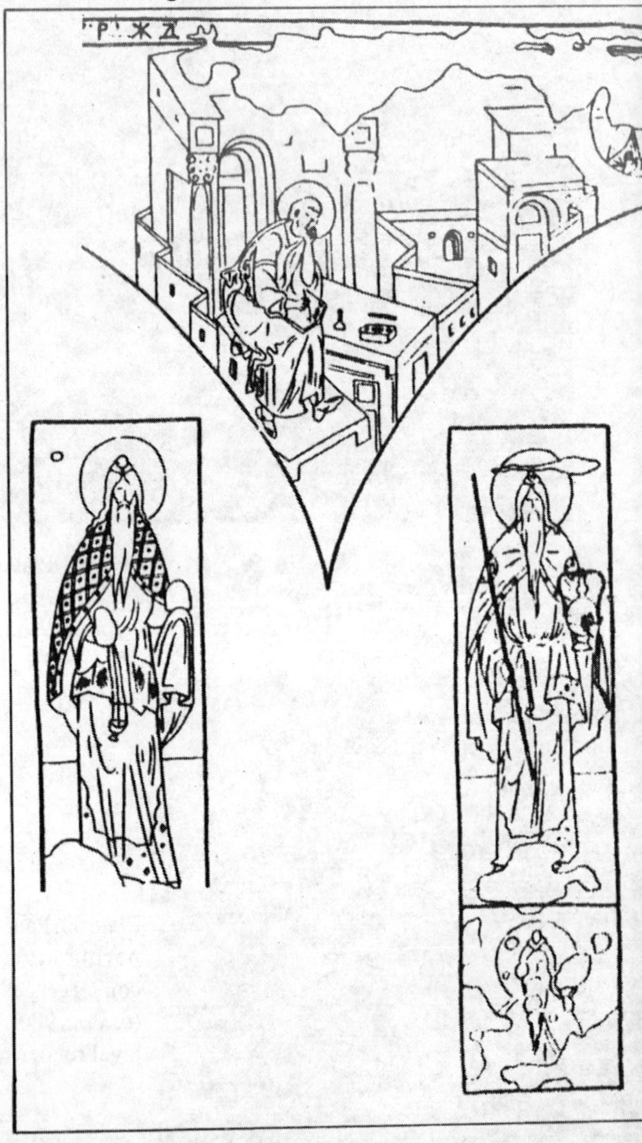

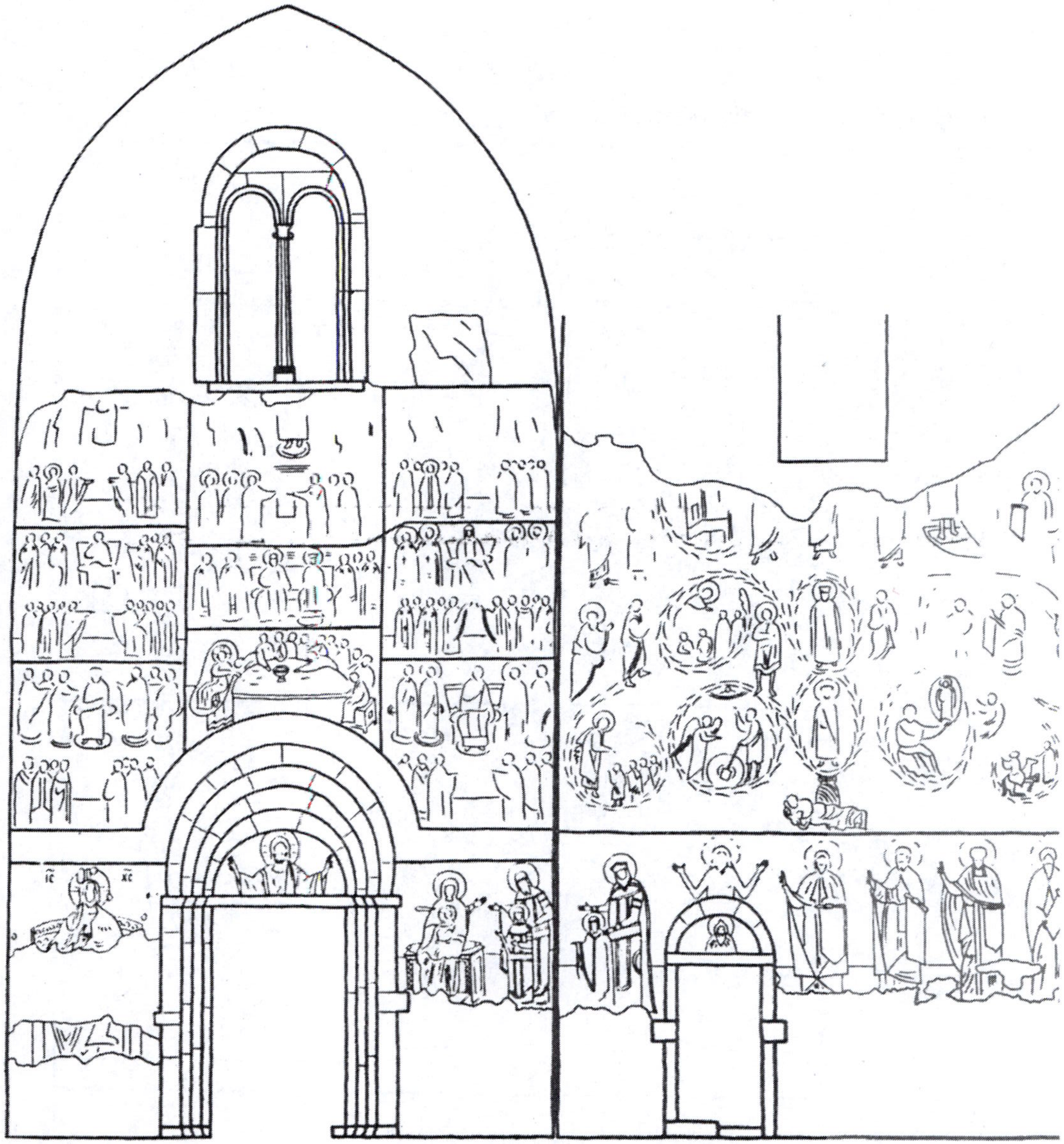

Plate 68. Sopoćani: Extendible grid-system and horizontal bands of narration (Narthex).

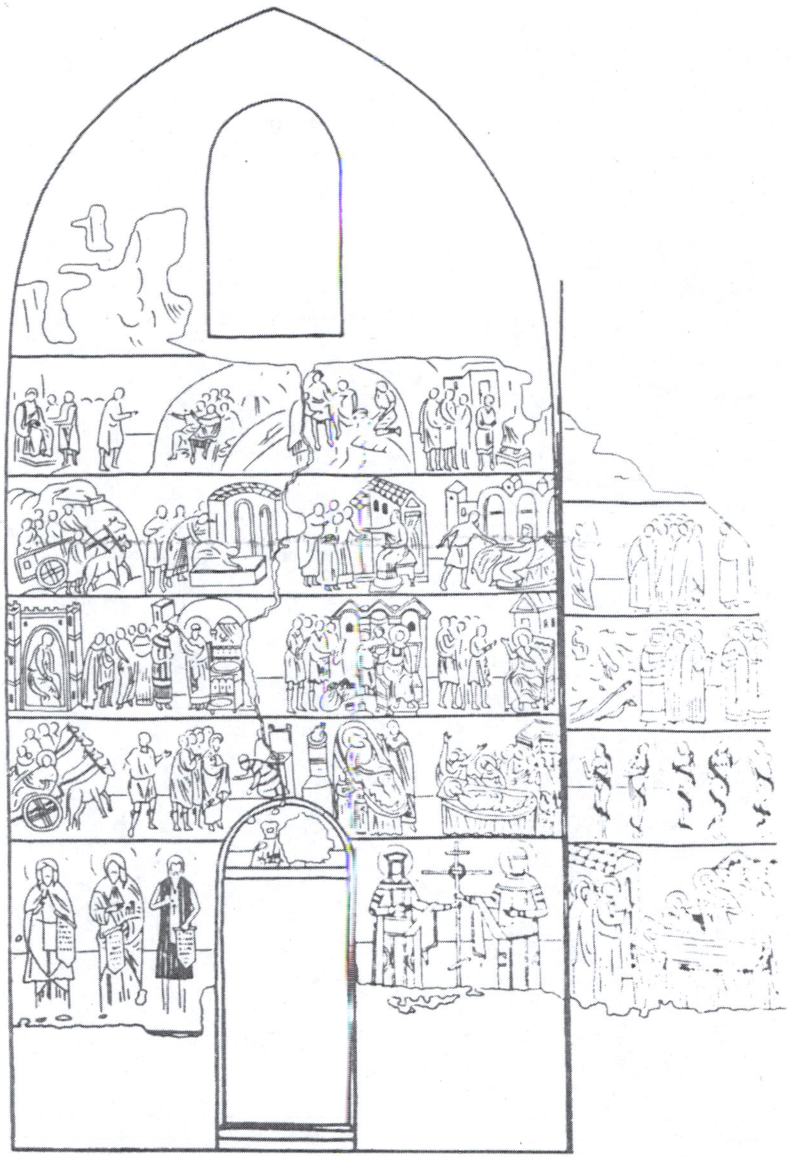

Plate 69. Sopoćani: Eastern Orthodox Cross held by Emperor Constantine and Empress Helena (Narthex).

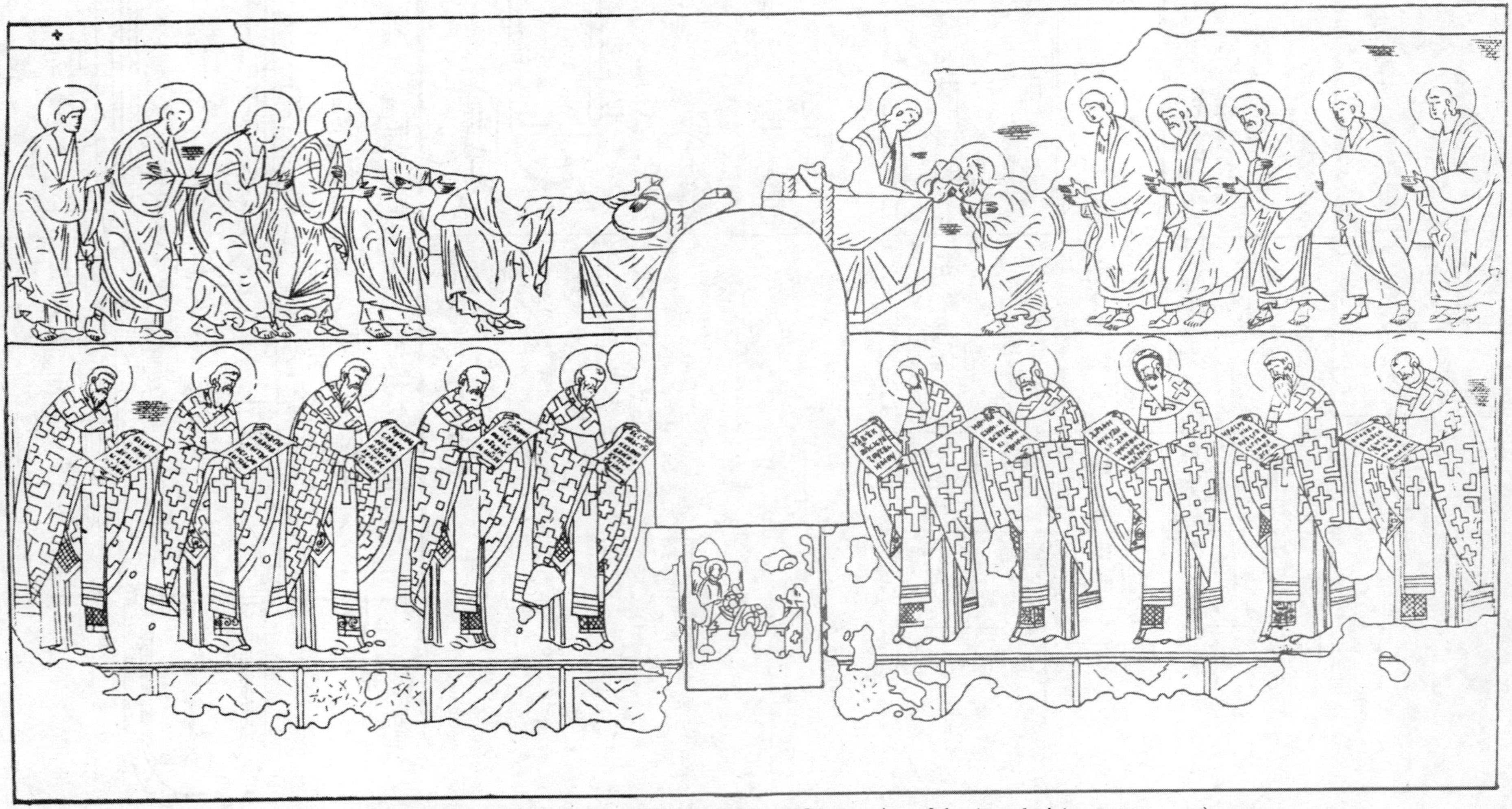

Plate 70. Sopoćani: Overlapping for spatial perception, 'Communion of the Apostles' (sanctuary, nave).

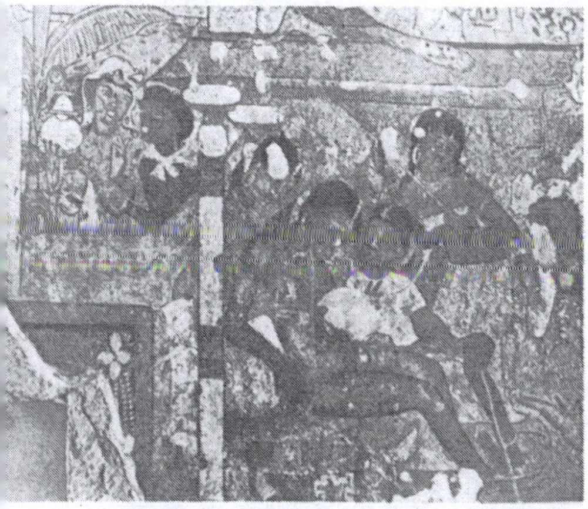

Plate 71. Ajanta: Inversed print of 'The Dying Princess' (cave 16).

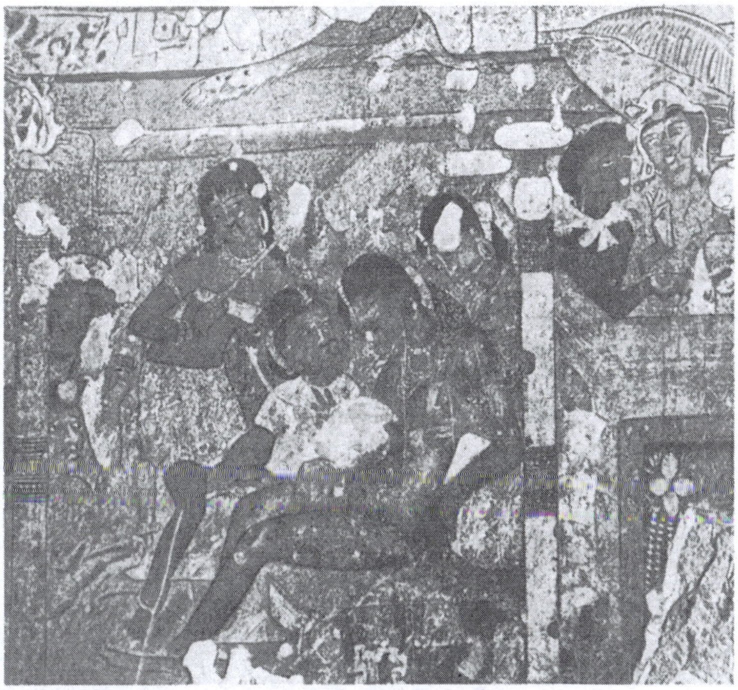

Plate 72. Ajanta: 'The Dying Princess' (cave 16).

Plate 73. Ajanta: Perceptual 'world-wheel' and spatial balance drawn over 'The Dying Princess'.

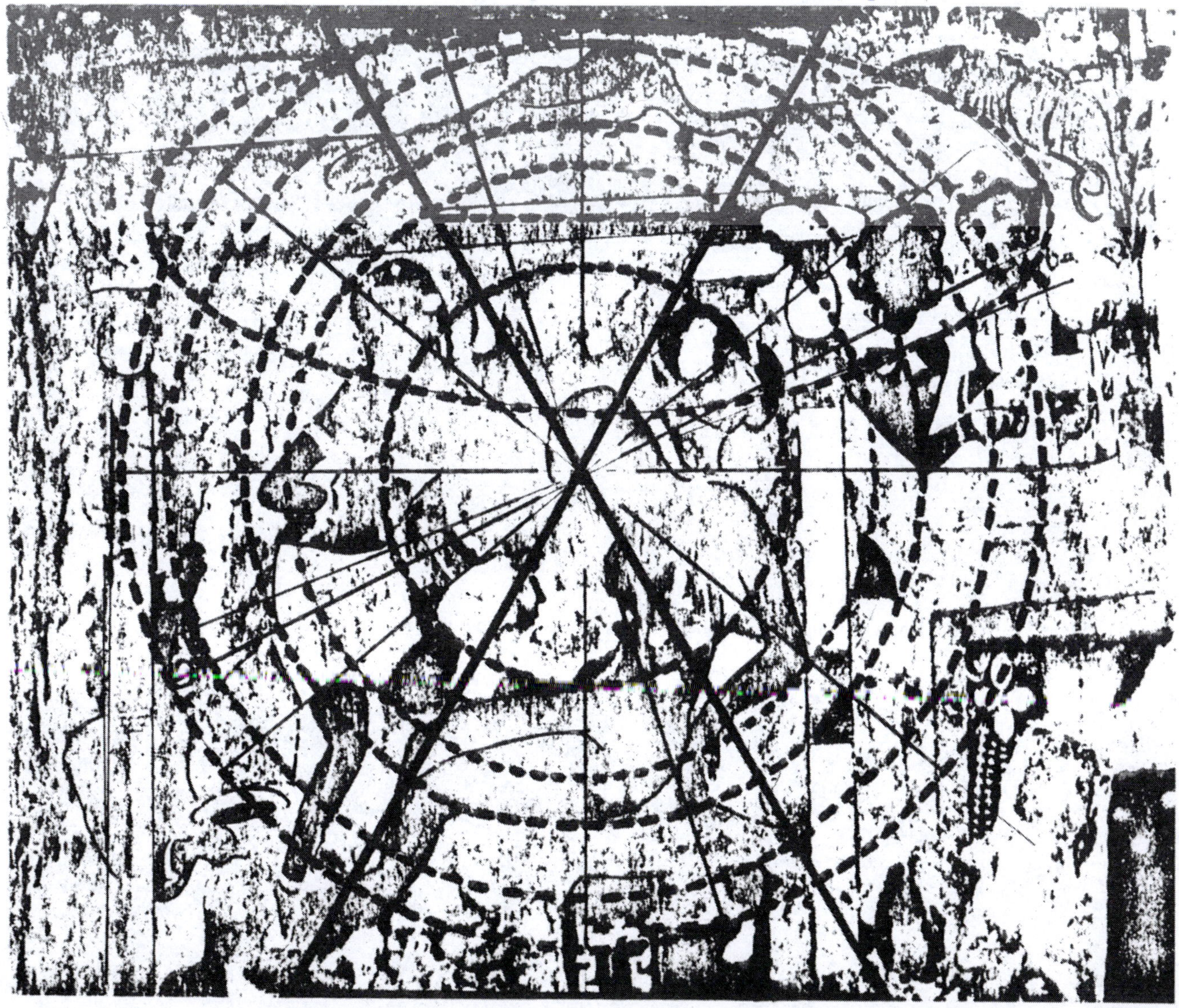

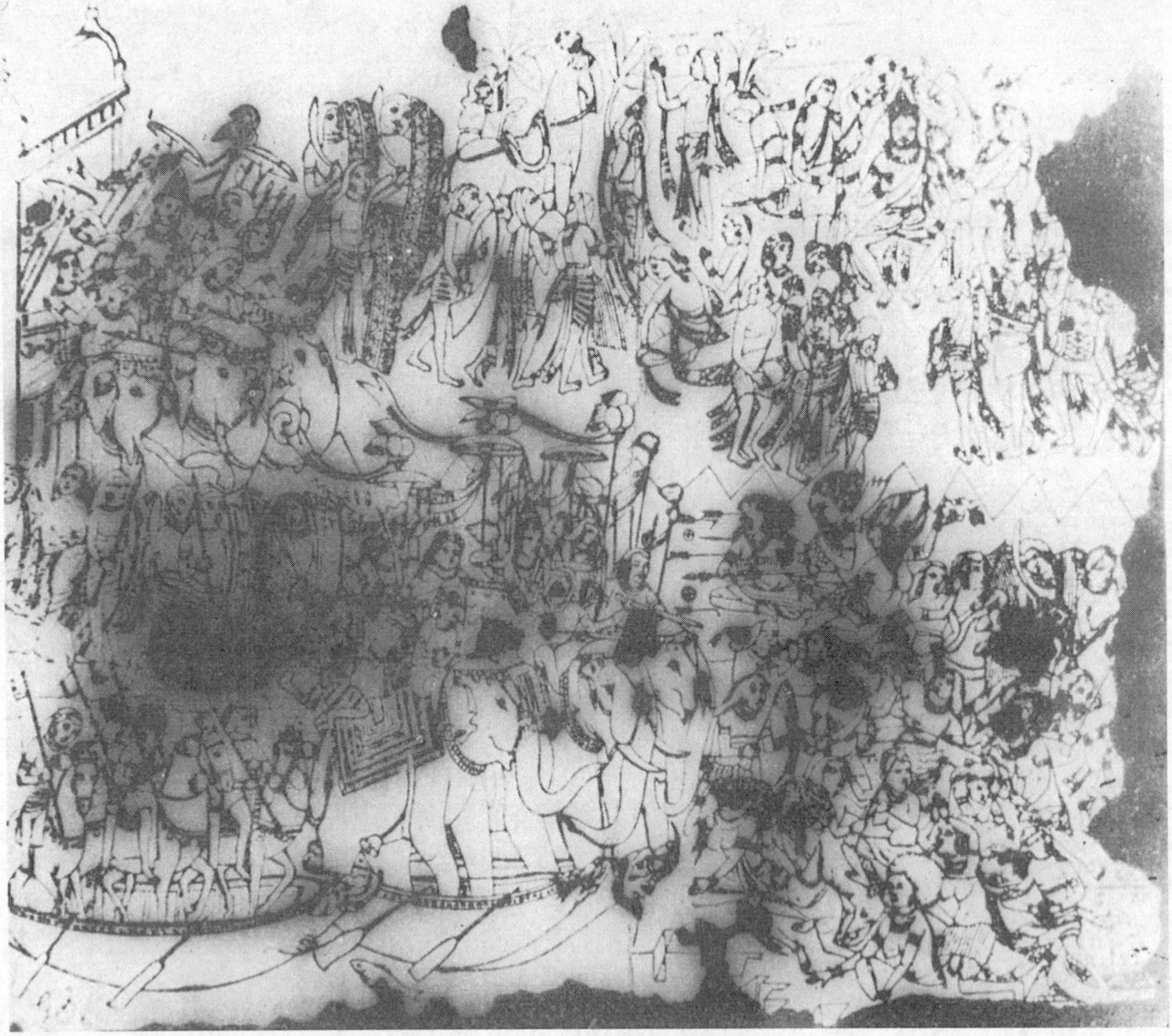

Plate 74. Ajanta: Simhala Avadāna (cave 17).

Plate 75. Ajanta: Horizontal narrative sequence, *Chaddanta Jātaka* (cave 10).

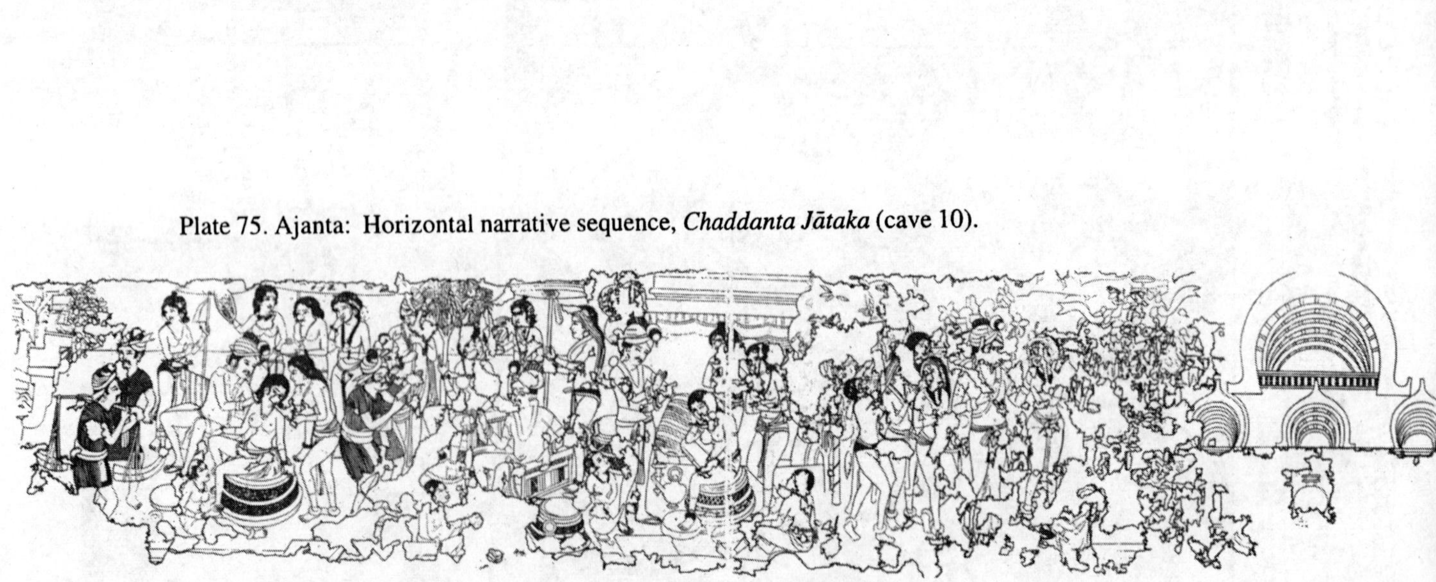

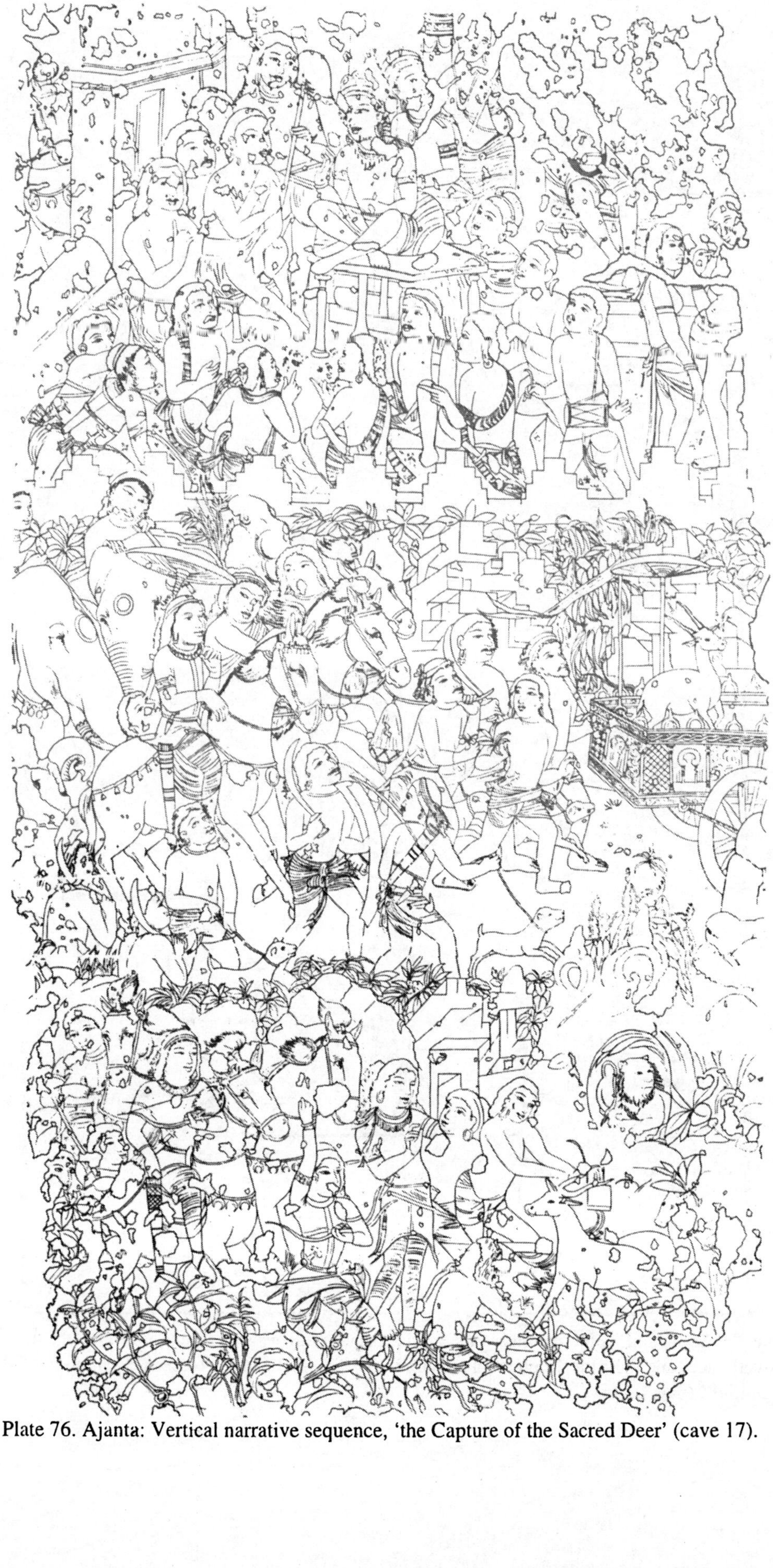

Plate 76. Ajanta: Vertical narrative sequence, 'the Capture of the Sacred Deer' (cave 17).

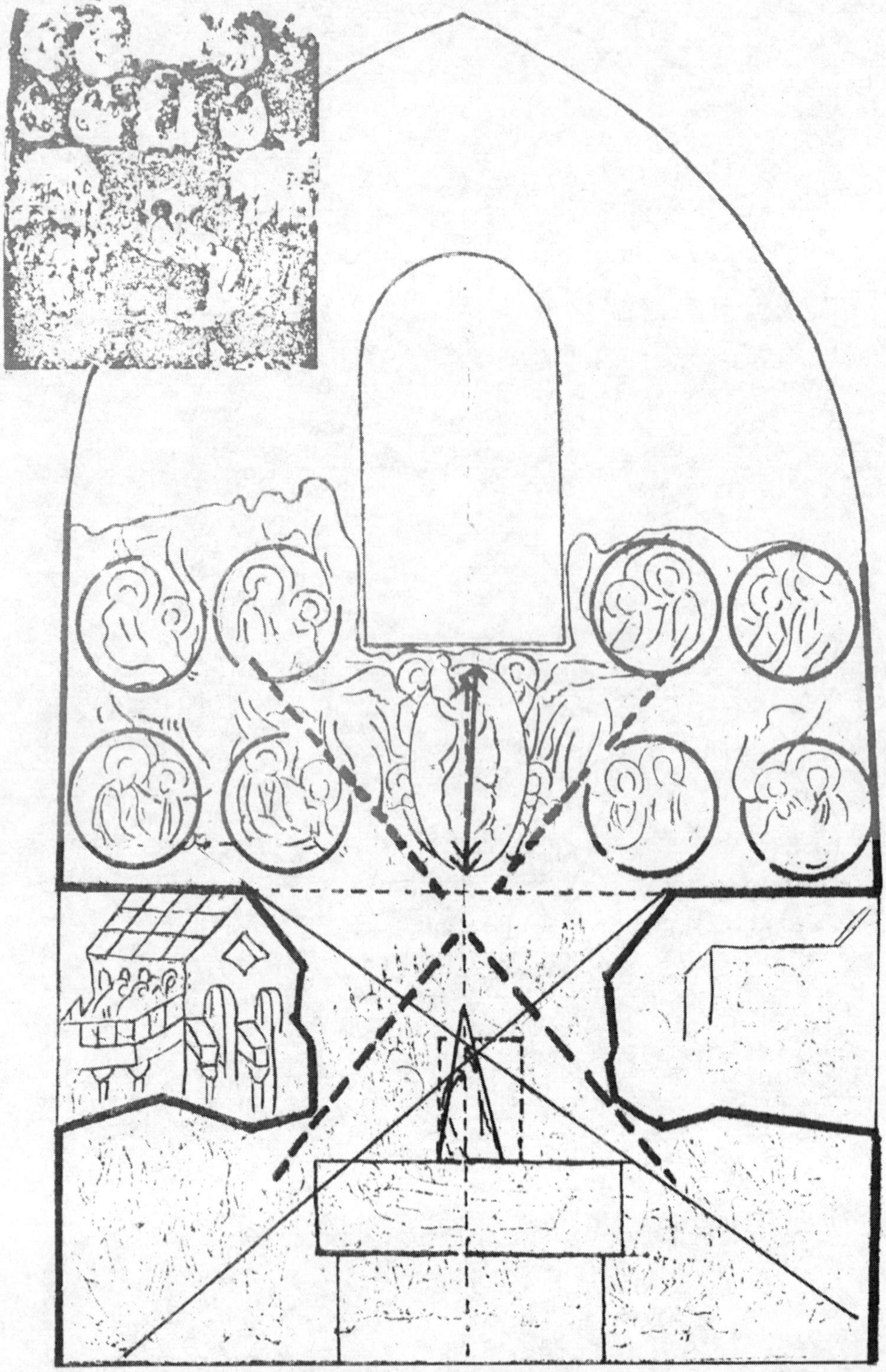

Plate 77. Sopoćani: Composition scandées, composition diffuses, crescendo of breadth, sharp convergences and their inversion for 'forthcoming' effect and gamma forces perceived in 'The Dormition' (nave).

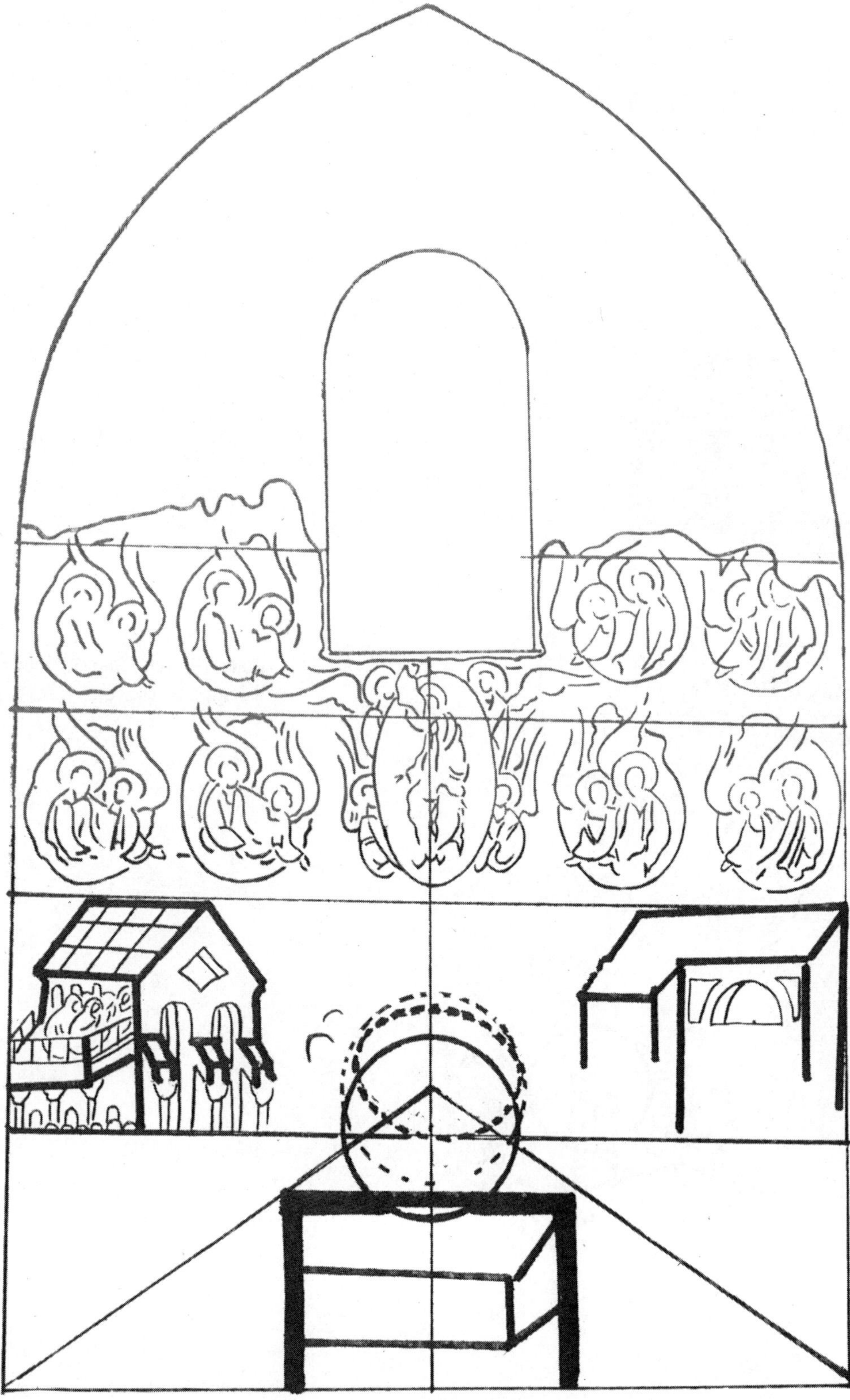

Plate 78. Sopoćani: Spatial balance in 'the Dormition' (nave).

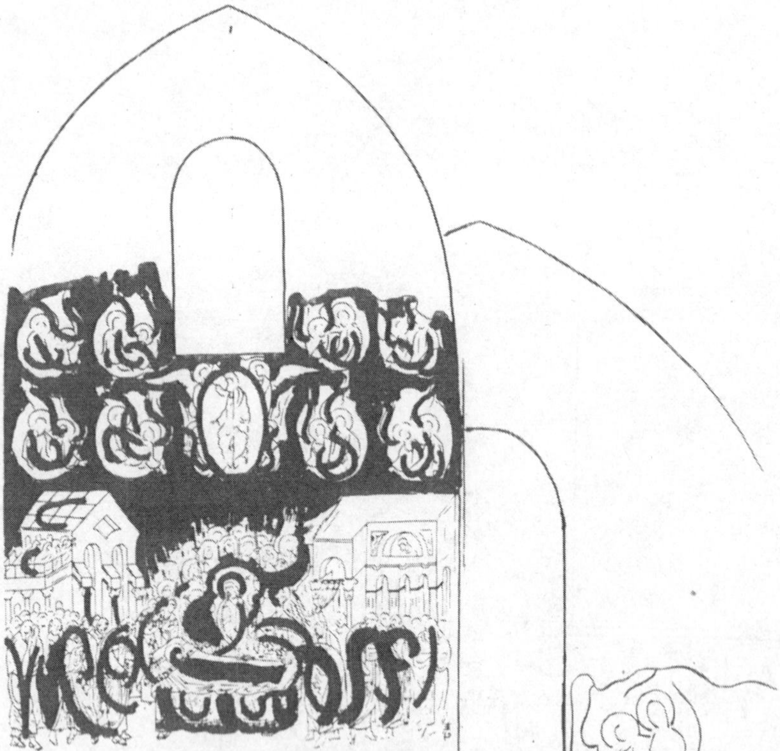

Plate 79. Sopoćani: Colour rhythms in 'The Dormition' (nave).

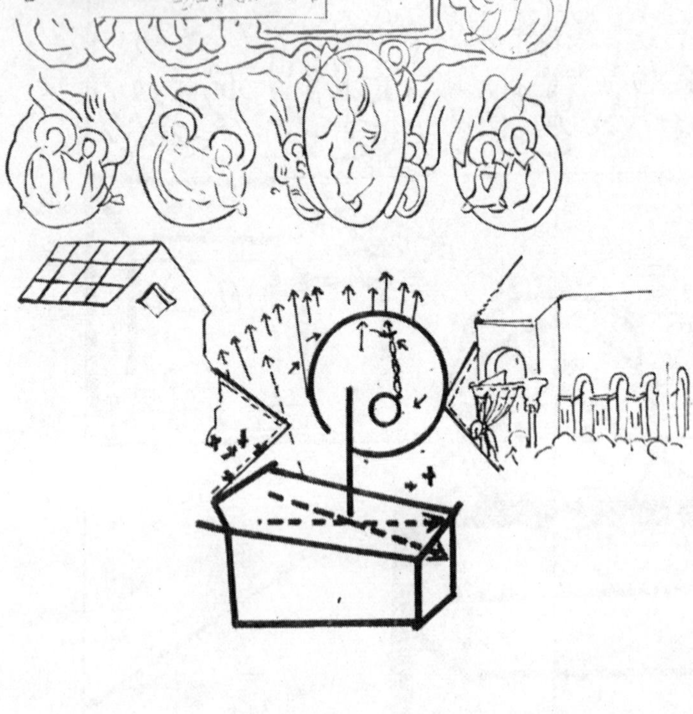

Plate 80. Sopoćani: Chi-Rho symbol wedged in the compositional scheme, 'The Dormition' (nave).

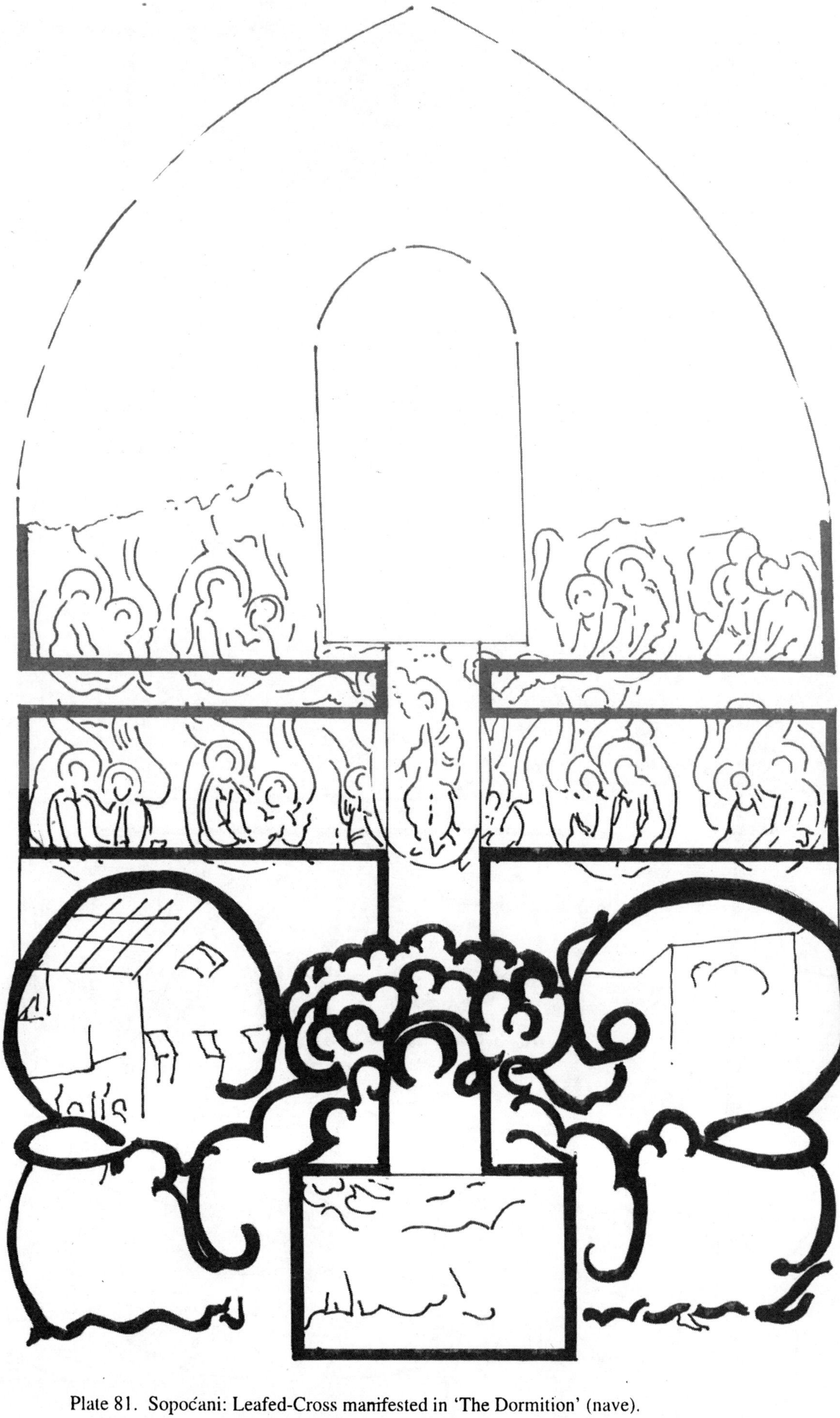

Plate 81. Sopoćani: Leafed-Cross manifested in 'The Dormition' (nave).

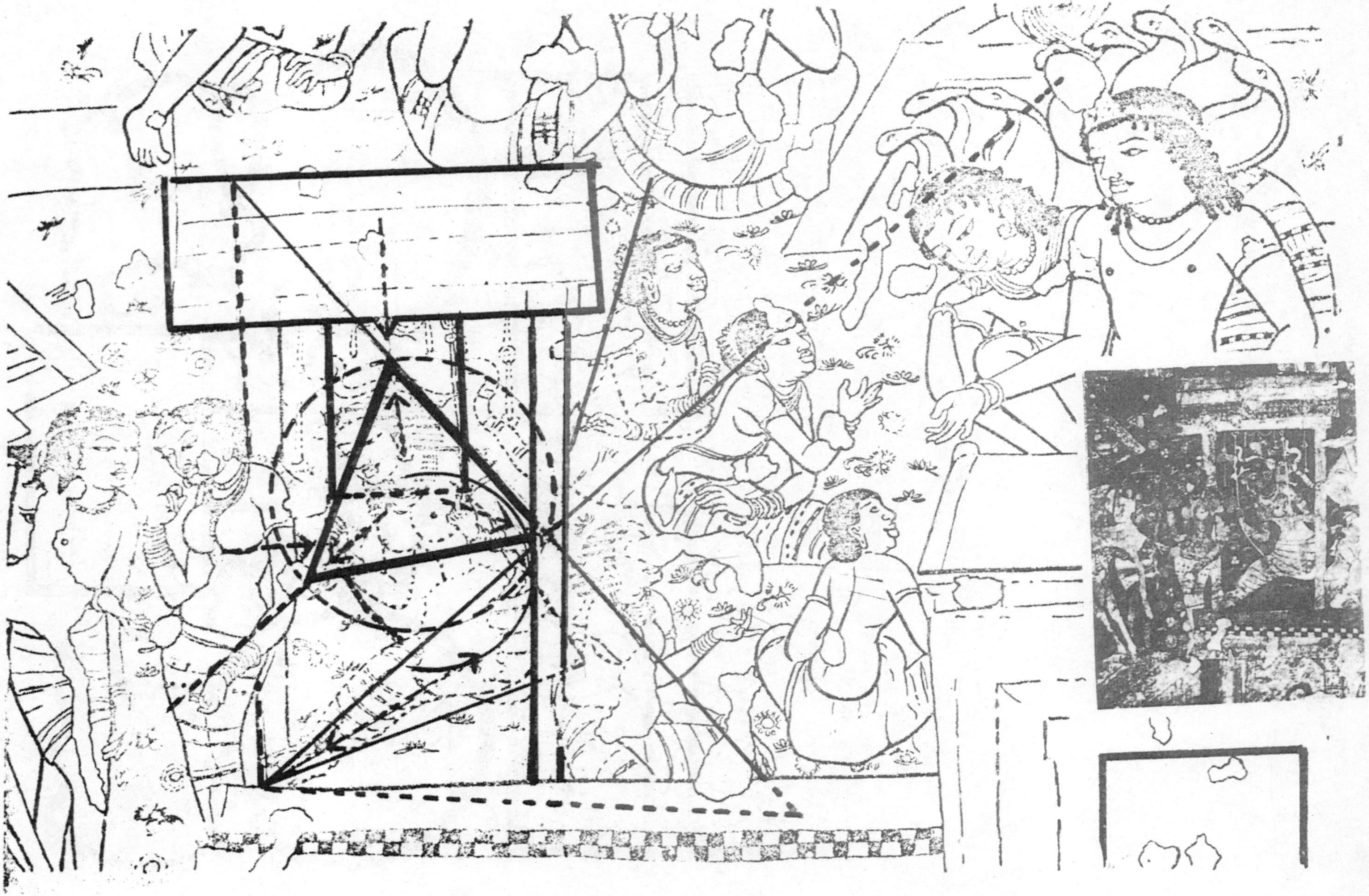

Plate 82. Ajanta: Perceptual balance in the dynamic composition of 'The Princess on swing' (cave 2).

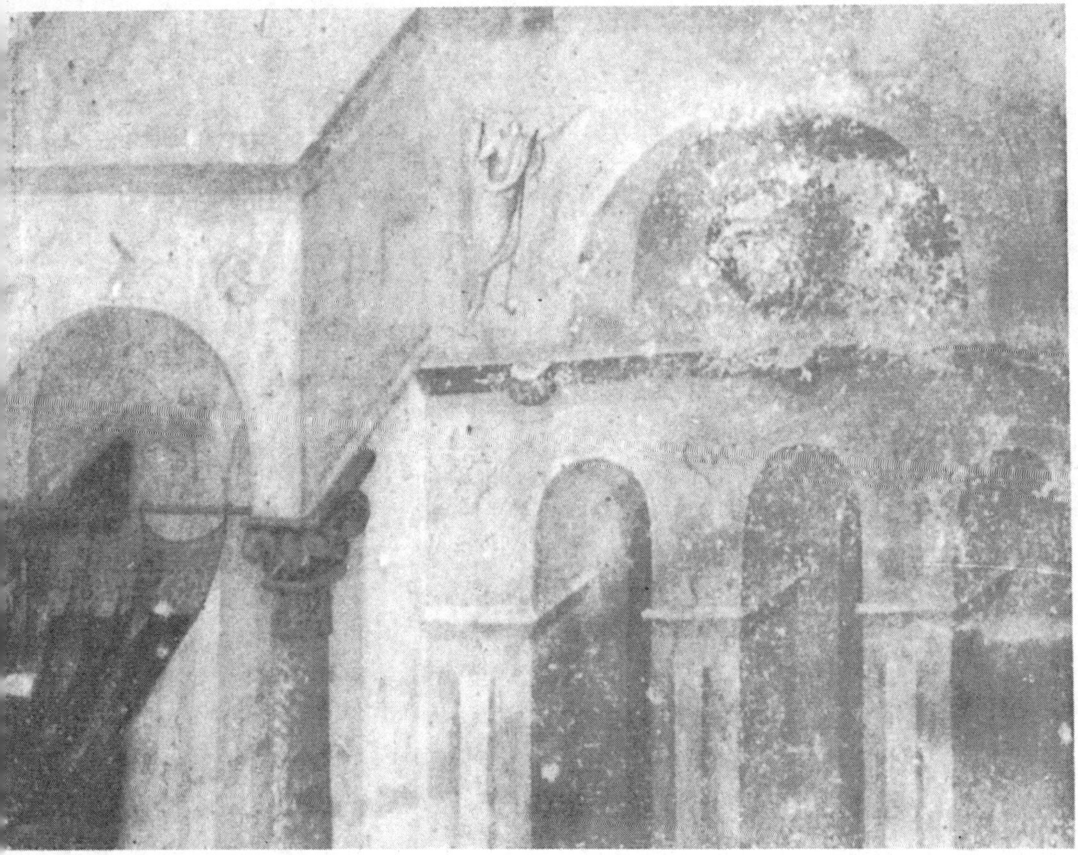

Plate 83. Sopocani: 'Modal-Conventions' in the (Saint's) attic-figure, a modulation on *Kausia* wearing figure and Corinthian capitals, 'The Dormition' (detail, nave).

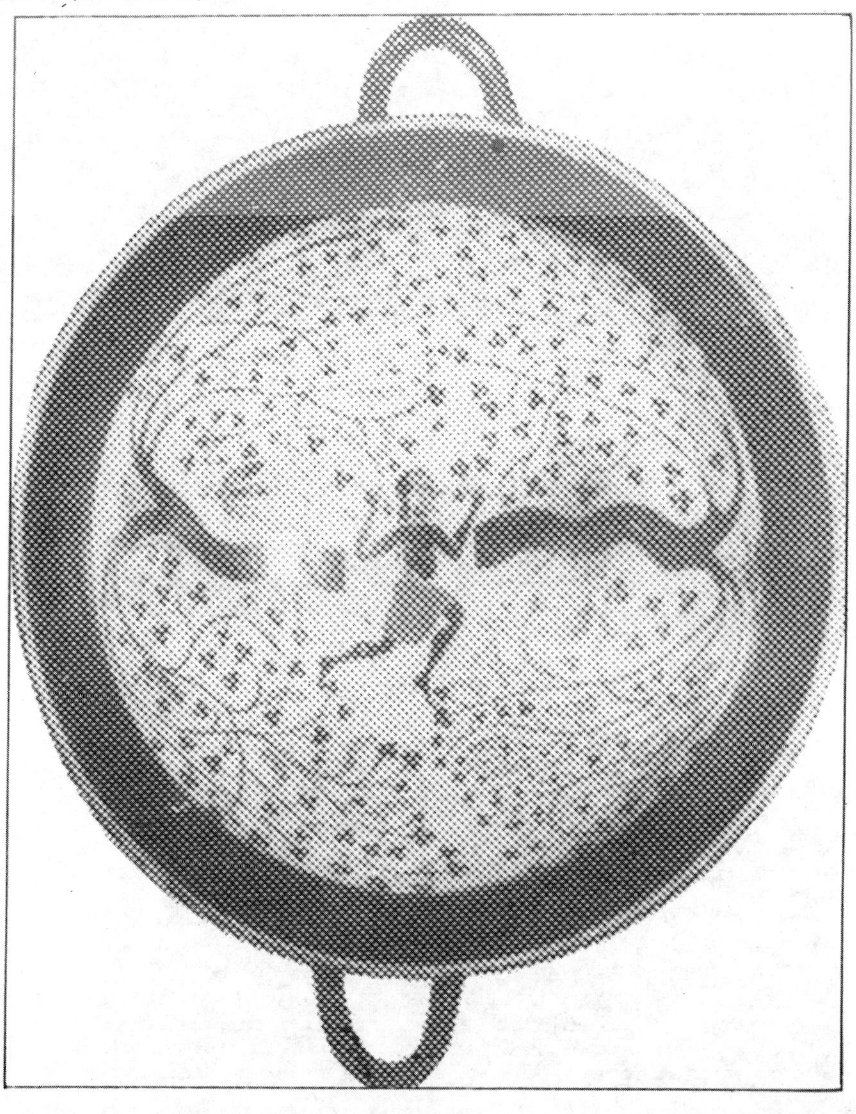

Plate 84. Greek Art, Archaic pd.: 'Man between Two Trees', painted inside an East Greek cup.

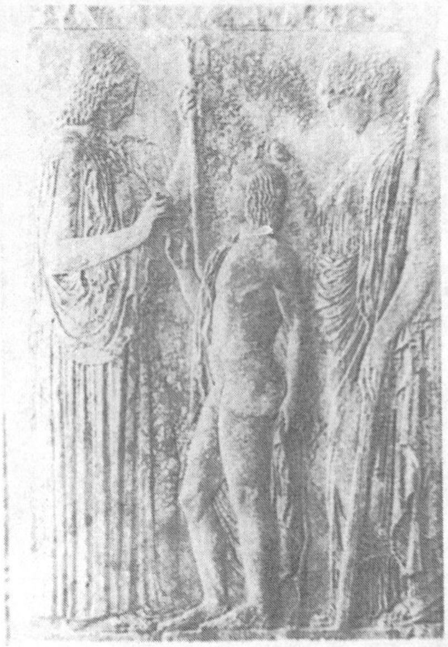

Plate 85. Greek Art, classical pd.: 'Relief of Elevsis' (B.C. 440-430).

Plate 86. Ohrid (Yugoslavia), Saint Sophia: The Archangel in 'Ascension' (detail, vault of the beam, A.D. 11th cent.).

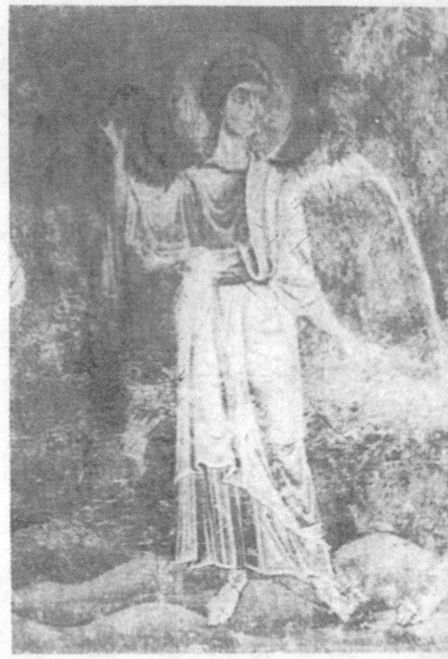

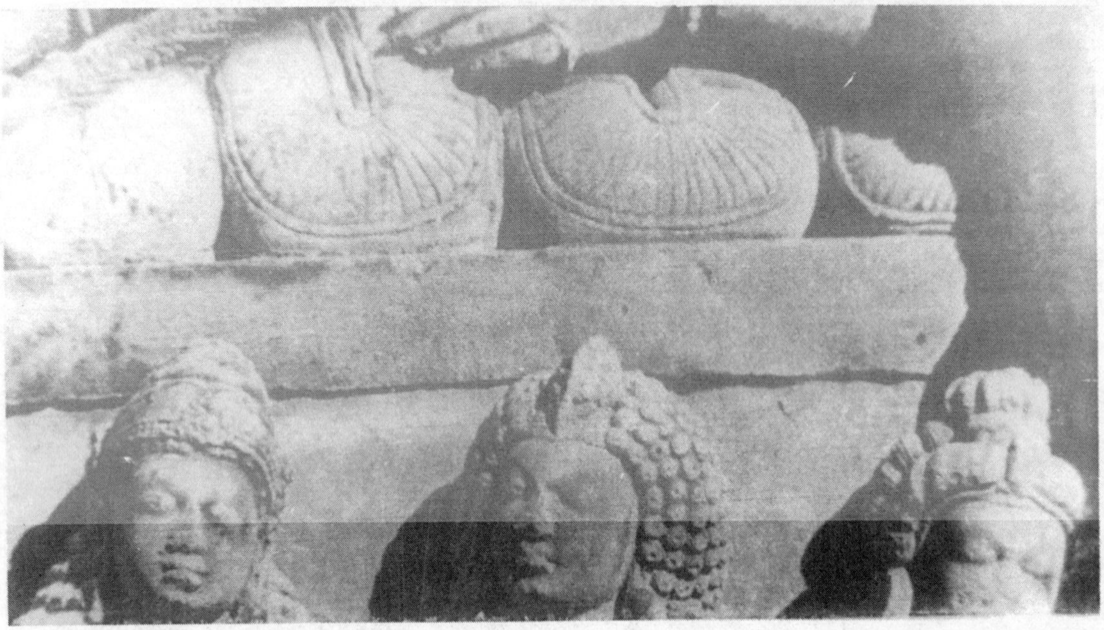

Plate 87. Deogarh (India), Daśāvatāra Temple: Viṣṇu Anataśayana' (detail, A.D. 5th cent.).

Plate 89. Sketches, cave 16, Ajanta.

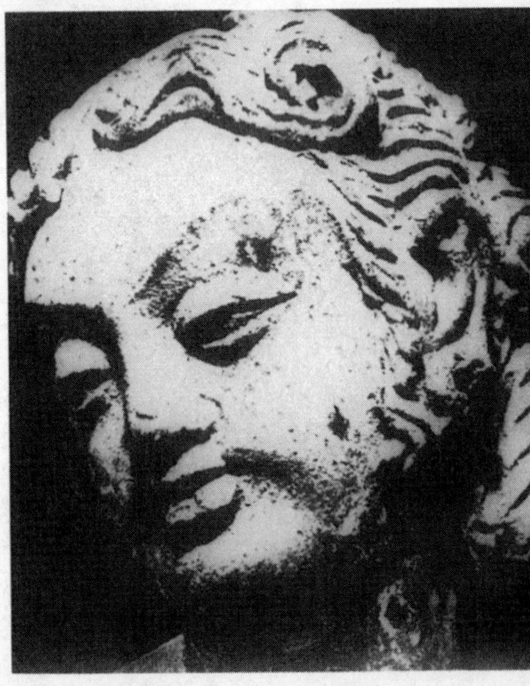

Plate 88. Ushkár, Kashmir (India): 'Bodhisattva' (A.D. 7th or 8th cent.).

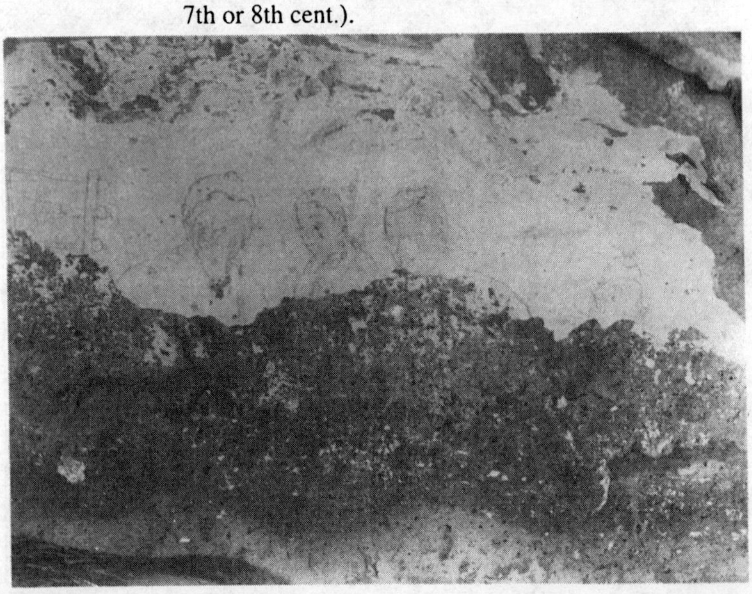

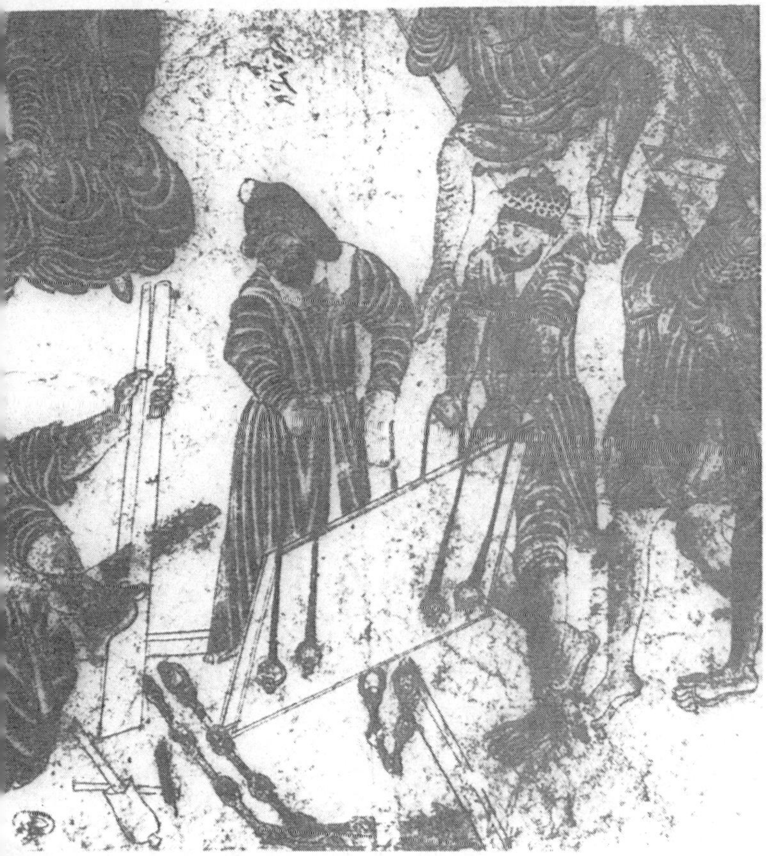

Plate 90. Siyah Qalem (Turkey): 'Group of men engaged in building work' (detail, A.D. 15th cent.): pub. in Graphic 189.

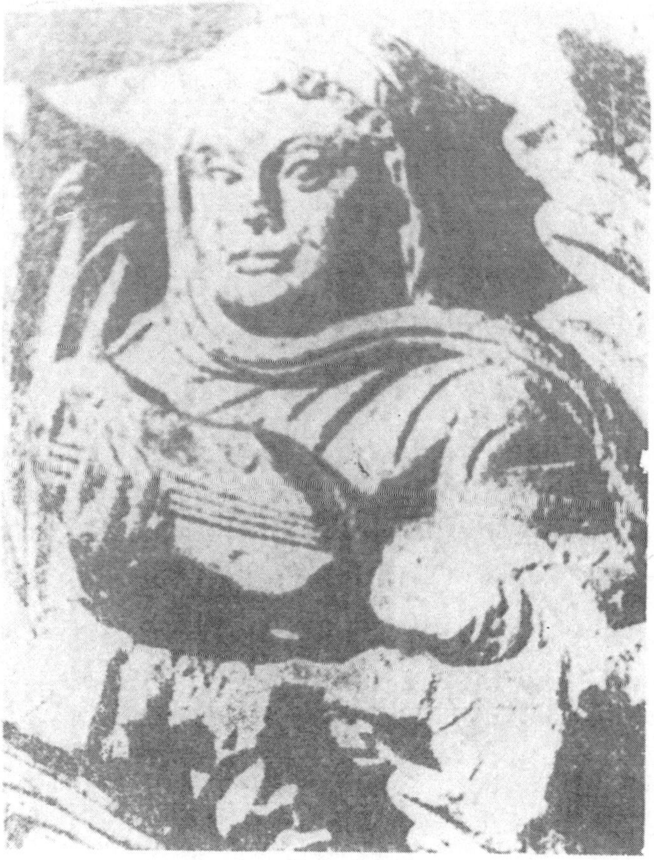

Plate 91. Ḳushan art (Airtam, Termez): 'Three Musicians' (detail c. 1st cent. B.C. to A.D. 1st cent.).

Plate 92. Ohrid (Yugoslavia), Church of St. Clement: 'Annunciation' (detail, A.D. 1295).

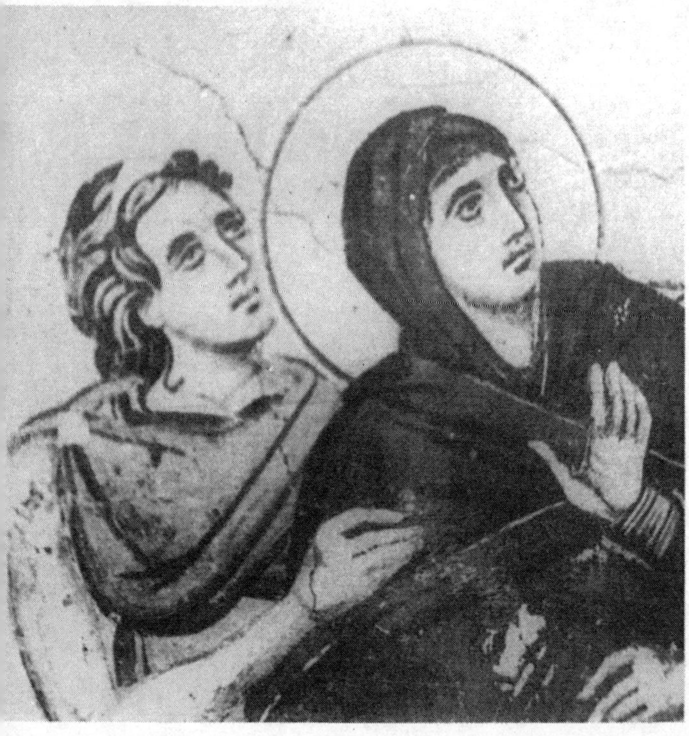

Plate 93. Rome, SS Cosmo and Damian: Forthcoming 'Christ' (apse, A.D. 526-30).

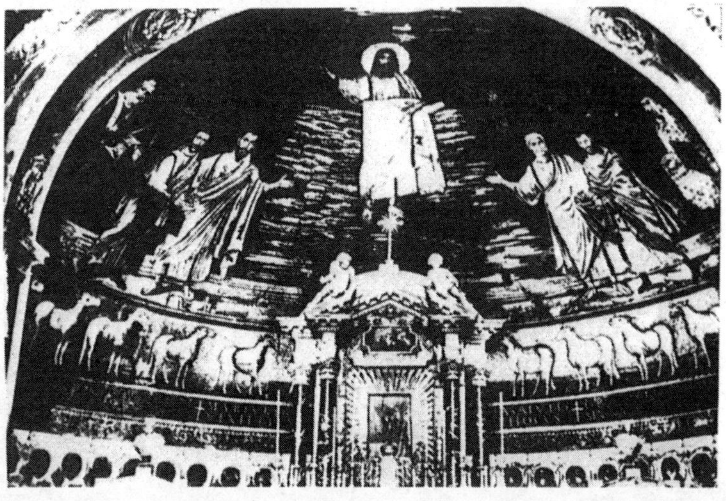

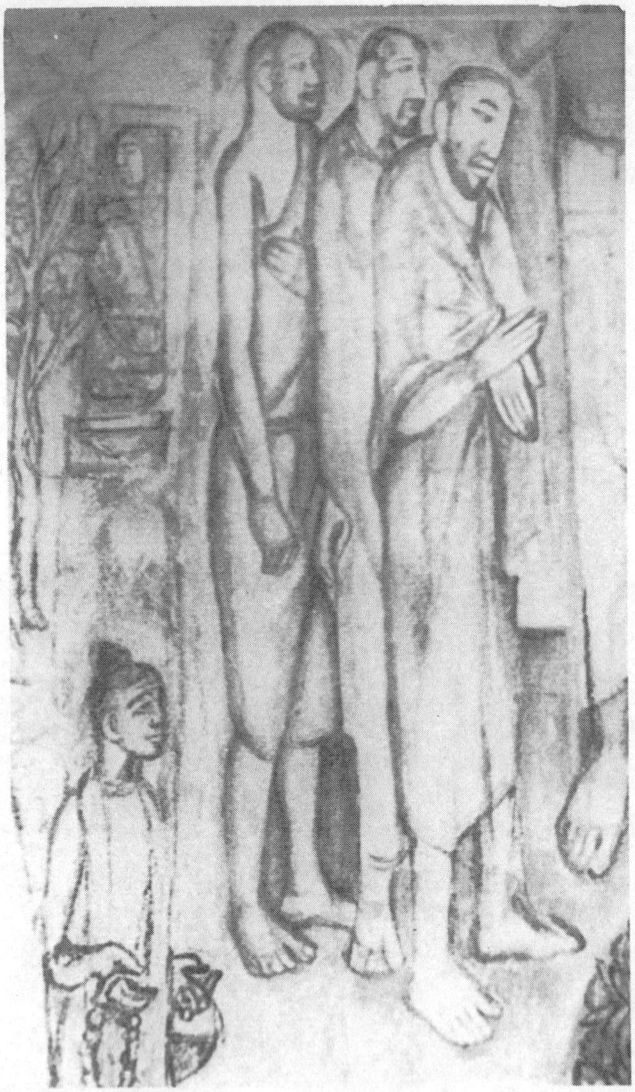

Plate 94. Binod Behari Mukerji, 'Medieval Saints' (detail, A.D.1947).

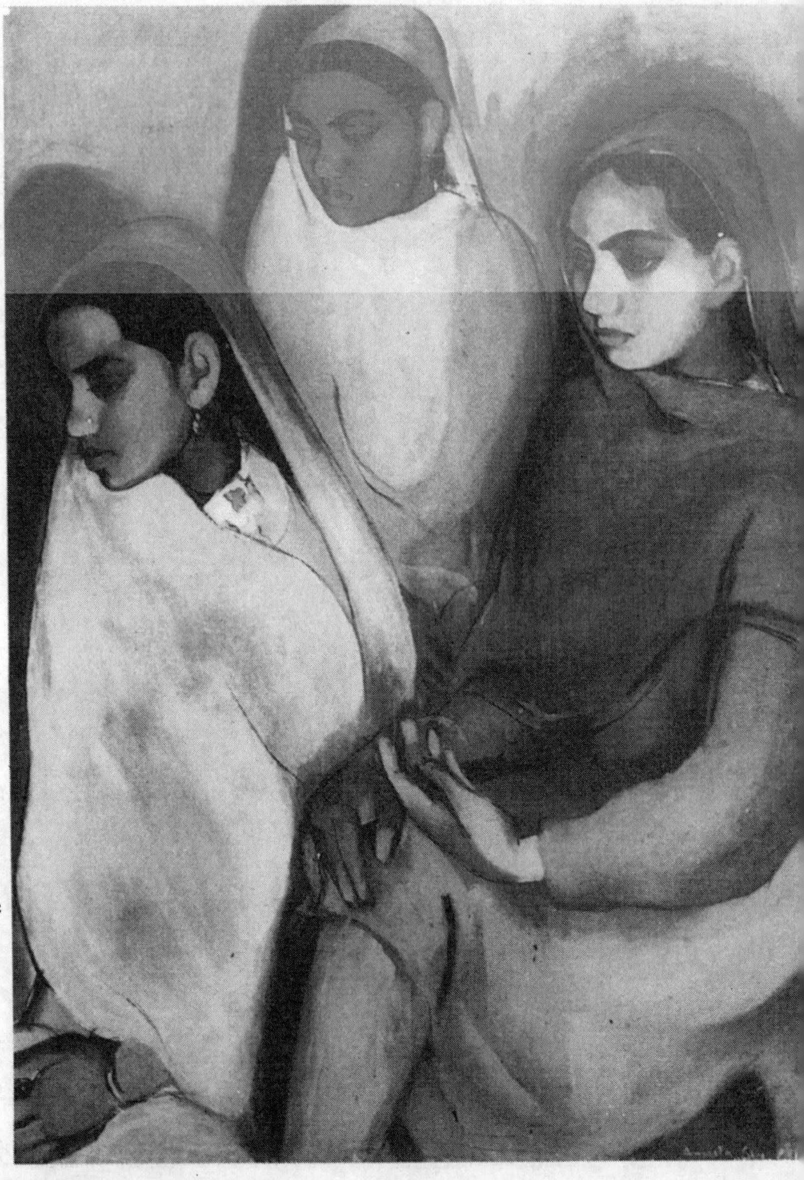

Plate 95. Amrita Sher-Gil, 'The Three Girls' (A.D. 1935).

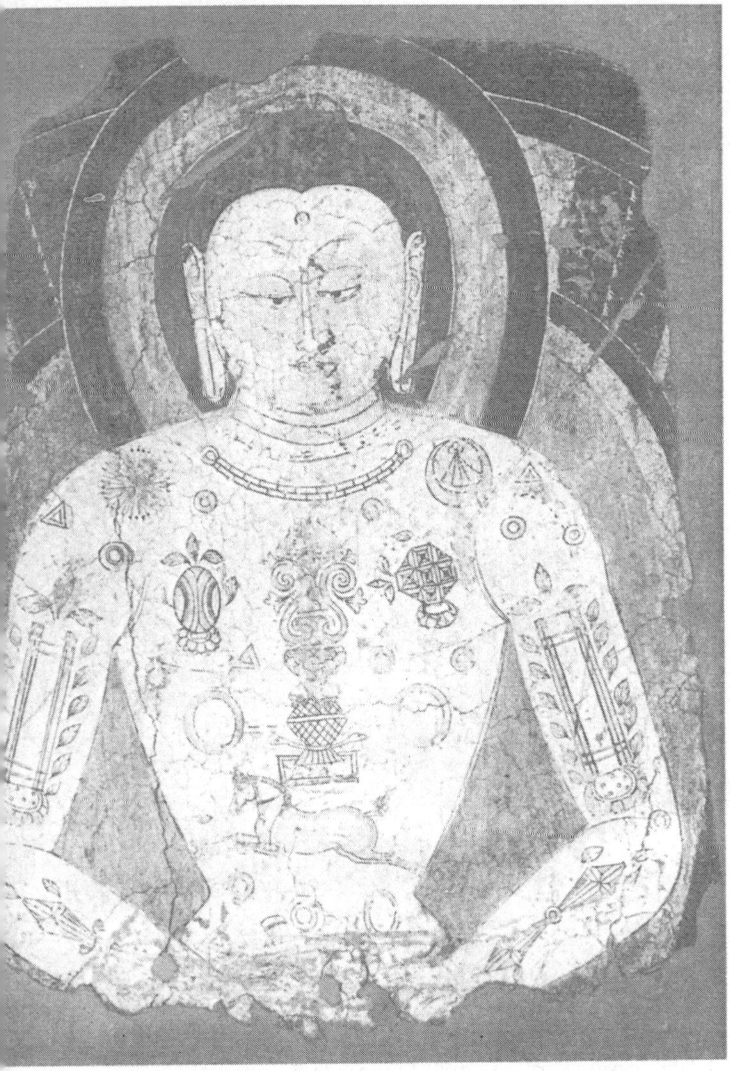

Plate 96. Belahan (Central Asia): Divine attributes on 'the Buddha' (A.D. 3rd-4th cent.).

Plate 97. Sopoćani: Divine attributes like *ūrṇā* on 'St. John the Divine' (diaconicon, A.D. 1263-68).

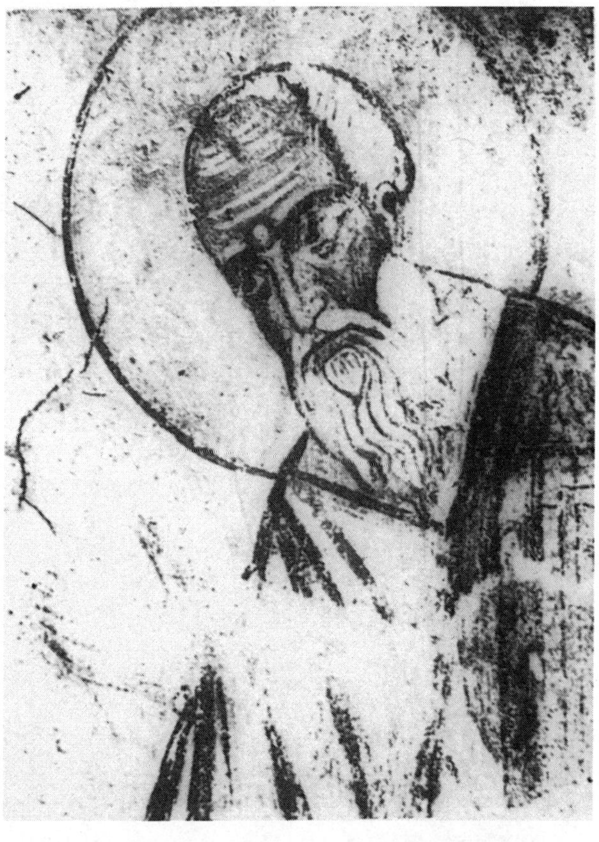

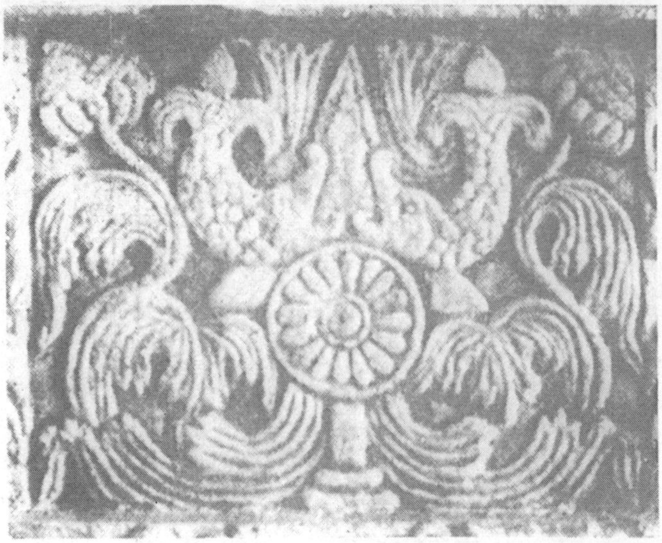

Plate 98. Amarâvati (India): Tri-Ratna (2nd cent. B.C.–A.D. 2nd cent.).

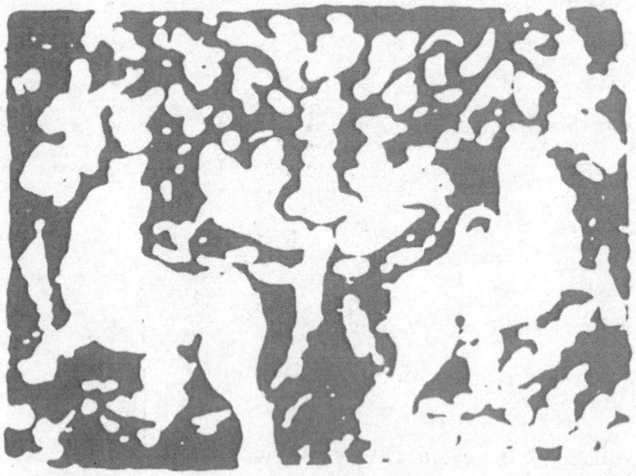

Plate 100. Ajanta: Kirtimukha (left centre pillar in back aisles, cave 4).

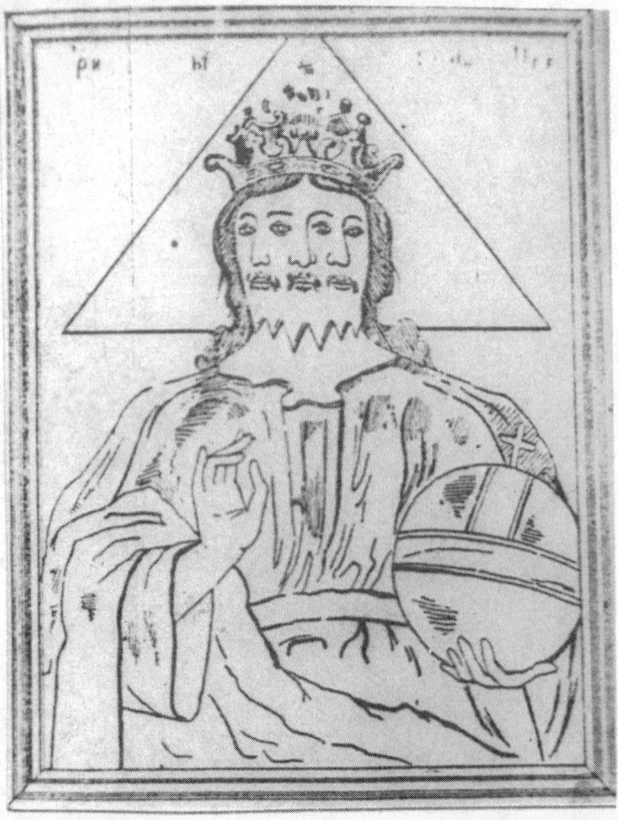

Plate 101. Sremu (Yugoslavia), village church: 'Saint Trinity' (c. A.D. 18th cent.).

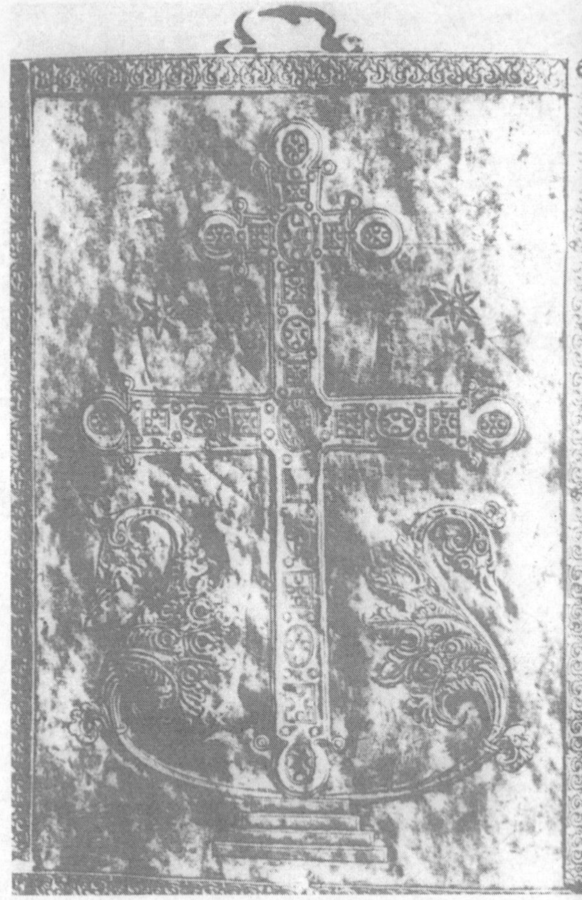

Plate 99. Germany, Metal back of the Limburg reliquary: Leafed Cross (Syrian) (c. A.D. 950).

Plate 102. Studenica (Yugoslavia): 'Kirtimukha' (detail on southern portal, A.D. 12th cent.).

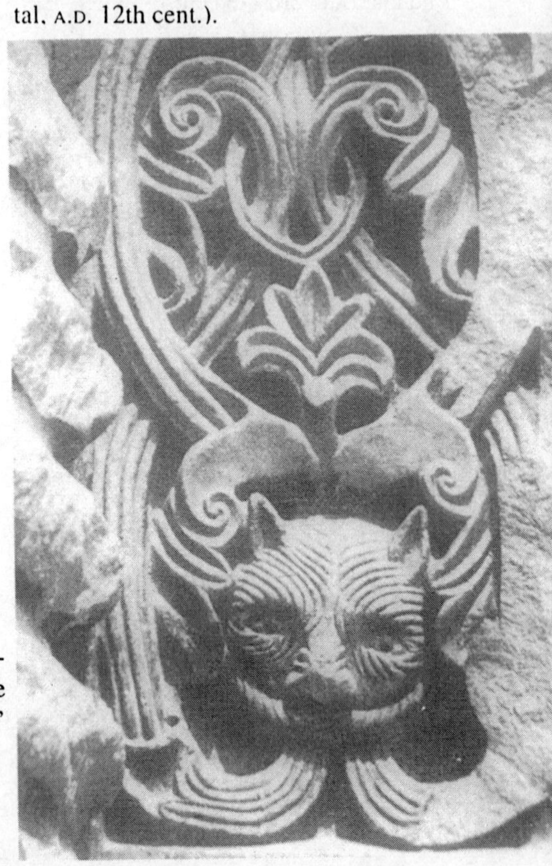

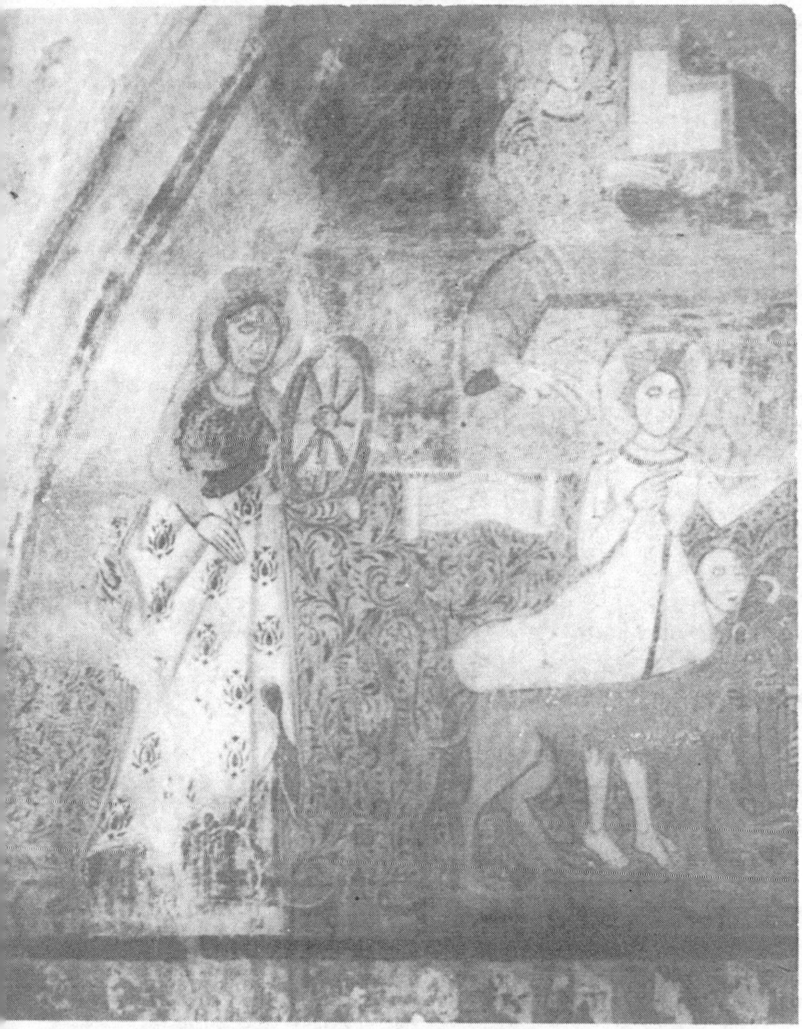

Plate 103. Linder (Istra, Yugoslavia) Church of St. Katarine, 'Wheel of life' in the hands of Mary detail of 'Living Cross' (A.D. 1400).

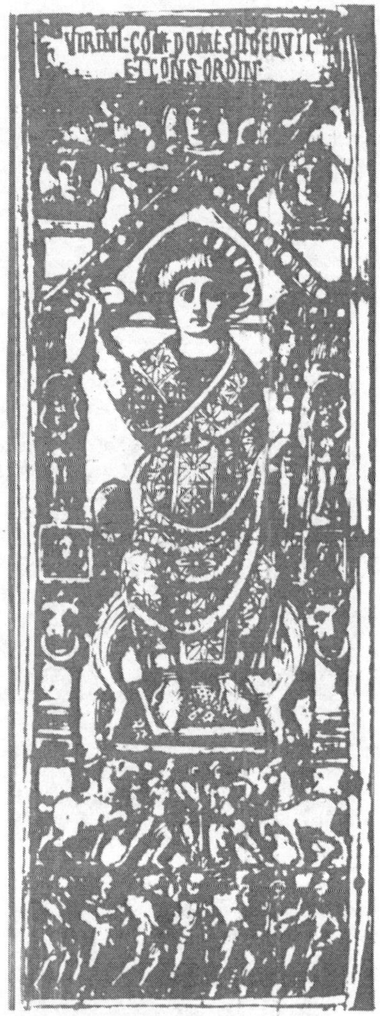

Plate 104. Byzantine, Consular diptych (ivory, Just after A.D. 500).

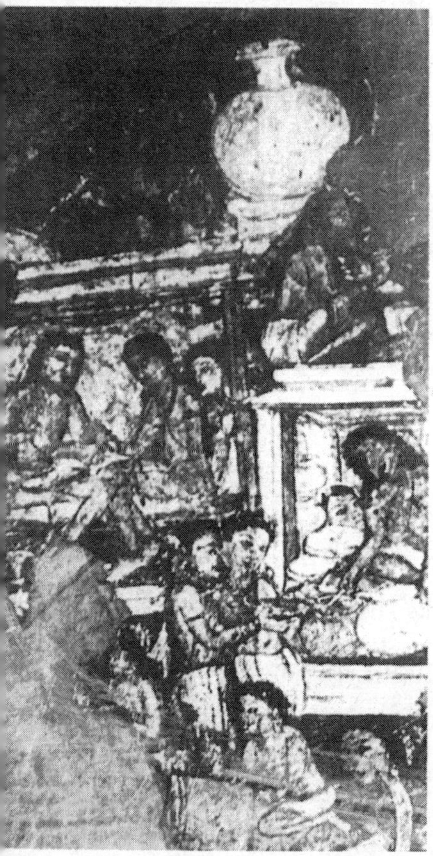

Plate 105. Ajanta: 'Wheel of Life' (detail, cave 17).

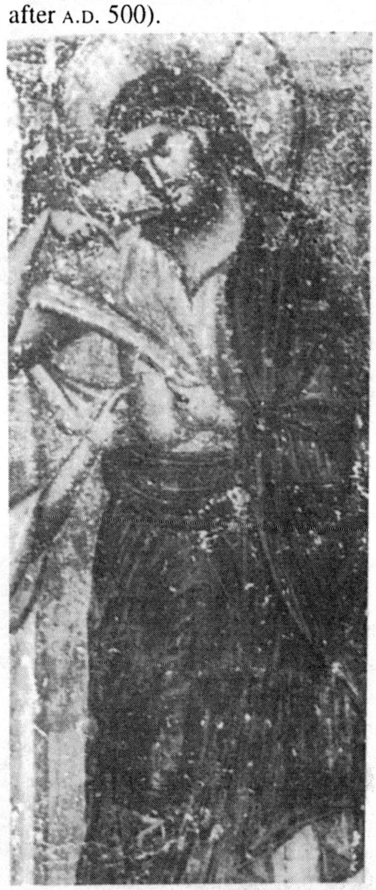

Plate 106. Sopoćani: Cakra (Crux Decussata) in the halo behind Christ, 'The Incredulity of Thomas' (detail, sanctuary, nave).

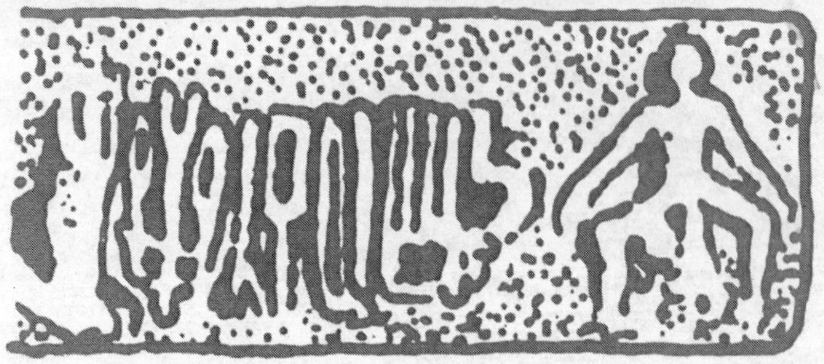

Plate 107. Mohenjo-Daro: Seal with plant issuing from the womb of a female (B.C. 2500).

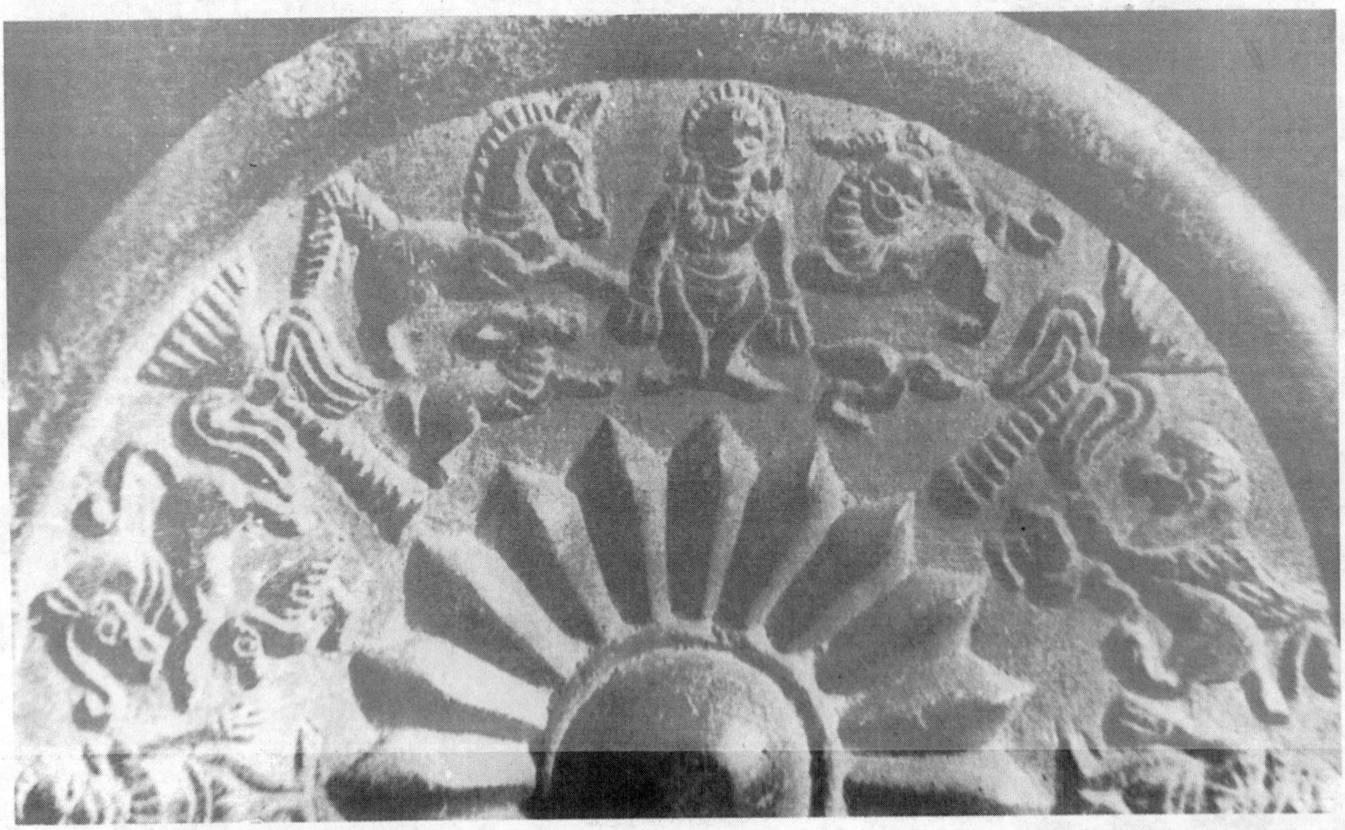

Plate 108. Murtaziganj (India): A panel or ringstone (c. 3rd to 1st cent. B.C.).

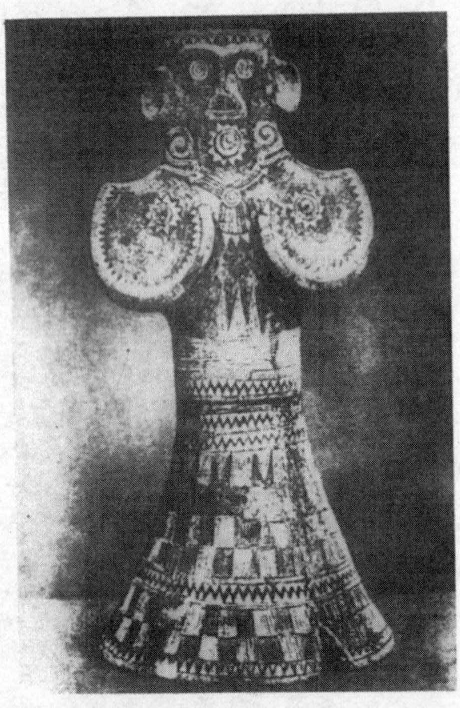

Plate 109. Yugoslavia: Mother Goddess (Bronze age).

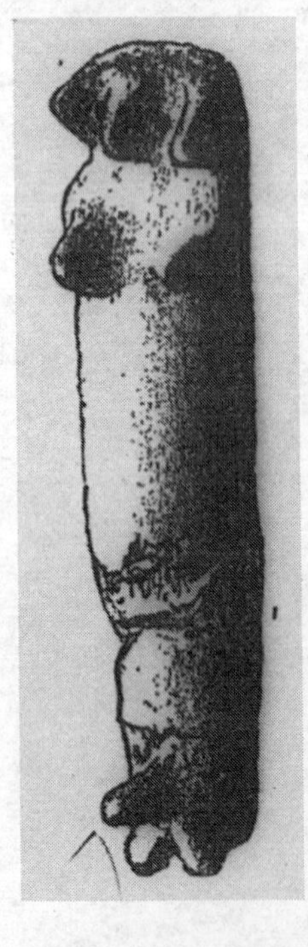

Plate 110. Yugoslavia: Hermaphroditic Idol (Bronze age)

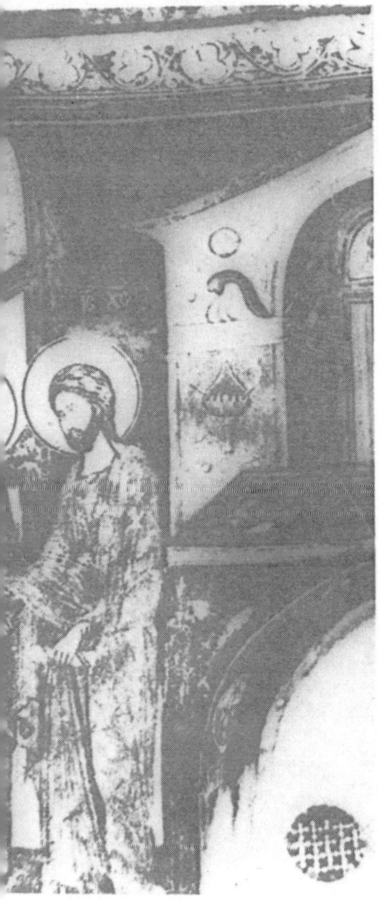

Plate 111. Peć (Yugoslavia), Church of St. Demetrius: Symbol of lotus with saplings shooting from top and flanking a pyramidal mountain with sun, 'The Communion of the Apostles' (detail, c. A.D. 1338-46).

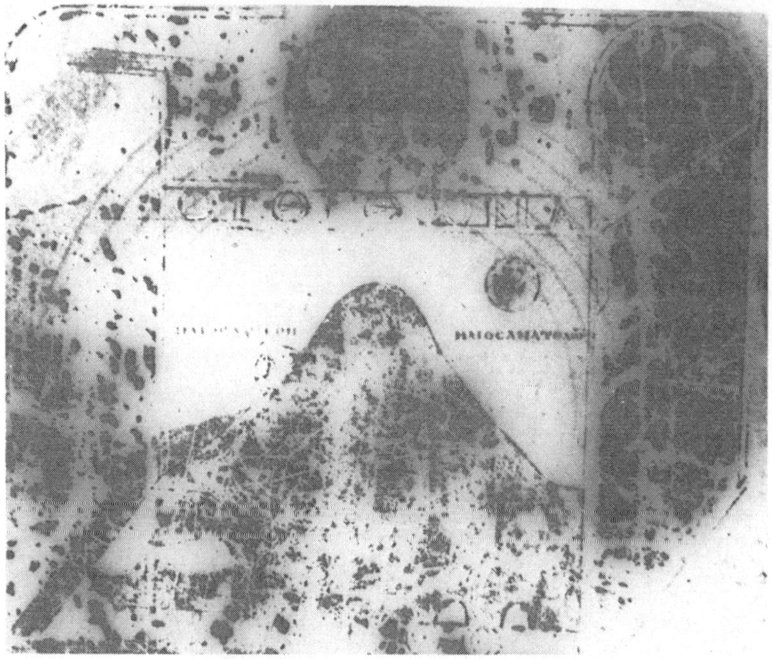

Plate 112. Byzantine: Illumination from the manuscript of Cosmas Indicopleustes showing Cosmological plan (A.D. 9th cent.).

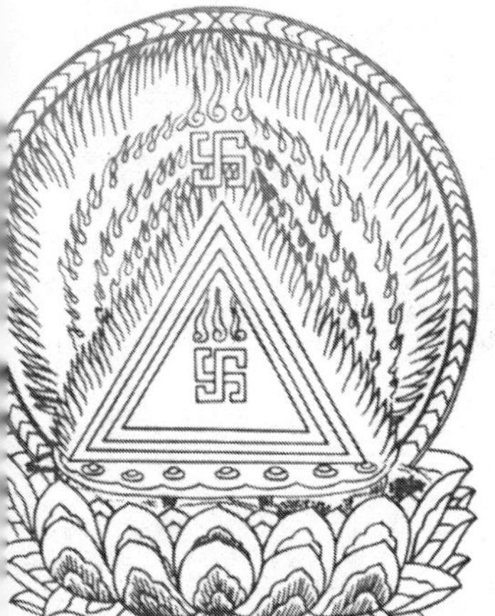

Plate 113. Buddhist Garbhakośa-dhātū maṇḍala (Shingon) illustrating The Doctrine of Prajñāpāramitā. The flaming equilateral triangle of universal potentiality (based on 'lotus' or 'ground') of the possible intellect is represented in the diagram.

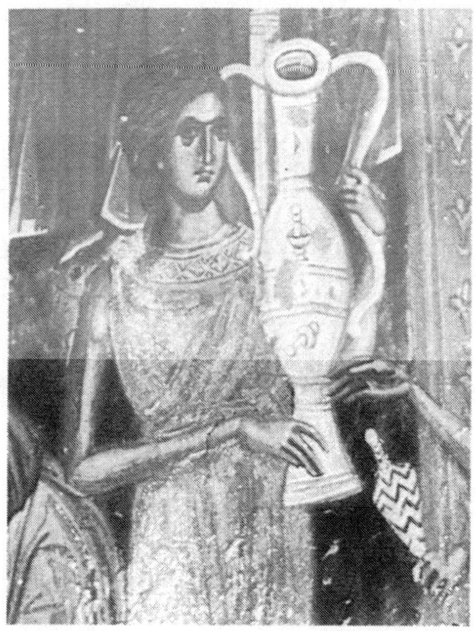

Plate 114. Peć (Yugoslavia), Church of St. Demetrius: Symbol of Agyieus and Phoebos pillars and Omphalos, the grave mound as navel of earth, painted over the amphora in the hands of the maid, 'the Birth of the Virgin' (detail, A.D. 1336-46).

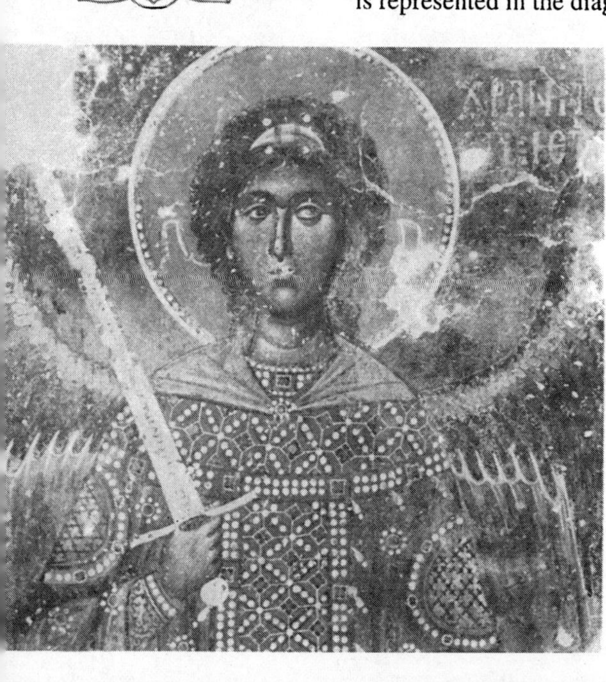

Plate 115. Sopoćani: The Archangel Michael as 'Guardian of the Holy Trinity' (Chapel of St. Stephen, A.D. 1263-68) with celestial attire of precious stones, etc.

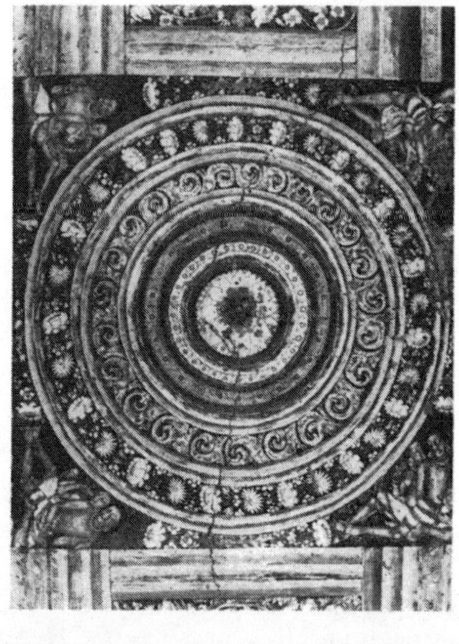

Plate 116. Ajanta: 'Cosmological plan', ceiling decoration (cave 2).

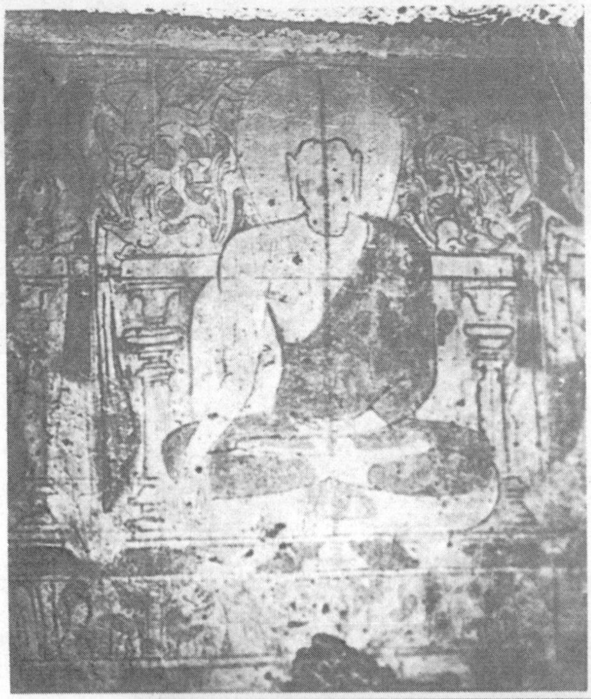

Plate 117. Kanheri (India): Grid-system as found on an unfinished fresco (A.D. 7th cent.).

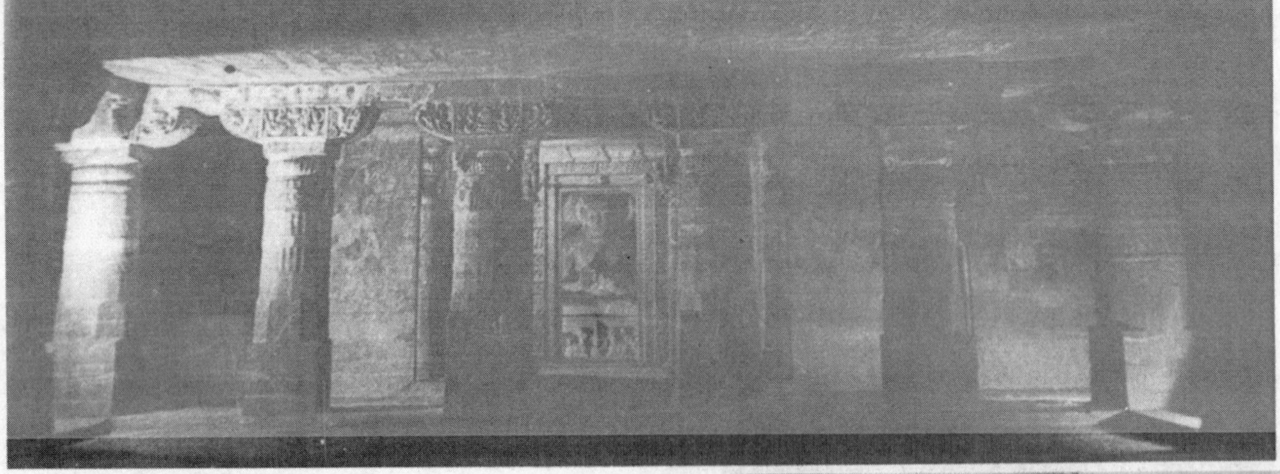

Plate 118. Ajanta: Interior of cave 1.

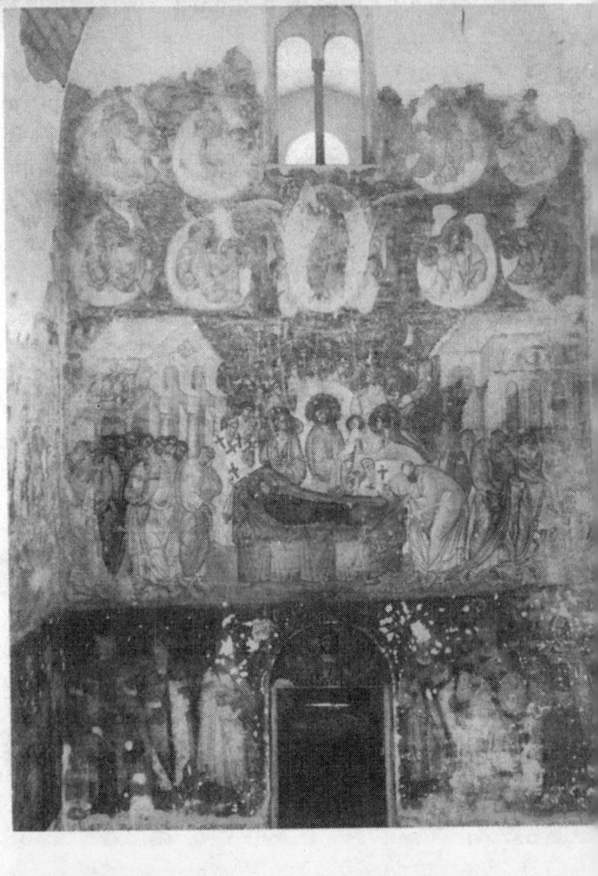

Plate 119. Sopoćani: Interior of nave.

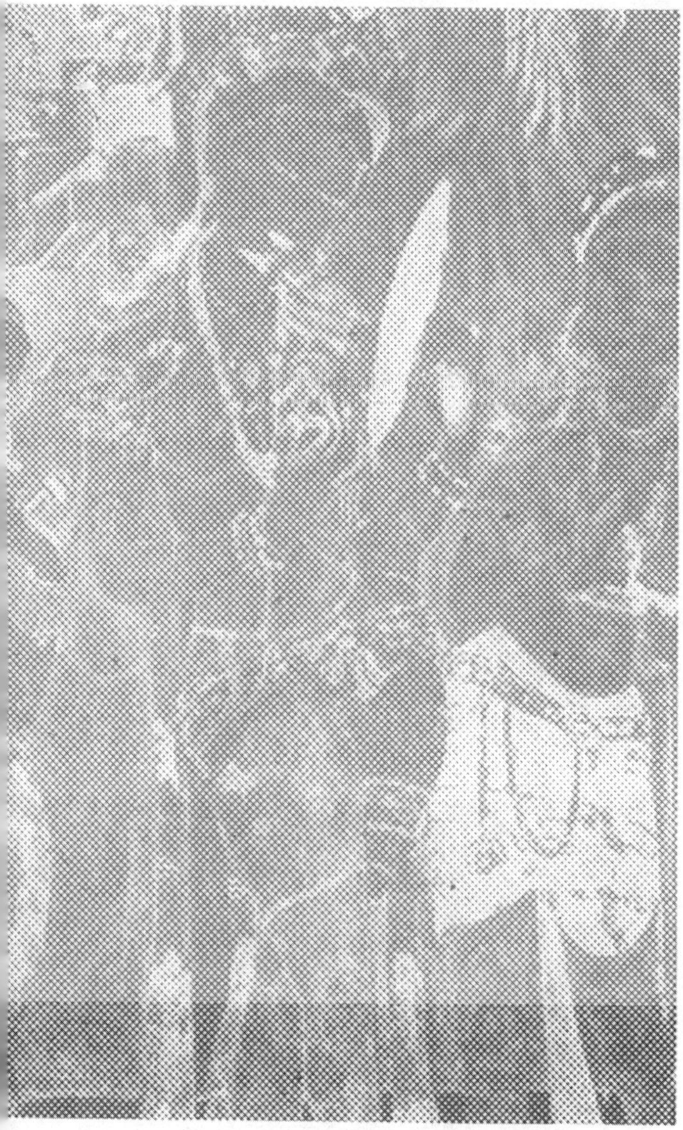

Plate 120. Ajanta: 'similarity of dominant' in 'earthy-tones' leaving germ-modules of fundamental colours, 'Princess at her toilet' (cave 17).

Plate 121. Ajanta: Early cubic-styles or 'Vanaspati' style of the tradition of Yakṣa sculptures, 'Raja with his retinue' (detail cave 10).

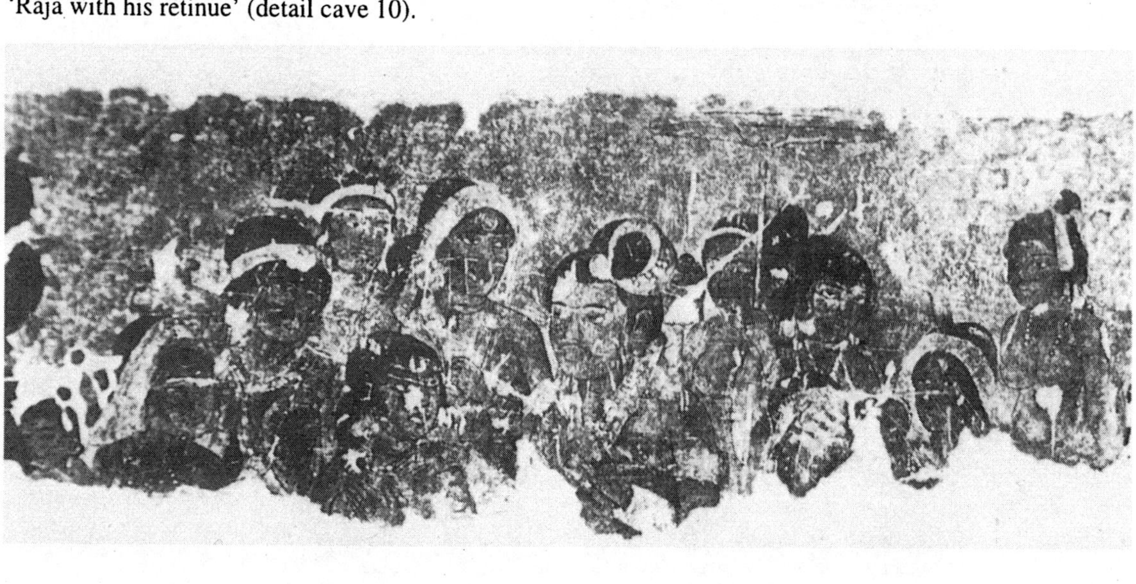

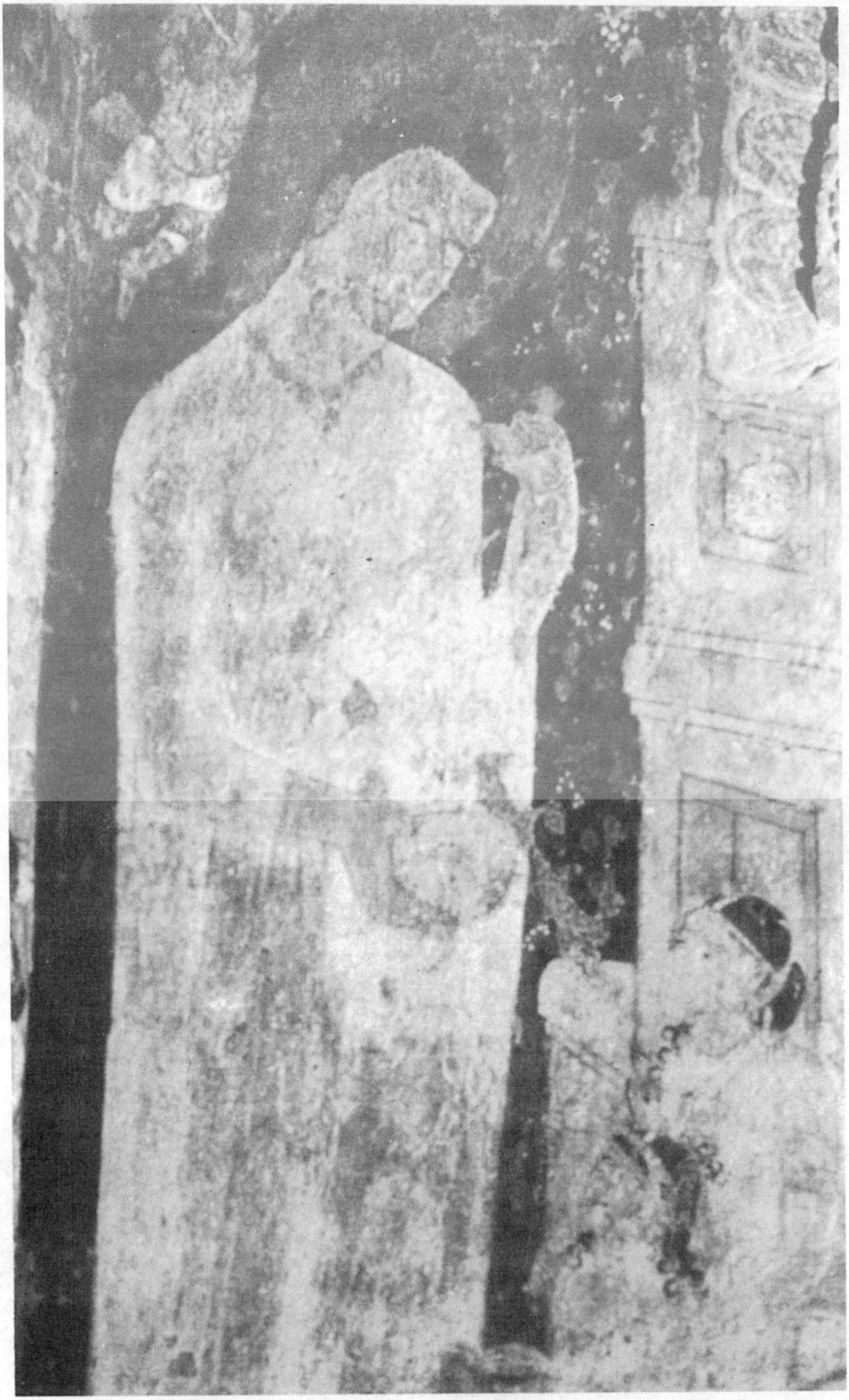

Plate 122. Ajanta: 'The Buddha in Kapilavastu' (cave 17).

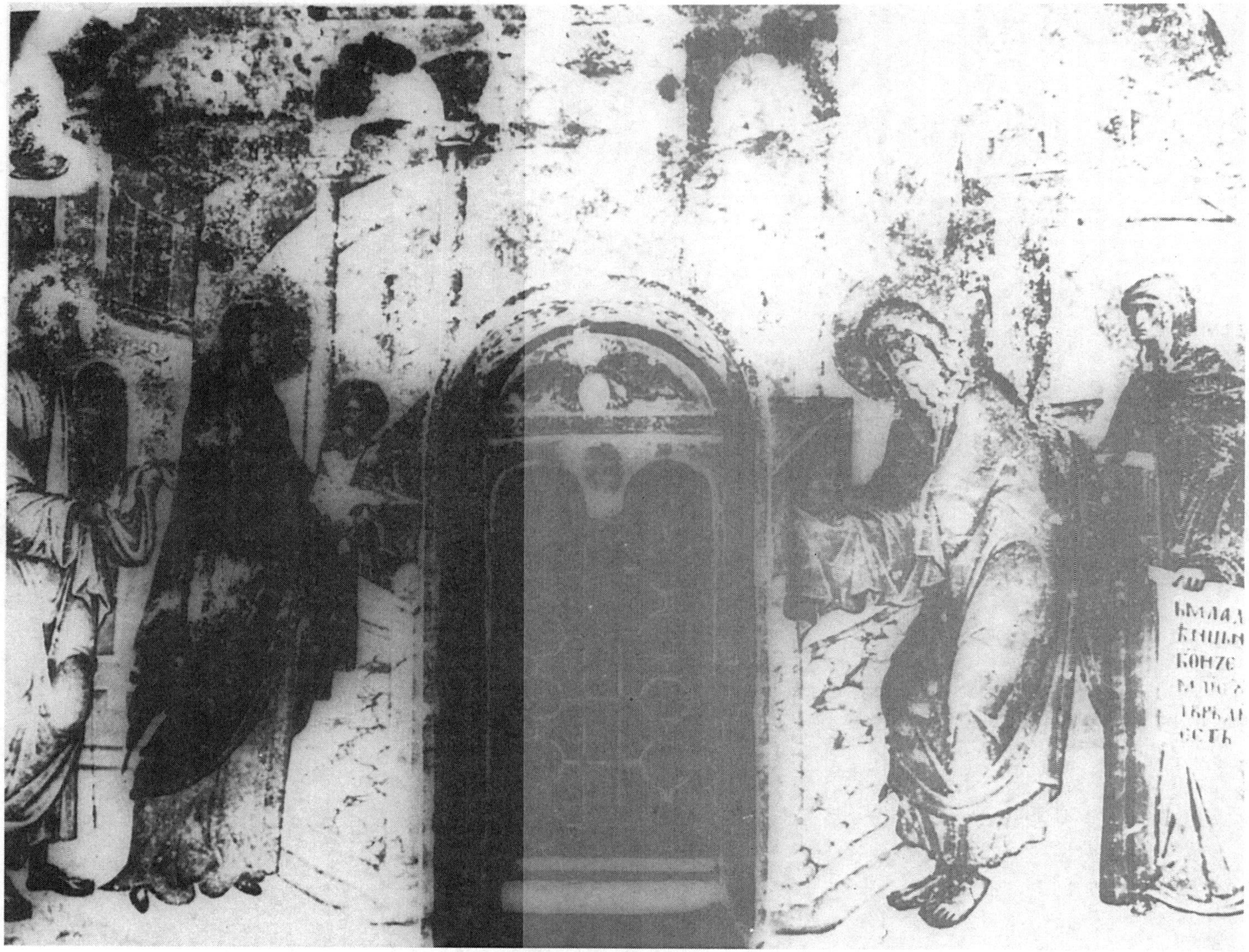

Plate 123. Sopoćani: 'The Presentation of Christ in the Temple' (nave).

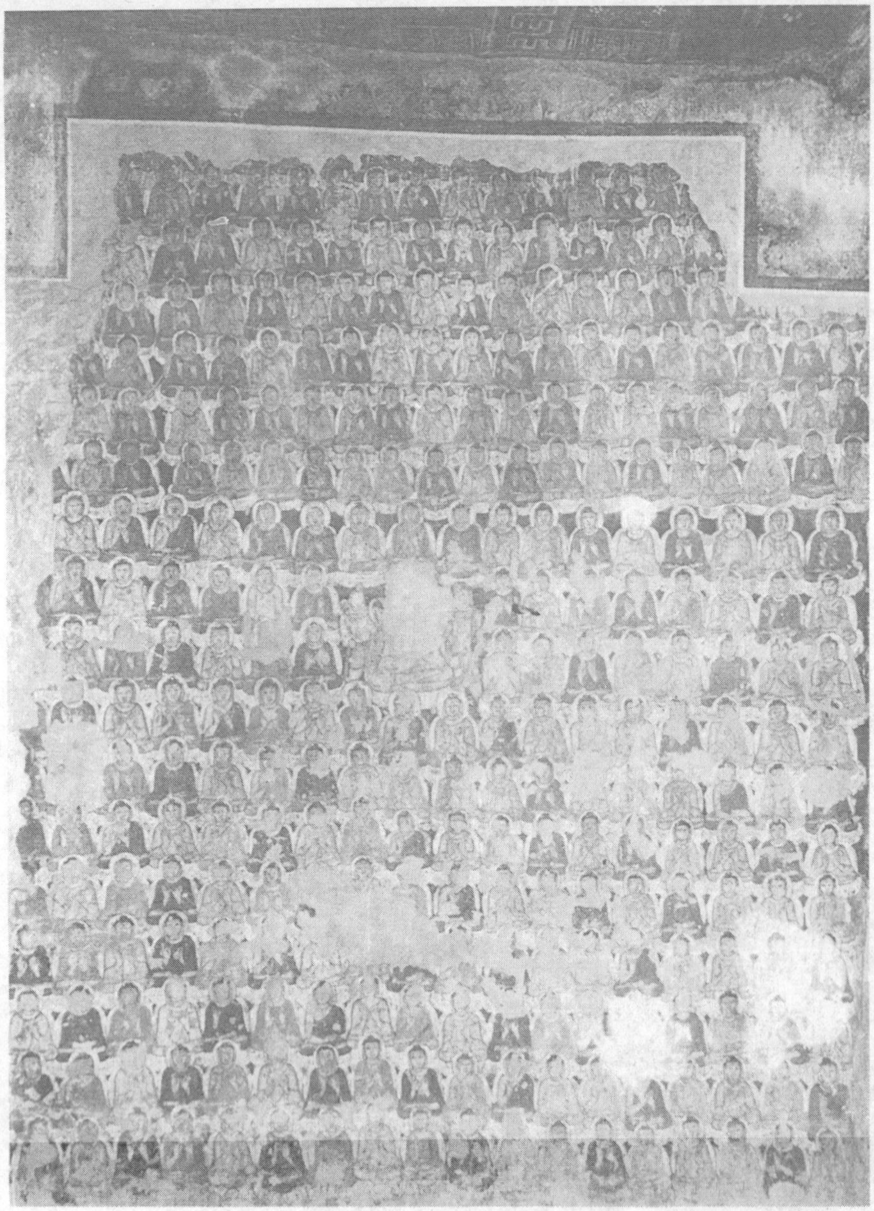

Plate 124. Ajanta: 'The Thousand Buddhas' (cave 2).

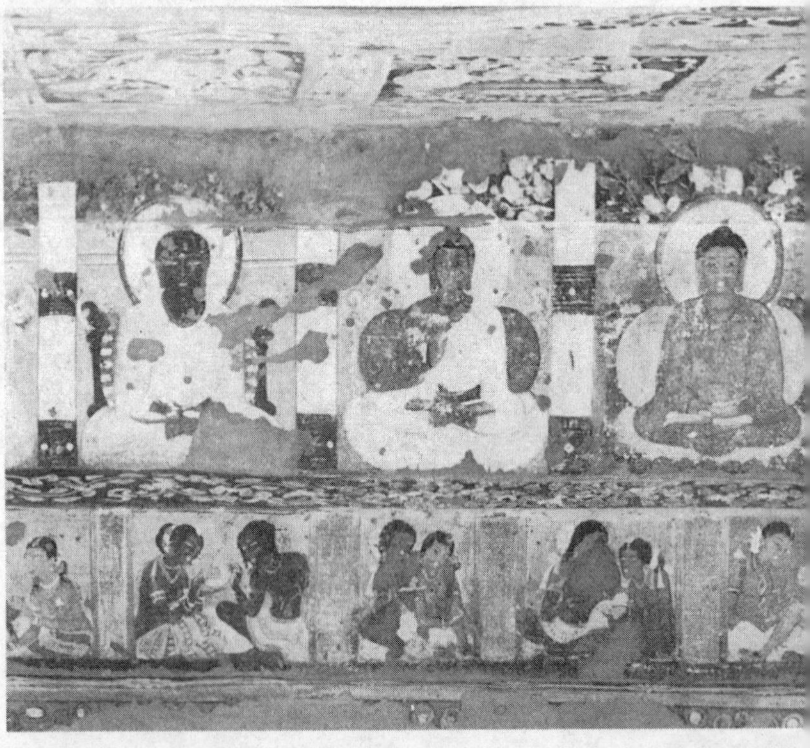

Plate 125. 'The Seven Mortal Buddhas' and the 'mithuna' figures (detail, cave17).

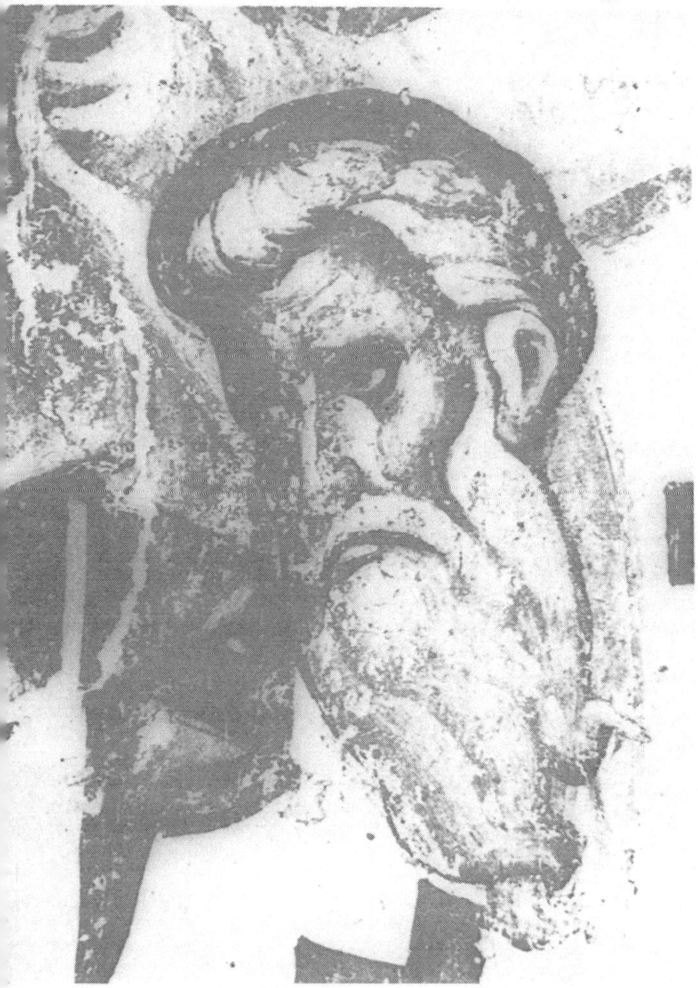

Plate 126. Sopoćani: Pope, 'the Dormition' (detail, nave).

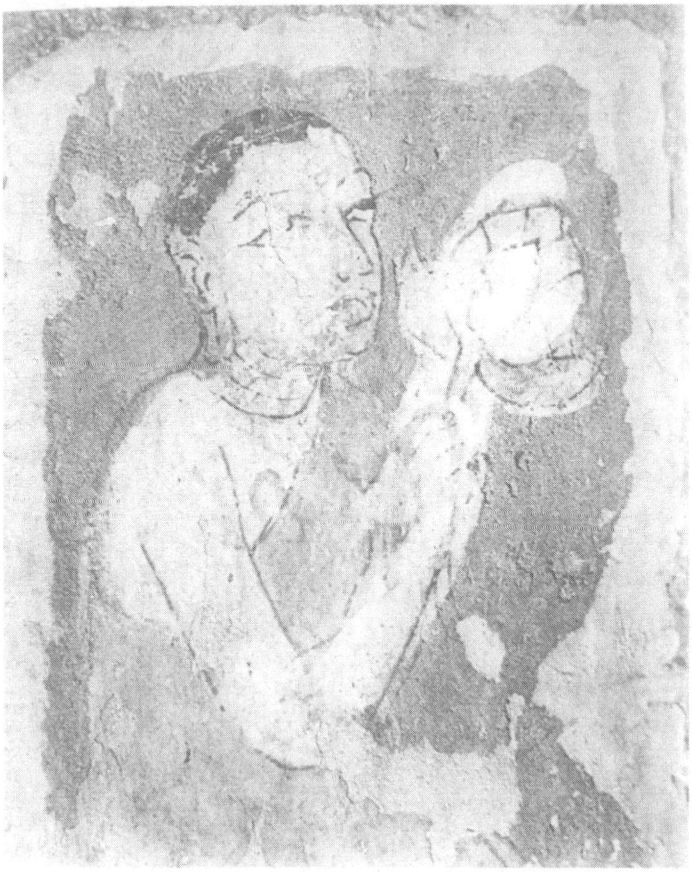

Plate 127. Ajanta: 'The Bodhisattva' (cave 2).

Plate 128. Ajanta: 'The Votaries with offerings' (side chapel, cave 2).

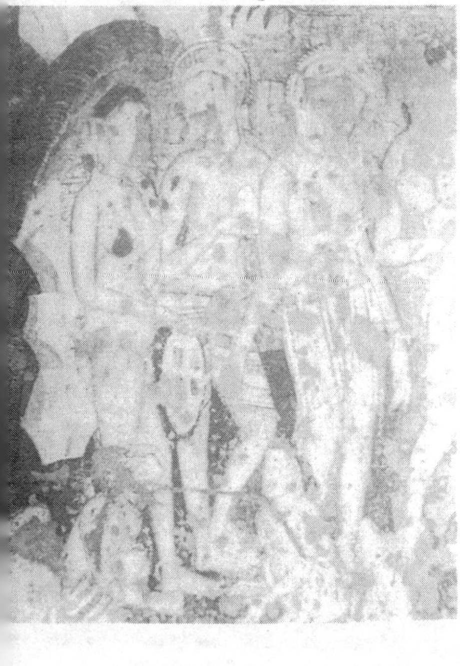

Plate 129. Sopoćani: The Last Judgment and 'the Death of Queen Anna Dandola' (Narthex).

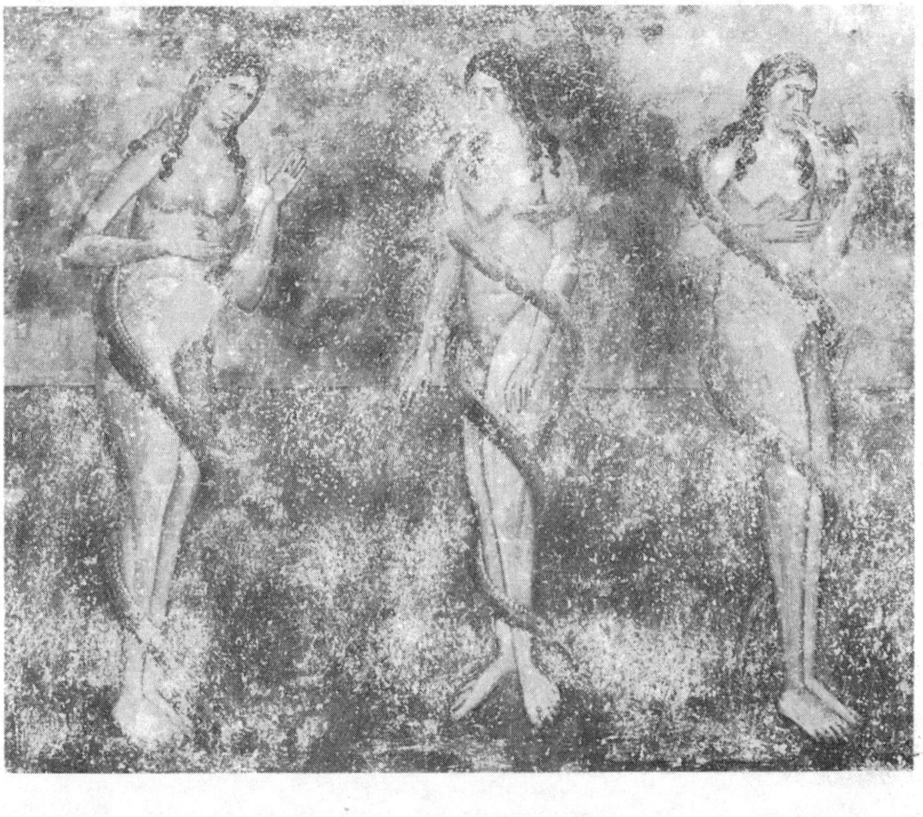

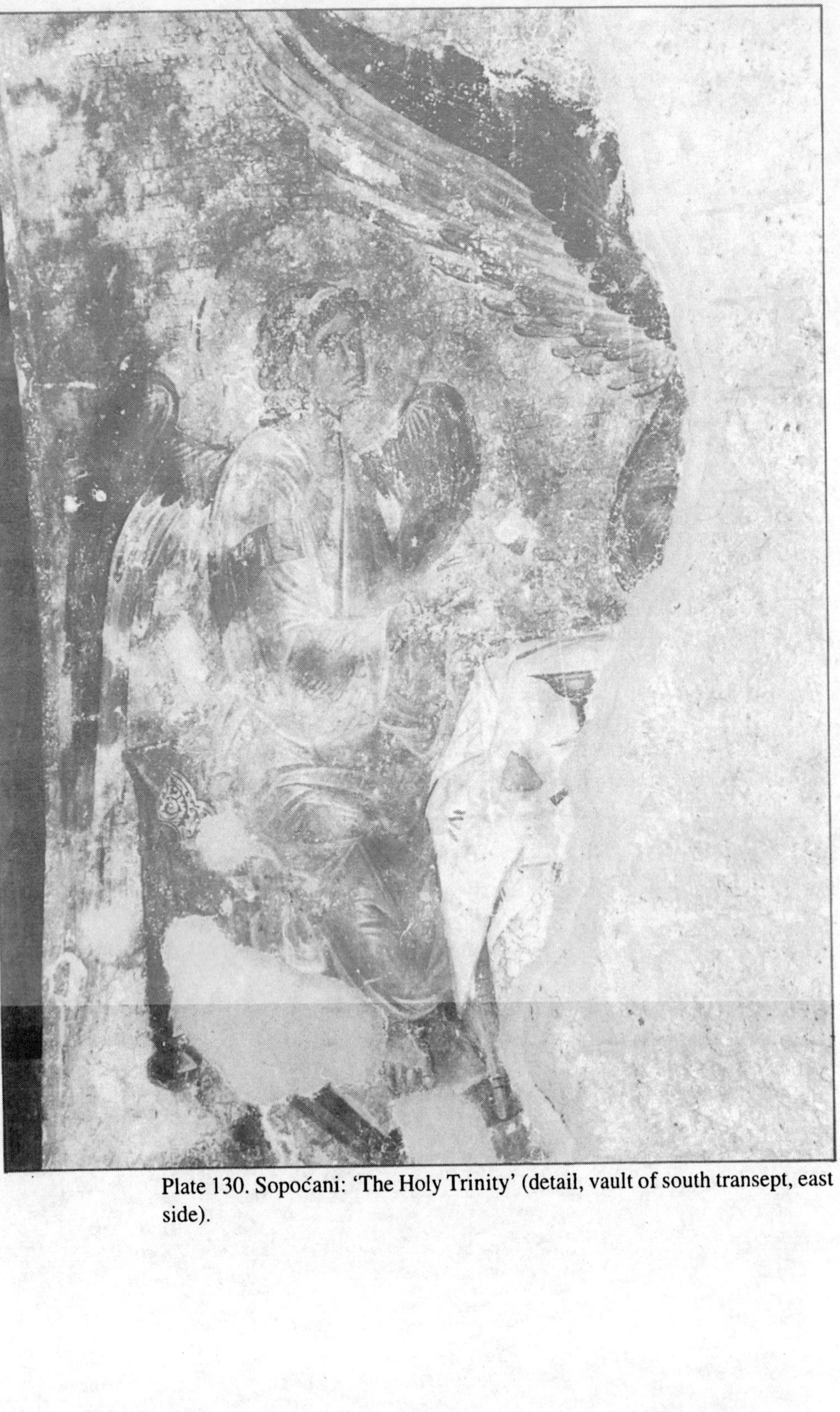

Plate 130. Sopoćani: 'The Holy Trinity' (detail, vault of south transept, east side).

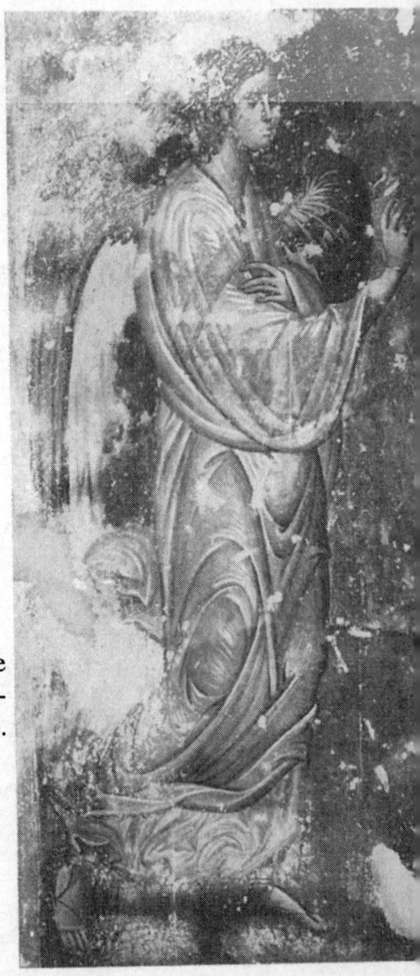

Plate 131. Sopoćani: 'The Archangel Gabriel, 'Annunciation' (detail, nave).

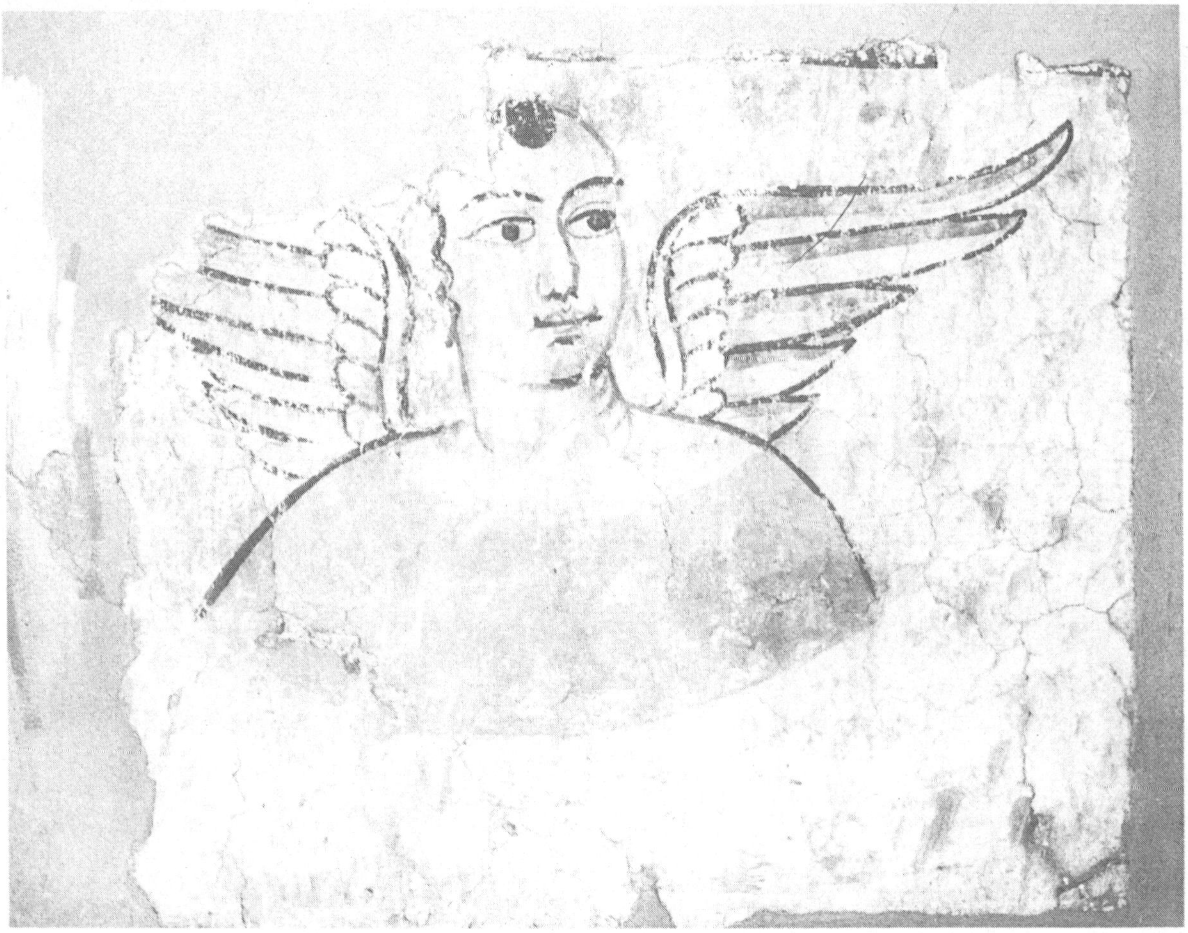

Plate 132. Miran (Central Asia) Shrine 3: Winged figure (A.D. second half of 3rd cent.).

Plate 133. Ajanta: Śṛngāra rasa in 'Simhal Avadāna' (detail cave 17).

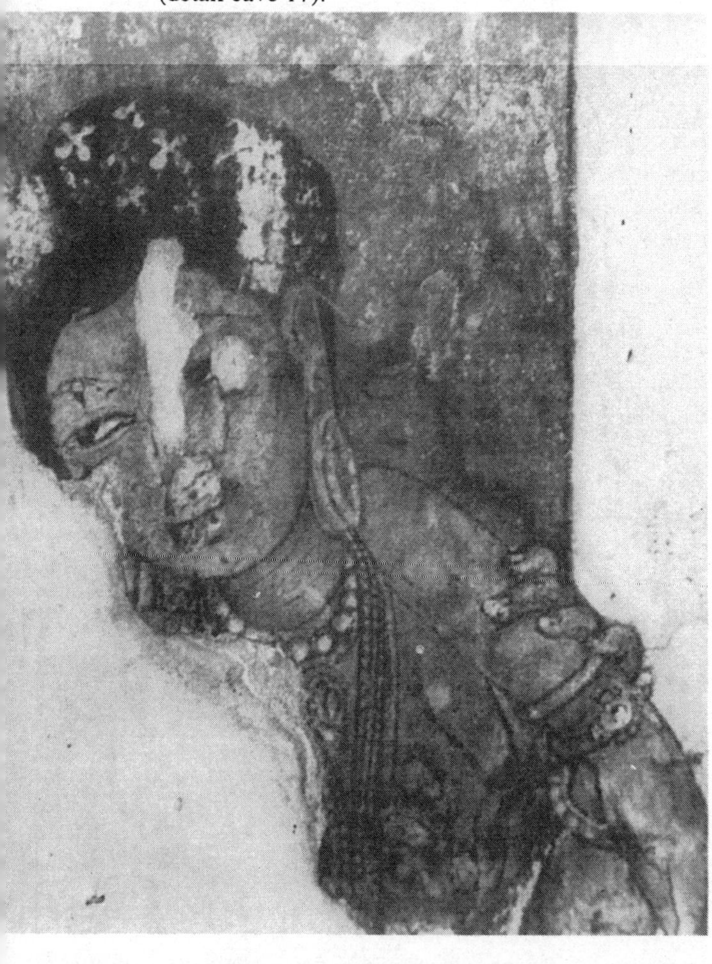

Plate 134. Ajanta: 'The Buddha' (cave 10).

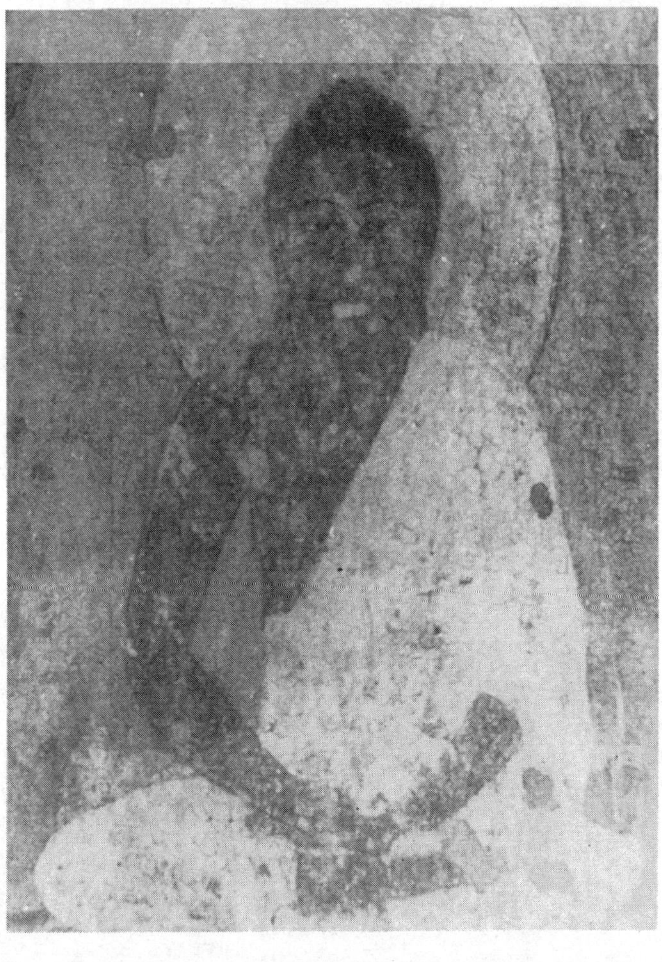

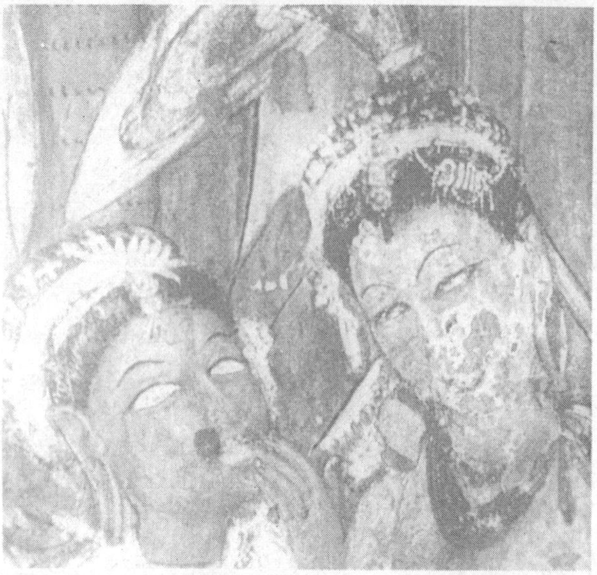

Plate 135. Ajanta: The Lady under parasol *Vessantara Jātaka* (detail, cave 17).

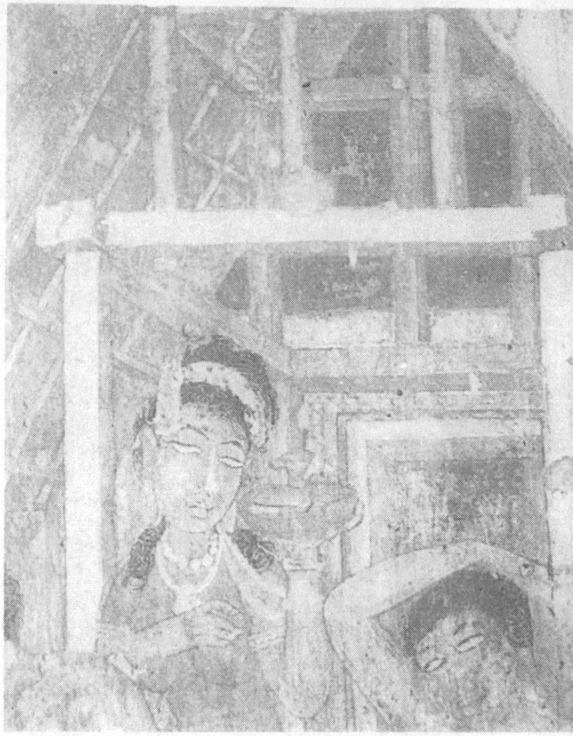

Plate 136. Ajanta: 'A Monastery' (cave 17).

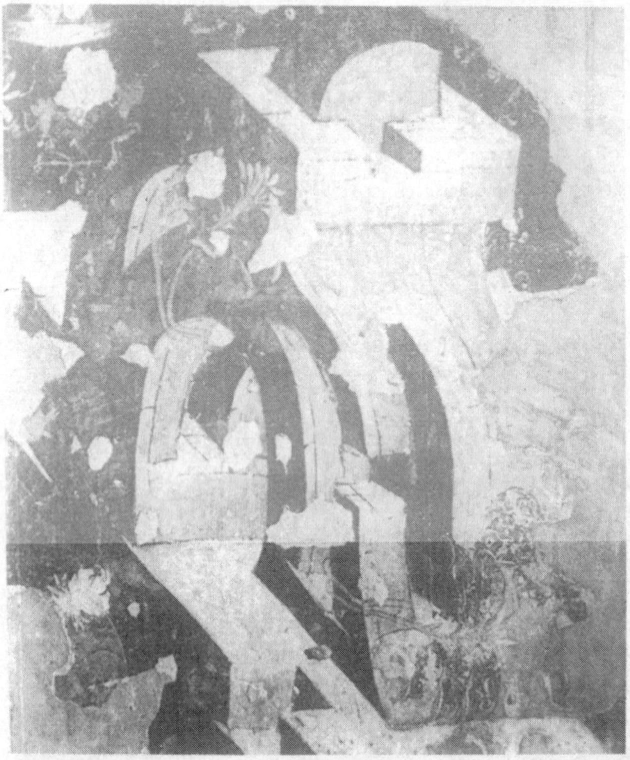

Plate 137. Ajanta: 'Gate in King Brahmadatta's Palace', *Mahāhamsa Jātaka* (detail, cave 2).

Plate 138. Sopoćani: Angel with candlestand 'The Dormition' (detail, nave).

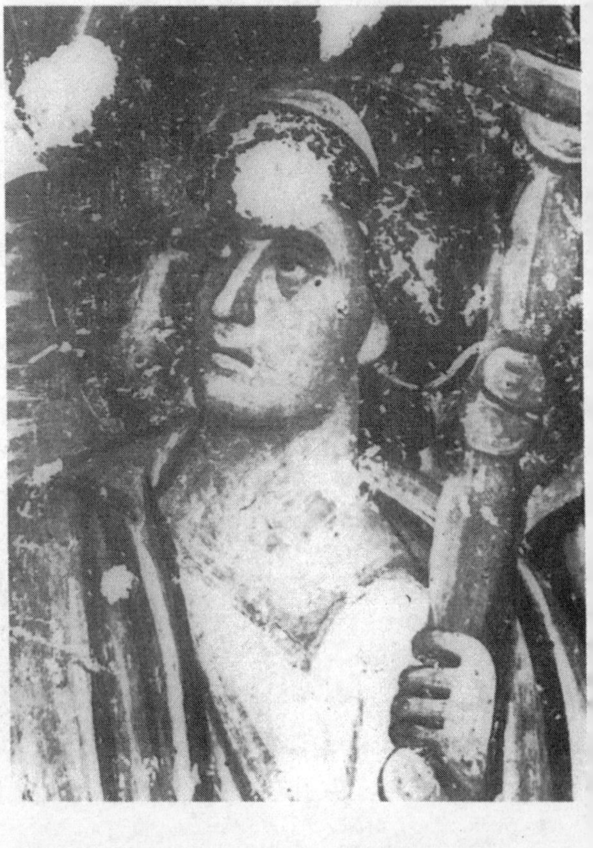

Plate 139. Sopoćani: 'The Nativity' (detail, nave).

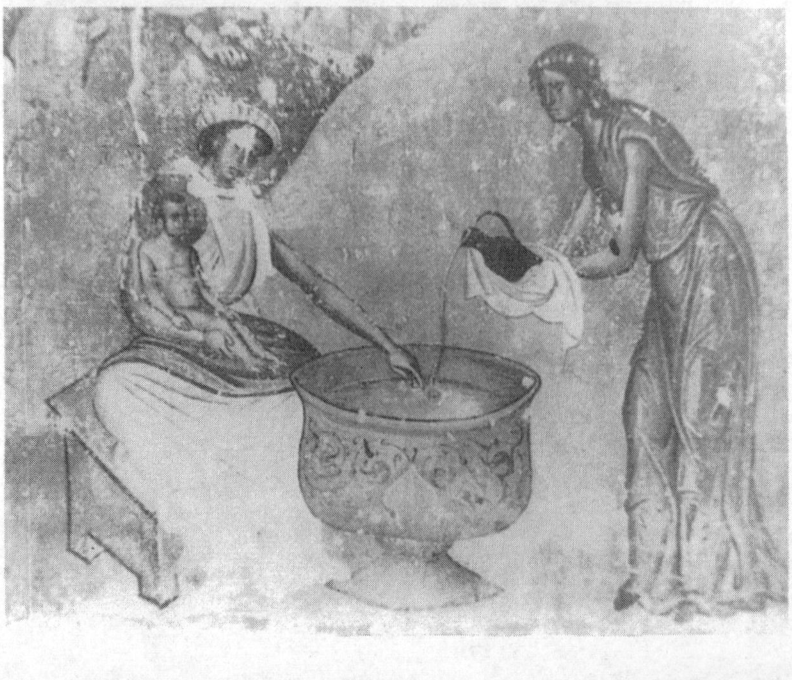

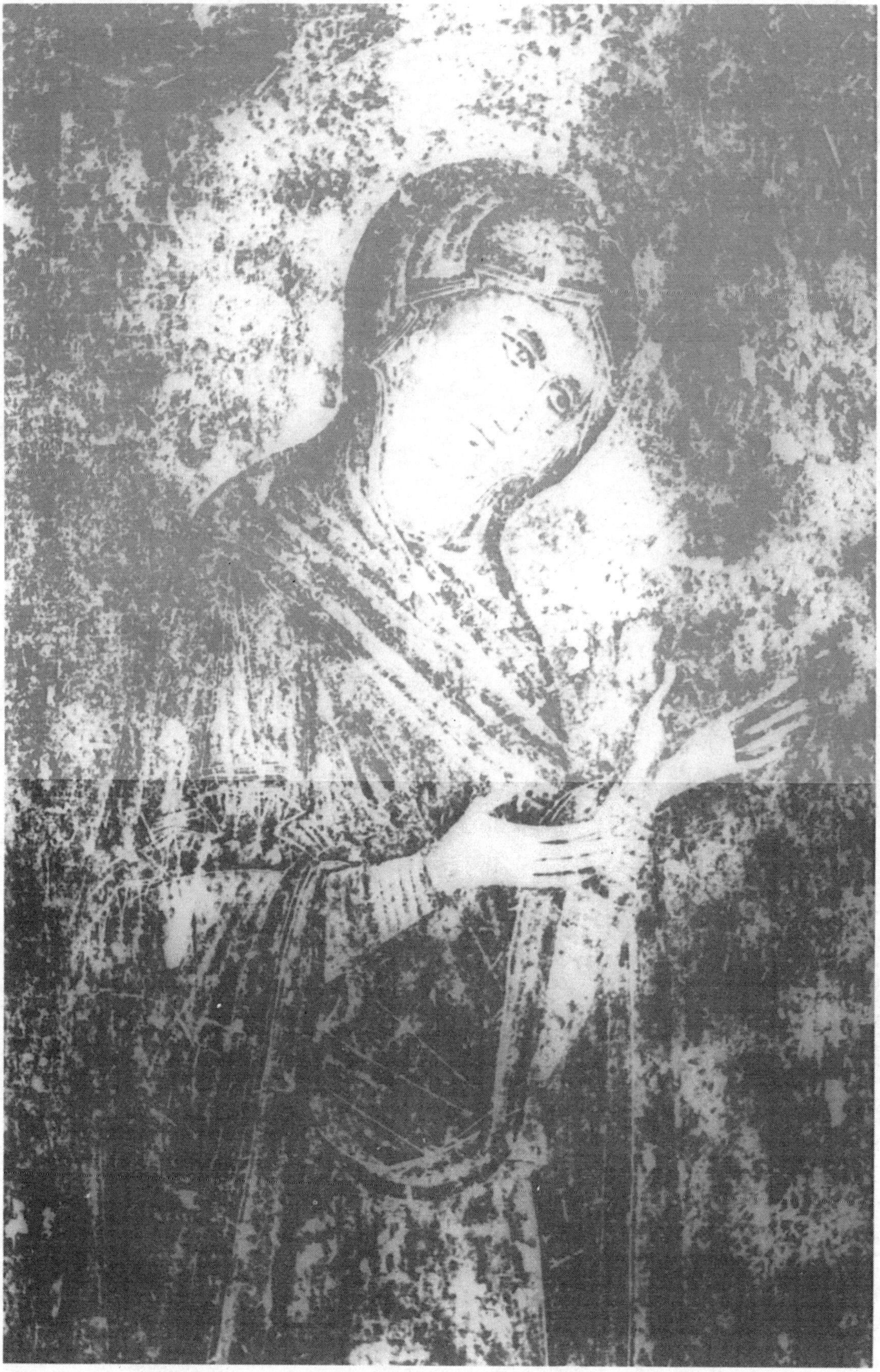

Plate 140. Sopoćani: 'The Virgin presentation of the Donor' (detail, nave).

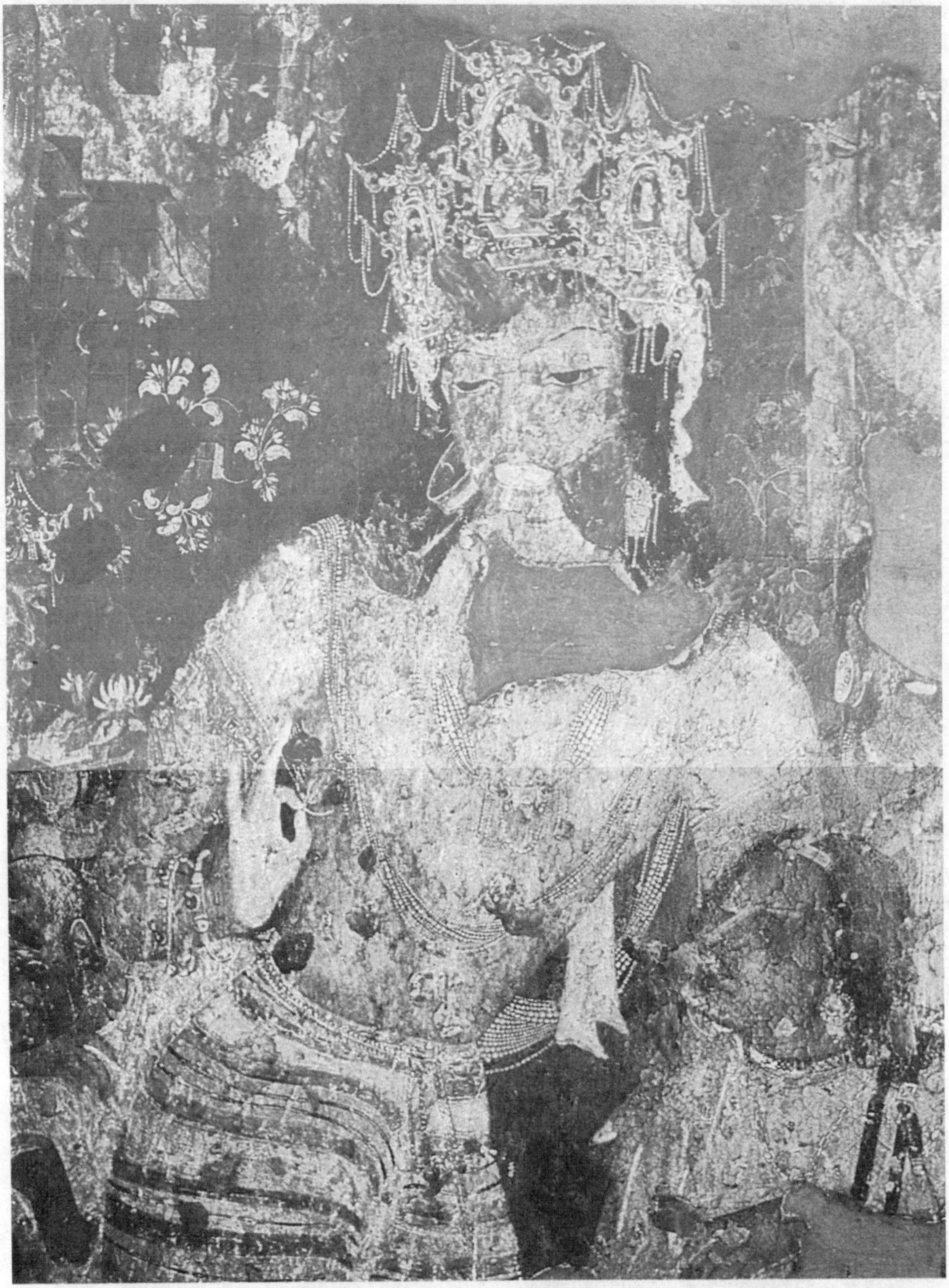

Plate 141. Ajanta: Luminosity gradients and structuring with colour, 'Bodhisattva Avalokiteśvara' (cave 1).

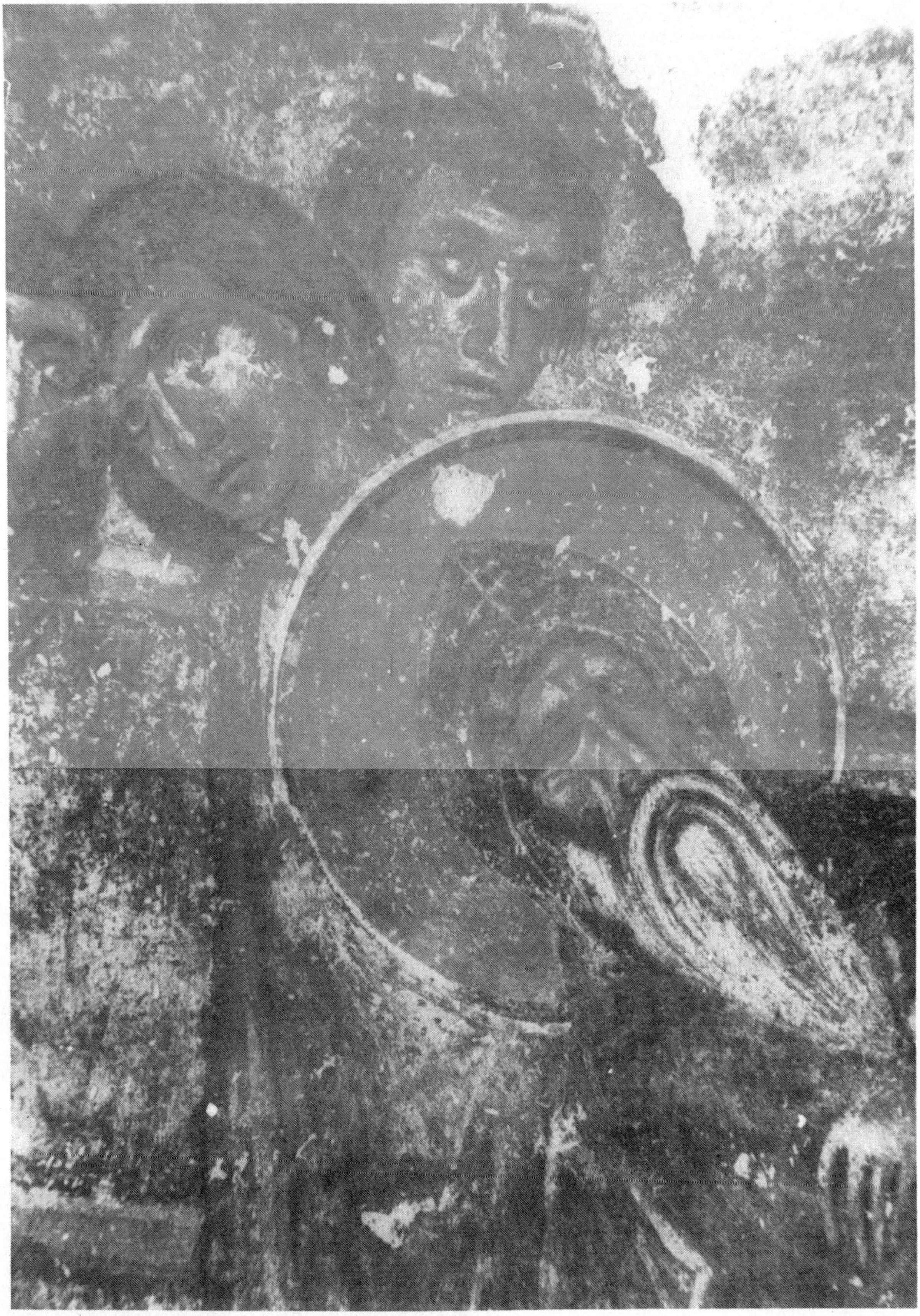

Plate 142. Sopoćani: Levelling efforts, luminosity gradients and structuring with colour, 'Transference of the relics of St. Simeon Nemanja' (Chapel of St. Simeon).

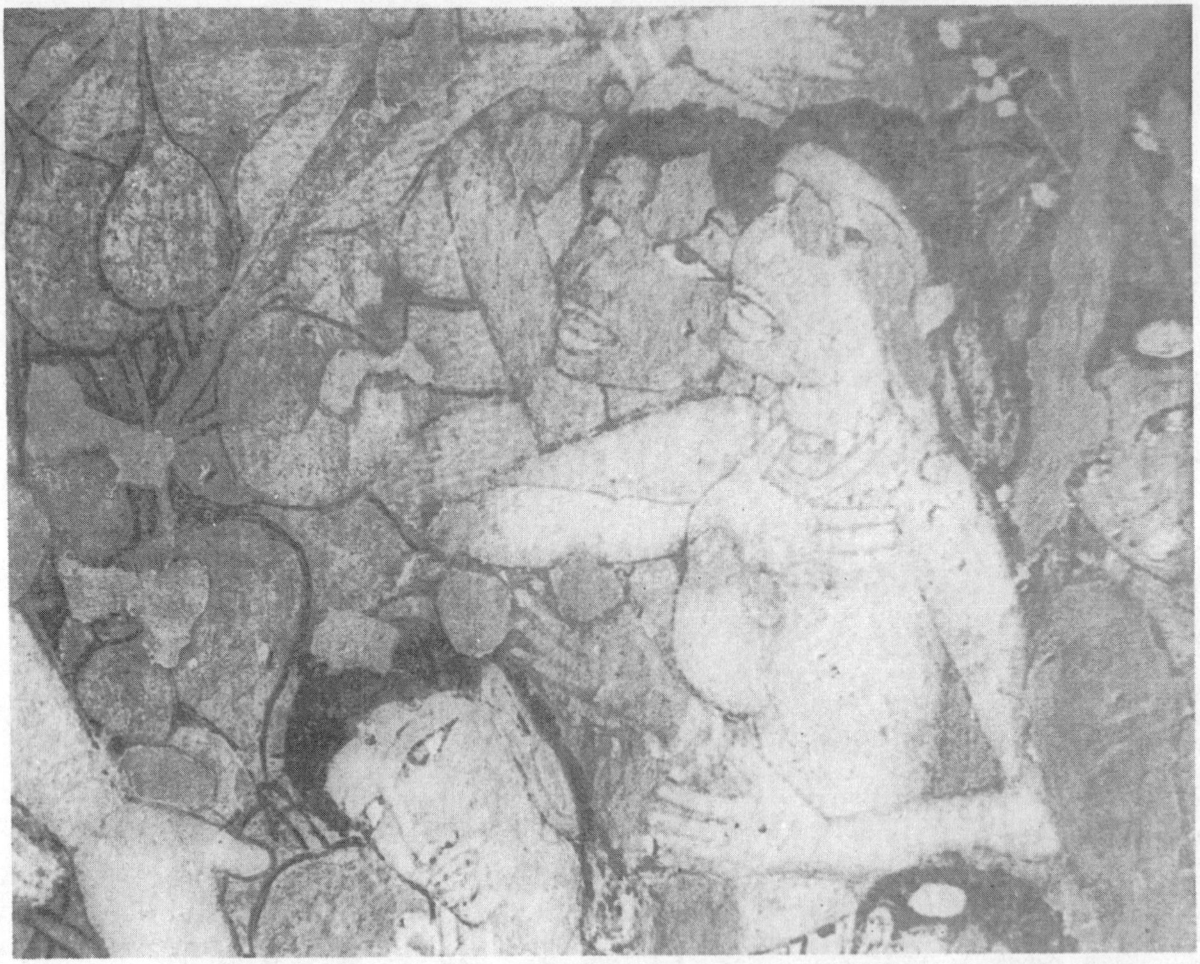

Plate 143. Ajanta: ' Levelling' efforts, the wailing women 'a Palace Scene' (detail, cave 1).

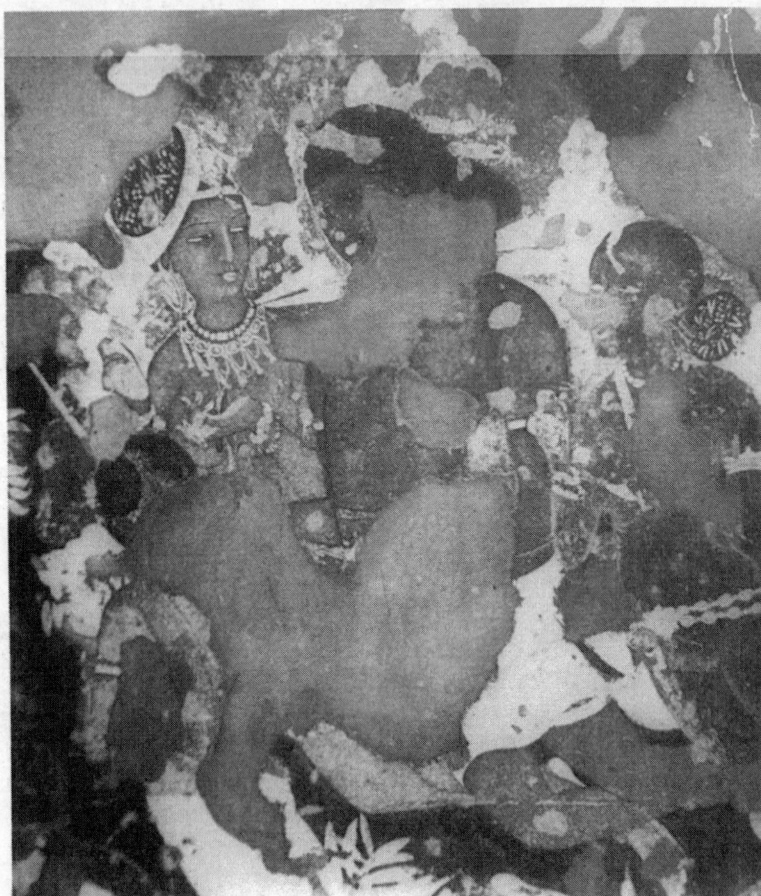

Plate 144. Ajanta: Periphery lighting and the levitating effects in 'the flying Apsaras and Gandharvas' (cave 17).

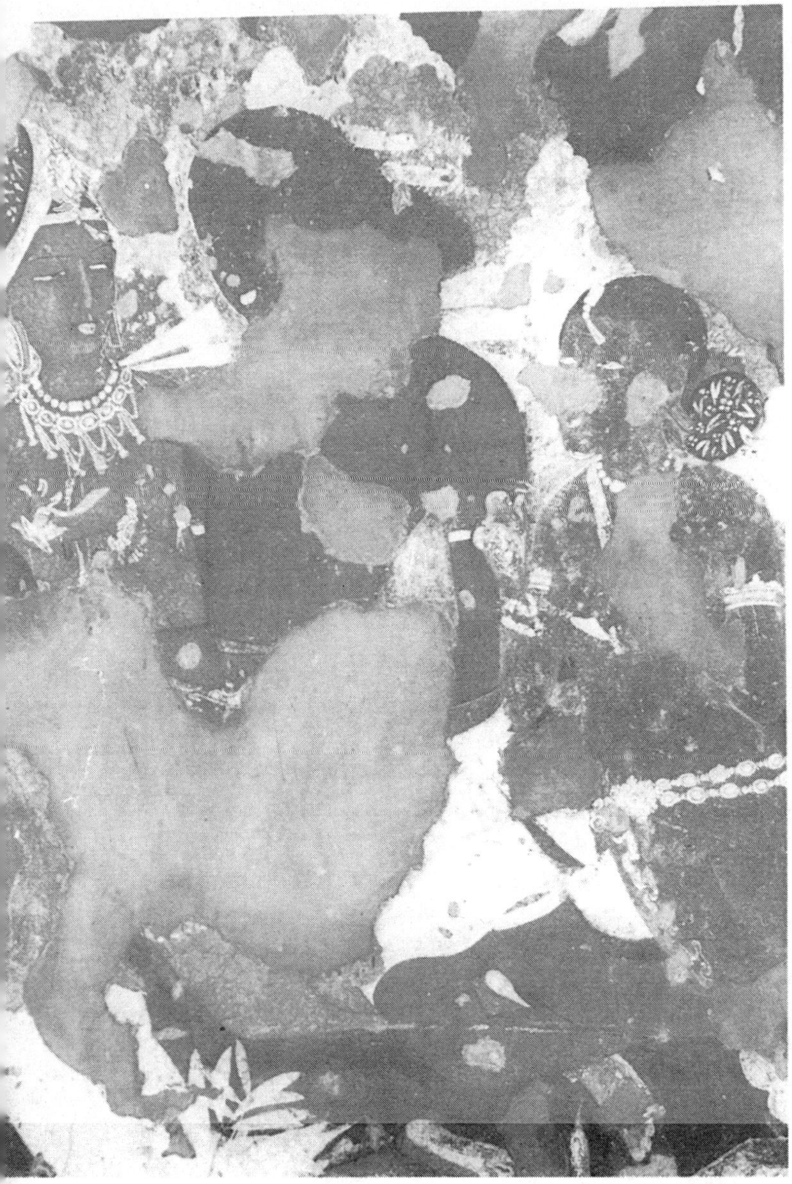

Plate 145. Ajanta: Periphery lighting and the levitating effect in 'The Flying Apsaras and Gandharvas' (cave 17).

Plate 146. Ajanta: 'Painterly style' of the woman with lotus a palace Scene (detail, cave 1).

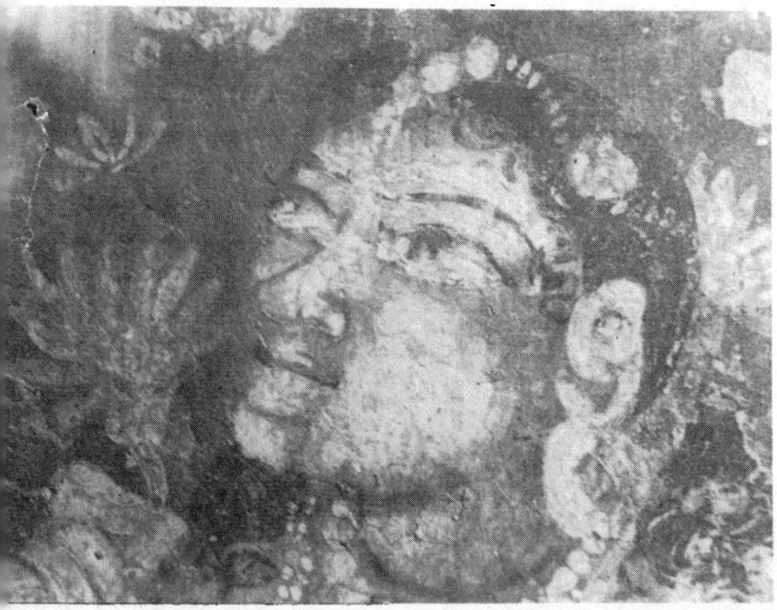

Plate 147. Alex Von Jawlenski, 'painterly style' in 'self-portrait' (A.D. 1912).

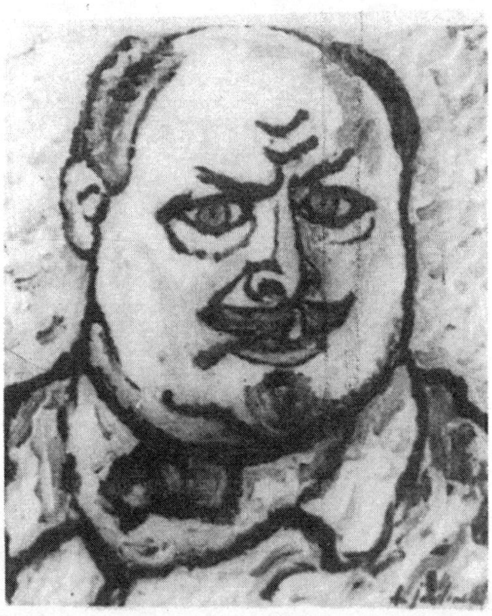

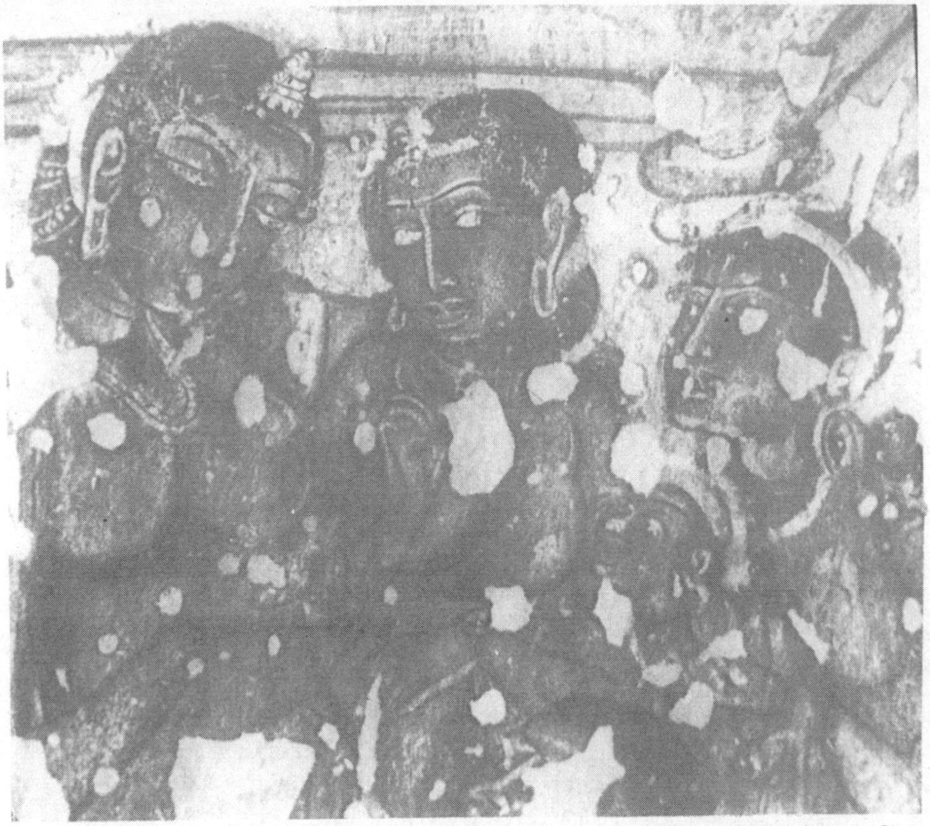

Plate 148. Ajanta: 'II Indian manner' of 'Votaries bringing offerings' (cave 2).

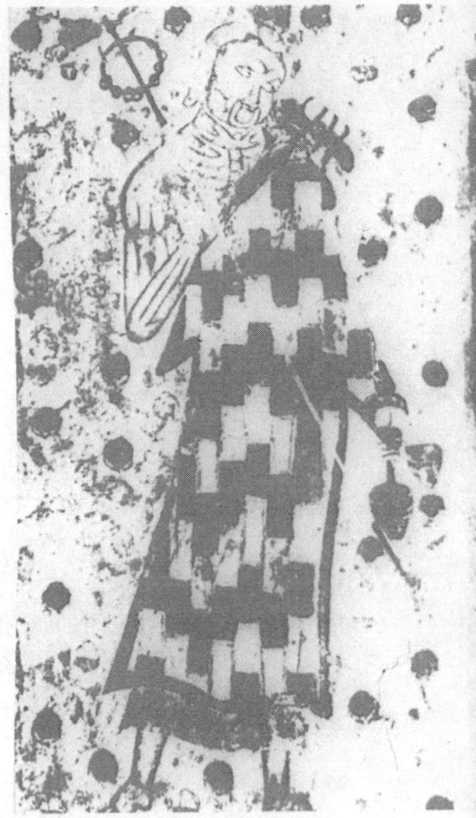

Plate 149. Qizl (Central Asia) Large cave: Mahākaśyapa (Arhat· A.D. 600-50).

Plate 151. Boško Karanovic: Study of a head (A.D. 1962).

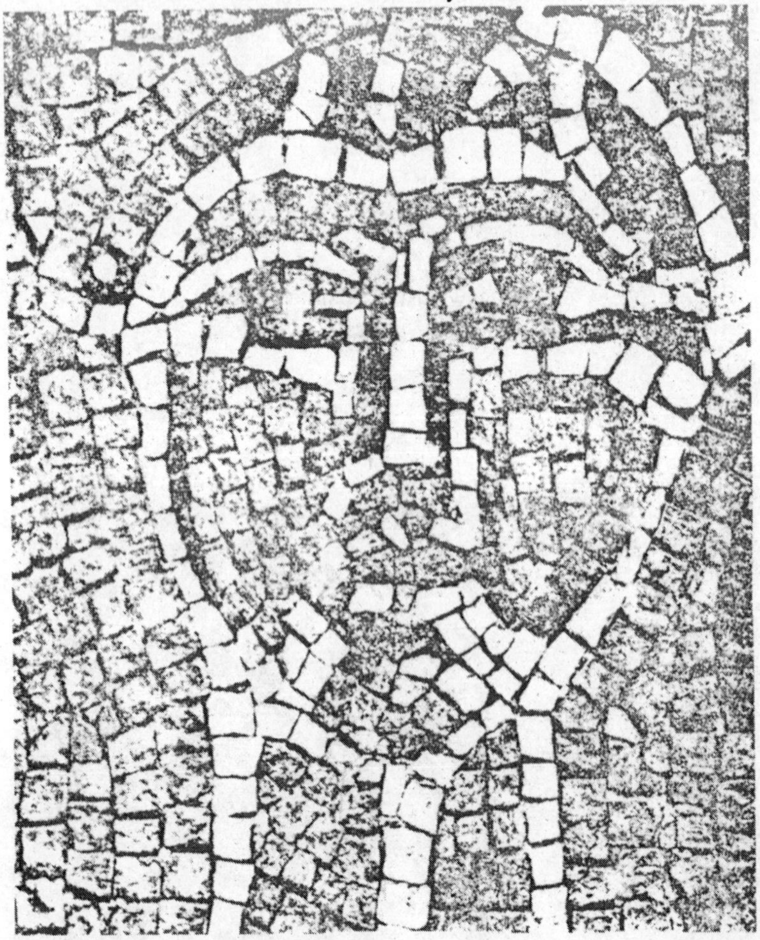

Plate 150. Sopoćani: Isocephelic array of patriarchs and saints (sanctuary, nave).

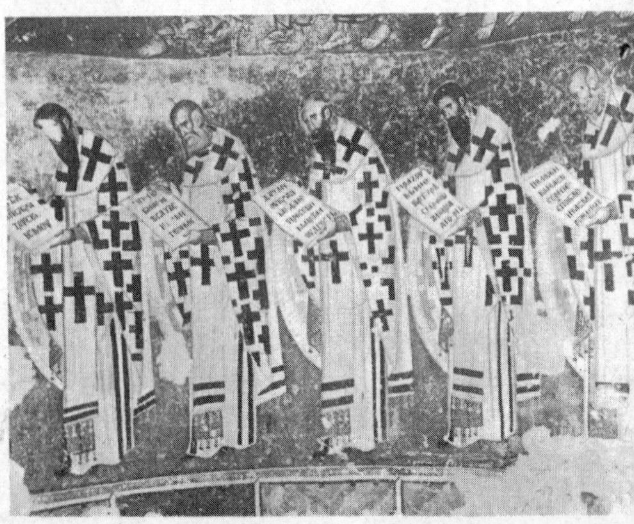

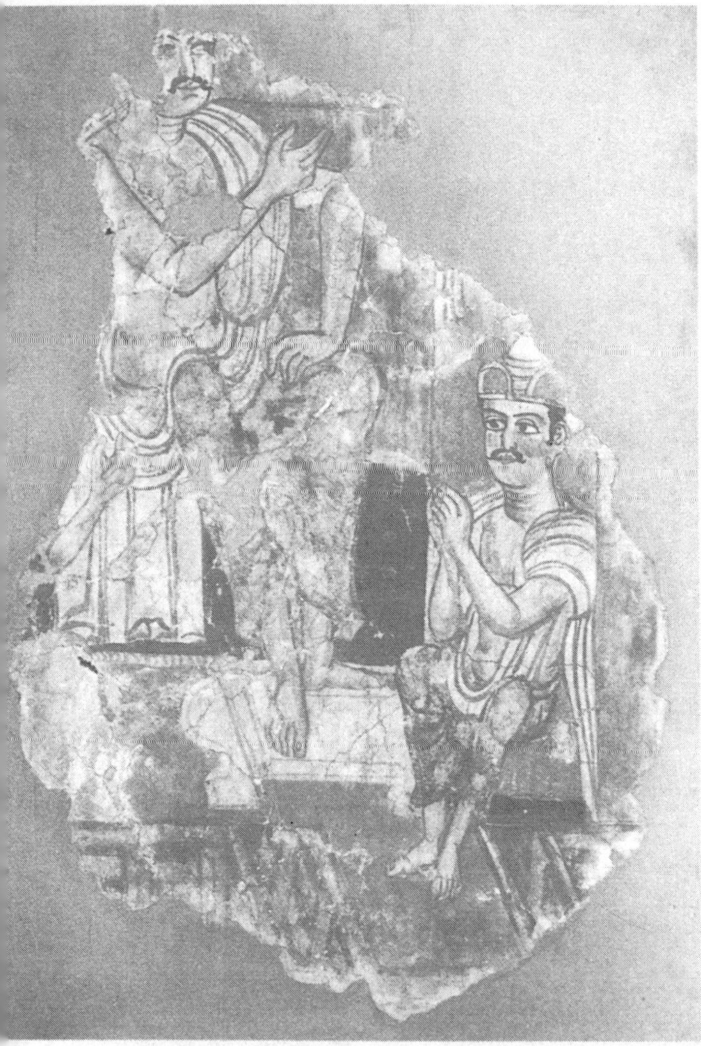

Plate 152. Miran (Central Asia): 'Royal figure praying' (fragment of an adoration scene, A.D. second half of 2nd century) Āhairikā Vartanā.

Plate 153. Ajanta: 'The Buddha and the one-eyed Monk' (cave 10).

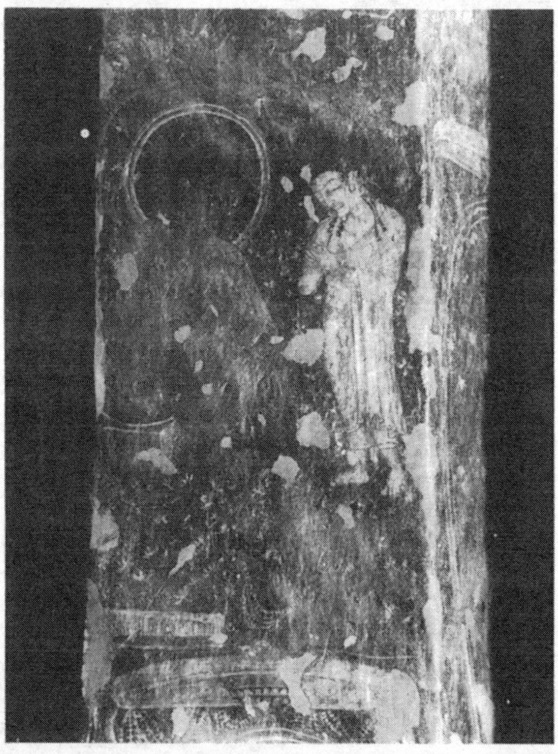

Plate 154. Sopocani: 'The Apostle Peter' (north transept.).

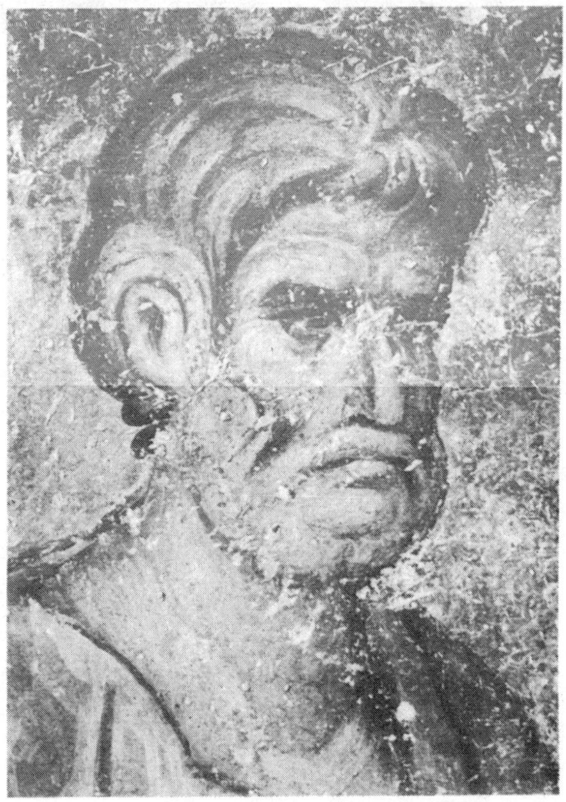

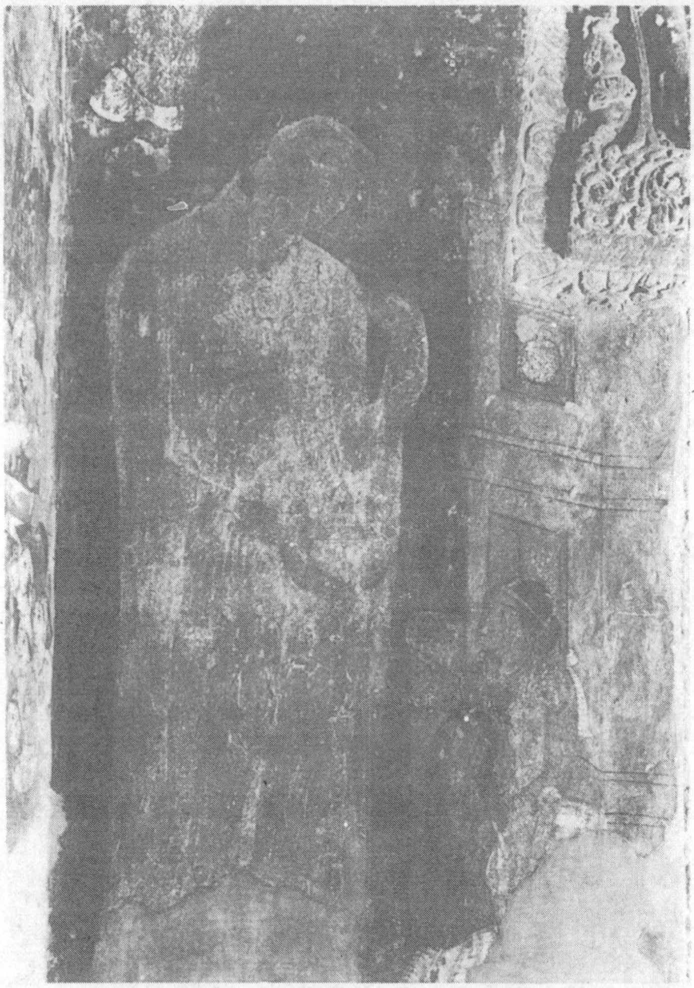

Plate 155. Ajanta: 'The Buddha in Kapilavastu' (cave 17).

Plate 156. Sopoćani: 'Joseph' in 'The Nativity' (detail, nave).

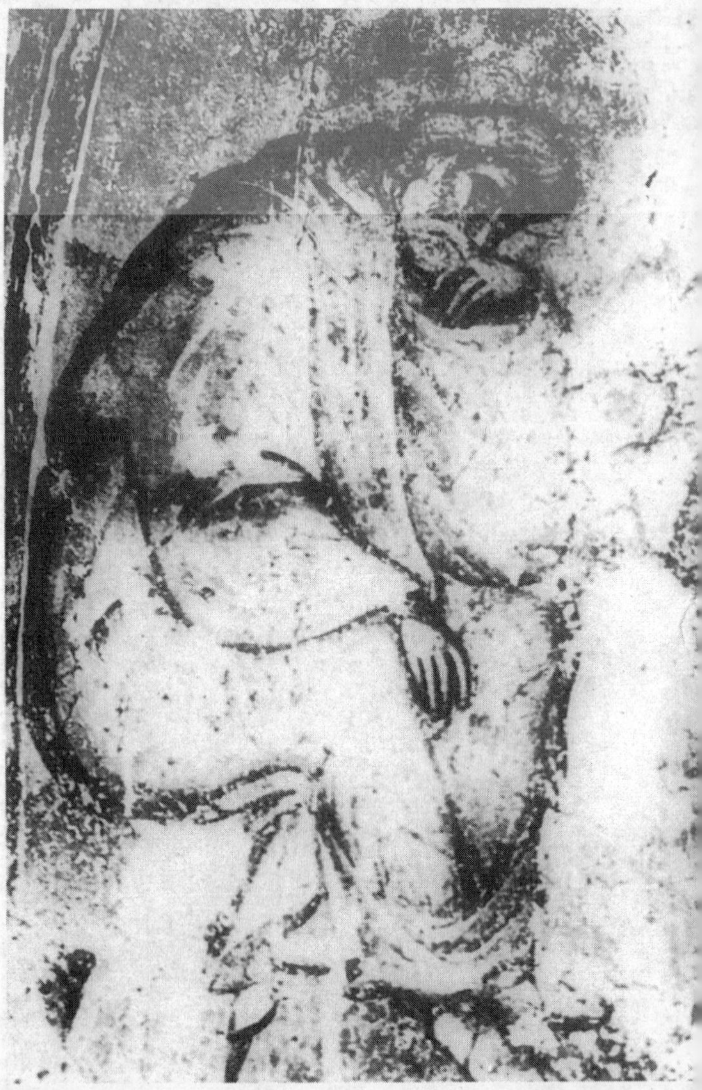

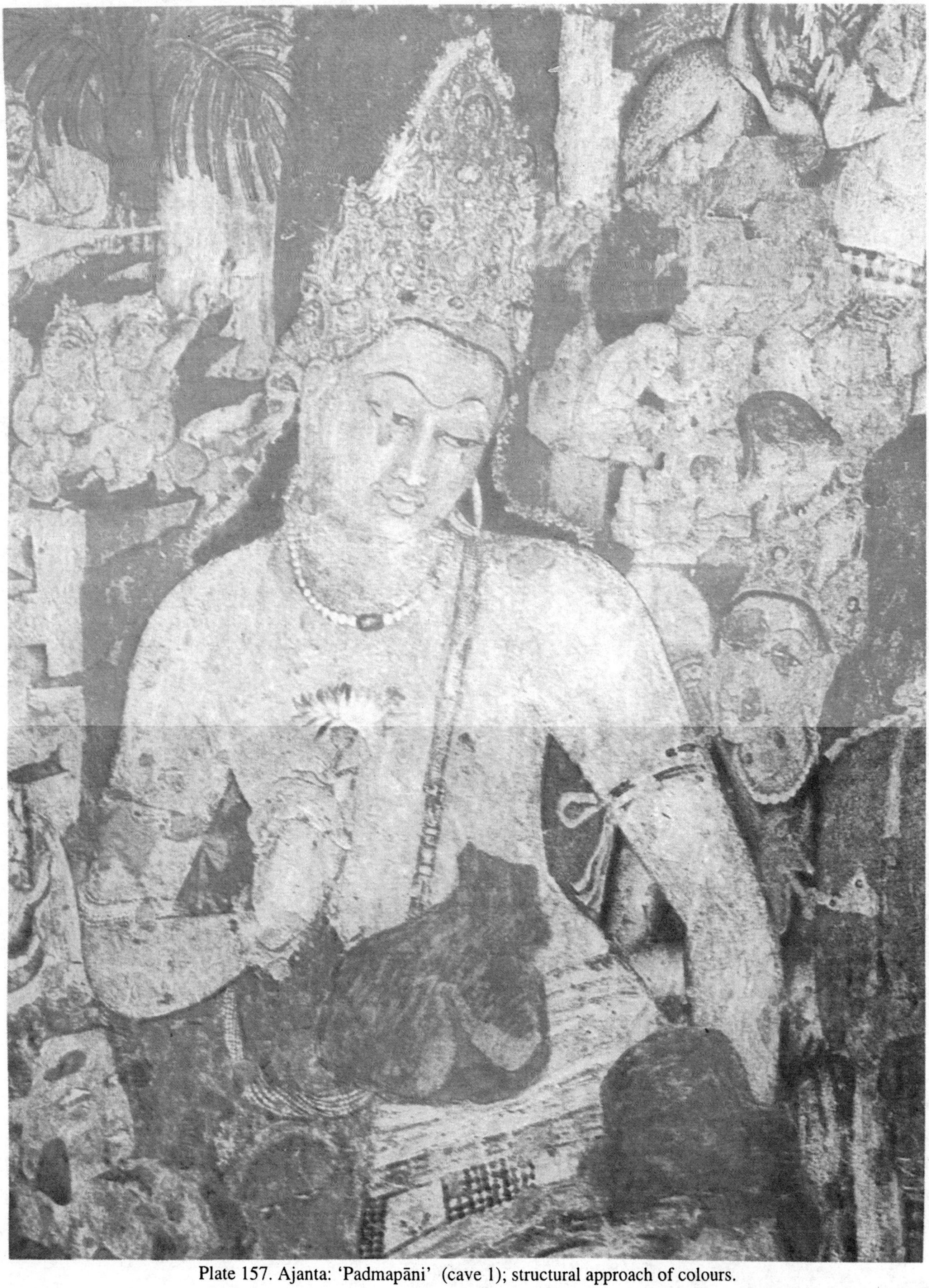

Plate 157. Ajanta: 'Padmapāni' (cave 1); structural approach of colours.

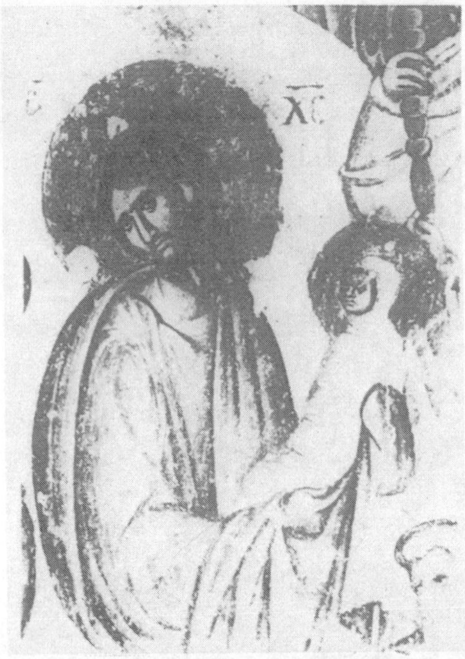

Plate 158. Sopoćani: 'Christ holding the spirit of Mary, The Dormition' (detail, nave).

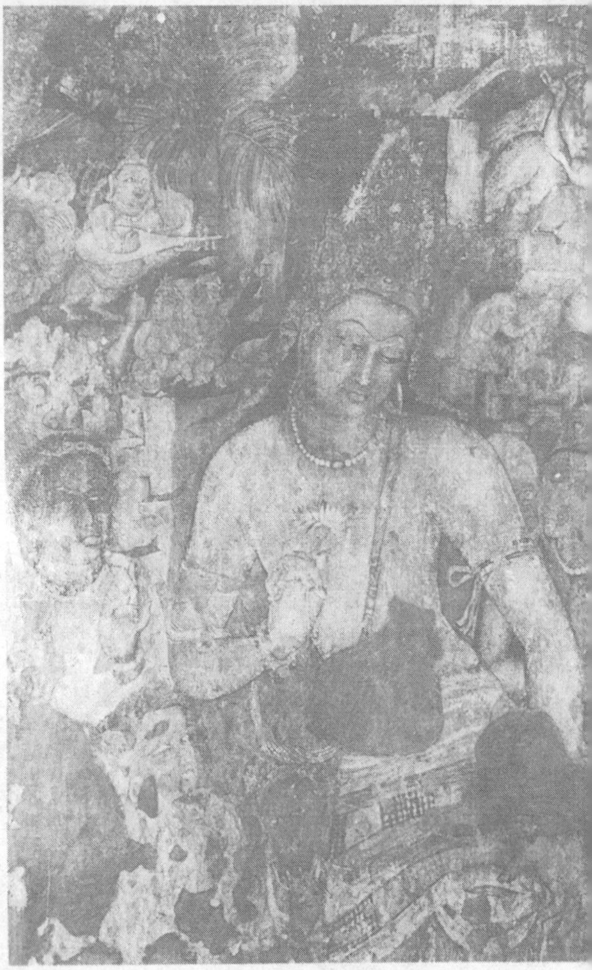

Plate 160. Ajanta: 'Padmapāṇi' (cave 1); showing '*ātmastha*' kind of *Dayā-Vīra* .

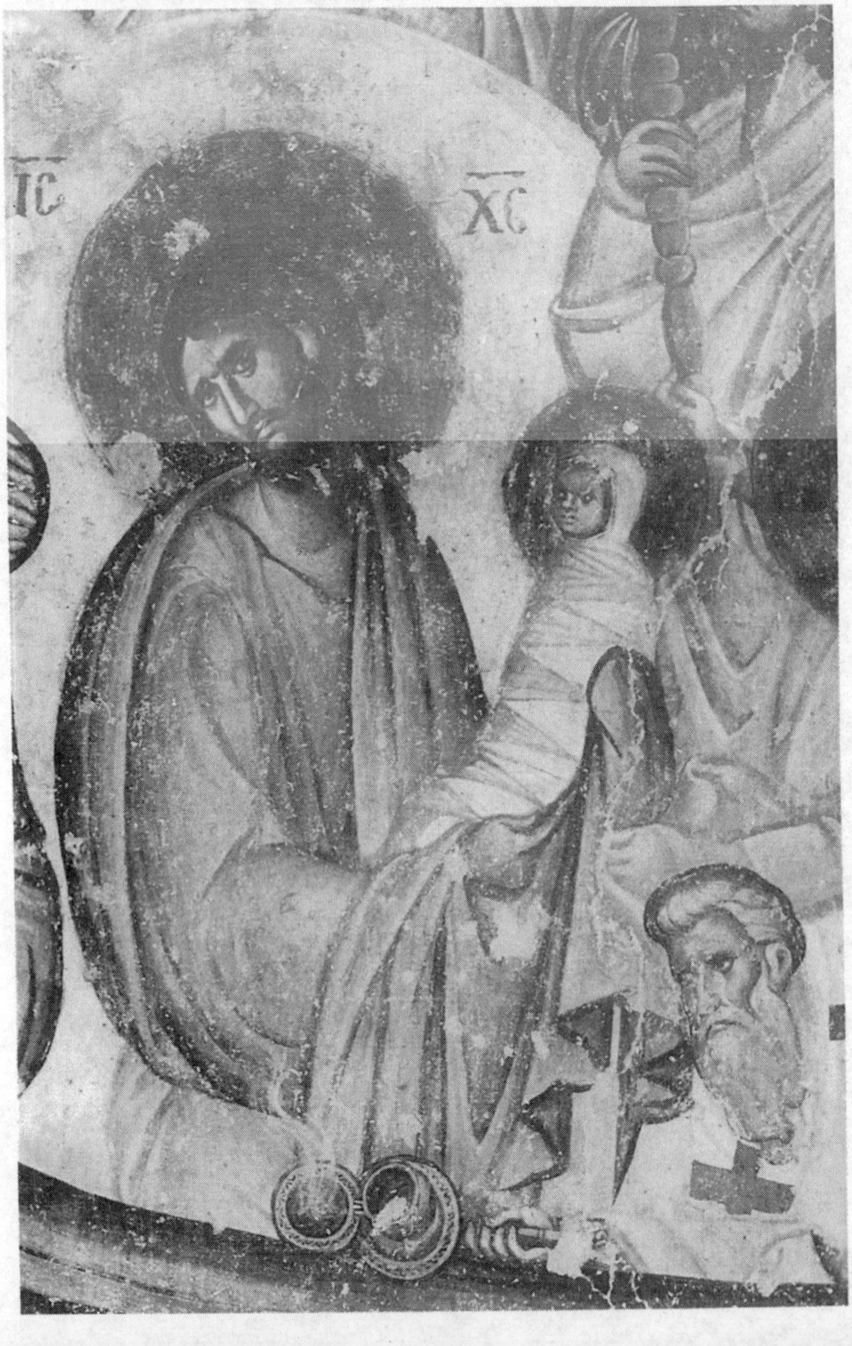

Plate 159. Sopoćani: Christ holding the spirit of Mary showing 'compassionate heroism'.

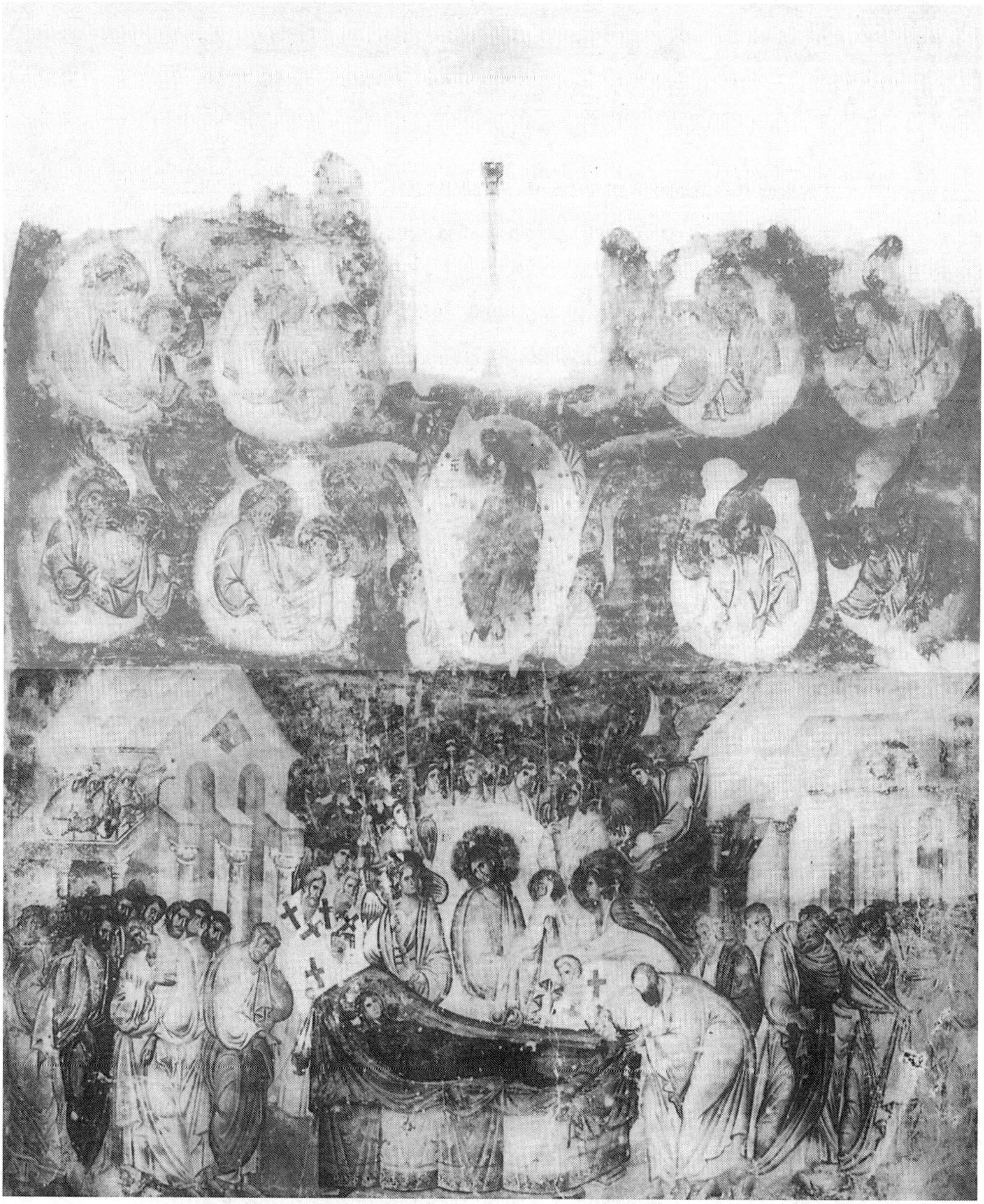

Plate 161. Sopoćani: 'The Dormition' or 'The Death of the Virgin' (nave).

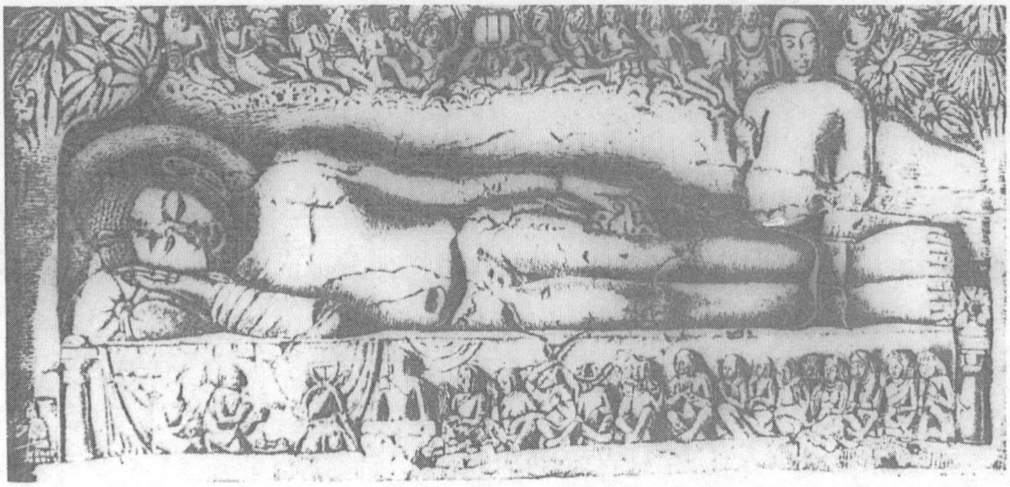

Plate 162. Ajanta: 'Parinirvāṇa of the Buddha' (cave 26).

Plate 163. Ajanta: A youth in an unidentified scene (cave 1).

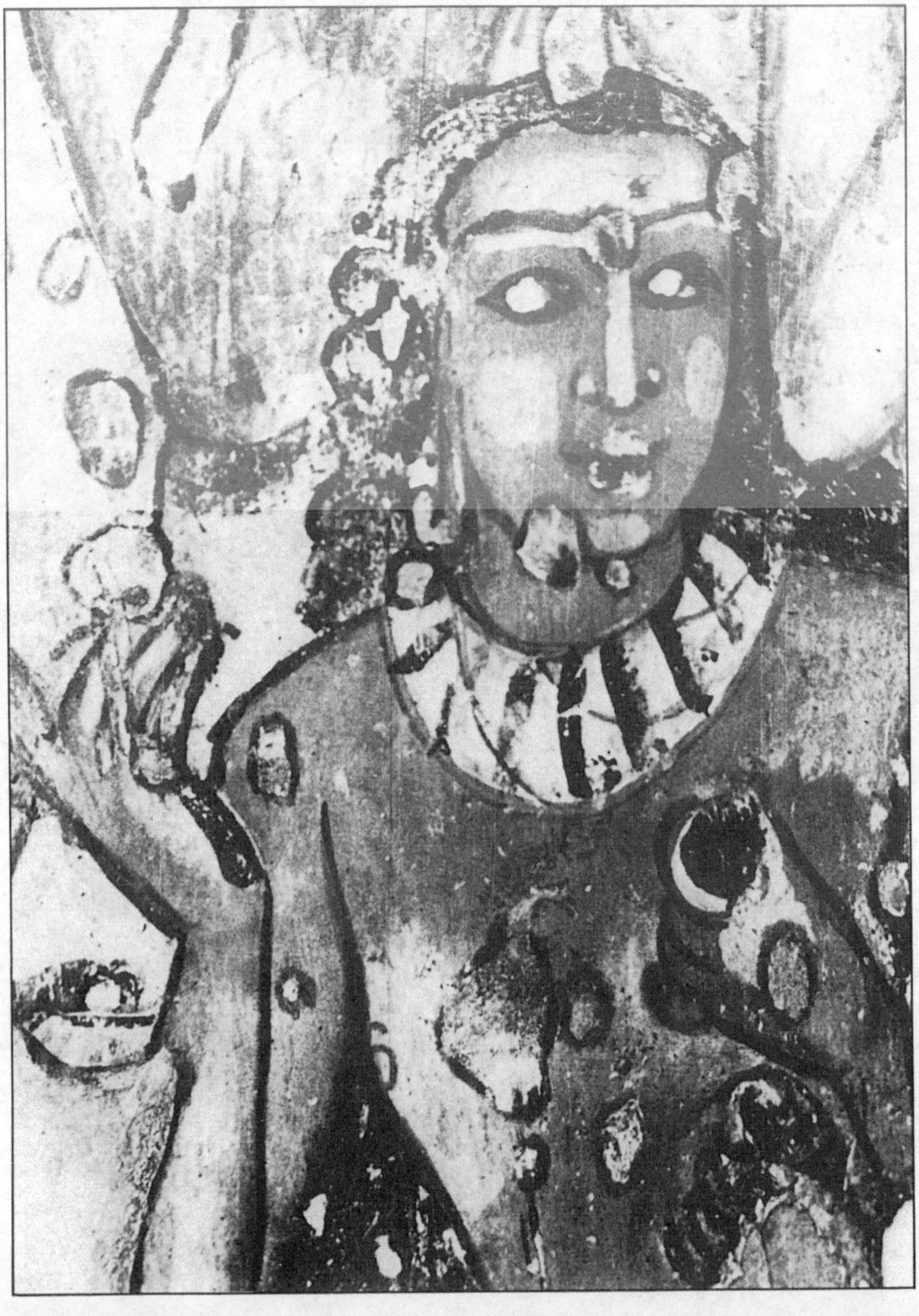

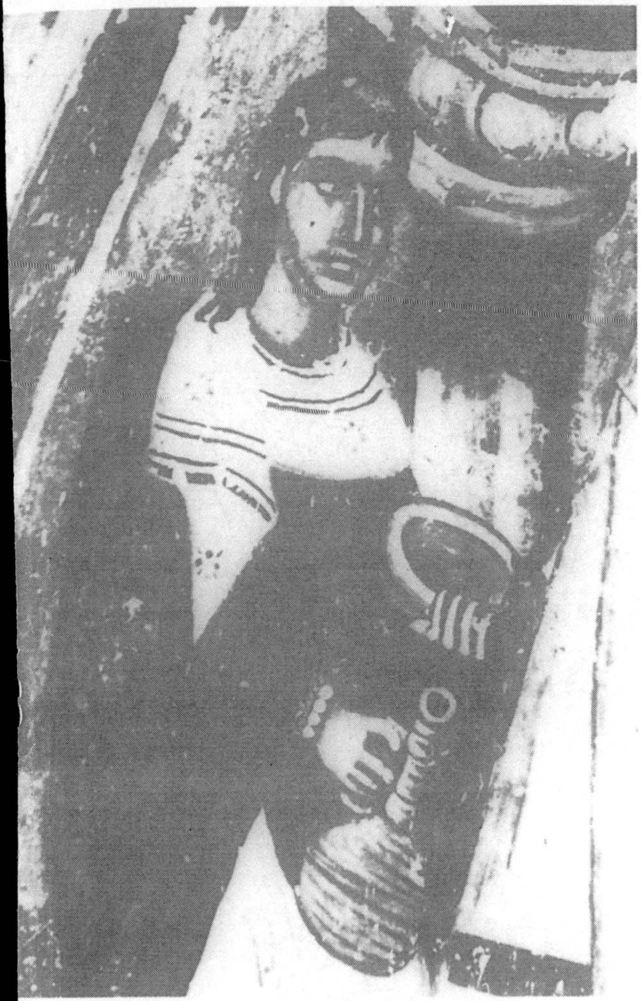

Plate 164. Sopoćani: 'St. Nicholas becomes a priest' (detail, chapel of St. Nicholas c. A.D. 6th or 7th decade of 14th cent.).

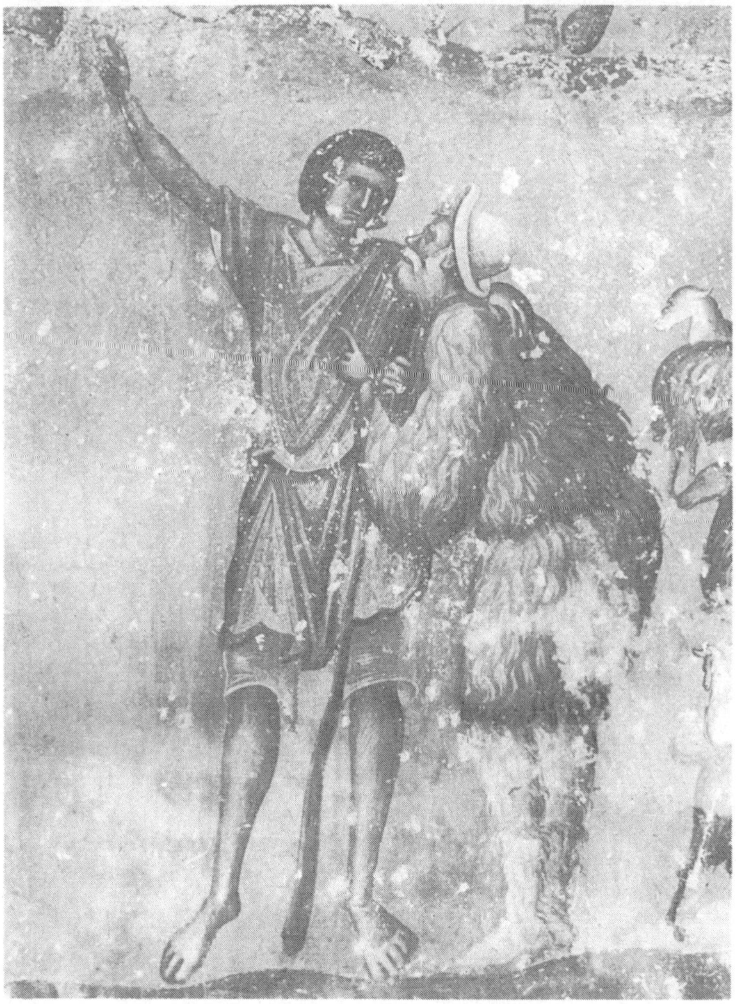

Plate 165. Sopoćani: 'Shephards' from 'the Nativity' (detail, nave).

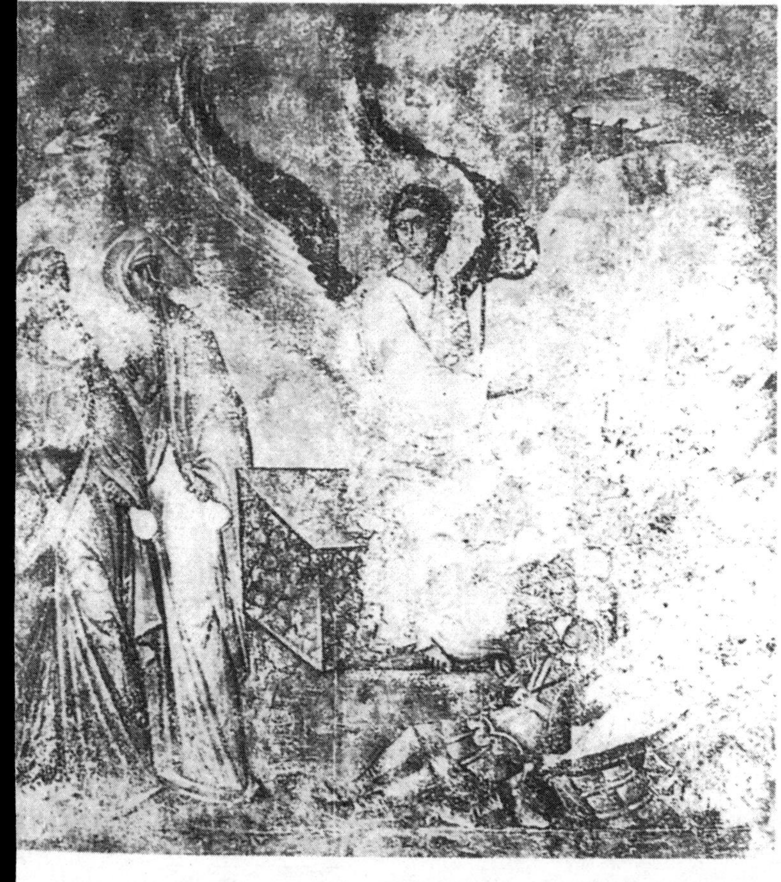

Plate 166. Sopoćani: 'The Marys at the tomb' (sanctuary, nave).